Fifth Edition

The Administration *and* Management *of* Criminal Justice Organizations

Fifth Edition

The Administration *and* Management *of* Criminal Justice Organizations

A Book of Readings

Stan Stojkovic
University of Wisconsin–Milwaukee

John Klofas
Rochester Institute of Technology

David Kalinich
Florida Atlantic University

WAVELAND
PRESS, INC.
Long Grove, Illinois

For information about this book, contact:
Waveland Press, Inc.
4180 IL Route 83, Suite 101
Long Grove, IL 60047-9580
(847) 634-0081
info@waveland.com
www.waveland.com

#SSI 122797

Contents

Section 2
The Individual in Criminal Justice Organizations   109

Section 3
Group Behavior in Criminal Justice Organizations   261

Introduction

The fifth edition of *The Administration and Management of Criminal Justice Organizations: A Book of Readings* represents a compilation of new articles and research on the operations of criminal justice organizations. As with the four earlier editions of the book, this edition focuses on innovative ways of viewing criminal justice administration and management. These ideas on criminal justice administration and management must be understood in the context of an ever-changing world and expectations for the criminal justice system. Since the fourth edition of this book, we have seen more emphases placed on capturing terrorists, an escalating war in Afghanistan, continued dwindling of federal and state funding for social service agencies, and a number of difficult problems facing states, including record budget deficits and shrinking local tax revenues due in large part to the greed of "Wall Street" financiers. In addition, the country has continued to respond to terrorist actions and threats by further supporting the Department of Homeland Security, representing an integration of over twenty federal agencies, tens of thousands of employees, and a budget in the billions of dollars. This department has been given broad authority to address the threat of terrorism and will require the direct involvement and assistance of criminal justice agencies. Even more recently, the judiciary has responded to governmental operations in addressing terrorism and has produced limits on the authority of the president to hold "enemy combatants" at the detention facility at Guantanamo Bay. Most notably, the most profound change in the United States has been the election of the country's first African American president, Barack Obama.

It is within this context that contemporary criminal justice administrators, managers, and employees have been asked to address crime and the nascent threat of terrorism. Many controversial ideas have been generated and proposed to improve the functioning of criminal justice organizations, and many prescriptions have specifically targeted practices and ways of doing business among criminal justice administrators. The fifth edition includes a representative sample of articles questioning the traditional methods and practices of criminal justice administrators. Whether discussing the politics of science and research in policing, the ever-changing environments of criminal justice systems, the influence of diversity in the criminal justice workforce, or the role of changing technologies in the transformation of police practices, criminal justice entities are being asked to improve the delivery of services to diverse and competing communities and constituent groups.

The fourteen new articles added to this edition of the book all address central concerns in how criminal justice organizations will function during very difficult times. These new additions to the book examine very important issues and concerns that will define criminal justice responses to crime. As organizational and political entities, criminal justice organizations oftentimes respond to crime based on changing environments, particularly as it relates to the pressure put on communities to develop strategies to address the reintegration of offenders back in the community. In Section 1, Leslie Smith (article 2) delves into how organizational environment influences the reentry process for offenders. Although we hope that with better knowledge, criminal justice organizations will improve their operations, this is not always the case. The marriage of science and politics is always a sticky one, as noted by Samuel Walker (article 5). His analysis shows how the relationship between science and politics in police research can be murky at best and sometimes problematical. Police organizations will have to respond to the changing nature of communities in order to fulfill their missions.

In Section 2, Susan Miller, Kay Forest, and Nancy Jurik (article 12) examine the diversity within police organizations by analyzing the unique experiences of lesbian and gay officers. They note the changing landscape of American policing and the issues faced by officers with differing sexual orientations. For some, such diversity represents a serious challenge as to how police organizations are managed. Micael Björk (article 13) addresses the ongoing problem of cynicism in policing and discusses the importance of self-motivation among police officers as a way to address this problem. In addition, this article provides a perspective on cynicism management through the efforts of individual officers in another country—Sweden. The lessons learned by Swedish police may be of value to police in America as they attempt to fight off the inclination toward cynicism in their work.

One of the most pressing questions faced by police and administrators is how changing technology has altered or transformed police practice. In Section 3, Janet Chan (article 14) examines modern police practices from a technological angle and its influence on Australian police. Chan discusses how technological changes have transformed police practices, but more importantly, how such changes have the potential to change police culture toward greater accountability and better services. Changes are always difficult and not always in the best interest of criminal justice organizations. Mitchell Mackinem and Paul Higgins (article 16) and Craig Haney (article 17) call into question some modern changes in how courts and prisons function. Article 16 questions the process of drug testing in drug courts, and article 17 explores the culture of cruelty found in supermax prisons. Both have been offered in the past decade as answers to two oftentimes intractable problems in criminal justice systems: a growing drug-offender population and difficult prisoner populations. In some cases, these two "remedies" to criminal justice problems have engendered other problems. As we have noted in earlier editions of this book, there are no simple panaceas to criminal justice problems. This is what makes criminal justice administration so challenging and difficult. It is also why processes are so critical to the management and administration of criminal justice organizations.

In Section 4, three new articles highlight the importance of decision making among criminal justice actors. Keith Wilmot and Cassia Spohn (article 19) discuss the issue of prosecutorial discretion, the role of charging, and the number of counts in determining the final sentence for an offender. Rachel Boba and John Crank (article 20) ask us to consider the adoption of problem-oriented policing (POP) as an organizational method of greater control in police departments. Originally targeting frontline officers as the implementers of POP has led to very few departments actually employing it as a police strategy. The efficacy of POP has to be questioned and the determination made as to what the real aims of police organizations are when implementing POP, especially if such innovative practices are directed downward in a police organization and do not include other important elements, levels, and processes within the organization.

In the end, criminal justice processes are about not only decision making but also how we "construct" offenders within the criminal justice system. Alexes Harris (article 23) delves into the social construction of juvenile offenders and the important role that judges play in this process. By focusing on waiver hearings, Harris was able to see how stereotypes, values, and assumptions influence what happens to a juvenile offender in a waiver hearing and how decision making must be understood within the context of an organizational framework. In all criminal justice organizations, the processes institutionalized are attempts by administrators to get a handle on what they do and how they do it. Any proposed change to existing processes is initially resisted and for good cause. Too often the desired change does not occur, and even worse, sometimes change produces unintended and deleterious consequences.

Section 5 features four new articles that examine change in criminal justice organizations. Allison Redlich, Henry Steadman, John Monahan, Pamela Clark Robbins, and John Petrila (article 26) provide a sobering analysis of mental health courts. They posit that very little is known about the growing number of mental health courts in this country. Without this added knowledge, mental health courts may not produce the change we seek in the management of mentally ill offenders. Edmund McGarrell, Steven Chermak, Jeremy Wilson, and Nicholas Corsaro (article 27) examine an innovative strategy to reduce homicide. Known as "lever pulling," this strategy attempts to improve the coordination of police efforts with other social service and correctional agencies to reduce homicide levels. These authors found that the strategy was successful in one city, but they caution its widespread use until we are able to move beyond single-city evaluations. In short, more multicity research is needed before we can say such an approach is effective in the reduction of homicides. Samuel Walker, Geoffrey Alpert, and Dennis Kenney (article 28) explore the topic of early warning systems in police organizations to identify officers with performance problems and develop a more systematic method of holding such officers accountable for their actions where appropriate. The authors discuss the many alternatives to early warning systems and suggest caution and awareness of the complexity of employing such systems within police organizations. Marvin Zalman (article 30) examines a growing problem for criminal justice administrators—wrongful convictions—focusing on the paucity of research available on the topic, and outlining an agenda for criminal justice research on what needs to be done to address this important social policy question.

Characteristics of Criminal Justice Organizations

Trying to address the many needs of both employees and offenders becomes one of the most central challenges faced by criminal justice administrators. Criminal justice administrators, politicians, and citizens often believe certain efforts will yield specific results, only to be thwarted by uncertainties, poor planning, and a host of unanticipated consequences (see Eugene Doleschal, article 24). Nevertheless, the criminal justice system continues to respond to crime, and criminal justice administrators are constantly reacting to the vagaries of their environments. As a police chief once told an editor of this volume, "The crime business is always going to be difficult and frustrating, but it is never boring." It is the ways in which these administrators respond to crime that this book was intended to address. As with earlier editions of the book, the collection of articles in this edition does reflect five specific characteristics, some of which are unique to criminal justice organizations, while others are common to all organizations. The reader is asked to consider these characteristics when reading the articles presented in this edition, which will serve as the foundation for understanding the complexity of criminal justice administration and management.

First, criminal justice organizations serve people. Whether it is a police officer diffusing a domestic violence situation, a parole agent supervising a sex offender, or a prosecutor presenting information to a grand jury, criminal justice administrators and employees work with people. Some of these people are offenders, while others may be concerned citizens or crime victims. The primary consideration for criminal justice administrators is how people are served by their organizations. Since an overwhelming majority of criminal justice agencies are public, they are held to standards of accountability by the citizenry they serve. Moreover, communities hold differing expectations of how criminal justice services will be delivered. A significant issue for criminal justice administrators is how they are *perceived* by their constituents, and fundamentally, this is predicated on both the quantity and quality of service citizens are provided. Social critic Jimmy Breslin is quoted as saying that many current "quality of life" programs initiated by police departments, for example, have inadvertently deteriorated into direct forms of brutality. To paraphrase him, "I want the quality of life to be improved by the police, yet what kind of quality-of-life effort includes torturing and brutalizing citizens?" Altering a negative perception of how people are treated by the criminal justice system is a constant effort for many criminal justice administrators.

A second characteristic of criminal justice organizations is a concern for efficiency and productivity. Efforts to reinvent government are good examples of a movement to increase the productivity of public agencies, and criminal justice organizations are no exception. The most visible component of the criminal justice system in its emphasis on greater efficiency and productivity in its operations is corrections. Private agencies are competing for tax dollars with traditional criminal justice agencies. Prisons are the most direct example. Private companies have entered the correctional domain and, in all likelihood, will be major players in corrections throughout the twenty-first century. Increased usage of private security forces in the police field, the computerization and modernization of court systems, and the growth in mediation centers to handle disputes that were formerly addressed by the criminal justice system are other good examples. Concerns over fiscal integrity, productivity, and efficiency in the private sector are shaping the contours of the criminal justice system in ways that were unheard of one or two decades ago.

Third, criminal justice organizations are also expected to accomplish conflicting and multiple goals. Examples are plentiful in criminal justice organizations: Prisons are expected to rehabilitate offenders while they are primarily structured to be secure facilities, police are expected to control crime while at the same time being sensitive to the rights of suspects, and courts are to guarantee due process rights to defendants while being cognizant of efficiency and case-processing issues in the dispensing of justice. For criminal justice administrators, meeting such multiple and conflicting goals is a challenging and daunting task. In fact, how criminal justice officials confront these challenges is what ultimately defines their character. It has been said that necessity is the mother of invention. This aphorism is true for criminal justice administrators who must come up with innovative ideas and approaches when addressing the many conflicting and multiple goals placed upon them by their communities.

Fourth, criminal justice goals are defined by external constituencies. Citizen groups demanding that something be done with a sexual predator in their community, politicians legislating that parole boards not release certain types of offenders, or business interests wanting more police protection during specific periods are all examples of how external constituents define goals for criminal justice organizations. For criminal justice administrators, many of the requests are not unreasonable. However, they must be understood within the context of finite resources chasing infinite demands. Administrators cannot respond to all requests for services; instead, they either respond to those that are the most "rational" from their perspective or try to share available resources with as many constituent groups as possible, thereby presenting an image that at least something is being done to meet the demands of the community. The result is that some groups win and get what they want from the criminal justice system; others do not. Most, however, get something. Moreover, all constituent groups are not the same. Some have more influence than others, and criminal justice administrators tend to respond accordingly. Gauging the political influence of external constituencies is a central activity of criminal justice administrators.

Finally, criminal justice organizations are composed of competing and conflicting internal constituencies. The level of conflict among the "rank and file" within criminal justice agencies has escalated over the past decade. The conflict is multidimensional. Take, for example, police organizations. The conflict may be split on the following dimensions: age, race, gender, educational level, years of service, and rank, to mention a few. For the twenty-first century police administrator the "troops" will be more diverse, making police administration more problematical and difficult. Similar concerns exist for correctional administrators and court personnel. Managing diverse organizations is becoming one of the most challenging tasks facing criminal justice administration.

The articles in this collection will reiterate these themes and characteristics. By keeping them in mind, readers will broaden their understanding and gain an appreciation for the complexity of criminal justice administration. Section 1 examines the nature of criminal justice organizations, placing them in the context of their structures and purposes. Section 2 stresses the importance of individual adaptation to organizational structure and demands. Section three expands the examination of criminal justice administration and management by looking at group behavior, with a particular emphasis on the interface between formal and informal elements within organizations. Section 4 highlights the importance of criminal justice processes to an understanding of criminal justice administration. The final section of the book, section 5, examines change within criminal justice organizations, noting that many reforms engender unintended consequences for both criminal justice administrators and society.

Acknowledgments

We would like to thank our families and colleagues who have assisted us with this edition of the book. Ilija Stojkovic, Milan Stojkovic, May Beth Klofas, and Carrie Kalinich have been instrumental in keeping the three of us together and producing new editions of the book. In addition, we want to extend our appreciation to valued colleagues, too many to mention here, who have been supportive over the past 25 years in the production of five editions of the book. Their assistance has been more valuable than they may realize. We can never thank them enough for their insight and encouragement over the years.

SECTION 1

THE NATURE OF
CRIMINAL JUSTICE ORGANIZATIONS

Responses to crime dramatically changed during the last decade of the twentieth century and continue to change into the twenty-first century. As a result, criminal justice administrators have to manage a much different criminal justice system. While there are still many functionally similar entities and purposes associated with criminal justice, there have been many changes occurring in how the system is structured and responds to crime.

Malcolm Feeley (article 1) offers a classic presentation of two competing models to understand the criminal justice organization. The differing models—crime control and due process—offer fascinating insights and implications for criminal justice administrators. Each model offers a look at criminal justice from different points of view. Feeley notes how criminal justice organizations must be understood as multidimensional entities. Changing or reforming them will depend upon the way you understand their nature and the way they function.

Leslie Smith's research (article 2) supports the hypothesis that the crime-control model of justice has negatively impacted state criminal justice systems. The implementation of the crime-control model has led to dramatic growth in incarceration of offenders and eliminated traditional offender reintegration systems such as discretionary parole. While effective planning has led to successful offender reentry systems, most states have done little to plan for the consequences of the crime-control model. Smith agrees that planning has been fragmented and that appeals for a unified or integrative method of criminal justice planning across the states presumably anticipates the consequences of the political environment. This will lead to a more unified system that would develop unified system goals.

Kevin Wright (article 3) applies a systemic examination of why goal conflict, while ubiquitous in criminal justice organizations, is actually a good thing. He examines how, out of primary concern for democracy and freedom, the criminal justice system should not be more rational and efficient. By introducing the principle of reflexive diversity, Wright encourages the reader to come to grips with the fact that there is no monolithic and unifying set of values in our society, nor should there be. He sees goal conflict within criminal justice organizations as both endemic and liberating at the same time. It represents both a check on the powers of criminal justice administrators and an opportunity for a diversity of ideas to be expressed within the criminal justice system.

John Klofas (article 4) explores the diversities of communities in his piece on metropolitan development and police organizations. Communities across the country are experiencing unprecedented urban sprawl and growth. Police organizations have not kept up with the changes found among these metropolitan communities. Klofas asks a central question regarding how police are to respond to changes in community organizations. More importantly, he paints a disturbing picture on the differences among police organizations in the "outer ring" of metropolitan communities and those in the inner circle or inner city. His analysis raises questions, not only about the purpose of police organizations but also about their role in the continued growth of metropolitan communities across the country.

Samuel Walker (article 5) proposes that external political factors have had a major impact on the police academy's research agenda. External forces have had a beneficial and enriching impact on police research as scholars were forced to examine important issues that had previously been neglected. For example, concerns about racial profiling generated a number of new issues and research questions about police and police operations regarding race. Conversely, police research has managed to affect the external political environment in that certain programs were found to be lacking in effectiveness when subjected to empirical testing. In some cases conventional wisdom and beliefs were undermined, which in turn created new opportunities for creative thinking for researchers and policy makers.

John Worrall (article 6) examines an unsettling but continuing practice found in law enforcement agencies to supplement, and in some cases augment, their budgets. Faced with dwindling resources, some law enforcement agencies have used the civil forfeiture laws created in the 1990s to meet their budgetary shortfalls. In this engaging piece, Worrall discusses the problems with the use of civil forfeiture laws to supplement and augment police budgets. The analysis underscores a more serious question concerning the usage of market-generated assets in public organizations. For decades, we have viewed criminal justice agencies as "nonmarket" entities; civil forfeiture laws have changed that focus and now enable police administrators to structure financial incentives into their calculations on how police services will be provided and the direction of police efforts. Should this be the case? The answer to this question cuts to the core issue of the nature of criminal justice organizations and how they are administrated and managed.

Two Models of the Criminal Justice System
An Organizational Perspective

MALCOLM M. FEELEY

Despite the scholarly and popular interest in the administration of criminal justice, there are few *theoretical* discussions of the process. Consequently, this article is an attempt to develop an explicit theoretical framework by which the practices in the administration can be depicted and explained. In it I characterize the criminal justice system in terms of the theory of large-scale organizations, and then examine some of the tasks of administration in terms of established concepts and criteria supplied by this perspective. Following Etzioni, by organization I mean "social units devoted primarily to the attainment of specific goals" (1961). In this case the formal task of the criminal justice system is to process arrests, determine guilt or innocence, and in the case of guilt to specify an appropriate sanction. The major actors in the organization include the defendant, prosecutor, defense counsel, judge, arresting officer, court clerk, and to varying degrees, other persons such as witnesses, additional policemen, clerks, parole officers, court psychiatrists and social workers, and the defendants' families and friends. A system of the administration of justice, whether it is adversarial or inquisitorial, entails the key elements of organization: institutionalized interaction of a large number of actors whose roles are highly defined, who are required to follow highly defined rules and who share a responsibility in a common goal—that of processing arrests.[1]

In this discussion, I will outline two models of, or approaches to, organizational analysis and then use them to characterize and evaluate much of the recent systematic research on the administration of criminal justice. Finally, some of the concerns raised by the theories of large-scale organizations generally, but which have been overlooked by students of the administration of justice, will be examined.

Two Models of Organization and a Modification

At the risk of oversimplification, let me suggest that a good portion of the systematic studies of the administration of justice in the United States can be classified into two general models of organization—models which I have adapted from Etzioni's discussion of organizational analysis. They are the *goal model* and the *functional-systems model* (1960). The former, he argues, is an approach which is concerned primarily with "organizational effectiveness," in which the criteria for the assessment of effectiveness is derived from organizational goals (Etzioni, 1960:257). Thus the announced public goals of an organization are usually regarded as the "source for standards by which actors assess the success of their organization" (Etzioni, 1960:257). This approach, its adherents claim, facilitates an "objective" analysis because it does not insert the observer's own values, but takes the "values," i.e., the goals, of the organization as the fixed criteria of judgment. On the other hand, Etzioni (1960:259) identifies what he has termed the functional-systems model of organizational analysis. It is sharply distinguished from the goal model in that:

> The starting point for this approach is not the goal itself, but a working model of a social unit which is capable of achieving a goal. Unlike a goal, or a set of goal activities, it is a model of a multi-functional unit. It is assumed *a priori* that some means have to be devoted to such non-goal functions as service and custodial activities, including means employed for the maintenance of the unit itself. From the viewpoint of the system model, such activities are functional and increase the organizational effectiveness.

The key difference between the models, Etzioni argues, is that the latter approach is more open-ended in its analysis of the function and "needs" of an organization than is the former, and the researcher is likely to be more attentive to a wide range of influencing factors and as a result apt to show a less biased point of view.

In applying this very general typology to a analysis of approaches to the study of the administration of criminal justice, I have made certain adjustments. In particular it seems appropriate to join the *goal model* with Weber's *rational-legal* model of organization, and produce what I call a *rational-goal model* of the criminal justice system. Etzioni has identified the key distinction between these two models. The rational model "differs from the goal model by the types of functions that are included as against those that are neglected. The rational model is concerned almost solely with *means* activities, while the goal model focuses attention on *goal* activities" (Etzioni, 1960: fn. 16, 263). In the administration of criminal justice, however, it is possible to join these two models, because means and goals merge. While on a highly abstract level, the goal—as opposed to the means—of the criminal justice system might be stated in terms of achieving justice, this goal has no clear empirical referent or context by itself. In the dominant tradition of the West at least, the goal, justice, usually acquires meaning in a normative, legal, and empirical context, only when operationalized in terms of procedure, i.e., means.[2] Thus, particularly in the administration of justice, the means become the end, at least in terms of viewing "organizational effectiveness" and "formal goal activities."[3]

The Rational-Goal Model

There is a large body of research focusing primarily upon means or formal goals of the administration of criminal justice. Although there is no consensus or common methodology among the writers adopting this rational-goal approach, their common theme is a primary concern with formal rules. One approach in this style of research is the logical analysis of the interrelationship of the rules of criminal procedure in order to identify and overcome problems of ambiguity, fairness, and discretion. These studies are analogous to the analysis and continuous refinement of formal organizational schema. Another form of research this model uses is the empirical description of practices in the administration of justice, which is then contrasted to the formal rules and goals of the system in an attempt to identify and measure discrepancies between reality and ideal.

This preoccupation with formal goals and rules has as its most eloquent theoretical spokesman Max Weber, who regarded the organization of the administration of justice in the West as the prime example of rational organization. According to Weber, the drift of history in the West has been an ever-increasing reliance upon rational modes of thinking, organization, and authority (1954). In terms of organization this has resulted in a system of depersonalized, rulebound, and hierarchically structured relationships, which produce highly predictable, rationalized, and efficient results. The system of the administration of justice, he argued, is an excellent example of this phenomenon (Weber, 1954:350):

> Above all, bureaucratization offers the optimal possibility for the realization of the principle of division of labor in administration according to purely technical considerations, allocating individual tasks to functionaries who are trained as specialists and who continuously add to their experience by constant practice. "Professional" execution in this case means primarily execution "without regard to person" in accordance with calculable rules. The consistent carrying through of bureaucratic authority produces a leveling of differences in social "honor" or status, and, consequently, unless the principle of freedom in the market is simultaneously restricted, the universal sway of economic "class position." The fact that this result of bureaucratic authority has not always appeared concurrently with bureaucratization is based on the diversity of the possible principles by which political communities have fulfilled their tasks. But

> for modern bureaucracy, the element of "calculability of its rules" has really been of decisive significance. . . . Bureaucracy provides the administration of justice with a foundation for the realization of a conceptually systematized rational body of law on the basis of "laws" as it was achieved for the first time to a high degree of technical perfection in the late Roman Empire.

On the formal level, and from a broad perspective, most legal scholars would tend to concur with this characterization of the administration of justice in the West.[4] However, on a more specific level, does this rational goal model characterize the actual organization of criminal justice? Weber has characterized the major components of all organizations as: (1) a continuous organization of official functions bound by rules; (2) a specific sphere of competence, i.e., a sphere of obligations, in the division of labor to be performed by a person who is provided with the necessary means and authority to carry out his tasks; (3) the organization of offices following the principle of hierarchy; and (4) a set of technical rules and norms regulating the conduct of the offices (Etzioni, 1964:43).

These conditions applied to the organization of the administration of criminal justice imply an elaborate apparatus which processes arrests according to highly defined rules and procedures undertaken by "experts" who perform the functions ascribed to them by highly defined formal roles, under a rigorous division of labor, and who are subject to scrutiny in a systematic and hierarchical pattern. This model seems to be the dominant view or ideal of the criminal justice process held by appellate judges and lawyers, and many of the academic students of the courts. Much of their discussion and research, therefore, has centered on the problems with the formal rules of operation, i.e., increasing the "rationality" by minimizing discretion and arbitrary administration, through specifying with increasing precision the roles of the actors. Lawyers under the auspices of the American Bar Association go to great lengths to articulate and refine the precise role of the advocate in criminal justice; many appellate court decisions are attempts at further defining and refining the rules and roles for the various actors in the organization; law journals and appellate court opinions are filled with discussions of the proposals for rules to minimize discretion and more completely define the rules of procedure; and social scientists continue to point out that no one is following the formal rules.

One form of planning by utilizers of the rational-goal model is to examine and explicate the operative rules to determine whether or not they are internally consistent. Abraham Goldstein's discussion of the rules of criminal procedure is an excellent example of this type of analysis (1960). He attempts to show by logical analysis and example that certain alterations of the rules of criminal procedure have the effect of undercutting other, more generalized and basic rules and norms of "equality" among the parties. Since the system is conceived of as a meticulous application of highly defined and prescribed rules, Goldstein can convincingly argue this point, that certain alterations in procedure undercut the power of the defense and thereby weaken or destroy the more fundamental rule of "balanced advantage" between the adversaries. An analogy is that the equilibrium or balance of power in a game of chess is disturbed if a new rule permits White additional moves that are not granted to Black.

The rational-goal approach has not, however, concerned itself entirely with speculative and logical analysis of the rules and norms of the system; it has an empirical component as well. As Etzioni has noted, one of the major objects of the empirical studies adopting a goal model approach is to measure organizational "effectiveness" by contrasting observed, actual behavior with the stated, formal goals of the organization, and a good deal of social science research has followed this pattern.

Lefstein, Stapleton, and Teitelbaum's study of juvenile court judges' compliance to the *Gault* decisions is one example of this research (1969). Their basic format was to outline the requirements and implications of the *Gault* and related decisions, and then identify the extent to which the actual practices of judges in various jurisdictions and types of cases conformed to them. While they have demonstrated quite convincingly that the *Gault* decision had a major impact on the administration of juvenile justice, their optimism regarding the eventual full compliance to the standards of that decision seems somewhat unwarranted when one considers the practices of the actors in the administration of justice generally. What is not found in this study is an examination of the variety of factors, goals, and incentives operative (and likely to remain so) for the various individual actors in the system. A skeptical social scientist might well ask of a lower court judge, "So the Supreme Court handed down a decision, why should it affect you?" A full analysis of the dynamics of compliance and a theory of organization effectiveness would have to address itself to this question which assumes that the Supreme Court decision is just one of a number of factors affecting the system.

Likewise some of the studies reporting the impact of the *Miranda* decision on police behavior follow a similar format (Wald, et al., 1966–67, and Medalie, et al., 1968). The requirements specified in the decision are regarded as the formal goals and then actual behavior is observed and contrasted with them. The studies report different levels of compliance and acceptance on the part of the police, but generally note a low level of effectiveness. Various factors are raised and suggested as possible bases for this less than complete compliance. The "newness" of the decision is one such mentioned factor. Another is the generally hostile attitude of the police toward the new requirements. These factors, however, are not examined systematically, nor are they—and others—incorporated into a dynamic model of organization which considers the multiplicity of goals and incentives operating simultaneously within the system.

My criticism of these types of empirical studies echoes Etzioni's criticism of the goal model approach in general. The preoccupation with a set of formal goals and the observation of behavior primarily in terms of how it squares with these goals (or how the rules have altered previous patterns of behavior) is not conducive to theory building and the explanation of the observed patterns of behavior. It tends to produce a *unidimensional* picture of the process by placing undue emphasis on one set of goals and rules without adequately considering other factors which are, perhaps, equally as important in shaping the behavior of the actors in the system. The shortcomings of this approach will become more evident as the functional-systems model is explicated and examples of it are discussed.

Functional Systems Approaches

Turning to the second model, the functional-systems model, a substantially different conception of organization is employed. A different set of practices tends to be focused on, and there is a far greater and explicit concern for "explaining" the behavior of the actors (as opposed to simply "contrasting" it). Etzioni has lumped together a wide variety of studies under the rubric of systems models, and here too, there is a wide variation in the approaches to the analysis of criminal justice which I have placed in this category. There are, however, a number of common and distinguishing characteristics and assumptions which are shared by most of them. They all tend to view the organization of the administration of criminal justice as a system of action based primarily upon *cooperation*, *exchange*, and *adaptation*, and emphasize these considerations over adherence to formal rules and defined "roles" in searching for and developing explanations of behavior and discussing organizational effectiveness. Rather than being the primary focus of attention, formal "rules" and "disinterested professionalism" are viewed as only one set of the many factors shaping and controlling individuals' decisions, and perhaps not the most important ones. The efficacious "rules" followed by the actors are not necessarily the ideal, professional rules; and the goals they pursue are not necessarily the formal "organizational" goals posited by the researcher or even the "public" goals posited by the leaders of the organization.

Rather the "rules" the organization members are likely to follow are the "folkways" or informal "rules of the game" within the organization; the goals they pursue are likely to be personal or sub-group goals; and the roles they assume are likely to be defined by the functional adaptation of these two factors. These three features of the organization then are the objects to be accounted for, and the functional-systems approach is likely to begin to identify and examine the adaptation of the actors to the environment, the workload and the interests of the persons placed within the system, i.e., other goals of the actors within the organization.

The idealized perspective of the *rational organization* pursuing its single set of goals is replaced by a perspective of the set of *rational individuals* who comprise the system, in this case the prosecutor, defense counsel, police, defendant, clerks, etc. pursuing their various individual goals. Unlike the rational-goal model, this model explicitly recognizes the "normality" of, and emphasizes the reality of, conflict between formal organizational goals, and the goals of the individual actors within the organization. According to this model, the "authority" of legal rules and "professionalism" is not automatically assumed to be efficacious. A more complete system of incentives is required.

In order to account for the actual behavior and practices of the organization, the scholars who to varying degrees utilize this functional-systems model of organization, describe the actual process and then begin to identify and examine the causes and conditions of the patterns of behavior of the various actors. In doing this they focus on the working conditions, the system of controls, incentives, and sanctions at the disposal of the various actors, and the larger environmental effects on the system. However, beyond these very general sets of concerns, there is little in common among the scholars who use this functional systems approach of criminal justice administration.

As with the rational-goal model, analysts utilizing a functional-systems model also tend to be motivated by normative concerns, but they are more likely to move beyond the contrasting of ideal goals with actual practices, to search for and identify the factors contributing to the observed practices. While perhaps personally accepting one set of goals for the system and giving expression to their own values, the functional systems approach is at least open enough to allow for and acknowledge the existence of other goals and not accept as "normal" the perfect coincidence of formal organizational goals with the goals of the individual actors within the system. Thus the perspective not only lends itself to accurate description of actual behavior but also begins to attempt to identify and account for the causes and conditions leading to this behavior.

Herbert Packer's . . . book, *The Limits of the Criminal Sanction* (1968), dramatically illustrates one of the major points of the functional-systems analysts. There can be many "goals" operating simultaneously—and at odds with each other—within any single system of organization, so that even to speak of "the formal goals" of an organization is likely to be misleading. He convincingly argues that there are at least two major sets of distinctly antagonistic values (the "due process" model and the "crime control" model) held by different actors responsible for administering criminal justice. One set emphasizes "due process," strict adherence to legal rules, and a full-fledged adversary relationship; the other emphasizes effective "crime control" for the community, and tends to minimize the concern for formality and individual rights. One's assessment of the "effectiveness" in achieving the "system's goals" would obviously depend upon which of the two sets of goals or models of values he subscribes to. Clearly any analysis of organizational behavior must be open-ended enough to identify and deal with the multiplicity of goals, values, and incentives of the various actors comprising the system. To do otherwise is likely to lead into the trap of reification and away from social theory.

Another body of research using a type of functional-systems approach tends to rely on an exchange model, adapted in varying degrees from Peter Blau's theoretical perspective (1964). The works of Jerome Skolnick (1966),

Herbert Packer (1968), Abraham Blumberg (1967), and George Cole (1970) all tend to utilize this framework. The most widely-read work by any of these scholars is Skolnick's *Justice Without Trial*. While it is primarily an analysis of the functioning of the police in the realm of law enforcement, it does touch on police-prosecutor-court relationships, and characterizes them as participating in an elaborate exchange and bargaining system. However, in a related study, he focuses directly on the administration of criminal justice, and in particular on the roles, behavior, and relationships of the public defender and the prosecuting attorney (1967). For purposes of analysis he has suggested that all institutions are based either on norms of cooperation or norms of conflict, and that a major task of the social analyst is to identify and analyze means for countering these norms. That is, in an organization such as the family or corporation, a major concern is maintenance of cooperation and procedures for cooperation, and in other organizations, such as the sporting event or the adversary system, a major concern is maintenance of the institutionalized conflict and procedures for conflict. In both sets of institutions, Skolnick argues, the social analyst is interested in identifying the "deviation" from these norms of cooperation or conflict and the conditions and principles accounting for such deviation (Skolnick, 1967:53). Thus his analysis focuses on the institutionalized and structural pressures to reduce the conflict between prosecutor and defense attorney, on the resulting functional adjustments, and also on the normative justifications that support these new practices which seem to violate the *formal* norms of conflict.

Skolnick (1967:53) identifies the main pressures for "deviant" cooperation in this system as *administrative concerns* of each of the sets of actors (e.g., the defense attorney wants to get the best deal for his client and also handle it in the most expeditious manner; the district attorney has many publics to satisfy, an enormous amount of work, and opportunity for a great amount of discretion in selecting cases and charges to develop). As a result, a strong tendency toward cooperation develops in the relationship that is theoretically portrayed as a zerosum game. Strong informal norms to enhance the smooth functioning of the system itself replace the norms of conflict and adversarial relationship (Skolnick, 1967:55). Thus, the main cause for the "deviation" from the conflict norms Skolnick identifies as administrative *convenience*, brought about through an elaborate exchange system of mutually advantageous benefits. Additionally, he notes that the prosecuting and defense attorneys (almost always young, inexperienced and idealistic lawyers) are usually "successfully" socialized into this through an elaborate system of informal controls, or are transferred out.

The main device in which all parties share an interest of administrative convenience is in settlement by a plea of guilty. This serves the administrative purposes of saving time, effort, and—the actors all usually emphasize—in "getting a better deal" for the accused. It also has the effect of replacing the adversary system's norm of "presumption of innocence" with a norm of "presumption of guilt." Skolnick, however, argues in regard to this point that cooperation does "not demonstrably impede the quality of representation," a phrase which is unfortunately quite vague.[5] The operating norms—which rationalize this "deviant" behavior—at least from the public's or layman's perspective—are those of "administrative efficiency" and the "interests" of the accused in securing a reduced sentence.

Similar themes are taken up by other writers, who supply additional evidence to support a functional-systems model of the administration of criminal justice. Cole, in an analysis of the defense counsel/prosecutor relationships in Seattle, describes a similar system of mutually advantageous exchanges which function to displace conflict with cooperation, and produce a smooth-running system which seeks to maximize the administrative and personal goals of the individual actors rather than the formal organizational goals of due process. Stefan Kapsch (1971), in an interesting analysis which characterizes the plea bargaining by prosecution and defense as a mixed-strategy game—rather than the zero-sum game of adversary theory—emphasizes the administrative goals (the reduction of decision-making costs) being served by this substitution of cooperation for conflict, and also goes one to develop an explicit justification for the practice.[6]

Another well-known study of the administration of justice—and virtually the only recent full-length sociological analysis of the operations of a criminal court—is Blumberg's book on the New York City criminal justice system (1967). Despite his strong adherence to the principles enunciated in the "formal organizational goals" and particularly full-fledged adversary proceedings, Blumberg undertakes a functional analysis attempting to identify *causes and conditions* leading to the actual practices. He does this by conceptualizing the organization (the court, as he terms it) as an elaborate system of exchanges by persons who can mutually benefit by cooperating. In a highly decentralized and complex organization, his model assumes that each of the actors will pursue more immediate goals and interests, and hence either the personal interests of the individual actor or the goals of and pressures for "production" and "efficiency" from his immediate supervisors and peer group will determine his actions. Thus, for example, the prosecutor's office wants high "batting averages," the defense counsel wants to handle cases as quickly as possible either for financial reasons or, in the case of the public defender, for administrative efficiency, and judges are constantly pressed to clear their calendars.

Blumberg identifies two main factors leading to the "displacement" of the formal, organizational goals by this system of mutual adjustment and exchange (1967).

> Intolerably large case loads of defendants which must be disposed of in an organizational context of limited resources and personnel. . . . As a consequence an almost irreconcilable conflict is posed in terms of intense pressures to process large numbers of cases on the one hand, and the stringent ideological and legal requirements of "due process" of law on the other hand. A rather tenuous resolution of the dilemma has emerged in the shape of a large variety of bureaucratically ordained and controlled "work

crimes" short cuts, deviations and outright rule violations adopted as court practices in order to meet production norms. (Blumberg, 1967a:22)

Thus he has identified the press of large case loads and the strains on the actors as perhaps the chief reason for the systematic violations and/or tendencies to deviate from the prevailing ideological rules and norms of the adversary system. This makes it literally impossible for the actors to perform their prescribed roles, even if they wanted to. While it is no doubt accurate to identify a crushing case load as one of the factors necessitating functional adjustments and violations of the due process norms, the implication of Blumberg's argument seems to be that, in the absence of heavy case loads, the actors would "naturally" tend to perform their "proper" adversarial roles as defined by the full-fledged fight theory of the adversary system, and as outlined in some of the rational-goal models of the process.

This position is in at least partial conflict with Skolnick's and Cole's analyses of the conditions for cooperation (as opposed to institutionalized adversarial conflict), which emphasize the structural factors of long-term interaction, acquaintanceships, and a variety of personal and administrative factors (including handling of heavy case loads) as the primary factors contributing to a system of cooperation and exchange. Also, there is some evidence to indicate that rapid processing of defendants (and presumably "corner-cutting" by the actors in the system) occurs in situations where the work-load of the court is not pressing (Mileski, 1971). Thus I suspect that Blumberg has somewhat overstated the importance of heavy case loads, and perhaps as well, over-inflated the efficacy of "professional norms" of lawyers, norms which he feels most criminal lawyers have been "forced" to abandon for the purposes of court-dictated expediency.

Blumberg is also interested in the defense counsel, whom he argues is ideally supposed to assume a highly defined "professional" role as advocate and champion of his client, but in fact is usually found—like the prosecutor, judge and other court personnel—to respond to more direct and immediate incentives than those of "professional duty" (Blumberg, 1967a:28).

> The strong incentive of possible fee motivates the lawyer to promote litigation which would otherwise never have developed. However, the criminal lawyer develops a vested interest of an entirely different nature in his client's case: to limit its scope and duration rather than to battle. Only in this way can a case be profitable. . . . In effect, in his role as double agent, the criminal lawyer performs an extremely vital and delicate mission for the court organization and the accused. Both principals are anxious to terminate the litigation with a minimum of expense and damage to each other.

This argument appears reasonable, and Skolnick's reports tend to corroborate it to some extent. However, one still wishes here that Blumberg had been more careful and systematic in collecting and evaluating his data and presenting his arguments on the incentives of defense counsel. His discussions of the two factors which undercut the full-fledged adversary role of the defense counsel, the heavy case load and the financial incentive to quick disposition of cases, tend to contradict each other. On one hand, he argues, the court, in an attempt to cope with the heavy case load, has "co-opted" the defense counsel and "forced" him into acting the part of a "confidence agent" in convincing his client to plead guilty. On the other hand, the discussion of the financial incentives indicates that regardless of the judge's and prosecutor's interests, it is still in the self-interest of the defense counsel to seek a quick termination of the case through a plea of guilty since he is usually paid a flat fee for representation. Consequently, the less time a case takes, the higher the volume of his income. If the financial incentive is an important one, then one would expect the defense counsel to willingly press for pleas of guilty regardless of case load before the court. Furthermore, it is not unreasonable to expect that up to a point, as case load diminishes, the defense counsel's desires for quick and cursory disposition of cases would tend to increase. If business is slackening, then one must hustle even more to maintain volume. Systematically gathered and presented evidence would go a long way toward resolving these rival plausible hypotheses and unsupported assertions. Still, on the whole, one is given the distinct impression from the works of Blumberg, Skolnick, and Cole that the defense counsel is not so much an unwittingly co-opted agent used by the self-serving court bureaucracy, as he is one of the key figures in an elaborate system in which everyone, including himself, has certain commodities to exchange in the pursuit of his own interests.

There is still another set of factors which has been identified and examined by many of the scholars adopting the functional-systems approach. This is the enormous amount of discretion possessed by most of the actors in the criminal justice system, and in particular, the police and prosecutor. Most analysts subscribing to the rational-goal model of the system make little mention of this, tending to emphasize the rational administration according to specified rules and assume that it is an "attainable goal." Likewise many "reformers" and advocates of increased "professionalism" (i.e., rule-following) avoid dealing squarely with the problem posed by discretion. Among those scholars who have focused on this problem, Joseph Goldstein (1969), Packer (1968), and Skolnick (1967) are the most prominent. What they have all noted is that the administrators of justice have tremendous leeway in defining a situation, a vast array of competing rules in their arsenal, and are placed in a situation where it is frequently physically impractical (if not literally impossible) to enforce or administer all, or perhaps even most, of the rules all of the time.

This problem of discretion has two main components: first is the problem of the sheer magnitude of substantive laws and procedural rules; second is the inherent ambiguity of rules. A moment's reflection tells us that it is physically impossible and undesirable in anything approaching a democratic society to attempt to enforce all rules—both substantive criminal law and due process norms in the administration of justice—all the time. There are simply too many rules, and it would require a police state, a totalitarian bureaucracy, and a highly costly apparatus to begin even to approach total enforcement. Therefore, given the virtual impossibility of faithful adherence to and enforcement of all the rules, there is considerable room for discretion in the enforcement and administration of the rules. Discretion in such circumstances is inevitable, and because of the low visibility of most of the criminal activities and administration, it falls primarily on the hands of the police and prosecutors, and is not subject to much public attention and continuous supervision.

The second component of discretion—the ambiguity of rules and the subsequent leeway in defining an action—is more complex and perhaps more philosophically intriguing. For instance, if a person is arrested for burglary, he could also be charged with intent to commit burglary, illegal possession of burglary tools, illegal entry, possession of stolen property, and numerous other criminal violations. In short, a single action can be defined and interpreted in a number of ways. The ambiguity of "facts," of course, further complicates the picture and enhances discretionary practices. The process of selecting which "facts" to consider and which "rule" to apply to define the activity is in itself a discretionary matter of considerable importance. The variety of available "legal" alternatives allows the actor a wide latitude for discretion, and of course a very valuable commodity to bargain with in the system of exchange. In this view the interpretation and use of the rules themselves are viewed as instruments of rationalization, not application. That is, the rules are selected and used as weapons or supports at the whim of, and in the particular interests of, the various actors in the system. Thus ambiguity and discretion are inherent to the very nature of all elaborate systems of rules, and "force" enforcement and administrative officials—the so-called rule "appliers"—into a position of making "lawless" decisions. This poses a major problem in the administration of justice, as Herbert Packer (1968:290) has noted:

> The basic trouble with discretion is simply that it is lawless, in the literal sense of that term. If police or prosecutors find themselves free (or compelled) to pick and choose among known or knowable instances of criminal conduct, they are making a judgment which in a society based on law should be made only by those to whom the making of law is entrusted.

To the extent that this in fact is the case—for the reasons just outlined—a faithful adherence to rational-goal model of the criminal justice system is *impossible* in practice and in principle.

Considerations for Reform

While analysts using the rational-goal model have tended to emphasize the set of formal goals, ideals, and rules which they suggest should be operating in the administration of justice, and have examined the consequences of non-performance of these goals in terms of the normative ideals and consequences to individual rights, they have frequently ignored the factors and conditions contributing to the displacement, violation, and non-performance of these goals, ideals and rules.[7] On the other hand, the functional-systems approach has gone a long way toward identifying the causes and conditions accounting for the observed behavior, and toward demonstrating that there is no particular reason to expect individuals' behavior to coincide with the behavior prescribed by the formal goals of the system. Formal rules and norms obviously affect and guide the behavior of the actors, but they are only one set of considerations among several.

It is therefore unreasonable to expect a perfectly "effective" system for administering criminal justice. This, of course, does not preclude the adoption of policies and practices which incrementally increase the system's "effectiveness." Additional rules of clarification and procedure, reducing the reliance on the criminal sanction, more and better trained personnel, more space, and improved calendars, are all frequently mentioned as measures of reform, and there is little question that their adoption would result in improvement. However, running through such proposals is the assumption that if these steps were taken, the actors in the system would somehow *naturally* begin to assume stronger commitments to the formal goals and rules of the system and act accordingly. This tends to underestimate, I think, the very real and strong individual and subgroup incentives, goals, and values, and underestimates as well the saliency of the "crime control model" as the operative normative ideal among many persons involved in the system. Clearly it is more than a problem of overcoming work-load so that good men can do good work. There exist strong competing norms and incentives which act at cross-purposes to the system's formal goals and norms. The task of institutionalized reform rests squarely on the generation of mechanisms which strengthen the position of the organizational goals and norms vis-à-vis the competing subgroup and individual goals.

At this point it is particularly useful to return to the concerns of the theorists of large-scale organizations, and begin to consider some of the structural features of the system, particularly the compliance-inducing mechanisms. What emerges from the analysis of the operations of the criminal justice system is a clear picture of an organization which has highly specified rules and goals, but has virtually no instruments by which to enforce them. Rather than the highly rationalized rulebound and bureaucratically structured system that Weber depicted the process to be, one finds a highly decentralized and decidedly non-hierarchial system of exchange, in which there are virtually no instruments to supervise practices and secure compliance to the formal goals of the organization. In the absence of such efficacious compliance securing mechanisms, institutionalized long-term reform is unlikely.

Only two mechanisms are institutionalized to induce actors to comply with the formal rules and goals of the criminal justice system—normative inducements accruing from *professionalism* and the *appellate procedure*—and neither is very effective in relation to the countervailing incentives.

Appeal to the normative considerations of professionalism is a key source of control in many organizations composed of highly trained and skilled personnel, and in many instances is a highly successful instrument. Certainly the guild-like pride and clannishness of the legal professional generally and bar associations in particular act as a powerful influence on lawyers. Legal training is marked with a continuing emphasis on the professional responsibilities of the lawyer and one might expect all these factors to act as a substantial "professionalizing" influence on the actors in the criminal justice system. However, a great many students of professional organizations have noted that the importance of professional norms—in the absence of direct supervision and other formal means of control—are not as powerful as they are popularly believed to be.

This downward revised assessment would particularly seem to be the case in the administration of criminal justice. There is little disagreement among knowledgeable observers that the criminal lawyer—including the office of prosecutor, defense lawyer, and not infrequently the criminal court judge as well—holds the status of anchor-man within the legal profession. This certainly acts to reduce the importance of the norm of "professionalism" as a compliance-inducing mechanism. Likewise, the low visibility of the administration of criminal justice and the generally "low" status of its clients tends to further erode the "professional" environment and leads to a lack of concern on the part of the more prestigious legal professional organizations and the public generally, further undercutting one of the major sources of inducement to professionalism.

The other mechanism—the only formal one—institutionalized to induce compliance to formal organizational norms on the part of the actors within it, is the appellate process, and the continuing opportunity for appeal. This, however, is a highly ineffectual instrument in that it is relatively passive, extremely expensive, can be instituted only at the insistence of a convicted defendant, and usually only if it is pressed by his defense counsel. At best it is a passive instrument, which might function to curb some of the most flagrant violations of administration, but is hardly a powerful and systematic instrument of control in most instances.

In short, what one finds in the system of criminal justice is a highly formalized and defined set of rules, norms, and goals, but also an organization which possesses no corresponding set of incentives and sanctions which act to systematically enforce them. Any far-reaching discussion of reform and proposals for change in the administration within the American system of criminal justice would have to deal with this problem of the nature and distribution of compliance-including mechanisms.[8] Ironically, it seems to lead to a solution requiring more bureaucracy, not less.

Endnotes

[1] I have been criticized on this point by some persons who argue that the American adversary system cannot be considered an "organization," and in fact is designed explicitly to avoid "organizational" and "bureaucratic" processing of cases on a routine basis. The argument is that the adversary system protects individual rights by institutionalizing the lack of an organization to "process" cases, in contrast to (to varying degrees) many of the countries relying on inquisitorial methods. While there are certainly differences between European and American

practices in the administration of criminal justice, I think that these differences are easily contained within an organizational framework. One system may be more centralized and hierarchically organized than another, but in all cases there is a group of institutionalized interacting roles which in principle are expected to work together (whether through conflict or cooperation) toward a common set of goals.

[2] Herbert Packer (1968) makes a similar point in his discussion of the two models of criminal justice, the "due process" model and the "crime control" model. He suggests that among academic lawyers, the former tends to be regarded as the "goals" of the system. Likewise John Rawls has made a similar point (1958).

[3] No doubt one of the major reasons for concentrating almost exclusively on "means"—aside from their connection with the concept of justice—in analyzing the activities of the criminal justice system is that there is no way of measuring effectiveness in terms of deciding guilt or innocence, another activity which might reasonably be identified as the "goal" of the organization. That is, if one posed this as the goal of the organization, there would be no reliable measure which would allow him to contrast the "ideal" with the actual in that there is no way of always knowing *factual* guilt or innocence.

[4] This position, on a general level, reflects Maine's (1963) celebrated observation that the "movement of the progressive societies has hitherto been a movement from Status to Contract." Likewise similar division of labor and specialization of the administration of justice has been demonstrated systematically in the work of Schwartz and Miller (1964) and Schwartz (1954). On the other hand, many scholars question the extent to which all this has in fact taken place. The legal realists have rather successfully demonstrated the ambiguity of legal rules and the flexibility of rule-application (Llewellyn, 1964). Likewise the judicial behaviorists have rather convincingly demonstrated a relationship between judicial backgrounds and judicial behavior (see Schubert, 1965, and Nagel, 1970). Also, Friedman (1966) has challenged and at least modified Weber's arguments regarding the nature of "rational" legal reasoning, and along with Joseph Goldstein (1969) and others has shown the increasing utilization of discretionary, non-rule specified powers within the "modern" law. Kadi-like justice seems not to have disappeared either in theory or in fact.

[5] At any rate, this argument should have been dwelt on in more depth. He offers no real evidence for it, nor does he attempt to operationalize "quality of representation," and it remains an undemonstrated assertion. It is, I think, an example of the conservative bias, i.e., the acceptance of the *status quo* once one "understands" it, which if not inherent in the logic of functional analysis generally is certainly reflected in a good deal of functionalist literature.

[6] I think that his is a tortured reading of the traditional theory of the adversary system and the administration of justice, but nevertheless it is one of the few thoughtful discussions of the practices—one that moves away from implicit normative support of the practices, and begins to offer an explicit justification of them.

[7] This language assumes that if there is widespread consensus that these are, in fact, the actual goals of the organization, and that they once were—or could have been—achieved. Packer's persuasive analysis of the two models of criminal justice points up the existence of a multiplicity of goals within the organization, and shows that they frequently lead to cross purposes.

[8] For an elaboration of the problem of individual incentives and compliance inducing mechanisms, see my discussion of law as a "public good," and the subsequent problem for an explanation of individual incentives and compliance (Feeley, 1970). For a general exposition of the problem of incentives and compliance to organizational goals by "rational actors," see Downs (1967).

References

Blau, P. (1964). *Exchange and power in social life*. New York: John Wiley.

Blumberg, A. (1967). *Criminal justice*. Chicago: Quadrangle Books. (1967a). The practice of law as a confidence game. *Law and Society Review, 1*, 15–29.

Cole, G. (1970). The decision to prosecute. *Law and Society Review, 4*, 331–345.

Downs, A. (1967). *Inside bureaucracy*. Boston: Little Brown.

Etzioni, A. (1960). Two approaches to organizational analysis: A critique and a suggestion. *Administrative Science Quarterly, 5,* 257–278.

Etzioni, A. (1961). *A comparative analysis of complex organizations.* New York: Free Press.

Etzioni, A. (1964). *Modern organization.* Englewood Cliffs: Prentice-Hall.

Feeley, M. (1970). Coercion and compliance. *Law and Society Review, 4,* 505–519.

Friedman, L. (1966). On legalistic reasoning—a footnote to Weber. *1966 Wisconsin Law Review,* 148–171.

Goldstein, A. S. (1960). The state and the accused: Balance of advantage in criminal procedure. *Yale Law Journal, 69,* 1149–1199.

Goldstein, J. (1969). Police discretion not to invoke the criminal process: Low visibility decisions in the administration of justice. *Yale Law Journal, 69,* 543–594.

Kapsch, S. (1971). *The adversary system and the assistance of counsel.* Unpublished Ph.D. Thesis, Department of Political Science, University of Minnesota.

Klonoski, J., & Mendelsohn, R. (Eds.). (1970). *The politics of legal justice.* Boston: Little Brown.

Lefstein, N., Stapleton, V., & Teitelbaum, L. (1969). In search of juvenile justice. *Law and Society Review, 5,* 491–563.

Llewellyn, K. (1960). *The common law tradition.* Boston: Little Brown.

Maine, H. (1963). *Ancient law.* Boston: Beacon Press.

Medalie, R. J., et al. (1968). Custodial police interrogation in our nation's capital: The attempt to implement *Miranda. Michigan Law Review, 66,* 1347–1422.

Mileski, M. (1971). Courtroom encounters. *Law and Society Review, 5,* 473–538.

Nagel, S. (1970). *The judicial process from a behavioral perspective.* Chicago: Dorsey.

Packer, H. (1968). *The limits of the criminal sanction.* Stanford: Stanford University Press.

Rawls, J. (1958). Justice as fairness. *Philosophical Review, 67,* 164–197.

Schubert, G. (1965). *The judicial mind.* Evanston: Northwestern University Press.

Skolnick, J. (1966). *Justice without trial.* New York: John Wiley.

Skolnick, J. (1967). Social control in the adversary system. *Journal of Conflict Resolution, 11,* 52–67.

Schwartz, R. D. (1954). Social factors in the development of legal control. *Yale Law Journal, 63,* 471–491.

Schwartz, R. D., & Miller, J. (1964). Legal evolution and societal complexity. *American Journal of Sociology, 70,* 159–169.

Wald, M. S., et al. (1966). Interrogations in New Haven: The impact of *Miranda. Yale Law Journal, 76,* 1521–1648.

Weber, M. (1954). Rational and irrational administration of justice. In M. Rheinstein (Ed.), *Max Weber on Law in Economy and Society.* Cambridge: Harvard University Press.

2

The Organizational Environment and Its Influence on State Criminal Justice Systems within the United States and the Offender Re-Integration Process

LESLIE J. SMITH

The 1990s were a decade of dramatic growth in the United States' incarceration population. In 1990, there were 1.1 million US citizens incarcerated in federal, state and local facilities but by the year end 2000 that number increased to 2,071,686 (Beck and Paige, 2001). The Bureau of Justice Statistics reports that the rate of incarceration increased from 292 inmates per 100,000 US residents in 1990 to 478 at year-end 2000. Of these incarcerated offenders 90 to 95 percent will eventually be released and nearly 600,000 of these offenders will return to our communities each year (Petersilia, 2000), by comparison, fewer than 170,000 were released in 1980 (US Department of Justice, 2000). Approximately 20 percent of these offenders will be released from prison *without* a comprehensive plan addressing post-release supervision and will receive no services (Petersilia, 2000). This increase in the movement from prison to the community comes at a time when traditional systemic mechanisms for managing re-entry have deteriorated due to decisions that

Leslie J. Smith, *Criminal Justice Studies*, Vol. 16(2), pp. 97–112, © 2003 by Taylor & Francis. Reprinted by permission of Taylor & Francis.

have led to the abolition of discretionary parole and parole boards that over-see the processes of re-integration (US Department of Justice, 2000). There-fore, it can be argued that the re-integration of these prison-hardened offenders to the community and in such large numbers poses unprecedented challenges to all aspects of the criminal justice system and the community.

Effective planning is crucial when trying to identify strategies that can address the offender re-integration process. During the last decade, there has been an emphasis on incarceration with a political mandate to "get tough on crime" as opposed to using alternative sanctions. This effort has failed to offer a comprehensive and organized approach for effective transitional services. Initiatives such as adjudication partnerships, considered important when developing comprehensive and effective responses to complex problems such as re-integration and recidivism, are slowly developing. Programs of this type actively seek representatives from each criminal justice system agency to join together in multiagency task forces, steering committees or planning groups to identify problems, develop goals and strategies for addressing the problems and to oversee implementation plans to manage or solve the problems (US Department of Justice, 1999). The literature suggests that justice partnerships of this type can address specific problems within the criminal justice system such as offender re-integration more efficiently and will minimize the impact of the changes that occur in the organizational environment, such as legal and political influences. The literature also suggests that as a result of these planning groups, overall improvements can be seen in the systemic relation-ship between each agency in the criminal justice system: the police, prosecu-tion, courts and corrections, thus, improving *system outcomes.*

Effective criminal justice planning has also led to the development of inno-vative and successful programs that address re-integration through restorative justice and re-entry models. Restorative justice involves returning to the ancient view that redefines crime more as an injury to the victim and commu-nity than as an injury to the government. It views the criminal justice process more comprehensively by including the victim, the offender and the community in its processes in a "community building" process (Bazemore, 1995). The com-munity is a responsible partner in the offender re-integration process and is actively involved in planning the restoration process as opposed to being a pas-sive participant. To further enhance this comprehensive approach, re-entry court models have been introduced with the role of re-entry management assigned to the sentencing judge, whose duties would be expanded to create a "re-entry court." At the time of sentencing, the judge would also convene meet-ings with the stakeholders who would be responsible for the offender's re-entry.

The US Department of Justice has also introduced a more comprehen-sive approach to criminal justice planning through a guide entitled *Guidelines for Developing a Criminal Justice Coordinating Committee* (January, 2002) which delineates the advantages of criminal justice planning partnerships and how they result in a better understanding of crime and criminal justice problems, greater communication and cooperation among agencies and units of local government, improved analysis of problems, clearer objectives and priorities, more effective resource allocation, and improved programs, services and personnel. It was further indicated that these results could, in turn, increase public confidence and support for the criminal justice processes, enhancing *system performance.*

In a study released by the US Department of Justice in June 2002, entitled *Recidivism of Prisoners Released in 1994*, it was found that of the nearly 300,000 prisoners released in 15 States in 1994, 67 percent were re-arrested within three years. A study of 1983 releases estimated that 62 percent were rearrested. Based on this data it can be argued that US criminal justice systems continue to perform at unacceptable levels and that improved planning is essential to assist in bettering system performance. This study reviews the current state of academic literature as it pertains to the organization's environmental influence, the primarily legal and political influences, on US criminal justice systems resulting in systemic fragmentation and poor performance, it qualifies that most state criminal justice experts support this premise and that improved planning efforts will result in strategies that can prompt the system to perform more efficiently resulting in improvements in the offender reintegration process.

The Organizational Environment

A system's organizational environment is described as any external phenomenon, event, group or individual which is composed of technological, legal, political, economic, demographic, ecological and cultural forces (Kolfas *et al.*, 1990). Kolfas and colleagues (1990) affirmed that as environmental conditions change, demands for service, legal resources and positions on policy and programs of both public and private organizations may change (p. 19). They further explained that adapting to these new demands, constraints and pressures may alter the mission or policy of the organization (p. 19). For example, increasing the number of arrests as a result of an increase in crime and public pressure will impact on the criminal justice system. The populations of jails will increase and court dockets and caseloads of prosecuting attorneys will expand (p. 29). Another good example of how the organization's environment (for example, the political climate) can affect the organization is through direct pressures from constituents and clients and indirectly through governmental action (p. 25). The government's response to political conditions can be passed on to the organization and other agencies within the system. Governments can be influenced to change budgets and mandates, and to alter the composition of top administrative personnel. These situations normally result after elections or after legislation is written that changes the purpose or power base of a bureaucracy (p. 25). It was also found that changes in organizational environments have led to a variety of justice models being used over the years. Cole and Smith (1998) identify seven justice models used from the 1600s through to the 1990s: the colonial, penitentiary, reformatory, progressive, medical, community and crime control (p. 456).

As the political climate changed in the 1970s and 1980s, a renewed emphasis on the crime control model of corrections developed. The crime control model emphasizes efficiency and the capacity to catch, try, convict and punish a high proportion of offenders; it also stresses speed and finality over the caution against the possibility of innocent people being adversely impacted (Cole and Smith, 1998, p. 9). It can be argued that the above mentioned components of the crime control model are actually deficiencies and may be the reasons why most US criminal justice systems are fragmented and not functioning at optimum levels. It can also be argued that these alleged deficiencies have impaired the offender re-integration process, which has prompted the need to explore new or a combination of justice models that will be more flexible and work more efficiently to improve the administration of justice.

Herbert Packer (1968) explains that the crime control model competes with the due process model, a model that encourages the adversarial process, the rights of defendants, and formal decision-making processes. He emphasizes that no one official agency functions according to one mode or the other, and elements of both models are found throughout the system. However, as indicated above, the crime control model that has been identified as the predominant model results in a philosophy that encourages police and prosecutors to decide early on whether a defendant is innocent or guilty, leaving the possibility that more procedural errors may ensue. In contrast, the due process model encourages conclusive evidence in order to minimize error (Packer, 1968). Although the philosophy of the crime control model and due process are polarized, it can be argued that the due process model emphasizes the goal of doing justice, where the crime control model considers justice more as an objective, thus, deeming the due process model a more appropriate model to use when addressing programs such as offender re-entry because it emphasizes the needs of the individual offender.

The Planning Process and Systemic Fragmentation

Systemic fragmentation, as defined in this article, is when the criminal justice system's planning processes are inadequate, which adversely impacts the relationship between its agencies and their overall mission, goals and objectives, the development of a unifying criminal justice philosophy and the system's expected outcomes. The review of existing literature revealed that all state criminal justice systems were found to be systematically fragmented at certain stages in the process and deficient in continuity, thus producing systems subdued in differences and occasionally deemed non-systems (Wright, 1994).

Criminal justice systems within the United States are designed sequentially with interrelated parts. For example, decisions in the criminal justice system are made in a specific order (Cole and Smith, 1998, p. 22). The police must make the arrest before the offender is prosecuted, the prosecutor's decisions determine the nature of the court's activity, prosecutors and judges cannot bypass the police and make arrests, and corrections officials cannot punish anyone who has not been through the earlier stages of the process (p. 22). This process creates an exchange relationship among the key decision makers in the criminal justice system that could impact goals, objectives and policy development (p. 22). The literature suggests that a "cause and effect" relationship exists for every decision made by system members that, in turn, can impact on system outcomes.

Much of the debate on criminal justice systems outcomes focuses on whether the systems' *planning processes* are adequate in addressing these issues or if there is a lack in unifying philosophy thus fragmenting the system's goals and objectives (Hahn, 1998).

Differing goals of retribution, deterrence, incapacitation and rehabilitation create differing operating policies that have an adverse effect on the offenders and their return to the community. As a result of these inequities, offenders do not feel obligated to make amends because they view themselves as victims of injustice (Carey, 1996). The literature suggests that criminal justice professionals are also becoming more cynical about the systemic functions of the criminal justice system, which in recent years have become more preoccupied with case processing efficiencies (p. 161). Criminal justice experts argue that the criminal justice system is not a system at all but a sequence of autonomous agencies and activities, each one generating a caseload for another, and each one competing for adequate resources from the public purse (Smith, 1996). There is a universal dissatisfaction among all players in the system: offenders feel injustices, which hinders rehabilitation; victims are re-victimized by the system because of inadequate coordination of services; the public believes that justice was not done; and criminal justice professionals are cynical because case processing supersedes the preferred system outcomes (Carey, 1996, p. 152–155).

Conceding to the argument that criminal justice systems are functionally fragmented and deemed non-systems, there has been a growing obsession with the creation of a monolithic system for the administration of criminal justice (Wright, 1994, pp. 19–31). This obsession has been reflected in many writings, yet a common theme is found throughout criminal justice literature: "if criminal justice is to fulfill its function of crime control, then a transformation must occur which will require devising a process that will develop a rational, well integrated system in which a set of common goals can be pursued through a compatible set of planning strategies and techniques" (pp. 19–31). The following paragraphs address these issues by first describing the functional components of the criminal justice system (in other words, police, prosecution, courts and corrections), with recommendations on how to improve their interrelationship.

Police

Most police departments function within the crime control model, and remain enforcement oriented. The priorities of most police departments are largely independent of the influence of the police agency's external environment (Zhao and Thurman, 1997, p. 345). Regardless of the rate and types of crime a police jurisdiction experiences, police administrators view protecting the public from crime as a priority, with *less interest* in providing services or order maintenance functions (p. 345). This crime control approach is narrow but popular and *neglects* the community-based service and order maintenance activities (pp. 345–347). Therefore it can be argued that the crime control philosophy of police and the influence of the crime control model itself exacerbate police operating policies and contribute to certain levels of systemic fragmentation.

It can also be argued that the social service and problem oriented policing approach is the planning strategy that can be considered most effective when trying to control the influences of the organizational environment and that the *care* taken by these "problem oriented" police officers in the processing of the arrest and investigative practices is paramount for their role in the justice process and the offender re-integration process.

Prosecution

The literature suggests that the crime control model of justice also impacts on the prosecutorial component of the criminal justice system. The literature suggests that contemporary prosecutorial systems focus on mass case processing because of the influence of the crime control model. It requires prosecutors and judges to work too closely together in an attempt to achieve case processing efficiency. The crime control model compels judges to adhere to the sentencing recommendations of prosecuting attorneys, pre-sentence recommendations can develop into recommendations from the prosecutor, and probation officers' pre-sentence reports become incidental (Rosecrance, 1985). Therefore, it can be argued that since the prosecutor drives the criminal case, this process could have an adverse impact on individual rights, due process and the effective overall effective administration of justice.

In order to counterbalance the impact of these above conditions, it can be argued that adjudication partnerships have emerged resulting in community-based prosecution and defense teams. Hahn (1998) explains that as community-based policing becomes more common in this country, community prosecution and defense teams now complement it.

In late 1990, Multnomah County, Oregon's district attorney assigned a senior deputy to work for one year on a neighborhood-based prosecution project in one of Portland's inner city districts. This idea of a special prosecutor caught on, and other neighborhood district attorneys (NDAs) were formed. The NDAs were effective in creating two-way communication to link themselves to both citizens and police officers (Boland, 1996). These neighborhood defense teams also represented individuals accused of crimes who could not afford private lawyers and were based in the community. Instead of waiting for the court to assign legal representation to the client, the defense teams encouraged residents to call the office at any time, and the client was represented by the entire legal team, contrasting with the usual practice of assigning a client to a single attorney (Stone, 1996). The literature suggests that the results of programs of this type disclose a more just and comprehensive approach to addressing crime and criminal behavior. This approach not only benefits targeting the individual problem defendants and the events leading to the development of criminal cases, but the necessary legal defense services and representation that, in the past, were neglected. It is implied through the review of this literature that community prosecution and defense may be used in the continuing debate concerning the crime control model of justice. The literature suggests that these types of justice teams can be used as another planning strategy to mitigate the influence of the crime control model and minimize systemic fragmentation.

Courts

As previously indicated, it can be argued that as the crime control model impacts on the prosecutorial processes, it can also have an impact on court systems. It influences the mass production and prosecution of criminal cases and requires judges to act jointly with prosecutors. The literature suggests that these exchanges could lead to breaches of due process and individual rights, and have an adverse impact on the effective administration of justice.

The majority of American trial courts are highly decentralized in order to be close to the people and responsive to their values (Cole and Smith, 1998, p. 257). Local judges decide cases that pass through the courts and also administer the court. These courts are subject to local political influences and community values (Cole and Smith, 1998). The courts are structured intentionally for these reasons and in the process each court develops its own legal culture with differing ways to administer rules, procedures and justice. There are many differences among local legal cultures that result in differing court decisions (for example, sentencing offenders), duplication of process and the poor use of legal resources (p. 257). It can be argued that although these conditions are customary and necessary, they can lead to more systemic fragmentation if not administered properly.

It was found that judicial court administration might be the most effective judicial planning strategy used to resist the influences that the crime control model of justice imposes on the courts. Robert Wessels (1992) describes judicial court administration as one of the most effective administrative elements that will eliminate most of the inefficiency found in the courts. It minimizes the preoccupation with case processing and allows judges to stay focused on the assigned court cases (pp. 3–18). Elimination of these administrative duties placed on the judge will result in more *individual attention* provided to each case and more quality time can be spent reviewing other relevant reports (pp. 3–18). The literature suggests that additional time saved can now be expended on the development of justice teams such as courtroom workgroups, re-entry courts and community-based justice coalitions, all of which allow for more individual attention. As previously indicated, groups of this type normally require judicial involvement and supervision of the offender throughout the sentence and reentry process, thus establishing a more comprehensive criminal justice process. These models feature an ongoing central role for the judge, a commitment between the court and offender, and judicial discretion within the sentencing process (US Department of Justice, 1999, pp. 2–8). Therefore, it can be argued that improvements in court planning and administration may minimize the impact of the crime control model, reduce systemic fragmentation and contribute to the improvement of the offender re-integration process.

Corrections

Most contemporary correctional institutions continue to be ineffective and a destructive form of punishment in promoting community safety. Creative punishments must be used that provide adequate retribution for offending behavior, together with reasonable levels of protection from further offending at a cost that is not out of proportion to that spent on other social programs. Correctional policy must be removed from the political arena so as to facilitate more rational and consistent policy development and implementation (Brownlee, 1998).

Since the correctional component of the criminal justice process is the last phase of justice administration, the literature suggests that correctional systems must be prepared to manage the offender population that is furnished to them by the court phase of the criminal justice process. Therefore, based on the existing literature, it can be argued that correctional systems serve as reservoirs of "systemic fragmentation" and these inequities adversely impact on the behavior of offenders and their eventual re-integration to the community. It can also be argued that one of the solutions to this problem is for a planning process that provides continuity between the administration of punishment and the correctional institution's ability to receive it.

The literature also suggests that alternatives to incarceration (in other words, intermediate sanctions) such as house arrest, electronic and global positioning monitoring, intense supervision parole and restitution centers are becoming more attractive than the costly and ineffective option of incarceration. They show evidence of being accepted as sufficiently punitive from the perspectives of victims and criminal justice professionals, while reducing recidivism, and may be the solution to the numerous problems associated with the correctional system.

These creative punishment strategies have been defined as an attempt to design a mode of constructive punishment that considers the needs and characteristics of the offender and their motivation. The strategies make use of professional knowledge, such as psychology, which is useful in the sentencing process. They also accentuate the differences between the handling of both violent and non-violent offenders with a sufficient punitive element that can satisfy the demand for justice and reduce recidivism (Henderson, 1982).

Planning

Planning can be defined as a decision-making process that involves politics and an effort to accomplish goals by increasing awareness and understanding of that process (Dahl, 1959, pp. 340–350). The politics of planning is the total behavior of the political order within which planning takes place. For example, to understand the politics of fiscal planning in the United States, one needs to understand the country's political processes. Therefore, planning is regarded as a rational social action and as a social process for reaching a rational decision (Dahl, 1959). Therefore, it can be inferred by this premise that to understand the politics of state criminal justice planning, one needs to understand the politics of planning at the state, county and local levels in order to facilitate an effective decision-making process.

Local and state criminal justice systems are constantly under pressure to plan more efficiently and effectively without diminishing the quality of their services (US Department of Justice, 1999). Problems associated with backlogged dockets, crowded jails, and recidivism is becoming commonplace. Collaborative efforts are becoming more important for mounting an efficient and effective response to these problems (p. 1). The creation of a cooperative planning partnership with independent agencies, although an arduous task for many jurisdictions, emerged as one of the solutions to improve communication among these agencies in order to deal with these complex issues (US Department of Justice, 1999).

Important ingredients for the development of successful collective planning and decision-making partnerships that are deemed consensus builders are (US Department of Justice, 1999):

1. *Leadership:* Key individuals in the justice system must provide leadership in giving direction. Leaders from one or more key agencies must step forward to assemble a team of leaders and managers from other criminal justice agencies that are concerned about issues facing their jurisdiction.

2. *Research and evaluation:* This group of individuals (in other words, a steering committee) must use research and information on the best practices to guide program development as well as the use of objective data to evaluate its' programs.

3. *Broad support:* Partnerships of this type must seek community support. They must provide information about the focus of their group and improve the communication process by seeking community input on identifying and addressing problems.

Criminal, justice leaders in many jurisdictions continue to be successful in bringing together key players to tackle difficult problems (U.S. Department of Justice, 1999, p. 2). Adjudication partnerships in other jurisdictions have been organized that include representatives from primary players in the adjudication process: the prosecution, the defense and the court. The participation of other criminal justice agencies such as law enforcement and corrections are also included (p. 2). Through a national mail survey, 103 well established and successful adjudication partnerships were identified (pp. 4-8). These programs were found in Buffalo, New York; Los Angeles County, California; Cedar Rapids, Iowa; Dakota County, Minnesota; Rochester, New York; San Jose, California; and Corvallis, Oregon. These coalitions are examples of criminal justice planning groups that have been deemed successful for many years. However, it can be argued that "state specific" methods of planning and a lack of means to communicate these efforts have hindered the successful outcomes of these programs.

As previously indicated, criminal justice partnerships are an intricate component of the planning process. It was found that community can also be a significant influence in shaping criminal justice policy and that new planning strategies should be developed that include collaborative efforts on behalf of the community and justice agencies (US Department of Justice, 1997).

For many years the community as an environmental force has failed to be an influence on the criminal justice system (US Department of Justice, 1997, p. 1). The police, prosecution, courts and corrections systems have become increasingly modernized in recent years, but they often fail to meet the needs of the justice system's primary consumers; the *communities* that experience crime problems on a daily basis (see for example p. 1). This problem was first addressed by the advocates of community-based policing. They argued that police officers could address crime problems more effectively if they established closer relationship with the community. As a result of these efforts, community-based policing became a reality and these "community-based" concepts of "community justice" have spread to other branches of the justice system including courts, probation departments, prosecutors and corrections offices (p. 1). The literature suggests that as local concerns grow about the offender's eventual return to the community and recidivism, the community and community justice planning groups are beginning to have a greater influence in shaping criminal justice policy and programs related to these issues.

Planning and the Punishment Process

After reviewing the available literature, it can be argued that there is a lack of understanding of the concepts of punishment and how to plan and administer its fundamental principles which, in turn, impacts on offender, institution and the community. The literature also suggests that punishment is the most complex process within the criminal justice system and the inconsistencies associated with comprehending these processes may be reasons for the development of more systemic fragmentation. For example, the concept of punishment is more socially than individually based. A useful place to begin to describe this phenomenon is with Kant's explanation of deserved punishment (in other words, retribution) (Von Hirsch, 1996). He based his concept of punishment on fairness. When someone infringes another's rights, the person gains an unfair advantage over others in society. The punishment for this act imposes a counterbalance disadvantage on the offender and restores balance (p. 147). The literature suggests that the fairness concept can be also applied to decisions made within the criminal justice system. It can be argued that if the social control agents are unjust regarding the administration of punishment (in other words, it is undeserved, unfair, unnecessary or extreme) a "social crime" may be perceived by the offender, therefore the offender perceives society as having an unfair advantage. As a result of these actions, social retaliation could be committed by the offender, in the form of prejudice, hostility, resistance, a criminal act and other acts of deviance in order to maintain the social equilibrium.

Understanding that the above viewpoint is purely speculation derived as a result of this study, it was found that offenders who regarded punishment as a "deserved" misfortune for their own wrongdoing were more susceptible to rehabilitation (Toby, 1964). In fact, the way punishment is practiced in Western societies it is usually an obstacle to rehabilitation (p. 58). It was found that if the disposition of convicted offenders were more commensurate with the gravity of their crime, even if greater or less austerity would promote other goals, the likelihood for successful treatment strategies and reduced recidivism would follow (Von Hirsch, 1996, p. 152). Therefore, based on this principle, it can be argued that understanding of the concepts of punishment may lead to social prerequisites for justice that may be more "solutions-based" whereas deterrence, incapacitation and rehabilitation are more subsequent strategies for the "control" of crime.

It was found that a planned system of sentencing guidelines may be considered one of the solutions to finding this fair and equitable distribution of punishments (US Department of Justice, 1997). For example, in many states, commissions have plans in place addressing the integration of intermediate sanctions into sentencing guidelines and are devising systems of interchangeability between prison and non-prison sanctions (pp. 29–30). The literature also suggests that sentencing guidelines may be another solution to the problem of disparities found in the judicial sentencing process. For example, statistical comparisons of sentencing tendencies in various jurisdictions show that disparities are widespread. In the Detroit Recorder's Court, sentencing dispositions were sampled from ten judges over a 20 month period. Findings revealed that one judge imposed prison terms upon as many as 90 *percent* of the defendants he sentenced, while another judge ordered prison sentences on 35 percent of similar cases (Inciardi, 1993). The literature suggests that the impact of these sentencing practices *increase* prison populations but the most significant finding is that when prisoners compare their sentences, if they deem their sentences unfair or if they see themselves as a victim of judicial prejudice, [then] hostility, resistance to correctional treatment and even a riot-prone environment can exist (p. 452). Obviously, these conditions will not lead to a successful offender re-integration process. In fact, this is a good example of injustices prompted by poor planning leading to what was previously identified as "reservoirs of systemic fragmentation" found within our correctional institutions.

Through an effective planning process, North Carolina and Ohio have adopted sentencing guidelines and have incorporated the use of intermediate sanctions that are interchangeable between prison and non-prison sanctions. Pennsylvania and Massachusetts redesigned their sentencing guidelines for the same reasons (US Department of Justice, 1997). The North Carolina model suggests that sentencing guidelines with the incorporation of intermediate sanctions can work. The North Carolina sentencing guidelines cover all felonies and misdemeanors with an attempt to increase use of prison sentences for violent crime. They reduced prison use for non-violent crimes by using intermediate sanctions. In 1995, after the first full year of operation under this system, 81 percent of violent felons received prison sentences, up [from] 67 percent in 1993. Twenty-three percent of non-violent felons were sent to prison, down from 42 percent in 1993. For all imprisoned felons, the mean time to be served increased from 16 to 37 months (US Department of Justice, 1997). In this case, sentencing guidelines provided the necessary vehicle for "fitting the punishment to the crime." The literature suggests that improved criminal justice planning was a key component to "fighting crime" by developing an improved sentencing process that not only was fair but by using intermediate sanctions for non-violent crimes, the violent criminals received longer prison terms. This analysis also suggests that more collaborative planning between the police, prosecution, courts and corrections could lead to a more unifying philosophy resulting in the development of a common mission. Furthermore, it was inferred that these changes could lead to resolution of those issues deemed "inequitable." prevent systemic fragmentation associated with the inconsistencies found when attempting to manage punishment and improve the offender re-integration process.

The Planners' Perspectives and Methodology

The previous information is a literature review qualifying data collected from various professional journals, observational notes as a participant, review of public documents, examination of videotapes, textbooks and Internet resources relating to the operations of state criminal justice systems. The planning and systemic functions of state criminal justice systems were examined and compared by conducting a content analysis. The planning processes examined were long- and short-term goals of the criminal justice system, and cohesive and non-cohesive planning. The systemic functions examined were the criminal justice system's strategies of police enforcement and investigation, prosecution policy, judicial court administration and process, and the management of correctional institutions. The impact of these factors was weighed against the offender re-integration process and community safety.

A survey instrument was also provided to the National Association of Criminal Justice Planners (NACJP) and representatives from state criminal justice planning agencies across the United States to provide additional support to this study. It should also be noted that there were only 27 criminal justice planners listed in 27 different states throughout the United States.

Therefore it can be speculated that there is a deficient number of criminal justice planners across the US, they are not participating in the planning association, or they exist and are not active organizations.

The perceptions of criminal justice planners addressing the same categories were measured by conducting a one-shot case study that evaluated the opinions of criminal justice planners currently practicing within the US criminal justice system. The survey was divided into two sections and comprised of 14 questions. The first section consisted of 10 questions that addressed the systemic functions of the criminal justice system and how these processes affected the offender re-integration process and community safety. The second section consisted of four questions addressing criminal justice planning processes. A frequency distribution was processed that measured the perceptions of criminal justice planners regarding the planning and systematic processes of the criminal justice system in their state and its impact on the offender re-integration process and community safety.

Fifty surveys were mailed to each state within the United States. The first set of surveys was mailed directly to known criminal justice planners that are listed as current members of the National Association of Criminal Justice Planners[1] in 27 different states. These states were Colorado, Kentucky, Louisiana, New York, Florida, Tennessee, Arizona, Ohio, Maryland, Texas, Minnesota, Michigan, Pennsylvania, Nevada, Oregon, South Carolina, Alabama, Hawaii, Washington, D.C., Iowa, New Mexico, California, Washington, Wisconsin, Virginia, Nebraska and Illinois. The remaining surveys were mailed to the remaining 23 states in the United States. It was not known whether these states had criminal justice planners, therefore the survey was forwarded to the governor's office with instructions requesting that a criminal justice professional should complete the survey.

Findings

Criminal justice planners from 15 states responded to the survey,[2] which resulted in a 30 percent response rate. The meager response rate may be indicative of the lack of governmental organizations addressing criminal justice planning which supports this study's hypothesis. For the purpose of clarification, the study's hypothesis is repeated in this section.

Hypothesis

This study reviews the current state of academic literature as it pertains to the organization's environmental (for example, legal, political, economic and cultural) influence on U.S. criminal justice systems resulting in systemic fragmentation and poor performance, it qualifies that most state criminal justice experts support this premise and that improved planning efforts will result in strategies that can prompt the system to perform more efficiently and improve the offender re-integration process. This study addresses these efforts.

It should be noted that there were only 27 criminal justice planners listed as members of the National Association of Criminal Justice Planners, representing 27 different states. Therefore, considering that only 11 of the 27 NACJP members responded (41 percent response rate) and 5 of the 23 non-NACJP planners responded (32 percent response rate), the 16 states that responded represent a 59 percent response rate from known planners across the US. The non-NACJP states that responded to the survey were Rhode Island, Wyoming, North Carolina Massachusetts and Mississippi.

When asked about the planning and management processes of their state's criminal justice system, the survey (see Table 1) showed that the majority (24 percent) of the respondents indicated that the criminal justice system in their state was not functioning effectively; 16 percent verified that there was no cohesive planning process; 18 percent indicated that their criminal justice system was not unified and structured on mission, goals and strategic planning; and 18 percent believed that their criminal justice system was fragmented and lacked a system-wide agreement of mission, goals and strategic planning (see Figure 1).

When asked questions regarding the systemic processes of the criminal justice system in their state as it relates to the offender re-integration process, the majority of the respondents (22 percent) indicated that law enforcement did not contribute to a successful re-integration process. The majority (24 percent) believed that prosecutors failed to address re-integration: 14 percent of the judiciary and corrections neglected the re-integration process, and the majority (24 percent) failed to have a pre-adjudication offender re-integration plan in place (see Figure 2).

It was found that 14 percent believed that judicial sentencing practices contributed to a successful re-integration process, 16 percent favored probation department programs, 14 percent believed that management of correctional facilities led to successful re-integration, 22 percent believed that incarceration work programs[3] contributed to offender success, 18 percent favored parole's efforts, and 14 percent believed that community safety was not in jeopardy.[4] (See Figure 3.)

Table 1   Survey Results

Questions	Yes	No	No Rpl	Rate
Systemic Functions (Section One)				
1. Do you believe that law enforcement practices within your state criminal justice system lead to the successful re-integration of the offender to the community?	4 (8)	11 (22)	35	–
2. Do prosecution policies within your state's criminal justice system lead to a successful offender re-integration process?	3 (6)	12 (24)	35	–
3. Does the internal management of judicial court functions within *your* state's criminal justice system lead to a successful offender re-integration process?	7 (14)	7 (14)	36	+–

Questions	Yes	No	No Rpl	Rate
4. Does your state court system develop a pre-adjudication re-integration plan before the sentencing phase of a trial?	2 (4)	12 (24)	36	–
5. Do judicial sentencing practices within your state's criminal justice system lead to a successful offender re-integration process?	7 (14)	6 (12)	37	+–
6. Does your state's probation departments have re-integration plans that lead to a successful offender re-integration process?	8 (16)	5 (10)	37	+–
7. Does the management of correctional facilities within your state's criminal justice system lead to a successful offender re-integration process?	7 (14)	7 (14)	36	+–
8. Do incarceration work programs within your state's criminal justice system lead to a successful offender re-integration process?	11 (22)	2 (4)	37	+
9. Do your state's parole departments have re-integration plans that lead to a successful offender re-integration process?	9 (18)	4 (8)	37	+
10. Do your state criminal justice system's offender re-integration programs have a positive impact on community safety?	7 (14)	6 (12)	37	+–
Planning and Management (Section Two)				
11. Does your state criminal system require a cohesive planning process that is considered community-based (for example, inclusive of community advocates, prevention organizations, state and local political representatives, and educational institutions)?	6 (12)	8 (16)	36	+–
12. Do you believe that your state's criminal justice system is unified and structured to establish system-wide agreement on missions, goals and strategic planning?	5 (10)	9 (18)	36	–
13. Do you believe that your state's criminal justice system is fragmented and lacks a system-wide agreement on missions, goals and strategic planning?	9	5	36	–
14. Do you believe that your state's criminal justice system is functioning effectively and no changes are necessary?	2 (4)	12 (24)	36	–

Note: percentages appear in parentheses

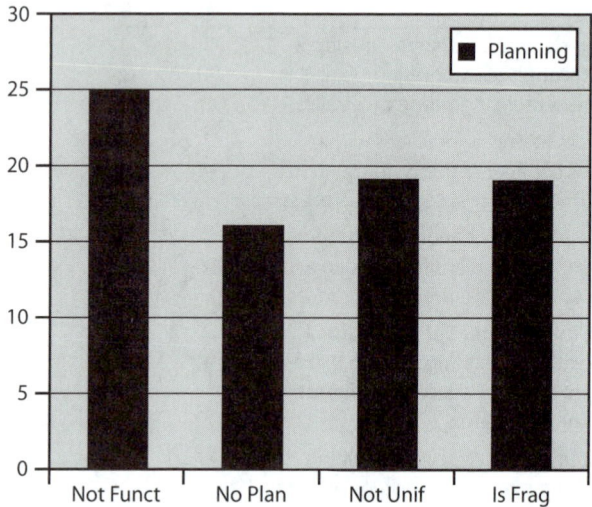

Source: Original research based on a 30 percent response rate (November 2000). This information was compiled from a survey that I designed and disseminated and which was completed by the members of National Association of Criminal Justice Planners (NACJP) in the United States. Members of criminal justice planning offices not associated with NACJP were also surveyed.

Figure 1   Planning Functions within United States Criminal Justice Systems.

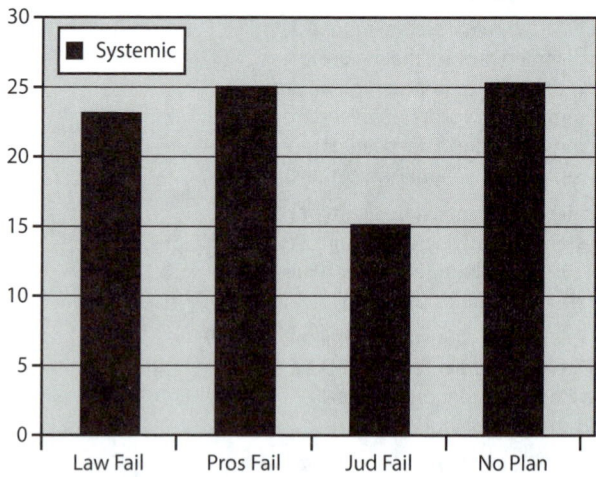

Source: Original research based on a 30 percent response rate (November 2000). This information was compiled from a survey that I designed and disseminated and which was completed by the members of National Association of Criminal Justice Planners (NACJP) in the United States. Members of criminal justice planning offices not associated with the NACJP were also surveyed.

Figure 2   United States Criminal Justice System: Systemic Functions Relating to Re-Integration.

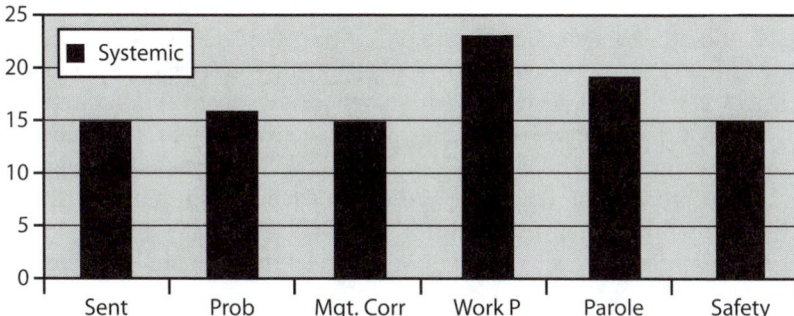

Source: Original research based on a 30 percent response rate (November 2000). This information was compiled from a survey that I designed and disseminated and which was completed by the members of National Association of Criminal Justice Planners (NACJP) in the United States. Members of criminal justice planning offices not associated with NACJP were also surveyed.

Figure 3   United States Criminal Justice System: Systemic Functions Relating to Re-Integration.

Conclusion and Policy Implications

The literature review and findings support the hypothesis that the organizational environment has impacted state criminal justice systems and fragmented its internal and external systemic functions and planning strategies, which has impacted adversely the effectiveness of the criminal justice system's expected outcomes as they relate to offender re-integration and community safety. A lack of a criminal justice planning processor was found to be the central problem contributing to a fragmented system of justice.

Information which contributed to the development of this research paper proposes that multiple approaches to the mission of US criminal justice systems have led to the erosion of a common purpose, resulting in a mix of both efficient and inefficient systems. This study has brought forth information that has clarified the argument that states have failed to plan collectively resulting in a fragmented system of justice. This departure has led to "state specific" methods of criminal justice processes that have had a widespread adverse impact on the offender, the re-integration process and community safety across the United States. The lack of collaboration and cooperation within law enforcement, prosecution and the judiciary and corrections is evident and must be improved. It is speculated that if the collective planning processes are improved, the relationship between systemic areas of the criminal justice process will improve. As a result of these efforts a more positive impact on offender reintegration and community safety might emerge.

This literature review and findings also suggest that one must begin to understand the concepts of punishment, and place an emphasis on how to punish versus whether to punish. US society has failed to understand and accept that other forms of punishment (for example, intermediate sanctions) can be utilized and are equivalent to, if not more effective than, prison. The lack of understanding of concepts of punishment factors has created social injustices as well as unprecedented and unnecessary incarceration rates.

Through the influences of an organizational environment, the crime control model of justice was found to be prevalent and also suspected in complicating judicial process, hindering due process, stagnating program development and hindering the effective administration of justice. Therefore, it is implied that it is essential to develop a new justice model that is more integrated and adaptable to its organizational environment.

Criminal justice systems must improve planning and communication strategies in order to monitor changes in the organization's environment and be prepared to implement needed changes when necessary. Successful programs should be replicated and programs that have failed should be discontinued. These conditions, led by poor planning and communication, emerge into systemic fragmentation and this essential programmatic information is not disseminated among criminal justice agencies. These conditions prevent successful programs from reaching offenders within their own states across the United States. Through poor planning offenders are not given the opportunity to successfully change their behaviors. This impacts adversely on the offender re-integration process and community safety. Therefore, policy development addressing improved planning and communication processes within the criminal justice system should occur, which will lead a more unified system of justice.

I suggest the development of a new and more integrated justice model which is a combination of previously described justice models that have been used throughout our history. I suggest that the benefit of a more integrated model is its adaptability to its ever-changing organizational environment. Although the crime control model has been defined as the barrier in this study it will not be eliminated from this new integrated approach. It will simply be used when necessary to expedite the flow of those offenders that are deemed chronic and regular clientele of the criminal justice system, thus negating the need to provide extensive inquiry into their background.

Although improvements in the planning process are described as a means to assist in this transition, the political and social influences bear a greater weight. As described throughout this study, the internal organizational units of the criminal justice system are embedded within their own organizational cultures and personalities. There will be resistance to this "integrated" model and a more unified system of justice because of tradition. The crime control model of justice compels most US court systems to manage traditionally, which minimizes a collaborative and cohesive planning process. However, once the public understands the need for a more comprehensive form of justice that is "results" oriented, empirically based, and that level of recidivism is the actual measure of effectiveness, the internal administration of the justice process will be more responsive to change. When a new criminal justice model is introduced to the public that is less competitive, that encourages cooperation among all agencies and is community-based, the influence of the organizational environment's social and political climate will eventually foster the reality of these changes.

Notes

[1] *The National Association of Criminal Justice Planners 1999 Directory*, Washington, D.C.
[2] See detailed survey in Table I.
[3] In the article provided by the National Criminal Justice Reference Service (NCJRS) entitled "Work Release: Recidivism and Corrections Costs in Washington State Entry Courts" (December 1996:1–2), work release programs provided nearly a quarter of all prisoners released in Washington with a successful transition to the community. Fifty-six percent of the work releases in the cohort study incurred no program infractions or arrests. The jobs selected by releases were restaurant and construction jobs. Incarceration work programs were viewed as successful by the majority of criminal justice planners surveyed (22 percent) in this study. Although work programs were considered significant in this study, this high success rate was a complete surprise.
[4] A 14 percent satisfaction with community safety implies that approximately one-half of the respondents believe that communities are unsafe. Considering the weight of community safety factors, these findings suggest that a community safety problem exists.

References

Bazemore, G. (1995). Beyond rehabilitation and retribution: a new framework for juvenile justice. Paper presented at the conference of the Campaign for an Effective Crime Policy, Washington, DC, January.

Beck, A. and P. Paige (2001). Prisoners in 2000. *Bureau of Justice Statistics Bulletin*, US Department of Justice, August.

Boland, B. (1996). What is Community Prosecution? *National Institute of Justice Journal* 231, 35–40.

Brownlee, I. (1998). *Community Punishment: A Critical Introduction*. Harlow, UK: Addison Wesley.

Carey, M. (1996). Restorative justice in community corrections. *Corrections Today*, 58, 152–155.

Cole, G. F. and C. E. Smith (1998). *The American System of Criminal Justice*, 8, 22–40, 143–257, 456.

Dahl, R. A. (1959). The Politics of Planning. *International Social Science Journal*, 340.

Hahn, P. H. (1998). *Emerging Trends in Criminal Justice*, 10–11:158–160.

Henderson, J. H. (1982). Interface between law enforcement and psychology: a case study of creative punishment and alternatives to incarceration. *Police Journal*, 55(3), 285–290.

Inciardi, J. A. (1993). *Criminal Justice*, 4th ed. San Diego, CA: Harcourt Brace College Publishers, pp. 451–452.

Knight. K. N. (1994). The desirability of goal conflict within the criminal justice system. *The Administration and Management of Criminal Justice Organizations*, 2nd ed. Lon Grove, IL: Waveland Press, pp. 19–31.

Kolfas, J., S. Stojkovic, and D. Kalinich (1990). Defining the environment of the criminal justice system. *Criminal Justice Organizations Administration and Management*. Belmont, CA: Wadsworth, pp. 18–30.

Packer, H. L. (1968). *The Limits of the Criminal Sanction*. Stanford, CA: Stanford University Press.

Petersilia, J. (2000). When Prisoners Return to the Community: Political, Economic, and Social Consequences, Sentencing and Corrections: Issues for the 21st Century, November. Washington, DC: U.S. Department of Justice.

Rosecrance, J. (1985). The probation officers' search for credibility: ball park recommendations. Crime and Delinquency, 31(4), 539–554.

Smith, M. E. (Ed.) (1996). Who wants an effective crime policy and can deliver one? In campaign for an effective crime policy. Crime and Politics in the 1990s: Three Perspectives. Washington, DC: Campaign for an Effective Crime Policy.

Stone, C. (1996). Community defense and the challenge of community justice. National Institute of Justice Journal, 231, 41–45.

Toby, J. (1964). Is punishment necessary? Journal of Criminal Law, Criminology, and Police Science, 55, 332–337.

US Department of Justice (Bureau of Justice Assistance) (1997). Responding to the Community: Principles for Planning Creating a Community Court, November [On-Line serial] NCJ 166821, p. 1.

US Department of Justice (1997). Intermediate Sanctions in Sentencing Guidelines, OJP, May, NCJ 165043, pp. xii, 29–30.

US Department of Justice (Office of Justice Programs, Bureau of Justice Assistance) (1999). Key Elements of Successful Adjudication Partnerships, May [On-Line serial] NCJ 173949, pp. 1–11.

US Department of Justice (Bureau of Justice Assistance) (2000). But They All Come Back: Rethinking Prisoner Reentry. [On-Line serial] No.7, NCJ 181413, pp. 1–11.

US Department of Justice (National Institute of Corrections) (2002). Guidelines for Developing a Criminal Justice Coordinating Committee, January.

US Department of Justice (Bureau of Justice Statistics) (2002). Recidivism of Prisoners Released in 1994, June [On-Line serial] NCJ 193427, pp. 1–16.

Von Hirsch, A. (1996). Doing justice: the choice of punishments. Criminal Justice, 3, 147–152.

Wessels, R. (1992). The Court Administrator: A Manual, NACM. Williamsburg, VA: National Association for Court Management, pp. 3–18.

Wright, K. N. (1994). The desirability of goal conflict within the criminal justice system. The Administration and Management of Criminal Justice Organizations, 2nd ed. Long Grove, IL: Waveland Press, pp. 19–31.

Zhao, J. and Q. C. Thurman (1997). Community policing: where are we now? Crime and Delinquency, 43(3), 345–357.

3

The Desirability of Goal Conflict within the Criminal Justice System

KEVIN N. WRIGHT

Conflicting Goals in the Non-System

Experts in the field of criminal justice have recently displayed a growing obsession with the idea of creating a monolithic system for the administration of justice. This obsession is reflected in a diversity of writings, yet a common theme can be found throughout the literature: if criminal justice is to fulfill its function of crime control, then a transformation must occur which will create a rational, well-integrated system in which a common set of goals can be pursued through a compatible set of strategies and techniques.

One source of this trend is found in the various theoretical and philosophical treatises which are intended to serve as a framework for revamping the criminal justice system. Duffee (1980:4) has succinctly described the nature of these works:

> Whether the analysis of criminal justice has been done by radicals, liberals or conservatives, most analysts from van den Haag, to Packer, to Quinney have assumed that centralized planning and program development dealing with criminal justice can or could influence significantly the frequency with which crime is committed, the proportion of offenders who are apprehended, and the degree to which punishment for crimes would feedback upon the political, economic and social conditions which give rise to crime and the means with which society responds to it.

Radicals such as Quinney (1969; 1974 and 1977) and Chambliss (1969; 1971; 1972; 1975 and 1979) generally perceive the existing system to be

Reprinted from *Journal of Criminal Justice*, Vol. 9. Kevin N. Wright, "The Desirability of Goal Conflict within the Criminal Justice System." pp. 209–218, 1980, with permission of Elsevier.

coherent in that the system functions to protect the interests of the powerful, and individuals are punished for the inequities of society. Change of the system is considered in terms of broader social change but is aimed at creating a new form of coherence. Conservatives such as Packer (1968), van den Haag (1975), and Wilson (1975) and liberals such as Clark (1971) and Menninger (1969), on the other hand, generally perceive the existing system as lacking coherence and continuity in that a single set of goals is not pursued. Each indicates, however, that coherence could be built into the system and the problem of crime control resolved.

A second source of advocacy for a monolithic system can be found in the structural analyses of the organizational aspects of the criminal justice system as reflected in the work of Skoler (1977) and Kellogg (1976). These assessments focus on the inability of the "system" to function as a true system, i.e., one which is coherent and well integrated and has a unitary set of goals. Consequently, this group of analysts refer to the criminal justice system as a "non-system." Criminal justice is characterized by conflicting goals, a lack of integration, and overlapping jurisdictions which promote inequities of justice and create inefficiencies which result in higher costs of operation:

> Official decisions affecting the criminal offender are made by a patchwork of separate jurisdictions, in a system of independent prosecutors, judges, prison administrators, and parole and probation officers. Respective policies vary arbitrarily from place to place, or even from time to time within the same place. Sentencing decisions within the same jurisdiction, not to mention among different ones, vary widely with the attitudes of individual judges. Decisions are based upon limited and inconsistent information, generally without adequate explanation to benefit other officials in the decision-making process. (Kellogg, 1976:50)

In fact, the components of criminal justice are characterized as being noncooperative and even hostile toward one another. It has been suggested that the inability of the criminal justice system to function as a true system results in a fragmented output and often an undesirable outcome (Skoler, 1977; Kellogg, 1976; O'Neill, et al., 1976:4–17).

Unlike the theoretical and philosophical treatises which propose frameworks for revamping the system, the structural analysts focus their attention on remedial structural changes. In other words, the structural analysts concentrate on the mechanics of change rather than the content and direction of change within the system. Various proposals (see Skoler [1977] for a comprehensive review) have been made to alleviate the problems of conflict and fragmentation within the criminal justice system. Such suggestions range from integration and cooperation to direct unification of the system. However, more attention has been given to the former than the latter. Statewide and comprehensive planning and fiscal incentives have been advocated as mechanisms for integration. Structural change has also been suggested as a mechanism for integrating the components. Reorganization of state government is quite often cited as a potentially effective method of structural change. Skoler (1977:289) has even suggested that the "fragmented, duplicative, and uncoordinated character of criminal justice services" can best be resolved through the consolidation and unification of the system's components. Services should be combined and centrally administered.

The inherent desirability of creating a monolithic system for the administration of justice, however, deserves further consideration. As suggested above, the lack of integration, coordination, and goal and technique compatibility within the criminal justice system seems to be quite inefficient and ineffective. The system lacks the rationality associated with systemic organization. Additional assessment, however, may not support this conclusion. Proposals for unification seem to ignore the environment in which criminal justice exists. Furthermore, there are at least three reasons why goal conflict within the system is desirable. The purpose of this article is to consider these factors in order to assess the desirability of a monolithic system.

The Sociopolitical Environment

The theoretical and philosophical treatises and the structural analyses which advocate a monolithic criminal justice system seem to have conveniently ignored the sociopolitical environment in which the system exists. Such an oversight may be helpful in gaining public attention to one's ideas but is most unfortunate from a practical and pragmatic standpoint. The essence of a system as complex as criminal justice simply cannot be understood from the perspective which considers it as an isolated system. Nor can any proposal for significant planned change of the system claim any validity without considering the effects and constraints of the environment on that system.

In order to understand fully the implications of this idea, it is necessary to assess what type of a system criminal justice is. Numerous authors (Emery and Trist, 1965; Terryberry, 1968; March and Simon, 1958; Cyert and March, 1963) have argued that there are at least two types of social systems: simple and complex. In a simple system, goals can be specified, tasks to accomplish those goals can be undertaken, and progress can be monitored so that the system is self-regulating. These activities are possible because the internal and external environments of the system are relatively stable. It is this model of the criminal justice system which the theoretical and structural analysts noted above have used. A complex system, on the other hand, does not exist in stable environments but rather finds itself in a complex and rapidly changing, or turbulent, environment which produces unpredictable changes within the system itself. This situation precludes rational, long-range, and macro-planned change. Because the environment is turbulent, and thus drastically and dynamically affecting the system, it is simply impossible to identify and specify a set of goals and to bring about some change to remodel the system (Emery and Trist, 1965, Terryberry, 1968). Duffee (1980:101) has made a very strong case that criminal justice is in fact a complex system:

There is a wide variety of information available pertaining to the fact that criminal justice is not a monolithic, commonly conceived routine exercise. Criminal justice may well have different meanings in different places, or behave differently under contrasting conditions. Before we attempt to change actual operating agencies so that they might conform to a unitary motive of criminal justice operation, we may wish first to ask why such variations occur, whether these variations are functional equivalents, or whether the contrasting practices provided to the locality in which they are observed contributions to social order that might be lost if all criminal justice agencies behaved appropriately to the expectations of the analyst.

Duffee goes on to argue that criminal justice is, in fact, an institution much like the family or religion, and that its existence and what happens to it are unrelated to goal accomplishment.

Just as Duffee noted that there is a wide variety of information which indicates that criminal justice is not a monolithic system, there is, in particular, considerable information which indicates the political nature of criminal justice. Both conservatives and radicals concur that the basis of criminal justice, criminal law, is generated within an interest structure (see Pound, 1943; Quinney, 1969:20–30.) Society is characterized by an interest structure in which various kinds of interests are distributed throughout that structure. Laws are the product of different interest groups vying for power to see their interests represented or realized. Theorists differ, however, in their perceptions concerning the output of the process as to whether the result is a product of compromise or domination.

Beyond the law, the actual administration and allocation of justice can also be viewed within the political context. Cole (1973:15–16) has provided one of the most concise reviews of this idea:

> Rather, like all legal institutions, the criminal justice system is "political" since it is engaged in the formulation and administration of public policies where choice must be made among such competing values as the rights of defendants, protection of persons and property, justice and freedom. That various groups in society interpret these values differently is obvious. Decisions result from the influence of the political power of decision makers and relative strength of competing elites.

Cole (1973:16) continues by noting that there is a wide range of discretion within the administration of justice. Laws are often ambiguous and full enforcement of them is neither possible nor desirable. Decisions must, therefore, be made within the context of the community and its interest structure. Legal personnel, judges and prosecutors, must operate within a political environment. Their decisions must rest on the selection among competing dispositions which reflect dominant political interests. The actions of police executives are similarly influenced by the political nature of the position. To summarize, "in many ways the administration of criminal justice is a community affair; political influentials and interest groups work to insure that the law will be applied in ways consistent with their perception of local values" (Cole, 1973:17). (For an excellent discussion of the political reality of the administration of justice see chapter 4, "The Making of Criminal Justice Policy" in Levine, Musheno, and Palumbo, 1980.)

Suggestions to create a monolithic, unified system deny the very existence of an interest structure characterized by a specific distribution of power. Therefore, to analyze the criminal justice system as if it did not exist within a political environment seems to be particularly naive. There are actors within the system who have a vested interest in its organization and operation, as well as influential persons within the community who want to see their particular interests represented. We know that interests vary from area to area. What is "justice" in an urban area may not be similarly perceived in a rural area. We know that what is "justice" to a police officer may not be "justice" to a young offender and his or her liberal public defender.

Radicals, to a degree, seem to understand the political context of the administration of justice in that their proposals for change are couched in terms of broader social changes. They realize that massive change in the system rests on social change. For example, the proponents of prison abolition fairly consistently advocate such change within a proposal for the creation of a society characterized by pervasive equality. (See Hawkins, 1976; 5–12 for a review of the abolitionist movement.) Radicals, however, often fail to consider the likelihood of drastic social change.

Liberals, conservatives, and structural analysts virtually ignore the political environment. They propose massive change in the system without considering the possibility that actors within the system as well as politically influential persons would resist that change. They fail to see that criminal justice is as it is for a reason, that there is a certain rationality in the seemingly structural irrationality of the system. (See Diesing's *Reason in Society* [1962] for a discussion of this conceptualization of rationality.) To create a monolithic, unified system would require a compatible set of values to serve as its basis; our complex society is not constituted in such a manner. Individuals working in the various components of the system, personnel in various jurisdictions, and influence bearers who have an interest in the administration of justice are extremely unlikely to agree on a single set of values. Levine, Musheno, and Palumbo (1980:38, 150) in their introductory textbook make this fact clear when they conclude:

> In short, the public interest is constantly being defined and redefined. The balance among its various facets is always shifting. As is true in any area of public policy, the choice of ideals in criminal justice is the result of an unpredictable, ever-changing and very intricate political process. . . . This often means that only incremental rather than sweeping changes can be made.

Furthermore, there are at least three reasons why goal conflict and fragmentation are advantageous to the processes and functioning of the system. Conflict makes it possible to represent and protect different societal interest, establishes a system of checks and balances, and promotes a smoothly operating offender-processing system.

Reflective Diversity

Underlying the ideas of unification and the creation of a monolithic system for the administration of justice is an assumption that there is a compatible set of values, or if you please, a single culture, from whence unification can proceed. As suggested above, there is considerable theoretical and empirical evidence that indicates the existence of a diversity of values within the criminal justice environment. The fragmentation and lack of integration within criminal justice would thus seem possibly to allow different interests to be incorporated into the system. As such, different societal interests may be reflected or represented by the different, and often conflicting, goals within criminal justice. This idea has been verified on a number of different levels.

First, the representatives of different interests can be seen among different jurisdictions. Wilson's study of the police (1968) indicated that styles of law enforcement vary from community to community. While the day-to-day routine of police work was not directly affected by political influence, the political culture of the community was found to influence directly the style and policies of the department. Similarly, Levin (1980) found in his study of criminal courts that the handling of defendants varied according to the political culture of the community. The lack of consistency between judicial decisions in Pittsburgh and Minneapolis was explained by their different political systems. If it is assumed that the political culture and public interests vary from area to area, then the seemingly fragmented system of justice may serve to fulfill those diverse interests. This conclusion is reflected in the research of both Wilson and Levin. For example, the influence of both a middle- and lower-class culture in Pittsburgh as opposed to a predominantly middle-class cultural influence in Minneapolis was found to be reflected in judicial practices.

On a second level, different interests can be represented by the fragmentation and inconsistencies within a single component. This situation is evidenced in the corrections' search for an alternative to rehabilitation. Certain interests are advocating community supervision and reintegration, while other groups stress increased incapacitation and retribution. These considerations are further complicated by new demands for lowering state budgets with correspondingly rising cost of incarceration and demands for the protection of the rights of offenders. Trends seem to be toward greater use of community supervision with simultaneous specification of mandatory sentences for particularly "fear-invoking" offenses. We thus see quite different and conflicting interests being considered, incorporated, and implemented within corrections.

A study by Cole (1980) of the Office of the Prosecuting Attorney in King County, Washington also supports the contention that different interests are represented within the seemingly conflicting processes of a single agency. Cole's research indicated that the prosecutor's office could be viewed as an organization within an exchange system that operated in a marketlike fashion. The decision to prosecute or not to prosecute could occur at various times during processing and was often based on the influence of a variety of officials. In this manner, the prosecutor could only exercise discretion within the exchange framework. As Cole (1980:166) points out, "the police, court congestion, organizational strains, and community pressures are among the factors that influence prosecutorial behavior."

In a most informative paper, Ohlin (1974) has outlined the manner in which conflicting interests influence organizational objectives and policy. (While Ohlin focused his analyses on correctional organizations, his ideas seem to be applicable to all criminal justice components.) Ohlin notes that interest groups arise when they feel that particular issues will directly affect them. The group may perceive that existing or possible activities will serve as a means to the achievement of its own objectives, it may be threatened by some existing or proposed activity, or it may view support of some issue as a way to fulfill some other obligation to another group. (See Bauer, 1968:17 for a discussion of obligatory activities which develop between interests groups.) A group's involvement in a particular issue will be determined by the advertency, saliency, and potency of the issue to that group. If the issue or activity is deemed important enough for the interest group's involvement or influence, the group can either try to obtain representation in the decision-making process or to support or penalize the organization for its particular decision. Over time and issues, the influence of various interest groups will change. As Ohlin (1974:149) describes, "the old, routinized ways of doing things gradually create problems. These problematic situations become the focus of new conflicts of interest, out of which new patterns of activity emerge."

The activities of an organization cannot be understood without considering the influence of interest groups. In that policies and activities of the organization reflect the influence of different interest groups, they may appear actually to conflict with one another, yet that conflict may be necessary in mediating among conflicting values within the community. The nature and activities of the organization may vary considerably as control passes from one group to another and as the interest structure shifts. Such dynamics are imperative for organizational survival in a complex environment.

On a final level, it would also seem possible that different interests are represented by the different components of criminal justice. Unfortunately, there is a lack of empirical analysis of this possibility, yet some support for the proposition can be inferred from what we know about the system. As suggested throughout this article, it is certainly reasonable to suggest that various aggregates of society desire different things from the justice system. The American Friends Service Committee seem to have a very different set of values than law-and-order traditionalists such as the International Association of Chiefs of Police. In attempting to see that their respective values are realized, these two groups advocate very different justice policies. However, each group tends to concentrate the exertion of its influence on a different component of the system, corrections and law enforcement respectively. In respond-ing to the interests of these and similar groups, it is quite possible for the components to focus on different and conflicting goals.

It is clear that criminal justice incorporates a number of different goals, including crime prevention, public tranquility, justice, due process, efficiency, and accountability (Levine, Musheno, and Palumbo, 1980:19–35). It is also known that the components differentially incorporate these goals into their operations. For example, it is often noted that the police tend to be more concerned with efficiency than due process, while the courts tend to focus on due process over efficiency. The different orientations of the police and the courts may very well make it possible to represent different interests within the community.

The apparent incoherence of the criminal justice goals does seem to serve a useful function when we view the environment in which the system exists. That environment is characterized by different values and interests. The frag-mentation among jurisdictions, the goal conflict within a single component of the system, and the conflict among components allow different interests to be incorporated into the system. As we will see in the following section, the existence of goal conflict allows for continual mediations of interests and adaptability of the system.

Mediations of Interests and System Adaptation

A second advantage of conflicting goals within the criminal justice system is that they promote a process of checks and balances within the system. Frag-mentation ensures that no single component of the system can dominate all other components, nor can any unitary interest be overemphasized. The vari-ous components can and do influence the operations of the other elements.

As Coser (1956) has demonstrated, conflict establishes and maintains a balance of power within the structure of the system. To make oneself under-stood and to achieve at least partial realization of goals, power must be exer-cised. Specifically, one's interest will not be considered in the negotiating process unless that individual's presence is felt. As Coser (1956:137) has stated, "struggle may be an important way to avoid conditions of disequilib-rium by modifying the basis for power relations. . . . Conflict, rather than being disruptive and dissociating may indeed be a means of balancing and hence maintaining a society as a going concern." In an environment which is characterized by a high degree of diversity of interest, conflict may well serve to produce an equilibrium, a balance, rather than a state of disequilibrium. Interest groups are forced continually to negotiate and compromise. Differ-ences are thus mitigated, and the system changes and adapts over time. Given the high diversity of attitudes about justice and its administration, the con-flicts and fragmentation within the criminal justice system probably provide the only means of maintaining equilibrium among the various interest groups. Thus, a strong law enforcement orientation can exist in a system which is also committed to a program of diversion. Lack of specificity is thus an effective device that allows various and diverse interests to be presented.

Lack of integration allows the system to adapt to special problems. For example, in reacting to public sentiment a local prosecutor may attempt to see that a particular offender is sentenced to a very long period of incarceration. Other than promoting the goal of retribution, such a sentence may be incongruent with other criminal justice goals. In a fragmented system, corrections may modify the prosecutor's action through some form of early release. The correctional decision as such directly conflicts with the values and goals of the local prosecutor and the public which he or she represents but may be consistent with contemporary trends of corrections and justice.

Blumstein and Cohen (1973) have suggested that levels of punishment are consistent over time within cultures. They contend that as crime increases the boundaries of criminality and the severity of punishment will be modified in order to maintain a consistent level of punishment. Lack of unification within the criminal justice system seems to serve a similar function. Discretion, such as corrections mediating a prosecutor's long sentence, allows for an equalization process to occur. In this manner, the motivation of police is modified by the decision of the courts as to what crimes will be prosecuted. Corrections monitors and modifies court decisions by implementing forms of early release, thus mitigating the overemphasis of incapacitation and retribution. The police and the courts monitor correctional decisions by being particularly attuned to previous offenders. This interactive process within the system makes it possible, at least to some degree, to maintain levels of punishment at consistent levels.

It is important to realize that the influence which components exert on one another is less than total domination. Because of the circular nature of influence, each component has the ability to modify the output of every other component and consequently that influence can be reciprocated. Also, no single component can totally reverse or change the action or activity of another component. Therefore, influence is limited to a specific extent. In this manner, the courts' insistence on police practices which are consistent with due process does not eliminate the law enforcement orientation toward efficiency. Efficiency is simply pursued within the boundaries of the courts' influence. This reality is critically important in that different components may represent different interests. The provision for diversity prevents any single interest from becoming dominant. Unification and the pursuit of a monolithic system would reduce discretion and limit the ability of the system to respond to aberrations and peculiarities. Fragmentation, on the other hand, allows the components to check the behavior of one another and to promote a balanced or equitable system of justice.

Thus, by allowing different interests to be present within an agency or a component, conflict may be played out and resolved among different jurisdictions and among the different components. Negotiation and mitigation may occur. Allowing fragmentation to exist and conflict to surface provides the system with the ability to adapt and evolve over time. Specifically, the system can experiment; it can act and react to the influence of different societal interests. The impetus and implementation of change develops slowly with a unified and monolithic system; a more fragmented system can rely on and use conflict as an impetus for change.

Offender Processing

The final advantage of goal conflict and fragmentation within the criminal justice system is that they may actually promote and support rather than retard and hinder the processing of offenders. This suggestion is contrary to most contemporary claims. For example, Kellogg (1976:50) suggests that "the system functions best when all of its parts most rationally and consistently assess offenders and their offenses, match these with the most appropriate responses, and administer the activities required to maintain the process." To the contrary, the lack of unity may be essential for the smooth operation of offender processing whereby the system is able to move a person through its various stages.

Recent research behind criminal justice consolidation has questioned the assumptions, theory, and evidence and has suggested that polycentricity is actually better than unity and centrality. Skoler (1977:300) has summarized the works of these researchers as follows:

> They cite, variously (and persuasively), emerging knowledge on organizational design and behavior, the cost and inefficiency of layered and complex public bureaucracies, new insights on where economies of scale and public service systems are illusory or nonexistent, and a theory of governmental responsiveness and efficiency which suggests greater "payoff" from less orderly, sometimes overlapping, and locally autonomous service units than from large, centralized, policy-uniform hierarchies. New theories of organizational behavior seem to suggest that large centralized organizations are less effective than smaller more autonomous organizations.

Ostrom and Parks (1973), in examining the merits of small versus large police departments, found that the public generally favors small departments, that efficiency is not gained with greater departmental size after a certain point, that fragmentation of agencies within a metropolitan area does not necessarily reduce the service, and that bureaucratization may reduce effectiveness more than increase it (Skoler, 1977:300). There seems to be little evidence that suggests that bigger, more centralized, and more unified systems or organizations are better; most evidence runs to the contrary.

In an attempt to unify a system, it is difficult, if not impossible, to anticipate all idiosyncrasies and probable changes and to formulate rules which will accommodate these future events. A nonunified system can change and make necessary adaptations to events which were not anticipated. Similarly, it is difficult to conjecture how the interest structure will develop and be modified in the future. A formalized and necessarily unified system will have difficulty in adapting to these changes.

Hasenfeld (1974:67–68) noted that the components of the criminal justice system depend on each other for validation of their claimed competence. The police depend on the conviction of apprehended offenders by the courts in order that their action be effective. The criteria that the police use for deciding which suspects to introduce formally into the system are partially defined by the behavior of the courts. Lack of unification within the system provides for the interaction between the various elements of the criminal justice system in this manner and allows the system to make changes in order to maintain a smooth flow of clients. As the use of marijuana became more widespread, the system adapted; courts ceased prosecuting users and the police responded by no longer arresting minor offenders.

Conclusions

Based on the arguments made above, the long-term implications of increased integration and unification cannot be regarded as favorable. Unification would create inequities to the extent that any new structure could not accommodate the diverse interests which currently have an impact on the system. The complex and dynamic process of negotiation which occurs within the decision-making environment of offender processing would accordingly be limited. Any system which exhibits high diversity, even in the form of fragmentation, allows conflicts to be played out and resolved on a continual basis. Any degree of centralization and unification, on the other hand, promotes rigidification and creates bureaucracy which is known to be an inefficient structure for change. A more unified criminal justice system would be more static, less able to respond to various interests. Greater investments of time and energy would be required to change the system.

As Coser has shown, conflict provides system stability rather than reduces it. The dynamic quality of a fragmented criminal justice system promotes a balance of power between antagonistic interests as it encourages adaptation and change. As societal attitudes and values fluctuate, the system can make corresponding changes. Unification would limit the ability of components to adjust their outputs to specific individual cases, to changes that occur over time, and to overreactions and mistakes by the other components. Furthermore, the balance which results from the exertion of influence on components by other components would be limited.

References

Bauer, R. A. (1968). The study of policy formation: An introduction. In R. A. Bauer & K. J. Gregen (Eds.), The study of policy formation (pp. 1–26). New York: Free Press.

Blumstein, A., & Cohen, J. (1973). A theory of the stability of punishment. Journal of Criminal Law and Criminology, 64, 198–207.

Chambliss, W. J. (1969). Crime and the legal process. New York: McGraw-Hill.

Chambliss, W. J., & Seidman, R. B. (1971). Law, order and power. Reading, MA: Addison-Wesley.

Chambliss, W. J., & Seidman, R. B. (1972). The state, the law and the definition of behavior as criminal or delinquent. In D. Glazer (Ed.), *Handbook of criminology.* Chicago: Rand-McNally.

Clark, R. (1971). *Crime in America.* New York: Irwin and Schuster.

Cole, G. F. (1973). *Politics and the administration of justice.* Beverly Hills: Sage.

Cole, G. F. (1980). The decision to prosecute. In G. F. Cole (Ed.), *Criminal justice: Law and politics* (pp. 155–166). North Scituate, MA: Duxbury.

Coser, L. A. (1956). *The functions of social conflict.* Glencoe, IL: Free Press.

Cyert, R. M., & March, J. G. (1963). *A behavioral theory of the firm.* Englewood Cliffs, NJ: Prentice-Hall.

Diesing, P. (1962). *Reason in society.* Westport, CT: Greenwood Press.

Duffee, D. (1980, reissued 1990). *Explaining criminal justice.* Long Grove, IL: Waveland Press, Inc.

Emery, F. E., & Trist, E. L. (1965). The causal texture of organizational environments. *Human Relations, 18,* 21–31.

Hasenfeld, Y. (1974). People processing organizations: An exchange approach. In Y. Hasenfeld & R. A. English (Eds.), *Human service organizations* (pp. 60–71). Ann Arbor: The University of Michigan Press.

Hawkins, G. (1976). *The prison: Policy and practice.* Chicago: The University of Chicago Press.

Kellogg, F. R. (1976). Organizing the criminal justice system: A look at "operative" objectives. *Federal Probation, 40,* 50–56.

Levin, M. A. (1980). Urban politics and policy outcomes: The criminal courts. In G. F. Cole (Ed.), *Criminal justice: Law and politics* (pp. 336–361). North Scituate, MA: Duxbury.

Levine, J. P., Musheno, M. C., & Palumbo, D. J. (1980). *Criminal justice: A public policy approach.* New York: Harcourt Brace Jovanovich.

March, J. G., & Simon, H. A. (1958). *Organizations.* New York: John Wiley.

Menninger, K. (1969). *The crime of punishment.* New York: Viking.

Ohlin, L. E. (1974). Conflicting interests in correctional objectives. In Y. Hasenfeld & R. A. English (Eds.), *Human service organizations* (pp. 135–152). Ann Arbor: The University of Michigan Press.

O'Neill, M. E., Bykowski, R. F., & Blair, R. S. (1976). *Criminal justice planning.* San Jose: Justice Systems Development.

Ostrom, E., & Parks, R. (1973). Suburban police departments: Too many and too small? In Masotti & Hadden (Eds.), *The urbanization of the suburbs: Vol. 7.* Beverly Hills: Sage.

Packer, H. (1968). *The limits of criminal sanction.* Stanford: Stanford University Press.

Pound, R. (1943). A survey of social interests. *Harvard Law Review, 57,* 1–39.

Quinney, R. (1969). *Crime and justice in society.* Boston: Little, Brown.

Quinney, R. (1974). *Critique of legal order: Crime control in capitalist society.* Boston: Little, Brown.

Quinney, R. (1977). *Class, state and crime.* New York: Longman.

Skoler, D. L. (1977). *Organizing the non-system.* Lexington, MA: Lexington Books.

Terryberry, S. (1968). The evolution of organizational environments. *Administration Science Quarterly, 12,* 490–613.

van den Haag, E. (1975). *Punishing criminals: Concerning a very old and painful question.* New York: Basic Books.

Wilson, J. Q. (1968). *Varieties of police behavior.* Cambridge, MA: Harvard University Press.

Wilson, J. Q. (1975). *Think about crime.* New York: Basic Books.

4

Metropolitan Development and Policing
The Elephant in the Living Room

JOHN M. KLOFAS

Introduction

It may seem obvious that the social conditions of American communities have important implications for policing those communities. That theme has been prominent in classical as well as contemporary investigations of police problems including subcultures (Westley, 1970) and the misuse of force (Skolnick and Fyfe, 1993:104): It was also the most pronounced theme in the report of the President's Commission on Law Enforcement and Administration of Justice in 1967.

Ironically, however, although changes in social conditions are widely recognized, these important elements of the context of policing have been largely neglected in the intellectual foundation as well as the practice of many contemporary approaches to policing. Concentrated poverty and racial isolation have become the "elephant in the living room"—obvious and omnipresent but often unacknowledged or ignored. This article will examine recent changes in communities and discuss their possible implications for policing. This will be done by focusing on medium- and small-sized cities in New York State.

Policing Then and Now

In 1967 the President's Commission contrasted the "old model," in which policing was regarded as a contest between the officer and the criminal, with a "new model" in which there emerged a role for police in maintaining order

John M. Klofas, "Metropolitan Development and Policing: The Elephant in the Living Room," *Criminal Justice Review*, Volume 25 No. 2, Autumn 2000, pp. 234–245. Reprinted by permission of *Criminal Justice Review*.

in communities. The commission focused on urban policing and identified social conditions in communities as a primary ingredient defining the nature of the police role. Its members wrote, "It is in the cities that the conditions of life are the worst, that social tensions are the most acute, that riots occur, that crime rates are the highest, that the fear of crime and the demand for effective action against it are the strongest" (1967:91).

In its report, the President's Commission elaborated a consistent perspective on the tasks facing criminal justice and the police in particular. It was based on a broad understanding of the causes of crime and included a prominent concern with changing social conditions in America's cities.

Although some have argued that the roots of modern policing can be found in the Commission's report (Walker, 1994:29), its concern with objective, definable conditions of communities does not seem to have the same place in discussions of contemporary policing. Instead, community policing discussions have often invoked idealized visions of self-regulating communities. These discussions, however, have been criticized as ignoring the economic and physical conditions of decline in communities (Buerger, 1994) and even as being circumlocutions designed to conceal the traditional police function (Klockars, 1999).

The literature of community policing pays little attention to the objective condition of communities despite its frequently expressed concern with the quality of life in those communities (Skolnick and Bailey, 1986). The focus of discussion is often internal, on the police and on how to change organizations and implement new strategies (Sparrow, 1999). In the language of management, this might be viewed as tending towards a closed-system perspective (Katz and Kahn, 1978) in which organizational analysis pays little heed to environmental factors.

It is, however, not simply ironic that community policing largely ignores objective community conditions. The theoretical justification for this seems to be the belief in the ability of good policing to overcome the power of other community forces such as poverty, poor housing stock, and racial and economic segregation (Kelling, 1998; Kelling and Coles, 1996). These beliefs are even more pronounced in some other contemporary strategies, most notably those emphasizing quality-of-life arrests.

Thus the contemporary view seems to be that good policing, albeit with strong community support and involvement, can counteract the impact of community conditions. Under this view, the most important condition is the quality of policing. By contrast, the perspective of the President's Commission in 1967 was that problems of crime and order, and ultimately the role of the police, would be shaped by the conditions of communities.

There are at least two possible implications of the contemporary view of the limited relevance of community conditions. First, the assumptions behind the contemporary strategies may be supported or refuted as crime is or is not controlled despite community conditions. That is an empirical question that is beyond the scope of this article.

The second implication may be more relevant to the regular operation of the police. Inattention to community conditions may mean that policing is influenced by forces unseen and that it is shaped in unanticipated and thus unplanned ways. A more open-systems analysis may avoid this outcome. The goal of the rest of this article is to reconsider the perspective of the President's Commission in which contextual variables were seen as relevant and to describe ways in which those variables may influence policing today. The goal is to talk about "the elephant in the living room," as we did in 1967, and to discuss its possible implications for the police in the twenty-first century.

From Urban to Metropolitan Communities

The 1992 presidential election was a milestone in electoral politics. It was the first such election in which a majority of the votes came from suburban communities rather than from cities and rural areas (Schneider, 1992). That was an important landmark in the movement of the population of the nation from a primarily urban to a metropolitan population. It signaled a sea change in American society similar to that when the country moved from a rural and agrarian nation to an urban one a hundred years ago (Jackson, 1985). Just as those early changes had broad implications for communities, so does the metropolitanization of much of American society. There are at least six trends that characterize this shift and that can be illustrated by examining upstate New York cities.

Shrinking Cities—Expanding Suburbs

Many small and medium-sized cities, particularly those in the northeast, have seen dramatic population shifts. For example, peak population levels for upstate New York cities were reached with the 1950 census. An examination of U.S. Census data shows that over the next 40 years the populations of Buffalo, Rochester, Syracuse, Utica, and Albany, declined by between 25% and 43%. The largest loser has been Buffalo. Its population fell from 580,000 to 328,000 during this period. In Rochester the population fell by more than 140,000.

While city populations fell, their suburbs grew, spurred on by highway construction and favorable financing and tax policies (Jackson, 1985). Buffalo's suburbs grew by 100% between the 1950 and 1990 censuses. As the city of Rochester lost nearly one third of its population, its suburbs grew by more than 200%. In 1950 two thirds of all Rochester area residents lived in the city; by 1990 that situation was reversed and two thirds of area residents lived in Rochester's suburbs. As the cities shrank and their suburbs expanded, other changes also occurred.

Increased Racial Segregation

The movement to the suburbs has not been uniform, across demographic groups. Analysis of census data reveals that whites fled many cities in remarkable numbers over the past 40 years. In Buffalo 1 out of every 1.6 whites left the city. In Rochester 1 of every 1.8 whites left. As whites left the cities the nonwhite population grew as a proportion of the total city population and in real numbers.

A nonwhite migration into the cities, by blacks and later by Latinos, has been masked by the overall decline in city populations. As late as 1950 nonwhites composed only 3% of the population of the city of Rochester. That rate was 40% in the 1990 census. From 1950 to 1990, the nonwhite population grew by more than 200% in Buffalo and by more than 350% in Albany. As the proportion of nonwhite residents of the cities grew rapidly, the suburbs remained almost exclusively white. The upstate suburban towns and villages have generally stayed below a level of 5% nonwhite.

Increasing Concentration of Poverty in Cities

As overall city populations fell and their minority populations grew, cities also saw dramatic increases in their rates of poverty (Wilson, 1987). Between, 1970 and 1990 poverty levels increased by 2 to 3 times across the four New York cities. According to the Census Bureau, more than one quarter of Buffalo's population fell below the poverty level in 1990. The other cities all saw poverty levels of around 20%.

In Rochester, half of all census tracts are now classified as "high poverty" tracts where 20% or more of the population live below the federal poverty level. The region's extreme poverty tracts, with poverty levels of 40% or more, are all located in the city of Rochester.

As with the racial gap between cities and suburbs, the poverty gap is also growing. Suburban poverty levels have changed only slightly as urban poverty has grown. Only Utica's suburbs reach as high as 8%. The other metro area suburbs had poverty rates of 4% or 5% for the last census.

Strain on Urban Institutions

A fourth trend associated with the metropolitanization of communities involves the strain that this places on urban institutions. Institutions that functioned for an urban society may not serve their new metropolitan communities as well. The best example may be public education. Many urban school systems appear to be failing as they are overwhelmed by the concentrated poverty of the urban core (G. Orfield, 1997).

The Rochester school system provides an illustration. Although city poverty levels are at the 25% mark, the figure is much higher for children. According to census figures, 38% of Rochester's children fall below the poverty line. That figure is still much higher when the public school system is considered. As late as 1980, 22% of Rochester School District children were from families who met income requirements to participate in the free and reduced-cost lunch program. In 1998 the figure had risen, to 90% (New York State Department of Education, 1999).

Those high poverty levels have also been tied to failing student performance. City schools do not compare well in educational outcomes with their suburban counterparts. Analysis of state education data (New York State Department of Education, 1999) shows that in the Rochester area, out of 100 suburban students entering high school, 85 can be expected to graduate in four years. In the city school district, however, that figure is just 27. And only 5% of city students as compared with 50% of suburban students will earn Regents diplomas—the highest standard in New York and the standard currently being phased in as a general graduation requirement for all students.

The situation in Rochester is not unique. According to Gary Orfield (1997), urban education across the country suffers similar problems. Although there are classrooms and even schools that fair better, no school district as a whole has made significant progress in the face of such high poverty levels.

Spread of Effects to Inner Ring

Movement to the suburbs actually began in the 1930s but escalated dramatically after World War II. The early suburbs that grew on the outskirts of cities were the first of expanding bands of development that now reach many miles out around most cities. And now those early inner-ring suburbs are showing many problems that were once regarded as limited to cities. Increasingly those suburbs are being plagued by decaying infrastructures, faltering local economies, and growing pockets of poverty.

A pattern being repeated around the country shows a decline of many inner-ring suburbs as wealth and resources move ever outward, often clustered in one direction, which has been referred to as a community's "golden crescent" (M. Orfield, 1997). There executive homes, office parks, and upscale retailing thrive while drawing resources from the central city and now the inner suburbs as well. But those inner suburbs lack even the strength of the city's business district or the concentration of social services found in cities, and so they may decline farther and faster than even the urban core (Rusk, 1995).

The trend is illustrated by the condition of Rochester's inner ring of suburbs. The oldest suburbs are seeing population declines and very slow rates of economic growth. The tax base of the city of Rochester has not grown in more than 20 years and is beginning to show significant declines (Metropolitan Forum, 1998). Total assessed value fell by 13% in the most recent year of available data. In fact, the county now provides more funds to the city budget than is raised by property taxes within the city itself.

But problems are also found in the suburbs. In the inner ring of suburbs, tax base growth has averaged 32% over the past 20 years while it has been 132% in the fastest growing "golden crescent" suburbs (Metropolitan Forum, 1998). What were once regarded as differences between cities and their suburbs are now surfacing in the form of disparities across suburbs.

Sprawl to Outer Ring and Rural Areas

The final trend, which can be recognized as part of the metropolitanization of communities, is the continued sprawl of suburban development. In many areas the pace of low-density development of the American landscape around cities has escalated. Since 1970 the population of the greater Rochester metropolitan area, for example, has grown by a mere 30% but the overall urbanized land use has grown by more than 100%. Similar patterns are found for other cities across the country. Recognition of urban sprawl has spawned concern with a wide range of issues including environmental degradation, loss of productive farmland, architectural aesthetics, increased transportation and utility costs, and the impact on rural culture. In recent years many initiatives have begun to try to slow or reverse these trends through preservation of farmland and protection of undeveloped land (American Farmland Trust, 1998).

Implications for Policing

An open-system perspective would suggest that the six trends that characterize metropolitan development have important implications for policing. Furthermore, consideration of contemporary growth patterns suggests that the effects on policing may be related but different in urban, suburban, and rural areas. For urban policing the continued decline of living conditions and problems of maintaining order in poor neighborhoods are likely to be major sources of concern. In suburban communities, police are likely to confront fears about the spread of crime and they may need to address community members' efforts to isolate themselves from their impoverished neighbors. In rural areas the pattern of growth suggests increasing concerns with the spread of crime and criminals to rural areas and with clashes between development interests and agricultural and rural interests. With those broad implications of metropolitan growth in mind, it is possible now to consider several more specific implications.

Increasingly Mobile Crime Problem

One consequence of the metropolitanization of communities is that crime patterns will follow the population. As infrastructure moves outward crime is likely to follow.

In recent years there has been renewed attention to the subject of rural crime (Weisheit, Falcone, and Wells, 1999; Weisheit and Wells, 1996). The subject of crime and justice across metropolitan areas has received less attention. It is clear, however, that gang and drug problems are not limited to urban areas and the crime trends reflect current population shifts (Kleniewski, 1997). The organization of policing, however, continues to follow established patterns of population density. Rural departments are inevitably small, with few officers covering large geographic areas. Many departments also have little or no capacity for conducting investigations. Suburban departments may grow as populations shift but they too may have few resources. Metropolitan development will put additional demands on a fragmented structure of policing and particularly on suburban and rural departments.

Greater Demands for Order in Cities

As the poverty gap widens in metropolitan areas, city police are likely to face increasing problems associated with the concentration of poverty. Among those problems may be growing demands for the maintenance of order in poor neighborhoods. As the physical and social conditions of neighborhoods grow to reflect poverty conditions many neighborhood residents and community leaders may pressure police to do what may be necessary to maintain order. Many police leaders have supported aggressive police tactics (Bratton and Knobler, 1998; Kelling and Coles, 1996). Sweeps, undercover drug enforcement, and specialized units to address street crime have become common in cities. These and other forms of aggressive policing may increase under growing demands for order. In the face of the personal consequences of structural change in communities, some residents may pressure police for even more aggressive efforts. If left unchecked these may strain the bounds of legal authority.

Strain on Police Community Relations

Police in American society have always shared a complex role marked by competing demands and interests (Bitner, 1970). Metropolitan development is likely to provide further complications. Although support for aggressive policing may grow in some areas, that support is not likely to be universal. The tactics, therefore, will also create additional conflicts with some community members who see themselves as the victims of more politically powerful groups. In a democratic society, current patterns of metropolitan growth seem likely to lead to increasing conflicts over police use of force, surveillance, stop and frisk practices, and other similar tactics.

Increasing "Culture Conflicts"

The race- and class-related consequences of changing metropolitan communities also suggest that these characteristics may play an even greater role in future police controversies. The growing segregation by class and race that marks metropolitan communities can spawn conflicts across those social boundaries. Police are likely to find themselves drawn into these culture conflicts. Divisions between "good" and "bad" neighborhoods and between a city and its suburbs will increase demands on police to contain problems of crime and disorder. Suburban police, in particular, are likely to face public support for activities designed to identify and remove people who are not seen as legitimate members of the community. Race and class can play central roles in such "border patrol" activity. If left unmanaged, pressure to engage in such activity may very well strain the boundaries of legitimate policing.

Mission Creep

As urban institutions experience problems associated with increasingly concentrated poverty in cities, police will be under increasing pressure to respond. Demand for new police interventions will come from those community institutions where the consequences of metropolitan development are most obvious. In Rochester, for example, police officers have been assigned to all middle and high schools on a full-time basis. Unlike the "officer friendly" role of the past, however, these officers are expected to perform a role that emphasizes traditional law enforcement powers.

In addition to schools, police in other communities have expanded their roles in public transportation and in the protection of downtown businesses and entertainment sites. In these and similar areas, police can expect increasing demands for their intervention. Those demands may place police officers in roles that take them beyond traditional approaches to policing.

Growing Problems Associated with Budget Constraints

As urban and inner-ring suburban tax bases fail, police will find themselves facing problems associated with increasingly tight budgets. Thus, at the same time that demands for services are increasing, the traditional sources of police support will be failing. Those problems may first mean greater calls for accountability or reorganizational efforts that stretch resources by moving officers to the street from administrative responsibilities.

There may also be other implications. Police may be forced to seek other revenue sources, perhaps through greater use of forfeiture laws. Local police may also increase reliance on funds from other governmental or private sources. And, too, private agencies may bear an increasing share of metropolitan policing responsibilities. Such changes, driven by the changing structure of American communities, can have very significant implications for the nature of local policing.

Impact of Sprawl on Rural Police

Whereas some of the effects discussed above primarily influence urban and suburban policing, rural police may also be significantly affected by metropolitan growth. As development sprawls outward, clashes are likely between long-term rural residents and the increasingly suburban population. Conflicts over early morning farming, spreading manure near residential neighborhoods, and other farm practices have been documented in metropolitan areas around the country.

The Social Meaning of Metropolitanization

In the nineteenth century, as the nation raced from its agrarian roots toward urbanization, the reform of social institutions and the development of new ones was inevitable. Public health housing reform, and improved public education are only a few of the reforms that grew with burgeoning cities. In criminal justice, institutional treatment of offenders and, later, the juvenile court and alternative sanctions such as probation and parole were all tied to the great change in American society (Rothman, 1971, 1980).

In the midst of this tumultuous change, however, not everyone embraced the new urban America. In the late nineteenth century the Populist Party emerged as a reactionary force in American politics. Populists pushed an agenda of economic and social reform that was meant to support threatened agrarian and rural interests. By the turn of the century the Populist Party had all but disappeared, overwhelmed by the forces of industrialization and urbanization.

Today, a clear reform agenda addressing metropolitanization is only beginning to emerge (Rusk, 1999). As yet, no consistent national policy has developed and states and localities are struggling sporadically with initiatives such as Smart Growth, a planning movement intended to address urban sprawl (Bollier, 1998). Like the Populists of the nineteenth century, many city and suburban interests resist such an agenda and pray for a return to an earlier era.

Despite the modern populists, the social implications of this demographic shift are substantial. Left unchecked, many are also quite harmful.

The pattern of development in metropolitan communities has led many people to home ownership, fine schools, and rising property values. Many have gone to the suburbs in search of the American dream. And many, both whites and minorities, have found it there. But, at a time when technology is making the world smaller and bringing cultures together, this pattern of development also threatens to divide us. With the growth of metropolitan areas there has also been a growth in the distance, both physical and social, between our nation's poor and the middle and upper classes. As William Julius Wilson (1987) has pointed out, it is a distance with significant economic and cultural consequences. As it widens, a burgeoning underclass falls farther from the social mainstream.

Social divisions by class and by race can also be exacerbated as opportunities for success, through education for example, close or remain closed to succeeding generations of poor children. Conditions in poor neighborhoods are also likely to grow worse as local municipal budgets are strained.

The decline of the urban core and the spread to older suburbs cannot occur without still wider social consequences. The great question for the near future will be whether we can build communities without building barriers. Fear can strengthen psychological barriers and engender hostility and conflict in older suburbs. It can spawn gated communities in the developing outer ring and it can push aside the bucolic isolation of rural America as we sprawl ever outward.

Conclusion:
Police Management and Metropolitan Growth

People who study the future in earnest caution against peering too deeply into the crystal ball (Cole, 1995). The future is most likely to resemble evidence-grounded, short-term predictions. It may be tempting to view this article as an attempt to peer deep into the future. But that would be an oversimplification. The forces changing American society are clear and well documented. Perhaps their consequences read like prognostications, but in each case there is already evidence of those consequences occurring across communities. The only element of prediction may be in estimating the magnitude of the consequences if metropolitan changes go unmanaged.

Unlike some fanciful predictions of the future, the forces of metropolitan growth and development have been gathering momentum for some time. In 1967 the President's Commission identified questions of race and class as issues that were central to the field of criminal justice. It recognized the relationship between poverty, discrimination, and crime and it noted the impact that these conditions have on police community relations and on the role of the police.

Although many of the conditions cited by the Commission have gown much worse, academic discussion of these matters in criminal justice has been more reserved, sometimes to the point of ignoring them. Outside of the field, however, a growing body of scholarship has been concerned with the social consequences of metropolitan patterns of development. Scholars and policy makers have used this framework to examine and suggest reform in a broad range of areas including education (G. Orfeld, 1997), fiscal policy (M. Orfeld, 1997), employment (Wilson, 1997), politics (Rusk, 1995), land use (Porter, 1997), and environmental justice (Bullard, 1994).

For managers of the police there are advantages to an open-systems view that encourages them to consider what has become the elephant in the living room. An understanding of population demographics and their consequences can contribute needed information for decisions regarding the management of police resources. Metropolitan development can have implications for police recruitment, training, and deployment of officers. This perspective suggests, at a minimum, that police should adopt regional perspectives that encourage cooperation across urban, suburban, and rural departments. It suggests that managers should be proactive in examining the demands that they face and in planning for expansion of their mission. And it suggests the importance of maintaining and enforcing clear professional standards as police negotiate increasingly complex and competing demands.

The importance of understanding the patterns of change that are altering American communities, however, is not limited to managerial concerns. The focus returns us to a question considered by the President's Commission in 1967: "What . . . is America's experience with crime and how has this experience been shaped by the Nation's way of living?" (1967:v). Now, as then, asking such questions seems important to understanding basic ideas of order and justice in a democratic society.

References

American Farmland Trust. (1998). *Call to action: Farmland protection success stories in the Empire State.* Washington, DC: American Farmland Trust.

Bittner, E. (1970). *The functions of police in modern society.* Washington, DC: National Institute of Mental Health.

Bollier, D. (1998). *How smart growth can stop sprawl.* Washington, DC: Essential Books.

Bratton, W., & Knobler, P. (1998). *Turnaround: How America's top cop reversed the crime epidemic.* New York: Random House.

Buerger, M. E. (1994). The limits of community. In D. P. Rosenbaum (Ed.), *The challenge of community policing* (pp. 270–273). Thousand Oaks, CA: Sage.

Bullard, R. D. (1994). *Dumping in Dixie: Race, class and environmental quality.* New York: Westview Press.

Cole, G. (1995). Criminal justice in the twenty-first century: The role of futures research. In J. Klofas & S. Stojkovic (Eds.), *Crime and justice in the year 2010* (pp. 4–17). Belmont CA: Wadsworth Publishing Company.

Jackson, K. T. (1985). *Crabgrass frontier: The suburbanization of the United States.* New York, NY: Oxford University Press.

Katz, D., & Kahn, R. (1978). *The social psychology of organizations.* New York, NY: John Wiley & Sons.

Kelling, G. L. (1998). Crime control, the police and culture wars: Broken windows and cultural pluralism. In National Institute of Justice (Ed.), *Perspectives on crime and justice: 1997-1998 lecture series* (pp. 31–51). Washington, DC: U.S. Department of Justice.

Kelling, G. L., & Coles, C. M. (1996). *Fixing broken windows: Restoring order and reducing crime in our communities.* New York, NY: Touchstone.

Kleniewski, M. (1997). *Cities, change and conflict: The political economy of urban life.* Belmont, CA: Wadsworth Publishing Company.

Klockars, C. B. (1999). The rhetoric of community policing. In S. Stojkovic, J. Klofas, & D. Kalinich (Eds.), *The administration and management of criminal justice organizations* (pp. 19–36). Long Grove, IL: Waveland Press.

Metropolitan Forum. (1998). *The health of Monroe's suburbs: Stagnation in the inner ring.* Rochester, NY: Author.

New York State Department of Education. (1999). *The state of learning: Report to the governor and state legislature* (Chap. 655 report). Albany, NY: Author.

Orfield, G. (1997). *Dismantling desegregation: The quiet reversal of* Brown v. Board of Education. New York, NY: New Press.

Orfield, M. (1997). *Metropolitics: A regional agenda for community and stability.* Washington, DC: Brookings.

Porter, D. R. (1997). *Managing growth in America's communities.* Washington, DC: Island Press.

President's Commission on Law Enforcement and Administration of Justice. (1967). *The challenge of crime in a free society: A report.* Washington, DC: U.S. Government Printing Office.

Rothman, D. (1971). *The discovery of the asylum: Social order and disorder in the new republic.* Boston, MA: Little Brown.

Rothman, D. (1980). *Conscience and convenience: The asylum and its alternatives in progressive America.* Boston, MA: Little Brown.

Rusk, D. (1993). *Cities without suburbs.* Washington, DC: Woodrow Wilson Center Press.

Rusk, D. (1999). *Inside game/outside game: Winning strategies for saving urban America.* Washington, DC: Brookings.

Schneider, W. (1992). The suburban century begins. *Atlantic Monthly, 240*(1), 33–44.

Skolnick, J. H., & Bailey, D. H. (1986). *The new blue line: Police innovation in six American cities.* New York: The Free Press.

Skolnick, J. H., & Fyfe, J. (1993). *Above the law: Police and excessive use of force.* New York: The Free Press.

Sparrow, M. (1999). Implementing community policing. In S. Stojkovic, J. Klofas, & D. Kalinich (Eds.), *The administration and management of criminal justice organizations* (pp. 397–408). Long Grove, IL: Waveland Press.

Walker, S. (1994). *Sense and nonsense about crime and drugs* (3rd ed.). Belmont, CA: Wadsworth Publishing Company.

Weisheit, R., Falcone, D., & Wells, E. (1999). *Crime and policing in rural and small town America.* Long Grove, IL: Waveland Press.

Weisheit, R., & Wells, E. D. (1996). Rural crime and justice: Implications for theory and research. *Crime and Delinquency, 42*(2), 379–397.

Westley, W. (1970). *Violence and the police: A study of law, custom and morality.* Cambridge, MA: M.I.T. Press.

Wilson, W. J. (1987). *The truly disadvantaged: The inner city, the underclass and public policy.* Chicago, IL: University of Chicago Press.

5

Science and Politics in Police Research
Reflections on Their Tangled Relationship

As a member of the committee that produced the report, reading the final version of *Fairness and Effectiveness in Policing: The Evidence* (Committee to Review Research 2003) and having a chance to see it whole proved to be a curious experience. I take considerable pride in having contributed to what will stand for some time as the definitive review of what we know about policing. I am also proud of the fact that the report elevates concern for fairness to a level coequal with effectiveness in policing. This is a significant and overdue shift in emphasis compared with previous reports that have attempted to provide a comprehensive picture of American policing (President's Commission 1967a, 1967b; National Advisory Commission on Criminal Justice Standards and Goals 1973).

Reading the report, however, brought a nagging sensation that something important is missing from it. I finally concluded that the missing element is the dynamic aspect of police research in the United States. Although chapter 2 provides a comprehensive review of the nature and development of police research (Committee to Review Research 2003, 20–46), it now strikes me as missing an important aspect of how that research has developed over the years.[1] The driving force behind much police research has been the influence of external politics. The police stand at the center of several issues that touch raw nerves in American politics, most notably, race relations and the tangled relationship between race and crime, and public concern about these issues has greatly influenced police research.

Samuel Walker, *The Annals of the American Academy of Political and Social Science*, Vol. 593, pp. 137–155, © 2004 by Sage Publications. Reprinted by permission of Sage Publications.

Whether police research is more or less influenced in this regard than, for example, research on public education, family policy, or public welfare is an interesting question that merits examination. It is quite possible that research on all politically sensitive social issues such as crime, education, employment, and others is heavily influenced by the political environment. It is also possible that this is an inevitable feature of social science research and one that sets it apart from research in the natural sciences. These questions, however, go far beyond the scope of this article, which focuses on the nature of political influence on police research.

The relationship between police research and the external political environment is extremely complex and is by no means simple or one-directional. I will argue in this article that while external political factors have heavily influenced police research, it is also true that research findings have shaped the public discourse about policing and the direction of public policy. In addition, and perhaps more controversial, I will argue that the influence of politics on research has, in some very important respects, greatly enriched social science research on the police. I will develop my argument by positing four basic propositions and then illustrating them through discussions of a few selected episodes in the history of police research.

The observations in this article are in part a response to an unjustly neglected article by Lawrence W. Sherman (1974), which raised a number of important issues about the relationship between police research and police reform through the mid-1970s. Unfortunately, Sherman's article provoked no noticeable response, and the issues it raised have not been addressed in the intervening years. As a result, our understanding of the relationship between politics, research, and public policy is not as well developed as it might have been.

The idea that political influence could have a positive effect on police research, or any social science research for that matter, will undoubtedly strike many people as outrageous. The history of research in the entire criminal justice field is filled with stories of improper political influence. Completed studies have been suppressed by their sponsors (Martinson 1974), findings have been subtly or not-so-subtly designed to serve a political agenda or to make them politically palatable (National Institute of Justice 1983; Fyfe 1983), and studies where the researchers have deliberately avoided investigating certain issues or asking certain questions because the results would probably not please the sponsoring agency and/or the agency granting access to the data.[2] Indeed, self-censorship on the part of researchers may actually be a larger problem than overt censorship by public officials. A full-scale review of the various forms of improper political influence over research in criminal justice research would be a valuable and overdue contribution to our understanding of the enterprise of research in this politically volatile field.[3]

The political influence that I discuss in this chapter is of a very different sort. My discussion involves *agenda-setting* influence rather than *truth-suppressing* influence. As the case studies discussed below illustrate, agenda-setting influence occurs where external political influence causes researchers to undertake research on a subject or subjects they had previously neglected, with the result that the agenda of research is significantly altered. Agenda-setting influence in no way distorts truth (although it undoubtedly shapes research in certain directions with undoubted political ramifications), but as I will argue, it has in fact often enriched the study of policing in the United States.

The Argument: Four Propositions

Police research in the United States involves a complex interplay between science and politics. To make sense of this complexity, I posit four general propositions.

> *Proposition 1:* External political factors have had a major impact in shaping the agenda of police research. That is to say, many of the important research questions in policing that have preoccupied social scientists over the past half century have been, in the first instance, prompted by external political concerns.

This model of research is different from what might be considered the model of "normal science" as defined by Kuhn (1962) in his famous and enormously influential book *The Structure of Scientific Revolutions*. In the normal-science model, scientific inquiry is driven by the internal logic of science itself; research raises unanswered questions that stimulate further inquiry. Kuhn (1962, 43–51) further argues that scientific research is guided by a dominant paradigm that defines problems and directs scientific inquiry. A scientific revolution occurs when the prevailing paradigm is replaced by an alternative paradigm that redefines problems and redirects scientific inquiry. In my interpretation of the development of police research, external influences have introduced new topics for research, but only one change in police research in the past sixty years—the American Bar Foundation (ABF) Survey of the 1950s (discussed below)—rises to the level of a genuine paradigm shift (Walker 1992).[4]

> *Proposition 2:* Once a question or set of questions is introduced into police research—for example, the exercise of discretion by patrol officers, alleged racial or ethnic discrimination in traffic enforcement—the process of normal science begins to operate. Research findings raise unresolved issues that stimulate further scientific inquiry that may answer some questions but also generates new unresolved issues and additional inquiry. At this point in the process, the external political factors, while still present as part of the environment in which research is conducted and disseminated, cease to be a motive force.

> *Proposition 3:* The impact of external political influence on police research has often been extremely beneficial and has enriched it in important ways. External factors have forced researchers to confront important issues they had previously neglected and to wrestle with com-

plex and methodological issues that often have broader application. The most recent and notable example of this impact is the current controversy over racial profiling, which I discuss in the next section.

Proposition 4: In several subtle but nonetheless important ways, police research has influenced the external political environment and played a significant role in shaping public policy. Much police research produces essentially negative findings, in the sense that certain ideas, assumptions, or policy recommendations are not supported by empirical evidence. (Indeed, many readers will be struck by the recurring refrain in *Fairness and Effectiveness* that the evidence on various points is "inconclusive.") The external audience is often highly frustrated by this outcome. It much prefers what might be called positive findings, for example, a finding in the medical arena that a certain treatment has a significant impact in preventing or treating a major illness.[5] As I will argue in detail later, a number of important studies, including the Kansas City Preventive Patrol Experiment (Kelling et al. 1974), undermined conventional assumptions about policing and as a consequence opened the way for creative new thinking about public policy.

Case Study 1:
The Racial Profiling Controversy

The current controversy over racial profiling (Harris 2002) is a classic example of the extent to which external political factors have shaped the agenda of police research. This subject serves as a useful starting point for several reasons, even though it is out of chronological sequence with respect to other examples discussed here. The impact of external political factors in this example is both very clear and very strong. In this respect, the case provides a useful illustration of propositions 1, 2, and 3. In addition, the controversy is a matter of immediate concern and will be familiar to virtually all readers of this chapter. Subsequent case studies, on the other hand, involve events in the past with which not all readers will be as familiar. Finally, depending on how the response to the racial profiling controversy develops, it could eventually illustrate proposition 4 as well.

Racial profiling burst onto the national political and legal agenda around 1999, largely as a result of court cases in Maryland and New Jersey alleging systematic racial discrimination in traffic enforcement by state police officers (American Civil Liberties Union [ACLU] 1999). Law professor David Harris (1997) popularized (and possibly coined) the phrase "driving while black," first in a law review article and then in a report published by the ACLU (1999). The phrase—graphic and potent in its imagery—struck a nerve with the public, and with surprising speed, the issue of racial profiling became a national political issue.[6]

In part because of the key evidence introduced in the Maryland and New Jersey cases, civil rights activists made traffic-stop data collection their principal strategy for reforming the police and reducing racial discrimination in traffic enforcement (ACLU 1999). This choice of strategy involved rejecting other possible reform strategies, such as improved police training or administrative rule making (Police Executive Research Forum 2001, 49–114; Cohen, Lennon, and Wasserman 2000; Walker 2001a). The basic assumption underlying the data-collection strategy is that systematic data on traffic enforcement (including traffic stops, searches of vehicles, and the various outcomes of arrest, citation, or warning) will reveal whether a pattern of illegal discrimination based on race or ethnicity exists. Legislative bills to require data collection by law enforcement agencies were introduced in Congress (U.S. House of Representatives 1999) and a number of states. State laws with varying data-collection requirements have been enacted in an estimated fourteen states.[7] Meanwhile, beginning with the San Diego (CA) Police Department (2000), several hundred law enforcement agencies have undertaken voluntary traffic-stop data collection. Police chiefs undertook these voluntary efforts to be responsive to the minority communities in their jurisdictions (San Jose Police Department 1999; Walker 2001a).

The mandated and voluntary data-collection efforts have already produced a small flood of official traffic-stop data reports and promise to produce still more.[8] The data-collection movement presented police researchers with some formidable challenges, both scientific and ethical.[9] Some researchers have been directly involved in data collection and analysis efforts, including writing official reports (Missouri Attorney General 2002; San Diego Police Department 2002). Meanwhile, many other scholars have been asked to comment publicly on specific traffic-stop data reports or on the issue generally.

Traffic-stop data collection has forced police researchers to confront the basic question of what kind of data are sufficient to prove or disprove that a pattern of illegal racial or ethnic discrimination in enforcement exists. This question was not chosen by the research community but forced on them by the data-collection strategy itself, namely, the civil rights activists' assumption that enforcement data will reveal patterns of discrimination. The debate among researchers quickly narrowed into a consideration of what data could serve as the proper benchmark (or denominator or base rate) against which traffic-stop data can be analyzed (Fridell 2004; General Accounting Office 2000; Home Office 2000; Police Executive Research Forum 2001, 115–44; Walker 2001a). There are also related questions involving exactly what data on traffic stops are necessary and, most important, whether data on individual officers are needed.

In the politically driven rush to collect traffic-stop data, few people paused to reflect on the nature of the data entered in the Maryland and New Jersey cases and on the implications of the methodology used. As developed by John Lamberth (2000), the research design in those cases involved direct observation of driving patterns on the highways in question and collection of data on the racial composition of both the total driving population and those drivers observed to be violating a traffic law. In both cases, the Lamberth-based data were sufficient to persuade the courts that patterns of racial discrimination did exist (Harris 1997, 1999, 2002). It is important to enter the qualification that the evidence was persuasive to courts and, apart from expert witnesses on the other side, not to peers in the scientific community. Without entering the controversy over "junk science" (Huber 1991), it is sufficient to say that courts might not accept as persuasive much of the data that have appeared in official traffic-stop data reports.

The official traffic-stop data reports, however, have used official census data on the resident population as the benchmark or denominator (Missouri Attorney General 2002; San Jose Police Department 1999, 2000). Scholars and other commentators, however, wasted little time pointing out that census data are not a proper benchmark for proving or disproving the existence of a pattern of race discrimination in traffic enforcement. Census data do not represent the at-risk driving population by race or ethnicity, in terms of either the overall driving population or the observed law violators (General Accounting Office 2000; Home Office 2000; Walker 2001a). Thus, while virtually every official report has found racial disparities in persons stopped, relative to the resident population, none has been able to make a persuasive case that a pattern of racial or ethnic discrimination exists. In fact, it is questionable whether such data would be persuasive to a court of law, much less a peer-reviewed journal.

The racial profiling controversy has enormously enriched police research in several ways. First, it has forced police researchers to study traffic enforcement, a subject they had virtually ignored for decades. The one major previous study of the subject was John Gardiner's (1969) book. The implications of this neglect of traffic enforcement were heightened by release of the Bureau of Justice Studies (Langan et al. 2001; Schmitt, Langan, and Durose 2002) study of police-citizen contacts (itself a product of the external political forces), which found that half (52 percent) of all citizen contacts with the police occur in traffic stops.

Second, the debate over the proper benchmark or denominator has been intellectually extremely rich. It spawned a flurry of special conferences and sessions at regular scholarly meetings including three at the Northwestern University's Center for Public Safety, one at Harvard University Law School, regular sessions at the annual meetings of the American Society of Criminology, and most recently, a conference at Northeastern University that brought together most of the major researchers involved in the subject (Northeastern University forthcoming). The Police Executive Research Forum, in the process of developing two reports on the subject (Police Executive Research Forum 2001; Fridell 2004), has held several meetings bringing together academics and law enforcement officials. The International Association of Chiefs of Police held two national meetings and issued a formal policy statement (International Association of Chiefs of Police 2000).

Scholars and law enforcement agencies have wrestled with a number of alternatives to the basic census data on residential populations. In perhaps the first such effort, Harris (1999) attempted to develop estimates of licensed drivers by race. The San Jose Police Department (1999, 2000) offered an interpretation using a combination of official crime data by police district and police officer deployment patterns by district. Other efforts have sought to use traffic-accident data as a surrogate measure of the driving population by race. Walker (2001a, 2003) has proposed an internal benchmarking approach that compares officers with peer officers. In addition, the debate has prompted scholars to develop explicit theories that would explain racial profiling (Engel, Calnon, and Bernard 2002). A comprehensive discussion of alternative benchmarks is forthcoming from the Police Executive Research Forum (Fridell 2004).

In sum, the advent of the racial profiling controversy illustrates propositions 1, 2, and 3. It was forced on the research community by external political factors and has greatly enriched research on the police. Scholars have been forced to direct their attention to an important but neglected aspect of police-citizen interactions and have been forced to address difficult methodological issues related not just to the study of traffic enforcement but, far more important, to the larger issue of racial and ethnic discrimination.

While it is a bit premature to predict how events will unfold, the current research activity on racial profiling ultimately may illustrate proposition 4. It is entirely possible that the criticisms of census-population-based data-collection efforts may eventually convince policy makers that alternative approaches to addressing the problem of alleged racial profiling are appropriate.[10]

Case Study 2:
The ABF Survey and
the Creation of the Modern Paradigm

Sustained social science research on the police began with the ABF Study of the mid-1950s.[11] The operative word here is *sustained*. Westley's (1970) study of the police subculture in the Gary, Indiana, police department, which is generally recognized as the first academic study of the American police (Sherman 1974), was essentially stillborn. Although rich in provocative insights (even though one of the most important findings rested on two interview questions involving thirteen and fifteen officers, respectively!) (Westley 1970, 113–14), it stimulated no immediate research and was rediscovered only in the 1960s as a consequence of the police-community relations crisis.[12] Research interest in policing began to develop largely as an outgrowth of research on juvenile delinquency, one of the major concerns of criminology in the 1950s, and the impact of police actions on juveniles. Westley's study, in fact, is one of the few major police studies that would fit the model of normal science as defined by Kuhn (1962). It originated out of an ongoing body of research, in this case the sociology of occupations, and sought to extend that field of inquiry to a previously neglected occupation.

The ABF Survey originated outside the academic community for reasons related to political and legal concerns (Walker 1992). Leaders in the legal community became convinced in the early 1950s that a "crisis" in the administration of criminal justice existed. In light of the great crime increase and police-community relations crisis that began in the 1960s, their notion of a crisis seems almost laughable today. Nonetheless, their real concern that something was wrong prompted them to act. With funding from the Ford Foundation, the ABF undertook field studies of criminal justice agencies in three Midwestern communities as a pilot project that would set the stage for a more comprehensive study. The field studies involved the collection of qualitative data through direct observation of officials at work in law enforcement, prosecution, and the courts. These field studies represented the first systematic study of routine police work.

The field observations stunned the members of the research team with respect to their richness and complexity and soon forced a complete revision of the project.[13] Plans for further research were cancelled, and the pilot project became the final project. In a very Kuhnian (1962) sense, the observations shattered the paradigm of criminal justice under which they were working and prompted the development of a new one. A summer seminar with a number of scholars was organized to discuss and try to make sense of the observations (Walker 1992). This seminar led not just to a series of publications that were enormously influential on subsequent research (Goldstein 1977; LaFave 1965; Newman 1966) but to a new paradigm for criminal justice research.

With respect to the police, the new (and still prevailing) paradigm holds that the police are called upon to respond to a wide range of social problems, only some of which involve law enforcement in the strictest sense; that the police exercise very broad discretion in handling these matters; that this discretion is (or was at the time) almost entirely unguided; that the exercise of discretion reflects a variety of situational, personal, and bureaucratic influences, with arrest and prosecution being only one goal; and finally, that much police behavior is of questionable legality (Walker 1992).[14]

In part because of its association with the University of Wisconsin Law School, where that perspective had taken root, the ABF findings emerged within the framework of the "law-in-action" perspective. This perspective shaped not only the publications that emerged directly from the survey but also several other extremely important studies. These include Skolnick's (1965) classic study *Justice without Trial*, arguably the second major study of the police after Westley (1970), and Reiss's initial explorations of the mobilization of law (Reiss 1971, x). (It is important to be sensitive to the contingency of historical events. There was nothing inevitable about how the ABF Survey developed. Under different influences, it could have taken a very different direction, with an unknowable impact on the development of police research.)

The paradigm that emerged from the ABF findings has guided the research that is summarized in *Fairness and Effectiveness in Policing* (Committee to Review Research 2003). Indeed, it is difficult to imagine the present field of police studies without ultimate reference to the ABF Survey. In this respect, the story of the ABF Survey illustrates propositions 1, 2, and 3. The survey, which was prompted by forces external to the research community, redefined the research agenda in policing (proposition 1). Once that occurred, the process of normal science took hold and much of the subsequent has been driven by the internal logic of scientific inquiry (proposition 2). All told, this process has enormously enriched research on the police, forcing scholars to address both substantive and methodological issues of major importance (proposition 3).

One intriguing question is why social scientists had ignored the police prior to the ABF Survey. Why was Westley's (1970) earlier study stillborn? Why did the process of normal science not take hold, despite the important questions his study identified and the obvious limitations of his methodology? To be sure, there was some nascent interest in policing as a consequence of research on juvenile delinquency during the 1950s, but this was largely an adjunct of the criminologists' primary concerns about juveniles. These questions, however, are beyond the scope of this article and would require some review of and reflection on the sociology and political science professions and their respective priorities in the 1950s.[15]

Another profound impact of the survey was not on police research, broadly defined, but on the specific issue of the police role. This impact can be traced in the work of Herman Goldstein, who began his career in policing as one of the ABF Survey field researchers. Goldstein played a major role in disseminating the idea that the police role involves not narrowly focused crime fighting but a far broader and more complex role as peacekeepers and problem solvers who are asked to respond to an infinite range of social problems (Goldstein 1977). He advanced this view in chapter 2 of the President's Crime Commission *Task Force Report: The Police* (President's Commission 1967b, 13–41) and the American Bar Association's *Standards for the Urban Police Function* (1980, 1-1.1) and then in his book *Policing a Free Society* (Goldstein 1977). The basic insight about the complexity of the police role moved from an exciting new finding in the late 1950s to the conventional wisdom a decade later. Goldstein pressed forward on the implications of this point, and his thinking ultimately led to the idea of problem-oriented policing, which along with community-oriented policing is the most important new idea in policing (Goldstein 1979, 1990).

The line of thinking that flows through Goldstein from the original ABF Survey to problem-oriented policing illustrates our proposition 4 regarding the impact of research on public policy. Evidence emerging from research called into question the prevailing assumptions about the role of a major social institution and set in motion thinking that eventually led to a reconceptualization of that role. This development, however, is only one part of the larger story involving the development of community policing that is discussed in the next section.

Case Study 3:
The Origins of Community Policing and Problem-Oriented Policing

Our third case study, which illustrates proposition 4, involves the development of community policing (Greene 2000), which, along with its first cousin problem-oriented policing (Goldstein 1979), is arguably the most important development in policing in the past quarter century (Bayley 1994).

Often described by its advocates as representing a "new era" in policing, community policing rejects the professional model that dominated policing since the early 1900s (Kelling and Moore 1988). The community policing idea had its origins in a twofold crisis of legitimacy for the police. On one hand, there was a loss of public confidence in the ability of the police to control crime. At the same time, the police faced continuing problems with respect to racial and ethnic minority communities. Although there were only occasional civil disturbances after 1968, virtually every police department faced allegations of race discrimination, involving unjustified use of deadly force, excessive physical force, failure to provide adequate police services, and employment discrimination. The two prongs of the crisis of legitimacy coalesced in the politics of "law and order," with some Americans demanding more aggressive anticrime activities (and with fewer procedural restraints on police actions) and with others demanding greater restraints on the police to reduce discrimination and police misconduct (Walker 1998).

The crisis of legitimacy led to a major rethinking of the police role and took the form of what we know as community policing. For the purposes of this article, the important point is that the specific content of community policing was heavily shaped by the accumulated research on policing. The influential research findings were both negative and positive in nature: negative in the sense of undermining basic assumptions at the core of the professional model of policing, and positive in the sense of pointing in new directions for police policy.

Three studies with negative findings were particularly influential in shaping thinking about the police. The Kansas City Preventive Patrol Experiment found that changes in the level of routine patrol had little impact on crime (Kelling et al. 1974). Studies also found that decreasing police response time produced no benefits in terms of either more arrests or greater citizen satisfaction (Kansas City Police Department 1977; Spelman and Brown 1981). Finally, the RAND study of criminal investigations found that traditional investigation activities were highly unproductive, that the most powerful determinate of solving crimes were factors associated with the crimes themselves (and independent of police effort), and that the prospects for increasing clearance rates were very dim (Greenwood, Petersilia, and Chaiken 1977). These studies had a devastating impact in undermining the basic assumptions surrounding the professional model of policing. Particularly important was the impact of the Kansas City patrol study in undermining assumptions about the role of routine patrol that had guided police thinking since the days of Robert Peel.

At the same time, the development of the community policing idea was influenced by certain intriguing findings from other studies. The most important of these findings involved the heavy influence of citizens over police work. Citizen requests for service through the 911 system were found to be a major determinant of routine police work (Reiss 1971). Citizen preferences were found to be an important factor in influencing arrest discretion (Black 1980). Eye witnesses' identification[s], from either victims or observers, were the critical factors in solving crimes (Greenwood, Petersilia, and Chaiken 1977). Finally, and particularly intriguing, the Newark Foot Patrol Study (Police Foundation 1981) found that while increased foot patrol did not reduce crime, it did decrease citizen fear of crime and improve public perceptions of the police.

These findings coalesced into a more general insight that the police do not function as independent professionals who bring to bear their special skills on problems. Rather, the police are heavily dependent on citizens for the problems they face, how they respond to those problems, and the success of some of their most important functions. This insight eventually formed the core component of community policing: that to be successful, policing needs to be community oriented and that police departments need to develop the appropriate organizational and programmatic strategies to enhance their relations with communities and their residents. (Again, it is important to be sensitive to the contingency of historical events. The crisis of legitimacy that struck policing in the 1970s could have led in a very different intellectual and policy direction.)

The development of the community policing idea, in short, illustrates proposition 4. Insights from an established body of police research played an important role in shaping the development of public policy and, in this case, a complete reorientation of the role of a major social institution. To be sure, the demand for a redirection of policing was primarily a product of external political forces, but research findings played an important role in demolishing the assumptions of the traditional model of policing and developing an alternative model. This is no small accomplishment and one in which the police research community can legitimately take pride. When skeptics ask what useful purpose is served by the investment in social science research on the police, the case of community policing provides an eloquent reply.

Notes on Other Chapters in the History of Police Research

Space does not permit a full discussion of all of the relevant cases involving the interplay of external politics and police research. Nonetheless, several additional examples deserve brief discussion because they amplify aspects of our four propositions.

Race Relations and the Police

It almost goes without saying that the ongoing problem of relations between the police and racial or ethnic minority communities has been a major influence on police research. The police-community relations crisis of the 1960s had an enormous impact on police research at the time, defining issues for research and directly spawning innumerable studies. Indeed, this crisis led to the rediscovery and eventual publication of Westley's (1970) pioneering but neglected study of the police subculture. It is safe to say that the focus on fairness and legitimacy in the National Academy of Sciences report is a product of this influence. The racial profiling controversy and its impact on police research represents the latest chapter in this story. These events illustrate our proposition 1.

At the same time, in an illustration of proposition 4, it should be noted that the police research community has had some impact on public policy with respect to questioning the effectiveness of many and perhaps even most of the programs designed to improve police-community relations. As the police-community relations crisis of the 1960s unfolded, civil rights leaders and their political allies advanced three major reform proposals: employing more African American police officers, creating special police-community relations units, and establishing external civilian review boards (National Advisory Commission on Civil Disorders 1968; Walker 1998).

As the *Fairness and Effectiveness* report makes clear, there is no strong support for any of these propositions. Most notably, there is no convincing evidence that increasing the number of racial or ethnic minority officers—in and of itself—improves police-community relations. (Improving police-community relations is a different goal than complying with equal employment opportunity laws.)[16] Nor is there any research demonstrating the effectiveness of special police-community relations units (U.S. Department of Justice 1973). Nor have there been any studies even investigating whether external civilian review boards do a better job of either investigating citizen complaints or reducing officer misconduct (Walker 2001b).

In sum, the police research community has responded to external concerns about the crisis in police-community relations, and there is substantial research documenting the nature and depth of that crisis. Research has also played some role in not confirming the effectiveness of some of the most popular reform ideas.

The Police and Domestic Violence

The case of research on police response to domestic violence is particularly complex. The impact of external political factors, in this case the women's movement, has been very strong. There was little interest in the issue prior to the 1970s. The first published study of police response to domestic violence was Raymond Parnas's (1967) article, which was based on the ABF field studies. Morton Bard's (1970) crisis-intervention experiment was one of the most highly publicized reforms of the late 1960s and early 1970s and reflected the 1960s popularity of reducing the formal role of the criminal justice system.

Research on police response to domestic violence took a dramatic new direction in the late 1970s and early 1980s, largely as a result of the women's movement. The women's movement not only defined domestic violence as a major social problem but also effected a 180-degree reversal in the thinking about the appropriate police response. The movement identified police failure to arrest as a major contributing factor to repeat violence. (The extent to which studies such as Black, 1980, contributed to this is not clear.) Litigation and advocacy soon led to the popularity of mandatory arrest, or arrest preferred, as the preferred policy goal (Loving 1980; Sherman 1992). These events established the context for the Minneapolis Domestic Violence Experiment designed to test the deterrent effect of arrest for domestic violence (Sherman and Berk 1984).

The saga of the Minneapolis experiment is well known. The study found a deterrent effect for arrest (Sherman and Berk 1984). The highly publicized findings are believed to have contributed to the spread of mandatory-arrest or arrest-preferred policies (Sherman and Cohn 1989). Replications of the Minneapolis experiment produced very mixed findings, however. For this and other reasons, many people in the domestic violence reform movement have serious questions about the wisdom of mandatory arrest or are now opposed to it completely (Sherman 1992, 124–53).

For our purposes, the domestic violence issue contains two important points. First, the impact of external politics in the form of the women's movement on both policy and research agenda seems quite strong. Second, the impact of research on policy is far more complex and particularly intriguing. The impact of the Minneapolis experiment sparked a serious debate among scholars about the wisdom of basing social policy on a single study. Some critics argued that this is a very unsound way to develop social policy and argued that scholars should exhibit greater humility with regard to the policy implications of their research (Lempert 1984, 1989; Meeker and Binder 1990; Sherman and Cohn 1989).

This case of the impact of research on policy is more complex. There is good reason to argue—consistent with our first proposition here—that the emergence of mandatory-arrest policies (and statutes) was a response to political forces that were at work before the Minneapolis experiment and would have continued to influence policy even if the experiment had never been conducted. The published study added a nice scientific gloss to a political agenda but was not itself a crucial factor in policy making. The doubts about the deterrent effect of arrest that have been raised by the later studies have not notably affected public policy. Arrest-preferred policies appear to have remained in place across the country. A possible interpretation is that the political audience that eagerly received the initial Minneapolis experiment findings has been disinterested in contrary findings.

Discussion

In his review of the relationship between police research and police reform, Sherman (1974) argued that there should be a fruitful partnership between the two domains. He was careful to emphasize that each domain has its own responsibilities the other should respect and that social science research would betray its mission if it were wholly subservient to the interests of practitioners. The best result, he argued, would be a process in which researchers would address issues raised by police practitioners and police practitioners would value and use the fruits of scientific research.

Looking back over the intervening quarter of a century since Sherman's article, during which there has been a veritable explosion of research on the police (as the *Fairness and Effectiveness* report makes clear), I would argue that in some complex and imperfect way, Sherman's model has been achieved. The essence of proposition 1 is that police researchers have responded to issues raised by the external environment. And as proposition 4 asserts, the external world has, in some important respects, responded to the findings of police research. What Sherman did not anticipate in his article, however, is the beneficial impact of politically driven research issues on the research enterprise that I have defined in terms of proposition 3.

One important distinction between Sherman's article and my analysis needs to be made. When he talked about "police reform," he referred to people who were directly active as police administrators and others with some close relationship with them. My analysis broadens the picture to take into account the much larger political environment, which includes both elected officials and, particularly important, political activists who help to shape the political agenda. I would argue that the police administrators that Sherman cites are as affected by major developments in the political realm as are police researchers.

What, then, is the larger meaning of the analysis contained in the four propositions offered here? I think several observations can be made.

The first observation is that external political influence in shaping the agenda of police research is not only pervasive but probably inevitable, given the salience of policing and the volatile relationship between crime and race in American society. The intriguing question is whether policing (and criminal justice generally) is a special case in this regard. As I suggested at the outset, it is entirely possible that research on all politically sensitive issues is similarly influenced. These issues include, most notably, public education, employment and income, social welfare programs, and health care. In this regard, we should probably accept the fact that social science research will probably proceed in a very different way than does research in the natural sciences. I could be wrong on this and readily concede that I know little about the enterprise of natural science research. Several years ago, I read and enjoyed Richard Rhodes's (1986) prize-winning book *The Making of the Atomic Bomb*. One point that comes through most strongly in that book is the extent to which science has been mobilized to serve military ends. This is not to say that political considerations (war being politics by other means) shaped the agenda of research in physics, but it would be difficult to ignore the enormous influence of government funding in the sciences. A thorough review may find that perhaps the worlds of social science and natural science are not completely different with respect to agenda setting.

A second observation involves the different forms of politically driven agenda setting in police research. We should distinguish between two very different forms. The racial profiling controversy represents one form, where controversies in the streets or the courts thrust an issue onto the national political agenda and then onto the research agenda. A second form involves a conscious effort to promote certain policies by a presidential administration through the use of federal research funds. The Clinton administration (1993–2001), for example, made an enormous investment in police research as part of its effort to promote community policing. Other administrations, both past and current, use federal funds in a similar manner. Lyndon Johnson used both the Crime Commission and the Office of Law Enforcement Assistance to further criminal justice programs consistent with the larger assumptions of liberal social policy (Walker 1998). Ronald Reagan pursued different criminal justice policies. These efforts represent the legitimate prerogative of government officials to shape the direction of social policies they were elected to implement. We might disagree with the policy orientations of the Reagan or Clinton administrations, but I do not think we can question their right in a democratic society to advance their policies.

A third observation, involving proposition 4, is that despite the heavy influence of external politics on the research agenda, the case of community policing seems to indicate that research can shape public policy. This is a matter of considerable significance, particularly for all those involved in producing *Fairness of Effectiveness in Policing: The Evidence*. The underlying assumption of the report, and of the National Academy of Sciences itself, is not only that scientific research should guide public policy but that it can do so. One of the common refrains among social scientists (and among many critics of higher education) is that published studies remain buried in obscure academic journals with no readership—much less impact—beyond professional peers. My discussion related to proposition 4 suggests that in certain circumstances, some of the best scientific research in policing has had some notable effect on the external world and on public policy.

Concluding Thoughts

The relationship between police research and the external political environment has been extremely complex. In this article, I have attempted to sketch the main themes. While the word *politics* generally has a negative connotation, one of my main arguments has been that with respect to agenda setting, political influence on police research has often been highly beneficial. At the same time, research findings have had an important influence on the external world and on public policy. This is no small achievement.

This article has raised a number of important questions that merit further inquiry. Particularly important is the question of whether the agenda of police research is more heavily influenced by external political considerations than is the research agenda in other politically sensitive fields such as public education or social welfare. The impact of government policies (and war in particular) on research in the natural sciences is another intriguing question. Finally, the entire relationship between research and public policy and the larger political environment merits a far more detailed discussion than has been possible here.

Endnotes

1 As a member of the committee, I have to accept my own responsibility for whatever I now find missing or inadequate in the final report.

2 The highly influential Harvard Executive Sessions on Policing, which played a major role in advancing the idea of community policing, managed to avoid almost any mention of police misuse of force, corruption, or racism. This neglect finally prompted two participants to write an additional paper raising these issues (Williams and Murphy 1990). This author has always speculated that the omission was due to the fact that these topics were unpalatable to Attorney General Edwin Meese whose agency not only funded the project but actively participated in the sessions.

3 A related issue involves the actions by the current Bush administration in controlling the dissemination of research findings to advance specific policies. Some previously available reports have been removed from agency Web sites, while in other agencies, all research reports are now reviewed by politically appointed agency officials.

4 Even a study as important as the Kansas City Preventive Patrol Experiment (Kelling et al. 1974) would not qualify as effecting a paradigm shift, because the findings discredited prevailing assumptions about patrol but did not question its central role in policing.

5 Examples are listed by Sherman (1992, 55) in his discussion of controlled experiments on police response to domestic violence.

6 Harris (personal communication, 2003) recalls first hearing the phrase from a law client and possibly seeing it in an article by Henry Louis Gates in *The New Yorker* magazine. In any event, his journal article (Harris 1997) undoubtedly deserves credit for popularizing it among social scientists.

7 The most current data, including legislation and reports, are at http://www.racialprofilinganalysis. neu.edu.

8 There are now more reports than need be cited here. The most current source for these reports, together with other relevant materials, is the Web site maintained by Northeastern University: http:// www.racialprofilinganalysis.neu.edu.

9 Space does not permit a full discussion of the ethical issues raised by data collection. In brief, however, the key issue is whether a social scientist should participate in a study where he or she believes the nature of the data cannot answer the question under investigation (e.g., the methods used in a study are not capable of determining whether a pattern of discrimination in traffic enforcement exists).

10 This author is not a disinterested party in this process, having published criticisms of the use of census data and advocated the internal benchmarking alternative (Walker 2001a, 2003).

11 The National Research Council report tends to underplay the influence of the American Bar Foundation (ABF) Survey and trace the beginnings of sustained research with the President's Commission (1967a, 1967b) in the mid-1960s.

12 To be sure, there were some studies, notably, the neglected and virtually forgotten Kephart (1957). But they do not represent the kind of sustained field of study that we associate with normal science (Kuhn 1962).

[13] The original field reports and the commentaries on them by Frank Remington are fascinating to read. The original materials are available at the University of Wisconsin Law School Library.

[14] With respect to the entire criminal justice system, the new paradigm may be summarized as follows: the administration of justice can be conceptualized as a system, involving a series of discretionary decisions, influenced by a variety of situational and organizational factors that only partly represent strict matters of law.

[15] Donald Newman, who was only later brought in to write the book on plea bargaining based on the ABF field research, provided a telling anecdote. He wrote his sociology dissertation on plea bargaining at the University of Wisconsin. In later years, he recalled members of the sociology department, including some members of his committee, asking, "But is this Sociology?" Many sociologists now believe that the field ignored criminal justice in those years because of its association with police training and [because it] lacked sufficient theoretical rigor.

[16] Similarly, there is no evidence to support early assumptions that female officers would be more effective than male officers because, as women, they would be less likely to use force and be more skilled at negotiating conflicts.

References

American Bar Association. 1980. *Standards for criminal justice. The urban police function.* 2nd ed. Boston: Little, Brown.

American Civil Liberties Union. 1999. *Driving while black.* New York: Author.

Bard, M. 1970. *Training police as specialists in family crisis intervention.* Washington, DC: U.S. Department of Justice.

Bayley, D. 1994. *Police for the future.* New York: Oxford University Press.

Black, D. 1980. *The manners and customs of the police.* New York: Academic Press.

Cohen, J. D., J. Lennon, and R. Wasserman. 2000. *Eliminating racial profiling: A third way approach.* Washington, DC: Progressive Policy Institute.

Committee to Review Research on Police Policy and Practices. 2003. *Fairness and effectiveness in policing: The evidence.* Washington, DC: National Research Council.

Engel, R. S., J. M. Calnon, and T. J. Bernard. 2002. Theory and racial profiling: Shortcomings and future directions in research. *Justice Quarterly* 19 (June): 249–73.

Fridell, L. 2004. *By the numbers: A guide for analyzing race data from vehicle stops.* Washington, DC: Police Executive Research Forum.

Fyfe, J. J. 1983. The NIJ Study of the exclusionary rule. *Criminal Law Bulletin* 19 (May–June): 253–60.

Gardiner, J. 1969. *Traffic and the police: Variations in law enforcement policy.* Cambridge, MA: Harvard University Press.

General Accounting Office. 2000. *Racial profiling: Limited data available on motor stops.* Washington DC: Author.

Goldstein, H. 1977. *Policing a free society.* Cambridge, MA: Ballinger.

———. 1979. Improving policing: A problem-oriented approach. *Crime and Delinquency* 25 (April): 236–58.

———. 1990. *Problem-oriented policing.* New York: McGraw-Hill.

Greene, J. R. 2000. Community policing in America: Changing the nature, structure, and function of the police. In *Criminal justice 2000.* Washington, DC: National Institute of Justice.

Greenwood, P. W., J. Petersilia, and J. Chaiken. 1977. *The criminal investigation process.* Lexington, MA: Lexington Books.

Harris, D. 1997. Driving while black and all other traffic offenses: The Supreme Court and pretextual traffic stops. *Journal of Criminal Law and Criminology* 87 (2): 544–82.

————. 1999. The stories, the statistics, and the law: Why "driving while black" matters. *Minnesota Law Review* 84 (December): 265–326.

————. 2002. *Profiles in injustice.* New York: New Press.

Home Office. 2000. *Profiling populations available for stops and searches.* London: Author.

Huber, P. W. 1991. *Galileos's revenge: Junk science in the courtroom.* New York: Basic Books.

International Association of Chiefs of Police. 2000. *Policies help gain public trust: Racial profiling.* Gaithersburg, MD: Author.

Kansas City Police Department. 1977. *Response time analysis.* Kansas City, MO: Author.

Kelling, G. L., and M. Moore. 1988. From political to reform to community: The evolving strategy of police. In *Community policing: Rhetoric or reality?* edited by J. R. Greene and S. Matrofski. New York: Praeger.

Kelling, G. L., A. M. Pate, D. Dieckman, and C. Brown. 1974. *The Kansas City Preventive Patrol Experiment.* Washington, DC: Police Foundation.

Kephart, W. 1957. *Racial factors and urban law enforcement.* Philadelphia: University of Pennsylvania Press.

Kuhn, T. 1962. *The structure of scientific revolutions.* Chicago: University of Chicago Press.

LaFave, W. 1965. *Arrest.* Boston: Little, Brown.

Lamberth, J. 2000. *Statistical report.* New York: American Civil Liberties Union.

Langan, P. L., L. A. Greenfield, S. K. Smith, M. R. Durose, and D. J. Levin. 2001. *Contacts between police and the public.* Washington, DC: Bureau of Justice Statistics. NCJ 184957.

Lempert, R. 1984. From the editor. *Law and Society Review* 18 (4): 505–13.

————. 1989. Humility as a virtue: On the publicization of policy-relevant research. *Law and Society Review* 23 (1): 145–61.

Loving, N. 1980. *Spouse abuse and wife beating.* Washington, DC: Police Foundation.

Martinson, R. 1974. What works? *Public Interest* 35 (Spring): 22–54.

Meeker, J. W., and A. Binder. 1990. Experiments as reforms: The impact of the "Minneapolis experiment" on police policy. *Journal of Police Science and Administration* 17 (2): 147–53.

Missouri Attorney General. 2002. *Annual report on Missouri traffic stops.* Jefferson City, MO: Attorney General's Office.

National Advisory Commission on Civil Disorders. 1968. *Report.* New York: Bantam.

National Advisory Commission on Criminal Justice Standards and Goals. 1973. *Police.* Washington, DC: Government Printing Office.

National Institute of Justice. 1983. *The effects of the exclusionary rule: A study in California.* Washington, DC: U.S. Department of Justice.

Newman, D. 1966. *Conviction.* Boston: Little, Brown.

Northeastern University. Forthcoming. Report of the 2003 Conference of Racial Profiling.

Parnas, R. 1967. The police response to the domestic disturbance. *Wisconsin Law Review* 31:914–60.

Police Executive Research Forum. 2001. *Racially biased policing: A principled response.* Washington, DC: Author.

Police Foundation. 1981. *The Newark foot patrol experiment.* Washington, DC: Author.

President's Commission on Law Enforcement and Administration of Justice. 1967a. *The challenge of crime in a free society.* Washington, DC: Government Printing Office.

————. 1967b. *Task force report: The police.* Washington, DC: Government Printing Office.

Reiss, A. J. 1971. *The police and the public.* New Haven, CT: Yale University Press.

Rhodes, R. 1986. *The making of the atomic bomb.* New York: Simon and Schuster.

San Diego Police Department. 2000. *Vehicle stop study mid-year report.* San Diego, CA: Author.

———. 2002. *Vehicle stop study: Year end report, 2001.* San Diego, CA: Author.

San Jose Police Department. 1999. *Vehicle stop demographic study: First report.* San Jose, CA: Author.

———. 2000. *Vehicle stop demographic study: Second report.* San Jose, CA: Author.

Schmitt, E. L., P. A. Langan, and M. R. Durose. 2002. *Characteristics of drivers stopped by the police.* Washington, DC: Bureau of Justice Statistics. NCJ 19148.

Sherman, L. W. 1974. Sociology and the social reform of the American police, 1950–1973. *Journal of Police Science and Administration* 2 (2): 255–62.

———. 1992. *Policing domestic violence.* New York: Free Press.

Sherman, L. W., and R. A. Berk. 1984. The specific deterrent effect of arrest for domestic assault. *American Sociological Review* 49 (2): 261–72.

Sherman, L. W., and E. G. Cohn. 1989. The impact of research on legal policy: The Minneapolis domestic violence experiment. *Law and Society Review* 23 (1): 117–44.

Skolnick, J. 1965. *Justice without trial.* New York: John Wiley.

Spelman, W., and D. Brown. 1981. *Calling the police.* Washington, DC: Police Executive Research Forum.

U.S. Department of Justice. 1973. *Improving police/community relations.* Washington, DC: Government Printing Office.

U.S. House of Representatives. 1999. H.R. 1443. *Traffic Stops Statistics Study Act of 1999.*

Walker, S. 1992. Origins of the contemporary criminal justice paradigm: The American Bar Foundation Survey, 1953–1969. *Justice Quarterly* 9 (March): 47–76.

———. 1998. *Popular justice: A history of American criminal justice.* 2nd ed. New York: Oxford University Press.

———. 2001a. Searching for the denominator problems with police traffic stop data and an early warning system solution. *Justice Research and Policy* 3 (Spring): 63–95.

———. 2001b. *Police accountability: The role of citizen oversight.* Belmont, CA: Wadsworth.

———. 2003. *Internal benchmarking for traffic stop data: An early intervention system approach.* Omaha: University of Nebraska at Omaha. http://www.policeaccountability.org/racialprof.html.

Westley, W. 1970. *Violence and the police.* Cambridge, MA: MIT Press.

Williams, H., and P. V. Murphy. 1990. The evolving strategy of police: A minority view. *Perspectives on Policing* 13 (January): 1–15.

6

Addicted to the Drug War
The Role of Civil Asset Forfeiture as a Budgetary Necessity in Contemporary Law Enforcement

Introduction

Civil asset forfeiture allows for the seizure and forfeiture of property derived from or used to facilitate certain crimes (Kessler, 1993). It is used in a number of criminal contexts, but is largely designed to weaken the economic foundations of the illicit drug trade and assist law enforcement in reducing drug-related crime (Department of Justice, 1994a). There are literally hundreds of state and federal statutes (e.g., President's Commission on Model State Drug Laws, 1993) that authorize the seizure of assets linked to drug offenses (not to mention other types of crime), and courts have consistently ruled that such statutes are constitutional, but civil asset forfeiture continues to be one of the most controversial weapons in the drug war arsenal (Morganthau and Katel, 1990; Pratt and Peterson, 1991; Wisotsky, 1991).

One reason that civil asset forfeiture is controversial is that, depending on the forum in which forfeiture proceedings are pursued (local, state, or federal), law enforcement officials can share in the proceeds derived from forfeitures (Blumenson and Nilsen, 1998:52; Department of Justice, 1994b). This potential for "profit" in law enforcement, otherwise known as "equitable sharing," has contributed to a near decade-old intellectual and legal battle about the disposition and distribution of forfeited assets (e.g., Atkins and Petterson, 1991; Hawkins and Payne, 1999). The law enforcement view is that forfeited assets

Reprinted from *Journal of Criminal Justice* Vol. 29, John L. Worrall, "Addicted to the Drug War: The Role of Civil Asset Forfeiture as a Budgetary Necessity in Contemporary Law Enforcement, pp. 171–187, 2001, with permission of Elsevier.

should be reserved for law enforcement purposes. Alternatively, critics claim that the police should never view their duties as a means of raising revenue for government agencies (McNamara, 1999; Thomas, 1999; Zalman, 1997).

State and federal laws vary in terms of what, if any, proceeds derived from civil asset forfeiture can be returned to the law enforcement agency (or agencies) that initiated the forfeiture proceeding(s) (Blumenson and Nilsen, 1998:54). This has led to fears that state and local agencies are circumventing state requirements, especially state requirements that prohibit law enforcement officials from sharing in the proceeds derived from civil asset forfeiture (e.g., Levy, 1996). Critics have claimed that the state and local agencies that participate with federal officials in civil forfeiture actions inadvertently contribute to an expanded role of the federal government in crime control, a notion antithetical to the ideals of federalism (Blumenson and Nilsen, 1998).

An interesting issue raised by the potential for law enforcement to receive a "kickback" from forfeiture is the role civil asset forfeiture, particularly equitable sharing, plays as a budgetary supplement. There are at least three ways forfeiture proceeds can be viewed with respect to law enforcement agencies' traditional budgets. One view (perhaps the most common) is that forfeiture proceeds can help to assist law enforcement officials by funding continued drug war activities. Another view is that forfeiture can be seen, more generally, as a fortuitous source of income that helps compensate for budgetary shortfalls. A final, perhaps more insidious view is that law enforcement agencies may be coming to depend on forfeiture in light of the revenue that stands to be earned. The latter, dependence-oriented perspective was the focus of the research reported here.

If the amounts of money and property seized from civil forfeiture were scarce and dispersed, there would hardly be a cause for concern. However, because the proceeds from forfeitures run into the hundreds of millions, if not billions, of dollars annually, the potential for "addiction" is not to be taken lightly. For example, in fiscal year 1996 alone, the Justice Department's Asset Forfeiture Program controlled US$338.1 million dollars, not to mention tens of thousands of pieces of real property. That amount was actually down by nearly US$200 million from the year before (Department of Justice, 1991). During the *height* of the drug war the Asset Forfeiture Program routinely oversaw amounts larger than half a billion dollars each year (Hyde, 1995). And with respect to asset forfeiture activities at the state and local level, one researcher recently found that it is not uncommon for single law enforcement agencies in large counties and municipalities to receive tens of millions of dollars from civil forfeiture during relatively short periods of time (Worrall, 1999).

Clearly, civil asset forfeiture can be a useful alternative source of income for law enforcement agencies, but some supporters have gone so far as to claim that forfeiture can, and even should, *supplant* traditional budgets. For example, the Justice Research and Statistics Association has made the following observation:

> Asset seizures play an important role in the operation of [multijurisdictional drug] task forces. One "big bust" can provide a task force with the resources to become financially independent. Once financially independent, a task force can choose to operate without federal or state assistance. (Justice Research and Statistics Association, 1993:9)

Whether or not this is a suggestion that drug task forces should attempt to fund themselves is unclear, but it is not difficult to see what role pecuniary concerns can play when law enforcement officials aggressively target money and property tied to both alleged and actual criminal activity.

The findings from the Justice Research and Statistics Association's report hardly stand alone. Reports from some US Attorneys' offices have shown seizures equal to as much or all of their operating budgets (Hawk, 1993). According to US Attorney Frederick W. Thieman (Hawk, 1993:7), figures from 1993 demonstrated that ". . . $1.9 million in asset forfeitures . . . [paid] for the operation of the entire US Attorney's Office [of the Western District of Pennsylvania]. . . ." Moreover, in reference to a New York Law Journal article, Blumenson and Nilsen (1998:63) reported that "in an eight month period during 1989 . . . the United States Attorney's office in the Eastern District of New York collected $37,000,000 from civil forfeitures," four times its operating budget. Thus, forfeiture laws have permitted governments to become "full financial partners and participants in the drug business" (Kessler, 1993:1.01). And to the extent that law enforcement agencies come to expect revenue from forfeiture, it is possible that other goals (e.g., service and crime control) are compromised.

In light of the hotly contested nature of civil forfeiture, there have been virtually no empirical studies of civil forfeiture (the lone exception appears to be Warchol and Johnson, 1996). Moreover, the fiscal budgeting perspective on civil forfeiture has been ignored entirely. It would seem that additional *empirical* attention to civil asset forfeiture, especially to the pecuniary concerns associated with the seizure of money and property, would be a worthy pursuit. Research in this area may help allay (or reinforce) some of the widespread fears that civil asset forfeiture laws are being abused by law enforcement officials (e.g., Hyde, 1995; Levy, 1996).

In an attempt to fill the gaps left by previous forfeiture research, this article reports on a nationwide survey of 1400 law enforcement executives concerning their experiences with civil asset forfeiture. Specifically, data were gathered on "adoptive" forfeitures, that is, forfeitures where state and local officials participated with federal officials in order to receive a "cut" of the proceeds; amounts of proceeds received from forfeiture; and perceptions of civil asset forfeiture as a tool for managing fiscal constraints. Since there have been no surveys of law enforcement's experiences with civil asset forfeiture, it is hoped that the results of the survey reported here contribute something more than rhetoric to the debate over civil asset forfeiture, as much of the current concern and criticism is linked to "celebrated" cases (e.g., Hyde, 1995).

This article takes a step beyond mere reporting, however. Evidence is offered that, indeed, a substantial proportion of law enforcement agencies *are* dependent on civil asset forfeiture, that forfeiture is coming to be viewed not only as a budgetary supplement, but as a necessary source of income. Potential explanations for "addiction" to civil asset forfeiture are then introduced. These are based on three primary factors: (1) past experiences with civil asset forfeiture; (2) fiscal expenditures; and (3) state regulations concerning the disposition of forfeited assets to law enforcement agencies and other criminal justice entities. Empirical tests of these explanations—including agency size as a control variable—reveal that dependence on civil asset forfeiture is tied to past forfeiture activities and, to a lesser extent, on fiscal expenditures.

Background:
The Controversy Over Civil Asset Forfeiture

Civil asset forfeiture's supporters hail, not surprisingly, from all arenas of local, state, and federal government. Prosecutors, law enforcement officers, Justice Department officials, even US Presidents, as well as others, have supported civil forfeiture with near unanimous consensus. Supporters have argued that civil forfeiture is an essential law enforcement tool, and that the "war on drugs" will never be won so long as criminals profit from their enterprises (e.g., Asset Forfeiture Office, 1994; Department of Justice, 1990, 1994b, 1995; Drug Enforcement Administration, Strategic Intelligence Division, 1993, 1994; Executive Office for Asset Forfeiture, 1994a, 1994b; General Accounting Office, 1990, 1991, 1992; Myers and Brzostowski, 1982). As the President's Commission on Model State Drug Laws (1993:A-29) remarked, forfeiture serves three remedial goals: it "(1) removes financial incentive to engage in illegal activity; (2) restores economic integrity to the marketplace; and (3) compensates society for economic damages suffered due to illegal activity by rededicating forfeited property to socially beneficial uses."[1]

Of course, civil asset forfeiture has just as many, if not more, critics (e.g., NACDL, 1996; Rudnick, 1992). The practice has been attacked by an unlikely coalition of critics, including conservative politicians. Critics have sensationalized the "drug war's hidden economic agenda" (Blumenson and Nilsen, 1997), referring to the means by which forfeiture annihilates due process (Jensen and Gerber, 1996) and encourages egregious law enforcement blunders (Hyde, 1995). Critics have also maintained that civil forfeiture tramples the Bill of Rights, circumvents proper appropriations channels, threatens the freedom of law abiding citizens, and guarantees a conflict of interest between crime control and fiscal management (Levy, 1996).

Both sides have been extremely vocal on the subject of civil forfeiture, but the voices of critics have almost drowned out the competition (e.g., Bauman, 1995; Burnham, 1996; Chapman, 1993; Enders, 1993; Greenburg, 1995; Rosenburg, 1988). In addition to criticisms of equitable sharing, which I address later, the critics have attacked civil forfeiture for its allegedly "perverted procedures" (Hyde, 1995). These procedural matters deserve special consideration.

Procedural Controversies

Civil asset forfeiture should be distinguished from criminal forfeiture. Criminal forfeiture proceedings are in personam, which means they target criminal defendants. Criminal forfeiture proceedings "are implemented in conjunction with the criminal prosecution of a defendant" (Warchol, Payne, and Johnson, 1996:53–54), and criminal forfeiture can only follow a criminal conviction. Moreover, criminal forfeiture is not to be confused with restitution or fines as potential penalties for criminal conduct. Civil forfeiture proceedings, on the contrary, are in rem proceedings, meaning that they target *property*. Civil forfeiture does not require that formal adversarial proceedings be initiated, and the property owner's guilt or innocence is largely irrelevant.

Civil asset forfeiture can be traced to an "archaic and curious legal fiction that personifies property" (Hyde, 1995:17). The personification of property originated in biblical times with deodands, which were things "forfeited, presumably to God for the good of the community, but in reality to the English crown" (Levy, 1996:7). If, for example, an inanimate object was responsible for a person's death, then the object was held in forfeit—as a deodand—in response to the superstition that the victim's soul would not rest until the object was accused and subsequently atoned. The Supreme Court has stated:

> Traditionally, forfeiture actions have proceeded upon the fiction that the inanimate objects themselves can be guilty of wrongdoing. Simply put, the theory has been that if the object is "guilty," it should be held forfeit. In the words of a medieval English writer, "Where a man killeth another with the sword of John at Stile, the sword shall be forfeit as deodand, and yet no default is in the owner." The modern forfeiture statutes are the direct descendants of this heritage. (*United States v. United States Coin and Currency*, 1971)

The notion that property can be "animate" and somehow responsible for wrongdoing is manifested in administrative and civil judicial proceedings where the government essentially sues property. Consider the names of the parties in two representative cases: *United States v. One Mercedes 560 SEL* (1990) and *United States v. One Parcel of Land at 508 Depot Street* (1992). This is important because the in rem proceeding is what ignites civil asset forfeiture's critics. In rem proceedings are sometimes controversial because they can shift the burden of proof from the state to the property owner (Durking, 1990; Petrou, 1984). Such proceedings can require the property owner to demonstrate, among other things, that the property was not used to facilitate a crime, nor that it was derived from the proceeds of criminal activity.

Asset forfeiture has also been criticized because law enforcement officials often need only demonstrate probable cause that the property is subject to forfeiture, not proof beyond a reasonable doubt as in criminal cases. And as Yoskowitz (1992:575) has pointed out, "as a practical matter, the government usually meets the initial burden of proof of probable cause simply by filing a verified complaint." The courts have allowed the government to use hearsay, circumstantial evidence, tips from anonymous informants (*United States v. All Funds on Deposit or Any Accounts Maintained at Merrill Lynch*, 1992) or information that is obtained *after* the seizure to establish probable cause in hindsight, *even if the initial seizure was illegal* (Yoskowitz, 1992, emphasis added; see also *United States v. One 56-Foot Yacht Named Tahuna*, 1983; *United States v. One 1977 Mercedes-Benz 450 SEL*, 1983).

Civil forfeiture's critics also contend that the law is equivocal about what is subject to forfeiture. Federal civil forfeiture law provides for the forfeiture of property that "facilitated" a drug crime; however, there is not always a clear indication of what constitutes facilitation (e.g., Heilbroner, 1994; *US v. Real Property Located at 6625 Zumirez Drive*, 1994). Moreover, the growing scope of civil forfeiture laws has raised many questions. Federal civil forfeiture laws have evolved from a focus on property to money and, more recently, to all real property.[2] Burnham (1996) has criticized these legislative changes, claiming that law enforcement officials can justify seizures without demonstrating that the property in question is clearly linked to criminal activity.

The legislative progression does not stop with addition of real property, however. Hyde (1995:25) has pointed out that the offenses subject to forfeiture are also growing in number:

> The 1986 Anti-Drug Abuse Act expanded civil forfeiture to include the proceeds of money-laundering activity. Certain 1990 amendments to that act included proceeds traceable to counterfeiting and other offenses affecting financial institutions—a bow to the savings and loan scandals. Then in 1992 Congress added more categories of offenses and also covered proceeds traceable to motor vehicle theft.

This broadening progression of federal forfeiture law says nothing about state forfeiture laws. And to the chagrin of the critics, some cases seem to suggest that state laws allow authorities more latitude with forfeiture (e.g., *Bennis v. Michigan*, 1996).

The remedial options for individuals whose property is subject to forfeiture are sometimes problematic as well; all the weight of the justice system can be stacked against property owners (Goldsmith and Linderman, 1989; Kasten, 1991). Sometimes it is ". . . up to the owner to challenge the seizure in a costly and unpromising hearing" (Blumenson and Nilsen, 1997:47). Thus, in cases where the forfeited property is not very valuable, the owner may have to make a cost/benefit decision, grudgingly conceding that it is best to "let the property go" (Edwards, 1994; Yoskowitz, 1992) because attorney fees can be too costly. As might be expected, the majority of forfeitures go unchallenged (General Accounting Office, 1989).

Forfeiture at the federal level has also been criticized because property owners are allowed less than 2 weeks to file a claim in federal court to challenge a forfeiture, and, until recently, they were required to post a 10 percent cash bond based on the value of the property simply to have their day in court (Hyde, 1995). Furthermore, the government has not always been liable for damage, storage, and maintenance costs while property is in its possession (Hyde, 1995).

Civil forfeiture has also been problematic for innocent owners, again because the owner's guilt or innocence does not matter (see *Bennis v. Michigan*, 1996; Canavan, 1990; O'Brien, 1991; Saltzburg, 1992; Stahl, 1992; Zeldon and Weiner, 1991). If innocent owners can muster the resources to challenge the seizure of their property, they can sometimes raise a successful innocent owner defense. According to 21 U.S.C. § 881(a)(7), property cannot be forfeited if the criminal activity at issue was "committed . . . without the knowledge or consent of [the] owner" (e.g., *United States v. Bajakajian*, 1998). However, there is no such protection in the some 200 civil forfeiture statutes at the state level (Levy, 1996), although there are some exceptions. "The federal courts simply have not clearly or uniformly explained the innocent owner defense, and Congress has not intervened to settle the matter" (Levy, 1996:164). In addition, the innocent owner defense is only relevant if the forfeiture is challenged.

Still other questions have been raised concerning the propriety of civil asset forfeiture, including the so-called relation-back doctrine (Jankowski, 1990). The relation-back doctrine is embodied in 21 U.S.C. § 881(h) and provides that "all right, title and interest in property [subject to forfeiture] shall vest in the United States upon commission of the act giving rise to forfeiture" (e.g., *United States v. 92 Buena Vista Ave., Rumson*, 1993). Still other concerns have been raised about the significance of the Fourth Amendment in civil forfeiture activities (Nelson, 1992; Speta, 1990).

One of the most controversial aspects of civil asset forfeiture is, of course, equitable sharing. Many observers have become concerned that the profit motive is winning out over the nobler goal of crime control (Dortch, 1992; Shaw, 1990; Willson, 1990).

The Civil Asset Forfeiture Reform Act of 2000

As this article was under review, the Civil Asset Forfeiture Reform Act of 2000 (CAFRA) was signed into law by the President Clinton. This was a significant victory for civil asset forfeiture's critics. Among other things, the new legislation shifts the burden of proof in federal forfeiture proceedings from the property owner to the state, eliminates the cost bond requirement, provides for reasonable attorney's fees for property owners who prevail in forfeiture proceedings, and creates a uniform innocent owner defense for all federal forfeiture proceedings.

The new legislation certainly minimizes the procedural controversies associated with civil asset forfeiture. Unfortunately, however, CAFRA is binding only on the federal government. States can decide themselves whether or not to follow the procedures outlined in CAFRA or change their own laws. In addition, and more importantly still, CAFRA does nothing to change the law pertaining to equitable sharing. That is, the potential for law enforcement to profit remains unchanged. This controversial feature of civil asset forfeiture is the primary focus of the remainder of this article.

Potential Explanations for "Addiction"

The foregoing has illustrated some of the controversies and problems inherent with civil asset forfeiture. Much of the extant literature seems to suggest that pecuniary concerns can motivate forfeiture activities. This raises at least two questions. First, is law enforcement coming to depend on civil asset forfeiture? Second, to the extent "addiction" is present, what explains this state of affairs? It has already been indicated that the former question will be answered in the affirmative. First, however, potential explanations for the "addiction" are reviewed, as these were incorporated into the multivariate models of "addiction" reported below.

To its critics, civil asset forfeiture is particularly loathsome because the agencies participating in forfeitures can also share in the proceeds. Prior to the Comprehensive Crime Control Act of 1984, the profits from *federal* civil asset forfeitures were deposited in the general fund of the US Treasury. Nowadays, at least at the federal level, the money goes to the Justice Department's Asset Forfeiture Fund and to the Treasury Department's Forfeiture Fund [see 28 U.S.C. § 524(c)(4) (1988 and Supp. IV 1992)]. "The money is then supposed to be used for forfeiture-related expenses and general 'law enforcement purposes,' with no further necessity for congressional appropriations or authorization" (Hyde, 1995:30).

The "equitable sharing" provision of the Comprehensive Crime Control Act of 1984 allows federal agencies to divide the proceeds derived from civil forfeitures with all participating agencies. State laws vary as to whether they return seized assets to participating agencies, but under federal law, participating nonfederal agencies are entitled to a (legal) "kickback" that is currently 80 percent (Executive Office for Asset Forfeiture, 1994a). One of civil forfeiture's most ardent critics has made this observation:

> Nothing revolutionized forfeiture in this country as much as equitable sharing. Its impact has been enormous, because it provides an intense incentive for law enforcement agencies at the state and local levels to search for assets connected with crime and to seize them for forfeiture. The incentive is self-aggrandizement: what the police take they will likely get to keep for their departments under federal law. (Levy, 1996:147)

The potentials for abuse and conflict-of-interest are obvious—equitable sharing not only provides an attractive budgetary supplement, but it encourages the circumvention of state forfeiture laws, thereby expanding the jurisdiction of federal law enforcement officials (Blumenson and Nilsen, 1997). This technique of "federalizing" forfeitures, or giving them up for "adoption" (also known as adoptive forfeitures) has been the target of numerous legislative reform proposals (e.g., Hyde, 1995).

Thus, it is reasonable to assume that increased participation in adoptive forfeitures could be tied to a dependence on civil asset forfeiture. According to Blumenson and Nilsen (1998:51), "at a time when state and local government budgets are shrinking, equitable sharing offers a new source of income, limited only by the energy police and prosecutors are willing to commit to seizing assets." In short, it was predicted that *the incidence of federalized seizures would be positively associated with "addiction."*

Second, in cases where state and local law enforcement officials do not (or cannot) give up forfeiture cases for "adoption," there is still a potential to share in the proceeds derived from forfeiture. As pointed out earlier, state law varies in terms of what percentage of forfeiture proceeds (if any) can go to law enforcement. At least three varieties of state laws are favorable to law enforcement. Each of these are reviewed in detail below (and in appendix A), but for now suffice it to say that state laws governing the distribution of forfeited assets can be expected to related to dependence on forfeiture. For example, some states allow more than 80 percent of the proceeds derived from civil forfeiture to go to law enforcement. Other state legal requirements, found in states that require proceeds to go into the general fund, are less likely to contribute to the growing dependence on civil asset forfeiture. Thus, it was predicted that *state laws authorizing a substantial proportion of civil forfeiture proceeds to go to law enforcement will be associated with "addiction."*

Third, in light of the observations by Hawk (1993) and others that forfeiture can be used to augment, even supplant fiscal budgets in some instances, it is reasonable to expect that past experiences with forfeiture will also be tied to the potential for "addiction." Accordingly, it was predicted that *the proceeds derived from civil asset forfeiture would be positively associated with dependence on civil forfeiture.* Put another way, as agencies come to receive more money and property from civil forfeiture, the more likely it is that they will come to depend on the practice.

Of course, a measure of total proceeds received excludes, a priori, those agencies that are prohibited by state law from sharing in the proceeds obtained from forfeitures. Moreover, just because an agency does not receive forfeiture proceeds does not mean that the potential for "addiction" will be absent. Some law enforcement agencies never receive forfeiture funds but are nonetheless aggressive in seizing money and property. The sheer incidence of attempted forfeitures (i.e., seizures), therefore, can be expected to serve as a useful predictor of "addiction" to civil asset forfeiture. Accordingly, it was predicted that *the incidence of seizures (whether or not money was actually returned to the participating agency) would be positively associated with "addiction."*

Fifth, it was predicted that fiscal expenditures will be inversely related to "addiction." Blumenson and Nilsen (1998:40) have observed that "during the past decade, law enforcement agencies increasingly have turned to asset seizures and drug enforcement grants to compensate for budgetary shortfalls, at the expense of other criminal justice goals." Thus, it is reasonable to expect that agencies with limited or restricted budgets will come to rely on civil forfeiture more than agencies that are better off, at least insofar as Blumenson and Nilsen's (1998) observations are accurate. Either way, the research reported here predicted that *law enforcement agencies with a "fiscal advantage" over other agencies would be less reliant on civil asset forfeiture as a means to compensate for budgetary shortfalls.*

Finally, it is reasonable to expect that *agency size is associated with dependence on civil asset forfeiture*, although there is no theoretical justification for specifying the directionality of such a relationship. It could be that large agencies enjoy large budgets, thereby reducing the need for civil forfeiture. Alternatively, large agencies could be those most in need of supplementary income to finance drug task forces, narcotics squads, and the like. More likely is the latter perspective; large agencies are, on average, confronted with more serious crime problems, and must occasionally be creative and innovative in their endeavors to combat illegal activity. Agency size is thus an important variable that deserves to be included in any model of "addiction" to civil asset forfeiture.

Methods

This article has two interrelated goals. The first goal of this article is to offer evidence that a substantial proportion of law enforcement agencies is dependent on civil asset forfeiture. The second goal is to offer an explanation for this phenomenon. Accordingly, this section describes the sources of data, variables, and statistical techniques used to reach the conclusions that many law enforcement agencies are dependent on civil asset forfeiture and that the dependence is tied to past forfeiture activities and fiscal expenditures.

Sources of Data

Three data sources were used in the analysis reported here. The first data set was obtained from a national survey of law enforcement agencies conducted in 1998. The second source of data was actually several subsources, namely the various civil and criminal codes of the 50 states and the District of Columbia. The third source of data was the Law Enforcement Management and Administrative Statistics (LEMAS) data set for 1993, the most recent year for which data are publicly available. Data from these latter two sources were merged into the 1998 *Policing Issues Survey* data set.

Policing Issues Survey

Under the auspices of the Division of Governmental Studies and Services at Washington State University, a survey was sent to 1400 police executives and county sheriff's nationwide during 1998.[3] The population for the survey was all municipal police departments and county sheriff's executives appearing in the 1998 *National Directory of Law Enforcement Administrators*. Two survey samples were drawn from that source. One was a sample of 700 police agencies employing more than 100 full-time sworn officers/deputies. This first sample attempted to reach *all* agencies with more than 100 officers/deputies, and was patterned after the sample collected in the 1993 LEMAS survey conducted by the Bureau of Justice Statistics. The second sample was of all the municipal police agencies and county sheriff's agencies appearing in the *National Directory* that employed *less than* 100 full-time sworn officers. The second sample was stratified random based on the type of agency (municipal police, county sheriff), size of population served, and number of sworn officers/deputies. Both samples were chosen so that they could be merged with both the LEMAS sample and the *Policing Issues Survey* sample.

The civil asset forfeiture section of the *Policing Issues Survey* asked a series of questions. Municipal police chiefs and county sheriffs were asked several forfeiture-related questions, three of which are pertinent to the research reported here:

1. Of the total number of times in the *previous three years* that your agency seized money or goods through civil forfeiture, on how many separate occasions did federal agencies act in conjunction with your agency?;

2. Please enter the estimated value of money and goods received by your agency during the *previous three years* from civil forfeitures; and

3. Please provide your reaction to the following statement by checking the appropriate response: Civil forfeiture is necessary as a budgetary supplement for my agency.

The responses available for the latter question were "strongly agree," "agree," "neutral," "disagree," and "strongly disagree."[4]

Overall, the survey response rate was 55 percent (770 of 1400 agencies responding). The response rate for large agencies was 60 percent (417 of 700 agencies responding) and the response rate for the small agencies was 50 percent. A probable reason for the low response rate among small agencies was that many small agencies do not have the resources and/or personnel available to complete the survey. Other potential reasons for the overall 55 percent response rate were that the survey took some time to complete and that the questions asked were somewhat sensitive.

After comparing the characteristics of respondents with nonrespondents, it was determined that there was some nonresponse bias. To probe nonresponse bias, particularly regional nonresponse, the author calculated two logistic regression models with response/nonresponse as a dependent variable. The first model included both agency size and population size as independent variables. This first model was unable to predict nonresponse (the model was no improvement over a model with all coefficients equal to zero). The author then calculated a second logistic regression model, this time including the four main census regions (Northeast, Midwest, South, and West). These were coded as three separate dummy variables. This second model was a significant improvement over the model without region as an independent variable, that is, it was able to predict nonresponse. The author coded the Southern Census region as the reference category and found that, relative to Southern agencies, Midwestern and Western agencies were more likely to respond to the *Policing Issues Survey*. This could have been due to the location of the author's university, but this is nothing more than speculation. Accordingly, readers should be aware that there was *some* nonresponse bias in the results reported below.

State Forfeiture Laws

As indicated in the literature, varieties of state laws governing the disposition and distribution of forfeited assets are believed to be of particular relevance to the apparent dependence on civil asset forfeiture. Accordingly, the author reviewed the relevant statutory provisions for each of the 50 states and the District of Columbia (see appendix A).

It was predicted that the statutory provisions that were most favorable to law enforcement would be the most likely to contribute to dependence on civil asset forfeiture. The author categorized state forfeiture laws in 11 different ways (see appendix A for the categorization and relevant statutory citations). However, the three types of law governing the disposition and distribution of forfeited assets that were expected to contribute to "addiction" were as follows: (1) state laws where 80 percent or more of the proceeds go to law enforcement; (2) state laws that permit agencies to share in forfeiture proceeds based on their contribution; and (3) state laws that specify that forfeiture proceeds go into a crime control fund (e.g., a drug awareness and education fund).

There are various reasons why law enforcement stands to benefit from the three legal arrangements selected for analysis. The first category was chosen because there is arguably less of an incentive to pursue adoptive forfeitures (forfeitures with federal officials), especially if close to 100 percent of the proceeds can be returned to law enforcement. Concerning the second category, state laws that permit agencies to share forfeiture proceeds based on their contribution also have a potential to be rewarding, especially if only one agency initiates forfeiture proceedings. Finally, even though state laws that require forfeiture proceeds to go into a crime control fund do not benefit participating agencies *directly*, such legal arrangement still benefit law enforcement overall (especially when the revenue is used to fund programs such as DARE).

Law Enforcement Management and Administrative Statistics

The third source of data used in the analysis was the LEMAS survey. One variable from the LEMAS data set believed to have a bearing on dependence on civil asset forfeiture concerned total fiscal expenditures. As indicated, the author predicted that total fiscal expenditures will be inversely related to dependence on civil asset forfeiture. Another important LEMAS variable included in the analysis was agency size. The LEMAS data set contains one variable for the average number of sworn officers/deputies that was also used in the analysis, although primarily as a control variable.

It was possible to use the LEMAS data set because the *Policing Issues Survey* sample was patterned after the LEMAS sample. Unfortunately, the most recent publicly archived LEMAS data set is for 1993. The 1997 data are currently being compiled, and, as of this writing, are not available. Nevertheless, it is reasonable to assume that the fiscal expenditures figures reported in 1993 compared to those reported in 1997 are highly correlated. There is no way to know this for sure as of this writing, so the use of 1993 LEMAS data should be acknowledged as a potential limitation of the research reported here.

Variables and Coding

The *Policing Issues Survey* was used to measure the dependent variable (dependence on forfeiture) and two independent variables (incidence of federalized forfeitures and amounts received). Additional variables were measured from the two alternative data sources (state laws and LEMAS), all of which were merged with the *Policing Issues Survey* data set. The analysis of state laws was conducted in order to find state laws most conducive to dependence on civil asset forfeiture. The LEMAS survey was used to measure total fiscal expenditures and agency size.

The dependent variable, dependence on civil asset forfeiture, was coded on a five-point ordinal scale. This corresponds to the five potential responses to the statement: "Civil forfeiture is necessary as a budgetary supplement for my agency." (The ordered responses to this statement appear in table 1 in the Results section.) In terms of the multivariate model of dependence on civil asset forfeiture, a logistic regression model capable of dealing with ordered dependent variable responses was employed. (The results for this model appear in table 4.)

The independent variables were coded in two primary ways. First, the three categories of state laws (80 percent or more of proceeds to law enforcement; proceeds into a crime control fund; and sharing based on contribution) were coded as three separate dummy variables. The presence of one or other of these legal arrangements was coded with a one; zero served as the reference category.

All of the remaining independent variables were coded as continuous variables. The incidence of total seizures and the incidence of federalized seizures were count outcomes. Both included the incidence of total and federalized seizures for the past 3 years. The total forfeiture proceeds variable was measured by amounts in dollars and included the incidence of federalized seizures for the past 3 years. The total fiscal expenditure was measured in the same way—total amounts in dollars for fiscal year 1993. Finally, department size was a continuous variable representing the average number of sworn personnel in each of the responding agencies.

Results

The results of the analysis were summarized for presentation in three ways. First, evidence is offered that a substantial proportion of law enforcement executives is "addicted" to civil asset forfeiture. Second, the independent variables used to explain the "addiction" were summarized. Finally, a multivariate model of dependence on civil asset forfeiture is reported. This section concludes with a discussion of potential problems posed by multicollinearity in the multivariate analysis.

Addicted to the Drug War

Table 1 reports on law enforcement executives' perceptions of civil forfeiture as a *necessary* budgetary supplement. Fully 176 law enforcement supervisors agreed or strongly agreed that civil forfeiture is necessary as a budgetary supplement, almost 40 percent of all the responding agencies.

Table 1 also suggests that small law enforcement agencies are less likely to depend on civil asset forfeiture. Just over 31 percent of the small agencies agreed or strongly agreed that civil forfeiture is necessary as a budgetary supplement. Even so, whether the focus is on large or small agencies, an "addiction" is still apparent.

In short, a substantial proportion of law enforcement agencies reported that they are coming to *depend* on civil forfeiture. Such a finding gives some support to criticisms that pecuniary concerns may be motivating law enforcement to forfeit money and property tied to criminal activity. To the extent that most of the response were truthful, this represents a potential conflict of interest, seemingly confirming forfeiture critics' worst fears.

Table 1   Responses to statement: "Civil forfeiture is necessary as a budgetary supplement"

	Large Agencies			Small Agencies		
	Frequencies	**Percent**	**Cumulative**	**Frequencies**	**Percent**	**Cumulative**
Strongly disagree[a]	63	16.45	16.45	50	15.97	15.97
Disagree	65	16.97	33.42	71	22.68	38.66
Neutral	79	20.63	54.05	94	30.03	68.69
Agree	77	20.10	74.15	46	14.70	83.39
Strongly agree	99	25.85	100.00	52	16.61	100.00
Total	383[b]	100.00	—	313[b]	100.00	—

[a] Pearson's chi-square = 17.8111; $P = .001$. Rows and columns are independent at the .001 level of significance.
[b] Total number of responses with complete data (out of 417 large agencies and 353 small agencies).

Summary Statistics: State Law, Forfeiture Activities, and Fiscal Expenditures

Table 2 summarizes the three varieties of state laws used in the analysis. The frequencies reported in table 2 are, again, for individual agencies. For example, 68 of the large agencies that responded were from states where forfeiture laws allowed a substantial proportion of forfeiture proceeds to go to law enforcement, a proportion equal to or greater than that which could be obtained by participating with federal officials in civil forfeiture actions. Only 11 agencies in the large agency sample were from states that require that forfeiture proceeds go into a crime control fund. Other agencies were able to receive forfeiture proceeds based on their contribution, but most common among the state laws governing the distribution of forfeited assets was the provision that 80 percent or more of the proceeds go to law enforcement.

Table 2   Prevalence of selected state laws governing the distribution of forfeited assets

	Large Agencies		Small Agencies	
	Frequencies	**Percent**	**Frequencies**	**Percent**
Eighty percent or more to law enforcement[a]				
No	345	83.54	272	77.27
Yes	68	16.46	80	22.73
Total[b]	413	100.00	352	100.00
Proceeds into crime control fund[c]				
No	402	97.34	337	95.74
Yes	11	2.66	15	4.26
Total	413	100.00	352	100.00
Distribution based on contribution[d]				
No	360	87.17	312	88.64
Yes	53	12.83	40	11.36
Total	413	100.00	352	100.00

[a] Two-way Pearson's chi-square = 4.7055; $P = .030$. Rows and columns are independent at the .030 level of significance.

[b] Total refers to the number of responses with complete data (out of 417 large agencies and 353 small agencies).

[c] Two-way Pearson's chi-square = 1.4625; $P = .227$. Rows and columns are not significantly independent.

[d] Two-way Pearson's chi-square = 0.3997; $P = .527$. Rows and columns are not significantly independent.

A cursory examination of table 2 suggests that there are no *significant* differences in state law by agency size. This is understandable, since the data reported in table 2 are actually state-level data, specifically state laws governing the distribution of forfeited assets. Any number of large and small agencies can be found in each state throughout the union.

Table 3 reports on agency forfeiture activities and fiscal expenditures, specifically the incidence of federalized seizures, total proceeds received, and total fiscal expenditures. These were the other three independent variables believed to influence agencies' dependence on civil asset forfeiture. Because these three variables are continuous, averages are reported instead of frequencies. Additionally, table 3 includes minimums and maximums for each of the three variables.

Not surprisingly, the large agencies were more likely to receive forfeiture proceeds than small agencies. The t statistic reported in footnote c of table 3 supports this observation; large agencies received approximately US$887,000 from civil forfeiture, whereas small agencies only received an average of approximately US$22,000. Much the same relationships held for the incidence of federalized seizures and total fiscal expenditures. On average, large

Table 3 Agency forfeiture activities and fiscal expenditures[a]

Size/Federalized Seizures and Dollar Amount	Obs.[b]	Mean	S.D.	Min.	Max.
Large agencies					
Number of total seizures	413	179	390	0	4500
Number of federalized seizures	349	45	177	0	3000
Total proceeds received (US$)	294	886,838	3,511,927	0	45,000,000
Total expenditures	413	3.06E+07	9.90E+07	129,742	1.70E+09
Small agencies					
Number of total seizures	352	18[c]	30	0	300
Number of federalized seizures	297	2[d]	5	0	60
Total proceeds received (US$)	255	21,697[e]	52,998	0	410,000
Total expenditures	352	2.95E+07[f]	5.33E+08	4800	1.00E+ 10

[a] The figures reported in this table are rounded off to the nearest whole number.

[b] "Obs." refers to observations, the number of cases with complete data for this variable. Observations reported are out of 417 large agencies and 353 small agencies that responded to the *Policing Issues Survey*.

[c] $t = -7.7638$; $P < .0000$. Small agencies participated in fewer total seizures than large agencies.

[d] $t = -4.1299$; $P < .0000$. Small agencies participated in fewer federalized seizures than large agencies.

[e] $t = -3.7512$; $P = .0002$. Small agencies received fewer total proceeds than large agencies.

[f] $t = -0.0435$; $P = .9653$. Small agencies' total fiscal expenditures do not differ significantly from large agencies' total fiscal expenditures.

agencies were more likely to participate in federalized seizures than small agencies. They also reported greater fiscal expenditures than small agencies.

Though not reported in table 3, the mean size of the large agencies was 526 with a standard deviation of 1673.56. The low-end cutoff for large agencies was, of course, 100 sworn officers/deputies, but the largest of the agencies in the large agency sample was 31,000. The mean size of the small agencies was 22 with a standard deviation of 22.4. The smallest agency included in the small agency sample employed only one sworn officer/deputy. Agency size is an important control variable introduced in the multivariate model that follows.

Explaining the "Addiction": A Multivariate Approach

Table 4 summarizes the logistic regression models of dependence on civil asset forfeiture. The dependent variable was reported dependence on civil asset forfeiture. The independent variables were those variables believed (based on theory and intuition) to be associated with dependence on civil asset forfeiture.

The results reported in table 4 are simultaneously comforting and disheartening. On the comforting side, the incidence of total seizures and the incidence of federalized seizures were not associated with dependence on civil asset forfeiture. This helps quell critics' (e.g., Blumenson and Nilsen,

Table 4   Logistic regression models of dependence on civil asset forfeiture

	Large Agencies (n = 363)[a]		Small Agencies (n = 298)[a]	
	Logit	Odds	Logit	Odds
Total seizures[b]	– 0.0000 (0.004)	0.9999 (0.0004)	0.0041 (0.0051)	1.0041 (0.0051)
Federalized seizures	– 0.0007 (0.0022)	0.9992 (0.0022)	– 0.0077 (0.0174)	0.9923 (0.0172)
Total proceeds received[c]	8.44E – 07**	1.0000**	2.01E – 06**	1.0000**
	(2.51E – 07)	(2.51E – 07)	(5.93E – 07)	(5.93E – 07)
Total fiscal expenditures[c]	– 1.04E – 08*	1.0000*	8.05E – 10	1.0000
	(5.04E – 09)	(5.04E – 09)	(3.63E – 09)	(3.63E – 09)
Eighty percent or more			0.3412 (0.3023)	1.4066 (0.4252)
(0.3149)	0.9593 (0.3021)			– 0.0415
to law enforcement				
Crime control fund	0.5792 (0.6891)	1.7845 (1.2297)	0.1578 (0.6826)	1.1710 (0.7993)
Based on contribution	0.5226 (0.3214)	1.6864 (0.5421)	0.0274 (0.4146)	1.0278 (0.4262)
Agency size	– 0.0003 (0.0013)	0.9997 (0.0012)	0.0878 (0.0553)	1.0918 (0.0603)
Constant	– 0.4160	–	– 1.2873	–
Log likelihood	– 237.7430		– 177.9106	
– 2 ln L chi-square	26.74		21.67	
Probability > chi-square	.0008		.0056	
Goodness of fit chi-square	375.79		297.08	
Probability > chi-square	.2039		.3438	

[a] n refers to the number of agencies with complete data on all variables of interest.
[b] Coefficients are close to zero and odds close to one because the units of measurement are small (individual counts of the number of total seizures and federalized seizures).
[c] Coefficients are close to zero and odds close to one because the units of measurement are small (amounts in dollars).
* $P < .05$.
** $P < .01$.

1998) fears that federal agencies are meddling in the affairs of state and local law enforcement. Table 4 also suggests that state forfeiture laws have no statistically significant relationship to dependence on civil asset forfeiture. Thus, the law enforcement agencies that stand to benefit from state forfeiture laws are neither less nor more dependent on civil asset forfeiture as a tool to manage fiscal constraints. The relationships were in the hypothesized direction, however.

It also appears the agency size is not related to "addiction," but interestingly the logit coefficient suggests an inverse relationship. This would seem to indicate that larger agencies are less likely to rely on civil asset forfeiture, a logical conclusion since large agencies are more likely than small agencies to enjoy larger budgets. However, the presence of more crime in large jurisdictions would suggest an opposite effect.

Somewhat disheartening are the relationships between total proceeds received, total fiscal expenditures, and dependence on civil asset forfeiture. The highly significant relationship between total proceeds received and dependence on civil forfeiture suggests, reasonably enough, that the agencies that not only engaged in comparatively more civil asset forfeitures, but also received generous revenues from such activities, throughout the past 3 years, came to depend on the practice more readily. That is, the more certain law enforcement agencies received in the way of forfeiture proceeds, the more likely they were to depend on such revenues. This was the case for both the large and small agency models.

Similarly, the total fiscal expenditure variable was significant. It was also in the hypothesized direction, but only for the larger agencies. Large agencies (those with 100 or more sworn personnel) with greater fiscal expenditures were *less* likely to depend on civil asset forfeiture. This relationship suggests that law enforcement agencies have stumbled upon a creative solution to the fiscal constraints that continue to plague public agencies. At the least, this poses some conflict of interest problems.

It should be noted that the relationships reported in table 4 are not due to chance. For example, the model chi-square statistics for both the large and small agency models were both significant ($P = .0004$ and $P = .0038$, respectively). The goodness of fit chi-squares reported at the bottom of table 4 also suggest that both models fit the data relatively well (.2178 and .3681, respectively).

A Note Concerning Multicollinearity

Multicollinearity, or too-high intercorrelations among X variables, can cause trouble. Specifically, it leads to unreliable coefficient estimates and large standard errors (Hamilton, 1992). This is important because the incidence of seizures, whether overall or federal, can be expected to correlate with the amount of forfeiture proceeds received by particular law enforcement agencies. Accordingly, steps were taken to ensure that multicollinearity was not a serious problem in the multivariate model reported in the previous section.

There are several methods for diagnosing multicollinearity, two of which were employed in the research reported here. First, a matrix of correlations among X variables was constructed. Table 5 includes the pairwise correlations among the regressors. According to Gujarati (1995:335), ". . . if the pair-wise or zero-order correlation coefficient between two regressors is high, say, in excess of .8, then multicollinearity is a serious problem." Two pairwise correla-

Table 5   Correlation matrix of continuous *X* variables[a]

	Total Seizures	Federalized Seizures	Total Proceeds	Total Fiscal Expenditure	Agency Size
Total seizures	1.000				
Federalized seizures	.6496	1.000			
Total proceeds	.6829	.8512	1.000		
Total fiscal expenditures	.1257	.1461	.1659	1.000	
Agency size	.5728	.7282	.8547	.1793	1.000

[a] Three variables (80 percent to law enforcement, crime control fund, and based on contribution) were excluded from this table because they were coded as dummy variables.

tions broke the .8 threshold, thereby indicating relatively high multicollinearity. These were the correlations between total proceeds and federalized seizures and agency size and total proceeds. These high correlations would seem to call the multivariate results into question. However, the correlation matrix method has been deemed fallible for various reasons (Hamilton, 1992, p. 133; Gujarati, 1995, pp. 335–336).

An alternative technique for diagnosing multicollinearity makes use of auxiliary regressions. This involves regressing each X variable on all the other X variables and examining the resulting R^2 values. The resulting R^2 values are then subtracted from one to yield a "tolerance" estimate (Hamilton, 1992). With perfect multicollinearity, tolerance equals zero and regression is not possible. Low tolerance, according to Hamilton (1992), that is, tolerance below .2 or .1, ". . . does not prevent regression but makes the results less stable."

Table 6 reports the tolerance estimates for the continuous independent variables. The tolerance of each variable, also known as the independent variation, is reported in the second column of table 6. Only one of the continuous variables demonstrates low tolerance: federalized seizures. Accordingly, the coefficients on federalized seizures in the multivariate results section should be viewed with some caution. Indeed, *all* coefficients in the multivariate "addiction" model should be viewed in this fashion, especially because many of the "cures" for multicollinearity were not suitable in light of the research design. For example, dropping selected variables, a common remedial measure taken in the presence of multicollinearity, would have left theoretically important variables out of the multivariate model. Similarly, data transformations, attempts to gather new data, polynomial regressions, and other techniques (see Gujarati, 1995 for a review) were not viable alternatives.[5]

Table 6   Tolerances of continuous X variables[a]

Variable	Shared Variation	Independent Variation
Total seizures	.4864	.5136
Federalized seizures	.8544	.1456
Total proceeds	.7339	.2661
Total fiscal expenditures	.0340	.9660
Agency size	.7325	.2675

[a] Three variables (80 percent to law enforcement, crime control fund, and based on contribution) were excluded from this table because they were coded as dummy variables.

Summary, Conclusions, and Implications

This article has offered evidence that a substantial proportion of law enforcement agencies, particularly municipal police departments and county sheriff's agencies, are dependent on the revenue generated from civil asset forfeiture. I then attempted to explain dependence on civil asset forfeiture in terms of three primary factors: (1) fiscal expenditures; (2) past experiences with forfeiture; and (3) state regulations governing the disposition and distribution of forfeited assets. Multivariate tests of these and other explanations for "addiction" suggested that fiscal expenditures were inversely related to dependence on civil asset forfeiture, but only for large agencies. The results also indicated that past forfeiture experiences, namely total proceeds received, were also associated with dependence on civil asset forfeiture, but in the positive direction. The incidence of total seizures, the incidence of federalized seizures, state law, and agency size were not significantly related to "addiction."

The most important finding reported in this article is that many law enforcement agencies are dependent on civil asset forfeiture. Of course, this was not the case for all agencies, or even for the majority, and cross-sectional data cannot reveal trends over time, but nearly 40 percent of the large agency sample reported that forfeiture is *necessary* as a budgetary supplement. The 40 percent figure was for 1998, and could very well be dynamic and changing in either a positive or negative direction, but the results nevertheless seem to confirm forfeiture critics' (e.g., Hyde, 1995; Levy, 1996) worst fears. If law enforcement is "in it for the money," which some agencies clearly are (see Miller and Selva, 1994), then it is difficult to see how the "war on drugs" can ever be won. (Of course, given law enforcement's minimal success in the "war on drugs," it is quite possible the "war" can never be won, even if profit is not a consideration.)

Taking this idea one step further, the notion that law enforcement is coming to depend on civil asset forfeiture lends support to perspectives such as Reiman's (1995) Pyrrhic defeat theory, namely that the criminal justice system is designed to fail. It could be that law enforcement has a vested interest in there being a drug problem because of the money and resources that stand to be gained. Of course, there is no way to support this statement, and such an eventuality is as implausible as it is radical, but the "policing for profit" notion is nevertheless intriguing. Nils Christie's (1993) view of crime control as industry also sheds light on the findings reported here. As Christie (p. 14) states, the crime control industry ". . . provides *profit and work* while at the same time producing control of those who otherwise might have disturbed the social process" (emphasis added).

The second most important finding from the research reported here is that past experiences with civil asset forfeiture and fiscal expenditures were associated with "addiction." Of course, these two variables do not fully *explain* dependence on civil asset forfeiture, but it would seem that conflict of interest problems are present in the way civil forfeiture is currently being carried out. Insofar as fiscal expenditures are inversely related to dependence on civil asset forfeiture, it is plausible to conclude that crime control is not the *only* goal among contemporary law enforcement agencies. Organizational survival and fiscal stability are also important considerations.

The finding that past experiences with forfeiture are tied to dependence has important implications. Aside from conflict of interest concerns, this finding helps explain why the CAFRA was tied up in Congress for so long. Numerous forfeiture reform proposals were continually been beaten down by the law enforcement lobby, particularly the International Association of Chiefs of Police, the Fraternal Order of Police, and the Department of Justice. The struggle may have occurred because of law enforcement's apparent dependence on civil asset forfeiture, and because law enforcement officials saw the potential to lose a significant proportion of the revenue generated from civil asset forfeiture.

It is possible that CAFRA's requirement that the burden of proof shift to the state may now improve things, but since the law does not require that forfeiture proceeds be diverted into a general fund, then the revenues generated from civil asset forfeiture will, in all likelihood, remain substantial. Regardless of what legislative changes have occurred, law enforcement agencies (and, to an extent, prosecutors' offices) enjoy a source of revenue that is not available to other public agencies. Any proposed changes to *this* arrangement are likely to confront serious opposition.

Much research remains to be done. Asset forfeiture has been scrutinized on constitutional and procedural grounds, but most research on forfeiture has not been empirical. The handful of empirical studies on civil asset forfeiture (this article included) could be starting points for future research. A host of questions remain, some of which include: What determines forfeitures?; What are the theories and motivations behind forfeiture?; Is forfeiture an effective crime control policy?; and, Are the police, in an attempt to generate money from civil forfeiture, violating people's civil rights? An answer to the latter question could lend additional support to the findings reported here. Other questions include: Is there a time dimension to dependence on civil asset forfeiture?; Is law enforcement really "addicted" to the drug war?; and, Is the "addiction" growing? If so, what can be done to ensure conflict of interest problems do not become more serious?

In closing, the research reported here has substantiated *some* of the concerns raised by civil forfeiture's most ardent critics. Despite noble intentions to strike at the economic foundations of the illicit drug trade, many law enforcement agencies are coming to depend on civil asset forfeiture. Moreover, past experiences and fiscal constraints are intimately tied to that dependence. The most profound consequence of this is that, depending on such variables as leadership philosophy and location, civil asset forfeiture can provide an opportunity for law enforcement officials to behave unethically, circumvent constitutional protections, and act in self-interest rather than in the interest of crime control or public safety.

Despite a number of past and current reform proposals, and despite the heated debate that asset forfeiture inspires, law enforcement's "double-edged sword" (Miller and Selva, 1994) is here to stay. It also appears that equitable sharing will survive well into the future. Given the fact that law enforcement agencies will continue to be able to reap the benefits from civil asset forfeiture, then steps should be taken to ensure that the "addiction" is not irreversible.

Appendix A   Percentage of proceeds going to law enforcement: State law
categories and relevant statutory citations[6]

State

Alabama	5 [Ala. Code § 20-2-93(e) (1990)]
Alaska	9 [Alas. Stat. § 17.30.122 (1996)]
Arizona	7 [Ariz. Rev. Stat. Ann. § 13-4315 (1997)]
Arkansas	6 [Ark. Stat. Ann. § 5-64-505(k) (1993)]
California	3 [Cal. Health and Safety Code § 11489(a)(2)(A) (1997)]
Colorado	3 [Colo. Rev. Stat. Ann. § 1613-506 (1997)]
Connecticut	3 [Conn. Gen. Stat. Ann. §§ 54-36h(f), 54-36i(c) (1997)]
Delaware	1 (100 percent) [16 Del. Code Ann. § 4784(f)(3) (1995)]
District of Columbia	1 (100 percent) [D.C. Code Ann. § 33-552(d)(4)(B) (1993)]
Florida	11 (depends on agency; not for operating expenditures) [Fla. Stat. Ann. § 932.7055(3)–(6) (1996)]
Georgia	6 [Ga. Code Ann. § 16-13-49(u)(4)(B) (1996)]
Hawaii	4 [Haw. Rev. Stat. § 712A-16(2)(a) (1993)]
Idaho	1 (100 percent) [Ida. Code § 37-2744(e)(2)(C) (1994)]
Illinois	11 (depends on particular statute) [ILCS ch. 720 §§ 550/12(g), 570/505(g) (1997); ILCS ch. 725 § 175/5(g)—(h) (1997)]
Indiana	8 [Ind. Code Ann. § 16-42-20-5(e) (1997)]
Iowa	8 (no discussion of distribution) [Io. Code Ann. §§ 809A.16-809A.17 (1997)]
Kansas	1 (100 percent) [Kan. Stat. Ann. § 60-4117(c)–(d) (1994)]
Kentucky	11 (depends on type of property) [Ky. Rev. Stat. Ann. § 218A.435 (1995)]
Louisiana	3 [La. Rev. Stat. Ann. § 32:1550(k)(1) (1989)]
Maine	10 [Me. Rev. Stat. Ann. § 5821 (Supp. 1996)]
Maryland	1 (100 percent) [Md. Crimes and Punishment Code Ann. §§ 297(f),297(k)(3)(v) (1996)]
Massachusetts	3 [Mass. Ann. Laws ch. 94C, § 47(d) (1995)]
Michigan	1 (100 percent) [Mich. Comp. Laws Ann. § 333.7524 (1997)]
Minnesota	3 [Minn. Stat. Ann. § 609.5315(5) (1997)]
Mississippi	1 (80 percent) [Miss. Code § 41-29-181(2) (Supp. 1997)]
Missouri	9 [Mo. Const., Art. IX, § 7; Mo. Ann. Stat. § 513.623 (Supp. 1997)]
Montana	1 (100 percent) [Mont. Code Ann. § 44-12-206 (1995)]
Nebraska	7 (50 percent only) [Neb. Rev. Stat. §§ 28-431(4), 28-1439.02 (1995)]
Nevada	1 (100 percent, but not for normal operating expenditures) [Nev. Rev. Stat. § 179.1187(2) (1995)]
New Hampshire	4 [N.H. Rev. Stat. Ann. § 318-B:17-b(v)(a)(1) (1995)]
New Jersey	6 [N.J. Stat. Ann. § 2C:64-6(a) (1995)]
New Mexico	0 [N.M. Stat. Ann. § 30-31-35(E), § 22-8-32(A)(1) (1978 and Supp. 1992, 1997)]

(continued)

State

New York	11 (40 percent to drug fund; 75 percent of remaining balance to participating agency) [N.Y. Laws 1349(h)(i)]
North Carolina	0 [N.C. Const., Art. IX, § 7; N.C. Gen. Stat. § 90-112(d)(1) (1993)]
North Dakota	2 (100 percent up to US$500,000) [N.Dak. Cent. Code §§ 19-03.1-36(5)(b), 54-12-14 (1997)]
Ohio	1 (100 percent) [O. Rev. Code Ann. §§ 2933.43(D)(1)(c), 2925.43(B)(4)(c), 2925.44(B)(8)(c) (1992)]
Oklahoma	1 (100 percent, but only for enforcing controlled substance laws) [Okla. Stat. Ann. §§ 2503(D)–(F), 2-506(L)(3) (1997)]
Oregon	1 (100 percent, but only for enforcing controlled substance laws) [Ore. Rev. Stat. Notes Preceding ORS 166.05 §§ 10(1)(c)–11(b)(1)(b) (1995)]
Pennsylvania	11 (shared by D.A. and Attorney General) [Pa. Cons. Stat. Ann. § 6801(f)–(h) (1997)
Rhode Island	6 [R.I. Gen. Laws § 2128-5.04(b)(3)(A)(i) (Supp. 1996)]
South Carolina	3 [S.C. Code Ann. § 44-53-530(e) (Supp. 1996)]
South Dakota	7 [S.Dak. Code Laws § 34-20B-89(2) (1994)]
Tennessee	11 (depends on type of property) [Tenn. Code Ann. §§ 53-11-451(d)(4), 5311-452(h)(2)(A) (1991 and Supp. 1996)]
Texas	11 (based on agreement between state and local officials) [Tex. Crim. Pro. Code Ann. § 59.06(a)–(d), (h) (Supp. 1997)]
Utah	1 (100 percent, but only for enforcing controlled substance laws) [Ut. Code Ann. § 5837-13(8)(a) (1997)]
Vermont	9 [18 Vt. Stat. Ann. §§ 4244(d), 4247 (Supp. 1996)]
Virginia	6 [Va. Code § 19.2-386.14(AB) (1995)]
Washington	1 (100 percent, but only for enforcing controlled substance laws) [Wash. Rev. Code Ann. §§ 7.43.100, 43.10.270, 69.50.505(f)(i) (1992 and Supp. 1997)]
West Virginia	10 [W.Va. Code § 60A-4-403a(g) (1992)]
Wisconsin	3 [Wis. Stat. Ann. § 961.55(5)(b) (Supp. 1997)]
Wyoming	9 [Wyo. Stat. § 35-7-1049(e)–(j) (Supp. 1996)]

Key

0 = none
1 = 80 percent or more
2 = 80 percent or more with restrictions
3 = less than 80 percent, but more than 0
4 = less than 80 percent, but more than 0 with restrictions
5 = based on contribution
6 = based on contribution with restrictions
7 = paid into state/general law enforcement fund (e.g., antiracketeering fund)
8 = paid into nonlaw enforcement fund (e.g., school fund) or general fund
9 = left to discretion of some official with or without restrictions
10 = law does not specify
11 = other

Endnotes

[1] Interestingly, the President's Commission failed to notice that most of the proceeds obtained from civil asset forfeiture go to law enforcement, not "society."

[2] The Comprehensive Drug Abuse Prevention and Control Act of 1970 provided, in relevant part, for the forfeiture of ". . . equipment . . . [and] property which is used, or is intended for use . . . in any manner to facilitate the transportation, sale, receipt, possession, or conceal-ment [of controlled substances]" [21 U.S.C. § 881(a) (1988 and Supp. IV 1992)]. The act was amended in 1978, providing for the forfeiture of "[a]ll moneys . . . or other things of value furnished or intended to be furnished by any person in exchange for a controlled substance . . ." [21 U.S.C. § 881(a)(6) (1988)]. In 1984, the act was further amended (or broadened) to provide for the forfeiture of "[a]ll real property . . . which is used, or intended to be used, in any manner or part, to commit, or to facilitate the commission of a violation" [21 U.S.C. § 881(a)(7) (1988)].

[3] Although sheriffs and chiefs were asked to complete the survey, it was clear in some instances that a subordinate completed the survey.

[4] It is possible that some agencies had an incentive to claim that they were dependent on civil forfeiture, perhaps not wishing to lose future revenues.

[5] It has been said that if the goal of regression is prediction, then multicollinearity may not be a serious problem (see Geary, 1963).

[6] Categories 1, 2, 5, 6, and 7 were used in the analysis. The remaining categories were not used in the analysis either because the percentages going to law enforcement are relatively small or because there is no guarantee that *any* proceeds go to law enforcement. Categories 1 and 2 were used to construct the dummy variable specifying that 80 percent or more of proceeds go to law enforcement. Categories 5 and 6 were used to construct the dummy variable specifying that proceeds are based on contribution. Category 7 represents the third dummy variable.

References

Asset Forfeiture Office. (1994). *Asset forfeiture manual: Law and practice.* Washington, DC: United States Department of Justice.

Atkins, D. P., & Patterson, A. V. (1991). Punishment or compensation? New constitu-tional restrictions on civil forfeiture. *Bridgeport Law Review, 11,* 371–381.

Bauman, R. (1995, February 20). Take it away. *National Review,* 34–38.

Blumenson, E., & Nilsen, E. (1998). Policing for profit: The drug war's hidden eco-nomic agenda. *University of Chicago Law Review, 65,* 35–114.

Bumham, D. (1996). *Above the law.* New York: Scribner.

Canavan, P. M. (1990). Civil forfeiture of real property: The government's weapon against drug traffickers injures innocent owners. *Pace Law Review, 10,* 485–517.

Chapman, S. (1993, March 7). Seizing property: Law enforcement's dangerous weapon. *Chicago Tribune,* p. 3, sec. 4.

Christie, N. (1993). *Crime control as industry.* New York: Routledge.

Department of Justice. (1990). *Annual report of the Department of Justice Asset Forfei-ture Program.* Washington, DC: Office of the Attorney General.

Department of Justice. (1991). *Points in response to presumed guilty series.* Washington, DC: Office of the Attorney General.

Department of Justice. (1994a). *Annual report of the Attorney General of the United States.* Washington, DC: Office of the Attorney General.

Department of Justice. (1994b). *Guide to equitable sharing of federally forfeited property for state and local law enforcement agencies.* Washington, DC: Executive Office for Asset Forfeiture, Office of the Attorney General.

Department of Justice. (1995). *Audit report: Asset Forfeiture Program.* Washington, DC: Office of the Inspector General.

Dortch, S. (1992, August 19). 356 marijuana plants, hose, weapons seized. *Knoxville News Sentinel*, p. 1.

Drug Enforcement Administration, Strategic Intelligence Division. (1993). *Illegal drug price/purity report—United States: January 1990–March 1993*. Washington, DC: United States Department of Justice.

Drug Enforcement Administration, Strategic Intelligence Division. (1994). *Illegal drug price/purity report—United States: January 1991–June 1994*. Washington, DC: United States Department of Justice.

Durkin, C. (1990). Civil forfeitures under federal narcotics law: The impact of the shifting burden of proof upon the Fifth Amendment privilege against self-incrimination. *Suffolk University Law Review, 24*, 678–709.

Edwards, E. E. (1994). *Review of federal asset forfeiture program (Testimony before the Legislation and National Security Subcommittee of the Committee on Government Operations, House of Representatives, June 22, 1993)*. Washington, DC: U.S. Government Printing Office.

Enders, J. (1993, February 11). Opposition growing to nation's drug forfeiture laws. *Chicago Daily Law Bulletin*, 2.

Executive Office for Asset Forfeiture. (1994a). *Guide to equitable sharing of federally forfeited property for state and local law enforcement agencies*. Washington, DC: United States Department of Justice.

Executive Office for Asset Forfeiture. (1994b). *Annual report of the Department of Justice Asset Forfeiture Program*. Washington, DC: United States Department of Justice.

Geary, R. C. (1963). Some results about relations between stochastic variables: A discussion document. *Review of International Statistical Institute, 31*, 163–181.

General Accounting Office. (1989). *Asset forfeiture: An update*. Washington, DC: General Accounting Office.

General Accounting Office. (1990, June). *Asset forfeiture: Legislation needed to improve cash processing and financial reporting (GAOIGGD-90-94-144FS)*. Washington, DC: U.S. Government Printing Office.

General Accounting Office. (1991, September). *Asset management: Government-wide asset disposition activities (GAOIGGD91-139FS)*. Washington, DC: U.S. Government Printing Office.

General Accounting Office. (1992, September). *Real property dispositions: Flexibility afforded agencies to meet disposition objectives varies (GAOIGGD-92-144FS)*. Washington, DC: U.S. Government Printing Office.

Goldsmith, M., & Linderman, M. J. (1989). Asset forfeiture and third party rights: The need for farther law reform. *Duke Law Journal, 39*, 1253–1301.

Greenburg, J. C. (1995, June 22). Hyde: Easy recovery of seized property. *Chicago Tribune*, p. 14.

Gujarati, D. N. (1995). *Basic econometrics* (3rd ed.). New York: McGraw-Hill.

Hamilton, L. C. (1992). *Regression with graphics: A second course in applied statistics*. Belmont, CA: Duxbury Press.

Hawk, R. (1993, November 8). Western district office pays for itself and more. *Pennsylvania Law Journal*, 7.

Hawkins, C. W., Jr., & Payne, T. E. (1999). Civil forfeiture in law enforcement: An effective tool or cash register justice? In J. D. Sewell (Ed.), *Controversial issues in policing* (pp. 23–34). Boston, MA: Allyn and Bacon.

Heilbroner, D. (1994, December 11). The law goes on a treasure hunt. *New York Times*, p. 70, sec. 6.

Hyde, H. (1995). Forfeiting our property rights: Is your property safe from seizure? Washington, DC: Cato Institute.

Jankowski, M. A. (1990). Tempering the relation-back doctrine: A more reasonable approach to civil forfeiture in drug cases. *Virginia Law Review, 76*, 165–195.

Jensen, E. L., & Gerber, J. (1996). The civil forfeiture of assets and the war on drugs: Expanding criminal sanctions while reducing due process protections. *Crime and Delinquency, 42*, 421–434.

Justice Research and Statistics Association. (1993). *Multijurisdictional drug control task forces: A five-year review 1988–1992.* Washington, DC: Justice Research and Statistics Association.

Kasten, L. (1991). Extending constitutional protection to civil forfeiture that exceeds rough remedial compensation. *George Washington Law Review, 60*, 194–244.

Kessler, S. F. (1993). *Civil and criminal forfeiture: Federal and state practice.* St. Paul, MN: West.

Levy, L. W. (1996). *A license to steal: The forfeiture of property.* Chapel Hill: University of North Carolina Press.

McNamara, J. (1999, June 6). When the police take property, who do you call? *Orange County Register,* 5 [Commentary].

Miller, J. M., & Selva, L. H. (1994). Drug enforcement's double edged sword: An assessment of asset forfeiture programs. *Justice Quarterly, 11*, 313–335.

Morganthau, T., & Katel, P. (1990, April 29). Uncivil liberties? Debating whether drug war tactics are eroding constitutional rights. *Newsweek,* 18–21.

Myers, H. L., & Brzostowski, J. (1982, Summer). Dealers, dollars, and drugs: Drug law enforcement's promising new program. *Drug Enforcement,* 7–10.

National Association of Criminal Defense Lawyers. (1996). *H.R. 1916 ("Civil Asset Forfeiture Reform Act") and the current federal asset seizure and forfeiture program* [Oral testimony presented before the United States House Committee on the Judiciary, July 22, 1996.] Washington, DC: National Association of Criminal Defense Lawyers.

Nelson, W. P. (1992). Should the ranch go free because the constable blundered? Gaining compliance with search and seizure standards in the age of asset forfeiture. *California Law Review, 80*, 1309–1359.

O'Brien, A. M. (1991). Caught in the crossfire: Protecting the innocent owner of real property from civil forfeiture under 21 U.S.C. Section 881(a)(7). *St. John's Law Review, 65*, 521–551.

Petrou, P. (1984, September). Due process implications of shifting the burden of proof in forfeiture proceedings arising out of illegal drug transactions. *Duke Law Journal,* 822–843.

Pratt, G. C., & Petersen, W. B. (1991). Civil forfeiture in the second circuit. *St. John's Law Review, 65*, 653–700.

President's Commission on Model State Drug Laws. (1993). *Volume 1: Economic remedies.* Washington, DC: White House.

Reiman, J. H. (1995). *The rich get richer and the poor get prison: Ideology, class, and criminal justice* (4th ed.). Boston, MA: Allyn and Bacon.

Rosenburg, J. A. (1988). Constitutional rights and civil forfeiture actions. *Columbia Law Review, 88*, 390–406.

Rudnick, A. G. (1992). Cleaning up money laundering prosecutions: Guidelines for prosecution and asset forfeiture. *Criminal Justice, 7*, 2.

Saltzburg, D. G. (1992). Real property forfeitures as a weapon in the government's war on drugs: A failure to protect innocent ownership rights. *Boston University Law Review, 72,* 217–242.

Shaw, B. (1990). Fifth Amendment failures and RICO forfeitures. *American Business Law Journal, 28,* 169–200.

Speta, J. B. (1990). Narrowing the scope of civil drug forfeiture: Section 881. Substantial connection and the Eighth Amendment. *Michigan Law Review, 89,* 165–210.

Stahl, M. (1992). Asset forfeiture, burdens of proof, and the war on drugs. *Journal of Criminal Law and Criminology, 83,* 274–337.

Thomas, C. (1999, May 8). Civil forfeiture laws in desperate need of change. *Arizona Republic,* p. B6.

Warchol, G. L., & Johnson, B. R. (1996). Guilty property: A quantitative analysis of civil asset forfeiture. *American Journal of Criminal Justice, 21,* 61–81.

Warchol, G. L., Payne, D. M., & Johnson, B. R. (1996). Criminal forfeiture: An effective alternative to civil and administrative proceedings. *Police Studies, 19,* 51–66.

Willson, E. (1990, February). Did a drug dealer own your home? (Criminal assets may be seized). *Florida Trend,* 6–9.

Wisotsky, S. (1991). Not thinking like a lawyer: The case of drugs in the courts. *Notre Dame Journal of Legal Ethics and Public Policy, 5,* 651–700.

Worrall, J. L. (1999). *Civil lawsuits, citizen complaints, and policing innovations.* Doctoral dissertation, Washington State University.

Yoskowitz, J. (1992). The war on the poor: Civil forfeiture of public housing. *Columbia Journal of Law and Social Problems, 25,* 567–600.

Zalman, M. (1997, May 9). The insidious side of drug forfeiture laws. *Detroit News,* A11.

Zeldin, M. F., & Weiner, R. G. (1991). Innocent third parties and their rights in forfeiture proceedings. *American Criminal Law Review, 28,* 843–861.

Cases Cited

Bennis v. Michigan, 116 S.Ct. 994 (1996).

United States v. All Funds on Deposit . . . at Merrill Lynch, 801 F. Supp. 984 (E.D. N.Y. 1992).

United States v. Bajakajian, 524 U.S. 321 (1998).

United States v. One Mercedes 560 SEL, 919 F.2d 327 (5th Cir. 1990).

United States v. One 1977 Mercedes-Benz 450 SEL, 708 F.2d 444 (9th Cir. 1983).

United States v. One Parcel of Land at 508 Depot Street, 964 F.2d 814 (8th Cir. 1992).

United States v. One Yacht Named Tahuna, 702 F.2d 1276 (9th Cir. 1983).

United States v. Real Property Located at 6625 Zumirez Drive, 845 F. Supp. 725 (1994).

United States v. United States Coin and Currency, 401 U.S. 715 (1971).

United States v. 92 Buena Vista Ave., Rumson, 507 U.S. 111 (1993).

SECTION 2

THE INDIVIDUAL IN
CRIMINAL JUSTICE ORGANIZATIONS

Criminal justice organizations influence the individuals who work for them, both on formal and informal levels. How both supervisors and subordinates respond to their environments and work settings is a critical issue facing criminal justice administrators. Issues such as job design, supervisory styles, and organizational structure directly impact how individuals within the criminal justice system view their roles. More importantly, these issues also affect the administration and management of criminal justice organizations. The articles presented in this section examine how individual actors respond to and are influenced by the various structures and environments within and outside the criminal justice system.

Peter Kraska and Louis Cubellis (article 7) present a fascinating examination of the proliferation of police paramilitary units within police departments across the country at a time when crime rates are falling and police progressives are trying to promote more problem-oriented and community- policing approaches to their departments. The authors suggest that the development of such units is consistent with the paramilitary history and structure of police departments, yet a movement toward the creation of such units is viewed in stark contrast to other attempts by police organizations to get away from the trappings of a paramilitary structure. The article suggests that the further development of these units within police departments reflects an interest on the part of the state to further refine the administration of violence through increased bureaucratization consistent with the tenets of "high modernity."

James Fyfe (article 8), in contrast, argues that what is needed in "good policing" is the adoption of other approaches to police organization and structure. His view is that good policing cannot be defined outside the context of what the police themselves view as the most important principles and practices to provide optimal police service. Fyfe would agree with Kraska and Cubellis that the traditional police structure is the source of many problems, both organizationally and individually, for administrators and officers. He offers a simple and basic remedy to these problems by enlisting the views of regular cops as to how they would organize and deliver police services. In this way, the impossible mandate given to police might become more manageable for both police supervisors and their subordinates (the rank-and-file police officers).

Examining an often neglected area in criminal justice research, that being defense attorneys and the court settings in which they work, Lisa McIntyre (article 9) provides a very descriptive profile of the ups and downs of doing criminal defense work. Her analysis shows both the "do's and don'ts" associated with criminal defense work and the various moral dilemmas that defense attorneys face. Yet, the picture painted by McIntyre is revealing of how these dilemmas are addressed within the context of a courtroom work group—most importantly, how criminal defense work serves the purpose of upholding the law and guaranteeing that the playing field is, at least on the surface, even for all participants in the criminal court process.

Robin Shepard Engel (article 10) examines the supervisory styles exhibited among sergeants and lieutenants within police organizations. This topic has not received much attention in the literature, but it is the individual behaviors of police supervisors that are most critical to the effectiveness of police organizations. Engel stresses the importance of supervisory styles in influencing behaviors among individual police officers and the nexus between supervisory styles and organizational goals. Police supervision, therefore, is critical to how organizational goals are achieved. The implementation of specific styles of supervision will have a profound impact on the behaviors of police officers, the goals attained by police agencies, and the general quality of services provided to the community.

John Rosecrance (article 11) describes the effects of bureaucratization on the organization and individual. He brilliantly explores how the increased bureaucratization of a probation department engendered specific patterns of adaptation among probation agents. In the long run, the effect was that many of the old "prima donnas" were weeded out of the organization, but not all. Similar to what was found by Engel regarding the importance of a balance of supervisory styles within police organizations, Rosecrance concludes that a balance of various role types is essential to the effective functioning of probation departments. His analysis requires serious examination by criminal justice reformers and administrators who view greater "rationality" as the panacea to their problems.

Susan Miller, Kay Forest, and Nancy Jurik (article 12) address a subject rarely examined in criminal justice: lesbians and gays in policing. Using open-ended survey questions asked of officers who are "out" and some who remain "closeted" in a large Midwestern police department, the authors describe the police organizational culture which these individual officers must confront. The elements of that culture include norms of heterosexuality and concentrated masculinity, both of which threaten both lesbian and gay officers. These officers felt they were closely scrutinized by fellow officers, even though the "out" officers had some claim to power by virtue of special recruitment efforts by the administration. The closeted officers felt great pressure to conform to the dominant police culture. Although reporting that all police officers were trained in the same way, gay and lesbian officers also reported feeling pressure to prove that they could do the job as well as straight officers. Both out and closeted officers form their own identities to cope with their organizational culture. The officers all sensed overt sexism and anti-gay behavior; however, the closeted officers also experienced conflict over their apparent support for the dominance of the traditional model of police masculinity. The lesbian and gay officers also felt that they had a greater ability than other officers to relate to the community and particularly to a wider range of underprivileged community members. They were also concerned, however, that their perceived competence with some groups might be seen as due to their sexual orientation and thus their abilities might actually undermine other officers' perceptions of their role as police officers. The research provides a window into various ways that some individuals adjust to a strong organizational culture.

In article 13, Micael Björk, a researcher from Sweden, examines an issue that has received considerable attention in studies of policing in the United States. Björk's analysis focuses on cynicism among the police and, in particular, on the techniques and mechanisms officers use to prevent themselves from becoming cynical without becoming overly enthusiastic zealots. These officers adopt individualized approaches in seeking an equilibrium—in the author's words, "a culture of reserve"—that allows them to stay motivated and consider themselves as good cops. Some officers seek frequent transfers to specialized units to avoid cynicism; other officers seek lateral transfers in search of a fresh start when they feel their crime-fighting efforts are thwarted. Officers also adopt strategies to avoid getting mired in the big picture of social dysfunction. They may turn to humor or irony as a way of staying focused on outcomes that are within their control. Still other officers may move towards less aggressive policing approaches and adopt *pragmatic humanism* as a way of addressing the ambiguities of the job. This wide range of strategies, the author argues, can counteract the process of burnout and allow officers to maintain suitable levels of enthusiasm and commitment to the job. These adjustments round out our focus on the individual in criminal justice organizations.

7

Militarizing Mayberry and Beyond
Making Sense of American Paramilitary Policing

PETER B. KRASKA AND LOUIS J. CUBELLIS

Crime and justice studies have a fundamental interest in society's formal reaction to the breaking of laws (Sutherland, Cressey, and Luckenbill, 1992). Consequently criminologists have examined and debated the changing nature of the criminal justice enterprise. Some penological scholars argue, for instance, that correctional ideology and practice are aligning themselves more closely with the features of a postmodern or high-modern society (Christie, 1994; Feeley and Simon, 1992; Garland, 1990, 1995). Policing scholars, on the other hand, focus predominantly on the "quiet revolution" occurring within the modern police institution, namely community- and problem-oriented policing reforms (Kelling, 1988).

Despite the democratic rhetoric connected with this "revolution," the discourse associated with military activity and war remains a core feature of crime-control ideology (e.g., the war on drugs, crime fighters). Indeed the military model, the armed forces, and a fear of martial control have all been influential in the development of police (Bailey, 1995; Bittner, 1970; Enloe, 1980; Fogelson, 1977; Manning, 1977). Early police scholarship examined in depth the military model's theoretical and practical importance for civilian law enforcement (Bittner, 1970; Fogelson, 1977; Manning, 1977). Contemporary discussions, however, rarely include the military model as a central influence on the police institution.

Peter Kraska and Louis Cubellis, "Militarizing Mayberry and Beyond: Making Sense of American Paramilitary Policing," *Justice Quarterly*, Vol. 14 No. 4, December 1997, pp. 607–629. Reprinted by permission of the Academy of Criminal Justice Sciences.

An important exception is Skolnick and Fyfe's (1993) recent discussion, similar to Bittner's in 1970, of the continued harmful influence of the military paradigm in contemporary policing. They argue that despite the recent rhetorical turn toward democratic reforms, the military model still lingers as a central feature of police culture and operation. One important manifestation of this paradigm which Skolnick and Fyfe overlooked is the adoption of the military special operations model,[1] embodied in what the international literature calls police paramilitary units (PPUs) (Brewer et al. 1988; Enloe, 1980; Jefferson, 1990; Reiner, 1992). These units are known most commonly in the United States as SWAT or special response teams.

At first glance, the police paramilitary unit imagery exhibited at Waco and Ruby Ridge hardly appear to support the notion that a component of policing is moving toward a military approach. These events were sensational and alarming, but could be regarded as unique events that portended little about trends in law enforcement overall. Kraska and Kappeler (1997), however, in a national study of PPUs in medium-sized to large police departments, found that these units have not only grown in numbers but have become increasingly proactive.

The research presented here stems from a separate national survey of small-locality police agencies. Descriptive and longitudinal data on small-locality PPUs are presented, followed by the implications of these findings. In an effort to begin making theoretical sense of these data, we then situate the small-locality findings with the larger PPU phenomenon. We present additional analyses and discuss how the rise and normalization of PPUs correspond closely to macro-level changes in formal social control.

The Military Model and Paramilitary Units

In this study we shed light on two neglected areas of scholarship in criminology. First, Weisheit (1993:217) charges crime and justice studies with urban ethnocentrism when reviewing the scant literature on rural crime and justice issues. Although the literature includes some case studies of small police departments (Decker, 1979; Gibbons, 1972; Marenin and Copus, 1991), few systematic examinations of these agencies exist (Weisheit, Falcone, and Wells, 1996). The existing literature characterizes small-locality police as oriented toward crime prevention and social service.

Second, until recently no scholarly research on PPUs existed except in the international literature (Jefferson, 1990; Reiner, 1992).[2] Few police scholars have acknowledged that the military and the police have an inherent political connection: both possess a monopoly on and the prerogative to exercise the state-legitimized use of force (Bittner, 1970; Enloe, 1980; Kraska, 1994; Turk, 1982). Even internationally, police rarely organize and administer force along any other lines than the military-bureaucratic model, although the degree of militarization varies widely (Brewer et al., 1988; Chevigny, 1995; Enloe, 1980).

Police academics, however, have criticized the military model as playing a central role in numerous problems that plague policing (Angell, 1971; Bittner, 1970; Fogelson, 1977; Fry and Berkes, 1983; Klockars, 1985; Skolnick and Fyfe, 1993). The military-bureaucratic model, epitomized in the professional model of policing, acts as a barrier to police-community ties by fostering a "we/they" attitude. Military ideology and organization are also antithetical to more democratic approaches, both internal and external to a police agency. Finally, the military model encourages overemphasis on the crime-fighting function of police work and promotes a warlike approach to crime and drug problems.

In the "era" of community- and problem-oriented policing, it may seem inappropriate to examine trends toward rather than away from the military paradigm, particularly in smaller police jurisdictions. Yet today, the military model's influence on the police may be no less significant (Chevigny, 1995; Kraska, 1994; Skolnick and Fyfe, 1993).

Cop-on-the-Beat Police versus Police Paramilitary Units

It is important to distinguish traditional police from policing with PPUs. In the images constructed by the media, PPUs are highly trained and disciplined teams of police officers housed in the largest agencies, which respond to the rare hostage, sniper, barricaded person, or terrorist. Police paramilitary units can be distinguished from what Enloe (1980) calls "cop-on-the beat policing" most simply by their appearance, their heavy weaponry, and their operations.

For a more exact identification, we must clarify the term *paramilitary unit.* We must distinguish between indications that are *necessary* in applying the PPU label and those which would only *contribute* to labeling these units and their activities as paramilitaristic.

First among the necessary factors, the unit must train and function as a military special operations team with a strict military command structure and discipline (or the pretense thereof). Examples include the U.S. Navy Seals teams and foreign police paramilitary squads such as the British Special Patrol Groups. This status as a unique team within a larger organization perpetuates the belief that these units and their members are "elite," a sentiment supported by their administrators (Kraska and Paulsen, 1997).[3]

Second, the unit must have at the forefront of their function to threaten or use force collectively, and not always as an option of last resort (e.g., in conducting a no-knock drug raid).[4] Operationally, PPUs are deployed to deal with situations that require a team of police officers specifically trained to be use-of-force specialists. Historically they have operated as *reactive* units, handling only strictly defined, high-risk situations already in progress.

Finally, the unit must operate under legitimate state authority, and its activities must be sanctioned by the state and coordinated by a government agency. This criterion would exclude common thuggery, militia organizations, and guerilla groups.

Contributing indicators include the hardware they employ and their garb. These teams generally outfit themselves with black or urban camouflage BDUs (battle dress uniforms), lace-up combat boots, full-body armor, Kevlar helmets, and ninji-style hoods. PPUs' weapons and hardware include submachine guns, tactical shotguns, sniper rifles, percussion grenades, CS and OC gas (tear and pepper gas), surveillance equipment, and fortified personnel carriers.

It would seem improbable, given the crime prevention and service orientation attributed to small-locality police agencies, that they would want, need, or be willing to fund these expensive units.[5] Ethnographic research, however, uncovered a flourishing PPU movement in small-town police departments in the north central United States (Kraska, 1996); this work overcame our doubts about using resources and time to conduct a national survey of these agencies.

Methodology

We designed and administered a 40-item (100-variable) survey to collect data on the formation, prevalence, and activities of PPUs in small localities. We developed a sampling frame of all U.S. police agencies (excluding federal agencies), serving jurisdictions between 25,000 and 50,000 citizens.[6] This list yielded a population of 770 law enforcement agencies. In March 1996 we made an initial mailing of the survey to this population of police agencies; the mailing included a letter of introduction and a copy of the survey instrument. Because police agencies are secretive and suspicious (Manning, 1978; Skolnick, 1966; Westley, 1956), and because of the difficulty in researching sensitive topics in policing, the letter was written on a recognized sponsor's letterhead. It was signed by both the principal researcher (the first author) and the director of the professional organization that was sponsoring the research. It also noted the researchers' university affiliation. The language used in the survey encouraged respondents to recognize the study as administratively oriented. It is likely that this orientation, coupled with the authors' familiarity with PPU rhetoric and the promise of confidentiality and anonymity, aided our response rate.

Within five weeks, the first mailing yielded 433 completed surveys, a 56 percent response rate. After approximately six weeks, we mailed a second wave of surveys to the remaining 337 nonrespondents. In the second mailing we emphasized the high level of participation by other police agencies and urged cooperation from departments without a PPU. After six additional weeks, this follow-up mailing yielded an additional 119 surveys for a total response rate of 72 percent ($n = 552$).

Of the 552 returned surveys, we excluded 79 departments that employed more than 100 sworn officers, and thus obtained a more accurate representation of policing in small localities ($N = 473$).[7] The resulting sampler of departments contained an average of 62 officers and a median of 60.

Of the 473 agencies, we selected 40 to provide identification and telephone information for semistructured follow-up phone interviews. We sought information on missing data and inquired into some of the more sensitive

PPU activities, such as proactive patrol work. Interviews lasted five minutes to one hour; most lasted about 30 minutes.

Analysis and Results

Demographic and Descriptive Characteristics

Over 65 percent ($n = 311$) of the departments responded that they had a SWAT team. Of the remaining agencies (those without a PPU), 28 percent ($n = 46$) responded that they planned to develop a team within the next few years. The highest proportion of these agencies (24 percent) used the traditional acronym SWAT. Other departments employed an array of labels for the reorganized or more recently formed PPUs, including SRT (special response team, 21 percent) and ERU (emergency response unit, 15 percent).

Most of the units we surveyed were equipped with the latest "tactical gear." Over 80 percent of the departments had MP5 submachine guns, tactical semiautomatic shotguns, night vision equipment, sniper rifles, flash-bang grenades, tactical shields, battle-dress uniforms, and specialized "dynamic entry tools." Over 50 percent had electronic surveillance equipment, tactical helmets, tactical communication headsets, and a mobile command center (i.e., a SWAT van). Seven percent had armored personnel carriers.

Most of the officers responding to the survey were police supervisors. Thirty-eight percent ($n = 119$) could be categorized as high-level administrators (chief, sheriff, deputy chief, major, or captain); 50 percent were either sergeants or lieutenants ($n = 154$); the remainder were patrol officers or deputy sheriffs.

Because the departments were relatively small, it was important to understand how PPUs fit into these agencies' organizational structures. Seven percent ($n = 22$) of the PPUs were maintained full-time; 93 percent were classified as a part-time arrangement ($n = 288$). Almost 74 percent ($n = 230$) of the PPUs served only one department, while 18 percent ($n = 58$) were multijurisdictional. Follow-up phone interviews revealed that many extremely small departments offset the high costs of forming and operating a paramilitary unit by participating in regional units. Some of these multijurisdictional operations involved 50 to 60 smaller agencies.[8]

There were 17.7 paramilitary officers for every 100 sworn persons. We realize that this finding is due mainly to departmental size. As we discuss later, the proximity of paramilitary police officers to regular patrol officers (in fact, most officers in small-town PPUs function as both) is important in assessing the potential cultural and operational effects of these units on the larger organization.

PPU Activities over Time

Analysis of the longitudinal data revealed important trends in the periods during which PPUs were formed (see figure 1). Only 20 percent ($n = 63$) of today's PPUs existed at the beginning of 1980. By the end of 1984, the number had risen to 121, a 92 percent increase. This increase foreshadowed the developments in the second half of the 1980s. The number of PPUs formed between 1985 and 1990 increased sharply: 130 new units came into existence during this period, bringing the total to 251 and representing an increase of 107 percent. Between 1985 and 1995, the number of paramilitary units in agencies serving small jurisdictions. increased by 157 percent. This growth is likely to continue. If we consider that 46 of the departments surveyed responded that they would establish a unit within the next few years, three-fourths of departments employing 100 or fewer officers and serving 25,000 to 50,000 persons will have a PPU by the turn of the century.

The formation of numerous but relatively inactive units, however, would lessen the significance of these data. Therefore we collected baseline data on the number of call-outs performed by each department beginning in 1980; we requested longitudinal data from 1980 to the end of 1995. "Call-outs" included any activity requiring deployment of the unit, such as barricaded persons, hostages, terrorists, civil disturbances, and the serving of high-risk search and arrest warrants. These data do not include activities related to proactive patrol work by PPUs.

The number of call-outs from 1980 to 1984 remained relatively stable at an average of 3.6 to 3.8 per year (see table 1). Beginning in 1985, the mean number increased steadily from 4.5 in 1985 to slightly over 12 by the end of

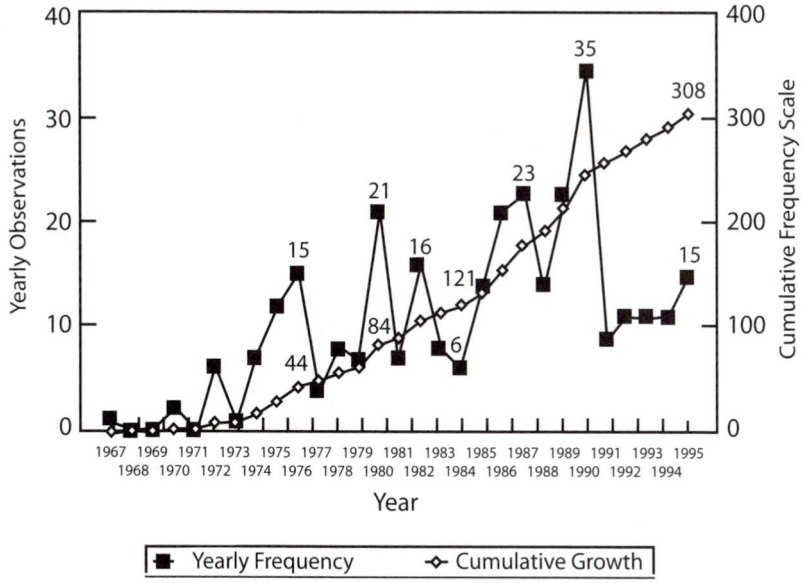

Figure 1   Cumulative growth of PPUs, showing number of new PPUs formed each year

1995. The median rose from 4 in 1985 to 9 in 1995. Between 1980 and 1995 the mean number of call-outs increased by 238 percent.

The total number of call-outs, because of the increase in the number of PPUs in the last 10 years, illustrates more clearly the aggregate rise in police paramilitary activities (see table 1). In 1980 the total was 220. By 1985 the number had more than doubled to 481, by 1988 it had quadrupled to 960, and by the end of 1995 it had reached 3,715, a total increase of 1,589 percent.

For 1995, traditional reactive functions associated with SWAT units accounted for a surprisingly small proportion of call-outs. Hostage situations (n = 193; 5 percent), civil disturbances (n = 52; 1 percent), and terrorist incidents (n = 5; .1 percent) were quite rare. Barricaded persons accounted for a higher proportion (n = 874; 24 percent). By far the most common use of these units was for executing search and arrest warrants: 66 percent (n = 466) of the units' call-outs belonged to this category.[9]

Figure 2 displays the number of departments each year that began using their paramilitary units to execute warrants. The total number of departments using PPUs for this purpose has increased steadily over the last 20 years, and increased exponentially (342 percent) between 1985 and 1995. Even though the overall number of units has increased, the percentage of units engaged in warrant work has grown significantly as well. For instance, as shown in table 2, only 40 percent of PPUs were used in this capacity in 1980. This number had risen to 49 percent by 1985, to 81 percent by the end of 1990, and to 94 percent by the end of 1995. These data indicate a dramatic shift in PPUs' activity.

Table 1   Selected characteristics of call-out data

Year	Mean	Median	Number of Call-Outs	Percentage Increase[a]
1980	3.7	3.0	220	N/A
1981	3.7	3.0	244	10.9
1982	3.6	3.0	274	24.6
1983	3.7	3.0	322	46.4
1984	3.8	3.0	350	59.1
1985	4.5	4.0	481	118.6
1986	5.5	4.0	685	211.4
1987	6.7	4.5	960	336.4
1988	7.1	4.0	1,151	423.2
1989	8.9	5.0	1,633	642.3
1990	10.3	5.0	2,311	950.5
1991	11.1	6.0	2,610	1,086.4
1992	12.1	7.0	3,052	1,287.3
1993	12.0	8.0	3,255	1,379.6
1994	12.2	8.0	3,452	1,469.1
1995	12.5	9.0	3,715	1,588.6

[a]Within the percentage increase column, 1980 is the base year for all calculations.

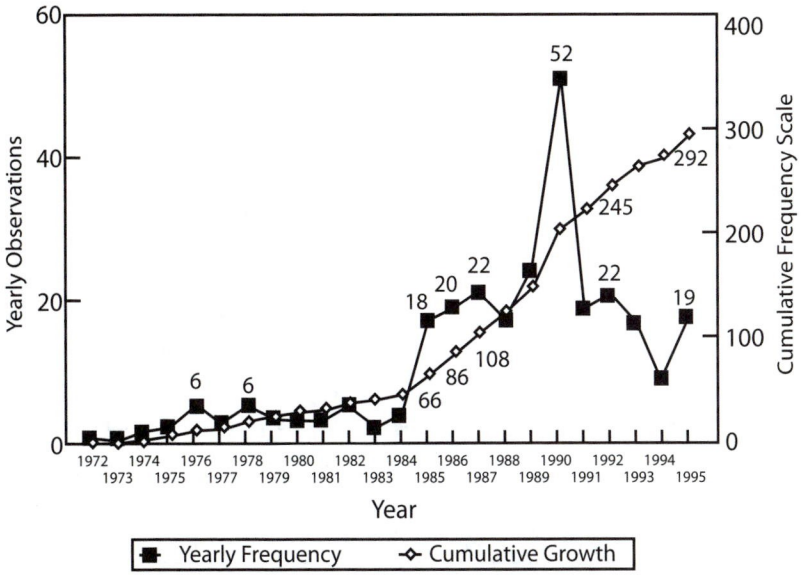

Figure 2   Years in which PPUs began warrant/drug raids

Serving warrants should not be interpreted as a "reactive" deployment of the unit when a felony arrest warrant is served on a high-risk suspect after a thorough investigation. Phone interviews revealed that warrant work consisted almost exclusively of proactive, no-knock "raids" for the purpose of investigating a residence and collecting evidence such as drugs, guns, and money. About 10 percent of the small-locality departments served 20 to 120 investigatory search warrants a year.

Possibly an even more controversial use of PPUs was their deployment as a patrol force. Seventeen percent of the departments with a paramilitary unit ($n = 55$) used the unit as a proactive patrol force in "high-crime" areas within their jurisdiction. Although a few PPUs performed this function before 1989 ($n = 6$), most of the increase has occurred since then ($n = 49$, a 717 percent increase; see figure 3). Phone interviewees described a variety of approaches used to deploy these units as patrol teams. Some PPUs patrolled in BDUs and

Table 2   Proportion of PPUs conducting warrant work for selected years

	Number of Units in Existence	Number of Units Used for Warrants	Percentage Engaged in Warrant Work
1984	121	48	39.67
1985	135	66	48.89
1990	251	203	80.88
1995	311	292	93.89

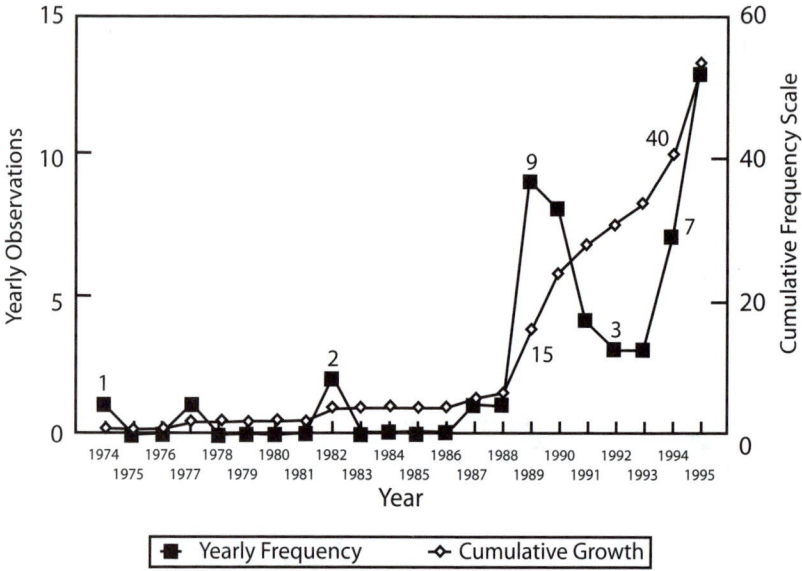

Figure 3   Years in which PPUs began proactive patrol

carried MP5 submachine guns. These units responded only to the most serious call for service; they spent most of their time conducting "terry-stops."[10] Other departments used similar tactics but dressed less like a military unit (in jeans and jackets identifying their unit) and carried only 9mm. service revolvers and semiautomatic shotguns.

Finally, the PPUs' training deserves mention. Training holds a central place in the police paramilitary subculture (Kraska, 1996; Kraska and Paulsen, 1997). As with military special operations teams such as the Navy Seals and the Army Rangers, these units' elite status is based in part on their reputation for receiving extensive training in "tactical or special operations."

In medium-sized to large police organizations, each officer in a paramilitary unit receives an average of 225 hours of formal training per year (Kraska and Kappeler, 1997). Most PPU commanders agreed that if a department is moderately active in conducting call-outs (two per month), a tactical officer needs at least 220 hours of training a year. If the unit conducts relatively few call-outs (three a year), it should provide at least an additional 50 hours of formal training per year. The PPUs housed in the small-locality departments studied here conducted a yearly average of only 106 hours of formal training per officer. Almost 53 percent of these departments conducted 100 or fewer hours of training per year; 20 percent provided their tactical officers with 50 or fewer hours.

Police paramilitary teams often draw their expertise and training from actual military special operations teams such as the Navy Seals and the Army

Rangers (Kraska and Kappeler, 1997). Surprisingly, even in these smaller jurisdictions, 32 percent ($n = 101$) of the respondents answered "yes" when asked whether they trained with active-duty military experts in special operations. Thirty-one percent ($n = 96$) responded that they were influenced by "police officers with special operations experience in the military." The two most popular sources of PPU training and/or expertise were the FBI and for-profit, tactical training schools. Forty-one percent ($n = 129$) of the PPUs worked with the FBI; 63 percent ($n = 196$) used private tactical schools.

Implications for Small Localities: The Dangers of Militarizing Mayberry

The data demonstrate a significant growth in the number of PPUs and a precipitous rise in PPU activity in small jurisdictions. Because small-locality PPUs engage in proactive patrolling and serve investigatory search warrants, these findings also document the normalization of the PPU approach into small-town police work. Most likely we captured these trends in the midst of their development.[11]

Previous research assessing macro-level shifts in police practices focused mainly on "big-city policy" (Fogelson, 1977). Our research adds a new dimension to the underresearched area of small-locality policing by raising questions about the assumption that these agencies are exclusively service-oriented. Paramilitary units in small towns are even more significant than in big cities because urban police officials and politicians can justify, at least partially, a paramilitary approach to crime and drugs in the media-constructed image of a hostile, crime-ridden, urban environment. How do we reconcile this same type of paramilitary policing imagery and activity in "Mayberry?"

It would be tempting to marginalize this paramilitary phenomenon as an interesting appendage of the multidimensional nature of modern police. Not only do the findings on the normalization of small-locality PPUs into routine police work neutralize this argument, it is also critical to recall that there are almost 18 police paramilitary officers for every 100 regular patrol officers in these small localities. Most of these PPU officers serve in the organization as regular patrol officers during their normal duties. In addition, police administrators view these officers as the "elite" or the "cops' cops" (see note 3). These factors add credence to the possibility that the paramilitary team model today represents a significant cultural and operational influence on small-locality police organizations as a whole (and possibly will do so more strongly in the future).

The small number of training hours in these PPUs raises another important issue: the degree to which these teams approximate the ideal of highly trained, proficient squads of use-of-force specialists. In keeping with the decentralized nature of American policing, departments form these squads in an ad hoc fashion, with no regulatory body or set of standards. Expertise in "tactical operations" often is gained from reading books, watching videotapes, and possibly visiting a 3- to 5-day for-profit, paramilitary training camp.

In view of these conditions, strict military discipline, a rigid command structure, and tight administrative oversight may not be the norm in Mayberry. PPU members in this study claimed autonomy from direct administrative supervision. As one team commander stated, "We're left alone. The brass knows that we know what we're doing more than they do. One of the reasons we're so effective is we have the freedom to handle situations and problems as we see best." Bock (1995) documents how the autonomy enjoyed by these PPUs, even at the federal level, carries high potential for abuse, particularly in serving no-knock search warrants.

Another development that must be tracked closely is departments' tendency to expand paramilitary units' range of applications, especially if we consider their high cost (see note 5) and the extreme concern about officers' safety in the police subculture (Skolnick, 1966; Van Maanen, 1978). PPUs are not only creeping into proactive functions; their existence in small localities also might be contributing to a broader definition of reactive situations requiring a paramilitary response. One small-locality SWAT commander gave the following justification for an inordinately large number of PPU deployments for barricaded suspects in relation to a departmental policy that requires patrol officers to ask "barricades" only once to surrender:

> If the subject refuses once, the SWAT unit is called in, and we almost always either gas 'em or toss in a flash-bang grenade. We're not gonna hang around for hours and beg, and we're sure not going to get killed because we're indecisive.[12]

Beyond Mayberry:
Explaining Paramilitary Unit Policing

Theoretical and Causal Analysis

To understand the PPU phenomenon more clearly, we must situate small-locality PPUs within broader changes in the police institution and in formal social control in general. We attempt here to make theoretical sense of the rise and normalization of paramilitary policing.

Trends in small-locality policing lag, by roughly three years, nearly identical shifts in larger departments (see Kraska and Kappeler, 1997). Small-locality paramilitary policing thus follows an even more significant movement in medium-sized to large police agencies. If we combine the data from larger departments with those cited in this study, we see that the paramilitary unit approach is becoming an integral part of contemporary policing in all departments serving localities with 25,000 or more people. In 1995 over 77 percent of police departments had paramilitary units, an increase of almost 48 percent since 1985. The returned surveys alone documented 29,962 paramilitary deployments in 1995, a 939 percent increase over the 2,884 call-outs of 1980. Over 20 percent of all departments with PPUs use the units for proactive patrol work, a 257 percent increase since the beginning of 1989.

Our assertion that these data represent a shift in the police institution should not be interpreted as the announcement of a mutually exclusive shift—that is, the only shift. The police institution has probably shifted as well toward the rhetoric and activities associated with community policing. National-level longitudinal data documenting the degree to which the police institution has structurally transformed and engaged in activities associated with community policing over time, however, have yet to surface (see Maguire forthcoming).[13] As we argue below, it is likely that the two approaches are increasing simultaneously.

As with any macro-social shift, an explanation for the rise of PPUs will likely involve a multitude of intersecting and overlapping factors forming a complex theoretical mix of social, political, economic, and cultural influences. Because of the shortage of relevant longitudinal, national-level data, valid theory testing and model building will be difficult.

Nonetheless we attempted to determine what factors accounted for variance in the dependent variables, paramilitary unit formation and paramilitary unit call-outs ($n = 846$). We collected 73 national-level independent variables that measured economic trends and trends in crime rates, drug use, fear of crime, and criminal justice activity. Using varimax factor analysis and multiple regression, as well as "differencing" to control for the influence of time (Lafree and Drass, 1996), we found that no single variable or construct accounted for a significant amount of variance in our dependent variables.[14]

The inability to account for variance by using these independent variables may be important in itself. We were especially interested in additional testing of the commonsense notion that the rise of PPUs represents a rational reaction by police to changes in crime. Therefore we tested, agency by agency, whether PPU activity corresponds to the occurrence of violent crime. We compared call-out rates from 1980 to 1995, for each jurisdiction, to a UCR violent-crime composite for each of those jurisdictions. We derived the UCR composite by summing the homicide, rape, and robbery rates for each of the responding locations for each year from 1980 through 1995. We excluded aggravated assault rates on the basis of recommendations in the literature (Gove, Hughes and Geerken, 1985; Lafree and Drass, 1996).

Because the data revealed time-based dependence, we differenced the call-out and crime measures at the first level to make them stationary (i.e., to remove the effects of time). A canonical analysis, using the 15 call-out variables and the 15 crime variables for each jurisdiction, revealed that the canonical correlation value of .59 differed significantly from zero at the .000 level. The Stewart-Love index of redundancy, which is directly analogous to the R^2 statistic in multiple regression and is interpreted similarly (Hair et al., 1995), allowed us to determine that only 6.63 percent of the variance in the call-out data was explained by the violent crime composites. Thus we could reasonably exclude changes in violent crime as an important factor explaining the activities of PPUs.

Beyond the Numbers: A Theoretical Exposition

To make sense of this phenomenon beyond the commonsense notion that it reflects a rational response to crime, we must first recognize that the specter of the military model still haunts the real world of contemporary policing, despite the recent rhetoric of democratic reforms. In learning that a component of the police institution is reorganizing itself and conducting operations that could be characterized as militaristic, we find strong support for the thesis that the military model is still a powerful force guiding the ideology and activities of American police. This should not be surprising considering the war/military paradigm remains an authoritative framework for crime-control thinking and action by politicians, bureaucrats, the media, and much of the public (Sherry, 1995).

To understand the revival of militarism in policing, we must point out the close identification between the police paramilitary subculture associated with PPUs and the recent growth of a larger paramilitary culture in the United States during the Reagan-Bush era, and especially since the end of the cold war (Gibson, 1994; Hamm, 1993; Kraska, 1996). Gibson (1994) believes that a ubiquitous culture of paramilitarism has arisen in the last 15 years. Indications include the popularity of paramilitary themes in films, movies, politics, and the news media during the 1980s; the rise of PPUs at the federal and local levels; the popularity of military special operations teams such as the Navy Seals, the Army Rangers, and the Delta Force; the rise of informal militia/paramilitary groups; and the paramilitarism found in some urban gangs (Gibson, 1994).

Within this larger culture, the police paramilitary subculture contains a status hierarchy with military special operations squads such as the Navy Seals at the top, followed by FBI, and BATF police paramilitary teams, large metropolitan paramilitary units, and, finally, PPUs in smaller jurisdictions (Kraska, 1996). In the past decade an enormous police paramilitary community has developed, which includes a 10,000-member professional organization, numerous periodicals, and even its own art work.

A complex of for-profit training, weapons, and equipment suppliers heavily promotes the culture at police shows, in police magazine advertisements, and in police paramilitary training programs sponsored by gun manufacturers such as Heckler and Koch and Smith and Wesson. As evidenced by data in this study, the U.S. armed forces also participate, particularly since the end of the cold war (Kraska, 1996). The allure of police paramilitary subculture stems from the enjoyment, excitement, high status, and male camaraderie that accompany the heavy weaponry, new technologies, dangerous assignments, and heightened anticipation of using force in most PPU work (Kraska, 1996; Kraska and Paulsen, 1997).

Ideologically the government's latest war on drugs, with its rhetoric and actions associated with doing battle (drug war boot camps, drugs as a threat to national security, and the use of the U.S. armed forces), dovetails nicely with Gibson's thesis on the growth of paramilitary culture. The drug war—beginning in the early 1980s, peaking in the late 1980s, and continuing through the 1990s—has profoundly affected all aspects of the criminal justice system (Irwin and Austin, 1997; Miller, 1996). It is no coincidence that the police cracked down on drugs in economically deprived areas concurrently with the great increase in investigatory, no-knock drug raids, conducted mostly by PPUs. Indeed, most of the increases in paramilitary deployments began in 1988, at the apex of drug war activity and hysteria. Nearly all police officials ($n = 126$) in small and large agencies explained in phone interviews that their agency either formed its PPU or dramatically increased the activities of its PPU to conduct raids on private residences in search of drugs, guns, and "drug money."

The escalation of the drug war and the increase in PPUs coincide as well with reformers' calls for the police to alter their operational focus. Reformers advocate a change from *reacting* to individual calls for service with one or two officers to adopting a *proactive* model, which establishes "teams" of officers that work collectively to "maintain order" or solve "community problems" (Goldstein, 1990; Kelling, 1988; Trojanowicz and Bucqueroux, 1990). As we found in this research, and according to data from larger departments (Kraska and Kappeler, 1997), police paramilitary teams are used as proactive patrol forces to "suppress" highly politicized problems such as guns, drugs, gangs, and community disorder in economically deprived areas. In fact, 63 percent of police agencies serving 25,000 people or more agreed or strongly agreed that PPUs "play an important role in community policing strategies." One PPU commander clarified the rationale behind this belief:

> We conduct a lot of saturation patrol. We do "terry stops" and "aggressive" field interviews. These tactics are successful as long as the pressure stays on relentlessly. The key to our success is that we're an elite crime-fighting team that's not bogged down in the regular bureaucracy. We focus on *"quality of life"* issues like illegal parking, loud music, bums, neighbor troubles. We have the freedom to stay in a hot area and clean it up—particularly gangs. Our tactical enforcement team works nicely with our department's emphasis on community policing (emphasis added).

At first glance one might assume that a trend toward militarization must be in opposition to the community policing "revolution." In the real world of policing, however, some police officials are interpreting the reformers' call to adopt a proactive stance, and to "actively create a climate of order" (Bayley, 1996), as requiring a more aggressive, indeed militaristic approach to enforcing law and order among the "dangerous classes." At least in their minds, PPUs do not supplant a CP or POP approach; they operate in harmony. This reasoning is exemplified most clearly in the recent crackdown on crime and drugs by New York city politicians and police officials.[15]

The rise and the normalization of PPUs, then, correspond to changes in popular culture, drug control operations, and police reform efforts. It should be apparent that a complex combination of factors plays a role in this phenomenon. To explain the final and perhaps most compelling way in which the rise of PPUs corresponds to larger shifts in formal social control, we must revisit the essence of paramilitary unit functioning: PPUs are deployed to deal with situations that police agencies perceive as requiring a team of officers with a strong focus on the threatened or actual use of violence. Street-level policing has always been individually based, discretionary, and unregulated (Bittner, 1970; Skolnick, 1966). Does this shift in policing, away from individual, situational uses of violence and toward the collective use of violence by "well managed" teams of officers, coincide with larger trends in formal social control?

A comparable development in scope, form, and function is occurring in corrections. It cross-validates the notion that paramilitary units may indicate *modernizing* changes in the handling of violence by social control agents in the larger criminal justice apparatus (Christie, 1994; Feeley and Simon, 1992; Garland, 1990). Correctional administrators have adopted the paramilitary unit model in attempting to *rationalize* (in the Weberian sense) correctional officers' use of violence through the establishment of "special operations" or "emergency response" teams. As has occurred in policing, "many departments of corrections created their own emergency response teams modeling them after Police SWAT Teams and military commando units such as the Army Green Beret Special Forces and the Navy Seal Teams" (Bryan, 1995:2). These units, originally designed to react to only the most serious inmate disturbances, have expanded their range of functions in the last few years to include cell searches, lesser inmate disturbances, "extractions" of inmates from cells, and the forced administration of medicines (Beard, 1994; Bryan, 1995).

Why is this paramilitary model so appealing to both corrections and policing? As noted above, part of the answer lies generally in the seductive powers of paramilitary unit subculture as promoted by for-profit industry. The techno-warrior garb, heavy weaponry, sophisticated technology, hypermasculinity, and "real-work" functions are nothing less than intoxicating for paramilitary unit participants and those who aspire to work in such units (Kraska, 1996; Kraska and Paulsen, 1997).

An additional source of allure is the hope that bureaucracies, by creating "violence specialists," can finally control, manage, and make more efficient the state-administered force which is their prerogative. This faith in professionalizing violence by adopting the military model has a long history in both corrections and policing. Thus, to much of the practicing criminal justice community, the recent implementation of the military special operations model represents not a regression in the administration of justice but a step toward further modernizing and refining state violence.

In sum, militarizing state force does not only signal a falling back on a culture of militarism and crude state power in the war on crime and drugs. It also corresponds closely to developments documented by Christie (1994), Cohen (1985), Ericson (1994), Feeley and Simon (1992, 1994), Garland, (1990, 1995), Manning (1992, 1993), and of course Foucault (1977). All of these scholars have theorized on what they view as an unpromising, fundamental shift in formal social control: an acceleration of criminal law agencies' uncritical implementation of practices consistent with the tenets of "high-modernity"—accentuated standardization, routinization, technical efficiency, scientificization, risk minimization, technologicalization, actuarial thinking, the "what works" fetish, moral indifference, and a focus on aggregate populations—in a quest to more efficiently manage those who threaten state order. The rise and the normalization of PPUs represents, therefore, an adaptation to conditions of high-modernity in the crime war.

Policy Science and General Schwartzkopf

We cannot assume, however, that this quest for rationality will lead to rational outcomes. Ritzer (1993:121) draws from Weber in asserting that "rational systems inevitably spawn a series of irrationalities that serve to limit, ultimately compromise, and perhaps even undermine, their rationality." The central policy issue related to PPUs is the degree to which this phenomenon constrains police violence, as intended, or escalates it. Except for individual departments, no systematic data have been compiled on the extent to which these units use force. The first author interviewed officials from large and small police departments who claimed that their units had never discharged weapons during a deployment; others stated that they often discharged their weapons on call-outs; some admitted shooting innocent people; and some described casualties to officers caused by "friendly fire."

The paramilitary community is adamant about PPUs' life-saving potential. Few could argue against using well-trained specialists to respond to serious terrorist or hostage situations. Even within these narrow reactive functions, however, we need only recall Waco and Ruby Ridge to appreciate what the adaptation of the paramilitary model implies for civilian law enforcement. Valid system-wide data on PPUs' use of force is needed but will be difficult to obtain.

To determine the rationality of this approach, however, we must consider issues broader than whether these units "save lives" and how often weapons are discharged. Researchers also must track and assess PPUs' "mission creep" into mainstream policing functions. As evidenced by the broad definition of "barricades" in some small-locality agencies, the normalization of the PPU approach carries high potential for expanding the use-of-force options available to the police and the circumstances in which they are utilized in a type of police violence net widening. "Less-lethal technologies," for instance, are becoming extremely popular among PPUs (Kraska, 1996).

These data also demonstrate the expansion of police power in conducting contraband raids. PPUs provide the police institution with a new tool for conducting a crude form of investigation into drug and gun law violations inside private residences. This new approach to drug and gun law enforcement is not necessarily a reaction to a dangerous existing condition (such as a hostage situation). Rather, it is a police-initiated proactive approach, which itself manufactures dangerous situations.

Policy research as it applies to police militarization, however, can provide only limited guidance. The debate on paramilitary policing in the British literature illustrates clearly that normative concerns play a central role in assessing its desirability (Jefferson, 1990; Reiner, 1992). This issue involves heartfelt beliefs, values, and morals. To many people, even among academics, the military model represents constraint, discipline, honor, control, competence, and even a type of patriotism. To others it stands for tyranny, state violence, human rights abuses, war, and an ideology which stresses that problems are best handled by technologized state force. Some will see the rise and normalization of PPUs as a necessary and rational approach to today's crime, gang, and drug problems; others will view it as bureaucracy building and as evidence of a government in crisis moving toward a police state.

Crime and justice academicians nevertheless must be careful not to succumb to what Ericson calls "General Schwartzkopf criminology": an uncritical policy science approach that emphasizes "how military-type bureaucracy, discipline, technology, deployment and coercion fight criminal sources of insecurity" (Ericson and Carriere, 1994:100). The ideological trappings of the General Schwartzkopf approach lie in its close association with military professionalism, scientific rationality, advanced technology, and expedient, value-neutral problem solving through the use or threat of force. Scholars must remain skeptical about applying these tenets of high-modern militarism to the criminal justice apparatus, and must watch closely for the irrationalities it is likely to spawn.

Endnotes

[1] For a more thorough discussion of the war/military paradigm and its connection to paramilitary policing, see Kraska (1996).

[2] The Iron Fist and the Velvet Glove (Crime and Social Justice Associates, 1983) was the first work to identify and critique the SWAT phenomenon. Chambliss (1994) conducted field research on the Washington, DC rapid deployment unit (RDU) and discussed its "repressive" tendencies. Stevens and MacKenna (1988) conducted survey research on PPUs in 1986, which yielded only a 40 percent response rate. Their research focussed on administrative issues.

[3] Ninety-six percent (n = 45) of the police chiefs responding to this survey agreed or strongly agreed with the statement "Being part of a tactical unit is a prestigious position in the department."

[4] One department of 75 officers sent us professionally made trading cards depicting its 15-man unit. One of the cards was a photograph of the SRT posed around an armored personnel carrier. Members were dressed in full tactical gear; nylon mesh masks covered their faces. The back of the card read, "When citizens need help they call the police. When the police need help they call SRT." The SRT's self-image as the cops' cops illuminates members' self-perception as specialists in the use of force.

[5] In phone interviews with two departments that had just established PPUs, the informants estimated that start-up and first-year costs of a 15-member unit would be $200,000 to $250,000. This figure includes all "tactical gear" and first-year training costs.

[6] The demographic literature makes the break between smaller and larger cities at 50,000 (McGregor-Matlock and Woodhouse, 1987; Shannon and Ross, 1977). In labeling this study

"small-locality," as opposed to "small-town," we included 37 county agencies that serve 25,000 to 50,000 people and employ 100 or fewer officers.

[7] Although the N is reduced by truncating the population subset at the 100-officer level, analysis of the larger data set revealed no appreciable differences in our findings.

[8] Some police administrators in small towns and rural counties are developing multijurisdictional PPUs by using existing arrangements designed to assist small communities in natural disasters. A paper agency is formed when departments participating in the disaster relief arrangement also donate one to three officers and associated funds to be a part of a fully operational 40- to 60-member PPU. Several interviewees claimed that their multijurisdictional PPUs gradually developed an independence from political and community oversight; this left them free to collaborate with state police agencies, with little political or community scrutiny.

[9] Three percent ($n = 125$) of call-outs were categorized as "other."

[10] Interviews revealed that when paramilitary units conducted proactive patrols, they were not required to answer routine calls for service. These units instead were deployed into "high-crime" neighborhoods to conduct street interrogations of "suspicious" pedestrians, occupants of automobiles, and even persons in "drug houses." Three departments said that it was not unusual for their units to conduct "warrantless dynamic entries" into private residences if they saw suspected drug dealers entering a residence to elude police interrogation.

[11] Evidence for this assertion includes the large number of police departments planning to establish a PPU in the future, the recent steep growth in PPUs doing warrant and patrol work, and the fact that much of these data comes from newly formed units.

[12] One of the anonymous reviewers of this paper claimed that similar changes are taking place in hostage/barricade situations:

> Instead of following the tried and true 25-year-old practice of negotiating for a bloodless resolution no matter how long it takes, some departments seem to have adopted the practice of turning scenes over to SWAT after a relatively short time.... SWAT then attempts to implement a "tactical resolution" which usually ends in one or more dead bodies. Indeed, members of one SWAT team even told me that their department has given up on negotiating for a bloodless resolution no matter how long it takes. Instead, they have adopted the "LA procedure" which consists of negotiating with hostage takers or barricaded persons for the purpose of putting them in position for a "tactical resolution": an "instantly catastrophic" shot by a sniper to the cerebral cortex.

[13] On the basis of data from 1987–1993, Maguire (forthcoming) finds no significant differences in the extent of structural change between agencies that identify themselves as community policing departments and agencies that do not.

[14] Currently we are collecting data relevant to social threat theory for each of the 846 jurisdictions for 1995. The objective is to determine which (if any) social threat variables account for the variance in paramilitary deployments across jurisdictions.

[15] NYPD officials, with support from the Harvard School of Government, are quite vocal in claiming that their unique brand of proactive, aggressive policing has reduced crime dramatically. In April 1996, NYPD launched a "3,000"-officer offensive to "crush drug trafficking and the drug business," employing the same tactics as discussed in this research (Kraus, 1996:1). NYPD is also aggressively marketing its "success strategy" to other police agencies via national conferences.

References

Angell, J. E. (1971). Toward an alternative to the classic police organizational arrangements: A democratic model. *Criminology, 9,* 195–206.

Bailey, W. G. (1995). *The encyclopedia of police science* (2nd ed.). New York: Garland.

Bayley, D. H. (1994). *Police for the future.* New York: Oxford University Press.

Beard, J. A. (1994, August). Using special management units to control inmate violence. *Corrections Today,* 88–91.

Bittner, E. (1970). *The functions of police in modern society.* Chevy Chase: National Clearinghouse for Mental Health.

Bock, A. W. (1995). *Ambush at Ruby Ridge: How governmental agents set Randy Weaver up and took his family down.* Irvine, CA: Dickens.

Brewer, J. D., Guelke, A., Hume, I., Moxon-Browne, E., & Wolford, R. (1988). *The police, public order and the state.* New York: St. Martin's.

Bryan, D. (1995). Emergency response teams: A prison's first line of defense. *Corrections Compendium, 20*(7), 1–13.

Chambliss, W. J. (1994). Policing the ghetto underclass: The politics of law and law enforcement. *Social Problems, 41,* 177–94.

Chevigny, P. (1995). *Edge of the knife: Police violence in the Americas.* New York: Free Press.

Christie, N. (1994). *Crime control as industry: Toward GULAGS, Western style.* New York: Routledge.

Cohen, S. (1985). *Visions of social control: Crime, punishment and classification.* Cambridge: Polity.

Crime and Social Justice Associates. (1983). *The iron fist and the velvet glove: An analysis of the U.S. police* (3rd ed.). San Francisco: Garret.

Decker, S. (1979). The rural county sheriff: An issue in social control. *Criminal Justice Review, 4,* 97–111.

Enloe, C. (1980). *Police, military, and ethnicity: Foundations of state power.* New Brunswick, NJ: Transaction.

Ericson, R. (1994). The division of expert knowledge in policing and security. *British Journal of Sociology, 45,* 149–70.

Ericson, R., & Carriers, K. (1994). The fragmentation of criminology. In D. Nelken (Ed.), *The Futures of Criminology* (pp. 89–109). Beverly Hills: Sage.

Feeley, M., & Simon, J. (1992). The new penology. *Criminology, 39,* 449–74.

Feeley, M., & Simon, J. (1994). Actuarial justice: The emerging new criminal law. In D. Nelken (Ed.), *The Futures of Criminology* (pp. 173–201). Beverly Hills: Sage.

Fogelson, R. M. (1977). *Big-city police.* Cambridge, MA: Harvard University Press.

Foucault, M. (1977). *Discipline and punish: The birth of the prison.* New York: Vintage.

Fry, L. W., & Berkes, L. J. (1983). The paramilitary police model: An organizational misfit. *Human Organization, 42,* 225–34.

Garland, D. (1990). *Punishment and modern society: A study in social theory.* Chicago: University of Chicago Press.

Garland, D. (1995). Penal modernism and postmodernism. In T. G. Blomber & S. Cohen (Eds.), *Punishment and social control: Essays in honor of Sheldon L. Messinger* (pp. 181–210). New York: Aldine.

Gibons, D. C. (1972). Crime in the hinterland. *Criminology, 10,* 177–91.

Gibson, J. W. (1994). *Warrior dreams: Manhood in post-Vietnam America.* New York: Hill and Wang.

Goldstein, H. (1990). *Problem-oriented policing.* New York: McGraw-Hill.

Gove, W. R., Hughes, M., & Geerken, M. (1985). Are uniform crime reports a valid indicator of the index crimes? An affirmative answer with minor qualifications. *Criminology, 23,* 111–120.

Hair, J. F., Jr., Anderson, R. E., Tatham, R. L., & Black, W. C. (1995). *Multivariate data analysis with readings* (4th ed.). Upper Saddle River, NJ: Prentice-Hall.

Hamm, M. S. (1993). *American skinheads: The criminology and control of hate crime.* Westport, CT: Praeger.

Irwin, J., & Austin, J. (1997). *It's about time: America's imprisonment binge*. Belmont, CA: Wadsworth.

Jefferson, T. (1990). *The case against paramilitary policing*. Bristol, PA: Open University Press.

Kelling, G. L. (1988). *Police and communities: The quiet revolution*. Washington, DC: National Institute of Justice.

Klockars, C. B. (1985). *The idea of police*. Beverly Hills: Sage.

Kraska, P. B. (1994). The police and the military in the post-cold war era: Streamlining the state's use of force entities in the drug war. *Police Forum, 4*, 1–8.

Kraska, P. B. (1996). Enjoying militarism: Political/personal dilemmas in studying U.S. police paramilitary units. *Justice Quarterly, 13*, 405–429.

Kraska, P. B., & Kappeler, V. E. (1997). Militarizing American police: The rise and normalization of paramilitary units. *Social Problems, 44*, 1–18.

Kraska, P. B., & Paulsen, D. J. (1997). Grounded research into U.S. paramilitary policing: Forging the iron fist inside the velvet glove. *Policing and Society, 7*, 253–270.

Kraus, C. (1996). NYC police to start big drug offensive using new approach. Posted on World Wide Web, April 4. *New York Times* Company.

LaFree, G., & Drass, K. A. (1996). The effects of changes in intraracial income inequality and educational attainment on changes in arrest rates for African Americans and whites, 1957 to 1990. *American Sociological Review, 61*, 614–634.

Maguire, E. R. (Forthcoming). Structural changes in large municipal police organizations during the community policing era. *Justice Quarterly*.

Manning, P. K. (1977). *Police work: The social organization of policing*. Cambridge, MA: MIT Press.

Manning, P. K. (1978). The police: Mandate, strategies and appearances. In P. K. Manning & J. Van Maanen (Eds.), *Policing: A view from the street* (pp. 53–70). Chicago: Goodyear.

Manning, P. K. (1992). Economic rhetoric and policing reform. *Criminal Justice Research Bulletin, 7*, 1–8.

Manning, P. K. (1993). The preventive conceit: The black box in market context. *American Behavioral Scientist, 36*, 639–650.

Marenin, O., & Copus, G. (1991). Policing rural Alaska: The village public safety officer (VPSO) program. *American Journal of Police, 10*, 1–26.

McGregor-Matlock, L., & Woodhouse, L. (1987). *The state of the small city: A survey of the nation's cities and towns under 50,000*. Washington, DC: National League of Cities.

Miller, J. G. (1996). *Search and destroy: African-American males in the criminal justice system*. New York: Cambridge University Press.

Reiner, R. (1992). *The politics of the police*. Toronto: University of Toronto Press.

Ritzer, G. (1993). *The McDonaldization of society: An investigation into the changing character of contemporary social life*. Thousand Oaks, CA: Pine Forge.

Shannon, J., & Ross, J. (1977). Cities: Their increasing dependence on state and federal aid. In J. Herrington (Ed.), *Small cities in transition: The dynamics of growth and decline* (pp. 211–229). Cambridge, MA: Ballinger.

Sherry, M. S. (1996). *In the shadow of war: The United States since the 1930s*. New Haven: Yale University Press.

Skolnick, J. H. (1966). *Justice without trial: Law enforcement in a democratic society*. New York: Wiley.

Skolnick, J. H., & Fyfe, J. J. (1993). *Above the law: Police and the excessive use of force*. New York: Free Press.

Stevens, J. W., & MacKenna, D. W. (1988). Police capabilities for responding to violent criminal activity and terrorism. *Police Studies, 11*, 116–123.

Sutherland, E. H., Cressey, D. R., & Luckenbill, D. F. (1992). *Principles of criminology.* Dix Hills, NY: General Hall Inc.

Trojanowicz, R., & Bucqueroux, B. (1990). *Community policing: A contemporary perspective.* Cincinnati: Anderson.

Turk, A. (1982). *Political criminality: The defiance and defense of authority.* Beverly Hills: Sage.

Van Maanen, J. (1978). Kinsmen in repose: Occupational perspectives of patrolmen. In P. K. Manning & J. Van Maanen (Eds.), *Police and policing: A view from the street* (pp. 28–39). Chicago: Goodyear.

Weisheit, R. A. (1993). Studying drugs in rural areas: Notes from the field. *Journal of Research in Crime and Delinquency, 30*, 213–232.

Weisheit, R. A., Falcone, D. N., & Wells, L. E. (1996). *Crime and policing in rural and small-town America.* Long Grove, IL: Waveland Press.

Westley, W. A. (1956). Secrecy and the police. *Social Forces, 34*, 254–257.

8

Good Policing

JAMES J. FYFE

According to Peter K. Manning (1977), the social mandate of the American police is a hodge-podge of conflicting duties and responsibilities that has developed with little input from the police themselves. He is correct. Firefighting, the uniformed public service frequently compared to policing, has a clear mandate that firefighters have helped to fashion: the fire service exists to prevent fires and to extinguish as quickly and as safely as possible all those it did not prevent. It is virtually impossible to derive a similarly succinct and comprehensive statement of the police role. Instead, it is safe to say only that police perform a variety of services that must be available seven days a week, 24 hours a day, that may require the use or threat of force, and that are not readily available from any other public agency or private institution.[1]

Doing What Nobody Else Does

Police responsibility for these tasks not handled by others has meant that the police sometimes are called upon to do the impossible or to attempt to provide services they have not been adequately prepared to perform. The historic reluctance of police to intervene in domestic disputes,[2] for example, probably has more to do with the difficulty of straightening out other peoples' arguments in the middle of the night than with the purported danger to police of such assignments. A line of research has recently demonstrated that *domestics* are not nearly the police job hazard they were assumed to be (see, e.g., Margarita, 1980; Konstantin, 1984; Garner and Clemmer, 1986). The difficulty of resolving these arguments while they are at flashpoint, however, has long been clear, and is a task that might better be handled by social workers provided with protective police escorts. Social workers understandably have not volunteered to play such a role. Consequently, the police have been

James F. Fyfe, "Good Policing," in Brian Forst, Ed., *The Socioeconomics of Crime and Justice.* Reprinted by permission of M. E. Sharpe, Inc., Armonk, New York 10504.

stuck with it on grounds that they are available and that their duties include order maintenance.

In the past, the ready, round-the-clock availability of the police has caused them to be assigned to many duties that fit under this *order mainte-nance* rubric only by the most liberal definition. In the late nineteenth cen-tury, Philadelphia police provided lodging for more than 100,000 people every year. Early in the twentieth century, New York police stations were the distri-bution points for food and coal doled out to the poor under "home relief" pro-grams (Monkonnen, 1981:81–106).

In addition, the close ties of the police to the powerful have, in many places, made police departments a major vehicle of job patronage. A major factor in historic analyses of policing is the great extent to which attainment of formally stated police goals has continually been affected by use of police departments as means of politically dispensed upward mobility for newly arrived ethnic groups and recently empowered racial minorities (Fogelson, 1977; Walker, 1977; Wilson, 1964).

The closeness of the police to communities and to politicians has also led to corruption, especially in inner cities where police have been charged with enforcing laws that had been enacted by conservative rural-dominated legis-latures, but that found little support in the hurly-burly of urban life. In such places, it became the job of locally controlled police to protect illegal busi-nesses—most notably, gambling and prostitution—from disruptions caused by both other law enforcement agencies and by unruly clientele who might scare off paying customers.[3]

This trend reached a peak during Prohibition, when official corruption became the standard operating procedure of many American police depart-ments (Citizens' Police Committee, 1969). By the time Prohibition ended, however, the United States was deep in the Great Depression, and a con-stricted job market made policing an attractive career option to well-educated people who in better times would have gone into more traditional white collar and professional work. In many cases, this new breed was repulsed by old school corruption and sought to turn policing into a respectable undertaking.

Police as Crime Fighters

Two icons of these new professionals were J. Edgar Hoover, whose FBI waged a bloody and successful war against the gangsters of the early 1930s, and August Vollmer, who earlier had made the Berkeley Police Department an exemplar of efficiency and technological excellence (Carte and Carte, 1975). These two role models led many local police to attempt to do away with the ambiguity of their mandate by redefining themselves first and fore-most as professional crime fighters. These new professionals among police believed that, like FBI agents, local police would win their war by adopting the selective personnel standards and high technology employed with such apparent success by both Hoover and Vollmer. Unfortunately, the police were to find over the long run that the experiences of Hoover and Vollmer were not readily generalizable to other times and places.

J. Edgar Hoover

Hoover's Depression-era successes came not in a broad-fronted war, but in a series of skirmishes against a small number of spectacular outlaws. When local police attempted to apply this same model of *the resolute and professional lawman on the track of bad guys*, however, they eventually became stymied. Police used this strategy over three decades and took great credit for the comparative domestic tranquility that then prevailed. Then, in the 1960s, American crime exploded. Since that watershed decade, the police have learned that the techniques that had been so useful to the FBI in its war against a few colorful characters meant little when a huge baby-boomer generation entered its crime-prone adolescent years, or in inner city crime factories that systematically turn out criminals in overwhelming numbers. Hoover could declare victory when his agents had rounded up or killed the likes of John Dillinger, "Pretty Boy" Floyd, "Babyface" Nelson, and other legendary bandits of the era. But no such easy victory is possible over the rampant and ubiquitous street crime that has literally consumed many inner cities.

August Vollmer

In the same way that police were misled by Hoover's victories, police attempts to emulate Vollmer's example generally have been based on an inexact analogy. Without question, Vollmer turned the Berkeley Police Department into the early twentieth-century American ideal. The Berkeley department was extremely selective, allowing only the very best young men to wear its uniforms. Under Vollmer, the department's apparent success in stifling crime, combined with its great responsiveness to the needs of the *good people* of the community, won it universal admiration at home (Carte and Carte, 1975). But history suggests that, like the "service" style police departments studied by James Q. Wilson during the 1960s (Wilson, 1968)—the Nassau County (NY) Police Department, for example—the Berkeley Police Department enjoyed such apparent success and exalted status largely because it was serving an ideal community that didn't need much from it.

When Vollmer was the police chief of Berkeley, the city was the fast-growing, prosperous, homogenous, and well-educated home to wealthy families who had been scared out of San Francisco by the crime, disorder, bawdiness, earthquake, and fire for which that bigger city on the Bay was best known at the time. Berkeley also was home to the first campus of the University of California, an industry of the type that did not draw employees or clients likely to cause the police much trouble. Indeed, if early twentieth-century Berkeley undergraduates sought to raise hell, it was easy enough for them to ferry across the Bay to the more exciting Sodom of San Francisco or to simply walk across the city line to the Gomorrah of Jack London's Oakland waterfront.

Wilson studied Nassau County, the Long Island suburb adjacent to New York City, when policing there was the same sort of cakewalk that Vollmer's staff had enjoyed a half-century earlier in Berkeley. Until World War II, Nassau County consisted largely of farms, a few small towns, and estates like those occupied by Fitzgerald's Jay Gatsby and friends. During the War, Long Island's expansion began with the growth of its defense industries and aircraft manufacturers. In the years immediately after the War, Nassau County became a booming suburb that, except for its larger population, was much like those that sprouted around Los Angeles at the same time. Generous GI financing, a new highway system, and quick construction methods combined with the desire for the good life—a patch of green away from mean city streets—overnight turned potato fields into tract housing. By the time Wilson observed its police department, the population of Nassau County had nearly doubled during the 1950s—to 1.3 million by 1960—and the county boasted a tax base larger than all but a small handful of U.S. cities. The non-white population in areas served by the county police (as opposed to the generally more exclusive towns policed by a few small independent departments) was 2.5%, and was located largely in a few small and long-established enclaves that had started as the homes for domestic help to the wealthy (Wilson, 1968:224). The county's homicide rate was less than one-sixth the national average and, despite the fact that its ratio of cars:population was far higher than the national norm, Nassau's vehicle theft rate was only one-third the national average (see Wilson, 1968:86–93). Like Vollmer's Berkeley Police Department, Nassau selected its officers carefully, paid and equipped them well, and asked them to give friendly service to a homogenous populace who sought to share peace, quiet, and stability with their neighbors.

Wilson's Nassau differed from Vollmer's Berkeley chiefly in size and by virtue of the high percentage of its population that wore blue collars at work. Both places enjoyed freedom from poverty, inequity, class and ethnic conflict, or social discord of any other type. Both had ideal police departments because both were populated by people of means who had chosen to move there from elsewhere in order to be part of an idyllic community.

In the years since Vollmer's tenure and Wilson's studies, both Berkeley and Nassau have changed. Neither has remained homogenous, uniformly prosperous, or untroubled by decay, conflict, social discord, homelessness, unemployment. Regardless of the quality and competence of its chief executives or what they may have accomplished since Vollmer's halcyon days, nobody in policing regards the Berkeley Police Department as *the* local American law enforcement agency that stands in a class by itself, *the* role model for professional policing. Nobody studies policing in Berkeley[4] and nobody in policing knows much about what may be going on there. Nor has any scholar recently studied police in Nassau County. There, while the number of residents has declined slightly over the last three decades, the population has grown much more heterogenous. The percentage of non-white residents has increased five-fold to 13.3 percent, and Hispanics—virtually unknown in the county at the time of Wilson's work—comprise another 3.3 percent (U.S. Department of Commerce, p. 72). In addition, crime rates have increased, closings of defense and aircraft manufacturers have severely hurt the economy, and even the most casual observer would not expect a replication of Wilson's work to come up with the same rosy picture he found a quarter century ago.[5]

Lessons Learned?

The two lessons of these experiences have not been easily digested by either the police or the public. The first of these lessons is that *neither the low crime rates during the golden years of J. Edgar Hoover and August Vollmer nor the great increases since then have had much to do with the police or law enforcement.* Despite Vollmer's good efforts, Berkeley boasted low crime rates during his years because it was a fast-growing, prosperous, homogenous, and highly-educated town in which the major employer was the state's flagship university. Around the country during the Depression years of Hoover's climb to fame, most people were concerned with putting bread on the table and were too beaten down to be aggressive. Thus, minor property crime was common but—except for a rash of well publicized kidnappings and one-man crime waves of the type he vigorously stifled—violent crime generally was not much of a concern.

With the exceptions of a few defense industry boomtowns, the home front remained quiet during World War II because most young men of crime-prone age were either in the military or busy working overtime to supply or fill in for the boys overseas. Crime remained low throughout the fifties, probably because the generation then at peak crime age (roughly 16–24) was small in number: it had been born in the Depression, when birth rates had dropped.

The sixties changed all this. Urban crime rates soared virtually everywhere regardless of whether police conformed to the ideal of professional-warrior-against-crime. The increase in crime was attributable to several converging forces, but two probably are most important. The huge baby-boom generation entered adolescence, so that an unusually large percentage of the population was in its most crime-prone years. In addition, cities changed. For years, blacks and Hispanics had steadily been replacing white city dwellers who had fled to suburbs like Nassau County, taking businesses, jobs, and the cohesiveness of their former neighborhoods with them. This pattern came to a head in the sixties: old communities broke up to be replaced by impersonal and densely populated projects. Racial, cultural, and class conflicts arose. Urban tax bases eroded, municipal services declined, and all the ills of the inner city flourished as they had not since the great waves of European immigration a half century earlier. Since the sixties, the death of Jim Crow, the increased mobility of the black middle-class, and cutbacks in social programs have aggravated these conditions. With few strong community institutions or positive role models for young people, inner cities have grown even more desolate and hopeless.

Thus, it is unrealistic to model the police on Hoover's FBI or, even, to think of the police as our first line of defense against crime. In large measure, the presence or absence of crime has nothing to do with the police. Indeed, even though many people continue to think of *police* and *law enforcement* almost interchangeably, the boom in scholarly studies of policing that began in the 1960s has shown with some consistency that only a small proportion of street police officers' time—in the neighborhood of a quarter—involves law enforcement or investigation of crime. Eric Scott, for example, studied more than 26,000 calls for police service in three urban areas. Two percent of these involved reports of violent crime; seventeen percent involved reports of non-violent crime, and five percent concerned people or circumstances that had aroused citizens' suspicions. The remaining 76 percent concerned interpersonal conflict (seven percent); requests for medical assistance (three percent); traffic problems (nine percent); dependent persons in need of police care (three percent); noise and other public nuisances (11 percent); calls for miscellaneous assistance (12 percent); requests for information (21 percent); provision of non-crime-related information (eight percent); and various police internal matters (two percent) (Scott, 1981:28–30; see also, Reiss, 1971; Webster, 1970; Wilson, 1968). In short, the clientele of the FBI consists almost exclusively of criminal suspects and victims and witnesses to crime, but most of the people with whom the police interact need help with problems not related to crime.

The second lesson is that *policing can probably be regarded as ideal only in places that are themselves idyllic and untroubled*. This is a message with important implications for police reformers, many of whom currently urge adoption of new *community-oriented* and *community-based* policing models. According to the first of Trojanowicz and Bucqueroux's three- paragraph definition (1990:5–6):

> Community Policing is a new philosophy of policing, based on the concept that police officers and private citizens working together in creative ways can help solve contemporary problems related to crime, fear of crime, social and physical disorder, and neighborhood decay. The philosophy is predicated in the belief that achieving these goals requires that police departments develop a new relationship with the law-abiding people in the community, allowing them a greater voice in setting local police priorities and involving them in efforts to improve the overall quality of life in their neighborhoods. It shifts the focus of police work from handling random calls to solving community problems.

Trojanowicz and Bucqueroux go on to say that this new model requires the designation of some patrol officers as "Community Policing Officers." Each of these CPOs should be assigned on a continuing basis to the same small geographic area. There, from their patrol cars and the responsibility of responding to radio calls, CPOs can then develop collaborative relationships with community members. These relationships, in turn, will allow "people direct input in setting day-to-day, local police priorities, in exchange for their cooperation and participation in efforts to police themselves" (Trojanowicz and Bucqueroux, 1990:5).

While there certainly is room for greater and more imaginative police interaction with the communities they serve, it often is difficult to distinguish these new community-oriented models from Wilson's *service* style of policing and from such police arrangements as the democratic team policing alternative of John E. Angell (1971) and neighborhood team policing (see Sherman, et al., 1973). Indeed, I can find virtually nothing in descriptions of recent community policing models that differs from my own experience in two New York City police precincts that included Neighborhood Police Teams more than two decades ago.

But these prior attempts to rearrange police departments and their relationships with communities have either been discarded or, as in the case of Wilson's service style, apparently have been feasible only so long as there exists a monolithic community to which the police can become oriented.[6] Unfortunately, in the areas most in need of high quality police services—however such quality be defined—the *community* and its needs are neither readily identifiable nor monolithic.[7] Instead, as Wilson suggested, such neighborhoods are marked by great social, racial, and political cleavages, and by divergent views about law enforcement and order maintenance policies and practices (Wilson, 1968:288–89; see also, Greenberg and Rohe, 1986). As long as this is so, virtually every police policy or action will offend some interests in the community and near unanimous approval of the police, as in Vollmer's Berkeley or 1960s Nassau County, will remain unattainable. Further, as long as communities define the police role in the expectation that police will merely respond unquestioningly to their wishes, the police mandate will continue to be amorphous and unclear.

Consequences of Unclear Direction

Priority Setting

The consequences of vague definition of the police role and minimal police participation in specifying it are widespread. Police have not been given much direction for setting priorities among the melange of duties and responsibilities they have been assigned. The police are expected both to maintain order and to enforce the law but, in important instances, these two obligations may conflict. Uniformed officers assigned in response to citizens' complaints that specific streets have become open air drug markets, for example, usually are instructed by their superiors to enforce the law aggressively. But officers who follow such instructions by arresting the first minor offender they see may find themselves off the street and caught up in the booking and court processes for hours. While these officers are gone, their beats remain open territory, dealers do uninterrupted land-office business, and law-abiding citizens wonder what happened to the cops they had asked for. The final frustration in such cases usually comes when arrestees are slapped on the wrist by the courts, treated like public nuisances rather than as the purveyors of poison that officers and residents see.

A better alternative might be to direct officers to avoid making arrests except in major cases and, instead, to attempt to drive dealers off the street by maintaining as high a degree of presence as possible. If this were done, police officers might rid their beats of drug trafficking and restore order to lawless streets, just as they routinely have done in neighborhoods marred by street prostitution and other annoying public order offenses. Importantly, however, such a strategy would generate little of the enforcement "activity" so often used to justify police budget requests (Rubinstein, 1973).

Trying to Quantify Quality

Quantitative measures of police activity—numbers of tickets, arrests, calls for service, minutes and seconds required to respond to calls—often mislead. They say nothing about the vigor or quality of police service or, as in this street drug dealing example, about whether the numbers presented have had any substantial effect on the problem the police were marshaled to address (see, e.g., Rubinstein, 1973). But, regardless of their limited usefulness as a measure of police effectiveness—or their questionable accuracy—numbers are part and parcel of American policing. From the annual figures of the FBI's Uniform Crime Reports through the flashy charts and bar graphs that characterize police departmental annual reports to the monthly activity reports of patrol officers and traffic cops, policing revolves around numbers.

Herman Goldstein (1979) called this tendency to measure police performance in quantitative terms a "means-ends syndrome." It exists, he suggests, because of the ease of toting up the frequency and rapidity with which police use the tools available to them—arrests, tickets, response time—and the difficulty of sitting down and resolving Manning's dilemma by clearly defining police goals, measures of the extent to which they have been achieved, and some notion of whether the police actions involved in doing so may have created or aggravated other problems. From a desk in police headquarters, it is very easy and often very convincing to report to a concerned city councilperson that the police response to complaints about drug dealing on 25th Street has resulted in n arrests. It is not so easy to go out and measure the level of apparent drug activity on 25th Street, or to determine whether police presence has displaced it to 24th Street. Even when such measures are attempted, the absence of impressive arrest numbers often makes them less than convincing.

Prevention and Apprehension

This situation is a conundrum and a contradiction of the principles enunciated by Sir Robert Peel when he established the first modern urban police in Dublin and in London (Palmer, 1988). Before Peel's "Bobbies," police forces existed in continental Europe, but these generally focused their activities on political criminals and on after-the-fact investigations of crime; the notoriously persistent Javert of Hugo's *Les Miserables* is a case in point. But Peel, inspired by the Enlightenment view of man as a rational and ultimately redeemable creature, designed the London Metropolitan Police to be *preventive* rather than punitive. The widespread presence on the streets of police in distinctive but purposely nonmilitary uniforms, Peel reasoned, would convince potential criminals that successful crime was impossible. Accordingly, Peel also reasoned, the best measure of police success in crimefighting would be the *absence* of crime, disorder, and related police business, rather than the measures of law enforcement activity currently in vogue in the United States.

Certainly, police today also are expected to prevent crime. A considerable amount of research, however, suggests that their ability to do so, especially in sprawling, multicultural American cities, is more limited than Peel, Hoover, or Vollmer believed (Kelling, et al., 1974; Police Foundation, 1981). Further, the incentive to develop more sophisticated prevention strategies is diminished by news and entertainment media that grant police their greatest glory for arresting those whom they have failed to deter in the first place. *Cops 'n' robbers* make for spectacular headlines and sensational docudrama, but the work of police crime prevention officers has never been the focus of any movie or TV series. This emphasis and glorification of apprehension over prevention spills down to the lowest level of policing, where the greenest beat cops learn early in their careers that "important arrests" are enthusiastically counted and rewarded, while nobody knows—or seems to care—how many crimes did not occur because of officers' vigilance.

On occasion, the consequences of this apprehension-oriented incentive system are bizarre and certainly not what Peel intended. In some departments, instead of cruising by bars at closing time to make sure that drunks do not attempt to drive home, officers hide in darkened cars a block or two away to catch them after they have gotten into their cars and driven off. In using this technique to gain credit for arrests, these officers allow drunks to commit the very same life-endangering acts one might expect the police to prevent. In Los Angeles, an elite squad has for years refrained from intervening while, as its officers anticipated, armed burglars and robbers have victimized unsuspecting citizens. Instead of preventing these victimizations, officers have stood by and watched in order to confront their quarry—often with bloody results—after all doubt about their intentions has been removed. "Public safety is certainly a concern," the unit's commander told the *Los Angeles Times*, "but we have to look beyond that because if we arrest someone for attempt, the likelihood of a conviction is not as great" (Freed, 1988; Skolnick and Fyfe, 1993).

Accusations of Discrimination

At the same time that police are charged to enforce the law firmly and fairly, they also are expected to be judicious and selective in their enforcement efforts. Unfortunately, the police have received little guidance in estab-lishment of criteria to distinguish between unfair discrimination and discretion that serves some legitimate social end. Consequently, "selective enforcement" often is little more than individual officers' *ad hoc* decisions about which driver should receive a ticket and which should not; which loud-mouthed kid should be arrested, which taken home to his parents.

Regardless of how judicious a police department may be, the absence of meaningful decision-making standards dictates that any agency that polices a pluralistic constituency will be the subject of regular criticism and dissatisfac-tion on the part of one or more subpopulations. Further, the absence of such standards means that the best-intended police officers in such a department will be left confused and vulnerable to accusations of arbitrariness. Motorists know that cops do not issue tickets for all the traffic violations they witness. Consequently, every experienced cop has heard bitter motorists allege that the tickets they have just been handed were motivated by questions of race or class rather than by the need to enforce laws against traffic violations that so many others commit without punishment.[8]

Further, in a society in which race and class are as closely related as ours, it often is hard to draw a line between discretion and discrimination. The fun-damental precept of the juvenile justice system—to *help and reform*, rather than to *punish*—generally dictates that police interventions into kids' minor delinquencies should be no more intrusive and formal than whatever may be necessary to accomplish two goals. First, the action selected—ranging any-where from warning through arrest and booking—should give officers some sense that the youngsters involved have learned the errors of their ways. Sec-ond, officers should be assured that, after they leave the scene, responsible parties will carefully supervise the miscreants and keep them on the straight and narrow. But when cops act on these precepts, their dispositions of juve-niles who have been involved in minor delinquencies result in numbers heavily skewed by class and, therefore, by race. Middle-class kids are skilled at ingratiating themselves to people who can affect their futures. When the police bring them home or to police stations after such kids have done wrong, the police meet concerned, stable families from nice neighborhoods. Most important, the police get convincing assurances from Moms and Dads that it will be a long time before Junior—who is by now teary-eyed and apologetic—has another opportunity to misbehave. Consequently, the police typically take no formal action, but leave such kids to the care of their parents.

Street kids learn early to challenge authority. In the ghetto, where life often includes no thoughts of the future beyond tomorrow, the middle class skill of ingratiating oneself to people who can affect one's future is meaning-less and denigrated. Often, ghetto kids come from home environments in which no meaningful control is exercised over their conduct. In such circum-stances, cops are likely to conclude that helping kids to find the straight and narrow can be accomplished only by invoking the formal juvenile justice sys-tem. This, of course, has two effects. First, it punishes these youngsters by attaching formal delinquent labels to them. Second, it generates statistics that can be used to put police on the defensive by those who claim that cops' decisions routinely are racist. In fact, the statistics may hide well-intended decisions to arrest or release juveniles that, like police and judicial decisions related to adults' bail and pre-trial release, appropriately are driven by variables independent of the instant offense. Judges' bail decisions and police releases on adult suspects' own recognizance are based on assessments of the probability that defendants will be back in court on schedule. Cops' decisions about what to do with young violators often are based on officers' assessments of the probability that police will have no further contact with the youngsters involved. Thus, the goals of these decisions—to achieve the hope of seeing subjects again in the first case; to achieve the hope of never seeing them again in the second—are different, but the criteria used in making them should be similar. Unlike police and court discretion related to adult criminal defendants (see, e.g., Thomas, 1976; Institute for Law and Social Research, 1980), however, police decisions concerning juvenile offenders generally are unbounded by rules or guidelines and, therefore, remain subject to criticism.

Defining Good Policing

The discussion to this point suggests the overarching dilemma caused by the absence of a clear police mandate: beyond some prescriptions for specific field situations in which closure is rapid and clearly identifiable, we have yet to derive a widely accepted definition of police effectiveness. Within policing, the absence of such a definition reverberates at every level. The requirements for entry into an occupation, for example, should be those that best predict satisfactory job performance. But the absence of clearly articulated standards for assessing police effectiveness means that police entry requirements can be no more than guesses about which candidates are likely to be abusive, to beget scandals, or, through physical disability or acts that create legal liability, to impose great financial losses on those to whom they have applied for employment. Some police candidates are screened out on the basis of bizarre personal histories or criminal records. Others, however, survive this screening and demonstrate their lack of suitability for policing only after they have been locked into it by civil service tenure. Equally important, the imprecision inherent in searches to fill jobs that are not clearly defined undoubtedly results in the loss of fine candidates whose membership in policing would undoubtedly increase its representativeness of the population.

The Absence of the Satisfaction of a Job Well Done

Those who make it through this screening find that police work carries many rewards. Although no honest police officer ever becomes rich, policing in most parts of the United States pays a decent wage which, despite the last couple of decades' police layoffs in financially strapped cities, also is very dependable. In the busiest jurisdictions, the police workday goes very quickly and, in the words of a recruiting poster in use when I began my police career, often includes "a view of life your deskbound friends will never see." Certainly, this view is not always pleasant or fulfilling: the things police see cause some to become chronically distrustful and hardened, ultimately leading to great problems in their private lives. Other officers, however, draw from their work greater appreciation of their own comparative good fortune. However trying, regular exposure to violence, exploitation, greed, madness, cruelty, poverty, hopelessness, addiction, and the rest of humankind's most serious ills puts into perspective and makes less insurmountable the annoyances of middle-class life.

Specific police actions—cracking a big case, pulling a driver from a burning car, talking an emotionally disturbed person out of a suicide attempt—also provide a great deal of satisfaction and official praise for police officers. But, absent the opportunity to engage in such heroics, cops may try their hardest to earn their salaries without ever knowing whether they are doing well or whether their work has made a difference, and without ever receiving formal acknowledgment of their efforts.

This issue involves much more than the salving of cops' tender egos. A quarter century ago, Arthur Neiderhoffer (1969:95–108) reported that New York City police patrol officers, the street cops who performed the most familiar but most ill-defined and least prestigious work in their department, had higher levels of cynicism than any other officers he studied. Over time, Neiderhoffer suggested, the intractability of patrol officers' work and their inability to get out of it and into more glamorous assignments may lead to a sense of frustration and victimization. These, in turn, may alienate officers—and, indeed, whole police departments—from the community, causing the dysfunctional *us and them* relationship between police and citizens found in many jurisdictions and manifested by incidents like the beating of Rodney King. It was no accident that the King incident involved the Los Angeles Police Department, the agency that, more than any other big city U.S. police department, had come to define itself as a beleaguered thin blue line that protects ungrateful and undeserving citizens from themselves (see, e.g., Gates, 1992).

Indeed, Carl Klockars (1980) suggests that the gap between what police are expected to achieve and what they can achieve encourages them to brutality, perjury, and other fabrications of evidence against guilty people who would otherwise go free. Anxious to achieve the noble end of seeing that offenders receive deserved punishment, good cops, asserts Klockars, become very frustrated by a criminal justice system that too often seems to dismiss cases for reasons that have nothing to do with whether arrestees actually committed the offenses of which they were accused. Then, like Clint Eastwood's movie character, "Dirty Harry" Callahan, some of these officers render a violent brand of street justice and/or lie from the witness stand in order to assure that the guilty get what they deserve. The now famous videotape showing Los Angeles police beating Rodney King while he is on his hands and knees memorialized the first half of such an episode. Absent George Holliday and his videocam, the episode's second half would have been the prosecution the police had initiated against Mr. King before they knew they had been caught by George Holliday and his videocam. At this court proceeding, the police who arrested and beat King would undoubtedly have offered perjured testimony to the effect that King was standing upright and physically attacking them when they used no more than necessary force to subdue him.

Cops' Rules

Elizabeth Reuss-Ianni (1984) has written that police estrangement may extend to conflicting "street cop" and "management cop" subcultures within police departments. Where these exist, street cops see themselves as excluded from a management system that espouses lofty ideals and that employs meaningless statistics and other forms of smoke and mirrors in order to give the illusion that these ideals are being achieved. Consequently, street cops see their leadership as an illegitimate and naive obstacle that must be surmounted if *real* police work is to be accomplished.[9]

Like the values constructed and honored by lower class delinquent boys in response to rejection by middle class teachers (Cohen, 1955), however, street cops' definitions of admirable behavior are developed without input from above and, in addition to serving as guideposts to survival in a harsh world, often are antithetical to those publicly espoused by official police spokespersons. Reuss-Ianni's astute observations of New York City police led her to formulate a list of the rules that govern street cops' interactions with each other and with their supervisors and administrators:

> Watch out for your partner first and then the rest of the guys working the tour [shift];
>
> Don't give up another cop;
>
> Show balls [physical courage];
>
> Be aggressive when you have to, but don't be too eager;
>
> Don't get involved in anything in another guy's sector [car beat];
>
> Hold up your end of the work;
>
> If you get caught off base, don't implicate anybody else;
>
> Make sure the other guys [officers, but not supervisors or administrators] know if another cop is dangerous or "crazy";
>
> Don't trust a new guy until you have checked him out;
>
> Don't tell anybody else more than they have to know, it could be bad for you and it could be bad for them;
>
> Don't talk too much or too little;
>
> Don't leave work for the next tour;
>
> Protect your ass;
>
> Don't make waves;
>
> Don't give [supervisors] too much activity;

Keep out of the way of any boss from outside your precinct;

Don't look for favors just for yourself;

Don't take on the patrol sergeant by yourself;

Know your bosses;

Don't do the bosses' work for them [e.g., let them discover miscreant officers without assistance];

Don't trust bosses to look out for your interest. (Reuss-Ianni, 1984:14–16)

The adversarial relationship between "street cops" and "management cops" suggested by many of these rules has its roots in the pyramidal, military style of police organization that so sharply distinguishes between administrators and those on the front lines.[10] Thus, as we see over and over again in both examples of great heroism and officers' reluctance to expose the wrongdoing of colleagues (Christopher, et al., 1992; Daley, 1978; Maas, 1973), street cops' primary loyalties are to each other rather than to the bureaucracies in which they work or to the taxpayers who pay their salaries. In the absence of formal recognition of what street cops justifiably regard as good work, street cops' reward systems consist primarily of their peer groups' status rankings of their members, and the highest status in this system is the recognition that one is *a cop's cop*. The irony that those who win this high accolade from their peers often are regarded with antagonism and suspicion by police administrators is evidence of the depth of the cleavage between management and street cops.

What To Do

Several scholars have suggested solutions to all or part of this dilemma of the vague police mandate. Manning (1978:374) argues that police should focus on enhancing their ability as crime-fighters and on delegating to other agencies as many of their traffic control and other non-crime related service tasks as possible. However easy this proposal might appear to make police lives and evaluation of police performance, it is unrealistic. There is no evidence that any other agencies are anxious to fill the police role as round-the-clock-first-responders to the wide variety of non-enforcement tasks currently handled by police. Further, it is not easy to distinguish in advance between crime-fighting and police non-crime service tasks. Most police services are rendered in response to citizens' telephone calls for help of some kind or other. In some cases, 911 operators can determine very quickly that those who respond to assist must be authorized and equipped to use force and to enforce laws. In most cases, however, this is not possible, and officials must actually arrive at the scene to determine whether calls for services of the types currently handled by police require use of force, law enforcement, or both. Hence, it probably is wishful thinking to plan for police delegation to other authorities of such non-enforcement tasks as handling domestic calls, resolving neighbors' disputes, chasing noisy streetcorner groups, dealing with emotionally disturbed street people, and responding to vehicle accidents.

Klockars sees severe punishment of officers who use dirty means to achieve noble ends as the appropriate approach to the "Dirty Harry Problem." But, paradoxically, even he recognizes that this solution is unsatisfactory:

> In urging the punishment of policemen who resort to dirty means to achieve some unquestionably good and morally compelling end, we recognize that we create a Dirty Harry problem for ourselves and for those we urge to effect such punishments. It is a fitting end, one which teaches once again that the danger in Dirty Harry problems is never in their resolution, but in thinking that one has found a resolution with which one can truly live in peace. (Klockars, 1980:47)

Klockars' realization that it would be difficult to live in peace with this resolution is correct, but for reasons he seems not to take into account. Punishment achieved by end runs around due process is no more an "unquestionably good and morally compelling end" than is family prosperity obtained by a breadwinner's thefts from his or her employer. In both cases, the most peaceful and satisfying resolution might be achieved not by punishing the wrongdoer, but by preventing the wrongdoing in the first place. This might be accomplished by demonstrating to the people on whose behalf the wrongdoing is likely to be conducted—the public in Klockars' case; the family in my analogy—that their desires are unrealistic and likely to impose other, unquestionably bad, costs.

Breadwinners usually can bring the desires of overly demanding families into line with reality by pointing out the limits of family resources and that the immorality and costs of stealing apply regardless of whether one is caught with a hand in the till. Public officials should make sure that their constituents know that the widespread desire to ignore constitutional limits so that *justice may be done* is oxymoronic and equally immoral and costly. Punishing wrongdoers without regard to the process that has been prescribed by 200 years of American experience weakens the entire society, perpetuates the myth that society can rely on the police as its primary defense against crime, and encourages society's policy makers to allow the continued festering of the social conditions that have turned our inner cities into crime factories. Unfortunately, in this era of concern over law and order and apparent resolve to address the crime problem by harshness alone, few public officials seem willing to bring forth this message.

Mastrofski's suggestions seem closer to the mark and are more strongly supported by the work and experiences of other scholars. He suggests that the broad and vague mandate of the police is here to stay. He indicates also that the extent to which it is accomplished is best assessed at close range, at the microlevel of the quality of police officers' daily encounters with citizens:

> . . . what police officers themselves know about good policing has to do with how officers respond to the particular circumstances they are called to handle. This is the craft of policing, about which a great deal is known, yet uncodified: making good arrests, deescalating crises, investigating

> crimes, using coercion and language effectively, abiding by the law and protecting individual rights, developing knowledge of the community, and imparting a sense of fairness by one's actions. (1988:63)

There is reason to believe that this is a feasible approach to the eventual derivation of a definition of *good policing*. As Bayley and Garofalo (1985) have reported, line police officers are excellent assessors of their peers' talents. These two researchers asked groups of street officers to identify the most outstanding of their number. Subsequently, Bayley and Garofalo observed both officers identified as outstanding and their colleagues at one of their most difficult police tasks, intervention in disputes. They report finding quantifiable differences between the manners and techniques employed by the *cops' cops* and the rest, most notably that the officers who had been identified as outstanding were less judgmental and more helpful than their peers in their dealings with disputants. Thus, even though the officers Bayley and Garofalo had asked to rate their peers had not been requested to specify *why* they thought some officers better than others, it appears that these officers had observed something different about the work of *cops' cops* that could subsequently be documented empirically.

Hans Toch and his colleagues (Toch, et al., 1975) had earlier approached much the same problem from a different angle (see article 28 of this volume). They identified a group of Oakland police officers who frequently were involved in on-the-job violence they seemed to provoke or manufacture. These violence-prone officers were themselves asked to analyze the problem of violence between police and citizens, and to develop solutions to it. The most intriguing result of this work was the creation by these officers of an officially approved Peer Review Panel, consisting mostly of violence-prone officers. This panel met regularly with officers whose apparent violent activities had been brought to light in incident reports or by supervisory referral, and was

> designed (1) to stimulate the subject to study his violence-related arrests over time and to help him tease out cues to his contributions to violent incidents and (2) to assist the subject to define and formulate alternative strategies for coping with violence-precipitating incidents. (Toch, 1980:60)

This program was, by all measures, a success. It allowed these most violent-prone street cops to diagnose their own problems, to analyze the more generic problem of police-citizen violence, and to devise solutions to it. It enhanced their analytic sophistication and helped to break down the adversarial relationship between street cops and management. Involvement in violent incidents by officers who participated in the program declined vis-à-vis that of other officers. Further, and just as important as substantive results, the Oakland work showed that:

> [p]rograms that are usually resisted as arbitrary interferences with the officers' autonomy can become experiments in whose outcome the officers have a proprietary interest and a substantial stake. (Toch, 1980:61)

This early exercise in what has since come to be known as *Problem-Oriented Policing*—identifying a problem and the most desirable outcome of attempts to resolve it; carefully analyzing the problem and devising appropriate means of resolving it (see, e.g., Goldstein, 1990)—was the basis for a project I subsequently directed in Dade County, Florida (Fyfe, 1988). There, a task force consisting of Metro-Dade Police Department street officers, trainers, investigators, and field supervisors was assembled and asked to analyze a random sample of reports of police-citizen encounters that had *gone wrong*, in the sense that they had resulted in citizens' complaints against officers, use of force by officers, or injuries to officers. The analysis required task force members to identify every decision and action of the officers in each encounter; to describe its effects (in terms of increasing or decreasing whatever potential for violence may have existed); and, where appropriate, to prescribe alternative decisions or actions that may have better served to defuse potential violence. The goals of this analysis were to identify the most satisfactory resolutions of several types of frequently encountered potentially violent encounters between police and citizens,[11] and to construct a detailed list of "Do's and Don't's" that would help officers to achieve these resolutions.

In other words, the project enlisted officers to define *jobs well done* in street cops' most challenging work, and to identify the steps most likely to help officers to do such jobs well. This project, conducted under rigid social science experimental conditions, eventually resulted in a five-day "violence reduction training program" that was delivered to all Dade County officers between February 1988 and February 1989. In the three years since then, Metro-Dade police records show that complaints against officers, use of force by officers, and injuries to officers all have declined between 30 and 50 percent.

All of this signals that street cops know more than anybody about what is *good policing* and who are the *cop's cops*. But, until the groundbreaking work of Toch, Grant, and Galvin, nobody had asked them. When they have been asked, street officers have responded with remarkable accuracy. In Oakland, street cops—notably, the *most violent* street cops—were empowered to address the problem of which they were the major part, and came up with solutions. Bayley and Garofalo asked street cops to identify the stars among themselves, and the answers appear to have been substantiated by observations of cops at work. I asked street cops, trainers, and supervisors below the policy making level to define *good policing* in a variety of challenging situations. The answers resulted in a course of training that has been followed by remarkable reductions in police-citizen violence in one of the country's most volatile policing environments.[12]

The implications seem clear. As Manning (1977) has noted, the police mandate is vague, internally inconsistent, and generally uninformed by the police themselves. If we are to derive a clear statement of the police mandate and how well it is accomplished, we should start by asking street cops to define *good policing* at the micro-level of their one-on-one interactions with citizens. Then, brick by brick, we will build meaningful macro-level definitions of the police mandate, good policing, good police department, and good cops.

Endnotes

[1] This definition owes much to the work of Egon Bittner and Herman Goldstein.

[2] Here, I distinguish between domestic disputes and domestic *violence*. In my view, the role of the police in situations involving violence of any kind is clear cut: to see that no violence occurs after the police have arrived on the scene, and to arrest those who have engaged in criminal violence before the arrival of the police.

[3] See, e.g., James Q. Wilson's description of "watchman" police agencies in *Varieties of Police Behavior* (Cambridge, MA: Harvard University Press, 1968).

[4] The most recent exception to my assertion apparently is a 1978 doctoral dissertation which compares dispositions of citizens' complaints in Berkeley, Contra Costa County (CA), Kansas City, Oakland, and San Jose (Perez, 1978).

[5] In addition to changes in Nassau County specifically, a more general trend to increased accountability for police actions has meant that activities regarded as acceptable at the time of Wilson's study would today be condemned as both indiscriminate and wasteful. Of Nassau County's special "burglary patrol," for example, Wilson noted:

> During 1965 this patrol, operating in high-risk areas of the county, stopped and searched over twelve thousand vehicles and questioned over fourteen thousand "suspicious persons." Eighty-six arrests resulted, but only nine were for burglary. (Wilson, 1968:204)

[6] The more successful of the two Neighborhood Police Teams in precincts where I worked was in Brooklyn Heights, a highly organized brownstone neighborhood populated largely by upper-middle-class residents who were very anxious to see that their community remained fashionable and expensive. The second NPT, in the tough Hell's Kitchen area of Manhattan's West Side, engendered considerably less interest and enthusiasm among residents.

[7] Monolithic community norms related to the police and their role in the community are not necessarily a good thing. In ethnically or racially changing neighborhoods, for example, the most powerful sentiment regarding the police may be a bigoted desire for their assistance in harassing the newcomers back to whence they came (Mastrofski, 1988).

[8] In my own 16 years of police experience, the specific race or class of the ticketed violator did not matter as much as the perception that police treated *others* with great leniency. I have heard whites claim that "you wouldn't give me this ticket if I were black" because, e.g., "you know they run this city," as often as I heard the converse claim from black violators. Similarly, obviously well-heeled violators bemoaned their tickets with claims that police enforcement efforts would be better directed at people driving dangerous "clunkers"; people in clunkers argued that enforcement should focus more heavily on luxury car drivers who "thought they owned the road" and could better afford tickets.

[9] Former Los Angeles police officer Mike Rothmiller has painted a similar picture of his department, where street officers used the pejorative term "pogues" to refer to their naive, and often venal, police supervisors and administrators (Rothmiller and Goldman, 1992).

[10] I have argued elsewhere that the military organizational model is a historical accident that probably is the single most inappropriate way to structure police organizations (Fyfe, 1992; Skolnick and Fyfe, 1993).

[11] The research showed that the most frequently encountered potentially violent encounters between Dade County police and citizens were routine traffic stops; responses to reports of crimes in progress or police investigations of suspicious persons; disputes; and "high-risk vehicle stops" of cars occupied by persons suspected of criminal activity (Fyfe, 1988).

[12] It is more than modesty that causes me to refrain from attributing this decline in police-citizen violence and tension exclusively to the project I directed. The training was part of a wide variety of personnel, training, and administrative changes that began in the early 1980s and that has resulted in a major philosophical shift in the Metro-Dade Police Department. It is today a much more community-oriented and representative police department than was true a decade ago.

References

Angell, J. E., (1971). Toward an alternative to the classic police organizational arrangements: A democratic model. *Criminology, 9,* 185–206.

Bayley, D. H., & Garofalo, J. (1989, February). The management of violence by police patrol officers. *Criminology, 27,* 1–25.

Carte, G. E., & Carte, E. H. (1975). *Police reform in the United States: The era of August Vollmer, 1905–1932.* Berkeley: University of California Press.

Christopher, W., et al. (1991). *Report of the Independent Commission on the Los Angeles Police Department.* City of Los Angeles.

Citizens' Police Committee. (1969). *Chicago police problems.* Montclair, NJ: Patterson Smith (Reprint of 1931 original).

Cohen, A. K. (1955). *Delinquent boys: The culture of the gang.* New York: The Free Press.

Daley, R. (1978). *Prince of the city: The true story of a cop who knew too much.* Boston: Houghton-Mifflin.

Fogelson, R. M. (1977). *Big-city police.* Cambridge: Harvard University Press.

Freed, D. (1988, September 25). Citizens terrorized as police look on. *Los Angeles Times,* pp. 1, 3–5.

Fyfe, J. J. (1988). *The metro-Dade police/citizen violence reduction project: Final report.* Washington, DC: Police Foundation.

Fyfe, J. J. (1992, August). Lessons of Los Angeles. *Focus.* Washington, DC: Joint Center for Political and Economic Studies.

Fyfe, J. J., & Flavin, J. (1991, June). *Differential police processing of assault complaints.* Paper presented at Annual Meeting of Law and Society Association, Amsterdam.

Garner, J., & Clemmer, E. (1986). *Danger to police in domestic disturbances: A new look.* Washington, DC: National Institute of Justice.

Gates, D. F. (1992). *Chief: My life in the LAPD.* New York: Bantam Books.

Goldstein, H. (1979, April). Improving policing: A problem-oriented approach. *Crime and Delinquency, 25,* 236–258.

Goldstein, H. (1990). *Problem-oriented policing.* New York: McGraw-Hill.

Greenberg, S. W., & Rohe, W. M. (1986). Informal social control and crime prevention in modern urban neighborhoods. In R. B. Taylor (Ed.), *Urban neighborhoods: Research and policy* (pp. 79–118). New York: Praeger.

Institute for Law and Social Research. (1980). *Pretrial release and misconduct in the District of Columbia.* Washington, DC: Institute for Law and Social Research.

Kelling, G. L., Pate, T., Dieckman, D., & Brown, C. E. (1974). *The Kansas City preventive patrol experiment: Summary report.* Washington, DC: Police Foundation.

Klockars, C. (1980, November). The Dirty Harry problem. *Annals of the American Academy of Political and Social Science, 452,* 52.

Konstantin, D. (1984, March). Homicides of American law enforcement officers. *Justice Quarterly, 1,* 29–37.

Maas, P. (1973). *Serpico.* New York: The Viking Press.

Manning, P. K. (1977). *Police work: The social organization of policing.* Cambridge: MIT Press.

Margarita, M. (1980, November). Killing the police: Myths and motives. *Annals of the American Academy of Political and Social Science, 452,* 72–81.

Mastrofski, S. D. (1988). Community policing as reform: A cautionary tale. In J. R. Greene & S. D. Mastrofski (Eds.), *Community policing: Rhetoric or reality* (pp. 47–68). New York: Praeger.

Monkonnen, E. (1981). *Police in urban America, 1860–1920.* Cambridge: Cambridge University Press.

Neiderhoffer, A. (1967). *Behind the shield.* Garden City, NY: Doubleday.

Palmer, S. H. (1988). *Police and protest in England and Ireland 1780–1850.* Cambridge: Cambridge University Press.

Perez, D. (1978). Police accountability: A question of balance. Ph.D. dissertation, University of California, Berkeley.

Police Foundation. (1981). *The Newark foot patrol experiment.* Washington, DC: Police Foundation.

Reiss, A. J., Jr. (1971). *The police and the public.* New Haven: Yale University Press.

Reuss-Ianni, E. (1983). *Two cultures of policing: Street cops and management cops.* New Brunswick, NJ: Transaction Books.

Rothmiller, M., & Goldman, I. G. (1992). *L.A. secret police.* New York: Pocket Books.

Rubinstein, J. (1973). *City police.* New York: Farrar, Straus and Giroux.

Scott, E. J. (1981). *Calls for service: Citizen demand and initial police response.* Washington, DC: U.S. Government Printing Office.

Sherman, L. W., Milton, C. H., & Kelly, T. V. (1973). *Team policing: Seven case studies.* Washington, DC: Police Foundation.

Skolnick, J. H., & Fyfe, J. J. (1993). *Above the law: Police and the excessive use of force.* New York: Free Press.

Thomas, W. H. (1976). *Bail reform in America.* Berkeley: University of California Press.

Toch, H. (1980, November). Mobilizing police expertise. *Annals of the American Academy of Political and Social Science, 452,* 53–62.

Toch, H., & Douglas Grant, J. (1991). *Police as problem solvers.* New York: Plenum Press.

Toch, H., Douglas Grant, J., & Galvin, R. T. (1975). *Agents of change: A study in police reform.* Cambridge, MA: Schenkman.

Trojanowicz, R., & Bucqueroux, B. (1990). *Community policing: A contemporary perspective.* Cincinnati: Anderson Publishing Co.

United States Department of Commerce. (1991). *1990 Census of population and housing, summary of population and housing characteristics, New York,* CPH-1-34. Washington, DC: United States Government Printing Office.

Walker, S. (1977). *A critical history of police reform: The emergence of professionalism.* Lexington, MA: Lexington Books.

Webster, J. (1970). Police time and task study. *Journal of Criminal Law, Criminology and Police Science, 61,* 94–100.

Wilson, J. Q. (1964, March). Generational and ethnic differences among career police officers. *American Journal of Sociology, 69,* 522–528.

Wilson, J. Q. (1968). *Varieties of police behavior.* Cambridge: Harvard University Press.

9

"But How Can You Sleep Nights?"

LISA J. MCINTYRE

Hardly anyone will take issue with the idea that everyone, guilty or innocent, is entitled to a fair trial. But beyond this, the views of lawyers and nonlawyers diverge. To the nonlawyer, a fair trial is one that results in convicting
the defendant who is factually guilty and acquitting the defendant who is not.
But it is the lawyer's job to do every possible thing that can be done for the
defendant, even when that means getting a criminal off scot-free. Loopholes
and technicalities are defense attorneys' major weapons. Lay people are
inclined to feel that using legal tricks to gain acquittals for the guilty is at least
morally objectionable, if not reprehensible. What many people want to know
is how defense attorneys can live with themselves after they help a guilty person escape punishment.

It might be supposed that lawyers are unimpressed by what, to the rest of
us, is the core dilemma of their profession—that is, how to justify defending a
guilty person. It might be reasoned that lawyers escape this quandary because
their legal training has taught them that it does not exist. In law school everyone learns that a defendant is innocent until proved guilty. Lawyers believe
this—and can act on it—because they have been taught to "think like lawyers." Legal reasoning, "although not synonymous with formal reasoning and
logic . . . is closely tied to them. Promotion of these skills encourages abstract-
ing legal issues out of their social contexts to see issues narrowly and with precision" (Zemans and Rosenblum, 1981:205).

Simply put, legal reasoning depends on a closed set of premises; some
propositions are legal, others are not. The nonlawyer can scarcely be expected
to appreciate or understand the difference, for it takes "trained men" to "win-

Lisa McIntyre, *The Public Defender: The Practice of Law in the Shadows of Repute*, pp. 139–170.
Copyright © 1987 by the University of Chicago Press. Reprinted by permission of The University of Chicago Press.

now one from the other" (Friedman, 1975:245). But lawyers, by virtue of this training, are expected to cope with complex issues, to detach themselves from difficult moral questions and focus on legal ones, to take any side of an argument while remaining personally uninvolved, and to avoid making moral judgments about their clients or their clients' cases. Thus—and this is a surprise to nonlawyers—the factual guilt or innocence of the client is *supposed* to be irrelevant. A lawyer is expected to take a point of view and argue it; a criminal defense lawyer is expected to put on a vigorous defense even when the client is known to be guilty.

On the other hand, however much their training sets them apart, there are some attorneys who cannot detach themselves, cannot overlook the social and moral meanings and consequences of their jobs. There are lawyers who in fact see the issues very much as nonlawyers do. Ohio attorney Ronald L. Burdge explained to columnist Bob Greene why he had given up defending criminal cases: "If your client is guilty and you defend him successfully, then you have a criminal walking the streets because of your expertise. I have a couple of children. I just didn't like the idea of going home at night knowing that I was doing something so—unpalatable. I found it difficult to look at my kids knowing that this was how I was making a living" (Greene, 1982:1).

A former assistant public defender who spent five years in the Cook County Public Defender's Office echoed Burdge when he explained his disenchantment with the job: "The public defender's cases are thankless: if you lose, society wins; if you win, society loses. I really began to feel as if I was doing a bad thing when I got someone off. They were dangerous people." Today, almost all of this attorney's clients are indigent, but criminal cases do not intrude into his practice.

In spite of their training, lawyers may find it difficult to focus only on the narrow legal aspects of their cases because they are rarely isolated from others who question the morality of the defense lawyer's job. Seymour Wishman, in his book *Confessions of a Criminal Lawyer*, says a chance encounter with one of these "others" marked a turning point in his career, made him rethink how he was spending his life. It happened in a hospital emergency room:

> Across the lobby, a heavy but not unattractive woman in a nurse's uniform suddenly shrieked, "Get that motherfucker out of here!" Two women rushed forward to restrain her. "That's the lawyer, that's the motherfucking lawyer!" she shouted.
>
> I looked round me. No one else resembled a lawyer. Still screaming, she dragged her two restrainers toward me. I was baffled. As the only white face in a crowd of forty, I felt a growing sense of anxiety.
>
> I didn't know what she was talking about. "Kill him and that nigger Horton!"
>
> Larry Horton . . . of course. Larry Horton was a client of mine. Six months before, I had represented him at his trial for sodomy and rape. At last I recognized the woman's face. She had testified as the "complaining" witness against Horton. (1981:4)

Wishman remembered how he had humiliated this woman when she tes-tified against his client, how by cross-examination he had undone her claim that she had been raped and had made her seem to be little more than a pros-titute. Seeing her rage started him thinking that society—and, more specifi-cally, the victims of those whom he had defended—were "casualties" of his skill as a defense lawyer. After years spent preparing for and practicing crimi-nal law, Wishman believed that he had to change: "I had never turned down a case because the crime or the criminal were despicable—but now that would change. I could no longer cope with the ugliness and brutality that had for so long, too long, been part of my life."

Encounters between defense lawyers and those who question the ethics of their work are seldom as dramatic as the one experienced by Wishman. But it is certain that such encounters occur with great frequency in the lives of defense attorneys. All of the current public defenders with whom I spoke and nearly all (93 percent) of the former assistants interviewed in my research agreed that people "constantly" ask public defenders, "How can you defend those people?" But the disenchanted public defender quoted above seems to speak for only a minority of lawyers. The overwhelming majority (97 percent) of former public defenders interviewed agreed that they had believed that they were putting their legal skills to good use by working as public defenders. Only five (8 per-cent) said that they would not join the office if they had it to do over again.

Given that the public defender's goal is to zealously defend and to work toward acquittal for his or her clients (even clients whom they themselves believe are guilty of heinous crimes), how do these lawyers justify their work? As I explain below, it is not as if public defenders harbor any illusions about the fac-tual innocence of the usual client; on the contrary, most will openly admit that the majority of their clients are factually guilty. If conventional morality has it that defending guilty people is tantamount to an obstruction of justice, how do public defenders justify their rebellion? How *do* they defend those people?

How can you defend people whom you know are guilty? Public defenders say that question is incredibly naive, that for the most part they have little patience with that question and little time for anyone who asks it. One sus-pects that they would like to answer with shock and outrage when asked how they do what they do—and sometimes they do answer like that. But usually they respond in a manner that is more weary than indignant:

> Oh God, *that* question! How do you represent someone you know is guilty? So you go through all the things. You know, "he's not guilty until he's proven guilty, until a judge or a jury say he's guilty, until he's been proved guilty beyond a reasonable doubt." I think everyone deserves the best possible defense, the most fair trial he can get. It's a guarantee of the Constitution, no more, no less.

> I tell them it's easy, and I give them a whole list of reasons why it's easy. . . . Everyone has a right to a trial, and with that right to a trial you have a right to a lawyer. I'm that lawyer. That's the American way.

I get asked that all the time, even by my family, even by my wife! The only answer I can give is just that everyone deserves somebody to stand up for them; everyone deserves a trial, a fair trial. They aren't going to get a fair trial unless they have someone like me.

Without exception the public defenders whom I interviewed all had spiels prepared for that question—another testimony to the fact that answering it is part of their routine. As a reporter who interviewed public defender James Doherty in 1983 observed, "If you don't ask him soon enough, he'll preempt you" (Spencer, 1984:1). Some lawyers even had two spiels, one for people who phrased it as a question and another for those who made it an accusation: "I have developed a patter that depends on how aggressively I am asked. When asked aggressively, I respond aggressively—'How can you possibly ask me such a question? Have you never read the Constitution?' It gets meaner. When I am asked, well, you know, in a relatively dispassionate way, a neutral sort of way, basically the response is, 'It makes no difference to me whether they are guilty or not, whether they have committed the offense or not, the person is entitled to have representation to protect his Constitutional rights.'" Simply put, public defenders believe that they come not to destroy the law but to fulfill it.

The sincerity of the public defenders' beliefs is compelling, but the persuasiveness of their arguments is less so. The litany of constitutional ideals rarely convinces the hearer any more (as I will suggest) than it emotionally empowers public defense lawyers to act zealously in the defense of their clients. Attorney Burdge, for example, states unequivocally that *he* still *believed* in the constitutional rights of defendants, that all he was abandoning was his personal protection of these rights: "I just think I'll let other lawyers defend them" (Greene, 1982:1).

Making a Case Defensible

Sociologist Emile Durkheim pointed out that conformity to and rebellion against conventional morality have much in common. The individual, he argued, can free him- or herself partially from the rules of society if there is a felt disparity between those rules and society as it is: "That is, if he desires a morality which corresponds to the actual state of society and not to an outmoded condition. The principle of rebellion is the same as that of conformity. It is the *true* nature of society which is conformed to when the traditional morality is obeyed, and yet it is also the true nature of society which is being conformed to when the same morality is flouted" (1974:65). If Durkheim is correct, public defenders who daily "flout" conventional morality by defending guilty people are perhaps no more focused only on the narrow legal issues than are those who are troubled by what public defenders do. In fact, if pursued (tactfully) beyond the obvious constitutional justifications, the question, How can you defend someone you know is guilty? uncovers the fact that other sorts of rationales are used. Although none of the lawyers went so far as to say, "Yes, I like putting guilty people back on the streets, and I am proud of myself each time I do it," they find justification for doing defense work precisely where Burdge and Wishman found justification for abandoning it—that is, in its social and moral (rather than simply legal) context. Of course, as one might expect, most public defenders stress a different kind of moral and social context than Burdge and Wishman emphasized.

Under some circumstances, mere empathy with the client's situation permits lawyers to feel justified when defending someone whom they know is factually guilty:

> Especially when I was in misdemeanor courts, I could see myself as a defendant. Sometimes you get angry enough at somebody to take a swing at them—if you had a gun, to take a shot at them. I could see myself doing that. . . . Just because somebody was arrested and charged with a crime doesn't mean they are some kind of evil person.

> Look, kids get into trouble, some kids get into serious trouble. I can understand that. In juvenile court our job isn't to punish, the result is supposed to be in the best interests of the minor. Here you've got to keep them with their family and give them all the services you can so they don't do this again.

Not unexpectedly, at some point the ability to empathize breaks down. This is especially true for public defenders who have passed through juvenile or misdemeanor assignments and into felony trial courts, where they are less able—or maybe less willing—to see themselves as being like their clients:

> They [the clients] are seedy and they tend to be, compared to the general population, they are seedier, dirtier, less intelligent, have less conscience, are more sociopathic, more inconsiderate of others, more violent, more poverty stricken and more schizophrenic.

> Your clients have no funds, they know witnesses who only have one name and not even an address because they all hang out on the streets. They don't have phones. They just don't have a life like the rest of us.

> They don't make their appointments; they aren't articulate enough to take the stand. All those things make it hard.

While the differences between attorney and client mean that the attorney sometimes has a hard time understanding his or her client (and especially the client's motive), *it does not mean* that the client cannot be defended:

> A guy hits somebody over the head and takes a wallet—no problem. A guy that gets into a drunken brawl—no problem. I understand that. Somebody that goes out in the street and commits a rape—I still don't know what goes on his mind. No, it doesn't make it harder to defend. There is *never* any excuse for a rape, but you don't have to understand what makes a rapist tick to defend him effectively.

> Sometimes I would question their motives—if it [the crime] seemed senseless, if it seemed particularly brutal or something like that. Then I

realized that those were really, for me, irrelevant questions. I still wonder, of course, but I don't ask anymore.

But the alien character especially of the crimes that their clients are alleged to have committed—and the sorts of attributions that they make about their clients because of their crimes—often mean that "you have to care more about your clients' rights than you can usually care about your clients."

A. The Moral Context of Public Defending

> Why do I do it? I do it because the day that I start laying down and not doing my job is the day that people who aren't guilty are going to be found guilty, and that person might be you because the whole system will have degenerated to the point where they can arrest and convict you on very little evidence. So I am protecting you, I am protecting the middle-class.

On the surface, what a defense lawyer does is simply protect the client's rights. But many lawyers transform the nature of the battle. They are not fighting for the freedom of their client per se but to keep the system honest: "It doesn't mean that I want to get everybody off. It means that I try to make sure the state's attorneys meet up to their obligations, which means that the only way they can prove someone guilty is beyond reasonable doubt, with competent evidence, and overcoming the presumption of innocence. If they can do that, then they get a guilty. If they can't do that, then my client deserves to go home."

The lawyers' way of "bracketing" their role (Weick, 1979), of focusing not on the guilt or innocence of their client but on the culpability of the state, transforms circumstances of low or questionable morality into something for which they can legitimately fight. They do not defend simply because their clients have rights but because they believe that those rights have been, are, or will be ignored by others in the criminal justice system. That their adversaries often cheat is taken for granted by public defenders. As one put it, "I expected a fairly corrupt system, and I found one. Here I am representing people who cheat, lie, and steal, and I find the same intellect represented in the police who arrest them, in some of the prosecutors and some of the judges as well." Even when not asked to provide examples, every public defender with whom I spoke offered examples of cheating. There was cheating by the police:

> When I was [working] in the state's attorney's office, I would have cops walking up to me as I was preparing a case and I would say, "Officer, tell me what happened." And they would say, "Well, how do *you* want it to have happened?"

> The biggest form of police dishonesty was this street files thing. They were hiding evidence that would get people off—or get the correct person. But they had decided in their own minds, "This guy is the guy I'm going after," instead of letting the court system decide who was right.

And there was cheating by state's attorneys:

> Sometimes you know it; sometimes you just suspect that they are kinking the case. One guy, fairly high up in the state's attorney's office, described one of their lawyers as naive because he'd been shocked to find a state's attorney had kinked the case. He said of the lawyer, "He thinks this is for real?"

> Q: Kinked the case?

> R: You might call it suborning perjury; you might call it jogging the memory.

> Q: Are you saying that state's attorneys are sometimes a little unprofessional?

> R: Yes, yes, yes! Lying, having witnesses lie; they lie themselves on the record, they make inferences that I'm lying. It's just a basic matter of cheating, of not being professional. Because they feel they *must* win the case and will do anything to win the case. . . . Their obligation is *not* to win; it is to make sure the law is upheld—and to make sure that my client gets a fair trial. And to them, *that* is a fallacy.

> I remember in that case the prosecutor basically pulled every trick she could: she argued things that were outside the record; she told the jury that [my client] had a record, that he had put a contract out on the witness. She would stop at nothing to win.

This is not to say that one can walk into a Cook County courtroom and expect to see public defenders and state's attorneys at each others' throats. That does happen (at least verbally) on occasion (as I illustrate below), but most public defenders say that they try to maintain a good rapport with their opponents—if only because it helps them do their jobs. And I was cautioned by some lawyers not to listen to those who would condemn state's attorneys universally. As one lawyer told me, "Most of them are not unreasonable; most of them are not [pause] dirty. Most of them are just doing their jobs as best they can."

Yet, scratch the surface just a little and it is likely that a great deal of tension will be uncovered. It can be noted too that this is not unique to Cook County. A study conducted in Alameda, California, found that relations between public defenders and prosecutors were "often characterized by hostility, suspicion, and conflict" and that "relations between public defenders and judges were not much better" (Lydon, 1973; cited in Utz, 1978:215).

Actually, public defenders in Cook County seem to be of two minds about their judges. On the one hand, they seem willing to trust the judges to do the right thing.

> If the facts are on your side then you usually take a bench trial. Because you know if you take it before a decent judge, he'll give you a not guilty.

> We win most of our bench trials; at least we get what we think the case is worth in most of our bench trials.

> I think if you stand up there and talk like you know what you are talking about, judges who don't know the law tend to listen to you. If you can present it in a fair-minded way and not ranting and raving and saying, "You idiot, you can't do that and you can't do that!" Sometimes it doesn't work, but, for the most part, it is better if you rationally and calmly explain why you are right.

On the other hand, one gets a definite impression that what public defenders trust about judges is not their fair-mindedness and good-will, but rather, in many cases, the judges' desire not to get into trouble by being overturned by a higher court. In any case, many public defenders told me that they just do not trust the judges' instincts:

> Knowing legal theory is important, I guess, but it doesn't do any good in Cook County courts, because the question is not Does the law apply? but Can you get the judge to obey it, even though his instincts are to fuck you?

> Oh, I wised up real quick and found that judges don't care about the law; they don't always follow the law.

> Q: Do they know the law?

> R: Sometimes . . .

> Q: But there's always a public defender there to teach them?

> R: Yea [laugh], but they don't usually care.

> I view judges as another state's attorney. I see judges as essentially enemies I have to deal with . . . most of them are just bangers.

> Q: Bangers?

> R: Someone who gives heavy sentences—oftentimes regardless of the facts of the case.

The sort of cheating to which public defenders attribute their hostility toward police, prosecutors, and judges is something that public defenders say they see a lot. And though such cheating may be expected, public defenders find it unacceptable—and are not afraid to say so. It is ironic, but listening to public defenders talk about their cases and why they do what they do is like listening to someone who has just been mugged. Public defenders do feel as if they are often mugged—by the legal system. There is a lot of real and passionate anger: "Some people said I'd become cynical after a while. Well, I might be more cynical about some things, but I don't think I have really changed my attitude. If anything, I might have become a little more gung ho. You see that there really is an awful lot of injustice. It becomes very real and it's scary. I find myself becoming very angry in this job, all the time."

There is good evidence that the things that public defenders cite when they complain about police, prosecutorial, and judicial misconduct do happen (and not just in Chicago [see, e.g., Alschuler, 1972; Dershowitz, 1983; Dorsen and Friedman, 1973; Friedman, 1975]), but it would be difficult, of course, to determine just how widespread such behaviors actually are. Yet, the real frequency of misconduct is beside the point. The point is that most public defenders *believe* that such things do happen "all the time. It's something you really have to watch for."

Whether or not public defenders are correct in their assumptions that police lie, that prosecutors will often do anything to win, and that judges do not really care or know enough to be fair, it is quite clear that the way in which the public defenders see the world not only excuses their work but makes it seem important. Their rationales are enabling mechanisms for the public defenders. But what ultimately pushes the lawyer to do the job is, I believe, something even more personal—the desire to win.

B. "Adversariness"

Perspectives on the criminal justice system sometimes make use of two ideal type models: the classic adversarial model, which is "couched in constitutional-ideological terms of due process" (Blumberg, 1979:291), and the "dispositional" or "bureaucratic" model, which serves only "bland obeisance to constitutional principles. It is characterized by the superficial ceremonies and formal niceties of traditional due process, but not its substance" (Ibid., 145). (See also Eisenstein and Jacob, 1977; Packer, 1964.) The difference between the two models is the difference between the presumption of innocence and the presumption of guilt.

It is significant that social scientists who study public defenders tend to discuss their findings only in terms of the second model—the bureaucratic or plea-bargaining model. Never is the matter of how public defenders measure up as trial attorneys studied. The stereotype of the public defender as plea bargainer is, to put it mildly, firmly entrenched in the literature (see, e.g., Blumberg, 1967, 1979; Eisenstein and Jacob, 1977; Heumann, 1978; Jackson, 1983; Nardulli, 1978; Sudnow, 1965).[1]

It is a fact that most cases that come into the criminal trial courts are disposed of through pleas of guilty; many of these are negotiated—that is, based on a reduction of charges or sentences. Kalvin and Zeisel's (1966) estimate that 75 percent of total criminal prosecutions are disposed of through pleas is now seen as conservative; more often the estimate is between 85 percent and 95 percent (depending on whether misdemeanor cases are included in the count) (see Blumberg, 1979:168). The National Advisory Commission on Criminal Justice Standards and Goals (1974:42) has estimated that in many courts the rate of guilty pleas is 90 percent.

Public defenders do not deny the importance of plea bargaining in their work; they openly and easily acknowledge that the greatest majority of their cases are ultimately disposed of through pleas of guilty. But, they stress, plea bargaining is not their reason for being there but is just a tool:

> Q: Now here you are telling me that you are a "trial attorney." How can you say that? To be fair, isn't most of your work really plea bargaining?

R: Plea bargaining is just part of procedure. Just like I wouldn't say, "I'm a procedural attorney." . . . It's part of what you go through, and it's one of the options available to my clients. You know, "If you in fact did this, and you want this deal, and you understand what you are offered, here is the deal."

In some cases, I was told, the structure that ostensibly exists to handle plea bargaining is used in the lawyer's trial strategy:

In most courtrooms you have a conference before the trial and lay out your case and say what you are going to do. This happens before the judge. Part of this is a function of State's Attorney Daley's office. The state's attorneys are very rarely giving very reasonable offers. They are putting it all on the judges; they make the judge make the decision.

So, in general what you do is ask for a plea conference. You go back with the state to the judge's chambers.

Supposedly, you are there for the state to say their side, for you to say your side, and for the state to make an offer.

What I'm finding though, is that you are trying your case that way—for the judge. We [public defenders] are stronger, better prepared. Even if I'm not getting an offer that my man is going to plead guilty to, I'm taking the case in front of the judge. It gives me an advantage in the trial.

The Role of Trials in Local Justice

The majority of their clients do plead guilty, but trials are not unimportant in the world of the public defender. They are important, on the one hand, because what happens during trials helps determine the outcome of cases that are plea bargained. For example, prosecutors wish to maintain a strong record of conviction at trial or else defendants who might otherwise opt for a plea bargain will seek acquittal at a trial. Rulings on evidence made by judges during trials also have an impact on the negotiating process. Attorneys from both sides will evaluate the strength of their positions by the standards evolved through trial court and appellate hearings; these rulings made by trial judges, as well as the sentences given to defendants found guilty, help parties in a plea bargain to determine what their respective cases are "worth" (Jacob, 1980:80).

But more fundamentally, trials are important in the public defender's world (and hence are stressed here) because, at least in Cook County, public defenders first and last define themselves as trial lawyers. Lawyers become public defenders primarily to gain trial experience; once they have become public defenders, performance at trial is much more crucial to attributions that they make about themselves and each other than one could ever guess given the relative frequency of these performances.

Public defenders often said that they like the trial work more than any other part of their job. Each one will admit, however, that there are some who do not feel that way.[2] These were pointed out to me as examples of bad public defenders or "kickers." "Sometimes we get a public defender that does not work. He'll force his guy to take a plea, finally on the last day before trial: 'Listen guy, you can take a plea which is the best thing you could do or you can go to trial. But I'm not prepared for trial and you're going to lose because you are *supposed* to lose this case—you know that too.'" Some public defenders are labeled as bad lawyers because they cannot hack it in the courtroom; the reason that they cannot hack it (it is said) is that they are afraid. As many pointed out, being "on trial" is scary. One veteran lawyer told me: "We lose a lot of public defenders because they can't handle being on trial."

But all of them, even the lawyers who love trial work, are ambivalent about it. Trial work, or so most of them acknowledge (in words, if not by deed), is as terrifying as it is exhilarating.

> You know [a lawyer who is now in private practice]? Now he is one of the better trial lawyers. But he used to throw up before final arguments. Once he did it right in front of the jury; he just went over to the wastebasket and threw up.

> Trials? *That's* when I can't sleep well at night; I'm too busy thinking. A trial is not one issue, it's many. It's win or lose; it's deadlines, organizing things, making sure your witnesses are ready, looking good in front of the jury, looking confident in front of the judge, watching everything you are doing, being alert, keeping a lot of things in your mind at once. And remembering that your client's freedom depends on your polish, how well you can bring it off.

Doing Trials

On television a defense lawyer confronts his clients with demands for the truth: "Okay, I'm your lawyer and you gotta trust me. If I'm going to do a good job I need to know exactly what happened. Don't be afraid to tell me, I can't defend you unless you are perfectly straight with me." The client is thus persuaded to tell all to his lawyer.

This sort of dialogue may appeal to the viewer's common sense—that is, of course the lawyer needs to know what happened and whether the client is guilty. But in real life, things do not happen that way—at least they do not happen that way when the lawyer is a public defender. Public defenders are quick to admit that they usually *do not* ask their clients whether they are guilty or innocent. Why not ask? The lawyers claimed that it was simply not relevant, that it was something that they did not need to know.

> I don't ask "Did you do it?" anymore. I realized it was irrelevant.

> I say to them first thing: "I don't care if you did it or not."

> I say: "I don't give a damn whether you did it or not. I'm not your judge, I'm not your priest, I'm not your father. My job is to defend you, and I don't care whether you did it."

It might be that public defenders do not ask because they know that their client is probably guilty and because, as one said, "they will all lie anyway." But there seems to be more to it than that. Many said that, when it comes down to it, they do not ask because they are afraid that the client will tell them the truth!

Q: Don't you ever ask your clients if they are guilty or innocent?

R: Never!

Q: Why is that?

R: Because, in the first place, it is irrelevant. It's not my role to decide whether they are guilty—in our sense of the term guilt.

Q: What about the "second place?"

R: Well, it is my role to fashion a defense and to be creative. If the person says to me "This is how I did it," it's pretty hard for me to come around and try to do something for them. In general, I fence around with some of my questions. I ask them about an alibi or something like that. But the more I think they are guilty, the less I will ask.

Public defenders do not begin their relationship with a client by asking awkward questions (e.g., Did you do it?) because once the client admits guilt, it limits what the public defender can ethically do:

> I don't ask them because you put them at a disadvantage if you ask them and they say they did it.
>
> I had a client once who was charged with battery, and he said, "Yea, I hit him, and I've been meaning to hit him for a long time. But it's just his word against mine, and I'm gonna say I didn't do it."
>
> And I said: "*Not* with me as your lawyer you're not! You are not going to say anything like that."
>
> So it's important to get the transcript [from the preliminary hearing] and look at the police reports and say "Look, this is the evidence against us" and then let him make up his own story. It's the only way to do it.

Being honest, ethical, and "scrupled" in a system that many of them believe is corrupt is very important to the lawyers with whom I spoke.[3] Although some (naive observers) may wonder at the fragility of this honesty, it is something in which the public defenders take pride:[4] "There aren't many public defenders—if any—that I can point to and say: 'that man is dishonest. He lied and distorted everything, just to get a client off.' That just doesn't happen. The same cannot be said for lawyers in the state's attorney's office. You test the state's evidence, you doubt it, you put it into its worst light. But that is not dishonest. Quite the contrary, that is how you get at the truth!"

Public defenders learn quickly that the tell-me-the-truth approach will only help defend an innocent person—the exceptional client. Public defenders argue that it is not their job to decide who is guilty and who is not. Instead, it is the public defender's job to judge the quality of the case that the state has against the defendant. If the lawyer does decide that the state has a case that cannot be called into reasonable doubt, then the lawyer will probably try to get the defendant to admit guilt so that pleading is more palatable—but usually *only* then.

Bad Cases and Good Lawyers

There is a saying in the office: "Good facts make good lawyers." A good lawyer, I think, is one who doesn't screw up a case. Someone who takes a case that's a winner—one that should be won—and wins it; gets a not guilty. A bad lawyer is a person who takes a case that should be won and loses it. A good lawyer isn't necessarily one that wins a loser case. You get lucky; you get a good jury and win a case that no one could possibly win. That doesn't prove anything; that is very often luck, and it doesn't mean anything.

In practice, a more diffuse yardstick is used: "competency is taking the right cases to trial and winning them." As I show below, the lawyers following this logic are in peril of succumbing to a painful tautological trap.

Public defenders try not to go into a trial with cases that cannot be won. Unfortunately, most of their cases are of this type—loser (or "dead-bang loser") cases, cut-and-dried situations in which the client was caught red-handed and "the state has everything but a video tape of the crime." In the face of overwhelming evidence, the lawyers will try to talk the client into taking a plea or "copping out." One reason for this is the knowledge that taking a loser case to trial will hurt the client:

My philosophy is that if you are going down and you know it, you should get the best deal for your client that you can. And you should try and make your client see the wisdom of that. It's better for your client. I could say "Sure, I'll take this to trial, sure I can use the experience," but that doesn't do your client any good if he's going down for more time.

I have a client who I have been dealing with just recently who, ah, I was his attorney and I told him he ought to plead guilty. I told him I got this *great* deal for him: I had packed up several cases he had pending in several courtrooms and got him two years. And he had been convicted before!

But he didn't like it. He got himself a private attorney who gave him a guarantee of probation or something. He calls me up and said the private attorney had come back to him with an offer of *six* years. He said to me: "You were right!"

In large part, being competent is being able to convince a client that it is not in his or her best interests to insist on a trial that cannot be won. One lawyer explained how he had learned this lesson back when he was assigned to a preliminary hearing court:

"Well, pal, listen. They caught you inside this guy's home, this guy held you down while his wife called the police. You are not going to get a chance to beat this case. You say you were drunk, but being drunk just isn't a good excuse anymore. It's up to you. The state is making you an offer and if you take it, you'll be better off than if you go upstairs [to the trial court]."

Everybody told you to say things like that and sure enough, when I got up to the trial courts, I realized it was true. The offers *are* much better in preliminary hearing courts.

But to confront those guys with that decision. It was incredible, it was so hard.

Now I can do it fairly routinely because I have been doing it long enough to have confidence in what I'm saying. I know it is true. And I learned that you aren't doing anyone a favor when you bring a loser case upstairs—it's no good for the client, it's no good for the lawyer. But then I felt incredibly guilty.

Once it is decided that they have a loser case, different attorneys have different ways of trying to "cool out" clients who want to go to trial. However, all of the attorneys with whom I spoke and all of the public defenders that I observed with clients seemed uncomfortable with the idea of forcing anyone to take a plea.[3] Most emphasized that they always tried to reason with their clients:

Most of our clients do feel that if you are a public defender you are not going to give it your all, because you have so many cases, or you just don't care, or whatever. They feel that you are just there to cop them out.

But my partner and I sit down with a guy and say: "Look, we are lawyers, and we are paid to analyze facts. After we have analyzed the facts we might say to you, 'we don't think you have a good case and we think you should cop out.' If you don't feel that way, it's up to you."

We let *them* make the decision.

I always leave it up to the defendant. I lay it out for him what the risks are, and if he asks me I'll tell him what his chances of winning are. But just like I can't play God and say if he's guilty or not, I can't play God and tell a guy "You go to trial," or "You don't go to trial."

I always tell them, "it's no skin off my nose whether you go to trial or not. I'll do the best job I can if you want to go to trial; I'll negotiate the best deal I can if you don't want to go to trial."

But, public defenders admitted, reasoning with a client does not always produce the desired result. One lawyer, now a supervisor, admitted that occasionally he would resort to a little "bullying."[6] What did he mean by that? "I would come in, and I would say things like, 'You know, you are a damn fool if you don't take this deal, because this is the best you are going to get. If you go on trial, in my opinion, you are going to be found guilty and you are going to get more time.' And then people would say—not often, but occasionally, the person would say—'I don't care; I didn't do it, and I want a trial!' And I would say, 'Okay, okay. If *that's* your attitude, let's go to trial!'"

If public defenders resist taking loser cases to trial because it will hurt the client, they resist too because it will be painful for the lawyer. One of the worst things about being a public defender, said one former assistant, was "not the realization that most of your clients were in fact guilty" but the fact that "there was very little you could do to get the system to give them a not guilty" or that, as another said, "your clients never had any real obvious defense and you [the attorney] were just stuck."

Ask any public defender "What was your worst case?" and you may or may not hear about some horrible crime; you may or may not hear about the case that lasted the longest or took the most preparation. Chances are, however, you will hear about a case that was a loser. Understanding the nature of a loser case is crucial, for embedded in the concept—and in the distinctions that lawyers make between losers and other sorts of cases—is the clue to what makes public defenders tick.

> The worst case is where the state has an overwhelming amount of evidence and there is nothing you can do with it. . . . It's a case where you are just overwhelmed by the state's evidence. It's a case where you get beat up in court. And that is just *no fun.*

> You are so relieved when a guy pleads out on a case that you know you can't win, and you are going to get your head beaten on, and the jury is probably going to throw rocks at you when you make the closing argument.

> My worst case was a very hopeless case, a rape and armed robbery, and the persons were captured by the police and they were contending that they were the wrong guys.

> Q: Why was that your worst case? You've defended people accused of murder before.

> R: The fact that the individuals were given reasonable offers and they should have copped pleas, because there wasn't a chance of their being acquitted. And they were going through the ordeal because they opted for a jury trial. It was just a very painful process; it was just an *absurd* situation.

> Q: Was it a particularly awful crime?

> R: No. Well, he just beat up his girlfriend; he didn't kill her or anything. The evidence was just overwhelming against him. He should have pleaded, and he wouldn't. He made me go to trial.

The opposite of a loser case is not necessarily a winner. It is a fun case, which in turn must be distinguished from a boring case.

> I don't like armed robberies because they are boring. There are only one or two issues—either the guy did it or he didn't—and that doesn't make for very interesting work.

> The case I am trying with _____ right now is a murder that is really a lot of fun.

> Listen to me! "A murder is a lot of fun." How can I say that? [Laugh] It's a murder of a baby, and here I am with my two little kids and you would think that I would feel terrible about that, wouldn't you?
>
> But it's an interesting case because the facts are such that they [the state] don't really have much evidence in the case—a lot of other people could have done it. It's all circumstantial evidence. That's fun. It's something for me to get excited about and get into, whereas a lot of cases—there are just no issues and that makes them boring.
>
> I don't know if I have a favorite kind of case, there are some that are a lot more fun to do—if you just think of it in those terms. I may sound horrible, but, just because of the circumstances, usually murder cases are kind of fun.
>
> Usually what kills you in a case is somebody is on the witness stand pointing a finger at your client, saying "that guy robbed me with his gun." Whereas in a murder case you don't have a victim.
>
> Q: What you mean is that you don't have a victim who can come to testify in court, right?
>
> R: Right, he's not there in court. And all the evidence—well, oftentimes you have a totally circumstantial case which gives you a lot to do.
>
> And rape cases. I hate to say it, but there's a lot to play with in a rape case: identification, consent, much more so than in your average armed robbery. You never, for example, you never have the issue of consent in armed robbery.

It is shocking to hear the lawyers talk about their favorite cases, and they are not unmindful of this. But the point is important: a favorite case is the opposite of a loser—a loser is not a loser just because it is a case that will be lost. A case is a loser when it leaves the lawyer nothing to do for the client.

The lawyers are possessed by the very human desire, as they put it, not to make "assholes" of themselves or be perceived as "jerks" in court. The jury may not really throw rocks at them but, what is worse (or so the lawyers think), will think that they are naive or stupid for "falling for what the defendant told them."[7] A case is fun to the degree that it allows the lawyers to act in the way in which they think that lawyers ought to act; a case is interesting when it gives them an opportunity to "comport yourself in a professional manner, to be an advocate for your client without looking *ridiculous* in the process, when you can get across to the jury that there is, at least, a *respectable* difference of opinion here."

Loser cases put the lawyer-as-a-professional at a terrible disadvantage:

> I had one case where the, one of the defendants shot the leg off a ten-year-old girl with a shotgun. You know, that's kind of rough.
>
> What are you supposed to say in defense of that? But because the state wasn't offering us anything decent in the plea bargain and we offered some pretrial motions that we could only preserve by going to trial, we had to go to trial.

The worst case is one where you just don't have anything. And you know you are just going to go out there and lose, and there is *nothing* you can do.

Like, they will have two counts and one will be for aggravated battery and one will be for robbery and [the state] will toss the agg. batt., drop it down to plain battery, if you plead. But if you don't, and if you go to trial, you get a finding of agg. batt.

Well, I had to go to trial on this case because the kid swears up and down that he didn't do it. But I haven't got *anything*! They've got two eyeball witnesses, and all I have is the kid saying, "But I didn't do it!" *And what am I going to do with that?*

And it's a sure loser, but I am going to trial because the kid won't admit.

The lawyers feel that, with a loser case, it is hard—if not impossible—to look respectable. With a loser case it is often difficult to look as if you are doing *anything*.

Losing

In his look at the legal profession, sociologist Talcott Parsons (1954) commented that adherence to procedure (i.e., doing everything that can be done when it ought to be done and as it ought to be done) protects lawyers from being devastated when they lose: "The fact that the case can be tried by a standard procedure relieves [the attorney] of some pressure of commitment to the case of his client. He can feel that, if he does his best then having assured his client's case of a fair trial, he is relieved of the responsibility for an unfavorable verdict" (1954:380).

One of the attorneys with whom I spoke seemed to confirm Parsons's hypothesis, at least with respect to loser cases: "There is a certain consolation of going to trial with a loser case. If I lose, what the hell. I gave it my best shot. If I lose, *it was a loser.* If I win, it's amazing."

Most of the attorneys, however, were not so sanguine and could not detach themselves from the outcomes of their cases so easily. Even losing a loser case, most of them said, is incredibly hard on the attorney.

> It's hard, you know? You can tell someone the facts of the case, and they say, "What did you expect? It was a loser." But that doesn't make me feel any better when I lose a loser. I want to win.

> Ah, idealistically I've talked about why I'm a public defender, about how I want to keep the state on the straight and narrow. And I *could* go home and say, "Well, I forced the state to prove their case beyond a reasonable doubt," but, ah, I still, that isn't what I *really* feel when I lose. What I *really* feel is just that I lost this case and I wanted to win this case.

The attorneys are not much comforted by the fact that the client was guilty—or probably guilty, anyway.

> Q: When you feel bad about losing a case, doesn't it help to know that the client was probably guilty anyway?

R: Yea [pause], maybe. But in the middle of the trial, it's you, you know? You are trying to make them believe what you are trying to sell them, and, if you don't win, it means that they don't believe *you*. That's probably one of the reasons that it doesn't help.

There was a case, not too long ago, that I really came to believe that they had no evidence on my man, and I fought very hard for him. We lost, and I felt very bad about that.

Afterward, he just fell apart, started screaming at me back in the lock-up. We had this big fight. And I yelled at him: "You know, I really put myself on the line too, and I did everything I could for you, and what are you doing yelling at me? Cause I really believed, and I worked hard."

And then I misspoke myself, because I said, "And I really believed that you didn't do this."

And he said, "Would it make you feel any better if I told you that I *did* do it?" [Laugh].

Q: How did you answer him?

R: [Laugh] I said, "I don't want to know; don't tell me!" I still don't want to know, and that's how it is.

Most telling is how these lawyers talk about doing trial work. They do not say, "I'm doing a trial now"; they do not ask, "Are you doing a trial this week?" They say, "*I'm* on trial"; they ask, "Are *you* on trial?"

Lawyers hate to lose because, although reason tells them a case is a loser, sentiment says that justice favors not the stronger case but the better lawyer. What makes losing any case, even a loser, so bad is their belief that, in the hands of a *good* attorney, there is really no such thing as a dead-bang loser case. One attorney told me: "Fewer and fewer of my cases are losers. . . . Because I am a better and better lawyer."

Most of the attorneys seemed to feel the same way:

One of the maxims I've learned is that the evidence is always better than the way it looks on paper. There is always some goof-up of a witness, something that comes up in the trial, so that you always have something to work with. Invariably that is so.

By the time I walk into the courtroom, even if rationally I sat down when I first heard the case and said "Well, there is no way I can win," by the time I walk into the courtroom I will figure out some way to argue to the judge or the jury that I think I can convince them. By that time, I believe I can win the case.

You start out thinking "I can't win this, no one can win this." Then you start to get a glimmer, a way out of it being a loser case. Then you think that, if only you can make the jury understand things the way you understand things, they will go along with you and give you a not guilty. Part of you knows—or at least that is what you tell yourself later—part of you knows you *can't* win, that you aren't going to win, but that gets lost in the part of you that wants so much to win this case for your guy—and to win this case for you.

Of course, you have to be good to take advantage of those goof-ups, those things that invariably come your way in the trial. Because of the suspicion that there is always something, when it cannot be found or when it does not work, the lawyer is apt to feel at fault. Even when they know that their client was factually guilty, public defenders are likely to feel, "I let my client down."

> The most stressful time is on a difficult case and you realize that, well, some other lawyer could win this, why the hell can't I? I will do everything I can, but there will still be something I miss. And yet, maybe nobody in the courtroom, not even my client, knows about it. But it can destroy our case. Then, when you lose, you feel the weight of your client's sentence on your shoulders. When my client gets sentenced, part of me is going with him.

> You go home and you have those "ah, shit! God damn, why didn't I? If I only would have, if I only would have spent ten more minutes, if I only would have asked him this, if I would have gone out and asked, or done more investigations. . . . Your mistakes? Your mistakes go to jail.

The stress of being on trial and the pain of losing are compounded on those rare occasions when the lawyer believes the defendant is innocent. For this reason, although the lawyers will say, "I don't care if he's guilty or innocent," their claim to neutrality is often a lie. When they say, "I don't care if my client is guilty," what they usually mean is, "I *prefer* my clients to be guilty."

> Most defense attorneys would rather not have a client they think is innocent, because it's just irrelevant. Because it's your job to fight the state's case no matter what. You *hate* to lose, and you are worried about losing just because it's your job to win. And if you think he's innocent, you worry more. And that is just aggravation, which is really irrelevant to your job.

None of the current public defenders with whom I spoke said they preferred innocent clients, and all but two said they actually preferred representing defendants whom they believed were guilty.[8] Many of the attorneys did not want to talk about such cases, even hypothetically. Most of them just said something like, "In my own gut I know I have a harder time defending people I know are innocent than people I suspect are guilty—the pressure to win is so much greater then," or "it is just harder to defend an innocent person because there is so much pressure." Although no public defender said as much, given what they did say, I suspect that what makes defending an innocent client so stressful is the fact that if one should fail to win an acquittal, it would be difficult to avoid the conclusion that it was the lawyer's fault (although in theory, this may not be true). In such cases, the weight of the client's sentence really hangs on the defender. One lawyer told me how he protected himself from the possibility of that kind of "incredible stress." He explained that he "tried not to think about having innocent clients [pause], but it's academic since they are all guilty anyway."

Coping with Losing

Losing is one of the costs of being an attorney; losing a lot (I was told) is one of the costs of being a public defender:

> You must try to convince the judge or the jury that what you are saying must be followed. But as a public defender, you get the realization that no matter how hard you do this, no matter how well you do this, you are probably not going to get it across. Or, even if you do, the judge or the jury is going to say no. You cannot be afraid to lose, because mostly it's a lost cause. You cannot have a personality where you must win or it's going to screw you.
>
> Sometimes it's just that you get rotten case after rotten case. It drives you crazy. What it does is it makes you think you can't win.
>
> When you lose a few in a row, you question yourself. And then it becomes real hard to go back into court and try again.

Public defenders do not like to lose—but said that one must just learn to accept it. Nevertheless, watching them try their cases and listening to them talk about their cases made it clear to me that the attorneys do not just accept losing. In many instances, the attorneys seemed to try to outwit defeat.

However it looks to the spectator—or, for that matter, to the defendant—public defenders can show you how a trial is not a zero-sum situation. Even when the lawyer does not win freedom for his or her client, *something* may have been won: "I don't feel defeatist. There is a lot you can do, even if you lose—like mitigate a person's involvement or partly win by getting a guilty on one charge and not on another."

Even when there is no way to mitigate the client's guilt or to partly win, there is such a thing as an almost win. Those count too—at least they are counted by the attorneys, especially if the case had seemed to be open and shut. There is a certain measure of satisfaction that can be drawn, for example, from keeping the jury out longer than could have been expected.

> It was a terrible case, a terrible case. It was a brutal, cold-blooded slaying of a ma-and-pa grocer. They had a witness, a flipper. The guy who drove the car flipped against them both. They found the guns in my guy's house; they had a dead-bang loser case against them.
>
> We tried to discredit the flipper and minimize the effect of the gun being found, saying that they couldn't absolutely prove that it was the same gun that had been used.
>
> We lost. We kept the jury out for about ten hours or so, and that was something. But we ended up losing.

We did a jury trial a few weeks ago—the case was a rape, a 14-year-old. Both my partner and I felt he would be found guilty and that he probably did it. But we tried that case *so* hard, then we lost it.

But we kept the jury out almost three hours. And we thought it was going to be like a 15-minute guilty verdict.

Moreover, the lawyers are helped some by their ability to distinguish a loss from a defeat. Even when they lose, public defenders search for evidence that they did a better job, that they "out-tried" the state's attorneys. Out-trying one's adversaries can mean anything from simply acting more professional to forcing your opponent to commit reversible error. Sometimes it just means making him or her look silly in court.

During long or tough cases the level of exchange between defense and prosecuting attorneys can destroy all ideals that one might have about noble adversaries. Attorneys (as they themselves admit) will sometimes bait each other, trying to force their opponents to do something regrettable. The following are snatches of dialogue from a death-penalty case. All these exchanges took place on the record (I have, however, changed the lawyers' names). Mr. Buford and Mr. Petrone speak for the prosecution; attorneys Carney, Stone, and Richert appeared for the defense:

[Time One]

Richert: [To the court] During Mr. Carney's remarks, Mr. Buford came to me personally and pointed to Mr. Stone and said, "Do you realize your partner looks like Lenin?" I would appreciate if the prosecutor would avoid interfering with my participation in proceedings such as these.

The Court: Which prosecutor? Who is he talking about? Who looks like Lenin?

[Later that day]

Carney: [To Buford] Oh, put your foot down [off the table]. Act like an attorney. What is wrong with you?

Buford: Come on.

Carney: Take your foot off the table!

Buford: You don't tell me what to do!

Carney: It insults me as an attorney.

Buford: I may do that, but you don't tell me what to do!

The Court: We will take a recess.

[Time Two]

Petrone: Let's go. We have been wasting seven months for it.

Stone: That's unprofessional.

Petrone: That's as unprofessional as you, Mr. Stone.

Stone: Wasn't it enough that we showed you how to pick a jury?

Petrone: You showed us how to pick a jury? You pleaded him right into the electric chair!

[Time Three]

Buford [in chambers]: I am at this time requesting that we go out in the court and requesting that—I just did—that we go on the record, because once again, I am not going to put up with any more of this state's attorney baiting or this other bullshit that's gone on here in chambers.

Carney: *That's on the record!*

Buford: Right; exactly. That has gone on here for eight weeks. I request that we go out in open court. Let the record reflect [pause]. [To judge] Look at Mr. Carney!

Carney: And I am looking at Mr. Buford, Judge. And I have never heard *that* word said in a court of law in eight years, Judge, by a state's attorney or any defense lawyer, and I am *really* shocked!

Buford: Look at these faces that they are making. I am asking that you hold them in direct contempt!

The Court: All right, but I just wanted to know what witnesses are you calling?

The defense lost the case. They had hoped to "win" by getting a life sentence, but their client was sentenced to death. To any observer, it was a total loss. After listening to testimony for several weeks, the jury took less than an hour and only one vote to make the decision unanimous. Still, the attorneys (Mr. Carney, in particular) appeared to derive a great deal of satisfaction from their belief that they had not been "defeated," that they had caused their opponents (Mr. Buford, in particular) to "lose it" several times during the case. The night before the case ended, Mr. Carney recalled what for him had been a major highlight of the case. "Lisa, you know what Buford said to me that first day? He said, 'Carney, I heard you were a choker; I *collect* chokers, Carney.' When Buford said 'bullshit' in chambers, I leaned over and whispered to him: 'C-H-O-K-E.'" After the end of the last day in court, after hearing that their client would be sentenced to death, at a dinner that could more properly be called a wake, a deeply depressed Carney repeated several times: "We sure got that bastard Buford; we sure beat their asses, didn't we?" "Yes," he was assured again and again, "we *sure* did."

In retrospect the attorneys seemed a bit childish, their bickering like juvenile acting-out. Yet when one is trying to salvage something that is a lost cause, anyway, every little bit seems to help.

It should be noted too that the above exchanges are unusual, a result of the fact that, in the attorneys' minds, baiting the state's attorneys could not make things any worse for their client than it was inevitably going to be—and might, if they could push the prosecutor far enough, win him a mistrial. Normally, the attorneys are mindful of the fact that acting out will probably hurt one's client. Even in this case, the lawyers (the defense lawyers, anyway) never got totally out of control. It should be noted that while all of these exchanges (and others like them) took place on the record, they took place out of the hearing of the jury.

But even if the public defenders do not usually feel free to really mix it up with the prosecutor in court, there is still an important kind of anticipatory satisfaction that emerges from knowing that oftentimes the "only reason the state wins is because the facts are on their side." The satisfaction comes from knowing that *someday* most of those prosecutors are going to leave the state's attorney's office, and many of them are going to turn their hands to criminal defense work. That day, believe many public defenders, will be the day when these prosecutors will get what is coming to them. Public defenders sometimes sound almost smug when they talk about what is in store for prosecutors: "One of the ways I deal with [losing], with when I have to look over at the state's attorneys as they gleefully congratulate each other on their records of victory, when I know I have out-tried them on a case, well, you just say, 'chalk it up.' They are going to leave the office some day; they are going to find out that they are not such hot shit. That's a *big* satisfaction, a very big satisfaction."

Perhaps the most important way in which they cope with losing is know-ing that they do not always lose. When I asked one attorney "How do you keep going when you lose?" he said: "Always remembering that there is a flip side of that—you feel great when you win. There is no feeling like it. And *that* wouldn't feel as good if it weren't so hard to win." In fact, the lawyers seem to go into each trial with great expectations of winning. The knowledge that the next case may be the one you win seems to keep them going.

Coping with Winning

> I do not apologize for (or feel guilty about) helping to let a murderer go free—even though I realize that someday one of my clients may go out and kill again. Since nothing like that has ever happened, I cannot know for sure how I would react. I know that I would feel terrible for the vic-tim. But I hope that I would not regret what I had done—any more than a surgeon should regret saving the life of a patient who recovers and later kills an innocent victim. (Dershowitz, 1983, xiv)

Doctors lose patients; lawyers lose cases. Failure is something with which every professional must cope. But implicit in the question, How can you defend those people? is the idea that public defenders ought to have trouble coping with winning.

The possibility of getting a guilty person off is not a specter that haunts public defenders, at least not to the extent that you would notice it. In misde-meanor and juvenile courts, the majority of defendants represented by public defenders are relatively innocent and/or harmless criminals accused of rela-tively innocent or harmless crimes. The lawyers are protected by the fact that they rarely win cases for clients who are horrible criminals; winning an acquittal for a burglar or even an armed robber is, for a public defender, hardly cause for intense introspective examinations of one's morality or personal guilt. It is not that they have lost all sense of proportion but that they have gained a new one—by the time that they get to felony courtrooms, the lawyers are, most of them, convinced that what they see happen to their clients in the jails or in the courts is as bad as or worse than most of what happens to victims out on the streets. There is, moreover, often a sense that the injustices perpetrated by the system are worse because they are committed by people who really ought to know better.

However rarely it occurs, the possibility of winning big someday and then having your client kill again exists in the future of every defense lawyer. It is not something that they seem to talk about very often. It is difficult to talk about it perhaps because there is so much emphasis on the importance of the defendant's right to a lawyer who will do everything possible to win a case. Moreover, in the tough, heroic world of the trial lawyer, it is perhaps difficult to conceive of feeling bad about winning.

A few years ago, an episode of the television show *Hill Street Blues* featured the story of a public defender who got a murderer freed on a "technicality." Some time later, the client murdered again. This time, the victim was a friend of the public defender, who, unable to deal with the guilt, quit the office.

At the time, many public defenders were avid fans of this television show, in large part (I thought) because the writers had created a very competent, tough, and sympathetic role for a public defender on the show. A few days after this particular episode aired, a group of lawyers in the office discussed the story-line and decided that it was unrealistic. I later asked one of them why. "Because the lawyer quit. That's just not the way it's done. You just move into the next case. As a lawyer you are very removed from the reality of it." Reflecting on his answer for a moment, I said, "I just can't believe that." "It's true," he assured me. I pushed him: "What would you do if it happened to you? What if you got a N.G. on a killer and he came around and killed again?" After a few moments he admitted that he "probably would move into another branch of law."

Most of the lawyers with whom I spoke said, as does Dershowitz, that it had not happened to them—and that while they hoped that it would not happen, they did not think that it would bother them. But one added: "As I say that, I am mindful of one public defender named _____, I think one of the reasons he left was that he managed to get a guy acquitted on a murder and the guy went out and committed another murder. That really got to him. And I watched him suffer with that, and I wondered if I would suffer like that, and I came to no conclusion."

A few of the lawyers admitted that they had come close to winning cases that, deep down inside themselves, they had not wanted to win: "I've never felt bad about winning a case. The last jury trial I did I almost won, and I was worried about that. It really bothered me. But all of it has to do with the relationship you have with your client. He was a real asshole and hard to deal with, and he was a mean son of a bitch."

Often it seemed that one of the things that helps the lawyer not to feel too bad about winning is one of the things that makes it so hard to lose—that is, their relationship with the client. Most of the lawyers said that usually, especially when they go to trial, they end up liking their clients. In most cases, the lawyers spoke with some affection about their "guys."

> There is in any human being a soul you can reach. [Pause] Now I use language like this hesitantly, you know, people usually look at you like you're crazy when you talk like this. But if you are willing to take the risk and open up your heart and reach into their hearts, you will reach it.
>
> You need to do that for yourself. You need to do that too because if you are going to try the case for either a judge or a jury . . . you have to make that person human. They are not some black or brown face—or white face, for that matter. They are someone. And that is what costs. 'Cause everytime you do that you are giving something of yourself away. You get something sure, but you give away a lot.
>
> [At first] I was a little leery. You wonder, "Can I talk to a guy like this?" And you find out it's real easy [laugh], you find out that they are real people, just like you. Well [laugh], maybe not *just* like you, but real people. And you come to like most of your clients [laugh]. That surprised me, still does.
>
> A lot of criminals I have gotten to like. There are some real nice human beings even if they are in real serious trouble.
>
> [Recalling his first murder case] It was funny—I liked the shooter. He was a real nice guy.

The danger, of course, is in getting too involved with your client, getting to like him or her too much. That is when you lose your sense of proportion. As one lawyer told me, you "must always remember that he is a defendant, and you must treat him as a defendant."

Two of the lawyers with whom I spoke had experienced what one called the "defense lawyer's nightmare." One would not talk about it; one would:

> Once on a case with _____, he came up with a brilliant idea about collateral evidence, and I wrote a brilliant brief. It persuaded the judge to dismiss the indictment—just unheard of.
>
> And three months later he killed three other people. He participated in a gang killing—didn't actually do the killing, but he was definitely part of it. That, of course, is the defense lawyer's nightmare.
>
> There are people who can—for example, my partner—who can say, "that's not my concern," but that is bullshit. That is why he is losing his hair and I'm not. You feel bad. You *have* to feel bad.
>
> *However*, the constitutional proposition was correct, and it made some important law in Illinois; and I would do it again. But I would not represent [that client] again. Because we could not wholeheartedly represent him zealously, we were let off representing him.

"How can you live with that?" I asked. "You either leave, stay and repress it, or you stay and cope. Sure you feel bad, but you deal with it by knowing that hopefully you are doing enough good to make you feel good about what you are doing."

At the time, that did not seem like much of an answer—but perhaps it is the only one.

Concluding Remarks:
Public Defenders and Their Society

Justifying the public defender's rebellion against society is, in fact, a strict adherence to important social values. They believe that it is right to defend "those people" because of the principle that everyone is innocent until proved otherwise and so everyone is entitled to a defense. More important, they also believe that it is right to defend even the guilty because their clients *need* someone to defend them against police, prosecutorial, and judicial abuse. Because of what they see happen in the system every day, public defenders would be the last to claim that defense lawyers are unnecessary luxuries for defendants (guilty or innocent) in our criminal courts.

Beyond these rationales, public defenders are motivated by the desire to legitimize themselves as professionals, to act as professionals, and, as final proof of their right to professional status and respect, to win. Their desire to win makes them look very closely at each client's case: Where has the state failed to make its case? Did the state make an error? Did the police mess up the arrest? Public defenders want to find those cases, because those are the kinds of cases that make them look good. The closer they look, the more they find, and this, in turn, reinforces their view that their work is essential.

In an important sense, then, there is a synergistic relationship between the public defenders' egoistic and altruistic concerns, their desire to win, and their view that they are needed. It is that synergy that no doubt accounts for the combative tone of most of their remarks. In theory this could spiral into a process that is out of all proportion to reality. In truth, the lawyers—especially when they are on trial—do seem to get carried away with what they do. But what prevents them from losing all touch with reality is, I think, the fact that they are not totally enclosed in the cognitive ghetto of public defending. Each is still a member of a society that suspects the morality of what they do; this attachment to society is shown in a process that some public defenders call "honking." By honking each other, public defenders remind one another how the rest of their society regards their work:

> There is a term that I didn't know until I came to this office, a thing called honking. And that is needling or giving someone a hard time, ostensibly in a friendly manner—but it can be very pointed, very barbed. It goes on a great deal. People will get honked for their pretentiousness, for their actual performance on trial.

And people will get honked *mercilessly* for things over which they have *absolutely no control*—the quality of the client, the heinousness of the act with which the person is charged. And people get honked for trying to defend people who really have hopeless legal positions.

Endnotes

[1] Importantly, not all who study plea bargaining necessarily regard it as a nonadvocacy—or even a nonadversarial—process. Feeley, for one, has cautioned us that "preliminary hearings, probable cause hearings, and informal discovery may serve many of the functions of a trial—to obtain and test crucial evidence and challenge assertions of fact and law—which may in turn lead to nolles, dismissals, or pleas of guilty in the face of an overwhelming case. To infer the lack of an adversarial stance and the existence of bargained settlement—for the pure purpose of administrative convenience—from the absence of trials is to ignore altogether the importance of these other 'truthtesting' and highly combative processes" (Feeley, 1979:29; see also Maynard, 1984, chap. 5).

[2] At some level public defenders seem to understand clients who think that public defense lawyers are unwilling to go to trial, are just "penitentiary dispatchers" interested in making deals for clients. Appearances can sometimes be deceiving—even to some lawyers: "Now _____, he was to me the epitome of the worst kind of public defender. From a distance, I got the feeling that he was just there to cop people out, and to run through cases with no sense of the client, no empathy with the person. I know now I was making a childish sort of judgment. It's a show he puts on, maybe to protect himself. In reality he practically weeps when he loses, not for himself, but for his client."

[3] For discussions of such ethical positions see Freedman (1975, chap. 5) and Hazard (1978, chap. 9).

[4] On the other hand, most of the lawyers admitted that, as public defenders, they are relatively protected from temptations to cheat. Whenever I asked them about this, the typical response was "Who would want to bribe a public defender? Anyone who could afford to bribe someone would have a private lawyer."

Once in private practice, these lawyers may not find it so easy to avoid what may be called the near occasions of sin that are apparently relatively common in Chicago. Recently, a former public defender was indicted for attempted bribery. He got a not guilty on a "technicality." Furthermore, five of the twenty lawyers alleged by the *Chicago Lawyer* magazine to be "Hallway Hustlers" were former public defenders. This label is applied to lawyers who hang out in misdemeanor courts and prey on unwary defendants—that is, take their money and render no or only dubious services.

[5] As a result of his nationwide survey of defense lawyers, Professor Albert W. Alschuler of the University of Chicago Law School noted that, in some measure, how the problem of the "innocent" defendant was handled helped to distinguish the strategies of public from private defense attorneys: "With only a few exceptions, public defenders refused to enter guilty pleas when their clients claimed to be innocent. Private defense attorneys, by contrast, were almost evenly divided between those who followed the same rule and those who maintained that 'guilt or innocence has nothing to do with it.' " (1975:1283).

[6] It should be noted that public defenders say that, when the occasion demands, they will work just as hard to convince a client with a good case that he ought to go to trial:

Some will say, "I'm guilty, and I'm going to plead." And if I think they have a good case, I'll say to them, "Look, I think we can win this; you have a good case."

It takes something out of you when you have a case you think you can win and you want to try, but the guy pleads.

The *worst* situation, though, is when you have a young kid with no record who can't stand it any more, being locked up and raped and beaten in jail, and they offer him a way out and he takes it—probation, or time served, or something. And you can't get him to trial fast enough; it's living hell for him in there.

[7] Despite the lawyers' insistence that they do not want to know, they are careful to learn enough so they will not look silly in court. That is one of the first lessons that public defenders learn. Ronald Himel, a former public defender, in 1971 assured a reporter from *Newsweek* that one just cannot afford to believe everything one hears: "My first case out of law school, the guy told me he walked around the corner and found the TV set. So I put that on [in court]. The judge pushed his glasses down his nose, hunched up and said, 'Fifty-two years I have been walking the streets and alleys of Chicago and I have never, ever found a TV set.' Then he got me in his chambers and said, 'Are you f____ crazy?' I said, 'That's what he told me.' The judge said, 'And you believed that s____? You're goofier than he is!'" (8 March 1971:29).

[8] Consensus was not as high among former public defenders. When asked whether they agreed with the statement "Contrary to what you might expect, I preferred cases where I thought my client was guilty to cases where I believed my client was innocent," almost a third (32 percent) refused to answer, saying that it was irrelevant. Among those who did answer, about half (49 percent) agreed that they preferred guilty clients. When I compared the answers of those who had worked in felony courts with the answers of those who had not, there was a significant difference. Among those who only worked in misdemeanor, juvenile, or appeals divisions, only 21 percent agreed that they preferred guilty clients. Among those who had worked in a felony courtroom, 71 percent said that, as public defense lawyers, they preferred guilty clients.

References

Alschuler, A. W. (1972). Courtroom misconduct by prosecutors and trial judges. *Texas Law Review, 50,* 629.

Alschuler, A. W. (1975). The defense attorney's role in plea bargaining. *Yale Law Journal, 84,* 1179–1313.

Blumberg, A. S. (1967). The practice of law as a confidence game: Organizational cooptation of a profession. *Law and Society Review, 1,* 15–39.

Blumberg, A. S. (1979). *Criminal justice: Issues and ironies.* New York: New Viewpoints.

Dershowitz, A. M. (1983). *The best defense.* New York: Vintage.

Dorsen, N., & Friedman, L. (1973). *Disorder in the court.* New York: Pantheon.

Durkheim, E. (1974). *Sociology and philosophy.* New York: Free Press.

Eisenstein, J., & Jacob, H. (1977). *Felony justice: An organizational analysis of criminal courts.* Boston: Little, Brown and Co.

Feeley, M. M. (1979). *The process is the punishment: Handling cases in a lower criminal court.* New York: Russell Sage Foundation.

Freedman, M. H. (1975). *Lawyers' ethics in an adversary system.* Indianapolis: Bobbs-Merrill.

Friedman, L. M. (1973). *A history of American law.* New York: Simon & Schuster.

Friedman, L. M. (1975). *The legal system: A social science perspective.* New York: Russell Sage Foundation.

Greene, B. (1982, November 3). Lawyer closes the book on criminal defense. *Chicago Tribune,* sec. 4.

Hazard, G. (1978). *Ethics in the practice of law.* New Haven, CT: Yale University Press.

Heumann, M. (1978). *Plea bargaining.* Chicago: University of Chicago Press.

Jackson, B. (1983). *Law and disorder: Criminal justice in America.* Urbana: University of Illinois Press.

Jacob, H. (1980). *Crime and justice in urban America.* Englewood Cliffs, NJ: Prentice-Hall.

Kalvin, H., & Zeisel, H. (1966). *The American jury.* Boston: Little, Brown and Co.

Lydon, S. T. (1973). The public defender as an adversary: The Alameda County public defender revisited. In *Alameda County public defender, forty-sixth annual report.* Oakland, CA: Alameda County Public Defender.

Maynard, D. (1984). *Inside plea bargaining: The language of negotiation*. New York: Plenum.

Nardulli, R. F. (1978). *The courtroom elite: An organizational perspective on criminal justice*. Cambridge, MA: Ballinger.

National Advisory Commission on Criminal Justice Standards and Goals. (1974). *Report*. Washington, DC: Government Printing Office.

Packer, H. L. (1964). Two models of the criminal process. *University of Pennsylvania Law Review, 113*, 1–68.

Packer, H. L. (1954). A sociologist looks at the legal profession. In *Essays in sociological theory* (pp. 370–385). New York: Free Press.

Spencer, J. (1984, January 8). No glamour, no money: Public defenders still seek justice for all. *Chicago Tribune*, sec. 2.

Sudnow, D. (1965). Normal crimes: Sociological features of the penal code in the public defender's office. *Social Problems, 12*, 255–277.

Weick, K. (1979). *The social psychology of organizing*. Reading, MA: Addison-Wesley.

Wishman, S. (1981). *Confessions of a criminal lawyer*. New York: Penguin.

Zemans, F. K., & Rosenblum, V. C. (1981). *The making of a public profession*. Chicago: American Bar Foundation.

10

Supervisory Styles of Patrol Sergeants and Lieutenants

ROBIN SHEPARD ENGEL

Introduction

Most scholars and practitioners agree that supervising patrol officers is a "challenging, and at times, insurmountable task" given the environmental constraints and general nature of patrol work (Tifft, 1971; Van Maanen, 1983). Although first-line supervision is critical to the success of police organizations, very little is known about the actual roles and activities street-level patrol supervisors perform. In addition, differences in supervisory styles have not been adequately described or examined. It is troubling that the policing community knows so little about the activities, roles, and styles of patrol supervisors, who are generally considered to be the backbone of American police organizations (Trojanowicz, 1980). In this era of community policing, as police departments are encouraged to move from traditional authoritarian bureaucratic models to flatter organizational structures with greater line-officer latitude, the importance of supervisory styles will increase. The promise of this research is that it identifies different supervisory styles that currently exist in policing and addresses how supervisors with particular styles differ. Implications for policy and future research are also addressed.

Literature Review

Some general propositions can be reached from a review of the literature written about police supervisors' responsibilities, activities, and roles. First, it

Reprinted from *Journal of Criminal Justice*, Vol. 29, Robin Shepard Engel, "Supervisory Styles of Patrol Sergeants and Lieutenants," pp. 341–355, 2001 with permission from Elsevier.

has been acknowledged that the performance of first-line supervisors is measured through the effectiveness of their subordinates' performance. This encourages supervisors and subordinates to engage in a reciprocity of informal "exchanges" (Brown, 1988; Manning, 1977; Rubinstein, 1973; Van Maanen, 1983). Furthermore, sergeants can use their specific daily tasks (e.g., scheduling of shifts, beats, assignments, etc.) to influence and control subordinate actions and behavior (Van Maanen, 1983, 1984). Finally, police sergeants are in a perceived position of conflict, caught between their responsibility *to* superior officers and their responsibility *for* subordinate officers. Faced with this conflict, individual sergeants adapt and define their roles differently (Trojanowicz, 1980; Van Maanen, 1983, 1984). Therefore, one would expect patrol supervisors to develop different supervisory styles, which influence their own behavior as well as the behavior of subordinate officers.

Several policing ethnographies have addressed the role of the police supervisor. Muir's (1977) work examining patrol officers' understanding of human kind and morality regarding the use of coercion suggested that patrol sergeants *could* have a fundamental influence on officers' development of both understanding and morality, and therefore on their behavior. Wilson (1968) also came to a similar conclusion, proposing that an administrator's preference has a varying influence on patrol officers' use of discretion in different types of citizen encounters. In contrast, Brown (1988:121) hypothesized that field supervisors and administrators have relatively little influence over patrol officers' behavior. His examination of survey responses of both patrol officers and supervisors indicated that "the routine actions of field supervisors have but a marginal impact on the way they [patrol officers] use their discretion." Other researchers have empirically tested the effects of supervision on patrol officer behavior (Allen, 1980, 1982; Allen and Maxfield, 1983; Brehm and Gates, 1993; Gates and Worden, 1989; Mastrofski, Ritti, and Snipes, 1994; Reiss, 1971; Smith, 1984; Tifft, 1971), but no firm conclusions have been reached. Much of this research has measured only the *quantity* of supervision (e.g., mere supervisor presence at police-citizen encounters, time spent at encounters, etc.) rather than the *quality* of supervision (e.g., styles of supervision, attitudinal and behavior differences among supervisors, etc.).

A handful of studies have examined different supervisory and leadership styles of patrol supervisors and administrators. Both Cohen (1980) and Pursley (1974) identified two types of police administrators based on survey data. Pursley's "traditionalist" and "nontraditionalist" police chiefs bear a striking resemblance to Cohen's "tradition-oriented" and "reform-oriented" commanders. Moreover, these classifications are similar to Reuss-Ianni and Ianni's (1983) identification of the "street cop" and "management cop" cultures. Van Maanen (1983, 1984) identified and described what he termed "street" sergeants and "station house" sergeants. His classification was based primarily on the activities of sergeants; active sergeants in the field who directly monitored subordinates (street sergeants) were contrasted with administrative sergeants who were more likely to remain in the station (station house sergeants). Van Maanen suggested that these two types of sergeants defined their roles differently.

In addition to these "police-specific" styles, leadership styles identified in the management literature have been applied to police supervisors. For example, the "consideration" and "initiating structure" styles of leadership developed through the Leader Behavior Description Questionnaire (LBDQ) (Halpin and Winer, 1957; Hemphill and Coons, 1957) have been applied to police supervisors (Aldag and Brief, 1978; Brief, Aldag, and Wallden, 1976; Pursley, 1974). Likewise, Blake and Mouton's (1978) managerial grid styles have been applied to police supervisors (Kuykendall, 1977, 1985; Swanson and Territo, 1982), as were Hersey and Blanchard's relations-orientation and task-orientation styles (Kuykendall and Roberg, 1988; Kuykendall and Unsinger, 1982). Furthermore, Jermier and Berkes (1979) have applied the supervisory styles developed in the path goal theory to police supervisors. Most of these studies sought to predict subordinate satisfaction and generally produced mixed results.

For a number of reasons, findings from this body of research should be interpreted with caution. First, the measures of supervisory styles are often based on subordinates' perceptions of their supervisors rather than supervisors' perceptions of themselves or their actual behavior (Aldag and Brief, 1978; Brief et al., 1976; Jermier and Berkes, 1979). It is also unclear if the subordinates were asked to, and were able to, answer the leadership questions about a particular supervisor, rather than simply describing supervision in general (Aldag and Brief, 1978; Brief et al., 1976). Many shifts are supervised by multiple supervisors, making it problematic to attribute subordinates' perceptions of supervision to a particular supervisor. Even studies that base measures of supervisory styles on behavior are limited because they use hypothetical vignettes rather than actual observed behavior (Kuykendall and Unsinger, 1982). Finally, while leadership questionnaires can generally be applied to most types of supervisors, they may not adequately capture the unique circumstances of supervisors in police organizations. Several scholars who applied these questionnaires to police populations reported findings that were somewhat different from results consistently reported in the management field (Aldag and Brief, 1978; Brief et al., 1976; Kuykendall and Unsinger, 1982).

In general, the police supervision literature is limited in scope and fails to answer many conceptual and empirical questions regarding field supervision. This is especially true of questions regarding differences in supervisory styles. As stated by Southerland and Reuss-Ianni (1992:177), "we need more broad-based research using a variety of methodological tools and conducted throughout a wide range of police agencies, not simply generalized from management studies conducted in business settings, to understand the current style and status of the police leadership and management." This article provides the first attempt to address this perceived need. The next section describes several underlying attitudinal constructs identified in the management and policing literatures that are combined to create four supervisory styles for a sample of patrol supervisors in two metropolitan police departments. These four styles are thoroughly described and their distribution among supervisors is explored.

Underlying Attitudinal Constructs

Since the 1930s, scholars focusing on leadership theories have described a variety of different leadership styles. Similarities among these theories are easily identified by examining their underlying attitudinal and behavioral constructs (Bass, 1990; Graham and Hays, 1993; Yukl, 1989). Indeed, there are strong similarities and one should expect a correlation between Lewin and Lippitt's (1938) "democratic" leaders, those leaders scoring high on the "consideration factor" created by the LBDQ (Hemphill and Coons, 1957), and Blake and Mouton's (1978) "concern for people" factor. The characteristics defining these types of leaders also correspond to Hersey and Blanchard's (1988) relations-oriented leader, McGregor's (1957, 1960) Theory Y managers, and Bass' (1985, 1990) transformational leader. Since many of the taxonomies of leadership behavior are similar, many of the leadership styles capture the same attitudes and behaviors. Yet, it is important to identify the actual individual constructs on which these leadership styles are based. Bass (1990) identified some individual attitudinal constructs underlying styles of leadership, each of which should be considered a continuum upon which leaders vary.

Rather than relying on styles identified in the management literature, this work identified underlying attitudinal constructs that were considered important for police supervision. Using Bass' (1990) work as a base, six underlying attitudinal constructs were identified and measured for a sample of police field supervisors: level of activity, decision making, power distribution, relations-orientation, task-orientation, and inspirational motivation. These constructs were later combined with three police-specific constructs (expectations for community policing, expectations for aggressive enforcement, and general views of subordinates), to create supervisory styles for police officers.

The first underlying construct, *level of activity*, examined the extent to which leadership was either avoided or attempted. This construct involved the relative distance and/or amount of supervision a leader employs. Early leadership research focused on three classic styles developed by Lewin and Lippitt (1938): authoritarian, democratic, and laissez-faire. One of the defining characteristics of these styles was the level of activity displayed by the leader. For example, laissez-faire leaders were described as inactive leaders that avoid or shirk their supervisory duties (Lewin, Lippitt, and White, 1939). In his discussion of Theory X and Theory Y management styles, McGregor (1960) compared close, controlling supervision to supervision that was more general and loose. Rather than simply identifying active or passive leadership as a dichotomy, a leader's motivation to manage can be measured along a continuum.

The second construct of leadership styles was based on *how leaders made decisions* (e.g., group decision-making, group input with one person deciding, one person deciding with no input, etc.). Tannenbaum and Schmidt (1958) examined how leaders made decisions and developed a continuum of autocratic and democratic behavior. Bass (1990) described the differences between directive decision-making and participative decision-making. The directive leader "plays an active role in problem solving and decision-making and expects group members to be guided by his or her actions," while participative leaders engage subordinates in the planning or decision-making process (Bass, 1990). Leaders have also been differentiated based on how they communicate the decisions they make to subordinates. Hersey and Blanchard (1988) have described four types of leadership styles—telling, selling, participative, and delegating—that are based in part on one-way and two-way communications between leaders and subordinates.

A third construct examined *how power is distributed* (i.e., who is in charge, how many share power, who makes the decisions, etc.). "Power" refers to the control of others, though it does not necessarily imply authority, or the legitimization of power in the eyes of followers (Graham and Hays, 1993). Authority is power that has been legitimized in the eyes of the follower. A leader may rely on other types of power that are not based on legitimate authority, for example, French and Raven (1960) identified five power bases that may be utilized by leaders: legitimate, reward, coercive, referent, and expert power.

The fourth and fifth underlying constructs, referred to as *relations-orientation* and *task-orientation*, involve the focus of the leader's attention (Hersey and Blanchard, 1988). These dimensions consider what needs are being met as determined by the particular focus chosen by the leader. Leaders who are more relations-oriented focus their attention on the well-being of their subordinates. These leaders pursue a human-relations approach and maintain supportive relationships with subordinates by building friendships and mutual trust. In contrast, task-oriented leaders are most concerned with the goals of the work group, means of achieving these goals, and the output produced. These leaders focus on production and achievement. Although these two dimensions share common elements, they are conceptually and empirically distinct. Therefore, a leader could simultaneously rank high (or low) on both dimensions. Relations-orientation and task-orientation are similar to the "consideration" and "initiating structure" dimensions identified through the use of the LBDQ (Halpin and Winer, 1957; Hemphill and Coons, 1957) and the "concern for people" and "concern for production" dimensions systematic arranged into the Managerial Grid (Blake and Mouton, 1978).

The final construct identified from the management literature, *inspirational motivation*, was a leadership dimension that refers to the potential range of team-building behavior that a leader may demonstrate. This dimension includes motivating and inspiring subordinates, arousing team spirit, and demonstrating commitment to goals and shared vision. Inspirational motivation is a form of transformational leadership (Bass and Avolio, 1994).

Research Sites

This empirical examination of supervision uses data collected for the Project on Policing Neighborhoods (POPN), a large-scale study of police behavior funded by the National Institute of Justice. Systematic observation of patrol officers and field supervisors (sergeants and lieutenants) was conducted during the summer of 1996 in the Indianapolis, Indiana Police Department and during the summer of 1997 in the St. Petersburg, Florida Police Department (see Parks, Mastrofski, DeJong, and Gray, 1999).

The Indianapolis Police Department serves the city of Indianapolis, which had an estimated population of 377,723 in 1995, including 39 percent minorities, 8 percent unemployed, 9 percent below the poverty level, and 17 percent female-headed households with children. The UCR Index crime rate in 1996 was 100 per 1,000 residents. During that year, the department employed 1,013 sworn officers—17 percent female, 21 percent minority, and 36 percent with a four-year college degree. The patrol division was divided geographically into four districts, all of which were studied during the project. Each district was unique in character, mission, and emphasis placed on community policing (for details see Mastrofski et al., 2000; Parks et al., 1999).

Supervisory structure and form differed across IPD districts and shifts. It was unclear if a direct supervisor-subordinate relationship actually existed because this department did not have a formal evaluation process in place. Each patrol officer in IPD was assigned one of three work schedules with rotating days off. On each shift in every district, a sergeant was assigned to a particular schedule. Therefore, each shift had three different squads supervised by different sergeants. This supervisory structure provided that sergeants work the same schedule as the group of officers (their squad) that they were responsible for. Officers working in specialized community policing units were directly supervised by one sergeant whose sole responsibility was to monitor and direct the activities of the officers in that unit. Three of the four observed districts had a community-policing unit, although the structure and emphases of these units differed. Finally, in the patrol division, one lieutenant was assigned to each shift in each district.

St. Petersburg, Florida is located at the southern tip of Pinellas County with a population of 240,318 in 1995, including 24 percent minorities, 5 percent unemployed, 6 percent below the poverty level, and 10 percent female-headed households with children. The UCR Index crime rate (per 1,000 residents) was 99 in 1996. During that year, the St. Petersburg Police Department had 505 sworn officers, 13 percent of whom were women, 22 percent minority, and 26 percent with a four-year college degree (Parks et al., 1999). The jurisdiction of this department was divided into three districts and forty-eight community policing areas (CPA) with a community policing officer assigned to each area.

The SPPD supervision structure had undergone tremendous change in recent years.[1] During the period of observation, it reflected a compromise between geographic deployment and a squad system. Sergeants were directly responsible for a "team" of officers on a particular shift working in a specific sector or geographic area (three sectors in each district), along with a handful of community policing officers assigned to a CPA. Each sergeant had responsibility for one or more CPAs (and the community policing officers working in those areas) within their sector. Sergeants were scheduled to work three "temporal" shifts (twenty-four hours) and then "flex" their schedule for the remaining sixteen hours each week. During a "temporal" shift, sergeants were responsible for the direct supervision of all patrol officers working that shift for the entire district, not just their sector. During "flex" shifts, sergeants were expected to work on problem-solving in their specific CPA, supervise their community policing officers, and complete administrative paperwork.

Methodology

Systematic observation was conducted in IPD with fifty-eight patrol supervisors (sergeants and lieutenants) during eighty-seven rides, totaling over 600 hours—78 percent of IPD patrol sergeants and lieutenants were observed at least once. In SPPD, systematic observation was conducted with twenty-six patrol sergeants, four patrol lieutenants, and eight patrol officers working as the acting temporal sergeant during seventy-two shifts—96 percent of patrol sergeants in SPPD were observed at least once. Data were also obtained through structured interviews with sixty-nine of seventy-four patrol supervisors in IPD and all twenty-seven patrol sergeants in SPPD. The interview captured demographic and background information along with supervisors' views in the following areas: perceived problems in their districts, training, subordinates, their role as supervisors, how they distribute and use power, patrol work, goals of policing, priorities of management, and problem-oriented and community-oriented policing.

In addition, field observation of patrol officers was conducted for over 5,700 hours in twenty-four neighborhoods across the two sites. In IPD, 194 patrol officers were observed during 336 shifts, while in SPPD, 128 officers were observed during 360 shifts. Combined, observers recorded information regarding encounters between officers and approximately 12,000 citizens (Parks et al., 1999).

The measures of supervision used in the following analyses are based on supervisors who were both interviewed and observed. Combining both sites, eighty-one supervisors are included in the analyses—seventeen lieutenants and thirty-nine sergeants from IPD and twenty-five sergeants from SPPD.[2] The demographic characteristics of these supervisors are displayed in table 1. The majority of supervisors in this sample were White (85 percent), male (85 percent), and with a four-year college degree (51 percent). The average supervisor was forty-four years old with nearly ten years of supervisory experience. Although supervisors reported receiving more *training* on issues related to supervision, management, and leadership compared to the concepts and principles of community policing, they reported having more *knowledge* about community policing issues.

Table 1   Supervisors' characteristics

Variables	Min	Max	Mean	Standard Deviation
Sup sex (1 =female)	0	1	0.15	0.36
Sup race (1 =nonwhite)	0	1	0.15	0.36
Supervisor age	31	70	44.07	7.99
Years experience as supervisor	1	33	9.94	7.13
Education (four-year college degree)	0	1	50.62	0.50
Amount training in concepts and principles of community policing	1	5	3.48	0.99
Amount knowledge of concepts and principles of community policing	1	3	1.72	0.60
Amount training in supervision, management, and leadership	1	5	3.70	1.07
Amount knowledge in supervision, management, and leadership	1	3	1.40	0.52

N = 17 IPD lieutenants, 39 IPD sergeants, and 25 SPPD sergeants.
Amount training: 1 (none), 2 (less than one day), 3 (one to two days), 4 (three to five days), and 5 (more than five days).
Amount knowledge: 1 (very), 2 (fairly), 3 (not very knowledgeable).

In the following analyses, the substantive nature of supervision is measured using the underlying attitudinal dimensions of supervisory styles identified from the management and policing literatures. Individual items are extracted from the supervisor survey and are intended to represent the supervisors' beliefs and attitudes (for a complete list of these items, see appendix A). Six additive scales are created to represent the attitudinal dimensions previously described: power distribution, decision-making, activity level, relations-orientation, task-orientation, and inspirational motivation.[3] These scales are further described in table 2.

Any examination of supervisory styles of patrol officers must also take police-specific attitudinal constructs into consideration. In addition to the six dimensions previously described, three police-specific constructs were examined: supervisors' expectations for community policing by subordinates, expectations for aggressive enforcement by subordinates, and their general views of subordinates (see table 2 and appendix A). These police-specific dimensions were believed to be important underlying components of supervisory styles.

The attitudinal constructs do relate to one another in a meaningful and interpretable manner. As expected, some scales do have significant correlation coefficients. For example, supervisors who are strongly relations-oriented also appear to have positive views of subordinate officers. Likewise, supervisors who score high on the community expectation scale tend to score low on the aggressive enforcement expectation scale. Indeed, all of the constructs correlate in the expected directions (see Shepard, 1999).

Table 2   Supervisors' attitudinal dimensions

Variables	Min	Max	Mean	Standard Deviation	Mean IPD Lieutenants	Mean IPD Sergeants	Mean SP Sergeants
Activity level scale	4	8	6.65	0.96	7.06	6.74	6.24
Decision-making scale	3	7	5.66	0.88	5.48	5.67	5.77
Power scale	17	32	24.38	3.12	25.65	24.51	23.32
Relations 1—friends	1	4	2.52	1.09	2.53	2.54	2.48
Relations 2—protect	1	5	2.68	1.46	3.00	2.74	2.36
Task-orientation scale	6	20	12.49	3.17	12.44	11.64	13.84
Inspirational motivation	1	5	4.09	1.23	3.94	4.33	3.80
Expect CP scale	20	36	27.21	3.90	27.41	27.51	26.60
Expect aggressive enforcement scale	4	13	8.62	2.32	8.82	8.05	9.36
View of subordinates scale	5	9	8.18	1.00	8.58	8.35	7.64

$N = 81$ supervisors.
Larger values represent higher levels of activity, more direct decision-making, more perceived power, and higher levels of relations-orientation, task-orientation, inspirational motivation, expectations for CP, expectations for aggressive enforcement, and more positive views of subordinates. Numbers reported in the table are unstandardized scores.

Findings

These nine constructs[4] are analyzed using exploratory factor analysis to identify underlying latent styles of supervision. Based on the sample of eighty-one supervisors, factor analysis reveals four significant factors with eigenvalues greater than one, which collectively explain 63 percent of the variance.[5] The factor loadings for each attitudinal construct are reported in table 3. Each of the four factors is considered a different "style" of supervision. The factor scores indicate the strength of each underlying attitudinal construct for each style. The four styles of supervision that emerge are labeled *traditional*, *innovative*, *supportive*, and *active*, respectively. Supervisors are classified with a particular style based on their highest factor score.

"Traditional" Supervisors

The first factor is dominated by an expectation of aggressive enforcement and attitudes indicating high levels of task-orientation. To a lesser extent, these supervisors report being more directive in their decision-making and have lower expectations for subordinates to engage in community policing activities. Supervisors who score high on this factor may be considered more traditional in their approach to supervision. This traditional style of supervision is characterized by supervisors who expect subordinate officers to produce measurable outcomes—particularly arrests and citations, along with paperwork and documentation. Traditional supervisors expect officers to patrol aggressively, but they do not expect officers to handle situations that

Table 3 Factor analysis—factor loadings

Variables	Factor 1 (traditional)	Factor 2 (innovative)	Factor 3 (supportive)	Factor 4 (active)
Power	– 0.102	0.640	0.124	0.250
Decision-making	0.261	0.008	– 0.002	0.279
Activity level	0.004	0.007	0.003	0.647
Relations-orientation (friends)	0.004	0.447	0.115	0.007
Relations-orientation (protect)	– 0.004	0.005	0.680	– 0.005
Task-orientation	0.617	– 0.204	– 0.402	0.007
Inspirational motivation	– 0.150	0.106	0.204	– 0.314
Expect community relations	– 0.328	0.608	– 0.184	– 0.004
Expect aggressive enforcement	0.980	– 0.167	0.008	0.002
View of subordinates	– 0.006	0.296	0.113	0.534

$N = 81$ supervisors.

involve order maintenance or quality of life issues. They are more likely to make decisions because they tend to take over encounters with citizens or tell officers how to handle these incidents.

The traditional style of supervision is what many expect in police organizations. The supervisor who places importance on measurable outcomes of police activities and aggressive enforcement is representative of the "traditional" style of supervisor. They are concerned with controlling situations and the behavior of their subordinates. This control is maintained through relatively traditional means within the department—checking paperwork, measuring output based on arrest statistics, and making decisions themselves so subordinates will not have the opportunity to mishandle a situation.

It is important to recognize the differences between this style and other "traditional" labels of supervisors or officers from past research. Readers may misinterpret traditional supervisors as shielding subordinate officers from punishment and being more tolerant of corruption. One aspect of traditional supervisors in this sample, however, is their no-nonsense approach to policing, along with their strict enforcement of rules and regulations. As an observer recounts about a traditional supervisor:

> S1 [the supervisor observed] was obsessed with the issue of respect. S1 expounded at length about the familiarity of the department and laxity of discipline. He blamed this initially on the academy training, then the demise of the military style, and societal erosion of respect for elders and authority. S1 cited the old-style policing when officers would never address their superiors by name but by rank and would hope against hope to not be called into a supervisor's office. Now, S1 claims that the officers seek out the district commanders personally instead of adhering to the chain of command (POPN).[6]

Just as traditional supervisors expect strict law enforcement on the street, they expect adherence to departmental rules including the chain of command. Emphasis of both discipline and respect are central to this style of supervision. As described by another supervisor:

> S1 [the supervisor observed] said that he will sanction individuals if necessary and that he has actually had someone fired for numerous small things that just seemed to add up. S1 noted that most other sergeants would not have sought action against this particular subordinate, but he believes that officers should follow the rules, and when given instructions, should follow those instructions. S1 said he was more upset that the officer in question did not submit to his authority than by his actual behavior. (POPN)

Traditional supervisors are also generally resistant to community-oriented policing or other new policing initiatives. They believe that community policing involves duties that should not be the responsibility of patrol officers. The following explanation by a supervisor is typical of a traditional supervisor's view:

> S1 [the observed supervisor] is a self-described "traditionalist and dinosaur".... S1 felt that management has a real problem as a result of bending and swaying too much with whatever prevailing climate is in existence concerning the community, media and politics. In attempting to demonstrate change, initiative, and forward movement they have jeopardized efficiency, true policing, and proficiency. (POPN)

Traditional supervisors are more likely to be supportive of new policing initiatives if they are in the form of aggressive law enforcement. Of those classified as traditional, 61.9 percent "agree strongly" that "enforcing the law is by far a patrol officer's most important responsibility," compared to only 13.6 percent of innovative supervisors, 10.5 percent of supportive supervisors, and 10.5 percent of active supervisors. They expect and encourage the "traditional" goals of policing and demand strict adherence to rules and regulations.

The observed behavior of traditional supervisors also varied in expected ways. Traditional supervisors spend significantly less time per shift engaging in encounters with citizens (2.0 percent compared to 5.4 percent). This behavioral difference reinforces the characterization of traditional supervisors. One might speculate that they spend less time engaging with citizens simply because they emphasize their role as supervisor rather than doing patrol work. Although they may take over some incidents and make decisions, they are less likely to engage in direct citizen contact on their own. Furthermore, because traditional supervisors do not emphasize community policing, they may be less likely to engage in these activities themselves, which translates into less casual citizen contact, less contact with victims, fewer meetings with community representatives, etc.

Other observed behavior provides further support for classification. Traditional sergeants and lieutenants are more likely to give advice or instruction to subordinates (6.4 times per shift compared to 4.6 times), but less likely to reward them (0.9 times per shift compared to 2.4 times). Traditional supervisors may be less likely to reward officers because they are less relations-oriented. Rather, they are concerned with controlling situations and task-related behavior. Instructing subordinates is a behavior consistent with their desire for control.

"Innovative" Supervisors

The second factor represents supervisors who score high on the power and community-relations expectation scales. This factor is also characterized by high relations-orientation (have more officers they consider friends), low task-orientation, and more positive views of subordinates. These supervisors are "innovative" because they are generally more supportive of innovative changes in policing. They are defined by their expectations for community policing and problem-solving efforts by subordinates. Furthermore, they are less concerned with enforcing rules and regulations, report writing, or other task-oriented activities that characterize traditional supervisors.

Innovative supervisors are more receptive of new policing initiatives, and as a result, may encourage their officers to embrace these new philosophies as well. As one supervisor explained to an observer:

> S1 [observed supervisor] said that he is not resistant to change because he enjoys seeing the department strive to produce better quality services for the community. S1 said that some policies are certainly more effective than others but without change there is no way to make progress. (POPN)

Supervisors' support for innovative strategies appears to extend to expectations for their subordinates. Innovative supervisors' high scores on the expectation for community policing scale show that they expect subordinates to perform community-related tasks and insist on better relations with the community. One innovative supervisor describes his expectations for subordinates:

> S1 [the supervisor observed] said that he expects his officers to be fair with citizens and act in a morally defendable manner. S1 said that the people in the community are important to him and that officers often forget that they are employed by these people. S1 said that he expects his officers will treat all citizens with dignity and respect and act in a "courteous and respectful manner." S1 was very sensitive to matters of ethnicity, race, and gender. S1 said that every officer brings something different to the job and that a good officer is one who recognizes and accepts differences among groups of people. He said that he expects that officers will interact with citizens from different groups in appropriate though perhaps different ways. (POPN)

These expectations are further evident through innovative supervisors' responses to individual survey questions. For example, 95.5 percent of innovative supervisors reported that they "agree strongly" that "a good patrol officer will try to find out what residents think the neighborhood problems are," compared to only 47.6 percent of traditional supervisors, 68.4 percent of supportive supervisors, and 68.4 percent of active supervisors.

One of the goals of innovative supervisors is to provide subordinates with the support to implement community policing and problem-solving strategies. Scholars have noted that supervisors in an era of community policing should assume a new role, which includes coaching, mentoring, and facilitating officers. Innovative supervisors are more likely to embrace this new role. As one innovative supervisor explained to an observer:

> S1 [supervisor observed] said that his role involves becoming a "teacher or educator" to the officers. S1 said that if nothing else, his many years of service have provided him with the opportunity to see a variety of situations. S1 said that this insight is only valuable if shared with other officers who may learn something from his experiences. S1 said that officers frequently come to him for advice or suggestions about how he would have handled a particular situation. He said that what he tries to teach officers is that every situation is different. S1 said that frequently officers will become so routinized in their responses to situations that they lump together as being identical. S1 said the key is to teach officers that although situations are similar, there are always different elements involved and that different ways to handle these situations may be appropriate. (POPN)

Unlike traditional supervisors, innovative supervisors generally do not tell subordinates how to handle situations or take over the situations themselves. Rather, they are more likely to delegate decision-making. Innovative supervisors have accepted a new supervisory role characterized by less control over subordinates' behavior and decision-making. They chose to guide and teach their policing philosophies rather than strictly control officers' behavior.

Some behaviors displayed by innovative supervisors differ significantly from behaviors observed for other supervisors. For example, innovative supervisors spend significantly more time per shift engaging in encounters with citizens (6.5 percent of the shift compared to 3.8 percent). Presumably, those supportive of innovative strategies would spend more time themselves engaging in community-policing types of activities, which include interacting with citizens. Innovative supervisors also spend more time engaging in other types of community policing activities, but these differences are not statistically significant.

Innovative supervisors also spend significantly more time per shift engaging in personal encounters (with citizens or other officers) than other supervisors (14.5 percent compared to 8.7 percent). This behavioral difference is also consistent with the descriptions of innovative supervisors. Those supervisors who emphasize and engage in community-oriented activities often have more unstructured time, and as a result, more time for personal activities.

"Supportive" Supervisors

The third factor is characterized by high scores on the "protect subordinates" relations-orientation scale and low scores on the task-orientation scale. Additionally, this factor is represented by higher levels of inspirational motivation. These supervisors support subordinates by protecting them from "unfair" discipline or punishment and providing inspirational motivation. Furthermore, supportive supervisors are less concerned with enforcing rules and regulations, paperwork, or making sure officers do their work.

Supportive supervisors show their concern for subordinates in a number of ways. They may provide a buffer between officers and management to protect against criticism and discipline. This gives their officers space to perform duties without constant worry of disciplinary action for honest mistakes. One example of this protective buffer is explained by a supervisor:

> S1 said that he also feels his role is to take care of his officers and be their advocate in front of the administration . . . S1 explained that it is almost like a plea bargain in court. S1 said that during administrative proceedings against his officers, he often concedes that they have done something wrong, but also tells the mitigating circumstances and tries to sell the officer's good points. (POPN)

Alternatively, supportive supervisors may simply encourage officers through praise and recognition, or show support by establishing good relations with subordinates, acting as counselors and showing concern for subordinates' personal well-being. Furthermore, supervisors can become "career counselors" in a sense, looking out for the well-being of subordinate officers within the organization.

In some cases, supportive supervisors do not have strong ties or positive relations with management. They often view the police administration as something that patrol officers need to be shielded against.

> S1 [observed supervisor] said that from management's point of view, the sergeant is the person that they will "hang out to dry" as an example and to rid themselves of responsibility. S1 said that his true role is to protect officers from the whims of management and also to make sure that the officers are doing their jobs and back up one another. (POPN)

As a result, some supervisors classified as supportive may actually function more as a "protector" than strictly a "supporter." Of the supportive supervisors, 68.4 percent reported that "protecting their officers from unfair criticism and punishment" is one of their three most important functions, compared to only 9.5 percent of traditional supervisors, 4.5 percent of innovative supervisors, and none of the active supervisors. These findings relate to Reuss-Ianni and Ianni's (1983) description of two predominate cultures in policing, street-cop culture and management-cop culture. Supportive supervisors appear to adhere to street-cop culture by aligning themselves with their subordinates against administrators. They are management cops only in the sense that their rank is higher than entry level.

This protector role adopted by some supportive supervisors has the potential to become problematic. As has been noted in recent history, shielding officers from accountability mechanism within the department often leads to police misconduct (Christopher Commission, 1991; Mollen Commission, 1994). Supervisory protection of officers has also been associated in other research with promoting police solidarity and secrecy, which cultivates an atmosphere where police abuse of power, misconduct, and corruption are tolerated (Crank, 1998; Kappeler, Sluder, and Alpert, 1998; Skolnick and Fyfe, 1993).

Systematic observation of supportive supervisors reveals only one significant difference in behavior. Supportive supervisors praise or reward subordinate officers significantly more often during an average shift than do other types of supervisors (3.0 times per shift compared to 1.7 times). Intuitively, one would expect this behavior from supportive supervisors who are concerned with relations-orientation and inspirational motivation.

"Active" Supervisors

The fourth factor is characterized by high levels of activity and positive views of subordinates. To a lesser extent, this factor is also represented by high scores on decision-making, high levels of perceived power, and low levels of inspirational motivation. The active supervisor can be compared to Van Maanen's "street" sergeant. These supervisors are often in the field, directive in their decision-making, and have a relatively positive view of subordinates.

One characteristic of active supervisors is working alongside their subordinates in the field. Among active supervisors, 94.7 percent report that they often go on their own initiative to incidents that their officers are handling, compared to only 23.8 percent of traditional officers, 54.5 percent of innovative supervisors, and 68.4 percent of supportive supervisors. Another goal of active supervisors is to control subordinate behavior, as shown with their high scores on the decision-making and power scales.

In addition, active supervisors also give importance to being in the field and engaging in police work themselves. The same supervisor explained:

> S1 indicated that he does not follow the popular opinion that "I got my stripes so I don't need to do patrol work anymore." S1 indicated that he still does traffic stops, takes his own calls, and goes on calls when he is not required. When I got in S1's car to begin the ride, he had two traffic tickets that he had written on his way to work. I also saw him stop two people on traffic violations. (POPN)

Active supervisors attempt to achieve a balance between being active in the field and controlling subordinate behavior through constant, direct supervision.

Even though active supervisors believe they have considerable influence over subordinate decisions, low scores on the inspirational motivation scale show they are less likely to help them work on problems. One possible explanation is their reluctance to be too controlling and therefore alienate subordinate officers. As one active supervisor explained to an observer:

> S1 [supervisor observed] told me that he is the type of supervisor who likes to "get involved" and "be there" for his officers. S1 stated that he loves being on the streets. I asked S1 if he considered himself to be a "hands-on" manager. S1 thought about it for a moment, and then shook his head [no]. S1 commented that he associated "hands-on" with a

supervisor who would get "too involved," not trusting his subordinates to do the job correctly or with a supervisor who was a control freak . . . S1 stated that he would describe himself as a sergeant who did his best to be available to his officers and as someone who was there to back them up. At this time, S1 told me that he would take calls and volunteer as backup, so his officers would know that he was not "above" working alongside them. (POPN)

As evident by this supervisor, there is a fine line between active supervisors and those who are perceived as overcontrolling or micro-managers by their subordinates.

Active supervisors spend more time per shift engaging in general motor patrol (33.0 percent of a shift compared to 25.7 percent) and traffic encounters (3.9 percent compared to 2.1 percent). Active supervisors are also less likely to engage in work-related discussions regarding crime or disorders with subordinate officers (4.7 times per shift compared to 8.0 times). This is probably due to the amount of time supervisors spend in the field and not in direct contact with officers in the station where most of these conversations are likely to occur. Again, the differences in behavior lend support to the classification of these supervisors.

Distribution of Supervisory Styles

The distribution of supervisory styles for this sample of sergeants and lieutenants is reported in table 4. There is a roughly equal distribution of each style, however, when the styles are examined for each department separately, significant differences emerge. Traditional supervisors are significantly overrepresented in SPPD, while active supervisors are underrepresented. Supervisors in IPD are evenly distributed across all styles, however, IPD lieutenants are slightly more likely to be classified as innovative and less likely to be classified as traditional.

Also reported in table 4 are the differences between male and female supervisors. Female supervisors represent a disproportionate number of traditional supervisors (50 percent of female supervisors are classified as traditional supervisors). With this exception, few other differences in classification are apparent. There are no statistically significant differences in classification with regard to the supervisors' race, rank, age, years of experience, or educa-

Table 4   Supervisory styles

Variables	Overall ($n=81$)	Males ($n=69$)	Females ($n=12$)	White ($n=69$)	Nonwhite ($n=12$)	BA degree ($n=41$)	IPD Lts ($n=17$)	IPD Sgts ($n=39$)	SPPD Sgts ($n=25$)
Traditional style	0.26	0.22	0.50	0.26	0.25	0.24	0.12	0.18	0.48
Innovative style	0.27	0.30	0.08	0.26	0.33	0.27	0.35	0.28	0.20
Supportive style	0.23	0.25	0.17	0.25	0.17	0.20	0.24	0.26	0.20
Active style	0.23	0.23	0.25	0.23	0.25	0.29	0.29	0.28	0.12

Numbers in the cells are means representing the percent of supervisors with that predominant style.

tion. The four types of supervisors also do not differ from one another in their reported views of the importance of promotion or moving to a specialized unit, and their amount of training and general knowledge of the principles of community policing. Innovative supervisors, however, reported receiving significantly more training in supervision, management, and leadership.

Discussion

Using six underlying constructs identified from leadership theories and three underlying constructs identified from police ethnographic research, four different styles of police field supervisors are identified. These supervisory styles are evenly distributed among the sample of eighty-one supervisors, however, significant departmental differences exist. Nearly half of SPPD supervisors are traditional, compared to only 16 percent of IPD supervisors. Likewise, only 12 percent of SPPD supervisors are active, compared to 29 percent from IPD. Differences also emerge when the supervisor's sex is considered. Fifty percent of female supervisors are traditional supervisors, compared to only 22 percent of male supervisors. Furthermore, only 8.3 percent of female supervisors are innovative, compared to over 30 percent of males.

One explanation for these differences is the nature of the traditional supervisory style. Traditional supervisors are primarily concerned with controlling subordinate behavior. This is accomplished by demanding compliance with rules and regulations, monitoring work output measures, and using discipline. Van Maanen (1983) speculated that supervisors often focus on rules and regulations because they are concrete and can be controlled in a work environment that is unstable and difficult to regulate. Female supervisors, perhaps seeking to gain legitimacy in their supervisory roles, may be more likely to use rules and regulations as a means to control their officers. They rely on what French and Raven (1960) have termed a "coercive" power base (power taken from subordinates' perceptions of a leader's ability to mediate punishments given to them). In contrast, male supervisors are more likely to rely on "legitimate" power (based on subordinates' perceptions that the leader has a legitimate right to direct their actions) or "referent" power (based on subordinates' identification with leaders).

This explanation also accounts for the higher percentage of traditional supervisors in SPPD. Many of the SPPD supervisors complained that the supervisory structure and goals had changed several times in recent years due to administrative turnover and the implementation of innovative strategies. Many supervisors were unclear what their roles in the organization were, or what management expected of them. In fact, 72 percent of SPPD sergeants indicated during observation sessions that the structure of supervision and other departmental policies limited their ability to assess subordinate behavior and perform supervisory functions. Only 4 percent of IPD supervisors indicated similar feelings. It is likely that supervisors in organizations with changing structures, priorities, and strategies emphasize the one familiar element of their supervisory role—controlling subordinate behavior by enforcing established rules and regulations.

The implications for day-to-day operations and relationships with citizens for departments having a majority of supervisors with a traditional style are unknown. The present research has firmly established differences in supervisors' attitudes and behaviors; however, whether or not these differences have an influence over subordinates' behavior on the street is an empirical question that should be explored. That is, to better assess the implications for policy and future research, the influence of these particular supervisory styles on *subordinates'* attitudes and behaviors need to be examined. Although most scholars and practitioners agree that one role of police field supervisors is to control the behavior their officers, the degree of control that supervisors actually have continues to be a matter of debate (Allen, 1980, 1982; Allen and Maxfield, 1983; Brehm and Gates, 1993; Gates and Worden, 1989; Mastrofski et al., 1994; Reiss, 1971; Smith, 1984; Tifft, 1971).

Based on their reported attitudes and observed behavior, one might expect that each of these four types of supervisors would have influences over subordinates' attitudes and behavior that differ significantly in form and substance. For example, one might speculate that officers with traditional or active supervisors would be more likely to engage in aggressive enforcement activities in an effort to produce measurable output (arrests and citations). As a result of this aggressive enforcement, officers might be involved in more conflicts with citizens and perhaps be more likely to use force. Analyses have shown that at least one supervisory style (active) has a significant influence on the increased likelihood of patrol officers' use of force. Analyses also show, however, that patrol officers with active supervisors spend significantly more time engaging in police-initiated and problem-solving activities, and have higher rates of arrest (Engel, 2000; forthcoming).

It will also be important to test whether or not innovative supervisors have an influence over the acceptance and utilization of community policing and problem-solving techniques. One might speculate that officers supervised by an innovative supervisor would spend more time on problem-solving activities. Alternatively, these officers might take their cues directly from innovative supervisors by spending more time conducting personal business or otherwise neglecting their duties. Finally, future research should examine the influence that supportive supervisors have over police misconduct. The protector role that some supportive supervisors embrace might be directly related to problematic subcultural norms including isolation, secrecy, and solidarity.

Although identifying supervisory styles and examining differences in supervisors' behavior have provided interesting findings, caution should be exercised when interpreting them. The data used in this study of police supervision were limited in several ways. The POPN utilized a data collection design created for systematic observation of encounters between patrol officers and citizens. The study of patrol supervision did not fit neatly into this scheme. Although systematic observation and surveys provided a descriptive slice of police work, they often did not provide detailed information about long-term patterns of police behavior or the effectiveness of long-term policies and strategies. The study of patrol supervision might be better captured by some type of modified ethnographic research design where detailed information about the actual patterns (especially the underlying rationales, objectives, etc.) of supervisory practices could be collected. While the POPN research design did have a partial ethnographic component with detailed information collected during each ride, the ability to describe long-term patterns of supervision and the structural, environmental, and political factors affecting these patterns was somewhat limited. Future research on police supervision should address these issues.

Nonetheless, the implications for policy were clear. Police administrators who wish to establish particular policies and procedures within their departments need to recognize the differences in first-line supervisors. None of the four supervisory styles identified in this research should be considered the "ideal" standard for police supervision. Each style was associated with both benefits and problems. The appropriate supervisory style for departments will differ based on their organizational goals. Police administrators should recognize the need for better training of first-line supervisors to achieve these organizational goals.

Appendix A:
Individual Survey Items

Decision-Making (2 items):

1. When you are on the scene of an incident with your officers, how frequently do you tell them how to handle the incident? Never [1], rarely [2], sometimes [3], or often [4]

2. When you are on the scene, how frequently do you take it over and handle the incident yourself? Never [1], rarely [2], sometimes [3], or often [4]

Power Distribution (11 items):

How much influence do you usually have over each decision: Hardly any or none [1], some [2], a lot [3].

1. Which officers are assigned to your unit.

2. The specific CPA or job assignments your officers receive.

3. Whether one of your officers is permitted to go out of service to do problem solving or other special tasks.

4. Whether your officers are disciplined for minor rule infractions.

5. Whether your officers receive assignments to specialist units when they ask for them.

6. Whether one of your officers is authorized to work overtime.

7. Whether one of your officers is approved for off-duty work.

8. Your officers' prospects for promotion to higher rank.

9. Department policies about patrol operations.

Never [1], seldom [2], sometimes [3], usually [4], always [5]

10. When you have asked for resources needed to do a job, how often have you been given what you requested?

11. When you have made decisions about how to do patrol operations, how often have your decisions been supported by higher-ups?

Relations-Orientation 1 (one item):

1. How many officers in your unit would you consider to be your friends? None [1], a few [2], about half [3], all or most [4].

Relations-Orientation 2 (one item):

Out of a list of ten items, indicate the three that you think are the most important for you to perform as a first-line supervisor [5], and three that are the least important [1].

1. Protecting subordinates from unfair criticism or punishment.

Task-Orientation (4 items):

Out of a list of ten items, indicate the three that you think are the most important for you to perform as a first-line supervisor [5], and three that are the least important [1].

1. Making sure that reports are properly completed.

2. Enforcing department rules and regulations.

Out of a list of seven goals indicate the two you believe are the most important for patrol officers with 911 assignments [5], and two that you think are the least important [1].

3. Handling calls for service to their assigned area.

4. Making arrests and issuing citations.

Level of Activity/Relative Distance of Supervision (2 items):

Never [1], rarely [2], sometimes [3], always [4]:

1. How frequently do your officers ask you to come to the incidents that they are handling?

2. Other than when it is required by department policy, how frequently do you go on your own initiative to incidents that your officers are handling?

Inspirational Motivation (1 item):

Out of a list of ten items, indicate the three that you think are the most important for you to perform as a first-line supervisor [5], and three that are the least important [1].

1. Helping officers to work on problems in their assigned areas.

Expectations for Community Policing (9 items):
Indicate your level of agreement with the following: Disagree strongly [1], disagree somewhat [2], agree somewhat [3], agree strongly [4]

1. Police officers have reason to be distrustful of most citizens [values reversed].

2. Assisting citizens is just as important as enforcing the law.

3. A good patrol officer will try to find out what residents think the neighborhood problems are.

How often should patrol officers with 911 assignments be expected to do something about each of the following situations: Never [1], sometimes [2], much of the time [3], always [4]

4. Public nuisances (loud parties, barking dogs)

5. Neighbor disputes

6. Family disputes

7. Litter and trash

8. Parents who don't control their kids

9. Nuisance businesses that cause lots of problems for neighbors

Expectations for Aggressive Enforcement (3 items):
Indicate your level of agreement with the following: Disagree strongly [1], disagree somewhat [2], agree somewhat [3], agree strongly [4]

1. Enforcing the law is by far the patrol officer's most important responsibility.

2. A good patrol officer is one who patrols aggressively by stopping cars, checking out people, running license checks, and so forth.

Out of a list of seven goals indicate the two you believe are the most important for patrol officers with 911 assignments [5], and two that you think are the least important [1].

3. Making arrests and issuing citations.

Endnotes

[1] Supervision was previously organized as a "squad system," where one sergeant was directly responsible for a fixed group of officers who worked the same schedule. After a change in administrative personnel, SPPD implemented a supervisory structure that focused on geographic deployment. Each sergeant in the department was assigned to a particular geographic area (CPA) that they were directly responsible for. As a result, sergeants were responsible for supervising patrol officers and community policing officers who were assigned to their areas across every shift. After about a year, this structure of supervision was reorganized because of the unrealistic demands it placed on sergeants.

[2] Supervisors were excluded from the analyses if they were not both interviewed and observed (sixteen sergeants and lieutenants from IPD and three sergeants from SPPD). Also, eight patrol officers acting as temporal sergeants in SPPD were excluded as were all the lieutenants from this department. Lieutenants from SPPD did not engage in direct field observation of subordinate officers.

[3] Specific items with serious questions regarding their reliability or validity were eliminated from the composite scale measures. Where appropriate, a single item was used to represent an attitudinal dimension rather than an additive scale.

[4] The two relations-orientation items did not strongly correlate (Pearson's $r = .11$) and reliability analysis suggested that they do not belong in an additive scale (coefficient = .19). At face value, the items tap different issues. The number of officers that supervisors consider their friends does not appear to influence their reported importance of protecting officers from unfair criticism or punishment. As a result, these two items are entered separately in analyses, with both representing different aspects of the relations-orientation construct.

[5] This factor analysis is performed using the maximum likelihood extraction technique because its overall objective is "to find the factor solution which would best fit the observed correlations" (Kim and Mueller, 1978:23). An oblique rotation method (direct oblimin) is selected because "it does not arbitrarily impose the restriction that factors be uncorrelated" (Kim and Mueller, 1978:37). For a more detailed information on extraction and rotation methods, see Kim and Mueller (1978).

[6] For this and all subsequent quotes from supervisors, references to gender were reported in masculine form to further protect the identities of supervisors.

References

Aldag, R. J., & Brief, A. P. (1978). Supervisory style and police role stress. *Journal of Police Science and Administration, 6,* 362–367.

Allen, D. (1980). *Street-level police supervision: The effect of supervision on police officer activities, agency outputs, and neighborhood outcomes.* Ph.D. dissertation, Indiana University. Ann Arbor: University of Michigan Press.

Allen, D. (1982). Police supervision on the street: An analysis of supervisor/officer interaction during the shift. *Journal of Criminal Justice, 10,* 91–109.

Allen, D., & Maxfield, M. (1983). Judging police performance: Views and behavior of patrol officers. In R. Bennett (Ed.), *Police at work: Policy issues and analysis* (pp. 65–86). Beverly Hills, CA: Sage Publications.

Bass, B. M. (1985). *Leadership and performance beyond expectations.* New York: Free Press.

Bass, B. M. (1990). *Bass and Stogdill's handbook of leadership: Theory, research and managerial applications* (3rd ed.). New York: Free Press.

Bass, B. M., & Avolio, B. J. (1994). *Improving organizational effectiveness through transformational leadership.* Thousand Oaks, CA: Sage Publications.

Blake, R. R., & Mouton, J. S. (1978). *The new managerial grid.* Houston, TX: Gulf.

Brehm, J., & Gates, S. (1993). Donut shops and speed traps: Evaluating models of supervision on police behavior. *American Journal of Occupational and Organizational Psychology, 67,* 69–78.

Brief, A. P., Aldag, R. J., & Wallden, R. A. (1976). Correlates of supervisory style among policemen. *Criminal Justice and Behavior, 3,* 263–271.

Brown, M. K. (1988). *Working the street: Police discretion and the dilemmas of reform.* New York: Russell Sage Foundation.

Christopher Commission. (1991). *Report of the independent commission on the Los Angeles Police Department.* Los Angeles, CA: The Commission.

Cohen, B. (1980). Leadership styles of commanders in the New York City police department. *Journal of Police Science and Administration, 8,* 125–138.

Crank, J. P. (1998). *Understanding police culture.* Cincinnati, OH: Anderson Publishing.

Engel, R. S. (2000a). Patrol officer supervision in the community policing era. *Journal of Criminal Justice* (forthcoming).

Engel, R. S. (2000b). The effects of supervisory styles on patrol officer behavior. *Police Quarterly, 3*(3), 262–293.

French, J., & Raven, B. (1960). The bases of social power. In D. Cartwright & A. F. Zander (Eds.), *Group dynamics* (2nd ed., pp. 607–623). Evanston, IL: Row, Peterson, and Company.

Gates, S., & Worden, R. (1989). *Principle-agent models of hierarchical control in public bureaucracies: Work, shirking, and supervision in police agencies.* 1989 Annual Meeting of the American Political Science Association, at the Atlanta Hilton and Towers, August 31–September 3.

Graham, C. B., Jr., & Hays, S. W. (1993). *Managing the public organization* (2nd ed.). Washington, DC: Congressional Quarterly Press.

Halpin, A. W, & Winer, B. J. (1957). A factorial study of the leader behavior descriptions. In R. M. Stogdill & A. E. Coons (Eds.), *Leader behavior: Its description and measurement*—51). Columbus: Ohio State University, Bureau of Business Research.

Hemphill, J. K., & Coons, A. E. (1957). Development of the leader behavior description questionnaire. In R. M. Stogdill & A. E. Coons (Eds.), *Leader behavior: Its description and measurement*—38). Columbus: Ohio State University, Bureau of Business Research.

Hersey, P., & Blanchard, K. H. (1988). *Management of organizational behavior* (5th ed.). Englewood Cliffs, NJ: Prentice-Hall.

Jermier, J. M., & Berkes, L. J. (1979). Leader behavior in a police command bureaucracy: A closer look at the quasimilitary model. *Administrative Science Quarterly, 24,* 1–23.

Kappeler, V. E., Sluder, R. D., & Alpert, G. P. (1998). *Forces of deviance: Understanding the dark side of policing* (2nd ed.). Long Grove, IL: Waveland Press.

Kim, J., & Mueller, C. W. (1978). *Factor analysis statistical methods and practical issues.* Newbury Park, CA: Sage Publications.

Kuykendall, J. L. (1977). Police leadership: An analysis of executive styles. *Criminal Justice Review, 2,* 89–100.

Kuykendall, J. L. (1985). Police managerial styles: A grid analysis. *American Journal of Police, 4,* 38–70.

Kuykendall, J. L., & Roberg, R. R. (1988). Police managers' perceptions of employee types: A conceptual model. *Journal of Criminal Justice, 16,* 131–137.

Kuykendall, J. L., & Unsinger, P. (1982). The leadership styles of police managers. *Journal of Criminal Justice, 4,* 311–321.

Lewin, K., & Lippitt, R. (1938). An experimental approach to the study of autocracy and democracy: A preliminary note. *Sociometry, 1,* 292–300.

Lewin, K., Lippitt, R., & White, R. K. (1939). Patterns of aggressive behavior in experimentally created social climates. *Journal of Social Psychology, 10,* 271–301.

Manning, P. K. (1977). *Police work.* Cambridge: MIT Press.

Mastrofski, S. D., Snipes, J. B., Parks, R. B., & Maxwell, C. D. (2000). The helping hand of the law: Police control of citizens on request. *Criminology, 38*(2), 307–342.

Mastrofski, S. M., Ritti, R. R., & Snipes, J. B. (1994). Expectancy theory and police productivity in DUI enforcement. *Law and Society Review, 28,* 113–148.

McGregor, D. M. (1957). The human side of enterprise. In J. M. Shafritz & A. C. Hyde (Eds.), *Classics of public administration* (3rd ed., pp. 217–223). Belmont, CA: Wadsworth Publishing.

McGregor, D. M. (1960). *The human side of enterprise.* New York: McGraw-Hill.

Mollen Commission to Investigate Allegations of Police Corruption. (1994). *Commission report*. New York: The Mollen Commission.

Muir, W. K., Jr. (1977). *Police: Street corner politicians*. Chicago: University of Chicago Press.

Parks, R. B., Mastrofski Muir, S. D., DeJong, C., Gray, M. K. (1999). How officers spend their time with the community. *Justice Quarterly, 16*, 483–518.

Pursley, R. D. (1974). Leadership and community identification attitudes among two categories of police chiefs: An exploratory inquiry. *Journal of Police Science and Administration, 2*, 414–422.

Reiss, A. J., Jr. (1971). *The police and the public*. New Haven, CT: Yale.

Reuss-Ianni, E., & Ianni, F. (1983). Street cops and management cops: The two cultures of policing. In M. Punch (Ed.), *Control in the police organization* (pp. 251–274). Cambridge: MIT Press.

Rubinstein, J. (1973). *City police*. New York: Ballantine.

Shepard, R. L. (1999). *Street level supervision: Styles of patrol supervisors and their effects on patrol officer behavior*. Ph.D. dissertation, University at Albany. Ann Arbor, MI: University Microfilms International.

Skolnick, J. H., & Fyfe, J. J. (1993). *Above the law: Police and the excessive use of force*. New York: Free Press.

Smith, D. (1984). The organizational context of legal control. *Criminology, 22*, 19–38.

Southerland, M. D., & Reuss-Ianni, E. (1992). Leadership and management. In G. W. Cordner & D. C. Hale (Eds.), *What works in policing? Operations and administration examined* (pp. 157–177). Highland Heights, KY: Academy of Criminal Justice Sciences and Anderson Publishing.

Swanson, C. R., & Territo, L. (1982). Police leadership and interpersonal communication styles. In J. Greene (Ed.), *Managing police work* (pp. 123–139). Beverly Hills, CA: Sage Publications.

Tannenbaum, R., & Schmidt, W. H. (1958). How to choose a leadership pattern. *Harvard Business Review, 36*, 95–101.

Tifft, L. (1971). *Comparative police supervision systems: An organizational analysis*. Ph.D. dissertation, University of Illinois at Urbana-Champaign. Ann Arbor, MI: University Microfilms International.

Trojanowicz, R. C. (1980). *The environment of the first-line police supervisor*. Englewood Cliffs, NJ: Prentice-Hall.

Van Maanen, J. (1983). The boss: First-line supervision in an American police agency. In M. Punch (Ed.), *Control in the police organization* (pp. 275–317). Cambridge: MIT Press.

Van Maanen, J. (1984). Making rank: Becoming an American police sergeant. *Urban Life, 13*, 155–176.

Wilson, J. Q. (1968). *Varieties of police behavior*. Cambridge, MA: Harvard University Press.

Yukl, G. A. (1989). *Leadership in organizations* (2nd ed.). Englewood Cliffs, NJ: Prentice-Hall.

11

Getting Rid of
the Prima Donnas
The Bureaucratization
of a Probation Department

JOHN ROSECRANCE

The pervasive influence of bureaucracy in Western society is a central theme of twentieth-century social science. In the field of criminal justice, theorists have identified bureaucracy as the "single most important variable in determining the actual day-to-day functioning of the legal system" (Chambliss and Seidman, 1971:468). Criminological researchers have described the effects of bureaucratization upon probation recommendations (Hagan, 1977), juvenile court procedures (Tepperman, 1973), sentencing decisions (Reiss, 1974), police tactics (Littrell, 1979), plea bargaining (Rosett and Cressey, 1976), judicial processing (Blumberg, 1979), and parolee recidivism (McCleary, 1978). Bureaucratization of American criminal justice agencies typically involves shifting from a traditional authority system to a rational-legal one (Udy, 1959). Weber, a seminal source of modern bureaucratic concepts, observed that the bases of order and authority in traditional organizations are precedent and usage, while in rational-legal systems they are derived from formal procedure (Pugh, Hickson and Hinings, 1985:16–17). Although bureaucratization "is a somewhat nebulous concept" (Meyer, 1979:24), in this article it is the process whereby authority based upon formal rules and discipline is imposed upon an informal organization where authority had depended upon technical expertise (Blau, 1974:33).

While the increasingly bureaucratic nature of criminal justice components has been well documented, employee reactions to shifts in authority

John Rosecrance, *Criminal Justice and Behavior*, Vol. 14 No. 2, pp. 138–155, copyright © 1987 by Sage Publications. Reprinted by permission of Sage Publications.

structure have not been prominently identified. The expansion of bureaucracy invariably means the displacement of previously entrenched power bases, and is "always seen as a loss of prestige or actual power by both small and large groups of individuals" (Jacoby, 1973:14). The reactions and accommodations of criminal justice personnel to bureaucratic organization are an important but often overlooked phenomenon. The purpose of the present study is to describe and analyze the accommodations made by probation officers to the bureaucratization of their department. An understanding of this accommodation process, while of historical interest, can also provide valuable insight into organizational dynamics prevailing in contemporary probation practices. The types of employees who are able to adapt successfully to bureaucratic imperatives continue to shape the organizational milieu of today's probation departments. This article will also provide a glimpse of the real-world work experiences of white-collar correctional employees.

In the space of five years, the organizational dynamics prevailing in a California probation agency employing approximately 60 line officers and located in Pacific County (a pseudonym) were significantly altered by a change in administration. A new probation chief imposed a system of formal rules and central authority upon a department that had been run in an ad hoc, fragmented manner. In the process, probation officer discretion and individual decision making were restricted. Bureaucratic administrators were able to establish legal authority over work performance through the development and implementation of a department manual. Individualized work styles and expertise that officers had developed over the years were subordinated to formal procedures mandated by bureaucratic guidelines. Probation workers were discouraged from advocating controversial positions by an administration that emphasized smooth work flow and trouble-free relationships with other criminal justice agencies. Changes in the probation department authority structure occurred despite resistance from some of the existing probation staff. However, most of the probation officers satisfactorily adjusted to the bureaucratization of their department and relations between them and the administration were generally harmonious. The patterns of individual accommodation manifested by probation officers were similar to a tripartite typology identified by Presthus (1962). A delineation of these patterns will demonstrate how probation officers responded to a bureaucratic environment, and why certain types are well suited to such a setting.

The research methodology for this project involved a historical accounting based upon qualitative data drawn from probation sources and personal field notes. An ethnographic perspective was particularly suited to this type of analysis (Scott, 1965). The research data indicate that while bureaucratization can improve efficiency and lead to improved worker-organization relations, there can be problematic consequences. Those probation officers most adaptable to bureaucratic dictates are not likely to be sources of independent reporting or agents of change. This finding has import for those seeking to understand the reluctance of many probation departments to implement meaningful change in their operational practices (Glaser, 1985; Walker, 1985).

Methods

Much of the data for this research project was collected using a participant's perspective. For almost 15 years I was employed by Pacific County as a probation officer. I had worked there for seven years when the longtime probation chief, who had run the department on an informal basis, was replaced by an administrator who strongly advocated a formal hierarchical structure. For the next several years I witnessed the adjustments of probation officers to increasing bureaucratization. My particular adaptive pattern to bureaucratization, because of my interests outside of the work environment, was a passive noncontentious one. In the Presthus typology I would have been considered an "indifferent." By the time I left Pacific County the bureaucratic machinery was firmly in place and functioning smoothly. During this period of employment I kept field notes of my activities with the probation department. Subsequently these notes proved to be valuable in developing an accurate portrayal of events during the period of emerging bureaucratization.

When I began a historical accounting of this period I conducted interviews[1] with the current and former probation personnel (administrators, supervisors, and line officers) who were participants in the changing organizational structure. I had left the probation department under amicable conditions (to attend graduate school) and maintained generally good relations with both probation officials and line staff. During these interviews I queried probation sources on their views of and reactions to the formalized procedures instituted by the new administrators. I interviewed other criminal justice people such as judges, district attorneys, and public defenders regarding their recollections and observations of the events that occurred during the changing organizational structure of the probation department. Because of our common experiences, the respondents were generally candid and cooperative, and I was able to collect qualitative data unavailable to other researchers.

The method I used to analyze the data was similar to the grounded theory techniques of Glaser and Strauss (1967). I sought to develop analyses that were generated from the data. In the initial stages of the investigation I adopted a flexible and unstructured approach. As the data accumulated generalizations and propositions emerged; these were modified, compared, and, in turn, formed the groundwork for future data collection.[2]

Findings

An analysis of accumulated data revealed that accommodations by probation officers to bureaucratization tended to fall into one of three general patterns. These accommodations were similar to the ideal types posited by Presthus (1962): (1) upward mobile, (2) indifferent, and (3) ambivalent. A discussion of the three types will serve to clarify this finding. Since the Presthus typology is an empirical generalization with a sometimes accentuated set of criteria, the accommodation patterns of individual probation officers will vary from the type. However, each pure type can serve as a base line for gauging potential and actual deviations. In order to understand the responses of the probation officers it is necessary first to describe some procedures instituted by the bureaucratic administration. Several significant changes were brought about with the implementation of probation guidelines. The new administrators introduced a manual that eventually served to legitimate their actions in attempting to control dissension and divergence among the probation staff. From a Weberian standpoint the existence of written rules is the core of bureaucratic administration (Littrell, 1979:2). In this case the manual provided both instrumental and symbolic acceptance of rational-legal authority.

When the chief probation officer who had held the position for 20 years resigned under pressure, a judicial hiring panel charged his successor with the task of modernizing a probation department that was considered poorly managed, wasteful, inefficient, and "behind the times." The new chief probation officer had worked in a much larger and presumably more efficient probation department. He was given carte blanche (including the right to "kick ass") in his effort to improve Pacific County's probation department. Some probation workers were pleased with the change in leadership, as they had considered the former chief to have been capricious, unprofessional, and guilty of cronyism. The following quotes were taken from interviews with such probation officers:

> The old boy just wasn't consistent. He ran the place according to how he felt on that particular day.

> The chief got the job before civil service and he had no concept of professionalism.

> Chief _____ promoted only his buddies. He never paid attention to who was doing a good job; only to who was loyal to him.

The new chief probation officer took over an agency comprised of individual units such as adult supervision, adult investigation, juvenile intake, and juvenile supervision that had been functioning independently of departmental authority. Over the years probation officers had developed individual styles for managing their assignments. Those employees who had gained reputations for expertise were given wide discretion in handling probation cases and were subject to only minimal departmental supervision. Some officers had developed such credibility that their decisions were rarely questioned by supervisory staff. Characteristically, probation officers felt a greater responsibility to their individual units than to the department as a whole.

The new chief's first major undertaking was the centralization of authority, which meant breaking up the power bases that had developed under the traditional ad hoc system of his predecessor. The wide discretion and latitude that had been afforded individual officers were replaced with department regulations. Probation officers, regardless of their expertise, were required to adhere to the policies of the new probation administration. As the administration began to assert authority, it developed a rational justification for this action. Because there was no formal written policy governing employee job performance, the new chief probation officer developed a manual specifically delineating a department policy on this subject. Formal guidelines helped to temper criticism that the administration (consisting of a chief probation office, his appointed assistant chief, and four division heads left over from the previous administration) might be acting arbitrarily and set the stage for the curbing of individual discretion and decision making. During a staff meeting the assistant chief succinctly described the task facing the administration: "For the good of the department we've got to get rid of the prima donnas around here."

The new administration initiated two wide-ranging tactics as a first attempt to gain authority over the staff: transfers and mandatory staffing. Probation officers were transferred[3] "in the best interests of the department" and all pending court cases (that previously had been the responsibility of the individual officer) were to be staffed with supervisors. Buttressed by new departmental policies, wholesale transfers and innumerable case conferences commenced.

Probation officers who had worked in the same unit for several years were transferred to new and often unfamiliar assignments. Those who remained at their same job locations were patently aware that they too could be transferred. The staffing of every court case (holding a case conference) with supervisors enabled departmental authority to be reinforced on a continuing basis. Soon after mandatory staffing became a reality the administration indicated that in the future all court recommendations—the most visible aspect of probation work—were to be departmental rather than individual recommendations. In cases of disagreement between supervisor and officer it would be the supervisor's recommendation that was filed with the court. Individual officers were expected to subordinate their personal views in order to support departmental recommendations. The probation administration, through its supervisors, sanctioned adherence to prevailing sentencing guidelines and actively discouraged controversial court recommendations. Probation officers were expected to provide ballpark recommendations (Rosecrance, 1985) that, as one officer stated, "would not ruffle the feathers of judges or district attorneys." Officers who were reluctant to go along with the new administration's policies reported that they were transferred to unfavorable assignments or were not promoted.

When the new policies first took effect employees recalled that they had "chaffed" under regulations they believed severely limited their discretion. While there was a period of unrest, the department's authority came to be accepted as legal and binding through a combination of bureaucratic winnowing, attrition, and acquiescence. Eventually, employee relations with the administration improved as staff transfers slowed considerably, disputes over court recommendations gradually diminished, and department guidelines were rarely questioned. In most cases probation officers had accepted department policies to such a degree that the regulations now appeared logical and appropriate. The administration's noncontroversial stance also came to be accepted by the officers and discussions of divergent perspectives were rare. The completed department manual established formal regulations for the orderly operation of a probation department. After initial employee resistance to the administration ameliorated, there was little active dissension in the department. It was no longer necessary for the administration to assert its authority overtly on a staff that had embraced bureaucratic procedures. In effect, the bureaucratic system had become self-regulating. In order to understand how this occurred, it is necessary to describe the accommodation patterns of probation officers to a changing organizational structure.

Patterns of Accommodation[4]

Upwardly Mobile

According to Presthus (1978:182–183) the sine qua non of those who adopt an upwardly mobile pattern of accommodation to bureaucratization is their pragmatic willingness to accept organizational dictates. Upwardly mobile individuals are determined to make the most of opportunities for advancement in their organization (Terkel, 1975). This type of officer "does not need perfect causes" (Presthus, 1978:183) to support wholeheartedly organizational goals. Typically they find a bureaucratic setting congenial and the accommodation process is nonproblematic.

While the probation department was undergoing bureaucratization, some officers responded to the new procedures in a manner characteristic of Presthus's upwardly mobile type. This group of officers readily accepted central authority and were quick to adapt their work routines to the new guidelines. Their court reports generally adhered to the administration goal of noncontroversy and their recommendations were in line with informal judicial and prosecutorial expectations. Upwardly mobile types perceived their job as an extremely important part of their lives. They were concerned with maintaining stable employment and did not see themselves as agents of change. They generally had not been openly critical of the former chief probation officer. However, they were compatible with a bureaucratic structure and soon became strong supporters of the new administration. The following statement is representative of an upwardly mobile pattern of accommodation:

> I'm basically a team player. When the new chief took over I was a little nervous about the change. But when I could see the new administration was up-front about what it expected, I became a real fan. The new rules didn't bother me, some of them were long overdue. A few of the p.o.s had been getting out of hand. They were doing their own thing to such an extent that you hardly knew they worked for the probation department.

Officers who opted for this pattern of accommodation characteristically viewed the changing organizational structure as an opportunity to advance their careers. They were quick to scrutinize the new job requirements in order to render themselves promotable. The remarks of a probation supervisor are typical of this perspective:

> I sure like the changeover. Under _____ I never knew exactly what was expected of a p.o. But when the new job specifications and duties were clearly spelled out we all knew exactly what they wanted from us—and I liked that. I knew what it took to qualify for the supervisor's job, and I got the promotion. In the old regime I'd still be a p.o. wondering how to get ahead.

Since upwardly mobile probation officers frequently were rewarded with promotion, the bureaucratic nature of the probation department was maintained and strengthened.

Indifferent

The leitmotif of those who have adopted an indifferent accommodation pattern is "coming to terms with their work environment by withdrawal and by a reduction of their interests toward off-the-job satisfaction" (Presthus, 1978:186). When faced with bureaucratization, many probation officers in Pacific County decided the most appropriate course of action was acquiescence and compliance. While not wholeheartedly supporting the new organizational structure (as did the upward mobiles), they felt it was easier, as one officer put it, "to go along rather than swim against the current." In several instances the officers had manifested a similar pattern of disinterested compliance in dealings with the former administration. Their adjustments to a new organizational structure were a continuation of an established job outlook.

Indifferents tended to perceive their jobs as a necessary, but not the most fulfilling, aspect of their lives. They had developed interests or hobbies outside their work environment, and while demonstrating a superficial commitment to department regulations, they were not emotionally caught up in a changing department structure. The observation of an officer who chose an indifferent accommodation is representative:

> I saw a lot of dissension and scrambling resulting from the "new probation department." But to tell the truth it never really affected me. I just came in to work and did what they wanted me to do. I never took it all that seriously. You know I'm a real scuba nut—that's what turns me on. This job is not all that important. It pays the bills but it's not that big a deal for me.

Some in this category either were not concerned with occupational mobility or had become disenchanted with their promotion prospects and they were content to "draw a salary without working up too much sweat." Klockars (1972:551), in his typology of probation officers, labeled these types as "time servers." A probation officer who had been passed over for promotion (after the new administration had taken over) subsequently opted for an indifferent accommodation and indicated:

I'll give them [the department] eight hours per day, but no more. I don't get worked up over the job anymore. I'll follow their rules; but I'm not going out of my way any more. I don't need the hassle. I already paid my dues and I'm sure not going to bust my ass.

For various reasons indifferents chose not to become actively involved in the bureaucratic process and adapted to the new regulations with resignation and while not embracing the new organizational dictates, neither did they oppose them. The opposition was to come from another group.

Ambivalent

One group of probation officers found it extremely difficult to adjust to increasing bureaucratization. Their patterns of accommodation were similar to the ambivalent type described by Presthus (1978:228):

Creative and anxious, their values conflict with bureaucratic claims for loyalty and adaptability. While the upward mobile finds the organization congenial and the indifferent refuses to become engaged, ambivalents are a small residual category who can neither reject its promises of success and power nor play the roles required to compete for them. In the bureaucratic situation the ambivalent is a marginal person with limited career chances.

Under the informal policies of the former chief some probation officers had worked out accommodations whereby adequate job performance would allow them to have a good measure of independence. Officers with acknowledged expertise had the opportunity to individualize their reports and case recommendations without fear of department censure. They had been permitted relative freedom in handling their probation cases and in making recommendations to the court. It was generally understood "that as long as you got the job done, the chief didn't ask questions." A frequent observation among officers was "the chief didn't know much about probation but at least he left us alone."

The new regulations limiting discretion caused a small group of probation workers to question seriously administration dictates. These officers found the mandatory staffing of court cases particularly objectionable. They resented attempts by supervisors to influence the final court recommendation and balked at the administration's desire for noncontroversial reporting. These officers prided themselves on being independent and "telling it like it is." One ambivalent stated: "Those jerks in administration who didn't know shit about doing a probation report were trying to tell me how to do my work!" In the process of conducting investigations the officers often revealed information that, while germane to the case, raised questions about the appropriateness of plea bargaining agreements. Their recommendations, sometimes at odds with current sentencing guidelines, caused judicial questioning, and on occasion drew complaints from either prosecution or defense. Officers who strove to maintain independent reporting frequently caused problems for an administration bent on facilitating a routine, noncontroversial work flow. An administrator stated: "The prima donnas were a big pain in the ass. They pissed off the judges and caused everyone a lot of trouble. They only could see things their own way."

At first the dissatisfied officers took their complaints about the new procedures directly to the administration. Some examples of these confrontations with the administration included filing a union grievance over transfers, airing objections to mandatory case conferences at staff meetings, complaining to supervisors and unit heads about loss of discretion, and sending a delegation of officers to the chief probation officer to complain that the new policies were extremely unpopular. One of the rebellious officers summed up these efforts:

> By God, we tried to work within the department. We wanted to keep our bitches in-house. We did everything to convince them to change some of the new policies. But the administration turned a deaf ear. It was hopeless. They just ignored us. We had to take more direct action.

As their disagreement with the new administration worsened, the ambivalents openly rebelled against the new regulations by refusing to sign court recommendations with which they disagreed and by being contentious in dealing with supervisors during the staffing of cases. On occasion these officers complained to sources outside the probation department such as judges, public defenders, district attorneys, or members of the board of supervisors about the restrictive policies and loss of an objective perspective. Administration responded to these actions by quietly transferring the dissident officers to less visible assignments, such as juvenile hall counselors or supervisors of large write-in case loads. These jobs usually required little or no report writing, and the officers no longer had a viable work-related forum for expressing viewpoints differing from those sanctioned by the administration. The out-of-favor officers reported that they were watched carefully by their supervisors and indicated they frequently had been cited for minor violations of department regulations. None of the officers' names appeared on promotion lists. When questioned about these situations a supervisor replied:

> Of course they weren't promoted, and yes we did watch them carefully. What did they expect? Remember they were trying to wreck the department. What should we have done—rewarded them for being real assholes? No way! They got what they had coming to them. You can't have it both ways.

The rebellious officers exhibited ambivalence toward their employment by demonstrating both a strong liking for probation work and an impatient frustration with a system that (from their standpoint) made it difficult for them to perform their job responsibilities adequately. Other officers did not join or support the dissident officers. Gradually the protest lost its impact and administration policies were rarely challenged by probation staff. Eventually most of the group retired or left for other jobs while one member, frustrated by her inability to alter administration mandates, opted for noninvolvement and accommodated to bureaucracy through indifference. She recalled: "I got tired of beating my head against the wall. The administration wasn't going to change—regardless of our protests. So I said fuck it; I got a family to support. I stopped fighting and just did my job." Approximately one year after the abortive protest a probation administrator commented, "We finally got rid of the prima donnas in this department and everything's running smoothly."

Summary and Conclusions

In this article I have described the bureaucratization of a probation department. After initial employee protest was overcome the organization's rational-legal authority was established and bureaucratization proceeded smoothly until it became virtually self-regulating. While the study was concerned with a single, medium-sized probation department, the findings provide additional insight into the effects of organizational dynamics upon the behavior of probation personnel. My research has identified the fact that accommodations of probation officers to rational-legal authority help to maintain a bureaucratic structure. This factor has not been researched adequately and needs further study and clarification. However, preliminary indications from the present study reveal that prevailing accommodation patterns influence significantly the operations of probation departments.

I have demonstrated how the indifferent and upwardly mobile types of probation officers are able to survive and flourish in a bureaucratic setting. They adapt comparatively easily to organizational dictates by integrating their personal opinions with departmental goals. The ambivalents face a more problematic situation. They find it difficult to make necessary adaptations to organizational imperatives and inevitably are forced to leave probation work or to alter drastically their accommodation patterns. However, by actively discouraging the presence of ambivalents the probation bureaucracy has removed sources of balance, independence, and change.

In the absence of the balance provided by ambivalent officers who espouse varied and divergent perspectives, probation departments can be co-opted by more powerful organizations such as the court or district attorney. Probation officials and officers view judges as powerful figures who exert considerable influence upon their careers, and they have learned to "appreciate the importance of the breezes which blow from the judges' chambers" (Goldsborough and Burbank, 1968:109). Judges typically demand court reports that facilitate a smooth work flow, expect probation officers to sanction all preplea agreements, and favor recommendations that reflect their sentencing philosophies. Without officers who are willing to maintain differing viewpoints, many probation departments acquiesce to judicial demands and their court reports are structured accordingly (Blumberg, 1979).

Prosecuting attorneys can be an influential force in the decision making of probation officers (McHugh, 1973). Members of the district attorney's office frequently remain personally involved with criminal cases through sentencing and have few reservations about complaining to the probation administration concerning the way a particular case is being handled. Much of the information needed for court reports—for example, police reports, criminal records, and legal proceedings—is obtained from the district attorney's office, and provides an opportunity for prosecutors to influence probation officer investigations. While ambivalent officers often reject such influence, other types are more likely to be swayed. Frequently, overt and subtle attempts by prosecuting attorneys to influence probation officers result in court recommendations generally favorable to the prosecution (Hagan, Hewitt, and Alwin, 1979).

Ambivalents tend to put independence ahead of department loyalty. While this approach can be disruptive, it does have its place in probation work. In some situations the probation department is well served by officers who are willing to take a controversial stand. An administrator admitted to me that although the prima donnas were "no fun to be around," they did provide sources of strength in the probation department. She indicated that many of the present probation officers "caved in too easily" and could not be "counted on" to maintain firm convictions about their cases. However, the ambivalent's desire for independence is a crucial factor in the group's inability to survive in a bureaucratic milieu. The remaining probation officer types (upwardly mobile and indifferent) working with a departmental orientation, in the main, relinquish their independence to expedite a routinized work flow.

Ambivalents provide an important ingredient in an organizational structure by serving as agents of change. Those who have chosen upwardly mobile and indifferent types of accommodation tend to be so well integrated into the bureaucratic system that they cannot see the need for flexibility. On the other hand, ambivalents have not conformed fully to bureaucratic guidelines and are inclined to express criticism and to seek changes in departmental policies. The very fact that some questioning occurs can be a positive organizational dynamic (Scott, 1981). The need for flexible probation policies and procedures seems especially salient in light of the generally accepted caveat that probation services have failed to satisfy either public or organizational expectations (Conrad, 1985; Glaser, 1985; Petersilia, Turner, Kahan, and Peterson, 1985).

A retired supervisor described the dilemma facing many probation departments: "Every department needs a few prima donnas—but not too many. The trick is to find the right mix."

Endnotes

[1] My interview schedule included the following contacts:
(A) Line officers: 27
Current (still working at the department): 18
Former (no longer working at the department): 9
(B) Supervisors: 6
Current: 3
Former: 3

(C) Administrators: 5
    Current: 3
    Former: 2
I also talked to four judges, three district attorneys, and two public defenders.

[2] An example of this process occurred early in my analysis when I tried to "make sense" of the data. Originally I attempted to categorize adjustments to bureaucratization on the basis of personality traits such as aggressiveness, passivity, or competitiveness. These tentative generalizations and propositions proved invalid since I was unable to find traits that were manifested in a regular pattern. Upon further observation I found that adjustments fell into three patterns and when I compared them to the Presthus typology there was an obvious "fit."

[3] Several sources told me that the new chief probation officer frequently stated: "Transferring p.o.s keeps them off balance and easier for me to control."

[4] Out of the 60 officers in Pacific County during the reorganization I estimated that 17 could be classified as upwardly mobile, 28 as indifferent, 10 as ambivalent, and 5 who didn't fit into these categories.

References

Blau, P. M. (1974). *On the nature of organizations*. New York: John Wiley.

Blumberg, A. S. (1979). *Criminal justice: Issues and ironies*. New York: New Viewpoints.

Chambliss, W., & Seidman, R. (1971). *Law, order, and power*. Reading, MA: Addison and Wesley.

Conrad, J. P. (1985). The penal dilemma and its emerging solution. *Crime & Delinquency, 31*, 411–422.

Glaser, B., & Strauss, A. (1967). *The discovery of grounded theory*. Chicago: Aldine.

Glaser, D. (1985). Who gets probation and parole: Case study versus actuarial decision making. *Crime & Delinquency, 31*, 367–378.

Goldsborough, E., & Burbank, E. (1968). The probation officer and his personality. In C. Newman (Ed.), *Sourcebook on probation, parole, and pardons* (pp. 104–112). Springfield, IL: Charles C. Thomas.

Hagan, J. (1977). Criminal justice in rural and urban communities: A study of the bureaucratization of justice. *Social Forces, 55*, 597–611.

Hagan, J., Hewitt, J., & Alwin, D. (1979). Ceremonial justice: Crime and punishment in a loosely coupled system. *Social Forces, 58*, 506–527.

Jacoby, H. (1973). *The bureaucratization of the world*. Berkeley: University of California Press.

Klockars, C. (1972). A theory of probation supervision. *Journal of Criminal Law, Criminology and Police Science, 63*, 550–557.

Littrell, W. B. (1979). *Bureaucratic justice: Police, prosecutors, and plea bargaining*. Newbury Park, CA: Sage.

McCleary, R. (1975). How structural variables constrain the parole officer's use of discretionary powers. *Social Problems, 23*, 209–225.

McCleary, R. (1978). *Dangerous men: The sociology of parole*. Newbury Park, CA: Sage.

McHugh, J. (1973). Some comments on natural conflict between counsel and probation officer. *American Journal of Corrections, 35*, 34–36.

Meyer, M. (1979). Debureaucratization? *Social Science Quarterly, 60*, 25–34.

Petersilia, J., Turner, S., Kahan, J., & Peterson, J. (1985). Executive summary of Rand's study, granting felons probation: Public risks and alternatives. *Crime & Delinquency, 31*, 379–392.

Presthus, R. (1962). *The organizational society: An analysis and a theory*. New York: Knopf.

Presthus, R. (1978). *The organizational society* (Rev. ed.). New York: St. Martin's.

Pugh, D. S., Hickson, D. J., & Hinings, C. R. (1985). *Writers on organizations*. Newbury Park, CA: Sage.

Reiss, A. J. (1974). Discretionary justice. In D. Glaser (Ed.), *Handbook of criminology* (pp. 679–704). Chicago: Rand McNally.

Rosecrance, J. (1985). The probation officers' search for credibility: Ball park recommendations. *Crime & Delinquency, 31*, 539–554.

Rosett, A., & Cressey, D. R. (1976). *Justice by consent*. New York: Lippincott.

Scott, W. R. (1965). Field methods in the study of organizations. In R. E. L. Fairs (Ed.), *Handbook of organizations* (pp. 485–529). Chicago: Rand McNally.

Scott, W. R. (1981). *Organizations: Rational, natural and open systems*. Englewood Cliffs, NJ: Prentice-Hall.

Shover, N. (1979). *A sociology of American corrections*. Homewood, IL: Dorsey.

Tepperman, L. (1973). The effect of court size on organization and procedure. *Canadian Review of Sociology and Anthropology, 10*, 346–365.

Terkel, S. (1975). *Working*. New York: Avon.

Walker, S. (1985). *Sense and nonsense about crime*. Monterey, CA: Brooks/Cole.

Udy, S. (1959). Bureaucracy and rationality in Weber's organizational theory: An empirical study. *American Sociological Review, 24*, 791–795.

12

Diversity in Blue
Lesbian and Gay Police Officers in a Masculine Occupation

SUSAN L MILLER, KAY B. FOREST, AND NANCY C. JURIK

The struggle for social acceptance and equal rights for lesbian and gay Americans has been a long one. Recent battles over laws that would specifically prohibit hate crimes, the legality of same-gender marriages, the adoption and custody of children by gay and lesbian couples, and a wide range of state-level antigay and antilesbian initiatives have garnered massive public attention. The widely publicized debate over gays in the military also aroused intense sentiments both supportive of and opposed to the expansion of the rights for gays and lesbians in the workplace. Despite controversy and numerous setbacks, lesbians and gay men are now more visible to mainstream America, have come "out" in political leadership, and forcefully challenge old barriers (Harvard Law Review 1990; Marcus 1992).[1]

Social institutions have varied tremendously in their acceptance of gays and lesbians. The criminal justice system is still dominated by a white, masculine, and heterosexual ethos (Messerschmidt 1993). As threats to dominant groups, people of color and/or women seeking police positions faced tremendous obstacles (Martin and Jurik 1996). Racist (Leinen 1984; Christopher et al. 1991) and sexist (Martin 1980, 1990; Pike 1991) attitudes and behavior remain a problem in many departments.[2] Employment of lesbians and gay males as police officers is especially threatening to an occupation that values "traditional masculinity and middle-class morality" (Shilts 1980).

This article explores how gay and lesbian police officers construct their identities within a traditionally masculine, heterosexually dominated police organizational environment. Through this exploratory study, we hope to gen-

Susan L. Miller, Kay B. Forest, and Nancy J. Jurik, *Men and Masculinities*, Vol. 5, pp. 355–385, © 2003 by Sage Publications. Reprinted by permission of Sage Publications.

erate hypotheses and theory that will be useful in future research efforts. In the first section of the article, we discuss our conceptual framework, which posits the social construction of identities along gender, sexual orientation, racial, and ethnic lines. This "doing" of identity occurs within specific organizational and societal contexts. Work environments such as policing are gendered, sexualized, and racialized. Such environments shape gay/lesbian officers' construction of identities and shape their strategies for confronting potentially hostile work environments.

After discussing our framework, we turn to an analysis of survey data from gay and lesbian police officers. Our data draw from a series of open-ended questions designed to address gay and lesbian officers' perceptions of (1) stereotypes surrounding gender identity and sexual orientation, (2) the working environment, and (3) their strategies for coping with workplace barriers. The survey also explored the ways in which multiple identities of race, ethnicity, gender, and other dimensions contribute to officers' choices of the "best" strategies for doing their jobs and surviving a hostile organizational milieu.

The Social Construction of Gender and Sexuality in Work Organizations

We conceptualize gender and sexuality to be integrally connected parts of human identity. Along the lines of Candace West and Don Zimmerman (1987) and others (e.g., Connell 1987; Lorber and Farrell 1991; West and Fenstermaker 1993; Messerschmidt 1993; Martin and Jurik 1996), we view these identity components as ongoing social productions that emerge through social interaction. Moreover, individuals "do gender" and simultaneously "do sexuality" with an awareness of dominant societal norms and in anticipation of the judgments of others (West and Zimmerman 1987, 127; West and Fenstermaker 1995; Omi and Winant 1994; Messerschmidt 1997). Thus, identities are accomplished in everyday social interactions framed by larger social structures (Giddens 1979, 1984).

Robert Connell (1993) wrote that some images of gender—in particular, hegemonic masculinity and emphasized femininity—predominate over others. Hegemonic masculinity is most closely associated with the ideal mode of conduct for elite, white men in Western capitalist society. It is based on authority, aggressiveness, technical competence, and heterosexist desire for and domination over women (p. 615). In contrast, emphasized femininity is defined by and subordinate to hegemonic masculinity. It is organized around themes of heterosexual receptivity to men, dependence, and motherhood, and is most readily associated with middle- and upper-class white women in Western societies. In this regard, predominate images of gender implicitly include other social dimensions, including race, ethnicity, class, sexuality, and physical ability/disability, to name a few.

Together, gender, sexual orientation, and other dimensions of social difference serve as organizing features of work organizations (Connell 1987;

Martin and Jurik 1996; Britton 1997). As such, work organizations are sites of the social production of difference. Joan Acker (1990) argued that organizational policies and interactions control, segregate, exclude, and construct hierarchies of workers. Qualifications for particular jobs are infused with conscious and unconscious images of the appropriate gender, race, ethnicity, class, and sexual orientation of the "winning" applicant. Individuals who deviate from the prescribed social type for their job and/or organization may confront formidable barriers to successful work performance. Rosabeth Moss Kanter (1977) identified several such structural barriers.[3] Socially deviant workers are more visible than those of the dominant social type. Their performance is subject to intense scrutiny, and they must excel to be deemed competent. Members of the dominant social group may exclude deviant types, remind them of their difference, or stereotype them (Kanter 1977). Organizational practices and policies also may restrict the work assignments and organizational power allocated to deviant social types (see Martin 1980; Jurik 1985). Job expectations and performance evaluations often reflect the dominant social type; to succeed, deviant types must emulate the socially dominant category (Zimmer 1987).

Not surprisingly, norms of heterosexuality permeate most work organizations, especially those in the criminal justice system (Messerschmidt. 1993; Cockburn 1991; Buhrke 1996). Policing, in particular, "is defined culturally as an activity only 'masculine men' can accomplish" (Messerschmidt 1993, 175). This masculinity depends on the devaluation of all femininities as well as subordinated masculinities, including "gay masculinities" (Connell 1992). Historically, police work has been associated with images of working-class masculinity that emphasize physical strength and aggressiveness. Thus, the dominant ideal of police masculinity typically deviates from modern hegemonic masculinity, which emphasizes managerial and technical dominance. This hegemonic ideal is most closely associated with the behavior of elite white men (see Messerschmidt 1993; Jurik and Martin 2001).

Police Organizational Culture

Since the rise of American crime fighting in the 1930s, police departments have been white, working-class male enclaves (see Miller 1999; Appier 1992, 1998; Martin and Jurik 1996; Schulz 1995). White women were also present in this early history. In fact, the early police matron's movement was initiated during the social reform era of the nineteenth century. Early policewomen were associated with social service and crime prevention models of policing (Appier 1992). Yet their duties focused on the traditional female roles of service, nurturing, and protecting morals and virtues; as such, they did not threaten male police officers' terrain (Schulz 1995; Miller 1999).

In contrast to the police matron, the ideal male police officer emerged in the early decades of the twentieth century as the tough, fearless calorimeter, "the fierce warrior-robot, devoid of emotions. . . . Policemen relied on technology, expertise in marksmanship, and their courage to bring criminals to justice" (Miller 1999, 83; Appier 1992). Over time, policing recruitment and selection practices effectively excluded outsiders. These included physical requirements (to exclude women), written tests or educational requirements (to exclude blacks), and "background investigations and personal interviews [that) further screen out candidates who failed to express the 'correct' attitudes toward the meaning of masculinity, including an aura of toughness and aggressiveness" (David and Brannon 1976, quoted in Martin 1992, 286).

The relegation of white female officers to peripheral reform activities continued until the 1970s. At this time the Johnson administration urged police departments to increase hiring racial minority, female, and college-educated officers for patrol, vice, and investigative divisions (Miller 1999). In succeeding years, a growing number of gay men and lesbians also entered the policing ranks (Meers 1998; Miller 1999). As of 1992, ten departments directly recruited gay and lesbian officers: Boston, Minneapolis, Madison, Seattle, Portland, Atlanta, Philadelphia, San Francisco, Los Angeles, and New York City (Leinen 1993, 11). Chicago has also initiated efforts to recruit officers in gay and lesbian communities.

Policing Sexualities: Chilly Climate Control

In combination, reform and resistance can be understood as tensions in the social production of difference within police organizational culture, especially the construction of subordinate masculinities and emphasized femininity. As the number of outsiders increased within policing, the stable production of hegemonic masculinity was challenged and triggered the hostility of many traditional white male officers (Hunt 1990).

The hiring of men of color became one of the first challenges to the all-white male work organization. As a group, men of color, especially African Americans, are still likely to be suspected of criminal activity by the police, and are highly likely to be arrested and prosecuted (Coleman and Cressey 1999). Thus, their arrival on the police force contradicted a long-held antagonism between the hegemonic crime fighter and the subordinated criminal. Not surprisingly, policemen of color have struggled against exclusion, harassment, and limited advancement (Buhrke 1996; Alex 1969). In addition, reform professionalization strategies also increased the number of more highly educated officers from middle-class backgrounds (Jurik and Martin 2001), a practice that challenged the working-class dimension of police culture. On both counts, outsiders have now made inroads into police organizations.

When women were integrated into patrol jobs, the traditional association of police work with masculinity was further threatened (Martin 1992; Hunt 1984, 1990). Women's presence has been met with covert and overt hostility. Policemen try to create differences between themselves and female officers by emphasizing women's "femininity" (Messerschmidt 1993, 182). Yet women are not treated uniformly. For example, white male officers might attempt to shield white women from the dangers of the job, while black women may not be accorded such protections (Martin 1994). Suspected lesbians may also be treated with less protection and increased hostilities (Judge speaks out 2000; Martin and Jurik 1996). As a result lesbians may feel pressured to demonstrate their conformity to ideals of emphasized femininity in order to avoid animosity (Schneider 1988).

Gender and sexual identities are closely intertwined in their production. In particular, an emphasis on sexuality serves as a significant component of gender subordination: "Enforced heterosexuality has been identified as a primary mechanism for subordinating women at home and at work" (Rich 1980, 633; Cockburn 1991). In part because police departments regulate heterosexuality in society, they exude exceptionally strong norms of compulsory heterosexuality. Female police officers may endure questions about (or charges regarding) their sexual orientation. For example, according to a 1998 study by the National Center for Women and Policing, 80 percent of female police officers have been sexually harassed at work, including explicit lesbian-baiting and lewd commentary by male colleagues (Purported male deputies 1999; Judge speaks out 2000). Still other "women [officers] have been threatened with death, falsely accused of crimes like child abuse and drug violations, and alienated from colleagues" (Women face 1999).

Masculinity is further traditionally conferred on male officers through the policing of gay men, especially because police often view hate crimes committed against homosexuals as "harmless pranks or as an acceptable form of behavior" (Berrill 1992, 31). Gay bashing by police symbolically confirms a police officer's heterosexual status. Again, this gendered aspect of policing permits the police to "construct a white, heterosexual, hegemonic masculinity through the authorized practice of controlling 'deviant' behavior of 'inferior' men," practices which leave little room for the legitimization of other sexualities (Messerschmidt 1993, 184).

In fact, until recently, being an openly gay or lesbian officer meant dismissal from the job (Doss 1990). The daily reality of conventional policing, as part of a gendered and a sexualized institution, entails homosociality—"men generating a closeness between men" for informing, socializing, and mentoring (Britton 1990; Cockburn 1991, 189). Any suggestion of traditionally "feminine" traits, such as gentleness or sensitivity, encourages colleagues to brand men as "sissies" or "faggots" (Blumenfeld 1992). Thus, questioning a worker's sexual orientation is a common tactic for devaluing the actions of male workers who fail to conform to popular macho models; those who favor police reforms or who support the inclusion of female officers may be denigrated and labeled homosexuals by defensive male coworkers (Martin and Jurik 1996). Closeted gay men may likewise feel pressure to engage in conversational banter with coworkers about heterosexual conquests to avoid being ostracized or labeled sexually suspect (Remmington 1981; Messner 1992; Messerschmidt 1993). Because racial subordination is intertwined with gender and sexual subordination, problems in the workplace associated with being gay or lesbian may be intensified for men and women of color (Rosabal 1996; Buhrke 1996).

Overall, homosexual police officers—regardless of race, ethnicity, or gender—are subordinated by the production of hegemonic masculinity (Connell 1987; Messerschmidt 1993). In this regard, lesbian and gay officers face barriers similar to those confronting racial-ethnic minorities and white women in policing, yet there are important differences (Leinen 1993; Buhrke 1996). Research suggests that homosexuals are the social group most disliked by police (Burke 1994). Such beliefs persist despite empirical evidence that lesbians and gay men perform police work as well as heterosexuals (Hiatt and Hargrave 1994). It is also still legal to deny employment on the basis of sexual orientation in most jurisdictions.[4]

With twenty-four states still criminalizing consensual same-gender sexual acts, gay and lesbian officers also occupy the ironic position of having to enforce penal codes that they themselves violate (Doss 1990; Leinen 1993). The hiring of lesbian and gay officers suggests to some that the "immoral behavior" of practicing homosexuals is condoned.[5] As a result, lesbians, gay men, and their allies in criminal justice fear for their jobs and sometimes even their lives (Buhrke 1996).

Workplace Strategies and Resistance: "Out" and "Closeted"

Gay and lesbian officers' adjustment to police or any other work is complicated by the issue of whether they will hide their sexual orientation (Schneider 1986; Taylor and Raeburn 1995; Woods 1993). As indicated earlier, some "closeted" gay and lesbian workers attempt to pass as heterosexual on the job (Burke 1994; Leinen 1993). Others may "come out" and openly define themselves as homosexual to varying degrees (Woods 1993). In fact, during the past twenty-five years, changes in police organizations have created some opportunities for gay and lesbian officers to work in "out" statuses in police departments. Recently, the formation of gay and lesbian police associations has challenged the compulsory heterosexuality of police organizations and police treatment of the gay and lesbian communities (Burke 1994; Buhrke 1996). These ongoing changes, in turn, inform the perceptions and strategies of gay/lesbian officers working within the police organizational context (Lamphere et al. 1993; Britton 1995).

The decision to be "out" as well as other workplace strategies is shaped not only by an individual's social location (e.g., gender, race, ethnicity) but also by situational factors, such as time on the job (Rosabal 1996). Organizational and community climates of support or hostility for gay/lesbian rights also shape individual and collective strategies for constructing sexual identity (Buhrke 1996; Bernstein 1997). For example, fears about coworker and supervisor hostilities, termination, loss of promotional opportunity, or denial of backup lead some officers to hide their sexual orientation (Burke 1994; Leinen 1993; Buhrke 1996). Tensions between the police and lesbian/gay communities encourage some officers to hide their occupation from gay/lesbian friends and acquaintances (Burke 1994). In either ease, hiding consumes energy, creates stress, and can erode job productivity (Powers 1996). And being "out" is not necessarily freedom from workplace stress but may encourage further self-consciousness and overachievement (Officer friendly Forthcoming).

The arguments surrounding the "explicit" inclusion of homosexuals on the police force are complex. Opponents of gay and lesbian officers claim that respect for police would decrease and that department morale would be harmed. They claim that heterosexual officers might not assist homosexual officers in danger and that unwanted sexual attention from gay officers might be forced on nongays (see Shilts 1980; DeMila 1978). Proponents of gay male and lesbian hiring argue that sexual orientation is unrelated to competent job performance. They propose that once gay and lesbian officers prove their abilities they will be accepted by their peers—as were white women and racial-ethnic minorities (Martin 1992)—and that police forces should reflect the diversity of the community (Shilts 1980; DeMila 1978). Some argue that gay and lesbian officers promote improved relations between police and the homosexual community, even though after decades of gay bashing and repression by police, many in the homosexual community view gay and lesbian officers to be traitors (Buhrke 1996).

In the absence of protective federal legislation, some courts have ruled in favor of gay/lesbian employment rights (Buhrke 1996, 20). Despite continuing organizational pressures, these changes have provided an opening for workers to resist the pressures of hegemonic police masculinity or emphasized femininity. Some workers may consciously or unconsciously construct masculinities or femininities that oppose dominant ideals such as openly opposing macho, tough-guy styles of policing, or opposing men's protection of female officers. Others may conform to dominant ideals or develop identities that are more covertly oppositional.

It should be noted as well that traditional masculinist police culture is not without its costs. Between 1990 and 1999, for example, the city of Los Angeles paid out $63.4 million for lawsuits involving excessive force, sexual assault, and domestic violence by male police officers (Gender differences 2000). National and international studies of police brutality show similar patterns (Scandal highlights need 2000). As more police departments explore the benefits of community policing models, the inclusion of gay and lesbian police officers may represent more than a human rights effort; these nontraditional police officers may bring a range of roles and skills that can enhance the flexibility of police work without sacrificing its crime-fighting mission.

The Present Study: Gay and Lesbian Policing in a Midwestern City

In 1992, the new police superintendent of the Midwestern Police Department promised zero tolerance for insensitivity to and discrimination against lesbian and gay police officers; he also actively recruited gay men and lesbians (Griffin 1992). Within this supportive environment and with the culmination of almost a year of informal planning, the only two "out" homosexuals on the Midwestern police force—joined by two "closeted" police officers—formed a gay and lesbian police officers' association. The association's goals are to provide support for other gay and lesbian police officers, develop a recruiting program for "out" gay and lesbian officers, educate heterosexual officers, dispel the fears of members of the gay and lesbian community about police officers, and improve police-community relations. Although all four founding members were from the Midwestern City Police Department, membership in the Lesbian and Gay Police Alliance (LGPA) is open to law enforcement officers across the state. The formation of this coalition parallels the efforts of lesbians and gay men in other police departments and occupations (Taylor and Raeburn 1995; Burke 1994; Buhrke 1996).

This research first examines how police organizational climates inform workplace perceptions and experiences of gay and lesbian officers. Second, it describes how gay and lesbian officers produce policing identities and perceive that their multiple identities affect job performance. Third, it discusses different strategies or levels of being "out" and how these strategies affect officers' perceptions of inclusion and exclusion, including multiple identities of gender, race, and ethnicity.

Method

Data Collection

This study uses a sample of gay and lesbian police officers ($n = 17$) working in a large Midwestern city that has twelve thousand police officers. To make contact with gay and lesbian officers, we approached the cofounder and current codirector of the LGPA in the Midwestern Police Department with our ideas. She agreed to assist us in distributing the survey to all law enforcement members of the LGPA ($n = 25$). She also vouched for our support, objectivity, and sensitivity, which may have played a part in generating such strong cooperation from the members. Although there are currently fifty members of the LGPA, only twenty-five are police officers from the Midwestern Police Department; the remainder are from suburbs and other cities and towns in the state, as well as a few members from other Midwestern states. Thus, the sample was not randomly selected; individuals volunteered to participate. All data were gathered through survey questions rather than by direct observation. The in-depth nature of the questionnaire resulted in respondents offering a [more] vast amount of material than would have been gained if the survey were close-ended. To fully capture the extent of gay and lesbian officers' perceptions, beliefs, and experiences, we designed a twenty-two page questionnaire consisting of primarily open-ended questions. Questions addressed officers' perceptions about stereotypes surrounding gender identity and sexual orientation, officers' working environment, and officers' strategies for coping with workplace barriers.[6]

There was ample space for responses, and the respondents were encouraged to provide as much detail as they wished. We provided the home phone number of one of the authors in case a respondent felt reluctant about participation and needed reassurance. We also asked the respondents to provide their phone numbers if they felt comfortable being contacted by us for clarification purposes. Five respondents did include their numbers and were contacted by one of the authors to provide further information on topics that were unclear or incomplete.[7]

Respondents answered the questions with very lengthy discussions. We also maintained contact with the gay male and lesbian cofounders of the LGPA, and they served as cross-check verification on information. We received seventeen completed surveys, giving us a 68 percent completion rate from the Midwestern Police Department members of the LGPA. The sexual orientation of eight officers in our sample is known at work. To assure confidentiality, self-administered questionnaires and postage-paid return envelopes were used, with the guarantee of respondent anonymity.[8] Despite what might seem like a small sample, given the relative rarity of gay and lesbian officers willing to discuss their sexual orientation and careers, the data are invaluable in contributing to our understanding of gay and lesbian police officers. Although there is an inevitable bias presented by using self-report surveys with sensitive populations, even when open-ended questions are constructed, we made every effort to minimize bias by cross-validating information with our (gay) contact officers and telephoning respondents to probe for additional information when we were able to do so. Since our sample includes officers who have varying "out" and "closeted" statuses, as well as varying racial and ethnic identities, we can be reasonably sure that their responses capture the gamut of possibilities among this population.[9] The 68 percent response rate is sufficiently robust, given the sensitive and hidden population (Renzetti 1992).

Sample

Nine lesbian officers completed the questionnaire. Seven are white and two are Latina, and their ages range from twenty-five to forty-two years. Two are single, while seven are engaged in long-term live-in relationships with their partners. Eight women indicated that they had some college education, and one had received a BA. Together, they have had between two and thirteen years of experience on the Midwestern police force, and all except one has served in the capacity of patrol officer.

Eight gay male police officers also completed the questionnaire. Three are white, one is black, three are Latino, and one is Asian. Their ages range from thirty to forty. Two officers are single, while the remaining six are in long-term live-in relationships with their partners. Four officers completed some college, two have associate's degrees, one graduated from a four-year college, and another has completed a master's degree and is continuing with additional postgraduate study. All together, they have between one and twenty-six years of experience on the police force, and all served in the capacity of patrol officers (although two have achieved a rank above patrol officer positions). We discuss the degrees to which officers' sexual orientation was known in the police department in the findings section.

Findings

In this section, we discuss our analysis of gay and lesbian officers' open-ended survey responses. Our discussion focuses on (1) respondents' orientation to the job, including their perceived reception and experiences within the police organizational culture; (2) how gay and lesbian officers produce policing identities; and (3) how different job strategies or levels of being "out" affect officers' perceptions of inclusion and exclusion across multiple identities of gender, race, and ethnicity.

Experiencing the Police Organizational Culture

Policing is traditionally gendered and sexualized. As such, police culture typically embraces symbols of aggressive masculinity, such as toughness and physical strength, which are reinforced by practices that also confirm an officer's heterosexual status (Blumenfeld 1992; Burke 1994; Messerschmidt 1993). The latter can include dominating behaviors toward women and various forms of gay bashing, such as ridicule and overt harassment. Yet the more recent inclusion of outsiders within policing has challenged this hegemonic masculine solidarity and generated tensions between traditional police officers and those who represent reform efforts. The organizational reforms mandating zero tolerance of discrimination in this particular department have provided an avenue for officers to more openly challenge and question hegemonic masculinity and its links to police work.

Our sample responses indicate that most gay and lesbian officers experience what Kanter (1977) referred to as the increased visibility of minorities in work organizations; they are constantly scrutinized by others around them. In addition, the socially dominant group—in this case, heterosexuals—may try to establish boundaries between themselves and gay/lesbian officers through techniques of exclusion or verbal reminders of difference and subordinating stereotypes about their social category.

Every officer in the sample indicated that they had heard or been the target of antigay or lesbian jokes or derogatory slang and that they had seen antigay graffiti or cartoons around the station house, particularly in the locker room or on bulletin boards. Most of the "out" officers said that they had been excluded from "the grapevine" gossip, and they had not been invited to informal social activities, parties, or events. One "out" gay male officer (Wayne) explained, "Sometimes I'm excluded from social circles because some coworkers are uncomfortable about me being gay or are afraid of saying the wrong thing around me. Sometimes they treat me like I am sick." "Closeted" officers described their concern about how their current friendships and working relationships would suffer if their coworkers found out they were gay:

> Many of the guys I like at work are ardent followers of Rush Limbaugh and make anti-gay comments on an almost daily basis. I would be ostracized. (Cody)

"Closeted" officers also seemed to feel pressured to conform to models of hegemonic masculinity:

> On the surface, it appears that most of my colleagues are either married or think that they are a gift to women. Most of that (straight) pressure is very uncomfortable because if I don't join in I would be viewed with suspicion. (Tim)

To demonstrate conformity to the dominant police culture, many officers utilized boundary maintenance activities: "And, as you well know, everyone wants to be accepted and if making fun of gay people gets you accepted, then you make fun of them" (Kelly). The frequency of such activities suggests that social-cultural diversity of any sort is not easily tolerated in most police departments (Martin and Jurik 1996; Leinen 1993); as one of our respondents said, "Anytime someone is different in any way, police officers tend to ridicule them" (Rosa). However, two gay male officers seemed to believe that once individual gay or lesbian officers became known and respected, other officers might become more aware and show tolerance:

> Most speak from fear or lack of information. They say the things they say to conform to the larger group. If most knew about me, I think they would change their thinking after some soul-searching. (Gene)

In analyzing the stereotypes held by their straight coworkers, respondents linked the police organization context to larger societal patterns:

> Their homophobia forms a framework which negatively affects how they view everything gays or lesbians do or say. However, that's true for society as a whole. Police officers are products of our society and reflect society's ignorances [sic] and prejudices. (Wayne)

Lesbian officers were asked if they thought it was harder to break into the male world of policing or into the heterosexual world of policing. All of the respondents felt it was more difficult to break into the male world, particularly when there are still older men on the force who remember when most police were men. All of the lesbian officers' responses suggested that, as one officer put it, "The good ol' boys' network still runs smoothly" (Jen).

> I feel it is much harder to break into the male world of policing. I think a lot of men become police officers for some sort of macho trip. The fact that women can then do the same job is a slap in the face. Misogyny is alive and well in our culture and the police culture is no different. (Michelle)

Some lesbian officers felt a common bond with heterosexual women in combating sexism on the force:

> It is the male world that most females have a problem with, whether gay or straight, this job in particular invites a macho-man attitude. It is a fact that men receive more privileges and receive a higher rating for the same job. A female on this job must do twice as much to prove herself. (Kelly)

Barriers to promotional opportunities have been a frequent problem for social minority groups in policing. We asked our sample of gay and lesbian officers if they felt that promotions were made using the same criteria as promotions for heterosexual officers, or if there would be any difference in the process because of sexual orientation. There was considerable variation in officers' perception about promotional opportunities and the best strategy for obtaining them. In fact, the officers in the Midwestern Police Department recommended a variety of strategies across the lines of rank, seniority, and gay versus "out" status. Half of the officers believed that being "out" could have a direct and negative effect on promotions. As one officer put it, "The 'don't ask, don't tell' policy works if you are seeking rank" (Tim). Another gay male officer, Jake, said, "You have to be married or perceived as marriageable to be promoted. They believe you can't be led by a fag."

In contrast, about one-third of the officers believed that advancement opportunities might be enhanced for gay and lesbian officers in certain contexts, although they disagreed on the exact nature of the context in which opportunities were enhanced: "Advancement chances may be better because 'out' gay/lesbian officers will be more visible and probably move up faster, so the superintendent can say, 'look, I've promoted gays/lesbians' for visibility" (Annie). One gay male officer (Michael) said, "It may actually be better since I'm the only "out" gay in my district and I understand people are 'afraid' of me because I am out and do my job well. So, politically, for the department, promoting me may 'look good.'" Several respondents indicated that advancement opportunities would compare similarly with heterosexuals only if an officer was publicly known to be gay or lesbian because then the department might face public pressure from the gay and lesbian community if the gay officer was not promoted simply because of his or her sexual orientation. However, the pattern that emerged from the responses suggests that the officers who believed that advancement chances were similar for gays and straights were primarily officers who had fewer years of experience as police officers, were assigned to desk duties, were not "out" to their coworkers, or had the longest amount of time on the force before coming "out." Thus, this perception may be based on ignorance or lack of experience.

In their assessments of workplace interactions, these officers point to the ways that the relationships between hegemonic and subordinate masculinities are maintained within police culture. Widespread ridicule of "others" is used to solidify power relations among dominant heterosexual males (Kaufman 1998). In this context, being a "closeted" gay officer thus becomes the most subordinate masculinity, silenced by the threat implicit in homophobia humor and exclusion by the collective masculinity (Connell 1998). Paradoxically, "out" gay and lesbian officers may have increased power due to shifts in organizational hiring priorities; however, our data suggest that this power is relative and based more on speculation than reality. Also noteworthy is the fact that all of the lesbian officers saw the male world, and not compulsory heterosexuality, as the greater barrier to advancement.

Overall, many of these lesbian and gay officers believed that their socially deviant statuses influenced assessments of their policing skills held by other officers. Such influence could work either negatively or positively for the gay or lesbian officer. Literature assessing the performance of minority social groups in the workplace consistently uses the performance of those in the majority social group as a baseline of comparison for new entrants (Zimmer 1987). The following section, however, reveals the extent to which there were considerable variations among gay and lesbian officers in constructing their policing identities.

Performance Strengths and Pressures: Producing Policing Identities

Within our sample, officer sexual orientation and gender were closely intertwined salient features of the social construction of policing identities. Like arguments made by Patricia Hill Collins (1990) who critiqued "either/or" dichotomous thinking and called for a "both/and" approach, officers in our sample viewed themselves and their job performance as similar to and different from heterosexual officers. For some, these differences include unique abilities derived from the hard lessons of social marginalization.

Because not all of our sample was "out" on the job, the visibility issue is not the same as those surrounding race, ethnicity, and gender minority statuses. In cases of "closeted" officers, visibility concerns have more to do with fear of coworker suspicions regarding their sexual orientation. Sexual suspicions are pervasive in police work, especially for female officers of any sexual orientation (Martin 1980). "If a female works with a female, then the other police officers may think they're both gay" (Kelly).

Lesbian officers described sexism as well as homophobia as creating barriers to their success in policing. They heard heterosexual officers make statements about the problems a lesbian officer might face when searching female suspects, including accusations of sexual harassment if the citizens were cognizant of the officer's lesbian identity. A few lesbian officers felt that, despite the sexism they must combat on the force, they could more easily gain acceptance as "out" lesbians than could "out" gay men. As Rosa, a "closeted" female officer summarized, "The guys already assume you're gay if you are a woman who wants to be a police officer, so you should just focus on being the best officer you can be." Another lesbian officer said,

> I know male cops who work with me willingly but [who] quite honestly state that if I was a gay man, they couldn't work with me. It still comes down to straight men being terrified of gay men. (Michelle)

Two "out" gay male officers disagreed. They felt that "out" gay men were more easily accepted by straight male officers than were "out" lesbian officers. As Jake, a fully "out" gay officer suggests, "There's still the male bond; my police partner and I both talk about our dates in the same way, even though he is straight."

In contrast, most gay male officers believed that once their sexual orientation was known, they had or would have much difficulty proving that they were sufficiently tough for the job. In other words, their masculinity was questioned. One officer said that if his sexual orientation was known, he would have to "work twice as hard to be considered half as good" (Gene). Another officer explained that he had established his reputation as a tough cop before he revealed that he was gay. He said that stereotypes of effeminate gay men would negatively influence other officers' assessments of his policing abilities if the first piece of information they had about him were that he was gay. Still another officer argued that all officers, regardless of gender and sexual orientation, had to establish "masculinity" on the job:

> Not necessarily harder, but certainly necessary to prove [masculinity] nonetheless . . . but this may be true for *any* new cop, gay or straight, male or female. (Michael)

Thus, proving masculinity was a recurrent theme in our responses. Respondents perceived that there was little room for alternative or oppositional forms of masculinity. Yet one man, Jake, who conformed to some key aspects of hegemonic masculinity, felt that he had little problem in this regard: "I am quite big, athletic, and it is known that I will take no shit and can physically back that up." It may be that Jake's conformity to some dimensions of police hegemonic masculinity (i.e., his sheer size, physical strength, and aggressive qualities) offers some shield against challenges to his masculinity.

Despite concerns about gender and sexual identities on the job, the lesbian and gay officers in our sample believed that they were highly effective on the job; they also felt that they brought unique abilities to policing. In related research, studies on the integration of men of color and women into police work find that they perform similarly to and as well as white male officers (Morash and Green 1986; Alex 1969). Some researchers argue further that, by virtue of their marginal or oppressed status in society, the pool of new entrants bring "special" talents and insights to police work that will improve services to victims and offenders and promote better police-community relations (Crites 1973; Alex 1969).

Our respondents were asked whether they believe gay and lesbian officers use any different methods to accomplish policing goals (such as crime fighting, crime prevention and deterrence, maintaining order, and providing public safety and service). They emphasized that all police officers—regardless of sexual orientation—are taught the same methods at the academy; these methods are subsequently reinforced on street patrol. There was no disagreement about general policing goals. This uniformity in responses is consistent with the loyalty to the police occupation and subculture that so typically characterizes police officers (Skolnick 1994).

Yet greater visibility and boundary maintenance may also stimulate a heightened performance pressure to "prove" that gay and lesbian officers (the social minority) can do the job as well as social dominants—in this case, as heterosexuals. Many officers described themselves as perfectionists or over-achievers, stating that they worked harder on the job so that their performance would be above scrutiny or so their effectiveness would not be challenged if their sexual orientation were to become known.

> The gay cops I know are mostly more dedicated to the job. I think it's because they have to be above criticism. (Cody)

> I think in a way [they are] even more effective because they are always aware of themselves. They don't tend to take things for granted. Always trying to do better so that their sexuality doesn't interfere with their performance as a police officer. (Kelly)

Although the above performance assessments represent the officers' own perception, all of the lesbian officers and seven of the eight gay male officers in our sample reported that they have received rewards, honors, or special recognition for their work in policing. Two officers (one male and one female) were valedictorians of their police academy classes. According to our contact on the force, it is fairly common for officers to receive honorable mentions (e.g., reflecting solid, good police work in making burglary or robbery arrests) and letters of commendation. The officers in our sample, however, received more infrequently awarded honors, such as the outstanding community service award, various commendations for taking actions beyond the call of duty, lifesaving award, and the class commander in academy (meaning that the officers achieved the highest academic standing in their group). Such information lends additional credence to their overall performance assessments. It is not clear, however, that work performance strengths translate into formal work rewards, particularly for "out" gay males and lesbians (see Croteau and Lark 1995; Levine and Leonard 1984).

More explicit differences were raised when the gay and lesbian officers were asked if they bring any unique abilities, skills, and life experiences to the job of policing. Their perceptions of differences covered two categories: dealing with the general citizenry and dealing specifically with gay and lesbian citizens.

> I believe if gay or lesbian officers have a political consciousness and understand the dynamics of homophobia and bigotry, they can bring a certain sensitivity and patience to the job. (Michelle)

> Being a "minority" you see both sides of the coin. And if you work in the gay community, citizens will explain more to you than they would to a straight cop. (Jake)

Three of the officers in our sample were members of citizen-police liaisons within the gay and lesbian community, including groups focused on hate-bias crime reporting prior to joining the police force. In dealings with the general public, respondents believed that their own experiences of marginalization provide them with increased sensitivity and tolerance. They believed that, relative to most heterosexual officers, they were better able to transcend strict gender role dichotomies and meet the needs of a diverse citizenry more effectively.

> I believe that knowing how a society can push you aside and not care about you helps especially when dealing with lower income families and minorities, in general. (Jen)

> As an "out" gay cop I know first-hand the feeling of being oppressed and victimized. Not only will I do the job well, but it will be done compassionately (within reasonable limits). . . . I think by virtue of my personality and gayness I bring more efficacy to public relations as "a cop who cares." (Michael)

As several gay male officers stated, "Gay people who have come to terms with being gay are survivors—we have had to struggle against the norms and are stronger, more independent people because of it" (Wayne), and "We bring a rich life experience different in a host of ways from straight folks that enable us to deal with the public in our own unique way" (Charlie).

Even as lesbian and gay officers bring unique strengths to policing, they may also have to adjust their workplace behaviors to compensate for homophobic tensions and a persistent degree of exclusion by heterosexual coworkers (Powers 1996). We asked our respondents if their sexual orientation inhibits their job performance. Noting that heterosexual officers also made statements that suggest the danger of lesbian and gay officers being around children, one lesbian officer remarked, "Heterosexual people are of the opinion that gay people are sick, loose, and have no morals (even though most pedophiles are heterosexual)" (Kelly). Gay male police officers echoed some of these concerns: "I'm cautious about being alone with kids for fear of misconduct accusations by malicious coworkers" (Jake). And as Michael says, "Fear of contracting AIDS is very real in the police community and gay officers are sometimes treated as though we're all plague carriers."

Officers utilized a variety of strategies for survival in the police organization. The opportunities and selection of these alternatives are often intertwined with rank, seniority, gender, and racial-ethnic dimensions of policing identities. Organizational and community climates also serve to shape differing opportunities for and choices of strategies in doing police work. Perhaps the greatest variations can be seen in the constructions of "out" versus "closeted" identities. In the following section, the constraints of police hegemonic masculinity on the expression of alternative sexualities become most evident.

Survival Strategies and Resistance

The choice of "out" or "closeted" status in the department is not a mutually exclusive dichotomy. Being "closeted" or "out" is more of a continuum of openness with considerable variability from one individual to the next. All of the lesbian officers in our sample said that their sexual orientation was known to other gay or lesbian officers but that they were more protective of this information with heterosexual officers on the force. Two lesbian officers indicated that their sexual orientation has been complete public information on the police force since the beginning of their careers (at the training academy).

Three other officers indicated that their sexual orientation is known to only some people for the past two or three years; these are also the three women who have served the longest as police officers, spending at least half of their careers "closeted." It may be that they already had established their reputations as competent officers prior to coming "out" as lesbians. For the remaining four officers, two have not come "out," but believe some coworkers are beginning to suspect (one of these officers indicated that she would like to come "out" but does not want to implicate her lover, who is a very "closeted" police officer not in our sample). The other two officers are only "out" to their police patrol partners.

Interesting racial-ethnic differences are also present. The two women of color in our lesbian sample are the most "closeted" to other members of the force, yet they did disclose their sexual orientation to their police partners, who are also women of color and/or lesbian. These officers' reticence to disclose their sexual orientation to any other officer may reflect their triple-minority status on the force: Latina, woman, and lesbian (Rosabal 1996). These multiple disadvantaged statuses may also help explain why the lesbian officers were able to disclose to their police partners, who also had marginalized statuses in the department and therefore might be seen as more trustworthy than the dominant members of the force.

Similar to the lesbian officers, all the gay men acknowledged that their sexual orientation is known to a few other gay or lesbian officers, but it is not necessarily common knowledge in the department at large. In fact, only four of the eight officers indicated their sexual orientation is widely or completely known at work. One of the officers came "out" on his resume when he applied for the job, while one of the other gay officers came "out" after eleven years, another came "out" the first year of his career, and another has been "out" for several years after serving on the force for nine years as a married heterosexual officer.

Again, interesting racial differences emerge. All of the white gay men are completely "out" at work, while four of the five men of color are closeted. The only gay man of color whose sexual orientation is public knowledge was also married to a female police officer for many of his early years on the force (and they had children together). These patterns appear to illustrate the hegemonic protections of race and gender. For those who retain protection in either racial status (i.e., white) or former and demonstrated heterosexuality, sexual orientation may be less dangerous to acceptance in police culture.

We asked all gay and lesbian officers who were not "out" to other officers to discuss the risks that surround disclosure of sexual orientation and describe the current climate or working environment (with regard to sexual orientation) they experience. Overwhelmingly, the "closeted" officers stated that the biggest fears that prevent them from coming "out" involve safety and trust issues. Safety issues included the possibilities of being physically or verbally abused, as well as fear that backup would be slow. As half the officers mentioned, "You could get killed because [of] lack of backup if the other officers knew of your sexual orientation" (Ryan). Trust issues included the reactions of coworkers, who would withdraw support and friendship, and the fear that their moral authority in the eyes of the community would diminish. As one fully "closeted" gay male stated, "The weight of any judgment calls or discretionary decisions I made would be diminished by people who disagreed because they would think: 'He's just a fag'" (Cody).

> The guys would treat me differently, especially in the locker room. My current friendships would be detrimentally affected because friends would feel pressure to conform to other officers who have a problem with gays. (Gene)

The psychological costs of a "false front" are extraordinarily high in a job that is already very stressful (see Goffman 1963; Powers 1996). These costs include the belief that "if police officers think they've discovered a secret someone is trying to hide, they can be very cruel—they perceive it as a weakness if you're trying to hide it" (Michelle). All of the closeted officers described the stress of hiding part of their identity and of hiding their significant relationships. The "closeted" lesbian officers were especially fearful of losing the respect of coworkers once their sexual orientation became known, particularly if the coworkers felt that the "closeted" officers had lied to them (see Rosabal 1996). Respondents envied the heterosexual officers who never experienced the burden of having to pretend their private lives did not exist or had no effect on their public lives. Yet the risks of social and professional ostracism seemed too high.

In spite of these fears of revelation, however, the benefits reported by "out" officers, as well as the benefits of being "out" projected by "closeted" officers, are many:

> I am able to talk about my personal life openly. (Paula)

> I can be myself. (Jen)

As has been found in other research (e.g., Burke 1993; Leinen 1993), "out" respondents were pleased to reduce the disjuncture between their work selves and private selves:

> I could stop bringing a "fake date"—like my cousin—to work-sponsored dinners, dances, or parties. . . . The further you advance, the more separate you become unless you have a partner of the opposite sex and therefore "fit in" with the brass. (Lisa)

> Freedom to be me. Freedom to talk about my social life, to flirt with guys I meet on the job—just like the straight men flirt with women, the chance to educate coworkers about what being gay is about. (Wayne)

> I can talk about my lover. I am no longer invisible. I can receive and make phone calls. I can share my life as they [straights] do. (Ben)

Being "out" was also believed to reduce work-related stress:

> You can relax; you are not always worrying about saying something that would give you away as a lesbian. (Annie)

> Being "out" would let me relax and stop hiding who I am. When the subject of significant others comes up, I'm tired of referring to "he" instead of "she." (Rosa)

Although research suggests that the motivations for coming "out" in recent years are often more personal than political (Taylor and Raeburn 1995), several respondents went beyond the personal advantages to discuss the political importance of coming "out" on their job:

> Benefits include helping other gays or lesbians (cops or citizens). I am looked up to for guidance. (Jake)

> They called me to handle the victim of an antigay attack because they knew I was gay. That made my very short (so far) career worthwhile . . . and the victim called brass the following day to thank them for sending me. (Michael)

Despite these advantages, the racial differences and varying seniority among more "out" versus closeted officers suggests the complexity surrounding the decision to come "out" of the closet.

Not surprisingly, there was some tension between "out" and "closeted" officers, particularly when identity ambivalence may encourage "closeted" officers to attempt to normalize behavior to reduce visibility (Burke 1994, 198). The following response speaks clearly to the continuing pressures for some to reproduce hegemonic masculinity and emphasized femininity as a survival strategy:

> The "closeted" gay male officers try to act more macho and tougher and turn me off as a person. "Closeted" lesbians try to act more (hyper) feminine and it's very false looking. These stereotypical appearances hurt all gay officers and make it harder to come "out." (Annie)

Although difference in the construction of "out" and "closeted" identities may create tensions within and among gay and lesbian officer groups, our respondents perceive that the lesbian and gay officer coalition and their department's zero tolerance policy have improved the climate for them within the police force. These organizational-level changes provide gay and lesbian officers with additional avenues for confronting harassment and other workplace barriers. One-third of the officers indicated that, since the new police superintendent's appointment and his publicized zero tolerance policy toward gay and lesbian discrimination, they believed their concerns would be taken more seriously by supervisors, even though homophobic attitudes might remain unchanged. If the climate continues to improve, more officers may feel comfortable with coming "out" to a greater degree.

Despite these perceived improvements, situational context and harassers' status within the department still shaped the decision to report or not to report an incident: "It depends on who was doing the harassing . . . if it was an officer who already has a reputation for being a 'dog,' the other officers would probably be supportive of you. However, if the harasser was a well-liked officer, it could alienate other officers from you" (Michelle). The fear of retaliation also influences reporting decisions: "If you reported harassment from coworkers to supervisors, the harassment would stop but then you'd get no back-up" (Ryan).

Discussion

In this article, using a sample of "out" and "closeted" gay and lesbian police officers, we explored officers' perceptions about how their sexual orientation affects their success in a hypermasculine subculture and occupation. Overall, our findings indicate that these officers sense patterns of social exclusion as well as overt sexist and antigay behavior within the police organization. At the same time, the data also support a profile of our respondents as loyal to the police profession, committed to many traditional police goals, and striving to be recognized as competent officers within the organization. Finally, these officers support a caring and humane approach to policing and see themselves as particularly qualified to work within marginalized communities because of their greater perceived ability to connect with citizens. Department policies of zero tolerance for discrimination based on sexual orientation may have provided gay and lesbian officers with an organizational space from which to challenge the hegemonic link between heterosexism, masculinity, and effective police work.

Earlier research found that some female police officers de-emphasized their femininity while employing stereotypic masculine traits such as verbal and physical aggressiveness as a way of gaining acceptance in a traditionally male occupation (Gross 1981; Berg and Budnick 1986). Some lesbians in our sample believed that they were able to "do gender" in the masculine tradition of policing without threatening heterosexual male officers to the extent that heterosexual women do (see Burke 1994). Paradoxically, their sexual orientation may offer a waiver from social pressures to enact emphasized femininity to reproduce traditional masculinist police culture. To avoid association with subordinate forms of masculinity, some gay male officers overemphasized their toughness and strength to facilitate acceptance into a profession that values and expects such macho attributes (see Officer friendly Forthcoming). Relative to gay male accounts, lesbian officers' comments focused as much on their experience of gender-related as on sexual orientation-related barriers. These experiences were conditioned by their degree of "outness."

Gay and lesbian officers also described efforts to reshape their roles as police officers. This transformation includes a heightened sensitivity to the needs of those citizens who are most disenfranchised from society—and who often feel most alienated from police officers. Although observational data are needed to confirm these perceptual findings, these subjective claims are supported by officers' reports of informal and official departmental recognition for "going the extra step" and for being able to establish a more mutually respectful rapport with community members. Of course, our sample may not be representative of all gay and lesbian police officers. Moreover, too much emphasis on the heightened sensitivity and tolerance of gay and lesbian officers as a group can ignore the range of diversity of work orientation and other characteristics within groups of gay and lesbian officers. Such imagery may become just one more stereotype or essentializing discourse to restrict individual gay and lesbian officers' behavior. The limitations raised by survey data also temper the generalizability of our findings.

Despite the barriers of homophobia and accompanying visibility, boundary maintenance, and stereotyping that tempered full acceptance, the gay and lesbian officers in our sample struggled to balance job demands with sexual orientation. The data suggest that "being out" removes some of the pressure of having to participate in a compulsory heterosexualized department culture. "Closeted" officers appear to not feel as free, although being "out" appears to benefit lesbian more than gay officers. Moreover, self-imposed compensatory overachievement may further dilute the advantages of being open. In short, remaining "closeted" supports—however unintentionally—the social dominance of the traditional model of police masculinity, a construction that requires the silence of alternative sexualities to survive (Messerschmidt 1993).

Skin color privilege—being white—also shapes acceptance into the hegemonic traditions of the police world. White heterosexual men are simply granted more legitimacy—and thus power—within the departmental structure (as evidenced by promotions to higher ranks; see Pike 1991; Martin 1994) and by society at large (see Messerschmidt 1993). For men of color whose homosexuality becomes known, this recognition might jeopardize their already tenuous alliances with the predominately white straight police force. With our data, this possibility is apparent: the "out" officers typically possess statuses that accord them legitimacy through other personal characteristics, such as skin color or gender privilege.

Several of the "out" gay and lesbian respondents in our study believed that their promotion opportunities were equal to or better than those of heterosexual officers. They attribute this possibility to the current political climate and leadership that is striving to embrace a more diverse police force. At the same time, these officers acknowledge that advancement is also linked to test performance. Yet if promotion of gay and lesbian officers is perceived to be tied to sexual orientation, not competence, this raises concerns that there may be a backlash against gay and lesbian officer progress. In related research on race, gender, and policing, Martin (1994, 388) found that white officers (particularly males) felt victimized by affirmative action programs if the promoted officers scored lower on exams, even when the exams are found to provide "advantages or disabilities in ways that are both gendered and racially biased."

Given the progress of gay and lesbian officers in the Midwestern Police Department and elsewhere around the country, it is important to assess continued efforts by administrators to ensure equal treatment and advancement opportunities for "out" officers. For example, Martin (1994, 388) contended that despite the visibility of recent affirmative action policies, the continuity of "old boy networks" and informal sponsorship across traditional white, heterosexual male lines goes unnoticed.

Overall, our study reveals considerable diversity among lesbian and among gay male officers, even given our small sample. Despite the variation across individuals of different gender, race, ethnicity, rank, seniority, and "out" versus closeted status, we also observe important, recurrent themes. Officers in our sample are loyal to many norms and goals of traditional policing subculture (such as crime fighting, crime prevention and deterrence, maintaining order, and providing public safety and service). Yet the majority of officers' responses also suggest that the inclusion of lesbians and gay men on the police force may bring new flexibility to the character of policing, particularly because their own experience in marginalized groups may facilitate greater ease in responding to the needs of other oppressed groups. At a time when improved community relations seems to be the direction of new policing policy (Alpert and Dunham 1986; Miller 1999), admirable qualities in officers are no longer aloofness and toughness, but qualities that express a more humane dimension (Manning 1984; Jurik and Martin 2001). As Bern (1974, 1993) argued two decades ago, rigid gender-role differentiation may have outlived its utility in a society in which human flexibility is increasingly associated with higher standards of psychological health, not to mention professional performance.

Although these findings are preliminary, given our small sample size, they indicate directions for future research. As Collins (1990) suggests, we need to look at a larger "matrix of domination," both within and across a variety of organizations, including intersections of race, gender, class, and sexual orientation. Martin (1994, 397) suggested that domination pervades "three levels at which people experience and resist it: the individual; the group or community; and social system." Following this guideline, future research could include these three dimensions. For instance, interviews with these community members (gay and straight) could explore if increased contact with gay and lesbian police officers decreases homophobia and intolerance as well as how gay and lesbian officers identify themselves as such to citizens.

Research could also address the process, and problems, of coming "out" in the course of one's career. It would also be important to explore the reasons why some gay and lesbian officers left the police force to determine if these factors are related to a homophobic environment, overt discrimination or even violence, or the emotional costs of maintaining a false front. This kind of research could also explore the resiliency of officers working with multiple identities, and the strategies they use to negotiate and secure their position within the police subculture. Research could also explore the correlations between stress and medical leave and "out" and "closeted" officers. In addition, gay men and lesbians are not the only individuals breaking out of gendered and sexualized social behaviors; further study could investigate other influences of a "modernized" policing approach, including the effects of greater contact with gay and lesbian colleagues on heterosexual officers (patrol and supervisors).

Parallel research could explore the career and promotion paths of "closeted" and "out" officers vis-à-vis heterosexual officers to determine any difference in the amount of time it takes to attain higher positions, controlling for performance evaluations, rank and years on force, and so forth. It may be that as police departments grow more diverse, the promotion process will reflect a receptivity to different officers, following the Good Cop Syndrome, as named by a chief inspector of the Metropolitan Police Force in England. This syndrome means that as long as odd individuals are seen as effective officers by others, they will be accepted and even respected (Burke 1994). A more policy-related suggestion is to encourage departments to place "out" officers with higher rank in training positions so that the newest recruits are cognizant of difference among respected leaders from their first exposure to the police environment in the training academy.

On one hand, findings from this study suggest the potential benefit gained if lesbians and gays endeavor to be more "out" to create increased visibility for the heterogeneity of gays as a group, thus challenging stereotypes. On the other hand, given the current stigma, stereotypes, discrimination, and possible violent consequences of being "out," gays and lesbians may be understandably reluctant to put themselves in a vulnerable position. The personal costs, real and perceived, of being "out" may be too dear. Yet the consequence of silence can be far-reaching: "Each time homosexuals deny their sexual orientation they hurt themselves slightly, which has a cumulative effect on their energies and vitality" (Wells and Kline 1986, 192). Clearly, given the high levels of fear associated with crime and police officers' professional responsibilities, what should be most salient is the quality and effectiveness of one's policing and not one's sexual orientation. In fact, the lesbian and gay police officers in this sample describe themselves as possessing the very qualities that increasing numbers of police departments are striving to establish as exemplary of first-rate officers to improve community-police relations. Being "out" can be very powerful and may interrupt the stronghold of hegemonic masculinity for all members of the police force through the contradiction of existing stereotypes by honest daily examples of the competency of gay and lesbian police officers. This visibility rests on the receptivity of a police subculture, however, that continues to embrace enduring images of tough, macho, hypermasculine officers.

Endnotes

[1] The concept of "out" or "being out" means that the respondent has personally acknowledged his or her own sexual orientation and that this status is known by others. "Closeted" refers to those respondents who identify themselves as lesbian or gay but do not disclose this status to others.

[2] Diversity on the police force—although supported by some—is viewed as undesirable by many and elusive by most: women comprise less than 10 percent of sworn police officers, and minority (primarily black) women make up 4 percent of all officers; minority women comprise 16 percent of all minority personnel, whereas white women constitute only 7 percent of white police personnel (Martin 1995, 395).

[3] We are aware of the criticisms of Kanter's (1977) structural theory of organizational disadvantage, in that she failed to recognize that dominant social groups such as white males are not disadvantaged when they occupy the position of proportional minority in organizations. The perceptual disadvantages that Kanter described so well accrue differentially to societally oppressed groups such as women, persons of color, and gay and lesbian workers (see Zimmer 1988; Williams 1989). Despite these problems, we find Kanter's discussion of perceptual barriers to be useful for describing the experiences of gay and lesbian police officers.

[4] In their rejection of hiring gays and lesbians as police officers in 1979, the International Association of Chiefs of Police stated that "every policeman should conduct his private life so that the public . . . regard(s) him as an example of stability, fidelity, and morality." Leinen (1993, 8) countered, "The inference, of course, is that gays are not stable, trustworthy, or morally principled."

[5] Difficulties for gay and lesbian police officers also stem from police policy precedents. To encourage community support, police administrators must "establish and maintain high standards of professional and personal conduct for officers under their command," and one potential area for scrutiny is the lifestyle choices of officers, including a range of behaviors from fitness, drug use, and financial status to sexual orientation or conduct (Doss 1990, 194–196). Sexual behavior that is criminal, such as sex on duty, sexual harassment, sexual assaults, sex with a suspect or prisoner, or any other similar behavior, would be illegal for any officer, regardless of sexual orientation. Although there has been some success in challenging regulations using rights such as privacy, due process of law, equal protection. and the freedom of association, the U.S. Supreme Court has not yet struck down as unconstitutional police department regulations stipulating "conduct unbecoming an officer" (Doss 1990). See also, Annotation, "Sexual Misconduct or Irregularity as Amounting to 'Conduct Unbecoming an Officer,' Justifying Officer's Demotion or Removal or Suspension From Duty," 9 A.L.R. 4th 614 (1981) and 9 A.L.R. 4th 41 (Supp. 1988). In 1986, the Supreme Court held in *Bowers Hardwick* (478 U.S. 186. 921–Ed. 2d 140) that homosexual behavior is not a constitutionally protected fundamental right and that homosexuals do not fall under a protected suspect class. Following the *Bowers* precedent, an Ohio court ruled that dismissal on the grounds of homosexuality was acceptable for military and law enforcement personnel (Doss 1990, 197). Subsequent court rulings have reinforced the assumption that a police officer's sexual orientation exerts a negative effect on the ability to perform effectively, the police department's morale, and the community reputation (Doss 1990). Suspensions, dismissals, and other sanctions have also been imposed on officers who engaged in sexual impropriety (such as cohabitation, adultery, use of prostitutes), although no evidence was used to demonstrate that these activities—occurring off duty—had any effect on officers' effectiveness or public service while on the job. As evidenced by the recent efforts to actively recruit lesbian and gay male officers, however, some departments have relaxed or changed policies deemed unrelated to job performance.

[6] For our purposes for this article, the analysis focused on the following items on the survey: work environment experience of bias against them, fear and consequences of being out, strategies used to maximize inclusion into subculture, the link between sexism experienced by women on the force and sexuality, and the construction of masculinity among men and how that may be exacerbated for gay men; performance: strengths and unique abilities brought to the job, pressures, job skills, extent of homophobia in their working environment, consequences of heightened visibility, perceptions of promotion process and how "out" status may affect it; and strategies of survival and resistance: convergence of gender, race, ethnicity, and sexuality, decisions about who to be "out" to, risks around disclosure, personal costs of false fronts, benefits of being "out," and tensions between "out" and "closeted" officers.

[7] The survey is available on request front the authors. The questions cover the following: demographics: relationship and family information: general occupational facts: work experience, years on force, trajectory of assignment and promotions, why did officer select this career, awards or honors received, special job duties—such as gangs, drugs, juveniles; social support network information across a range of issues: family, friends, children, and under what circumstance they came out to these people and their reactions (initial and current), and any consequences; career experiences: "out" status, anticipated problems, when did officer "come out" and the circumstances, responses, effects on others' assessments of officers' policing performance, benefits and risks of being "out"; job-related: examining gender versus sexuality—who is advantaged and disadvantaged and why, work expectations, comparison of opportunities between heterosexual and homosexual officers, consequences of being out in how other officers treat them, homophobic environment, assignments avoided because of sexuality or reactions of others, how to validate reputation; harassment: experiences, actions taken, consequences of actions taken, community bias against gay officers and reactions, responding to stereotypes and ignorance; differences and similarities: comparison of uniqueness versus sameness between heterosexual officers and homosexual officers, perception of effectiveness; social life: inclusion and exclusion into informal police culture, other social aspects; and general: examining masculinity construction and sexism and how they intersect sexuality within police profession, supportive responses to them after coming out.

[8] Although the cofounders and "out" officers were willing to reveal their identities, we choose to use pseudonyms for all of the officers so that potential homophobic backlash would not jeopardize their work environment.

[9] Our race/ethnicity analysis is limited to exploring patterns in the data, given the small sample.

References

Acker, Joan. 1990. Hierarchies, jobs, bodies: A theory of gendered organizations. *Gender & Society* 4:139–58.

Alex, N. 1969. *Black in blue: A study of the Negro policeman.* New York: Appleton-CenturyCrofts.

Alpert, Geoffrey P., and Roger O. Dunham. 1986. Community policing. *Journal of Police Science and Administration* 14:212–22.

Appier, J. 1992. Preventive justice: The campaign for women police, 1910–1940. *Women and Criminal Justice* 4:3–36.

———. 1998. *Police women: The sexual politics of law enforcement in the LAPD.* Philadelphia: Temple University.

Berg, B., and K. Budnick. 1986. Defeminization of women in law enforcement: A new twist on the traditional police personality. *Journal of Police Science and Administration* 14:314–19.

Bern, Sandra L. 1974. The measurement of psychological androgyny. *Journal of Consulting and Clinical Psychology* 42 (2): 155–62.

———. 1993. *The lenses of gender: Transforming the debate on sexual inequality.* New Haven, CT: Yale University Press.

Bernstein, Mary. 1997. Celebration and suppression: The strategic uses of identity by the lesbian and gay movement. *American Journal of Sociology* 103 (3): 531–65.

Berrill, Kevin T. 1992. Anti-gay violence and victimization in the United States: An overview. In *Hate crimes: Confronting violence against lesbians and gay men,* edited by Gregory Herek and Kevin Berrill, 19–45. Newbury Park, CA: Sage.

Blumenfeld, Warren J. 1992. *Homophobia: How we all pay the price.* Boston: Beacon Press.

Britton, Dana M. 1990. Homophobia and homosociality: An analysis of boundary maintenance. *Sociological Quarterly* 31 (3): 423–39.

———. 1995. "Don't ask, don't tell, don't pursue": Military policy and the construction of heterosexual masculinity. *Journal of Homosexuality* 30 (1): 1–21.

————. 1997. Gendered organizational logic: Policy and practice in men's and women's prisons. *Gender & Society* 11:796–818.

Buhrke, Robin A. 1996. *A matter of justice: Lesbians and gay men in law enforcement.* New York: Routledge.

Burke, M. E. 1993. *Coming out of the blue: British police officers talk about their lives in "the job" as lesbians, gays and bisexuals.* London: Cassell.

————. 1994. Homosexuality as deviance: The case of the gay police officer. *British Journal of Criminology* 34:192–203.

Christopher, Warren, J. A. Arguelles, R. Anderson, W. R. Barnes, L. F. Estrada, Mickey Kantor, R. M. Mask, A. S. Ordin, J. B. Slaughter, and R. E. Tranquada. 1991. *Report of the independent commission of the Los Angeles Police Department.* Los Angeles: City of Los Angeles.

Cockburn, Cynthia. 1991. *In the way of women: Men's resistance to sex equality in organizations.* Ithaca, NY: ILR Press.

Coleman, J. W., and D. R. Cressey. 1999. *Social problems.* 7th ed. New York: Longman.

Collins, Patricia Hill. 1990. *Black feminist thought: Knowledge, consciousness and the politics of empowerment.* New York: Routledge.

Connell, Robert W. 1987. *Gender and power* Stanford, CA: Stanford University Press.

————. 1992. *Gender and power.* Palo Alto, CA: Stanford University Press.

————. 1993. The big picture: Masculinities in recent world history. *Theory and Society* 22:597–623,

———— 1998. Masculinities and globalization. *Men and Masculinities* 1:3–23.

Crites, L. 1973. Women in law enforcement. *Management and Information Service*, 5.

Croteau, J. M., and J. S. Lark. 1995. On being lesbian, gay or bisexual in student affairs: A national survey of experiences on the job. *NASPA Journal* 32:189–97.

David, D., and R. Brannon, 1976. *The forty-nine percent majority: The male sex role.* Reading, MA: Addison/Wesley.

DeMila, S. 1978. Homosexuals as police officers? *New York Times*, 10 February, 25.

Doss, M. T., Jr. 1990. Police management: Sexual misconduct and the right to privacy. *Journal of Police Science and Administration* 17 (3): 194–204.

Gender differences in police brutality lawsuits: Men cost more. 2000. *Feminist Daily News Wire*, 18 September, Internet.

Giddens, Anthony. 1979. *Central problems in social theory.* London: Macmillan.

————. 1984. *The constitution of society.* Cambridge, UK: Polity Press.

Goffman, Erving. 1963. *Stigma: Notes on the management of spoiled identity.* New York: Simon & Schuster.

Griffin, J. L. 1992. Rodriguez says he won't allow police insensitivity toward gays. *Chicago Tribune*, 21 May, 2.2.

Gross, S. 1981. *Socialization in law enforcement: The female police recruit.* Final report. Miami, FL: Southeast Institute of Criminal Justice.

Harvard Law Review, eds. 1990. *Sexual orientation and the law.* Cambridge, MA: Harvard University Press.

Hiatt, D., and G. E. Hargrave. 1994. Psychological assessment of gay and lesbian law enforcement applicants. *Journal of Personality Assessment* 63:80–88.

Hunt, Jennifer. 1984. The development of rapport through negotiation of gender in field work among police. *Human Organization* 43:283–96.

————. 1990. The logic of sexism among police. *Women & Criminal Justice* 1:3–30.

International Association of Chiefs of Police. 1979. Gay police. *New Jersey Record*, 12 August.

Judge speaks out in case of harassed lesbian police officer. 2000. *Feminist Daily News* 29 September, Internet.

Jurik, Nancy. 1985. An officer and a lady: Organizational barriers to women working as correctional officers in men's prisons. *Social Problems* 32 (4): 375–88.

Jurik, Nancy C., and Susan E. Martin. 2001. Femininities, masculinities and organizational conflict: Women in policing and corrections occupations. In *Women, crime, and justice: Contemporary perspectives,* edited by Lynne Goodstein and Claire Renzetti, 264–81. Los Angeles: Roxbury.

Kanter, Rosabeth Moss. 1977. *Men and women of the corporation.* New York: Basic Books.

Kaufman, Michael. 1998. The construction of masculinity and the triad of men's violence. In *Men's lives* (5th ed.), edited by Michael S. Kimmel and Michael A. Messner, 4–16. Boston: Allyn & Bacon.

Lamphere, L., P. Zavella, R. Gonzales, and P. Evans. 1993. *Sun belt working mothers: Reconciling family and factory.* Ithaca, NY: Cornell University Press.

Leinen, Stephen. 1984. *Black police, white society.* New York: New York University.

———. 1993. *Gay cops.* New Brunswick, NJ: Rutgers University Press.

Levine, M. P., and R. Leonard. 1984. Discrimination against lesbians in the work force. *Signs: A Journal of Women in Culture and Society* 9:700–710.

Lorber, J., and S. A. Farrell. 1991. Preface. In *The social construction of gender,* edited by Judith Lorber and Susan A. Farrell, 1–5. London: Sage.

Manning, Peter K. 1984. Community-based policing. *American Journal of Police* 3:205–27.

Marcus, Eric. 1992. *Making history: The struggle for gay and lesbian equal rights, 1945–1990.* New York: HarperCollins.

Martin, Susan E. 1980. *Breaking and entering: Policewomen on patrol.* Berkeley: University of California Press.

———. 1990. *On the move: The status of women in policing.* Washington, DC: Police Foundation.

———. 1992. The changing status of women officers: Gender and power in police work. In *The changing roles of women in the criminal justice system: Offenders, victims, and professionals,* edited by Imogene L. Moyer. Long Grove, IL: Waveland.

———. 1994. "Outsider within" the station house: The impact of race and gender on black women police. *Social Problems* 41:383–400.

———. 1995. The interactive effects of race and sex on women police officers. In *The criminal justice system and women: Offenders, victims, and workers,* edited by Barbara Raffel Price and Natalie J. Sokoloff, 383–97. New York: McGraw-Hill.

Martin, Susan E., and Nancy C. Jurik. 1996. *Doing justice, doing gender: Women in criminal justice occupations.* Thousand Oaks, CA: Sage.

Meers, Eric. 1998. Good cop, gay cop. *The Advocate,* 3 March, 26–33.

Messerschmidt, James. 1993. *Masculinities and crime: Critique and reconceptualization of theory.* Lanham, MD: Rowman & Littlefield.

———. 1997. *Crime as structured action: Gender race, class, and crime in the making.* Thousand Oaks: CA: Sage.

Messner, Michael A. 1992. *Power at play: Sports and the problem of masculinity.* Boston: Beacon Press.

Miller, Susan L. 1999. *Gender and community policing: Walking the talk.* Boston: Northeastern University Press.

Morash, M., and J. Greene. 1986. Evaluating women on patrol: A critique of contemporary wisdom. *Evaluation Review* 10:230–55.

Officer friendly and the tough cop: Gays and lesbians navigate policing. Forthcoming. *Journal of Homosexuality.*

Omi, M., and H. Winant, 1994. *Racial formation in the United States: From the 1960s to the 1990s.* 2d ed. New York: Routledge.

Pike, Diane L. 1991. Women in police academy training: Some aspects of organizational response. In *The changing roles of women in the criminal justice system: Offenders, victims, and professionals* (2d ed.), edited by Imogene Moyer, 261–80. Long Grove, IL: Waveland.

Powers, Bob. 1996. The impact of gay, lesbian, and bisexual workplace issues on productivity. *Journal of Gay and Lesbian Social Services* 4 (4): 79–90.

Purported male deputies reveal hostilities in online forum. 1999: *Feminist Daily News Wire*, 8 April, Internet.

Remmington, Patricia W. 1981. *Policing: The occupation and the introduction of female officers*, Washington, DC: University Press of America.

Renzetti, Claire M. 1992. *Violent betrayal: Partner abuse in lesbian relationships.* Newbury Park, CA: Sage.

Rich, Adrienne. 1980. Compulsory heterosexuality and lesbian existence. *Signs* 5:631–60.

Rosabal, Gina S. 1996. Multicultural existence in the workplace: Including how I thrive as a Latina lesbian feminist. *Journal of Gay and Lesbian Social Services* 4 (4): 17–28.

Scandal highlights need for gender-balanced force/60 *Minutes* reports police family violence scandal. 2000. *Feminist Daily News Wire*, 29 February, Internet.

Schneider, Beth E. 1986. Coming out at work: Bridging the private/public gap. *Work and Occupations* 13:463–87.

———. 1988. Invisible and independent: Lesbians' experiences in the workplace. In *Women working*, edited by A. Stromberg and S. Harkess, 273–96. Palo Alto, CA: Mayfield.

Schulz, D. M. 1995. *From social worker to crimefighter: Women in United States municipal policing.* New York: Praeger.

Shilts, Randy. 1980. Gay police. *Police Magazine.* January, 32–33.

Skolnick, Jerome H. 1994. *Justice without trial: Law enforcement in democratic society.* 3d ed. New York: Macmillan.

Taylor, Verta, and Nicole C. Raeburn. 1995. Identity politics as high-risk activism: Career consequences for lesbians, gay, and bisexual sociologists. *Social Problems* 42 (2): 252–73.

Wells, J. W., and W. B. Kline. 1986. Self-disclosure of homosexual orientation. *Journal of Social Psychology* 127:191–97.

West, C., and S. Fenstermaker. 1993. Power, in-equality and the accomplishment of gender: An ethnomethodological view. In *Theory on gender/feminism*, edited by P. England. New York: Aldine.

———.1995. Doing difference. *Gender & Society* 9:8–37.

West, Candace, and Don H. Zimmerman. 1987. Doing gender. *Gender & Society* 1:125–51.

Williams, Christine. 1989. *Gender differences at work: Women and men in nontraditional occupations.* Berkeley: University of California Press.

Women face "blue wall" of resistance. 1999. *Christian Science Monitor*, 18 August, Internet.

Woods, James. 1993. *The corporate closet: The professional lives of gay men in America.* New York: Free Press.

Zimmer, Lynn. 1987. How women reshape the prison guard role. *Gender & Society* 1 (4): 415–31.

———. 1988. Tokenism and women in the workplace: The limits of gender neutral theory. *Social Problems* 35:64–77.

13

Fighting Cynicism
Some Reflections on
Self-Motivation in Police Work

MICAEL BJÖRK

Police work characteristically occupies areas on the "dark side" of social life. As the practical equivalent to political commentators and sociologists whose line of descent can be traced back to controversial thinkers such as Machiavelli and Hobbes, police officers could be said to "deal in darkness" (Oakeshott, 1991, pp. 225–228). Crime and criminals will not go away, nor will their victims or the underlying reality of brute force and the accompanying atmosphere of anxiety, grief, cruelty, misery, and pain. Even if comradeship and excitement on the job present their own rewards, much remains in the life of an officer that contributes to a sense of frustration, even failure, in the face of such inevitability; the feeling of fulfillment on the job seems placed permanently on hold. The imperative of perseverance amid all the "darkness" thus grows paramount for the police performance on the job. Although it is true that crime-related tasks are not always on the agenda (Waddington, 1999), consequences of crime permeate the parameters of police life in more ways than one. In consequence, self-motivation becomes crucial in the routine life of the force, helping to contain cynicism and its counterproductive effect on the ongoing day-to-day police practice (Manning, 2004; Maxwell & Klein, 2006).

In this article, I argue that police officers typically strive to avoid the temptations of cynicism, often managing to rein it in without at the same time falling prey to its opposite pole, represented by the enthusiasm of the bold and strong agents of law on a mission to wage a "war on crime" (McElhinny, 2003). Striking a balance between cynicism and zealotry in fact consti-

Micael Björk, *Police Quarterly*, vol. 11, pp. 88–101, © 2008 by Sage Publications. Reprinted by permission of Sage Publications.

tutes a response that is almost habitual in the police officer's way of life. It is precisely the mechanisms and techniques involved in this balancing act that I focused on during my 2 years of ethnographic field research among the gang units of the metropolitan police force in Gothenburg, Sweden's second largest city. In their daily life, officers of the city's police department use a set of sense-making techniques that I analyze as part of their *perseverance strategies* helping to achieve this balance; these techniques and strategies in turn give rise to a *culture of reserve* typifying the police practice in the department. At stake in these processes is the creation and maintenance of a workable balance between involvement and detachment, conducive to the operative expectations set for police performance and formed in response to concrete policing circumstances and the need to recreate the law in specific cases or diverse social locations (see Jonsen & Toulmin, 1988; Muir, 1977).

According to Barbara Czarniawska (1997, 1998), employees or groups of employees make sense of phenomena in their workplace by telling stories that articulate their personal experience of these phenomena. These sense-making practices, I argue, are relevant to our understanding of the processes that enhance self-motivation and effective professional conduct among police officers. Shared organizational tales form an important means of order construction in most organizations, and the stories narrated create a shared sense of reality; especially when the events they relate to are complex, even contradictory, and open to multiple interpretations, as is the case in most policing situations. Stories of this kind are performative: They involve not merely words; they actually take part or "happen" in composite social situations. In this way, most police work can indeed be said to be about managing ambivalence (cf. Åkerström, 2006).

In their specific role, the police remain outside of the ordinary system of government in the sense that their task is to invoke trust through institutionalized acts of suspicion. Somewhat paradoxically, then, state-sanctioned distrust in citizens, as represented by the very function of the police, is aimed at promoting confidence in civil society. This ambiguity is of vital importance for our understanding of police work. Its domain, moreover, is expansive in practice, because of the fact that the police, during their actual operations, must make decisions characterized by considerable freedom of action. Egon Bittner (1970) offered what is perhaps still the most clear-cut statement of the inherent element of discretion necessarily there in police work. In his words, "the role of the police is best understood as a mechanism for the distribution of non-negotiable coercive force employed in accordance with the dictates of an intuitive grasp of situational exigencies" (p. 46). Most policing activities presuppose a certain degree of freedom of action and reliance on discretionary choices made by police officers in diverse control settings (Emerson, 1981). In response to this need, sense-making techniques are employed where exercise of the freedom of choice and good judgment are called for. As, among others, Jonathan H. Turner (2003) has observed, legal systems in postindustrial societies enjoy a high degree of autonomy. "This autonomy," moreover, "is amplified as the practitioners of law—lawyers, judges and police—become more professionalized, since professionalism inevitably generates its own norms, values, ideologies and traditions that often deviate significantly from those of the broader society and culture" (p. 233). In this article, I want to argue that certain discretionary choices taken to counteract actual or potential cynicism contribute to the creation of a professional culture of reserve that, although detached on the surface, encourages vocational attitudes nourishing police desire and ability to work well in a western democratic society.

In what follows, I will briefly describe the ethnographic approach used in the research for this article before turning to the actual strategies of managing cynicism, focusing on what I call four perseverance strategies reconstructed from the materials collected during my fieldwork among the Gothenburg police. This main part of the article is followed by a brief discussion on police culture that draws some conclusions from the previous section and points to a need for a more nuanced understanding of this term, based on the irreducible aspect of ambiguity present in police practice. Finally, some implications of this discussion for proactive community policing and police training are considered.

A Note on Method

The research work for this article used participatory observation among police department gang units, involving also operations targeting the recruitment of young foot soldiers for criminal gangs. The fieldwork was carried out among the metropolitan police force in Gothenburg, the second largest city in Sweden, from early October 2004 through October 2005. A second round of fieldwork was conducted during the first half of 2006, including a set of supplemental interviews. The fieldwork phase covered a total of 400 hours of participant observation in police patrol and reconnaissance cars, witnessing individuals being taken into custody or involving various types of crackdown operations and responses to incidents of serious youth delinquency. A segment of the research was conducted following foot patrols in the city's hotspot areas (cf. Björk, 2006a). Given the "action" nature of the research, the quotations given below could be termed *vocabularies in action* (Skinner, 1989), represent[ing] as they do immediate articulations arising from actual police work. Although the supporting empirical evidence is presented in the form of "talk," most of my materials were obtained in actual real-life control settings. Last, in view of the contested nature of the field of my research, my analysis will be guided by the use of sensitizing concepts: concepts that "give the user a general sense of reference and guidance" (Blumer, 1954, p. 7). In these brief remarks outlining elements of the nature and significance of self-motivation in police work, I will therefore make no attempt at definitive conclusions or formal descriptions regarding the topic in my interest. References to my research material are given using annotations such as I: 99 or II: 213, indicating the page numbers in my digitalized first and second notebooks.

Policing and Perseverance Strategies

Techniques of self-motivation in police work represent a specific case of sense-making processes more generally. Hence, these motivational efforts can be viewed as perseverance strategies. Such strategies, and the techniques they rely on, are performance practices that evolve in daily considerations with oneself or in interaction with fellow colleagues, addressing the need of the police officers to stay motivated in an environment where the risk of disappointment and frustration runs high. Those expected to turn decent tend toward delinquency; communities with a chance to embark on a path to well-being continue to foster deviant codes of conduct; residential areas seemingly at the brink of prosperity keep veering toward criminality, persisting at low levels of collective efficacy (cf. Sampson & Raudenbush, 1999, pp. 609–613). At issue are the strategies providing an alternative to those for whom leaving the police force is not an option. How to stay motivated and continue being able to consider oneself a "good cop"? Here, the evidence gathered during my research points to the importance of the processes resulting in the creation of a specific culture of reserve. Below, I will try to outline some such responses, along with their constituent elements, thereby contributing to our understanding of the notion of democratic policing conforming to the moral standards of a highly skilled officer (Klockars, 1996; see also Manning, 2005, p. 24).

Alternative One: Relief through Lateral Job Mobility

Lateral job mobility is perhaps the most obvious means to affect the motivational element in police work; so at least we could interpret the quite common "here-and-there" fashion of advancing one's career and at times even of handling one's routine work assignments. An officer, for example, starts out in one division, say driving patrol cars or investigating human trafficking; 2 years later, the officer requests a transfer to a gang unit or the narcotics squad. After 2 more years, it is time to move on to the technical division analyzing evidence or providing high-tech support. Then, after an additional 2 years in the force, one might join the Special Weapon and Tactics team or the criminal investigation bureau or perhaps seek additional training in the hopes of a promotion. When both old and new police officers begin this way moving from position to position, it is not always in response to measures targeting flexibility in operational capability. One explanation behind this semi-institutionalized form of shuffling between positions and assignments may indeed have to do with the efficacy of internal recruiting and various other drafting mechanisms (Bayley & Garofalo, 1989). Yet these alone do not seem capable of accounting for the large number of police officers steadily seeking redeployment. Apart from the more trivial sentiments of being "fed up" with one's work, my assumption is that such mobility reflects a desire to maintain one's work motivation and a sense of its significance in the face of the "dark side" of police life already mentioned. In the words of two police officers,

> You can't stay for more than a year in an area where people keep throwing shit at you, where it's impossible to leave your car without having it getting thrashed. So I had to go someplace else after just one year. (II: 103)

> During my years on the beat, I got to hate human beings so deeply that I had to find another assignment before I would seriously hurt some junkie or another. (II: 152)

Police officers thus wish to become reassigned in the hopes of dissociating themselves from that aspect of human "darkness" they grow weary of or at least to vary its form and content. In other words, redeployment is sought partly to forget—and thereby to boost motivational energy during operational front line duties (cf. Brown, 2000). In the words of two officers being reassigned to their previous duties and commenting on a colleague seeking redeployment at another division,

> In our line of business, you have to be constantly in motion; otherwise, you stop functioning emotionally. Moving on to the narcotics division will be good for him. (1: 213–214)

An opposite alternative to seeking redeployment is to simply adjust and "do nothing particular." Within every profession in which a degree of discretionary freedom is allowed or even required, this remains a viable option that, however, will prove counterproductive from the point of view of efficient police work if it becomes the primary or even only option available for those in search for techniques to aid perseverance. It may still be functional for the personnel, allowing either the creation or the preservation of a degree of self-esteem on the job, provided that this form of inactivity remains limited by its temporal duration—a day every now and then—and the exercise of good judgment. It may take the form of transporting evidence or changing tires, for example, or servicing the patrol car in the afternoon. In these cases, paradoxically, such "doing nothing special" can be conducive to the maintenance of self-motivation on the job; "for your ability to go on," reported one gang unit officer on our way to the garage, "you need days like these" (I: 34).

Not every officer, however, makes an effort to change the perspective on daily routines through seeking reassignment within the department or by spending a day in informal idleness. Some choose to stay on in their specific division but focus their activities on other, less taxing neighborhoods within their district. This provides yet another option for the perseverance strategies among the police officers willing to use the discretionary element inherent in their job.

Alternative Two: Relief through Redeployment in Less Criminal Areas

The districts in the northwest and northeast of Gothenburg differ greatly from one another. Those in the northeast are characterized by large "Soviet style" public housing projects inhabited by the working poor and various immigrant communities. In contrast, the suburbs in the city's northwest consist mostly of privately owned residential areas bordering rural communities beyond the city's reach; the inhabitants are mostly White Swedish middle class. Crime in the immigrant communities of the northeast is predominantly gang related (Björk, in press). According to the police records, most of the serious crime involves interpersonal feuds among various street gangs and elements of organized crime such as the Albanian mafia and the Bandidos motorcycle club. In the "White" northwest, it is the industrious middle-class work ethic combined with heavy drinking that gives rise to restless youth groups and spontaneous delinquency mainly during the weekends. Such diversity within the same police district (northern Gothenburg) offers an opportunity for a change-of-place strategy. In practice, the police units, to a certain extent, have an option to choose to direct their patrols to the less troubled northwest when the situation in the northeast has become too "demoralizing"—when the police feel themselves constantly under attack and the workload becomes subjectively overwhelming because of occurrence of serious crime, witnesses who are threatened and refuse cooperation, and the like.

Speaking of a specific neighborhood in the northeast, a police officer, during a high-speed chase through the shady streets of the district, declared the street gang problem to be almost anarchic in the area. Against the background of several shootings, demolished police cars, armed robberies almost on a daily basis, and approximately 200 burglaries during the previous month, he defined the situation with a spontaneous "They'll eat us alive" (II: 7):

> Damn it, we are just scratching the surface. The silence is everywhere. Nothing is more frustrating than this feeling. It will take hold of you completely. In this kind of situations, I can never leave my job, not even in my dreams; everything's just going straight to hell! (II: 70)

Later, during another ride, I asked the same gang unit officer whether this sense of hopelessness was the reason for the many hours spent patrolling the northwest, chasing drunken teenagers and bootleggers. His answer was in the affirmative, although all in all, things had changed for the better thanks to some reinforcements received in the northeast:

> The biggest impact of the larger unit is the distance it gives between you and those kids. Without the new colleagues, you start feeling that every one of these goddamn gang-bangers is nothing but a pig, though that's of course not how it is in reality. (II: 70)

The need for shifting focus to another neighborhood or area of operation within one's precinct becomes more pronounced when there is a feeling that effective crime fighting is somehow hampered. The amount of crime in the northeast can then, in conjunction with the feelings of being "eaten alive" (caused for instance by unfilled vacancies at the local police precinct), bolster cynicism ("every goddamn gang banger is nothing but a pig"). Every police officer knows that the structure of feeling in evidence here will negatively affect both the overall job performance and the officer's own sense of satisfac-

tion on the job. Indeed, one of the prerequisites for a satisfactory job performance is the ability to "have your heart in it," or to go about doing it "in a
good mood and with respect for human dignity," as articulated by another
officer (II: 3). For this, however, a certain distance may be required. Such a
distance can, for instance, be created through redeployment in another
neighborhood or street, with the "fresh start" easing the burden and allowing
the return of a reinvigorated sense of self-motivation. The effectiveness of
this strategy was manifest in a statement by an officer standing amid a group
of approximately 80 beer-drunken teenagers at around midnight:

> It's nice to work these neighborhoods [the "White" northwest] from time
> to time. You see, here you can turn your back to the kids; you don't need
> to have it covered, the way you usually do in those parts in the northeast.
> (II: 99)

In this way, after occasional ventures out to the northwest, officers can
return to their tasks in the northeast, somewhat refreshed and better
equipped to meet the requirements of their job there and again handle it in a
humane fashion, "combining a tragic perspective with an integrated morality"
(Muir, 1977, p. 226). I will return to this balancing act characteristic of the
police culture of reserve below; first, however, I want to bring up yet another
way of managing ambivalence in municipal control settings. This technique
could be said to have to do with both the pragmatic humanism in the Gothenburg gang units and, probably, the reactive or contingent character of
nearly all modern police work (Manning, 2004); I will briefly return to this
issue in the conclusion.

Alternative Three: Relief through Particularization

Particularization as "self-policing" technique among the gang units of the
Gothenburg metropolitan police force is articulated in two versions: as a
peculiar form of reflexivity and through uses of irony. The former version was
captured well by an officer who, investigating serious gang-related crime,
stated that there is a "certain risk involved in broadening your scope" (I:
155). Digging deep in each case, and into important parallel cases, helps to
provide the impetus needed for her everyday work. At the same time, a motivated officer by necessity becomes privy to large amounts of information
about the background of the street players implicated in police work, their
networks of kinship, their crime records, debts, and other such circumstances
of interest to any law enforcement function. in crime prevention and crime
fighting, "understanding the social and cultural environment is vital" (I: 146),
as summarized by the same officer.

The risks entailed by such a broadening of the field of vision, however,
have to do with the way it encourages speculation about the perfectibility of
human society, which in turn will weaken the work commitment (Jackall,
2005, pp. 132–134). As regard its motivational bases, operational police culture is characterized by provisional goal fulfillment, not some wholesale prom-

ise of the elimination of all crime or a devotion to any associated "big issues" such as why there is lawlessness to begin with. An officer, to maintain his or her motivation at work, will shun away from the larger questions to which there are no easy answers, for it is the case that "enthusiasm at work comes from many solved cases and few high-minded reflections" (I: I55).

Irony provides an additional way of particularizing, or disengaging from, the potentially depressing "darkness" that provides law enforcement activity with the psychological undertone of its legitimate field. A dysfunctional mind-set may at times have to be fought with the help of sense-making techniques employed among colleagues backstage, that is, away from the streets and in the canteen area (Waddington, 1999). As a respected gang unit officer put it, "making fun of the disheartening aspects of our work must be an option for those on the job" (II: 119). Without laughter, the cynicism often associated with the clichéd version of police culture becomes front-stage reality, especially in the more discouraging settings such as work with gangs and troubled youth. However, during my research, I witnessed very little of this; respectful law enforcement runs as the dominant theme in my research notebooks, even when the night shift becomes scornfully summarized as so many sightseeing of "the decline of the West" (I: 201). Akin to an investigation conducted with great care, joke telling tends to split the social world into its fragments (Berger, 1997). These acts in tragicomedy serve the purpose of managing ambivalence in policing: in effect, they introduce moments of consolation that aid self-motivation in crime-fighting encounters:

> Our language may be rough and often there is much frustration that has to come out, and so we will have to be able to joke about some of the thugs—but only in the canteen, in the sauna, or in the cars, away from the streets. (II: 24)

Strategies of particularization in this vein have little to do with the idealizations of the image of the tough cop taking care of the "dirty work" (Manning. 2005, p. 31). Rather, they arise out of the need to survive operational shortcomings and handle some of the psychologically more taxing aspects of police work—in other words, to maintain functionality over long term. Through the relief provided by irony, cynical postures are temporarily driven back—not the other way around, as when backstage mockery engenders cynicism, "for the police know that the order that 'civvies' take for granted is always precariously teetering on the brink of a chaos" (Waddington, 1999, p. 299).

In the following section, I will argue that laughter, coupled with provisional goal fulfillment, is in fact an inherent aspect of the peculiar humanism in police work that I observed during my fieldwork in Gothenburg.

Alternative Four: Pragmatic Humanism as a Perseverance Strategy

Perseverance strategies are not techniques of neutralization; they are aimed at managing ambivalence. The talk and action drawn on in the techniques used for these strategies derive from the everyday experiences of the police. Societal despair and moral dilemmas in policing citizens can seldom be shielded behind delusive definitions of the situation, such as the "denial of responsibility" or "the appeal to higher loyalties," in the classical statements by Sykes and Matza (1957, pp. 667–669). However, with the help of different strategies and techniques of particularization, change of patrolling area, lateral reassignment, and possibly a promotion, the "dark side" of human condition confronting the police officers may be made more bearable. Together with one final element complementing this overall structure of feeling, they form what I address in my analysis as the police culture of reserve; we may term this element *pragmatic humanism.*

Examples of respectful control responses were frequently evident during my field research. One of such response types is closely connected with the techniques of individualization discussed above. Over the years, I witnessed many instances demonstrating the importance assigned by gang unit officers to not handling gang members uniformly but instead each time as an individual, even unique, case. In the interrogation room, reported one police officer, one always starts with the assumption that:

> In there, everyone is a person. not merely a member of some gang . . . [for] finding the right buttons to push, so to speak. is critical; deep down almost every one of the kids just wants to speak their mind, and in the conversation you want to treat him or her as a real person. (I: 147)

Treating aspiring gang members as real gangsters will probably also make them just that: this is a lesson worth learning for the police (Klein, 2004; Maxwell & Klein, 2006), and among the Gothenburg police gang units, the officers have done their homework. On the other hand, officers also know that conversations engaged in with the police can alone be grounds enough for a punishment fitting for code violating collaborators. Success in the interrogation room may thus breed failure in the streets as the "rat" back on the streets is met with the anger of the members of the gang. For a gang unit officer, this is a true dilemma, sometimes forcing him or her to pseudolegal accommodations. For example, the accused may be allowed to remain silent about the identity of his or her fellow criminals if willing to plead guilty to the charges put to him or her. To this extent, gang unit officers can be said to use "context, conditions, and common cultural knowledge as resources when they produce, manage and sustain a certain part of social reality" (Åkerström, 2006, p. 59). In this fashion, police knowledge may grow more complex and nuanced; the officers approaching certain neighborhoods as dangerous areas of operation will also know that the same streets provide a significant reference point for the charismatic relationships and sources of territorial power stamping the lives of their inhabitants:

> The attraction stemming from [the gang members'] own neighborhood is enormous. If you are 18, some of the investments in personal reputation and criminal identification may go back 10 years. The risks in "going straight" will then remain very high. (II: 102)

Reasoning of this kind is central to the police culture of reserve. As such, it promotes thinking and acting that could be characterized as multifaceted and not at all in line with the image of the stereotypical "gang cop" portrayed by Klein (2004)—a police officer straightforwardly sticking to the maxim of "tail-them, nail-them, and jail-them" when dealing with actors outside the normal moral order (cf. Emerson, 1981, pp. 7–9). Such ambitions are bound to become frustrated in any case, prompting the police officers I researched to adopt less aggressive approaches. In their worldview, citizens do not appear as enemies; and to continue interacting with diverse neighborhoods and understand the various intergroup conflicts among criminal elements, police officers need to develop perseverance strategies capable of fostering self-motivation at work. Pragmatic humanism as described above belongs to this set of discretionary skills.

> I recall one particular gang. some years ago, which we tailed almost every day—until I found out that the stickups that they carried out were in direct proportion to how much we "harassed" them. So I stopped using this tactic. Later on, one of the gang members told me that it was me and my unit who often triggered them. He said it became a kind of a sport for them [to respond to our initiatives with exactly the kind of actions we wanted to prevent in the first place]. (II: 145)

With these vocabularies in action in mind and against the backdrop of the four perseverance strategies outlined above, I will briefly comment on the notion of police culture before concluding with a few remarks on their repercussions for police training and problem-oriented community policing.

Self-Motivation and the Police Culture

Ever since its introduction by William Westley in 1953. the concept of police culture has become frequently used in the literature (see, e.g., Manning, 2005, pp. 31–34; Newburn, 2005; see also Ekman, 1999; Granér, 2004 on the Swedish police). To generalize on this body of research, "police culture" is characterized by tough-guy attitudes, missionary authoritarianism, resistance to change, and overt male chauvinism in its behavioral implications. As assessed by Steve Herbert (2006), its basic principles are crystallized in the precept "find the bad actors and punish them through ostracism" (p. 106). On the other hand, there is a wealth of ethnographic studies describing police conduct that conforms to another kind of approach, as exemplified by William Ker Muir's (1977) *Police: Street Corner Politicians*. On the whole, however, much of the literature on police culture can be said to have been motivated by the desire to "condemn a broad spectrum of policing practice" (Waddington, 1999, p. 287). In this article, I have followed the tradition going back to Muir, investigating the unique side of the police culture and its motivational aspects and the ways in which police personnel manage the ambivalence resulting from their "operational exposure to the difficult and dangerous" (Brown, 2000, p. 260). Although we can recognize some similarities here with other street-level bureaucracies (social workers and security guards), the intensity of the "darkness" facing the police in their everyday work is probably extraordinary, especially if we consider the irreducible and potentially violent element of decisionism inherent in the police practice itself (cf. Björk 2005, 2006b).

The police make decisions without knowing in advance whether these decisions will strengthen or weaken people's trust in the police; decisions simply *must* be made. An order to intervene in a certain neighborhood may thus be experienced, by commanders and the rank-and-file alike, as a need to "give oneself up to the impossible decision, while taking account of laws and rules," to use the words of Jacques Derrida (1992, p. 24). Discretionary judgment, furthermore, can only be exercised by someone who is relatively free, and the freer one is, the more of a concern does the reality of the uncertain become. For the police, it seems, "the undecidable remains caught, lodged, at least as a ghost—but an essential ghost—in every decision, in every event of decision" (p. 24). In other words, police culture is constructed in flux, and so are the sense-making techniques drawn on by professional police officers for the conduct of their work.

The inherent "darkness" that I have pointed out as something characterizing the experience of the police work and manifest in the spread of cynicism in the everyday attitudes and actions of the police may be held in check through the recourse to the four perseverance strategies discussed above. Such skills and knowledge deployed by the police officers, however, cannot readily be formalized as a set of theoretical principles lending themselves to training purposes. Policing citizens in diverse social settings always resembles something of a craft. Consequently, substantial parts of their motivational work can only be left for the law enforcement officers themselves, within a work organization that emphasizes self-motivation through a police culture of reserve.

Concluding Remarks

Through my ongoing research, I have attempted to contribute to an understanding of how certain social psychological responses are handled in the course of police work. My focus has been on how the ambivalence created by such responses is managed with the help of a set of sense-making techniques that render the ambivalence more conducive to the principles of democratic policing based on the ideals of the constitutional welfare state and characterized by a certain respectful code of conduct (Manning, 2005, p. 24). Lateral mobility, occasional forays into the "less criminal" neighborhoods within the precinct, keeping operational work separate from grand theorizing, and adherence to a humanistic style of policing citizens all represent perseverance strategies used by officers of the Gothenburg police department gang units to increase their motivation for the job and on the job in circumstances in which cynicism and distrust might otherwise prevail.

As implications of my investigation, I want to point to certain implications that the perseverance strategies discussed above have for the emerging style of community policing also known as *reassurance policing* (Fielding, 2005, pp. 463–465; Herrington & Millie, 2006, pp. 153–154; Holmberg, 2002, pp. 38–39). Reassurance (or proximity) policing calls for broad engagement in a residential area, relying on the same police officers coming back to social workers, civil associations, and businessmen in the neighborhood over a protracted period of time. If my analysis of the perseverance strategies employed by the police is correct, the techniques that help maintain a necessary culture of reserve will place constraints on this version of prolonged community policing. Their presuppositions, moreover, conflict not just with the familiarity requirement of community policing; self-motivational impasses will probably affect proactive efforts within reassurance policing as well, rendering the intelligence-led rationale slightly diffuse. In other words, problem-oriented features in a reassurance policing project will remain more or less reactive on the ground. However, I do not believe that this forms part of a wider policing crisis caused by officers who cannot "show themselves to be swift, flexible, or innovative" (Shearing, 2005, p. 61). Rather, it continues to form a culturally defined part of a police force destined to "deal in darkness," staying motivated in the face of persisting public order problems and acting with respect for the integrity of the citizens.

I wish to mention one last policy implication, regarding how the culture of reserve might be established, maintained, and strengthened in police organizations. More precisely, it is about police education. Given that the perseverance strategies seem constructive in terms of trust and confidence, the ambition to transform the current police training into a university degree (at least in the Nordic countries) might be reevaluated. Indeed, knowledge that is more theoretical could enhance the professional status of police education. However, too much academic idealism could hamper motivation on the job. Should the gulf between education and actual police work become too wide, that is, if there are only negligible opportunities for real-life experiences, one faces the peril of producing ex-policemen out of newcomers or police recruits. In short, their education risks not adequately equipping them for their life on the job. This is a well-known phenomenon among physicians (Ebaugh, 1988, pp. 52–65). To counteract in advance burnout processes among police officers, police training should include regular contact with the skills of craftsmanship in law enforcement, with its culture of reserve, and its concomitant not so rosy perseverance strategies. This, I argue, is a vital reminder from the streets, directed to police executives and political leaders trying to integrate police education with the larger university system.

References

Åkerström, M. (2006). Doing ambivalence: Embracing policy innovation at arm's length. *Social Problems, 53*, 57–74.

Bayley, D., & Garofalo, J. (1989). The management of violence by police patrol officers. *Criminology, 27*, 1–23.

Berger, P. L. (1997). *Redeeming laughter: The comic dimension of human experience.* Berlin: Walter de Gruyter.

Bittner, E. (1970). *The functions of the police in modern society: A review of background factors, current practices, and possible role models.* Chevy Chase, MD: National Institute of Mental Health.

Björk, M. (2005). Between frustration and aggression: Legal framing and the policing of public disorder in Sweden and Denmark. *Policing and Society, 15,* 305–326.

Björk, M. (2006a). *Ordningsmakten i stadens periferi. En studie av polisiära gänginsatser i Göteborg, 2004–2005* [Public order in the urban periphery. Gang-unit policing in Gothenburg, 2004–2005]. Eslöv: Brutus Ostlings Bokförlag Symposion.

Björk, M. (2006b). Policing agonistic pluralism: Classical and contemporary thoughts on the viability of the polity. *Distinktion: Scandinavian Journal of Social Theory, 12,* 75–91.

Björk, M. (in press). Wolves and sheepdogs: On migration, ethnic relations and gang–police interaction in Sweden. In F. van Gemert, I.-L. Lien, & D. Peterson (Eds.), *Youth gangs, migration and ethnicity.* Cullompton: Blumer.

Blumer, H. (1954). What is wrong with social theory. *American Sociological Review, 19,* 3–10.

Brown, J. (2000). Occupational culture as a factor in the stress experience of police officers. In F. Leishman, B. Loveday, & S. P. Savage (Eds.), *Core issues in policing* (pp. 249–263). Harlow: Pearson Longman.

Czarniawska, B. (1997). *Narrating the organization. Dramas of institutional identity.* Chicago and London: University of Chicago Press.

Czarniawska, B. (1998). *A narrative approach to organization studies.* London: Sage.

Derrida, J. (1992). Force of law: The "mystical foundation of authority," In D. Cornell, M. Rosenfeld, & D. G. Carlson (Eds.), *Deconstruction and the possibility of justice* (pp. 3–67). London: Routledge.

Ebaugh, H. R. (1988). *Becoming an EX. The process of role exit.* Chicago and London: University of Chicago Press.

Ekman, G. (1999). *Från text till batong* [From texts to nightsticks]. Stockholm: Handelshögskolan.

Emerson, R. M. (1981). On last resorts. *American Journal of Sociology, 87,* 1–22.

Fielding, N. G. (2005). Concepts and theory in community policing. *Howard Journal of Criminal Justice, 44*(5), 460–472.

Granér, R. (2004). *Patrullerande polisers yrkeskultur* [Police culture in the streets]. Lund: Socialhögskolan.

Herbert, S. (2006). *Citizens, cops and power. Recognizing the limits of community.* Chicago and London: University of Chicago Press.

Herrington, V., & Millie, A. (2006). Applying reassurance policing: Is it "business as usual"? *Policing and Society, 16,* 146–163.

Holmberg, L. (2002). Personalised policing: Results from a series of experiments with proximity policing in Denmark, *Policing, 25,* 32–47.

Jackall, R. (2005). *Street stories. The world of police detectives.* Cambridge, MA: Harvard University Press.

Jonsen, A. R., & Toulmin, S. (1988). *The abuse of casuistry. A history of moral reasoning.* Berkeley: University of California Press.

Klein, M. W. (2004). *Gang cop.* Walnut Creek, CA: Altamira Press.

Klockars. C. B. (1996). A theory of excessive force and its control. In W. A. Geller & H. Toch (Eds.), *Police violence: Understanding and controlling police abuse of force* (pp. 1–22). New Haven, CT: Yale University Press.

Manning, P. K. (2004). *Policing contingencies.* Chicago and London: University of Chicago Press.

Manning, P. K. (2005). The study of policing. *Police Quarterly, 8,* 23–43.

Maxwell. C. L., & Klein, M. W. (2006). *Street gang patterns and policies.* Oxford, UK: Oxford University Press.

McElhinny, B. (2003). Fearful, forceful agents of law: Ideologies about language and gender in police officers. *Pragmatics, 13*(2), 253–284.

Muir, W. K., Jr. (1977). *Police: Street corner politicians.* Chicago and London: University of Chicago Press.

Newburn, T. (Ed.). (2005). *Policing. Key readings.* Cullompton: Willan.

Oakeshott, M. (1991). *Rationalism in politics and other essays.* New and Expanded Edition. Indianapolis: Liberty Fund.

Sampson, R. J., & Raudenbush, S. W. (1999). Systematic social observation of public spaces: A new look at disorder in urban neighborhoods. *American Journal of Sociology, 105,* 603–651.

Shearing, C. (2005). Nodal security. *Police Quarterly, 8,* 57–63.

Skinner, Q. (1989). Language and political change. In T. Ball, J. Fan, & R. L. Hanson (Eds.), *Political innovation and conceptual change* (pp. 7–23). Cambridge, UK: Cambridge University Press.

Sykes, G. M., & Matza, D. (1957). Techniques of neutralization: A theory of delinquency. *American Sociological Review, 22,* 664–670.

Turner, J. H. (2003). *Human institutions: A theory of societal evolution.* Lanham: Rowman & Littlefield.

Waddington, P. A. J. (1999). Police (canteen) sub-culture: An appreciation. *British Journal of Criminology. 39,* 287–309.

Westley, W. A. (1953). Violence and the police. *American Journal of Sociology, 59,* 34–41.

GROUP BEHAVIOR IN CRIMINAL JUSTICE ORGANIZATIONS

One of the most fascinating areas within criminal justice administration is group behavior among employees. Much has been written about the power of socialization among officers within police departments, the influence of a "courtroom workgroup" on the court setting, and the ways in which correctional employees learn the ways of doing business within prisons. The extant literature has documented the nefarious side of criminal justice organizations, with very little examination of how and why employee behaviors are tied to the structural makeup of their organizations and influenced by group norms and values.

Janet Chan (article 14) examines the impact of technology on police practice. The author finds that new ways of implementing technology have changed many aspects of police work. Information technology has redefined the value of technical resources and institutionalized accountability and has restructured daily routines to some extent. As a result, police procedures have become more transparent, which is seen as an improvement in police services. Most officers surveyed in the research also appreciated the value of using technology-generated information for tactical and strategic purposes. However, technology seemingly has not impacted police discretion, and traditional policing styles have remained the same.

Mark Pogrebin and Eric Poole (article 15) analyze group dynamics within police organizations. They explore the lighter side of policing by discussing the role that humor plays within police work. Humor, according to the authors, relieves the stresses associated with the police occupation. Pogrebin and Poole place humor within a strategic and functional role that reveals the distinctive nature of patrol work. Such a revelation allows humor to be understood within the context of police operations, but more importantly, it has a specific impact on relations between supervisor and subordinate. Humor defines both acceptable and unacceptable behaviors on the part of officers while simultaneously affording the immediate supervisor (i.e., the sergeant) a reality perspective concerning the demands of patrol officers. The importance of sergeants to the delivery of services becomes critical for police administrators, since they are the nexus between the rank-and-file and commanders.

Drug courts are a recent development within the criminal justice system. Evaluating their effectiveness has been a popular pastime among scholars. Drug courts, like other treatment programs for offenders, look to outcome measures to gauge effectiveness. Mitchell Mackinem and Paul Higgins (article 16) take a deeper look at the construction of outcome measures in one drug court. They find that whether or not clients have successfully completed the program is not determined by clients' actions; rather, staff members produce the outcomes by interpreting clients' stories that explain incriminating behaviors (e.g., turning in "murky" or dirty urine samples, failing to keep appointments). In other words, if staff buy into clients' excuses for failing to comply with court rules and policies, they may not hold the clients officially responsible. As a result, a number of clients who "succeeded" are those whose reasons—"stories"—for failing to comply with the term of their treatment were accepted by staff as legitimate. Staff assumptions about drug abuse served as a basis for their reconstruction of the clients' behavior. For example, staff who believed that drug abuse was a medical problem or disease might see stressful family relationships as a reason for a return to drug use. The authors do a good job of examining who we are really evaluating with outcome measures: staff or clients.

Supermax prisons have been used to house prisoners referred to as the worst of the worst. The unintended but predictable consequence of creating the supermax system is well known to most criminal justice scholars and students. Craig Haney (article 17) provides an excellent description of how the supermax system is psychologically harmful to inmates and correctional staff. He argues that many of the behavior problems the system was designed to prevent are actually engendered by the harsh and brutal supermax environments. Haney refers to supermax systems as an "ecology of cruelty" in which men and women who work in the system are as much captives as the prisoners (i.e., the staff suffer the psychologically harmful effects of carrying out the cruelty). He argues that the harmful effects have become so well known that approval and use of supermax systems seem to be on the decline.

Michael Gilbert (article 18) describes the illusion of control within the traditional classical model of prison organization. Viewing prisons as places where discretionary authority is ubiquitous among officers, he suggests that the traditional approach to managing prisons is ineffective and insufficient to produce desired results. His critique points out that empowering traditional bureaucratic structures within prisons without being cognizant of the role and demands of correctional officers is pure fantasy. Correctional officers make the prison bureaucracy real; they enforce the rules, they negotiate with themselves and prisoners. Officer behavior is influenced more by group norms and their perception of what does and does not work in the prison than it is by administrative edict. Without this fundamental awareness, simply generating more rules makes the classical model of management illusory and potentially dangerous to all in the prison environment.

14

The Technological Game
How Information Technology Is Transforming Police Practice

JANET B. L. CHAN

> New technologies alter the structure of our interests: the things we
> think *about*. They alter the character of our symbols: the things we think
> *with*. And they alter the nature of community: the arena in which
> thoughts develop.
>
> —Postman (1992:18–20)

Introduction

Historically, technology has revolutionized police practices. The introduction of the telegraph in the late 19th century, and the use of two-way
radios, motor vehicles, and computer-assisted dispatching during the 20th
century have brought about dramatic changes in the organization of police
work (Manning, 1992a). There is, therefore, every reason to expect that the
latest round of technological change—the information technology revolution—would have an equally dramatic impact on policing. This article draws
on an Australian case study to examine the extent to which information technology has, as the above quotation from Postman (1992) suggests, altered the
structural, symbolic, and social organization of policing.

The latest round of technological changes in policing is driven by three
imperatives: to improve effectiveness and efficiency, to satisfy the demands of
external agencies for information, and to meet the requirements of new forms
of police management and accountability. The first imperative is technology-
driven: not only does technology promise to improve police effectiveness and
efficiency in controlling crime, it may also enhance their professional status

Janet B. L. Chan, *Criminology and Criminal Justice*, Vol. 1, pp. 139–159, © 2001 by Sage Publications. Reprinted by permission of Sage Publications.

and organizational legitimacy (Manning, 1992a; Ericson and Haggerty, 1997: 390). Given that information is the stock-in-trade of policing, police are investing in information technology to increase their capacity to store and process large volumes of data; improve their intelligence and investigative capabilities; and provide ready access to criminal records and other crime-related information. The need for technology that is compatible with other agencies is also an important driving force.

The second imperative is information-driven: police organizations regularly provide crime and accident data for external bodies such as road traffic authorities and insurance companies for their own management and risk assessment needs. Increasingly, police information is commodified and sold to external commercial institutions and individuals partly as a cost-recovery measure and partly to discourage frivolous requests (Ericson and Haggerty, 1997: 340–5). These external demands for police information are partly responsible for the need to improve information technology capacities within police organizations.

The third imperative is policy-driven. Police organizations' use of information technology to improve performance and management is the result of externally imposed demands for public accountability, in terms of cost-effectiveness, probity and procedural regularity. Since the 1980s, a new conception of public accountability has arisen in a number of western democracies such as Australia and Britain (Leishman et al., 1996; Power, 1997; Davids and Hancock, 1998; Chan, 1999). Traditionally, police practices and procedures are governed by laws and departmental rules, which are enforced by the courts and the police hierarchies respectively. The predominant mode of control is deterrence through legislation and rule making, investigation and enforcement, criminal sanctions and organizational discipline. The "new accountability," however, adopts the managerial techniques and administrative structures of private for-profit corporations, emphasizing cost control, efficiency, decentralization of management and the cutting back of the public sector, while creating market or quasi-market mechanisms, contracting out, performance indicators, risk assessment and audit procedures (Leishman et al., 1996; Power, 1997; Chan, 1999; Dean, 1999). In policing, the new managerialism has transformed the traditional police force into organizations with "mission statements," "business plans," "marketing strategies" and a new emphasis on "crime management," "customer service" and performance measures (Leishman et al., 1996; O'Malley and Palmer, 1996; Chan, 1997). Ackroyd et al. (1992) call it the "entrepreneurial revolution" in policing. Under this new order, police are being scrutinized *internally* by management systems, surveillance technologies, internal audits and investigations, and *externally* by "watchdog" agencies, public complaints systems, and central auditors. In effect, information technology provides a tool not only for the policing of citizens, but also for policing the police.

The Impact of Technology

The use of information technology has become part of everyday life in the 21st century for many individuals and the vast majority of organizations. It is therefore not surprising that a national mailed survey of US city police agencies in the mid-1990s found that only about 6 percent of the respondents did not have an in-house computer system (Mullen, 1996). Australian police forces, being typically much larger than American ones, have all adopted some form of service-wide computerized information system since the mid-1990s. But has the large-scale adoption of information technology made any difference to policing? Technology certainly has the capability to improve efficiency and enhance accountability, but whether this capability is realized in practice is not a foregone conclusion. Although there is now a growing body of research on technology-based organizational change (see Yates and Van Maanen, 1996), there have been very few research studies on the impact of information technology on policing (Manning, 1992a; Mullen, 1996).

Different perspectives have emerged from the available literature on the extent to which information technology has changed police practices. One view suggests that information technologies "have been constrained by the traditional structure of policing and by the traditional role of the officer" (Manning, 1992a: 350). Drawing on evaluation studies published in the 1970s and 1980s (e.g. Chaiken et al., 1975; Colton, 1978; Rheinier et al., 1979; Hough, 1980), Manning outlines the disappointing results of various technological innovations such as Computer-Aided Dispatch (CAD) systems, attempts to reduce response time, car locator and tracking systems, crime-mapping techniques and management information systems. He concludes that: "Such research as exists is often inconclusive or suggests that new technologies have less effect on police practices than their proponents predict or prefer" (Manning, 1992a: 382).

In contrast, studies conducted in the 1990s come to rather different conclusions. Harper's (1991) research on the use of a computerized crime-reporting system (CRS) by detectives in a medium-sized British police constabulary suggests that information technology has made a clear difference to detective work. Not only has the computerized information system made it easier and faster to access and retrieve information, it has transformed the "spatio-temporal context in which detectives operate": detectives no longer need to travel to different places to locate records and they have virtually 24-hour access to files. Although not originally intended by the technology, the crime-reporting system gave detectives an advantage over offenders when negotiating about "offences to be taken into consideration" (TICed) by "enhancing a detective's ability to bluff" (Harper, 1991: 300). This advantage is likely to be temporary, however, as suspects would eventually get used to seeing computers on the desk of detectives and no longer be intimidated by them.

Ericson and Haggerty's (1997) study of Canadian police organizations, carried out in the early 1990s, demonstrates that information technology has had a profound impact on the way officers think, act and report on their activities. The introduction of information technology has meant that individual police discretion is severely circumscribed by the rules, formats and technologies of the reporting systems, whereas supervision has been tightened both *prospectively* as details of police activities are embedded in the "required fields" of information technology systems and *retrospectively* as supervisors take more seriously their scrutiny of filed reports. The capability of information technology is such that it has become an effective tool for the surveillance of police supervisors, the detection of misconduct, and all types of audits, monitoring, and risk management (Ericson and Haggerty, 1997: 398–9). The researchers argue that:

> Communication technologies . . . radically alter the structure of police organization by levelling hierarchies, blurring traditional divisions of labor, dispersing supervisory capacities and limiting individual discretion. In the process, traditional rank structures of command and control are replaced by system surveillance mechanisms for regulating police conduct. (Ericson and Haggerty, 1997: 388)

Information technology has also created new cultures of policing and rendered police organizations more transparent (Ericson and Haggerty, 1997: 412).

The impact of information technology is, however, not always as intended. Ericson and Haggerty (1997) concede that police officers did actively resist some aspects of information technology through refusal to participate, aversion to use or other forms of subtle resistance. Resistance was likely where officers perceived that such technology was used as a surveillance mechanism by supervisors or where the systems were technically difficult or cumbersome. There were also unintended consequences such as the proliferation of "bootleg forms," an increase rather than a decrease in paper files and police work becoming even more office bound in some cases. As Manning (1992a) points out, the mere availability and accessibility of information does not necessarily mean that information is used effectively or appropriately by police officers and managers. In general, the use of computer technology may increase productivity without resulting in any gain in efficiency (see Henman, 1996).

Understanding Technological Change

Researchers who study the impact of technology on social life have long argued that technology should not be seen as consisting of a physical, material dimension only; rather, technology operates in a social context, and its meaning is perceived differently by people in different social and organizational positions (Ackroyd et al., 1992; Manning, 1992a; Orlikowski and Gash, 1994). While technological changes have the capacity to transform social and organizational life, it is important to recognize that technology is itself shaped by social and organizational conditions. The impact of a specific technology on social life is often determined by factors beyond its technical capacity—

factors which may be psychological, social, political, or cultural. Hence, technology may be constraining or enabling, but people have the ability to "adapt, bend, shape, develop, subvert, misuse and otherwise manipulate technological specifications for various purposes" (Ackroyd et al., 1992: 11). Orlikowski and Robey explain this as the underlying "duality" (see Giddens, 1984) of information technology:

> This duality is expressed in its *constituted* nature—information technology is the social product of subjective human action within specific structural and cultural contexts—and its *constitutive* role—information technology is simultaneously an objective set of rules and resources involved in mediating (facilitating and constraining) human action and hence contributing to the creation, recreation, and transformation of these contexts. Information technology is both an antecedent and a consequence of organizational action. (Orlikowski and Robey, 1991: 151)

Orlikowski has therefore argued that the impact of technological change on organizational structure, work practices, communication channels and performance cannot be understood in a *deterministic* or rationalist way (Orlikowski, 1996: 64). Instead, the consequences of information technology should be interpreted via an *interpretive* or *emergent* model, i.e. that they result from the "interplay among competing infrastructures, conflicting objectives and preferences of different social groups, and the operation of chance" and that information technology is open to interpretation during implementation and use (Robey and Sahay, 1996: 95). These models stress the active role of organizational members and the importance of social context and processes that produce the meanings of technology. From this perspective, technology is "an occasion for, not a determinant of, organizational change" (Barley, 1986).

Broadly speaking, we can distinguish three types of factors that influence the course of technological change and its impact on organizations: (a) *technical factors,* which include the nature of technology itself and how technological change is managed; (b) *cultural factors,* which include the assumptions inherent in the introduced technology and the extent to which these are congruent with those held by users within organizations; and (c) *political factors,* which consist of the interests at stake in technological change and the conflict or bargaining that may result.

Technical Factors

Technological change can have a large or small impact on organizations depending on the nature and design of the technology and the way in which technological change is managed. Ericson and Haggerty's (1997) research suggests that information technology has had a substantial impact on policing partly because of the design and implementation of a more coercive technology which is difficult to avoid or bypass: when the basic routines of police work are built into the system, officers are literally not able to work without using the technology (Ericson and Haggerty, 1997: 394). In fact, where systems are less coercive or less effective, technology can be called upon to correct the problem (Ericson and Haggerty, 1997: 414).

Sparrow has long emphasized the importance of managing information systems properly:

> [I]f badly managed, they can frustrate managerial purposes, enshrine old values, focus attention on outdated and inappropriate performance measures, give power to the wrong people, cast in concrete old ways of doing business, create false or misleading public expectations, destroy partnerships and impose crippling restrictions to new styles of operation—quite apart from their propensity to consume millions and millions of tax dollars. (Sparrow, 1991: 26)

Examples of technical and implementation problems of information technology in policing include flaws in system design which resulted in data of poor quality and the failure to build and maintain support for technology within police departments (Hough, 1980).

Cultural Factors

Technology is not simply an objective, physical given; people have to make sense of it and, in the process, "develop particular assumptions, expectations and knowledge of the technology, which then serve to shape subsequent actions toward it" (Orlikowski and Gash, 1994: 175). Orlikowski and Gash coin the term "technological frames" to describe a subset of the cognitive schemas shared by members of social groups (Schein, 1985; Sackmann, 1991). Technological frames can be both helpful and constraining: they can help "structure" people's experience and reduce organizational uncertainty, but they can also inhibit creativity and reinforce established assumptions (Orlikowski and Gash, 1994: 176–7). Technological frames generally vary between social groups, according to the "purpose, context, power, knowledge base, and the [technological] artifact itself" (Orlikowski and Gash, 1994: 179). In their case study, Orlikowski and Gash distinguished between three domains of technological frames: (a) the nature of technology—people's understanding of *what* technology is capable of; (b) technology strategy—their view of *why* technology was introduced in their organization; and (c) technology in use—their understanding of *how* technology is to be routinely used and the consequences of such use (Orlikowski and Gash, 1994: 183–4). The impact of information technology on organizations can then be explained in terms of the existence of *congruence* or *incongruence* in technological frames between social groups. Where incongruent technological frames exist, the introduction of technology is likely to encounter conflicts and difficulties.

The incongruence between the technological frames of information technology designers and those of the police was evident in the mismatch between the models of policing implicit in the technology introduced in the 1970s and the reality of policing:

> Most attempts to apply analytic techniques such as statistical modelling techniques to police administration are underpinned by a set of assumptions . . . (i) the primary objective of the police is crime control; (ii) police activity is one of the primary determinants of crime levels; (iii) the police are organised as a rational bureaucracy; (iv) police strategies are primarily those of deterrence. . . . That these basic assumptions are too inaccurate to pass muster even as a provisional statement is becoming increasingly clear. (Hough, 1980: 351–2)

Such incongruence can create tension in the workplace as workers seek to adjust their practices to conform to the system's requirements:

> . . . systems designers and implementers very often underrate, or even discount, the working context, its social organization, its tacit skills and knowledge, into which the system has to fit as a tool of that work. The result is often that working practices must be changed to accommodate to the system in some way (which may or may not be the intention behind the introduction of the system) and/or an uneasy tension is created between those who do the work and the requirements of the system. (Ackroyd et al., 1992: 119)

Sparrow (1991) shows the difficulty in trying to make a computer-aided dispatch (CAD) system designed for traditional-style policing serve a community-based, problem-solving style of policing that management in the Houston Police Department wanted to adopt. Problems of "call stacking" (holding calls for beat officers to deal with), "checking by" (allowing patrol cars to do proactive work instead of servicing non-urgent calls), "call histories" (the amount of time call information should be retained on-line) and "cherry picking" (officers taking the "good" calls and leaving the unpleasant ones) revealed the fundamental conflict between traditional-style policing where response time was a major concern and problem-solving policing where police were expected to do proactive work, analyze call histories and make mature, responsible decisions about their work. Sparrow even warns managers against leaving the design and implementation of information systems to technologists. This example illustrates the incongruence of technological frames between information technology designers and managers. If this example can be extrapolated, where information technology is designed to change management culture (Ackroyd et al., 1992), accountability procedures (Ericson and Haggerty, 1997) or rank-and-file work practices, clashes in technological frames would exist almost by definition. The result may be various forms of resistance, breakdown in communication, or even suspension of the information technology project itself (Orlikowski and Gash, 1994: 181).

Political Factors

Technological changes often "destabilize the power balance between organizational segments by altering communication patterns, roles relationships, the division of labor, established formats for organizational communication, and taken-for-granted routines" (Manning, 1996: 54). Since information itself is a source of power, information technology can lead to power struggles, adaptations or reactions which may subvert the original intentions of the new technology (Orlikowski and Robey, 1991: 155).

In policing, the introduction of information technology can restrict the discretion and autonomy of "street-level" police officers, while at the same time enhancing the status of information technology specialists (Ericson and Haggerty, 1997: 406). Such developments alter the balance of power between workers and supervisors and between sworn officers and civilians. When officers feel that their autonomy is threatened by internal surveillance or external interference, they are likely to resort to resistance or sabotage where possible. Ericson and Haggerty gave examples of patrol officers collaborating with dispatchers to avoid being tracked by computer-aided dispatch systems (1997: 414) as well as examples of officers refusing or resisting the mandatory reporting of family violence as an "externally driven surveillance technology based on an outlook of distrust" (1997: 386).

Dynamics of Technological Change

The above discussion may have presented an unduly static view of technological impact. The introduction of new technology is merely the beginning of a "technological drama" (Manning, 1992b, 1996) of normalization, adjustment, reconstitution and reintegration. The resultant reintegration and normalization may be manifested in various changes as well as continuities in organizational life. Orlikowski's (1996) "situated change" perspective of organizational change is similarly relevant for understanding the dynamic quality of technological impact. Orlikowski offers a view of organizational change which is emergent and continuous rather than rapid and discontinuous: "through a series of ongoing and situated accommodations, adaptations, and alterations (that draw on previous variations and mediate future ones), sufficient modifications may be enacted over time that fundamental changes are achieved" (Orlikowski, 1996: 66). Her study of the introduction of a call-tracking system of a customer support department in a software company found that the organizational structures and practices of the department had changed considerably over the two years following the implementation of the new technology, but the transformation, "while enabled by the technology, was not caused by it" (Orlikowski, 1996: 69). Rather, members of the department "attempted to make sense of and appropriate the new technology and its embedded constraints and enablements" and through their daily actions and interactions in response to the technology, they enacted "a series of metamorphic changes in their organizing practices and structures" (Orlikowski, 1996: 89).

The Technological Game

The above review suggests that technology should not be seen as purely technical and physical—it can shape social life but is itself modified by social and organizational conditions. The impact of technology on policing is dependent on how technology interacts with existing cultural values, management styles, work practices and technical capabilities. A useful way to conceptualize technological change is to examine its relationship to the "field" and "habitus" of policing (Bourdieu and Wacquant, 1992; see Chan, 1997). For Bourdieu, a field is like a game; it is a social space of conflict and competition, where participants struggle to establish control over specific power and authority. Central to Bourdieu's concept of field is the notion of "capital." Various forms of capital operate in different social fields—these include economic capital, cultural or informational capital, social capital and symbolic capital (Bourdieu, 1987: 3–4). Habitus is a "feel for the game." It is a system of dispositions which agents acquire either individually, through family and the education system, or as a group, through organizational socialization. Bourdieu's framework suggests that changes in the game (field) would create new necessities that may require the creation of new strategies (habitus) for coping. Technological change, to the extent that it redefines the game of policing, can bring about changes in the field (through various constraints and resources) as well as transform the habitus (e.g. classifications, assumptions and sensibilities).

An Australian Case Study

The following discussion is based on a recent study of an Australian police force (see Chan et al., 2001). There are only nine police forces in Australia, eight covering each of the States and Territories plus a federal force. The Eastern Police Service (EPS, a pseudonym) has several thousand sworn officers and provides service to several million people over a vast geographical area. Development of an information technology strategy began in the early 1990s following several public inquiries into the police force. The study was conducted in 1998–99. At the time, the EPS was in the middle of implementing an integrated computer system to incorporate several existing systems dealing with crime reporting, processing of offenders and criminal histories. In addition, a variety of computer-based facilities were operating, including electronic mail and bulletin board, computer-aided dispatch, traffic incidents and transport data, intelligence systems, electronic warrants and linkages to nationwide systems.

The research was designed to examine the extent to which information technology has modified the accountability structure, the occupational culture, and policing practices at the street, supervisory and management levels in the EPS. Several research techniques were used to obtain information on the development and implementation of the systems and their impact on policing: 23 interviews[1] with senior police and information technology specialists; 11 focus groups with a total of 106 participants including general duties officers, detectives, intelligence officers, officers in charge and information management personnel; a representative (but nonrandom) survey of 506 police officers[2]; approximately 30 hours of ride-along observation over eight half-shifts; and analysis of a large number of documents including annual reports, strategic and implementation plans and program specifications (see Chapter 2 in Chan et al., 2001 for further details).

Impact of Information Technology on the Field of Policing

Information technology had become an integral part of police life in the EPS by the late 1990s. Survey respondents[3] reported spending an average of three hours and 37 minutes per eight-hour shift using computers for administrative tasks. The vast majority (72 percent) of the respondents thought that information technology had made "a great difference" to police work, while a minority thought it had made "a little difference" (26 percent) or "no difference at all" (2 percent). This feeling was more prevalent among respondents who have had longer service in the EPS and those in higher ranks. The new technology has fundamentally altered the field of policing through the various resources (Bourdieu's "capital") it provided and constraints (Bourdieu's "necessities") it imposed on police work.

Technology as Resource

Effectiveness and efficiency. In spite of many complaints in the focus groups about various technical problems with the systems, EPS officers' assessment of the impact of information technology on their own work was generally positive. The majority of respondents indicated that information technology has allowed them to work more effectively (79 percent agreed versus 3 percent disagreed),[4] made their work easier (66 versus 7 percent) and helped them cope with the amount of information police needed to do their work properly (59 versus 10 percent). The gain in efficiency as a result of information technology was especially salient to police who had experienced the old technology. For example, one participant in a focus group of specialist investigators (FG9) said that five to six years ago, to type a record of interview for a large investigation would take five to six hours; now it could be done in half an hour from a taped record of interview.

Communication. Survey respondents also rated positively the impact of information technology on workplace relations and communication. The majority agreed that information technology has led to improved information sharing between workers (70 percent) and improved communication between workers (58 percent). Less than 10 percent of respondents disagreed with those statements. Similarly, respondents tended to agree that information technology has allowed people to work more cooperatively (47 percent agreed versus 7 percent disagreed) and created a more positive work atmosphere (30 versus 13 percent). Improvement in communication between workers was largely the result of the availability of electronic mail that facilitated teamwork, information gathering and sharing (FG5).

Technical expertise.   With the widespread use of technology in the organization, technical expertise became a much-valued form of cultural capital. The majority of survey respondents agreed that information technology has led to increased computer literacy among police (75 percent versus 5 percent disagreed) and enhanced the professional status of police (52 versus 9 percent). As one intelligence officer explained: "As intel officers we were considered the leaders in IT. We knew nothing, but we knew so much more than the basic [officer] who knew practically nothing. We were gods to them" (FG5). The growth in funding and staffing of IT-related functions within the EPS was a source of much envy and some bitterness among some officers. The ascendancy of officers with IT expertise may also threaten the traditional power structure of an organization where previously leaders were predominantly drawn from the criminal investigation branch (Interview 1).

Technology as Constraint

Time use.   A fairly substantial proportion of survey respondents thought that, as a result of information technology, they spent more time satisfying accountability requirements (41 percent); doing "paperwork" (36 percent); planning, organizing or analyzing information (30 percent); supervising or checking the work of staff (26 percent). In addition, a fair proportion indicated that they spent less time patrolling the streets (39 percent); interacting with members of the community in non-crime or non-emergency situations (30 percent); informing citizens on the progress of their case (25 percent); and responding to calls from citizens (20 percent). Respondents in the higher ranks (senior constable and above) were more likely to be affected. As an officer-in-charge in one of the focus groups explained:

> Eighty percent of our time is probably consumed in doing all this sort of stuff. . . . There's huge benefits in [information technology], but we haven't got time to use it. . . . There's accountability issues, . . . I could spend six or seven hours a day just doing compliance without even looking at police work. Officers-in-charge of bigger stations probably would need half a dozen staff to do that properly. Nobody does it properly—we're all aware of that. It's very frustrating. (FG6)

The issue of police spending more time in front of computers and less time on the streets was often raised in the focus groups. For example, a general-duties officer said that: "Technology has drawn a lot of people off the street and stuck them into offices"—even though there are a lot of police "on paper," very few are on the road (FG1).

Discretion.   Survey respondents were ambivalent about whether information technology has limited the amount of discretion police have—25 percent agreed, 17 percent disagreed and 59 percent were neutral. General duties officers were more likely to think that information technology has limited their discretion, compared with detectives. Similarly, officers in lower ranks were more likely than those in higher ranks to agree that their discretion was limited by technology. When the issue of discretion was raised in focus groups, one response was that it is a lot harder to write a file off because of insufficient evidence—a reason has to be entered. However, constables can still find ways of cutting corners, for example, in relation to whether a minor incident should be reported (FG5). Other police said that there are no shortcuts—the system was designed in such a way that it cannot be circumvented (FG4). In fact, the system is capable of monitoring shortcuts: "the shortcuts can now be assessed—if you are taking shortcuts, [it] can be seen that you are taking shortcuts" (FG5).

Routine operations. A substantial proportion of survey respondents thought that information technology has required police to follow unnecessary steps to get things done (43 percent agreed versus 13 percent disagreed). This feeling was particularly strong among detectives, with 59 percent agreeing and only 9 percent disagreeing. Responses also vary by rank—percentages who agreed went up from 35 and 36 percent among first-year constables and constables respectively to 51 percent for senior constables, 53 percent for sergeants, 47 percent for senior sergeants, and 60 percent for inspectors. Much of the focus group discussions centered on the additional steps officers had to follow to get their work done. For example, one general duties officer explained that the old way of doing the court brief was to put it in the typewriter and wind it on, but it was quicker because you knew exactly where you wanted to go, there was no need to wait for each screen to come up. Another participant said that on the old system, it would take 10 to 20 minutes to complete a court brief, whereas now it takes two to three hours (FG1). This view was supported by officers from other focus groups:

> When I was at [name of station] years ago we could . . . do a random breath test, pick up a drunk driver, take him into town, process him, . . . have him charged, have a [court brief] typed in the prosecutors box, have all the paper work done, be back on the road and the best we ever did it in was 40 minutes. . . . That was on a manual typewriter. Now, . . . by the time everyone does all their compliance with their custody indexes and all their indexes and does everything else, finally gets through to [crime reporting system] to get a number, then they sit down in front of the computer to do the [court brief] on the computer. And the [court brief] on the computer takes a lot longer than the old manual typewriter. So I'm looking at hours. . . . [Comments from the floor estimate that the process has gone from 40 minutes to two hours.] (FG6)

Accountability. There was a general feeling that with the advent of information technology came additional reporting and accountability requirements. Two-thirds of the survey respondents agreed that information technology has required them to report on their activities more frequently and made them more accountable for their actions. A number of focus group participants pointed out that it was in fact the need for accountability that caused the additional workload, not the information technology systems per se. As one specialist investigator said: "The amount of time spent on the computer isn't because of information technology, it's because of legislation that we've got to do" (FG9). Others added that: "If we didn't have the information technology to meet those regulations, we'd be even slower," or "We'd be stressed out that much that you'd have half the Police Service on stress leave." To achieve the same level of reporting using the old manual system would have been impossible (FG9).

The majority of survey respondents agreed that information technology has led to a closer scrutiny of their work by their supervisors (55 percent) and that information technology has made their supervisors more aware of their day-to-day activities and workload (52 percent). There is no doubt that information technology has given police supervisors a greater capacity to scrutinize the work of their staff, but whether this capacity has been utilized effectively is debatable. An officer in charge in a focus group explained that the new incident management system allows supervisors to check where their cars are, what their officers are doing, how far they have got in their crime report and whether they have done their job properly. However, this officer said that he does not really use the system, because he does not have time to do it (FG2).

Changes and Continuities in the Habitus

To what extent have these changes in the field made a difference to the habitus of policing, that is, the cultural assumptions about the aims of policing, appropriate ways of seeing and behaving and treasured values and beliefs? From the accounts of officers who took part in the study, it is possible to discern changes as well as continuities in the habitus that can be attributed to the use of information technology.

Policing Style and Practice

Information technology has had limited impact on the dominant style of policing in the EPS. Only 38 percent of the survey respondents agreed (52 percent were neutral, while 10 percent disagreed) that information technology has led to a more problem-oriented police service. Respondents in rural divisions were more likely (47 percent) to agree compared with respondents in metropolitan (37 percent), suburban (33 percent) and provincial city (35 percent) divisions. The idea of "smarter" policing strategies was raised in one of the focus groups. Some officers mentioned the potential of "intelligence-driven patrols," analysis of "hot spots" and repeat offenders and proactive crime investigations. Others were more skeptical: "Who gets time for that?" It was said that it does not happen—"never will," although in theory it could happen. One focus group participant explained the role conflict experienced by intelligence officers:

> Most of them are in Region Offices. Most of their time is [spent] putting stats together for bosses. But that's not their role. Their role is to look at

> the crimes that are going on to target areas or offences. They don't have time to do it because they are collating crime stats for a management meeting. Because intel officers aren't able to do their job, there's a whole bunch of baddies we can't get because they aren't looking at it. You might say we should do it, but where do we get time? (FG4)

Only 35 percent agreed that information technology led to better proactive policing, half were neutral and 18 percent disagreed. Information technology has given police the potential for crime prevention but, as a participant from a focus group pointed out, there were insufficient resources to realize this potential:

> From an intel perspective . . . . We can identify problems, we can predict where we believe where things are going to happen . . . and we can continue to say if we do this, then we should reduce crime. And we'll do it for six weeks, then stop because that's where the resources finish. And we've done that time and time again. So we've created this technology, or technology has helped us look at what's happened in the past and predict what's going to happen in the future crime-wise, but we don't have the resources to go to the next step. . . . We've got police collecting the information but not the time to actually go and act on what's been collected. (FG5)

One area where information technology has facilitated proactive policing in a dramatic way was the use of stand-alone computers in police cars to check for outstanding traffic offense warrants based on vehicle or boat license numbers, persons of interest and drivers licenses. As an illustration, during a five-hour period one of the researchers spent on the road with two officers, the officers executed the equivalent of approximately $5,500 worth of warrants (Legosz and Brereton, 2001). Focus group participants were enthusiastic about the system; officers said that they did about 1000 checks a week (FG6).

These findings would not have come as a surprise to the architects of the systems. Organizationally, the EPS was totally "immature" in the early 1990s, not only in relation to information technology, but more significantly, "there was really no management infrastructure to speak of at all," following the removal of top levels of management as a result of a damaging corruption inquiry (Interview 12). There was a deliberate strategy to secure support for, and ownership of, the system initially among operational police before targeting managers. The idea was to move gradually from an ad hoc, operationally oriented system to an integrated, tactically, strategically, and eventually policy-oriented system (Interview 1). However, this was expected to be a longer-term objective, as the organization has yet to move to the next level of maturity and capability. One of the barriers was precisely the "technological frame" of traditional culture that sees information as useful only if it leads to arrests:

> . . . even our intel people, even the high-end users, our power users, generally see information from an offender perspective—in other words, information analysis is all about how we can . . . find an offender . . . how

do you nick someone, and so that limits what becomes useful information. (Interview 1)

There was not a clear vision of what problem-oriented policing might offer; it was still seen as "soft" and marginal. Information technology has, in effect, "made things easier, rather than made things different" (Interview 1).

Reliance on Technology

Some officers were not entirely comfortable with the heavy reliance on information technology for information. As an officer-in-charge observed in a focus group discussion, because of the availability of electronic bulletin boards and databases, police no longer carry policing knowledge in their head (FG2). Reliance on information technology also meant the loss of "local knowledge," as one general duties officer remarked: "information technology is good for number crunching, but you don't know the face. You can drive around for whole shift and not see the same face twice" (FG1). Another officer-in-charge thought that police are not as directly involved with the public in criminal investigations as they used to be five to 10 years ago. Even though intelligence is extremely good, these officers felt that it will never take the place of basic hands-on traditional intelligence gathering—getting out on the street, talking to people, finding out what is going on (FG2).

Transparency of Procedures.   Survey respondents were generally positive about the impact of information technology on the quality of police service. Six out of 10 thought that information technology had led to improved police service to the public (62 percent agreed versus 12 percent disagreed) and improved police response to crime (59 percent versus 12 percent). Several groups mentioned that the crime reporting system has made a difference. With this system, police procedures are more transparent—the complainant can see the officer getting on the phone to file a report: "Now the public can see that something's really happening" (FG3). The system also allows victims and complainants to get faster feedback on the progress of their case by ringing up with a system number (FG2, FG8). Police can also respond better to customer inquiries as they can access information about the case and identify whom to contact (FG5).

Resentment towards Accountability Demands

When survey respondents were asked in general terms whether information technology has led to improved police accountability, six out of 10 agreed, although a similar proportion also thought that information technology has led to an *overemphasis* on accountability. Nearly four in 10 also thought that information technology has led to a less trusting or more paranoid organizational atmosphere. Accountability—internal and external—was a burning issue among many focus group participants. A familiar theme is that accountability has gone too far, and at the expense of doing the job:

> These days after [name of corruption inquiry] or what-have-you, the emphasis on accountability has become much higher, and in doing so they introduce 9321 different registers that's got to be filled out to maintain the accountability. But in doing that, you spend that much time becoming accountable and spend less time doing the job you're paid for. I think accountability is a good thing, but at the same time it's got to be weighed up between getting the job done. And trusting people too, you get to the point where you're so busy being accountable you feel that nobody trusts what you do . . . You've got to be given that trust and it be understood that you will do that job. (FG2)

Another concern was whether the information in the systems was going to be used for punishment (FG5). For example, with the crime reporting system, if there is a complaint about inaction on a crime report, the tools are there to find the individual officer responsible, and to show what the person did or did not do.

Some officers felt that "the Department has gone risk-management crazy" with new databases where it was no longer possible to "cut corners" (FG5). A participant from a group of detectives agreed: "It's about auditing and checking . . . and it's overdone . . . it's accountability and it's gone too far. . . . It's not being productive" (FG4). Other members of the group pointed out that many of the risk management or accountability exercises are "futile" and not worth the time. They argued that risk management should be about minimizing risk, but, according to one of the participants, the Police Service's idea of risk management is there should be no risk, no acceptable level of risk—"They haven't grasped the concept." Another officer agreed:

> The idea of risk management is to identify something everyone's doing wrong, e.g. entering an index wrong—not to check every index they're doing to make sure they're doing it. It's to check problems with the system, not as an accountability exercise, which is what they're using it as. (FG4)

A recurrent theme among focus group discussions relates to the abuse of technology-generated performance indicators. One example involved officers in a watchhouse who abused the system by putting in a computer entry every time they fed a prisoner, so that they got a new job number each time. Similarly, an officer can arrest someone with 100 warrants and enter the data for each arrest on each warrant to show how busy he has been (FG1). Another bone of contention was clear-up rates. Detectives blamed the crime reporting system data entry operators for not recording all their clear-ups, while others were concerned that monthly fluctuations in clear-up rates might give misleading indicators of performance (FG2).

Officers particularly resented demands for information and accountability from external organizations. It was said in one focus group (FG1) that a lot of police work is for the [watchdog organization], insurance companies, security companies, and other "vested interests." For example, the accident form is a very long form that has to be filled out by the police for every accident. Similarly, there were concerns that the [watchdog organization] has imposed a variety of reporting requirements that make officers' work more cumbersome.

Conclusion

These research findings are consistent with Ericson and Haggerty's (1997) conclusion that information technology has altered important aspects of the field of policing. In the case of the EPS, within a relatively short period of time following its introduction, information technology has redefined the value of communicative and technical resources, institutionalized accountability through built-in formats and procedures of reporting, and restructured the daily routines of operational policing. These changes in the field of policing have led to some changes in the habitus. For example, information technology has allowed police procedures to be more transparent at the level of "customer interface," and this transparency has become accepted as an indicator of good police service. Similarly, officers are beginning to appreciate the value of using technology-generated information for tactical and strategic purposes such as crime prevention, problem solving and resource allocation. Nevertheless, the dominance of traditional policing styles and values remains. Although information technology has given police the capacity to follow a "smarter" or more problem-oriented style of policing, this capacity has not been fully utilized. Even where technology facilitated proactive police work such as the checking of outstanding warrants, it has been used mainly to support a traditional law-enforcement style of policing focused on clear-up rates. The cultural suspicion and cynicism against management and external watchdogs is still very much alive, but this has been channeled into hostility towards the organization's "obsession" with risk management and external agencies' demand for data and accountability.

The case study sheds new light on the role of cultural factors in understanding the impact of technological change. There was undoubtedly a clash in "technological frames" (Orlikowski and Gash, 1994) between the users and the architects of the systems. Users of the technology, even the more advanced ones, expected it to make their work easier and more efficient, without their having to change existing policing and management styles. Architects of the systems, on the other hand, have intended the organization to move towards a more sophisticated mode of information usage—for resource management, tactical policing, strategic planning, and policy decisions. At the same time, governments and other external bodies continually demand new legislative and accountability requirements to be incorporated into the design, so that the capacity and functionality of the systems have to be constantly expanded. Yet the case study has shown that users' technological frames are not immutable. While police resent the additional workload generated by managerial and accountability demands, they have also become willing players in the new technological game. The coercive nature of the technology gave them no other alternatives. Thus, despite constant complaints about various technical problems, police have generally responded positively to the new technology. Ironically, rather than resisting the burden imposed by the technology, they demand more and better technology in the hope of lightening this burden. If Orlikowski (1996) is correct that organizational change is likely to be emergent and continuous rather than rapid and discontinuous, technology-based organizational change, by gradually and continuously altering the field of policing, will eventually have an impact on the deeply embedded assumptions of police practice.

Endnotes

[1] Twenty-three people were interviewed in 17 separate sessions.

[2] Partly a result of "survey fatigue," the response rates of random surveys carried out in the EPS during the 12 months prior to this project were around 20 percent. The research team therefore decided to follow an alternative strategy by targeting officers in selected training programs and police stations to ensure a high return rate and a representative sample according to rank, duty and location.

[3] Results are based on 506 respondents, although the actual number varies according to each item of the questionnaire depending on the number of missing values.

[4] Survey participants chose from a five-point likert scale (strongly agree, agree, neutral, disagree, strongly disagree) in response to various statements. Percentages in the text reflect pooled percentages that combined "strongly agree" and "agree," "disagree" and "strongly disagree." Percentages with neutral responses were not cited.

References

Ackroyd, S., R. Harper, J. A. Hughes, D. Shapiro and K. Soothill (1992) *New Technology and Practical Police Work*. Buckingham: Open University Press.

Barley, S. (1986) "Technology as an Occasion for Structuring: Evidence from Observations of CT Scanners and the Social Order of Radiology Departments," *Administrative Science Quarterly* 31: 78–108.

Bourdieu, P. (1987) "What Makes a Social Class? On the Theoretical and Practical Existence of Groups," *Berkeley Journal of Sociology* 32: 1–18.

Bourdieu, P. and L. J. D. Wacquant (1992) *An Invitation to Reflexive Sociology*. Cambridge: Polity Press.

Chaiken, J., T. Crabill, L. Holliday, D. Jaquett, M. Lawless and E. Quade (1975) *Criminal Justice Models: An Overview*. Santa Monica, CA: RAND.

Chan, J. (1997) *Changing Police Culture: Policing in a Multicultural Society*. Melbourne: Cambridge University Press.

Chan, J. (1999) "Governing Police Practice: Limits of the New Accountability," *British Journal of Sociology* 50(2): 249–68.

Chan, Janet, David Brereton, Margot Legosz and Sally Doran (2001) *The Impact of Information Technology on Policing: An Australian Case Study*. Brisbane: Criminal Justice Commission, forthcoming.

Colton, K. (ed.) (1978) *Police Computer Technology*. Lexington, MA: D.C. Heath.

Davids, C. and L. Hancock (1998) "Policing, Accountability, and Citizenship in the Market State," *Australian and New Zealand Journal of Criminology* 31(1): 38–68.

Dean, M. (1999) *Governmentality: Power and Rule in Modern Society*. London: Sage.

Ericson, R. V. and K. D. Haggerty (1997) *Policing the Risk Society*. Toronto and Buffalo: University of Toronto Press.

Giddens, A. (1984) *The Constitution of Society*. Cambridge: Polity Press.

Harper, R. R. (1991) "The Computer Game: Detectives, Suspects, and Technology," *British Journal of Criminology* 31(3): 292–307.

Herman, P. (1996) "Constructing Families and Disciplining Bodies: A Sociotechnical Study of Computers, Policy and Governance in Australia's Department of Social Security," Ph.D. diss., University of Queensland.

Hough, M. (1980) "Managing with Less Technology—The Impact of Information Technology on Police Management," *British Journal of Criminology* 20(4): 344–57.

Legosz, M. and D. Brereton (2001) "On the Road with Maverick: A Case Study of the Impact of Information Technology on Policing," paper given to the Australian and New Zealand Society of Criminology, Melbourne, February.

Leishman, F., B. Loveday and S. P. Savage (eds) (1996) Core *Issues in Policing*. London: Longman.

Manning, P. K. (1992a) "Information Technologies and the Police," in M. Tonry and N. Morris (eds) *Modern Policing: Crime and Justice, A Review of Research*, vol. 15, pp. 349–98. Chicago, IL: University of Chicago Press.

Manning, P. K. (1992b) "Technological Dramas and the Police: Statement and Counterstatement in Organizational Analysis," *Criminology* 30(3): 327–46.

Manning, P. K. (1996) "Information Technology in the Police Context: The 'Sailor' Phone," *Information Systems Research* 7(1): 52–62.

Mullen, K. L. (19961 "The Computerization of Law Enforcement: A Diffusion of Innovation Study," Ph.D. diss., University of Albany, State University of New York.

O'Malley, P. and D. Palmer (1996) "Post-Keynesian Policing," *Economy and Society* 25(2): 137–55.

Orlikowski, W. J. (1996) "Improvising Organizational Transformation over Time—A Situated Change Perspective," *Information Systems Research* 7(1): 63–92.

Orlikowski, W. J. and D. C. Gash (1994) "Technological Frames—Making Sense of Information Technology in Organizations," ACM *Transactions on Information Systems* 12(2): 174–207.

Orlikowski, W. and D. Robey (1991) "Information Technology and the Structuring of Organizations," *Information Systems Research* 2: 143–69.

Postman, Neil (1992) *Technopoly: The Surrender of Culture to Technology*. New York: Vintage Books.

Power, M. (1997) *The Audit Society: Rituals of Verification*. Oxford: Oxford University Press.

Rheinier, B., M. R. Greeless, M. H. Gibbens and S. P. Marshall (1979) *Crime Analysis in Support of Patrol. Law Enforcement Assistance Administration Report.* Washington, DC: U.S. Government Printing Office.

Robey, D. and S. Sahay (1996) "Transforming Work through Information Technology: A Comparative Case Study of Geographic Information Systems in County Government," *Information Systems Research* 7(1): 93–110.

Sackmann, S. (1991) *Cultural Knowledge in Organizations*. Newbury Park, CA: Sage.

Schein, E. (1985) *Organizational Culture and Leadership*. San Francisco, CA: Jossey-Bass.

Sparrow, M. (1991) "Information Systems: A Help or Hindrance in the Evolution of Policing?" *The Police Chief* 58(4): 26–44.

Yates, J. and J. van Maanen (1996) "Editorial Notes for the Special Issue," *Information Systems Research* 7(1): 1–4.

15

Humor in the Briefing Room
A Study of the Strategic Uses of Humor Among Police

MARK R. POGREBIN AND ERIC D. POOLE

Within various occupational groups humor represents a symbolic resource through which social meanings are created (Zijderveld, 1968). Certain types of humor actually come to characterize members of these groups. As part of the group subculture, humor entails a set of joking relations that support group values, beliefs, and behaviors.

First, through humorous exchanges group members find that they share common experiences and that they can raise a variety of both individual and group concerns that could not otherwise be addressed (Fine, 1983). Humor represents a strategic tool in testing the attitudes, perceptions, or feelings of other group members. By exploring some issue or concern through humor, people can gauge others' positions without having to take a stance themselves (Emerson, 1969).[1]

Second, humor promotes social solidarity. Through mutual ribbing, teasing, or pulling pranks, group members recognize that they can laugh at each other with no ill intent since they share a communal relationship (Coser, 1959, 1960). Shared laughter reflects a social benchmark of the group's common perspective. Joking relations among peers generate feelings of implicit understanding and camaraderie, thus strengthening group norms and bonds. Similarly, solidarity may be enhanced by directing humor at out-group members. This "laughter of inclusion" (Dupreel, 1928) affirms the group's social boundaries and moral superiority (Davies, 1982).

Third, groups utilize humor as a coping strategy in managing a variety of forces beyond their direct control. For example, gallows humor represents an

Mark R. Pogrebin and Eric D. Poole, *Journal of Contemporary Ethnography* (formally *Urban Life*), Vol. 17 No. 2, pp. 183–210, copyright © 1988 by Sage Publications. Reprinted by permission of Sage Publications.

attempt to transform crises or tragic situations into ones that are less threatening and thus more tolerable (Orbdlik, 1942). Although the humor may be morbid and cynical, group members are able to laugh at their plight, demonstrating *communities* and reinforcing group cohesion. Humor also helps to normalize crises by couching the threatening situations as routine occurrences; that is, as just part of the job. In this way humor fosters a sense of confidence that these problems can be handled (Holdaway, 1984).

In this article we extend the previous works on the role of humor in groups by exploring how police patrol officers incorporate humor as a strategic activity to ensure the integrity of their occupational work group. We seek to identify how various types of humor are used to define situations salient to police work; that is, we attempt to show how humor is situationally grounded in the social construction of reality of the police occupation. First, we describe our research methods. Second, we examine the strategic uses of four types of humor among patrol officers. Third, we discuss the role of institutionalized humorous communication in maintaining organizational relationships.

Methods

We collected data for the project during a year-long ethnographic study of a medium-sized metropolitan police department in Colorado. Our study began in June 1985 and ended in June 1986. Our objective was to examine the nature of interpersonal relations among patrol officers. We focused on humor and joking relations as complex, patterned constructions of interpersonal behavior and as strategic activities serving various functions for the group. We attempted to interpret and assign meaning to police humor by identifying how it was both responsive to a specific contextual situation and consistent with normative properties of the more general occupational structure.

Research Setting

The police department we observed is located in a community of approximately 90,000, part of the Denver Metropolitan Statistical Area. During the study there were 135 sworn personnel on the force, with 83 officers attached to uniformed street patrol. Patrol officers were assigned to one of three shifts for a 12-month tour, working a 10-hour day and a 4-day week. At the end of that time, a complex bidding process, based on seniority, was used to reassign officers across the three shifts; moreover, departmental policy prohibited any officer from serving more than two consecutive years on the same shift.

Every month we each took a different shift, rotating through all three shifts during the year. This procedure allowed us to return to the same shift every three months and provided the opportunity for both of us to spend four full months on each shift. It also ensured a more representative sampling of police activities across shifts and patrol assignments throughout the 12-month study. As observers, we kept field diaries, reviewed daily police logs, and conducted informal interviews. Our monthly rotating shift procedure provided the means by which we crosschecked our independent observations and field notes.

Our daily observations began in the briefing room, where all patrol officers met at the beginning of their shift. Based on officer deployment plans, we implemented a procedure whereby we rode with a different patrol officer every other day. Since we covered each shift on a three-month rotation, we were able to schedule our ride-along assignments so that both of us spent time on patrol with every officer during the year. On many occasions we spent the entire shift with the assigned patrol officer; on others, we were able to spend only a few hours on patrol. Our daily observations concluded with the debriefing sessions when the officers returned to the station house to complete their reports. Since our emphasis was on the role of humor among patrol officers, we focused our attention on the group interactions during the briefing and debriefing sessions.

Field Relations.   We made an intensive effort to get to know all patrol officers during the study. First, we sought to earn their respect through our personal commitment of time and energy in their organization. Second, we sought to gain their acceptance through our sustained collegiality and professional relations. As confidants, many officers kept us informed about the latest organizational rumor or personnel gossip, offered their personal views and assessments, and provided a wealth of "war stories"; others sought us out for information. While we gratefully acknowledged receipt of information, we were insistent that the code of ethics that governed our research prohibited our divulging any information that we received in confidence. This explanation was generally satisfactory to most officers; moreover, it reinforced the trust element that we worked hard to ensure in our field relations.

During the project we developed a working camaraderie with the officers, so that our presence on patrol or in the station house was taken for granted. We were viewed as part of the social organization of the department, having personally participated in the "routine" experiences of police work. Our personal acceptance in the police organization also led to our being invited by officers to off-duty social gatherings. The extension of these social relationships allowed us access to the private lives and personal histories of the officers. The mutual rapport and understanding that arose from such associations further supported our position in the police organization as "insiders." As a result, we feel confident that our observations and interpretations are reliable and valid representations of the phenomena under study.

Backstage Behavior in the Briefing Room.   While we were able to ride with and observe each officer on patrol, it was in the social context of the briefing room that groups of officers routinely exhibited the types of humor we focus on as part of the police occupation. The briefing room served as the primary setting where officers engaged in backstage behavior, that is, where the officers were not performing to a public or providing stereotyped scripts to outsiders (Goffman, 1959; Punch, 1979).

The briefing room represented what Lyman and Scott (1967:270) have defined as a "home territory... where regular participants have a relative freedom of behavior and a source of intimacy and control over the area." Ardrey (1966) has argued that control of territory is associated with maintaining identity. Backstage behavior reflects the subcultural group identity in contrast to the frontstage identity managed in public. As Goffman (1959) has noted, backstage identities are revealed in territories that are separated from public view.

In the station house a formal reception area served as a staging place where police appearance was managed for the public. It represented a screen or barrier for the backstage area where police could act in an uninhibited manner and not concern themselves with outside scrutiny. For each shift of officers, the briefing area offered a collective arena where they could talk about their street experiences to others who understood and appreciated their feelings and perceptions. Still, as members of a paramilitary bureaucracy, officers had to be careful to ensure that their manner of expressing these experiences was organizationally acceptable or tolerable. Humor provided a wide range for creative expressions within such organizational constraints.

The Briefing Room Routine.   When police officers arrived at the station house, they usually went directly to the locker room to change into their uniforms. The officers working a particular shift then proceeded to the briefing room for roll call and patrol assignments. During the 15-to-20-minute briefing session, officers also received current information on previous shift activities and communications on policy from the command staff. At times the shift sergeant cautioned the officers about some present dangers in the community, praised officers for their exceptional performance or related accomplishments, or called attention to particular problems officers might be experiencing.

At the end of a shift, officers returned to the station house briefing room to complete their paperwork. During this debriefing session, the sergeant reviewed the officers' reports, cleared up any questions that might arise, and offered officers constructive advice. The time required for debriefing all shift officers could range from a few minutes to over an hour, with officers leaving when their reports were filed and approved; however, officers typically remained in the briefing room long after their official duties were completed.

This informal period of officer interaction came to serve as a forum for officers to swap stories about individual work experience, allowing officers to "cool out" from a rough shift, to vicariously experience the highlights of fellow officers' calls, or to wind down before going home. It also provided an opportunity to discuss department policies, politics, and personalities. Rumors made their rounds at this time—with a few being squelched, several being started, and many being embellished. As Hannerz (1969) has observed, such informal gatherings of police officers foster highly stylized exchanges of information and forms of communication.

Like most groups characterized by informality, patrol officers have developed a set of joking references that require "insider" knowledge to be fully understood and appreciated as humorous.[2] After several weeks of riding with patrol officers and attending briefing and debriefing sessions, we began to discern distinct functions of joking relationships. The forms of humor we have identified are grounded in the natural work experiences of policing. We have classified police humor into four types: jocular aggression, audience degradation, diffusion of danger/tragedy, and normative neutralization.

Strategic Uses of Humor Among Police

In this section we will explore the strategic uses of the four types of humor. We begin our assessment of each type with a view of its functions in general; we then illustrate and examine the way each manifests itself within specific contexts of police work.

Jocular Aggression

Jocular aggression represents a humorous attack against supervisory or management personnel. It is a way subordinates in a group can collectively denounce departmental policies and regulations or the directives and orders of superiors in an acceptable manner. Jocular aggression thus avoids a direct confrontation with a superior that could lead to organizational sanctions.

Blau (1955) has contended that within bureaucracies individual complaints are often expressed and explored through joking relations in an informal work group. Jocular aggression reflects this type of joking relation in which discontent can be vented in a safe manner; that is, individuals are able not only to get their complaints out in the open but also to displace latent frustration and aggression via humorous expressions. In addition, jocular aggression serves to translate an individual concern into a group issue. In the group context the expression of an individual concern brings to bear the collective experience and advice of fellow workers. Individual problems may then be viewed from the perspective of the group.

The following problem incident involved a shift lieutenant who persisted in stopping drunk drivers and then calling for a patrol officer to respond to the scene and make the arrest. Such action involved the administration of a breathalyzer test, forced the officer to wait at the station until someone could come and take the drunk driver home, and required the completion of a lengthy offense report.

> Did you hear our favorite lieutenant on the radio tonight? He tied the fucking thing up so long we couldn't get through to anyone. Here we got both DUI cars tied up and that nut is running around catching four DUIs. It's dangerous to leave him out on the street. Why doesn't he sit on his ass in the station and pretend he's busy like the rest of the lieutenants do?

Another problem incident arose from the chief's new policy concerning relations with the minority community, whose spokespersons had met with the chief to complain about their treatment by patrol officers. The chief videotaped his new policy on minority-police relations and had it played for all shifts during briefing sessions. At one of the shift viewings, we observed the following. The officers were all seated, waiting for the tape to be played. One officer yelled out, "It's the Chief Marty Show; let's get some popcorn." As the tape played, officers made wisecracks, hissed, booed, and laughed; moreover, several officers threw paper airplanes at the screen. At the end of the video presentation, there was sporadic applause, and one policeman yelled out:

> This show was boring. . . . They should have sex flicks and make the Chief's show more interesting. Hell, I almost fell asleep.

Another officer joined in the chorus of criticism with a rather sarcastic observation:

> Now that was really a useful piece of shit. We all need to improve our community relations skills. Next thing they'll have us doing is asking a suspect for his permission before we can arrest him.

Jocular aggression reinforces the solidarity of the individuals within the group because it is based on shared experiences of the membership. Like jokes, it causes a collectivity of laughter that strengthens the group's social cohesion (Martineau, 1972). One such incident: An officer saw a young woman's car stuck in the snow and, after attempting to push her out, told the woman that he could do no more for her. After a short discussion in which the woman berated the officer for refusing to use his patrol car to pull her car from the snow drift, the officer told the woman to calm down and call a tow truck.

The woman subsequently filed a formal complaint against the officer with the department. Even though departmental policy prohibits the use of a police vehicle to remove a civilian's car (unless the car is impeding traffic), the officer received a three-day suspension without pay for the way he handled the incident. In assessing the implications of this administrative action, a fellow patrol officer presented his position to the shift:

> The next time it snows I'm going to help every goddam person stuck. Then when the dispatcher calls me on a case, I'm going to just say the chief wants us to help citizens get their cars out of the snow. I really have no time for the call.

Another officer followed up on this statement:

> And don't forget to tell them how grateful you are that you could be of help. You wouldn't want to leave a poor citizen stranded two blocks from home with groceries to carry.

The stories told in the briefing room tend to mediate the hierarchy of authority within the bureaucratic structure of the department. Such stories relate the patrol officer's perception of what "real" police work is all about.

These humorous tales often reflect frustrations experienced by officers who must rely on their own common sense in working patrol and then have their decisions second-guessed by a supervisor later on. Jocular aggression affirms the patrol officer's perceived superiority to management personnel who are far removed from the realities officers face on the street.

Because they must often deviate from administrative policies and procedural regulations in order to perform order-maintenance functions, patrol officers guard their autonomy and discretionary decision making. New sergeants have to adjust to this informal work norm. For these supervisors, learning the nuances of the shift's personality is critical to their success in effectively managing the officers' activities on patrol (Van Maanen, 1984).

Officers want and expect the sergeant to act in a consultative manner. They feel that because of the nature of their front-line work, they should initiate the bulk of their contacts with a supervisor as they deem necessary. As the following example reveals, supervisors must learn to accept and support the autonomy and discretion so valued by patrol officers. A new sergeant had been assigned to the swing shift (4 PM to 2 AM). Because he had worked for the preceding five years in the detective bureau, he had limited contact with those working patrol. Thus, the new sergeant was known to patrol officers only by reputation, although there were a few veteran officers who had worked with him when he was on the street in uniform.

Most officers contend that new supervisors have a tendency to become involved in too many radio-dispatched calls to patrol. On a busy night it is not uncommon for a rookie sergeant to be running from one side of town to another for what he believes to be necessary supervision of his shift. Since officers resent close scrutiny, they attempt to socialize new shift sergeants to the patrol norms stressing laissez faire supervision.

An example of this process took place in the briefing room after a busy Saturday night of calls for service. The new sergeant was obviously fatigued from attempting to be with his patrol officers at every call. He was seen as constantly invading officers' territory and interfering with the tactics each officer had developed for handling interactions with suspects and citizens. Jocular aggression was abundant that night, as evidenced in the remarks of one officer during debriefing:

> Hey, Sarge! Where were you when I got that call on those bikers' loud music complaint over on the East Side? I figure you could have made it there if you used your lights and siren. It was only about five miles from where you were. Hell, if you ran hot at 90 miles an hour, you could have been there to help me.

A veteran officer also raised the issue of the sergeant's intrusion into patrol work during that shift. He described an incident in which a male suspect placed under arrest for possession of an illegal weapon was refusing to come peacefully with his younger partner. The rookie sergeant arrived, took charge of the scene, and tried to convince the suspect to come to the station.

All attempts by the sergeant failed to resolve the situation, and the suspect became more agitated. At this point the veteran officer decided to intervene. He simply picked up the suspect and carried him back to the sergeant's car for transport to the station. At the debriefing, the officer gave the sergeant some friendly advice:

> Well, Sergeant, the reason I picked up that asshole at the apartment house and carried him to your car was that the bullshit that guy was giving you would have gone on forever. I figured you and Sam had talked enough; I just got tired of that runt's smartass manner. We got better things to do than listen to pukes like him. . . . Now don't you think I was professional?

In the following remark, we see how jocular aggression is used to address the larger issue of the new sergeant's attempts to supervise shift officers at every call:

> Now we all know that the city wants us to cut down on our driving time to save on gas expenses. Sarge, you must have put on over a thousand miles tonight. You better be careful or the city manager is going to get on your ass. You know you've got to help the city save money in these times of cutback management.

In short, jocular aggression provides a means by which subordinates can express dissatisfaction with superior officers or with the organization itself. However, those in subordinate positions must maintain the lines of authority that define the police structure. They must be careful not to cross the communicative boundary where jocular aggression becomes directly offensive to a superior, lest they suffer the consequences for violating organizational status (e.g., being perceived as insubordinate and sanctioned).

Audience Degradation

As we noted earlier, debriefing sessions present the opportunity for discussion of problems officers faced during the shift and feedback on how they were handled. Swapping stories about citizen encounters offered officers a chance to exploit the humor in the troubles and foibles of the public in general. Because the police saw themselves frequently called to intervene in conflicts between equally disreputable parties, they came to view the public in rather cynical terms. That is, they often failed to differentiate citizens in need of police services from individuals suspected of criminal involvement.

"Naming" refers to the process by which police classify people as social objects having certain stereotypical attributes and then act toward them on the basis of the identifying label (Lindesmith et al., 1977). Such standardized characterizations provide a common argot among police for conjuring up the appropriate images (e.g., demeanor, dress, speech, attitude) of individuals encountered. There is no need for further explanation when an officer refers to various persons contacted during the shift as "scumbag," "asshole," "puke," "bimbo," or other equally graphic appellations. One officer described his contact with a drunk couple as follows:

> I had a real good DUI tonight. I pulled behind a couple parked on the side of the road and they were drunk as well. When the driver got out, this bimbo also got out of the car and started yelling at me to leave the driver alone. There she is yelling at me about harassment, shit-faced and all, with her dress wide open. When I finally pointed this out to her, she sure as shit quieted down.

The use of the disparaging reference to the female suspect in this incident also reflects the frustration that officers experience in trying to protect citizens from themselves. Similarly, humorous remarks are used to belittle those individuals who create the "dirty work" that officers are called upon to perform. For example, one officer described the following encounter:

> A mental starts talking to me outside the station when I was coming to briefing. I can't understand what he's saying, but the next thing I know he pulls his pants down and exposes himself. At the same time all these women are coming out of city hall leaving work. . . . Hell, I don't know why he did that; there wasn't that much to show.

While most opportunities for backstage humor occur in the briefing room, many humorous stories about citizen encounters are told during slow times of a shift when patrol officers know that the supervisor is at the station or otherwise indisposed. These exchanges usually take place in isolated areas secluded from public view. A favorite spot for patrol officers to, as they put it, "shoot the shit" is behind shopping centers late at night. Usually two or three patrol cars will be parked parallel to one another, and officers will converse without leaving the vehicles. Such impromptu meetings of a few officers allow for more individualized sharing of work experiences that would not be suitable for collective discussion in the briefing room; moreover these brief storytelling sessions help break up the routine of a tedious shift. Comic relief provided by these occasions is illustrated in the following exchange among three officers:

> Officer Able: What was that call for over at the Sandstone apartments? It sounded like a good one.

> Officer Baker: There were some teenagers swimming naked in the pool, raising a lot of hell. When we rolled up, the boys ran but the chicks stayed. They came over stark naked and began to talk with Brewer and me; shit, they didn't bat an eye. It was hard not to look, believe me. . . .

> Officer Cruz: Damn, I never get good calls like that. If I did, by the time I was on the scene they'd probably be dressed.

The access the police had to individuals' personal problems caused them to make moral judgments on a regular basis. They were more often called on to perform social-service functions than law enforcement duties. They had to be counselors, mediators, arbitrators, referral agents, power brokers, and all-purpose consultants. To patrol officers oriented to "real" police work, many citizens calls for service seemed trivial, mundane, or unfounded. Officers came to view complainants as people who were too weak or ineffectual to handle their own problems. Responding to their calls was viewed as a waste of time and effort. In order to manage such distasteful situations, police recounted their encounters with citizens in humorously degrading ways, often poking fun at complainant misfortunes. As Goffman (1959:175) has pointed out, "Backstage derogation of the audience is another strategy that performance teams employ in order to maintain morale." Humorous putdowns of complainants served to promote the police sense of moral superiority and to maintain the dichotomy between police and policed.

Diffusion of Danger/Tragedy

Police are expected not to show fear in dangerous situations. Even to admit being afraid after threatening encounters is taboo. Displays of fear, although quite understandable under such conditions, are viewed as a sign of weakness. It is through humor that police can empathize with each other's feelings of fear and vulnerability. Joking relations concerning dangerous interactions provide a way for officers to express their emotions without damaging their professional image as confident and fearless. As Fine (1983:175) has argued, such humor fosters "a sense of social control for the participants on how to deal with these threatening or embarrassing topics."

In the following example, an officer conveyed the fear brought about by a highly threatening situation using joking references implicitly understood by other members of the group. The incident involved five patrol officers and one lieutenant who responded to a residential burglary-in-progress call. The six officers positioned themselves around the perimeter of the house and waited for the suspect to exit. An account of what occurred was provided by one of the patrol officers during the shift's debriefing session:

> There were six of us on the scene. The perpetrator is in the house and we've got the area covered. Everyone is in position waiting for the thief to come out. I'm in some bushes about 10 feet behind the lieutenant, who's standing behind a tree. The dude comes running out the back door, and the lieutenant is in the firing position and yells at the top of his lungs, "Hit the ground or I'll blow your fucking head off!" I thought the lieutenant was going to come in his pants right there. I couldn't tell who was more afraid—the bad guy or the lieutenant.

Every police officer is aware of the danger inherent in such incidents; moreover, apprehension is heightened by the possibility that the suspect is armed. The following incident illustrates how officers humorously reflect upon their own vulnerability in precarious situations. The call involved an officer dispatched to a residence for what was thought to be a minor domestic disturbance. Upon his arrival at the residence, the officer was met by a highly agitated male suspect wielding a shotgun. The officer immediately radioed for backup, took his shotgun from the cruiser, and positioned himself behind a tree in the front yard of the residence. The suspect demanded that the officer "get the hell off my property"; the officer ordered the suspect to put down his weapon. Neither complied, but the officer continued to talk to the suspect in an effort to calm him down. The backup officers arrived within minutes and assumed tactical positions behind their cars. After a 10-minute standoff, the suspect finally dropped his shotgun and surrendered to the first officer. At the debriefing one of the backup patrolman began gibing his officer:

> I thought you were going to be behind that tree all goddam night. That asshole didn't give a shit if you blew him to hell. I was going to bet Alex that you would shoot first. But you know him, he never carries more than a quarter when he's on duty.

Another backup officer joked about what could have happened:

> It's a good thing Wayne didn't have to shoot that scumbag, because we haven't qualified with the shotgun for I don't know how long. He would have shot and probably hit the front window, and that son of a bitch would have opened up on all of us.

This example reveals the importance of the officer maintaining control over his emotions; for had he "lost it" and overreacted, the consequences could have been disastrous. Yet the reality of such threatening situations cannot be denied, and the intense emotions must eventually be dealt with. Jokes can be used to focus on the uncomfortable topic of fear, allowing the group to deal collectively with an emotion that could not be expressible otherwise. When a fellow officer has confronted a life-threatening situation, the backstage humor of the briefing room promotes shared understanding of the experience and identification with the feelings of the officer. In this way, humorous debriefings help to manage the danger that is a part of police work.

Similarly to the way humor is used to diffuse emotions accompanying dangerous situations, joking relations also serve to temper tragic events experienced on the job. As trained professionals, police officers are expected to maintain a poised presence even under the most tragic circumstances. Their authority and effectiveness in handling such events would be compromised if officers could not control their own emotions. In the face of tragedy (e.g., victims of child abuse, rape, accidents), officers must maintain their composure, distancing themselves from the intense emotional reactions evoked in such encounters. To an outsider, the jokes that are told to diffuse tragedy may not seem humorous at all. In fact they can be perceived as cruel and insensitive; however, for patrol officers the callousness of such jokes actually helps lessen the emotional intensity elicited by tragic events. In this way humor allows the police to handle situations that would emotionally paralyze others.

One tragic event that occurred during our observational study involved the arrest of a middle-aged, white male suspect for driving under the influence of alcohol. After being brought to the police station and given a breathalyzer test, the suspect requested to see his "good friend" on the force, Lieutenant Williams. Although it was 2 AM, the lieutenant was called to the station. When the lieutenant arrived, he briefly talked with the suspect, explaining the procedures to be followed in DUI cases, then drove the suspect home. A few hours later the suspect committed suicide.

When the graveyard shift came off the street at 8 AM, Lieutenant Williams was in the briefing room and the discussion focused immediately on the suicide. It was soon learned that the suspect was not the lieutenant's close friend; rather, he was at best a casual acquaintance whom the lieutenant saw infrequently at a local stable where they both kept their horses. Once the relationship had been clarified, the patrol officers saw the opportunity to diffuse the tragic elements of the case for the lieutenant:

> I saw the guy in here when he was waiting to blow in the machine. He didn't look depressed. What the hell did you say to him to depress him to the point he blew himself away? You didn't bore him to death with all those horse stories you always tell?

After a few more speculative gibes concerning the role of the lieutenant in the suspect's demise, one officer offered the lieutenant some final advice:

> I tell you, Lieutenant, you really have to pick your friends more carefully in the future. You know, you could give the department a bad name.

In another tragic incident we observed during our study, a middle-aged white man walked into the police station around 3 AM on a Saturday and reported that he had just murdered his live-in girlfriend. When the graveyard shift returned for debriefing later that morning, the officers shared what they had learned about the bizarre event:

> The guy comes into the station, hardly anyone is around, and tells the desk clerk he needs to see a cop. I happen to pass the front desk and am told . . . that there is a man here who wants to speak to an officer. I take him back to the briefing room and he tells me he murdered his girlfriend and gives me the details. Then he says as calmly as hell he wants to speak to a priest, not a lawyer, but a priest! That's when I figure this guy's for real. Hell, it's too late to get religion.

One of the officers dispatched to the crime scene then described what he found:

> The door to the house was open and there to the left of the front door was the .22 [caliber] rifle, just like we were told by dispatch. We know right away this guy was not a mental. We go to the master bedroom and there is this broad with covers over her. We pull them back and, man, there are about five holes in her chest. She's deader than hell. Looks like the guy was trying to make her look like Swiss cheese.

The casual observer is likely neither to understand nor to appreciate the humorous social meanings created by these stories. But the appropriateness of joking depends on the situation; that is, there are contextual rules for joking that are often not explicit or even consciously recognized. They represent intricate functions of group processes. It is through the shared experiences of group activity that the standards by which humor is judged and interpreted evolve.

For police, backstage humor represents a strategic means of managing the consequences of tragic events. First, jokes allow officers to vent feelings in an acceptable manner. Second, joking relations provide for a collective diffusion of emotional responses (e.g., outrage, disgust, horror) to tragedies. Third, the humorous treatment of tragedy promotes its normalization as just part of the job. Humor thus supports emotional distancing, allowing officers to perform their jobs regardless of the situation.

Normative Neutralization

According to Reuss-Ianni (1983), the street-officer culture supports bending formal rules and procedures that may impede officers from doing their job as they deem necessary. Sometimes the law itself is seen by the police as getting in the way of the administration of justice (Skolnick, 1966); thus legislative and judicial constraints may have to be sidestepped by officers. When police "know" a suspect is guilty (i.e., factual guilt), they feel justified in violating procedural rules in order to obtain evidence that may better ensure a conviction. Similarly, if police perceive that a suspect who they feel deserves punishment is unlikely to be prosecuted or convicted, they may impose "street justice" (e.g., verbal or physical abuse). Street justice is also administered to belligerent suspects whom the police lack probable cause to arrest but whom the police feel need to be taught a lesson in proper respect for police authority.

We found patrol officers quite candid in describing street justice incidents to their peers. They often swapped humorous stories about these encounters during debriefing sessions, although they were discreet in the presence of certain supervisors. Such humorous accounts help to define the working ideology of patrol officers, providing examples of informal standards and expectations for behavior by which officers may be judged.

The following example shows how legal guidelines were compromised by one officer in adhering to the principle of street justice. This incident involved a veteran officer who was dispatched to a residence for a family disturbance call. After restraining the couple involved in the dispute, the officer learned that the wife had just returned home, having left her husband and two small children for a two-month hiatus with another man. This man had accompanied the wife to the home and was present when the officer arrived. The situation was further aggravated by the woman's agitated state and violent demeanor, a condition the officer judged to be drug-induced. Demanding that the officer arrest her husband, the woman then produced a court order awarding her temporary custody of the children, enjoining the husband to leave the home, and denying him child visitation rights until a subsequent court hearing was held.

The officer felt that the judge who issued the injunction was not fully cognizant of all the facts in the case; consequently he decided to ignore the court order. Instead, he lectured the woman on parental responsibility, told her and her boyfriend to leave the house without the children, and advised her to get an attorney. The officer then warned the woman that if she caused any more trouble that night, he would have her arrested for suspected drug use. The next day the woman filed a formal complaint against the officer at police headquarters.

When questioned about the incident by his fellow officers during the debriefing session, the veteran officer provided the following insight to his application of street justice:

> No sooner do I arrive on the scene when this hysterical asshole starts screaming at me to get her husband out of the house. There she is waving a court order in my face, screaming the judge wants him out. Then I heard from her old man that she returned after deserting the family for two months, leaving the two small kids at home with him and never leaving a note to explain where she was going and never contacting her husband while being gone. I told her what she could do with the court order. Then she gets real loud and starts cussing me out, all the while threatening to sue my ass. "Lady," I said, "you're high on drugs and I'm going to haul your ass in if you don't shut up and get out of here now." She saw I was pissed and she leaves with her boyfriend. No way I was going to throw that guy out and let that bitch stay with the kids, especially not in her condition. I just can't believe the judge knew what this case was about. But what the hell do they know anyway. When was the last time you saw a judge handle a domestic?

The working ideology of patrol officers is premised on the inherent superiority of their decision making and commonsense understandings that determine the appropriate course of action to be taken. By humorously degrading the demeanor of the wife and the wisdom of the judge, the officer justified both his negative assessment of her moral character and his refusal to abide by the court order. In this case, ensuring street justice was more important than abiding by the law. The legal constraints were thus neutralized by an appeal to higher loyalties (Sykes and Matza, 1957).[3] Although every shift member knew the officer would be subject to departmental disciplinary action, his example reinforced the preeminence of autonomy and discretion within the occupational ideology.

In addition to their resentment of legal constraints, patrol officers express frustration in following operational policies and procedures formulated by police administrators. Patrol officers often assert that management has lost touch with the realities of real police work and complain that many administrative directives are either intrusive or useless. Because officers view certain managerial policies as obstacles preventing them from being effective, they bend the rules and follow those procedures that have worked best for them.

In the following example one officer administered street justice to a suspect in direct contradiction to departmental policy concerning the handling of intoxicated individuals. The incident involved a routine investigation of a suspicious vehicle parked on the shoulder of a major thoroughfare early on a Saturday morning. The officer described the circumstances to the shift at the debriefing session:

> It's almost 2 AM and I came across this '85 Olds Cutlass on the side of Sheridan. The dome light is on and the driver's door is open, with a guy's legs hanging out. I wake up the dumb shit who's been sleeping one off and order him out of the car. Immediately he starts mouthing off, and really goes bat shit when I tell him I'm taking him to detox. . . . I told the asshole three times to shut up, but he keeps running his mouth. Fuck it. The puke goes to the county jail. . . . After I checked his license, I noticed it was his birthday and started feeling a little sorry for the guy. But I'm sure some of the inmates will have a few surprises for him this weekend.

In almost all cases when a person is found to be intoxicated but not driving a vehicle, departmental policy instructs that suspects be taken to the detoxification center, a county facility that holds drunken individuals for 24 hours and provides treatment on a voluntary basis. The policy calls for the use of the detoxification center in such situations in order to prevent the individual from getting injured or harming others.

In this case, the officer felt that the suspect had exceeded the bounds of acceptable demeanor to be exhibited in such encounters. He thus decided to arrest the suspect on a drunk and disorderly charge and have him jailed. In taking this action, the officer ensured a punishment more commensurate with the seriousness of the suspect's disregard for police authority. The officer's humorous account of the incident at the debriefing session served to justify his discretionary street justice superseding the departmental policy. Through humor the police reinforce their work perspective and organizational status, promoting a collective self-confidence conducive to the maintenance of group autonomy and the exercise of individual discretion.

Discussion

The four types of humor we have examined—jocular aggression, audience degradation, diffusion of danger/tragedy, and normative neutralization—reflect rather serious issues in policing. In considering the strategic uses of humor, we must address why officers choose to express such serious content in unserious forms. As noted above, joking relations provide a socially acceptable means to test the feelings of group members, one that allows denial of the serious implications of the humorous message if challenged. But the expression of serious concern in a humorous form may ensure more than a defensible posture in gauging others' sentiments.

First, a serious theme expressed in jest, rather than in earnest, may actually dramatize its message. The humorous expression, by providing amusement and eliciting overt reactions of smiling or laughter, symbolically commits the group to the position of the humorist. The impact of the message is also increased with the weight of consensual acknowledgment implicit in group laughter. If an overtly serious comment is offered, the group's response may be concealed by ambiguous silence or equivocally impassive faces.

Second, humor provides a forum for presentation of concerns without directly threatening the system that fosters them; that is, unlike the formal repercussions that could result from taking a serious position on an issue, humor affords expression (or even diffusion and defusion of concerns) without changing the terms of the organizational relationships. To this extent, then, the medium is the message. Humor is communicated and interpreted within the existing subcultural context (e.g., ideology, power, status, morality, norms, and values) of the police organization. Both the individual officers and the police organization benefit from institutionalized humorous communication. The status quo is preserved.

A final consideration of our findings deals with the use of jocular aggression aimed at superiors. We focus on this type of humor since previous studies have indicated that jocular aggression is directed either laterally or downwards through the organizational hierarchy; that is, individuals jokingly attack their equals or subordinates, but not their superiors. In two observational studies of joking relations in work settings, both Bradney (1957) and Coser (1959, 1960) reported no instance in which a subordinate worker used humor to express aggression or hostility to a superior face-to-face; humorous derision of superiors occurred only in their absence. In contrast, superiors publicly as well as privately, ridiculed subordinates for their failings or inadequacies.

The similarity of these findings, obtained in markedly different work settings (Bradney studied interactions of department store staff; Coser observed psychiatric staff meetings), supports the notion of asymmetrical access to jocular aggression. As the object of the hostile joking by subordinates, superiors have the authority to make reprisals. Subordinates subjected to humorous derision by superiors do not. Yet, in our observations of jocular aggression among police we have noted numerous occasions on which nonranking patrol officers directly ridiculed their first-line supervisors, the shift sergeants. To account for this joking relationship, we must examine the nature of the sergeant's position in the police organization.

Observational studies of police work have revealed that the exercise of authority in law enforcement agencies is primarily based on personal relationships with subordinates (Rubinstein, 1973; Muir, 1977; Van Maanen, 1984). This is because all supervisory personnel must rise from line-level positions in the police organization. The common occupational socialization experiences in the street culture of patrol work provided the basis for group solidarity and informal relations across departmental ranks.

At the same time, Van Maanen (1984) has pointed out that senior police administrators seek to promote individuals who are less likely to bring the "patrolman's mentality" to the supervisory role. The purpose of this selection strategy is to ensure that supervisors will supervise from a formal administrative, rather than an informal line-level perspective. Success in rising through the ranks is dependent, in part, on shedding the "street-cop" mentality. This promotional process thus serves to increase tension and social distance between supervisory and line staff.

Police sergeants, as first-line supervisors, occupy rather incongruous positions in the police organization. First, they are at the bottom of the supervisory hierarchy where policy and procedures developed from above must be implemented at the line level. But the ability of sergeants to implement policies and procedures is largely determined by the actions of line officers (Van Maanen, 1984). Sergeants have to earn the respect of their subordinates; it is not granted on the basis of rank alone.

Second, the relations between sergeants and patrol officers reflect a structured ambiguity. There is a mixture of camaraderie and antagonism, identification and rejection, and trust and suspicion. This ambiguity lends itself to a mutual testing of the boundaries of acceptable behavior in the roles of superior and subordinate. Under these conditions, subordinates are provided greater latitude in the expression of jocular aggression. For example, Radcliffe-Brown (1940) has argued that such joking relations are premised on institutionalized social ambiguity. That is, jocular aggression arises among individuals whose relationship is simultaneously conjunctive and disjunctive—having grounds for both solidarity and separation and reflecting "a peculiar combination of friendliness . . . [and] hostility" (Radcliffe-Brown, 1940:195). The terms of the joking relation allow a person to make fun of another who, in turn, is expected to take no offense. Since the police organization provides an analogous relation between sergeants and line officers, we can account for why, contrary to previous research, the subordinates in our study could direct jocular aggression at their superiors.

In this article we have explored the strategic uses of humor among patrol officers. We have emphasized the contextual aspect of humor; that is, we have focused on specific types of humor in relation to the distinctive nature of patrol work. It is hoped that future ethnographic research will build upon our efforts and move toward identifying the roles of individuals in the social organization of humor and the role of groups as humor repositories. In this way, a better understanding of the rules governing humorous interaction, communication, and transmission of group culture may be obtained.

Endnotes

[1] If the humorous remarks produce a positive response, one may assume that others share, or at least sympathize with, one's own viewpoint. On the other hand, if the humor is rejected, one may suffer the embarrassment of having told a bad joke but risk very little else, since the joker was, after all, only kidding.

[2] This is particularly important in relation to humor premised on an understanding of historical events within the department. Subtle or indirect remarks linking past experiences to present situations would be unrecognizable to those outside the work group. During the debriefing sessions, oral histories of the department are passed along to successive cohorts of police officers. Much of the localized culture is embodied in humorous stories and jokes that capture different aspects and reflect various versions of the department's history.

[3] One may argue that the officer also employed another technique of neutralization, denial of victim harm, in ignoring the court order; that is, the officer felt that the wife deserved the kind of street justice meted out because she had acted so irresponsibly.

References

Ardrey, R. (1966). *The territorial imperative*. New York: Dell.

Blau, P. M. (1955). *The dynamics of bureaucracy*. Chicago: University of Chicago Press.

Bradney, P. (1957). The joking relationship in industry. *Human Relations, 10*, 179–187.

Coser, R. L. (1959). Some social functions of laughter. *Human Relations, 12*, 171–182.

Coser, R. L. (1960). Laughter among colleagues. *Psychiatry, 23*, 81–95.

Davies, C. (1982). Ethnic jokes, moral values and social boundaries. *British Journal of Sociology, 33*, 383–403.

Dupreel, E. (1928). Le problème sociologique du rise. *Revue Philosophique, 106*, 213–260.

Emerson, J. P. (1969). Negotiating the serious import of humor. *Sociometry, 32*, 169–181.

Fine, G. A. (1983). Sociological approaches to the study of humor. In P. E. McGhee & J. H. Goldstein (Eds.), *Handbook of humor research* (Vol. 1, pp. 159–181). New York: Springer-Verlag.

Goffman, E. (1959). *The presentation of self in everyday life*. Garden City, NY: Anchor.

Hannerz, U. (1969). *Soulside: Inquiries into ghetto culture and community*. New York: Columbia University Press.

Holdaway, S. (1984). *Inside the British police*. Oxford: Basil Blackwell.

Lindesmith, A. R., Strauss, A. L., & Denzin, N. K. (1977). *Social psychology*. New York: Holt, Rinehart & Winston.

Lyman, S. M., & Scott, M. B. (1967). Territoriality: A neglected sociological dimension. *Social Problems, 15*, 236–249.

Martineau, W. H. (1972). A model of the social functions of humor. In J. H. Goldstein & P. E. McGhee (Eds.), *The psychology of humor* (pp. 101–125). New York: Academic Press.

Muir, W. K. (1977). *Police: Streetcorner politicians*. Chicago: University of Chicago Press.

Orbdlik, A. J. (1942). Gallows humor: A sociological phenomenon. *American Journal of Sociology, 47*, 709–716.

Punch, M. (1979). The secret social service. In S. Holdaway (Ed.), *The British police* (pp. 102–117). Beverly Hills, CA: Sage.

Radcliffe-Brown, A. R. (1940). On joking relationships. *Africa, 13*, 195–210.

Reuss-Ianni, E. (1983). *Two cultures of policing*. New Brunswick, NJ: Transaction Books.

Rubinstein, J. (1973). *City police*. New York: Farrar, Straus & Giroux.

Skolnick, J. H. (1966). *Justice without trial*. New York: John Wiley.

Sykes, G. M., & Matza, D. (1957). Techniques of neutralization: A theory of delinquency. *American Journal of Sociology, 22*, 664–670.

Van Maanen, J. (1984). Making rank: Becoming an American police sergeant. *Urban Life, 13*, 155–176.

Zijderveld, A. C. (1968). Jokes and their relation to social reality. *Social Research, 35*, 268–311.

16

Tell Me about the Test
The Construction of Truth and Lies in Drug Court

MITCHELL B. MACKINEM AND PAUL HIGGINS

Drug courts are popular and fast-growing court-supervised drug treatment programs. They began in Miami in the late 1980s as a response to the dramatic increase in cocaine and crack arrests (Murray 1994). More than sixteen hundred drug courts operate in every state, with a growing number operating or being planned in foreign countries (Huddleston et al. 2005). Drug courts have spawned a variety of problem courts that address public policy concerns including domestic violence, mental illness, drunk driving, gambling, homelessness, truancy, and gun possession (Huddleston et al. 2005). How drug-court staff members produce drug court has yet to be adequately investigated. Our discussion of how drug-court staffers construct the truths and lies told by drug-court clients when they confront clients with positive tests for illicit drugs is part of that larger project (Mackinem 2003).

Most of the research on drug courts has been done from a static stance and from the outside. First, the bulk of the research has focused on client and program characteristics to evaluate the efficacy of drug court, predict clients' completion of drug court, or examine program design (Government Accountability Office 2005; Belenko 2001). Second, comparatively few investigations have been field research studies (Burns and Peyrot 2003; Nolan 2001; Wolf and Colyer 2001). Finally, those studies conducted through field research have primarily focused on drug-court sessions, the most public, visible component of drug courts. While all of this research begins to inform us about drug courts, it cannot adequately explain what staff and participants do that is drug court.

Mitchell B. Mackinem and Paul Higgins, *Journal of Contemporary Ethnography*, Vol. 36, pp. 223–251, © 2007 by Sage Publications. Reprinted by permission of Sage Publications.

In the course of a multiyear investigation of three drug courts in a southeastern state, we explored how drug-court staff decides whether clients are telling the truth or lying when the staff confronts them with a positive test for drugs. As the court administrator in two of the drug courts and a professional colleague with staff in the third court, the senior author was able to examine the less public realms of drug court, where the staff does most of the work. The drug-court staff's construction of truths and lies is one occasion of many when staff members create moral identities for their clients and for those applying to be clients (Mackinem 2003).

Through an inside investigation that focused on the interpretations of staff, we are able to begin to understand how drug-court professionals produce the outcomes that other researchers, without examining the professional work that contributes to the production of those outcomes, attempt to predict (Loseke 1989). As do staff members in all service agencies, drug-court staff members produce client outcomes as they work within their organizations' policies and procedures, use their professional belief systems, and interact with a range of others to manage the demands of their positions.

In what follows, we first provide an overview of drug court. Next, we discuss the conclusions of three main categories of drug-court research, which are not based on field research, and examine the limitations of the small body of field research of drug courts. Third, we present how we conducted our multiyear, multisite study. We then explain the drug-court staff's professional belief system of drug addiction, treatment, and testing, within which staff members make judgments as to whether clients are telling the truth or lying when confronted with positive tests for illicit drug use. We follow with our discussion of how clients respond to accusations of illicit drug use and how the staff judges the clients to be telling the truth or lying.

We conclude by emphasizing that the outcomes of drug courts and other problem courts that have been spawned by drug courts, such as whether clients have successfully completed the program or not, are not determined by clients' actions. Staff members produce their courts' outcomes. One way they do so is by giving meaning to the stories told by clients who try to account for incriminating results or explain inappropriate conduct (Wines and Ulmer 1993). Investigating the interpretive work of court professionals is essential for understanding drug and other problem courts as it has been for understanding human service agencies (Lipsky 1980; Gubrium and Holstein 2001; Holstein 1993; Frohmann 1991; Higgins 1985).

Drug Courts

Drug courts are court-supervised drug-treatment programs. The participants in drug courts, commonly called clients, typically have a serious drug problem and a history of previous arrests. They are usually charged with felony crimes, such as possession with intent to distribute (PWID) crack cocaine or PWID marijuana (Belenko 2001).[1]

Drug court is composed of three elements: treatment services, drug testing, and judicial supervision. Treatment services include drug counseling, self-help meetings, such as Narcotics Anonymous, and perhaps other services, such as vocational and educational counseling. Staff members test clients for drugs, some as often as several times per week. In drug-court sessions, the staff reviews with the drug-court judge the clients' performance, reporting on the clients' drug-test results, attitude, and attendance at counseling and self-help meetings. Unlike in criminal court, judges in drug court come to know the offenders for months, even years. They monitor the clients' performance and encourage, praise, chastise, and warn them, among other responses. With the advice of program managers and treatment staff, judges may punish non-compliant clients with community service or jail time. As clients progress through the program, moving from an initial phase to the concluding phase, they may attend fewer counseling sessions and be drug tested less frequently (Burns and Peyrot 2003; Drug Court Program Office 1997; Goldkamp 1999). The three courts we studied fit this approach.

Although drug courts are popular, Nolan (2001) has criticized the intrusion of the growing therapeutic culture in America into drug court. This therapeutic intrusion allows for the courts to exercise increased control over the client's self as well as body, presumably for the good of the client. One of the consequences of such increased control is inadequate attention to the client's due-process rights. For example, since drug court is to be nonadversarial, the client loses the defense of his or her attorney. However, the good intentions of the staff do not compensate for a strong legal defense.[2] Or in traditional courts, urine testing can only occur if ordered by the court. A chain of custody must be maintained, and the defense is free to challenge the results. In drug court, none of this occurs; these due-process rights are waived.

Drug-Court Research

Most of the current research on drug courts is not field research. It focuses on client or program characteristics to evaluate the efficacy of drug courts compared to other programs, to predict which category of clients is most likely to complete the program, or to evaluate the design of drug-court programs. While valuable for beginning to understand drug courts, these three categories of drug-court research cannot explain how drug-court staff accomplishes drug court and produces its outcomes.

The research investigating the efficacy of drug court supports three conclusions. First, defendants in drug court participate in services longer and more consistently than those in voluntary programs. Second, while in the program, drug-court clients significantly reduce their drug use and criminal behavior when compared to match comparison groups. Finally, after graduation from the program, drug-court clients are rearrested at a lower rate than those defendants who received no services beyond supervision (Bedrick and Skolnick 1999; Belenko 2001; Brewster 2001; Deschenes and Greenwood

1994; Goldkamp 1999; Goldkamp, White, and Robinson 2001; Hora, Schma, and Rosenthal 1999; Longshore et al. 2001; Nolan 2001, 2002; Peters and Murrin 2000).

The latest review of studies investigating the efficacy of drug court, conducted by the Governmental Accountability Office, supports the earlier research, concluding that drug courts are effective in reducing recidivism both through reduction of in-program recidivism and postprogram recidivism (Government Accountability Office 2005). Because of the lower recidivism, drug courts also are cost-effective. How drug courts lead to less drug use and lower recidivism is not adequately understood.[3]

Studies investigating which clients are most likely to complete drug-court programs have examined the relationship of clients' characteristics, such as race, gender, criminal history, drug history, severity of drug use, and motivation, to the likelihood of completing the program. This research has revealed a complex and inconsistent picture of who was most likely to complete a drug-court program. Nonwhite participants, younger participants, and those whose drug of choice was crack cocaine have been found to be less likely to complete the program (Goldkamp and Weiland 1993; Senjo and Leip 2001; Butzin 2002). However, other research has found that race, gender, and drug of choice were not predictive of program failure (Brewster 2001). All the research on program completion is based on the assumption that defendant characteristics somehow produce outcome.

The smallest body of research examines program characteristics (Bouffard and Taxman 2004; Taxman and Bouffard 2003; Taxman 1999; Goldkamp, White, and Robinson 2001; Longshore et al. 2001; Wenzel, Turner, and Ridgely 2004). Given the many agencies that may be involved in a drug court, the flow of information and services between the entities is important. This research strongly suggests that programs that are closely integrated with court, case management, and intensive services are more effective than programs that are disjointed.

The comparatively few field research studies of drug court have relied heavily on observations during drug-court sessions (Burns and Peyrot 2003; Nolan 2001; Wolf and Colyer 2001). These studies begin to open up the black box of drug court. However, most of the work of drug court occurs outside the public court session and is not done by the drug-court judge. Within their particular responsibilities, program administrators, treatment counselors, and other professionals interview drug offenders in jail, talk with defense lawyers by telephone, meet with one another to staff clients' cases, provide treatment counseling in group meetings, test clients for drugs, and develop recommendations to give to the judge, among other drug-court activities. As in the criminal-court system, most of what occurs in drug court occurs outside the open court sessions. Even that which officials and other participants do in the courtroom can be adequately understood only through knowing what they do outside the courtroom and what beliefs they bring into the courtroom.

Setting and Methods

Our article comes from a larger project that explored how drug-court professionals transform drug-using offenders into drug-court clients through the social construction of the moral identity of offenders (Mackinem 2003). We studied three adult drug courts in a metropolitan region of a state capital in a southeastern state: one in an urban county in which the state capital is located, another in a suburban county, and the third in a farming county, which is in the same judicial circuit as the urban county. Mackinem served as the administrator in the urban-county drug court from its founding in 1996 to 2004, when it was folded into the farming-county drug court. He served as administrator in the farming-community drug court from its founding in 1998 to August 2005. He observed in the suburban-county drug court six times from August 1997 to July 1999.

In the following, we provide a portrait of the three counties in which the drug courts were located, discuss each drug court's type of court, present information about the drug court clients and staff, describe how we conducted our field research, discuss how we obtained and analyzed the cases of accusations of illicit drug use, and explore the strengths and challenges that occurred with Mackinem's being a key professional in two of the three drug courts we studied.

Although the three counties are in the same metropolitan area, they do differ. With professional, business, and white-collar workers living within the urban county, also home to a large state university, the county has one of the state's highest average incomes. Known as conservative and tough on crime, the suburban county, with many of its residents working in the capital city, is comparably prosperous to the urban county. The farming county, with agriculture and light industry, has an average income of several thousand dollars less than those of the other two counties.

Drug courts vary in how offenders enter the program after their arrest. The drug courts in the urban and farming counties were quasiadjudicatory programs. The defendants formally signed a stipulation of guilt before entering the program. Should clients then fail the program, they were subject to further legal action. In the suburban county's drug court, the first to be established in our southeastern state, clients entered through preadjudicatory and postadjudicatory paths. Preadjudicatory entrance provided diversion from the criminal court without any stipulation of guilt. Postadjudicatory participation occurred when judges ordered defendants into the program as a condition of probation.

The typical drug-court client for the urban and farming counties, where most of the research was done, was an under-thirty, African American male who used crack cocaine.[4] Since the beginning of these two drug courts, 61 percent of the 415 clients who have entered have been African American and 68 percent have been male. More than one-third of the clients were between the ages of twenty-two and thirty. Fifty-eight percent reported crack as their primary drug of choice. Nearly half spent more than three hundred dollars per week on drugs. Forty percent have graduated from drug court as compared to the national rate of 32 percent (Cooper 2001).[5]

Seventeen drug-court staff professionals across the three courts were significant participants in our larger investigation. The four drug-court judges were white males, each with more than fifteen years of judicial experience.

Mackinem, the only program coordinator for the drug courts in the urban and farming counties during our study, is a white male with more than twenty years of experience in drug counseling and now drug courts. Two program coordinators served the suburban county's drug court during our study—a white, male lawyer who began the program, and more recently, a white female with several years of experience in drug treatment. Of the four public defenders involved in our study, two were Black females and two were white females. Of the seven drug counselors who treated clients in the three programs, four were white females, two were Black males, and one was a white male. Their experience as counselors ranged from a few years to more than twenty years. One white female and the white male were recovering addicts.[6]

During the larger project, Mackinem produced more than four hundred pages of single-spaced field notes. He began by making notes about whatever he observed in his daily activities as program coordinator that occurred to him as potentially interesting. During the course of the project, he became more focused in his observations and note making. He created increasingly complex flow charts that showed the set of decisions the drug-court staff made about applicants and clients and used these flow charts, his discussions with the second author, and his emerging grounded analysis to guide his observations and noting (Glaser and Strauss 1967). Mackinem became increasingly attentive to recording the language used by the drug-court professionals, especially the terms used by staff to refer to failures and successes in drug court (Emerson 1969; Spradley 1979; Wider 1974).

In addition to numerous hours of observations, Mackinem interviewed eight drug-court professionals, developed key informant relationships with three professionals, taped seven drug-court sessions, and had access to a wide variety of documents. He interviewed two judges, one program coordinator, one public defender, and four treatment counselors, of whom three were interviewed together. Three of the interviews were taped and transcribed. Mackinem repeatedly discussed drug court with three key informants, two treatment counselors, and a program coordinator. With the permission of the judge in the urban-county drug court, Mackinem taped seven courtroom sessions and transcribed them. Finally, Mackinem had access to a wide variety of forms and documents used in drug court, such as arrest warrants, applications for drug court, and court notes from counselors, which were counselors' summary statements about how clients were participating in treatment.

Within this larger investigation of drug court, we explored how staff managed the responses of clients when confronted with a positive test for drug use. To do so, we analyzed seventy-eight documented accusations by drug-court staff of illicit drug use by clients, the clients' responses to the accusations, and the staff's reactions to the clients' responses, all of which we collected before we began writing this article.[7] All but a handful of the seventy-eight cases came from the drug courts in the urban and farming counties where most of our research was done. We collected the seventy-eight cases over eight years in two phases. During our larger study of drug court, Mackinem recorded information about accusations of illicit drug use, as he did any information that struck him as noteworthy. During this first phase, many of the accusations of illicit drug use occurred in the drug-court sessions that were taped and transcribed. Once we decided to focus explicitly on accusations of illicit drug use, Mackinem attempted to record all instances. Mackinem talked about clients' responses to accusations of illicit drug use with all three informants and in interviews with a coordinator, counselor, and judge.

In and out of drug court, the staff accused clients of drug use. In 65 percent of the cases, the accusation of use came in court. Mackinem was not the original accuser for any of these accusations. At times, he reported to the judge in court that a client had tested positive after the drug treatment staff informed him.[8]

We reviewed the instances of accusations independently, compared our coding of each instance, and were not surprised to learn that we coded each instance similarly as our categorizations were grounded in the field notes at a low level of abstraction. During the writing, we analyzed more than ten new accusations of illicit drug use that occurred in the farming county's drug court to check our analysis and to illustrate occasional points (Silverman 2000).[9] Our field research was opportunistic, with Mackinem using a complete membership role (Adler and Adler 1987; Riemer 1977). While the classical school of field research may criticize this approach because the investigator may be overly involved in the phenomenon, perhaps accepting uncritically the perspectives of the fellow members, field researchers have recognized the value of and encouraged fellow researchers to participate more intimately in the social worlds they study (Adler and Adler 1987; Adler, Adler, and Rochford 1986; Ellis and Flaherty 1992; Higgins and Johnson 1988; Jorgensen 1989; Lofland and Lofland 1995).

Being the program coordinator in two of the three drug courts studied provided opportunities and challenges for Mackinem. Most of the work of drug court occurs outside the public drug-court sessions. Mackinem participated in many less public activities of drug court: interviews of drug offenders in jail; courthouse conversations with lawyers; telephone conversations with distraught parents of defendants; meetings with treatment staff; precourt meetings with drug-court judges, public defenders, and treatment staff; and more. In these and the other places where the professional staff does the work of drug court, Mackinem had access not only to his experiences but also to the actions and talk of his colleagues, who knew of his research, and to the various reports written by himself and treatment staff (Snow, Benford, and Anderson 1986).[10]

Being a complete member also posed challenges (Adler and Adler 1987; Mackinem 2003). First, given his position as administrator, it was inappropriate to interview drug-court applicants and clients for research purposes. However, Mackinem informed all drug-court applicants that they were part of a research project on drug-court decision making. Second, as an experienced drug counselor, Mackinem at times found it difficult to notice the mundane in drug court and reflect on his observations and experiences. For example, Mackinem needed to work mindfully just to hear his colleagues or himself utter such mundane terms as *hit bottom*.

To address these challenges of being a complete member, Mackinem talked extensively with his coauthor, an experienced field researcher but an outsider to drug court. Field researchers have advocated this kind of team field research, which was effective for enabling Mackinem, the insider, to reflect on his experiences and observations as a drug-court administrator and to make them available for sociological inspection and analysis (Jorgensen 1989; Douglas 1970). The comments on a draft of this article from a scholar not directly involved with our project but who has written about drug court further enabled us to reflect critically on what Mackinem was learning as an insider.

Finally, Mackinem's complete membership role provided us the experiences and observations to decide that the drug-court professionals do not understand themselves as participants in the production of truths and lies. Instead, they understand themselves as recognizing the truths and lies told by the clients. Further, through making Mackinem's long-term experiences available for inspection, we concluded that the drug-court staff members' construction of truths and lies occurs within their professional beliefs about drug addiction, treatment, and testing, which we present later. The professionals typically do not reference these beliefs when discussing the clients' drug use and responses to accusations of drug use. The combination of an insider and an outsider enabled us to develop the grounded understanding that we present.

Belief System of Drug Addiction, Treatment, and Testing

Within their beliefs about drug addiction, treatment, and testing, drug-court staffers evaluate the clients' responses when confronted with positive tests for illicit drug use.[11] We take up each element of the professional belief system in turn. First, professionals view addiction as a compulsive behavior disorder in which the individual continues to use the substance despite significantly negative social, psychological, legal, and financial consequences. Whether it is useful to describe addiction as a disease, the disease concept is the dominant paradigm among drug treatment professionals today.[12]

Second, professionals regard the compulsion to use as a product of biological, psychological, and social drives (Lobdell 2004; Jellinek 1960). Biologically, the compulsion may be generated by the drug user's desire to avoid the painful symptoms of withdrawal. Professionals understand childhood traumas, emotional conflicts, shame, and guilt to be a few of the psychological conditions that may propel a person to use. Cognitive styles also may promote the use of illicit substances. Peer associations and membership in a drug-using subculture or network will socially promote the continued substance use. Professionals believe that all three compelling drives underlie the users' choice to continue using despite negative consequences of continued use. According to staff, the choice to quit using illicit drugs resides solely with the client.

Third, professionals believe that because of the biological changes created by the substance and the psychological accommodations associated with use, drug users cannot easily assess and evaluate their condition. Drug users lie both to themselves and to those around them, which is often called denial. Denial is not static. Drug users may have startling clarity into their problems at times but not see the most obvious aspects of their lives at other times.

Treatment attempts to change the drug user on biological, psychological, and social levels (NIDA 2000; White 1998). Treating an addiction is a process and not an event. The treatment intensity varies with the individual's progress. The services are divided into phases based on client progress, program length, and number of phases. The drug-court programs we studied varied from one year of services to almost two years for the majority of clients. All three programs used three phases. In Phase One, the most intense, clients spent nine to twelve hours in counseling per week. By Phase Three, clients spent two hours in counseling every other week. Phase One was the most intense because the clients were most likely to have trouble with program compliance and drug-use abstinence. Phase One commonly lasted three to five months in a year-long program. By the time a client moved to Phase Three, staff expected clients to be compliant with all program rules and to make substantial progress toward stable abstinence (Burns and Peyrot 2003).

The process of moving toward abstinence, called recovery, is characterized by periods of illicit drug use, which are called relapses. In the early stages of counseling, the staff and other group members seek to break through the denial and enable the drug users to define themselves as addicts. Once drug users come to accept the addict identity, the counseling moves to teaching the clients skills and techniques for avoiding future drug use (Burns and Peyrot 2003).[13] Treatment staff commonly referred to these as tools. Tools will include the activities and verbal skills needed to manage emotional upsets created by normal life, from such basics as learning to share intimacy to discussing childhood trauma to the more existential acceptance of life on life's terms. Tools may also include learning new cognitive skills (Kadden et al. 1995).

Treatment seeks to return addicted individuals to physical health and change their thinking about themselves and their use of mood-altering substances. Finally, treatment will seek to change the clients' social networks. Treatment staff pushes clients to avoid all former drug-using friends and associates, commonly called changing "playmates and playgrounds" (*Alcoholics Anonymous* 2001).

The staff expects specific client behaviors. First, addicts lie about drug use. Lying helps avoid stigma and promotes continued use (Furst et al. 1999).

Second, clients make bad decisions. When clients skip meetings, seek medical care, or go out on Friday night, the staff assumes clients are seeking drugs. Being late for a group counseling session could be a simple mistake or a sign that the client is returning to drug use. Third, despite the staff's best effort, clients are likely to relapse while in the program. Termed by the staff as a simple slip or a full-blown relapse, returning to illicit drug use is a normal part of the recovery process. Fourth, clients must change. Relapses and bad decisions are expected when clients first enter drug treatment. After sufficient time, the staff expects no additional relapses. It is within these expectations that the staff judged the clients' responses to accusations of drug use.

Drug Testing

Drug testing is a critical part of any drug court. Drug testing is necessary to catch the client using drugs (Borg 2000; Knudsen, Roman, and Johnson 2004; Yacoubian 2000; DeJong and Wish 2000). Since their inception, approximately 6 percent of drug tests conducted in the urban- and farming-county drug courts were positive. In all three drug courts, the staff fully trusted the drug-testing results. Never did staff members openly doubt the test. The science of drug testing supports such confidence. For example, neither secondhand smoke nor holding cocaine will result in a positive test (Hawks and Chiang 1986).

Not all drug testing is so clear, however. We identified three areas of subjective judgment within drug testing: levels, line identification, and dilution. In a levels test, the laboratory reports on the amount of drug in the drug user's body, usually in nanograms per deciliter.[14] The staff wrongly interprets increasing or decreasing levels in a series of drug tests as proof of new use or abstinence (Cary 2004). With counter-drug tests, the staff member places a small amount of urine on the test, observing to see if a line appears. Sometimes the line can be quite faint, and the staff member must evaluate how pronounced the line is before determining the results.[15] While any of these three areas might serve to fully illustrate the potentially subjective nature of drug tests, we will explore more fully the issue of dilution.

Diluted tests occur when clients have drunk such large quantities of fluids that the chemical and particulate matter in their urine samples are at such low concentrations that any finding of drug use is not possible. Treatment professionals commonly call drinking large quantities of liquids to hide drug use flushing. With water-soluble drugs, such as crack and crystal methamphetamine, flushing can be effective in hiding illicit drug use.

Many programs have policies that state that a diluted test is a positive test, although in none of the three observed programs was policy cited in discussion. Did the person drink excessive amounts of fluid to hide drug use, or is there some legitimate explanation? When one client told staff members after a diluted urine sample that he was on antidepressants, which commonly cause excessive dry mouth, they did not interpret the dilution as deceptive, nor did they interpret the client as having used illicit drugs.

Staff members judge other dilutions, however, as attempts to beat the test. In the following report to the judge during drug court, the counselor infers from the dilution level that the client was flushing.

> Counselor: His test on last Tuesday came back diluted! Critically diluted, chronically diluted. His diluted was Tuesday and came in at 17.7, a reading of 17.7. The cutoff is at forty, and the halfway point is twenty. He is even below that!

> Judge: I want you to tell this young man what you told us earlier.

> Counselor: To get to this level, you must be putting a garden hose in your throat and turning it wide open to flush your system. That is what it looks like to me. And I don't see it as anything but an all-out attempt to get this drug out of his system or whatever was there at the time. But as far as I am concerned, tested diluted at that level is the same as a positive test.

The counselor inferred that the client was trying to flush drugs out of his body. No science separates flushing from excessive drinking. The client's lack of an explanation for his diluted results bolstered the counselor's inference. The counselor concluded that the client was attempting to avoid detection, a sign of criminality.

Truths and Lies

Drug-court staff defines clients' responses when the clients are confronted with positive tests for illicit drug use as truths or lies. The staff creates the meaning for the clients' behavior (Gubrium and Holstein 2001; Holstein 1993; Miller and Holstein 1991). They encourage clients to tell the truth and they discourage lies. As one judge said, "All I ask is you tell the truth. The one thing I can't stand is a liar." Denials are claims by the clients that they did not intentionally use a mood-altering chemical. Clients who deny drug use often explain why the positive test result is inaccurate. Rarely do staff members believe them. Through confessions, clients admit to using mood-altering drugs willingly. Confessions may also include other elements that are congruent with the staff's professional belief system. Done well, confessions promote the clients' standing within the program. Staff members typically interpreted denials to be lies and confessions to be true. After discussing denials and the staff's response to them, we take up confessions.

I Swear, Judge, I Didn't Use!

Denial is a simple assertion that new use did not occur. Clients denied use in 32 percent of the accusations of illicit drug use. Denials conflict with the staff's unwavering belief in the drug-test results and match their understanding that addicts lie. For example, John had been in the program for several months when he tested positive for cocaine.

Judge: What happened?

Client: I didn't use. I don't know what happened, but I didn't use.

The client denied use but provided no explanation as to how he tested positive for cocaine. The staff easily dismissed the client as lying. The judge eventually expelled John from the program. John's denial is unusual in that it lacked an explanation for the positive test. More often, clients offer explanations such as faulting the test, residual use, incidental contact, or medical explanation.

When clients fault the test, they assert that positive results are in error because of a mistake with the test. They did nothing wrong. Clients have claimed that the sample cup was dirty or the lab must have confused their sample with another one.

Ronnie had tested positive four times and never admitted to using illicit drugs. On his fifth positive test, Ronnie vehemently claimed, "Something must be wrong with the test!" Ronnie tested positive two more times before the staff removed him from the program. Ronnie's attack on the test challenged the staff's belief in the infallibility of the test. His early failures to confess made him a liar, and the repetitions made him a criminal.

In a few cases, clients attacked the staff. Clients claimed that the staff was "out to get me" or that "someone must have put something in my test cup." Like Ronnie's attack on the test, these responses attempt to shift the focus onto others, a response comparable to Sykes and Matza's condemnation of condemners (1996). In the few documented cases, the staff reacts negatively to this attack. Such a response does not appear targeted to gain the judge's support but to diminish the accusation.

In referring to residual use, the client admits to the past use of drugs that the test has picked up but denies new use. If true, the results are inaccurate and the client is exonerated. Clients have claimed that cocaine was in their body three weeks after use, weak kidneys made the heroin last two months, or marijuana remained in the body more than six weeks. When deciding whether the claim of residual use is legitimate, staff members differentiate between marijuana—a long-lasting drug—and other drugs. Illicit drugs stay within the body for differing periods. Some illicit drugs, like marijuana, can last for several weeks in the body, while others, such as cocaine, last for a couple of days at most (Cary 2004; Hawks and Chiang 1986). Mackinem observed many clients trying to claim residual use weeks after any such drug residual would have left the body. With the exception of proximate positive tests for marijuana, the staff rejected the claim of residual use as absurd.

Frank admitted using cocaine at 3:00 AM on the Fourth of July. On the evening of the eighth, when he tested positive for cocaine, Frank claimed it was residual use from the Fourth of July. The claim was not congruent with the staff's knowledge of drug testing. Cocaine is a short-acting drug and leaves the body within seventy-two hours (Hawks and Chiang 1986). Even if Frank had used as late as the night of the fifth, the staff believed the drug should be out of his body. To the staff, Frank was lying.

In incidental contact, clients argue that they were exposed to drugs but did not intentionally ingest them. Secondhand smoke is a common claim of incidental contact. One client claimed, "I was in the car with my uncles and they were smoking weed." Other clients have claimed to have played catch with a bag of cocaine, kissed someone who used cocaine, or eaten crab legs boiled in beer to explain their positive tests. Incidental contact is often an awkward assertion. Clients admit to being in the wrong place with the wrong people with illicit drugs. If staff members were to accept the explanation of incidental contact, they might reduce the clients' moral responsibility for testing positive. However, the staff universally rejected the claim of incidental contact.

The staff occasionally accepted medical explanations as valid. Clients admitted to using drugs but only for licit purposes, not to get high. Clients have explained positive tests with reports of trips to the dentist, medication for migraine headaches, or menstrual medications.

Kelly had been in the drug-court program for more than six months and never tested positive. When it came time for her to provide a sample, she told the collector that she had taken migraine medication and offered to bring in the prescription bottle. Before court, the treatment-staff member informed the court of Kelly's explanation.

> Judge: You let us know way ahead of time of your medical situation. Thanks for letting us know before the test.

The client did test positive for barbiturates, but the staff never treated this as a violation of program regulations.

Other clients may claim a unique medical event. Henry, the counselor, reported that Alice, a client, had a highly suspicious test that was positive for alcohol. Until confronted in court, Alice had no knowledge of the counselor's suspicions or that her test for alcohol was positive.

> Client: Oh, my God. I knew about the test. It smelled bad, real bad. I have been drinking a lot of water. Been exercising; walks, runs, and biking. My dad is diabetic. All my relatives are on the needle. I haven't done anything wrong. I made the trip this morning to pay the bill, but the teller machine did not work. I would not have done all that if I was going to dilute my test. About the rest, I don't know.

> Judge: From now on, all tests will be observed.

Mackinem recalled that, under limited circumstances, the excessive sugar in the urine, common in diabetes, could ferment in the bladder and thereby produce alcohol. If not for Mackinem's recollection, the judge would have sent the client to jail.

Staff members are more likely to suspect clients who claim that their positive tests are because of medication received through emergency-room visits than those who point to preexisting medical conditions (Burns and Peyrot 2003). The staff frequently viewed dirty tests from emergency-room visits as attempts by clients to scam drugs.

Staff Judgment of Denials

When a client denies drug use after a positive test and is not believed, the staff can explain the denial in two ways: the client is incapable of telling the truth or unwilling to tell the truth. The illness, lack of tools, or distrust could lessen the client's capacity to tell the truth. Staff members know that addicts lie as part of the addiction disease. If the client is still sick, the staff can attribute the lie to the illness. Staff members marginalize the new client who denies drug use as too sick to tell the truth.

Staff members expect the worthy addict to progress toward recovery. A sign of progress is telling the truth. Staff members judge clients who are still lying after sufficient time in the program to be criminal, not sick. The amount of time that is sufficient is open to staff interpretation. The staff interprets the client's continued lying as a lack of commitment to change (Mackinem 2003; Burns and Peyrot 2003).

Staff members judge criminals as morally corrupt, deserving of contempt and punishment. They may become angry at such clients. In one staff note, Mackinem wrote, "You know he is lying because his lips are moving." Another staff member, a counselor, referred to a client as "Teflon Don," commenting, "if he would just take responsibility, I would keep him in the program." The staff eventually judged "Teflon Don" as a hopeless criminal trying to avoid punishment, not an addict struggling with a disease. Continued denial is a sign to the staff that the client is unworthy of further treatment.

I Won't Lie to You, I Used

Confessions are clients' admission of using illicit drugs to alter their mood. In 68 percent of the documented accusations of illicit drug use, the client admitted to use at some point after confrontation by a staff member. Staff members judge confessions to be telling the truth. Since lying is a sign of illness or criminality, telling the truth is a sign of progress and good character.

When clients offer a confession is important. Clients infrequently confess before staff members administer the drug test. Many confess when staff members confront them with the test results. Some confess to the judge after days of denial to treatment staff. Others confess between these extremes.

Staff members encourage clients to admit drug use before testing. When clients admit use before the test, they enhance their moral status, and the staff may reduce the sanctions. For example, after many violations, the staff discussed the removal of Chuck. A staff member harkened back to Chuck's earlier pretest confession as a sign of his potential and won the argument.

However, 92 percent of the recorded confessions occurred after the staff's accusation. We can only speculate as to why this is so. From the client's perspective, the results of the drug test may be far from certain. The test can be beaten. If a client used a water-soluble drug, like cocaine, on a limited basis and then drank excessive amounts of water, the test could be negative. The flushing would leave the body free of the drug and the client may have beaten the test. Alcohol is very difficult to detect in urine. A confession is certain punishment. A beaten test has no consequences.

Confessions range from the simple "I used" to admissions with multifaceted explanations, the latter being more common. Simple confessions admit to the accusation but do not express regret (Gold and Weiner 2000). Through responses that are more complex, clients can display behaviors congruent with the staff's professional belief system. The responses include mitigations, reports of changes made, and apologies.

Mitigation

Clients frequently attempt to mitigate their full responsibility for illicit drug use. They offer excuses such as the negative influence of peers, family stress, or a tragic incident. Some simultaneously state that the excuses are not justification for their illicit drug use. If staff members accept the clients' accounts, they may reduce the clients' culpability for their violation and enhance their moral identity (Scott and Lyman 1968; Hunter 1984).

The judge or other staff member often invites an explanation when he[16] asks, "Tell me about the positive test." In the suburban county's drug court, however, the judge did not ask clients to explain and appeared to assume the reported drug use was true and not worthy of discussion. Drug courts and drug-court staff may differ on which mitigations are accepted and which are rejected (Burns and Peyrot 2003).

We characterize the two most common forms of mitigations we observed as stress and peers. Thirty-four percent of the confessions that included explanations included references to stress and 25 percent included explanations about the influence of peers.

In their confessions, clients may point to the stresses of everyday life or the unique stress of an acute situation, such as romantic breakups, sick children, and parental conflicts, as triggers for their use. Stan had been in the program for more than six months when he first tested positive for marijuana.

> Judge: What happened?
>
> Client: I thought my girlfriend was pregnant. I have no real excuses. Yes, I thought she was pregnant, but that is not an excuse.

The staff judged Stan to be making progress. He admitted smoking marijuana, offered an explanation, and then showed insight by noting that his girlfriend's assumed pregnancy was not an excuse for his illicit drug use. To the staff, Stan was frankly honest, showing that he was not in denial and no longer thinking addictively. However, the staff did not reduce Stan's punishment, twenty-four hours in jail as prescribed in the policy manual. The judge and staff use more than the client's response to accusations of drug use when sanctioning the client (Mackinem 2003).

Gene points to the negative power of peers on his decision to use drugs. In his previous positive test, he initially denied use and blamed it on having contact with a girl under the influence. With the second positive test, however, he admitted his use.

> Mackinem: Your honor, I would like to call Gene. Gene tested positive for the presence of cocaine. I will let him explain the exact circumstances.
>
> Client: I made some wrong decisions, I can see that now. I made the decision to hang around the wrong people. Lesson learned.
>
> Judge: Gene, you have been in the program six weeks now.
>
> Client: Yes, your honor.
>
> Judge: You have heard this all before. I just want to make sure you understand. The first thing is, you see these people around you? You need to work with Mackinem and the counselors. This is very important. You must be truthful with these people. I rely on them. I will accept the recommendation of the solicitor and give you twelve hours of community service.
>
> Mackinem: Your honor, I would like to change the recommendation to four hours of community service since he was so forthright.
>
> Judge: Okay, I will accept that recommendation.

The staff judged Gene's response to be true and insightful. He pointed to the negative influence of others on his drug use but accepted responsibility for his decision to be with them. The staff and the judge rewarded the client for his truthfulness with a reduction in his community service.

Clients' confessions with reference to triggering conditions are successful when the staff judges clients to be showing insight about their motives but also accepting responsibility for their drug use. If the staff believes that clients are trying to deny responsibility for their illicit drug use because of triggering conditions, the staff may harshly judge the clients (Burns and Peyrot 2003).

Reports of Changes Made

Clients may report that they have made changes when they admit to using drugs. Such changes may include obtaining a self-help group sponsor, moving, or changing friends. Staff members routinely advise clients to dismiss drug-using friends. Staff members view clients' making changes as showing motivation, which they value.

After six weeks in the program, George again tested positive for drugs.

> Judge: What happened?
>
> Client: I just recently got rid of a lot of friends I used with. I feel that is going to improve my position.
>
> Judge: Your friends make you use? You got to say yes or no. These friends, you don't associate with them anymore?
>
> Client: That's right. I promise next time my levels will be lower.

Staff members see the client's motivation in the change made. Not only did the client display responsibility, he acted upon it! Ironically, while staff members believe clients lie, they took George's claim of changing friends to be true without any verification.[17]

Apologies

Through apologies, drug-court clients admitted responsibility for their drug use and expressed regret. Consider Carl, who had tested positive for cocaine and had another test that was diluted since he had last attended court.

"Tell me about your positive test," the judge asks.

"I had a relapse. I don't want to lie to you. I relapsed with cocaine," replies the client.

"What hours do you work?" asks the judge.

"I work 8:00 A.M. until dark, some Fridays and Saturdays, and no Sundays."

After a short discussion on when Carl would serve forty-eight hours in jail for testing positive for drug use, Carl adds, "I'm sorry for my problems, trying to take care of my family. I want to apologize to the court, my classmates. I am sorry. I tried to do too much."

Regret acknowledges the legitimacy of drug court and the trust of the drug-court staff or of the fellow clients that has been violated (Tavuchis 1991). The staff received apologies well.[18]

An apology may even counter a series of denials. Chet had been in the program for nearly eight months. During that time, he tested positive six times. Chet explained each incident with reference to his current medications. Eventually, the counselor hardly noted the positive results. Mackinem became suspicious, and with treatment staff, requested a more advanced drug-test method. The result conclusively showed a positive test for an illicit medication and not for one of Chet's prescription medications. When confronted, Chet denied all drug use despite drug tests indicating he had used a benzodiazepine, a legal but highly addictive drug. The judge removed Chet from the program for lying about his drug use.

Several days after the court, Chet called Mackinem and asked what he could do. Mackinem suggested he come to the next court and talk with the judge. The client came to the following court to ask if he could be allowed into the program. This was unusual, though it had happened a few times. In the staff meeting before court, the counselor commented with little enthusiasm that Chet had come as far as he was likely to go and he, the counselor, had little hope Chet would stay drug free.

Judge: Well what do you have to say?

Client: I want to apologize to you, my counselor, and Mr. M (Mackinem) for lying in court. I won't lie. I have been using Xanex on and off for three months. I don't know why I couldn't tell the truth last time. I have never done that before.

Mackinem: Your honor, he has been lying to us for months.

Client: I didn't mean lie in court like that. I knew it was wrong.

Judge: Are you ready to make a change? Because one thing I can't stand for is any more lying.

Client: I am. I want to apologize to the group for lying all that time.

After court, both the judge and Mackinem were impressed that Chet had told what they understood to be the truth. Chet showed he knew lying was wrong and that he had violated the trust of the court and its staff. The judge and the staff allowed Chet back into the program, and he graduated some months later. Accepted apologies can reintegrate the offender into the community.

Repeated Apologies

Apologies and confessions lose their power with repetition. Staff members question the sincerity of repeated apologies. If clients are sincere in earlier apologies, why did they not make the changes?

Charlie tested positive many times. With each positive drug test, Charlie apologized. After the third test in his short history in the program, all positive, Charlie explained,

> I did use the drugs. I apologize to you and my fellow group members. I have been having some family problems. I am not trying to blame them, but it has been hard.

When Charlie tested positive yet again, his apology forestalled his removal by the staff, which sent him to a residential treatment program. After his release from the residential program, Charlie immediately tested positive. Charlie offered yet another apology and explanation:

> I was in a bar having a few drinks and the cocaine was being passed around right under my nose. The temptation was too great, and I used. I have come to the realization that I cannot drink alcohol. I want to apologize to the court for putting myself in that situation.

The staff rejected Charlie's apology. They interpreted his realization after having been in the program for weeks that he cannot drink alcohol as trivial, not as a sign of an important change. Following the recommendation of the staff, the judge removed him from the program. Repeated apologies eventually may fail as staff members come to understand the client as either unmotivated or criminal.

Conclusion

Drug courts, a recent development within the criminal-justice system, aim to transform drug-using criminal offenders into drug-abstinent, noncriminal citizens. Present studies primarily attempt to determine which clients are likely to benefit from drug courts and to evaluate drug courts by focusing on characteristics of the offenders and/or of the program. The comparatively few field research studies that explore the work of drug-court professionals typically have focused on the drug-court session, the most public arena of drug court. While this research begins to help us understand drug court, it cannot adequately inform us of how professional drug-court staffers do the work of drug court.

How drug-court staff members decide whether clients are telling the truth or lying when they confront clients with positive tests for drug use, which we examined here, is part of that larger drug-court work. Staff members make their decision through the application of their professional beliefs about drug addiction, treatment, and testing.

Whether or not the clients have told the truth is not inherent in the clients' responses. The staff members construct the clients' responses as truths and lies. When they accept and reject the clients' denials, they are also constructing whether the clients have intentionally used illicit drugs to get high. They are producing, not merely recording, what they commonly understand to be a positive or dirty test, a significant drug-court outcome. They use this outcome in deciding how to manage the client.

Elements of the professional belief system held by the staff in the three drug courts we studied, such as the belief that drug addiction is an illness, are widely shared within the world of drug court. Other components may vary more among the staff, be more contested, or be less well supported by scientific evidence. For example, some drug-court staff members may interpret family stress as a reasonable trigger for drug use, though not exculpatory. Other staff members in the same court or in different courts may view the client's mention of family stress when testing positive for drugs as an attempt to deny responsibility. To some drug-court staff members, a diluted urine sample is an attempt to mask illicit drug use, but not all staffers make that assumption.

The drug-court staff's judgment as to whether clients are telling the truth or lying when confronted with a positive test for drugs is one occasion of many when the staff creates moral identities for its clients and for those applying to be clients. Are the drug-using offenders morally worthy drug addicts attempting to become sober, or are they unworthy criminals with no willingness to kick their habit? Staffers increasingly make these judgments as they evaluate the potential of drug-using offenders to participate successfully in drug court, as they monitor the progress of drug court clients in the program, and as they assess the performance of clients in deciding whether the clients will graduate or be removed from the program. For example, when clients miss appointments, skip counseling sessions, or fail to make payments, staff members judge the worthiness of the clients' explanations and of the clients. When clients attend counseling, humble themselves in the sessions, test negative for drug use, and make their payments, the staff also judges the worthiness of the clients. We see the moral identity in the names ascribed to clients.

Teflon Don, slimy, or *honest* all designate a moral identity. Staff members use these moral identities as they continue to work with the clients, making decisions about the clients' progress or lack of progress and about who has succeeded and who has failed. The staff's construction of clients' responses as truths and lies when it confronts clients with positive tests for illicit drugs is part of the staff's moral construction of drug-court clients, which we have taken up more thoroughly elsewhere.

Just as drug-court staffers construct the truths and lies that clients tell from the clients' responses when confronted with positive tests for illicit drugs, they produce the successes and failures of the clients out of the clients' participation. Working within their courts' policies and procedures and in interaction with each other, drug-court staff determines, for example, whether clients who have tested positive for illicit drug use, have missed meetings, or even have committed a new crime will be removed. The positive test, missed meetings, and even the new crime do not remove the clients.[19] The staff does (Higgins and Butler 1982).

However, evaluation and program-design research overlook this crucial point, and even if they did not, how it is presently conducted cannot adequately explore how staff members produce success and failure or any other outcome of drug court. To note that crack users fail in drug court at rates higher than clients who use other drugs implies that some characteristics of crack users are implicated in that higher rate of failure. Perhaps, but without exploring how drug-court staff manages clients, we cannot know.

With the rise of therapeutic jurisprudence has come the development of other specialty courts that handle problematic behavior, including domestic violence, mental illness, drunk driving, gambling, homelessness, truancy, and gun possession. The limited research and thinking about these problem courts, as they have with drug courts, focus on program design and evaluation and client outcomes. The research and discussion have largely overlooked the work of the staff in these problem courts. The staff produces the outcomes of these problem courts that the evaluation research attempts to predict (Berman and Feinblatt 2005). How the staff does so should appropriately concern us.

Staff members in all service agencies, not just in drug courts or in other problem courts, produce the client and organizational outcomes that become measures of their agencies. They do so as they work within their organization's policy and procedures; use their professional philosophy; interact with their colleagues, applicants, clients, and others; and manage the demands of their position. The characteristics and conduct of applicants and clients do not produce applicant and client outcomes. Staff members make important, sometimes fateful, decisions about applicants and clients who are understood by the staff to possess various characteristics or to have conducted themselves in various ways. The staff does so in part through interpreting the stories, explanations, and accounts told by applicants and clients. The staff turns stories into organizational facts (Maines and Ulmer 1993). Too often, the object of the staff's actions is mistaken for the cause of the staff's decisions.

Endnotes

[1] Some have commented that drug courts select only the highly motivated applicant, discarding the unmotivated or risky. Nationally, this is not always the case; many programs take those ordered by the court and have little say over the admission decision (Cooper 2001). In all three courts studied, violent offenders were excluded from the program, as were burglars in two of the programs. In the programs we examined, the staff sought to take drug addicts who were motivated to change.

[2] One of the professionals Nolan (2001) interviewed strongly disputed Nolan's characterization of her program in a conversation with Mackinem.

[3] While the Government Accountability Office (GAO) report echoes Belenko's earlier review, they both raise shortcomings. Less clear is whether the program reduces long-term drug use within participants. First, there is no clear evidence, according to the GAO report, on the effectiveness for specific drug-court components. Second, there is little research on the operation of drug courts or how the specific components of drug court contribute to the overall program. Questions about the effect of the judge in drug court, the impact of supervision, and the sufficient amount of treatment services remain unanswered. Some studies attempt to answer such questions, but no clear consensus has been reached (Banks and Gottfredson 2003; Marlowe, Festinger, and Lee 2004; Peters, Hass, and Hunt 2001).

[4] Drug-court clients varied among the three courts. In particular, drug-court clients in the suburban county, based on the first four years of operation, were 55 percent white and 44 percent African American. Forty-three percent of the clients in the suburban county drug court used powder cocaine as their primary drug of choice. However, we found no evidence in the cases that we analyzed that how drug-court staff handled clients' responses to accusations of illicit drug use varied by the social characteristics or drug-use preferences of the clients.

[5] Local arrest data for drug crimes did not include racial and gender breakdowns. Using state-level arrest data, of those arrested for crack-cocaine charges, African American males compose 81 percent of arrests for serious crack-cocaine drug crimes (including distribution, possession with intent, and drug sale), as compared to only 6 percent for white males. African American males are nearly three times more likely to be arrested for serious drug crimes, beyond crack cocaine, than white males. However, when one includes less serious drug crimes for all drugs (including simple possession charge and possession of drug paraphernalia), this difference disappears, and both males are equally likely to be arrested. For all types of drugs, only 13 percent of females of any race were arrested for any serious drug crimes (including distribution, possession with intent, and drug sale). The typical drug-court client in our study does not match the statewide arrest data; females and white males are overrepresented in drug court. This variation is probably because of differences in the criminal history of drug users, since none of the programs could take offenders with violent-criminal convictions in their history. Furthermore, all the programs studied avoided those charged with selling drugs.

[6] We have no evidence that the social characteristics of the counselors made a difference in how they handled clients' accounts. A recovering counselor was similar to a nonrecovering, as a female was to a male.

[7] The seventy-eight cases involved thirty-six different clients. Of the thirty-six clients, twenty were Black, thirteen were white, and three clients' races from the suburban county's drug court were unknown. Seventy-five percent of the clients were male.

[8] In three cases, clients admitted drug use before being accused. We reviewed these cases as part of a more comprehensive treatment of how drug-court clients respond to accusations (or potential accusations) of drug use and how the staff reacts to the clients' responses.

[9] While writing this article, Mackinem recalled several cases of accusations of illicit drug use that he had not recorded. While we did not base our analysis on these cases, we reviewed them as a further check on our analysis with the seventy-eight documented cases.

[10] Very likely, because of Mackinem's organizational position, treatment staff members and other drug-court professionals would not tell Mackinem some matters that they would tell a

trusted field researcher who was an outsider. For example, somewhat ironically, two counselors told Mackinem that they avoided telling him about some of the conduct of clients if they believed he would want to remove the clients from the program and they did not.

[11] Such a professional belief system is an ongoing product of personal experiences and history, education, professional training and socialization, experience, work group culture, and local theories of the office. Two of the counselors were recovering addicts. While the counselor's background did influence how the counselor explained client behavior, we found no evidence that leads us to believe that such a background influenced decision making.

[12] The disease concept is certainly highly debated (Peele 1989; Jellinek 1960).

[13] Sociologists have explored the importance of addicts' developing nonaddict identities for themselves during their recovery from drug use and the expectation of officials that addicts do so (Denzin 1987, 1993; McIntosh and McKeganey 2000; Peyrot 1985).

[14] In a lab test, the urine is mixed with a series of reagents that determine if a drug metabolite is present and the degree to which it is present. The degree to which a drug is present is a levels test. In a levels test, the number of nanograms per deciliter of urine is determined. As such, the results are less subject to interpretation. However, the levels test developed its own folk understanding. It was common practice to subject a client to a series of levels tests to see if the levels were coming down. Such a strategy involves biweekly drug testing. For example, if a client's results went from 330 nanograms at test one to fifty nanograms at test three, many staff members assumed that the client was not using new drugs and was getting clean. If the nanograms per deciliter increased over several tests, some staff members assumed that the client was using even when the test did not meet the level considered positive. These assumptions are not accurate.

[15] Coming in many different forms, the basic construction of these counter tests is a repository for the urine and a field where the urine interacts with chemical agents. A wicking agent absorbs and transfers the urine into the chemical field. The chemically embedded paper interacts with drug metabolites. If no drugs are in the urine, a line appears in the field. If the drug is present, no line appears in the field. Staff members may debate what constitutes a line.

[16] All observed judges were males.

[17] We speculate that staff members accept or at least do not dismiss the claim of change because such change fits their beliefs about drug addiction. The lack of contradictory indicators, either present or recalled, also appears to promote acceptance.

[18] As Carl's case illustrates, various elements can be added to an apology. For example, Carl added mitigation. Such addition may strengthen the overall effect of the apology.

[19] The staff considers the conditions under which clients commit a new crime and the crime committed. For example, staff removed a client charged with shoplifting after nine months in the program but allowed a client charged with driving while intoxicated to remain.

References

Adler, Patricia A., and Peter Adler. 1987. Membership roles in field research. In *Qualitative Research Methods*, vol 6. Newbury Park, CA: Sage Publications.

Adler, Patricia A., Peter Adler, and E. Burke Rochford. 1986. The politics of participation in field research. *Urban Life* 14 (4): 363–76.

Alcoholics anonymous: The big book, 4th ed. 2001. New York: Alcoholics Anonymous World Services, Inc.

Banks, Duren, and Denise C. Gottfredson. 2003. The effects of drug treatment and supervision on time to rearrest among drug treatment court participants. *Journal of Drug Issues* 33 (2): 385–412.

Bedrick, Brooke, and Jerome Skolnick. 1999. From "treatment" to "justice" in Oakland, California. In *The early drug courts: Case studies in judicial innovation*, edited by W. C. Terry. Thousand Oaks, CA: Sage Publications.

Belenko, Steve. 2001. Research on drug courts: A critical review, 2001 update. In *Research on drug courts.* New York: National Center on Addiction and Substance Abuse at Columbia University.

Berman, Greg, and John Feinblatt. 2005. *Good courts: The case for problem-solving justice.* New York: The New Press.

Borg, Marian. 2000. Drug testing in organizations: Applying Horwitz's theory of effectiveness of social control. *Deviant Behavior* 21 (2): 123–54.

Bouffard, Jeff, and Faye Taxman. 2004. Looking inside the "black box" of drug court treatment services using direct observations. *Journal of Drug Issues* 34 (1): 195–218.

Brewster, Mary P. 2001. An evaluation of the Chester County (PA) drug court program. *Journal of Drug Issues* 31 (1): 177–206.

Bums, Stacy Lee, and Mark Peyrot. 2003. Tough love: Nurturing and coercing responsibility and recovery in California drug courts. *Social Problems* 50 (3): 416–38.

Butzin, Clifford. 2002. Factors associated with completion of a drug court diversion program. *Substance Use and Misuse* 37 (12–13): 1615–33.

Cary, Paul L. 2004. *Urine drug concentrations: The scientific rationale for eliminating the use of drug test levels in drug court proceedings.* Alexandria, VA: National Drug Court Institute.

Cooper, Caroline. 2001. Drug court activities update: Summary information on all programs and detailed information on adult drug courts. Office of Justice Programs Drug Court Clearinghouse and Technical Assistance Project 2001. Retrieved February 26, 2003, from http://www.american.edu/justice/publications/allcourtactivity.pdf

———. 2002. Summary of drug court activity by state and county. American University, Drug Court Clearinghouse 2003. Retrieved November 17, 2003, from http://spa.ward.american.edu/justice/publications/adultchart.pdf

DeJong, Christina, and Eric D. Wish. 2000. Is it advisable to urine test arrestees to assess risk of rearrest? A comparison of self-report and urinalysis-based measures of drug use. *Journal of Drug Issues* 30 (1): 133–46.

Denzin, Norman. 1987. *The alcoholic self.* Newbury Park, CA: Sage.

———. 1993. *The alcoholic society: Addiction and recovery of self.* New Brunswick, NJ: Transaction Publishers.

Deschenes, Elizabeth, and Peter Greenwood. 1994. Maricopa County's drug court: An innovative program for the first time drug offenders on probation. *Justice Systems Journal* 17 (1): 99–115.

Douglas, Jack D. 1970. *Deviance & respectability: The social construction of moral meanings.* New York: Basic Books.

Drug Court Program Office. 1997. *Defining drug courts: The key components*, edited by Office of Justice Programs. Washington, DC: Government Printing Office.

Ellis, Carolyn, and Michael Flaherty. 1992. *Investigating subjectivity: Research on lived experience.* Newbury Park, CA: Sage Publications.

Emerson, Robert M. 1969. *Judging delinquents: Context and process in juvenile court.* Chicago, IL: Aldine Publishing Company.

Frohmann, Lisa. 1991. Discrediting victims' allegations of sexual assault: Prosecutorial account of case rejections. *Social Problems* 38 (2): 213–25.

Furst, Terry R., Bruce D. Johnson, Eloise Dunlap, and Richard Curtis. 1999. The stigmatized image of the "crack head": A sociocultural exploration of a barrier to cocaine smoking among a cohort of youth in New York City. *Deviant Behavior* 20 (2):153–81.

Glaser, Barney G., and Ansehn L. Strauss. 1967. *The discovery of grounded theory: Strategies for qualitative research.* Chicago, IL: Aldine Publishing Company.

Gold, Gregg J., and Bernard Weiner. 2000. Remorse, confession, group identity and expectancies about repeating a transgression. *Basic and Applied Social Psychology* 22 (4): 291–300.

Goldkamp, John. 1999. The origin of the treatment drug court in Miami. In *The early drug courts: Case studies in judicial innovation,* edited by W. C. Terry. Thousand Oaks, CA: Sage Publications.

Goldkamp, John, and Doris Weiland. 1993. *Assessing the impact of Dade County's felony drug court.* Washington, DC: National Institute of Justice.

Goldkamp, John S., Michael D. White, and Jennifer B. Robinson. 2001. Do drug courts work? Getting inside the drug court black box. *Journal of Drug Issues* 31 (1): 27–72.

Government Accountability Office. 2005. *Adult drug court: Evidence indicates recidivism reductions and mixed results for other outcomes.* Washington, DC: United States Government Accountability Office.

Gubrium, Jaber F., and James A. Holstein. 2001. *Institutional selves: Troubled identities in a postmodern world.* New York: Oxford University Press.

Hawks, Richard L., and C. Nora Chiang. 1986. *Urine testing for drugs of abuse.* Washington, DC: National Institute of Drug Abuse.

Higgins, Paul C. 1985. *The rehabilitation detectives: Doing human service work.* Beverly Hills, CA: Sage Publications.

Higgins, Paul, and John Johnson. 1988. *Personal sociology.* New York: Praeger Publishers.

Higgins, Paul C., and Richard R. Butler. 1982. *Understanding deviance.* New York: McGraw-Hill.

Holstein, James A. 1993. *Court-ordered insanity: Interpretive practice and involuntary commitment, social problems and social issues.* New York: Aldine de Gruyter.

Hora, Peggy, William Schma, and John Rosenthal. 1999. Therapeutic jurisprudence and the drug court moment: Revolutionizing the criminal justice system's response to drug abuse and crime in America. *Notre Dame Law Review* 74 (2): 439–537.

Huddleston, C. West et al. 2005. *Painting the picture: A national report card on drug courts and other problem solving court programs in the United States.* Alexandria, VA: National Drug Court Institute.

Hunter, Christopher H. 1984. Aligning actions: Types and social distribution. *Symbolic Interaction* 7 (2): 155–74.

Jellinek, Elvin Morton. 1960. *Disease concept of alcoholism.* New Haven, CT: Hillhouse Press.

Jorgensen, Danny L. 1989. Participant observation: A methodology for human studies. In *Applied Social Research Methods Series,* vol. 15. Newbury Park, CA: Sage Publications.

Kadden, Ronald et al., eds. 1995. Cognitive-behavioral coping skills therapy manual. Vol. 3 of the *Project MATCH Monograph Series,* edited by M. E. Mattson. Rockville, MD: National Institute on Alcohol Abuse and Alcoholism.

Knudsen, Hannah K., Paul M. Roman, and J. Aaron Johnson. 2004. The management of workplace deviance: Organizational responses to employee drug use. *Journal of Drug Issues* 4 (1): 121–44.

Lipsky, Michael. 1980. Street-level bureaucracy: Dilemmas of the individual in public services. In *Publications of Russell Sage Foundation.* New York: Russell Sage Foundation.

Lobdell, Jared. 2004. *This strange illness: Alcoholism and Bill W.* New York: Aldine de Gruyter.

Lofland, John, and Lyn H. Lofland. 1995. *Analyzing social settings: A guide to qualitative observation and analysis*, 3rd ed. Belmont, CA: Wadsworth.

Longshore, Douglas et al. 2001. Drug courts: A conceptual framework. *Journal of Drug Issues* 31 (1): 7–26.

Loseke, Donileen. 1989. Evaluation research and the practice of social services: A case for qualitative methodology. *Journal of Contemporary Ethnography* 18 (2): 202–23.

Mackinem, Mitchell. 2003. Judging clients: The creation of moral identity in a drug court. PhD diss., University of South Carolina, Columbia, South Carolina.

Maines, David, and Jeffery T. Ulmer. 1993. The relevance of narrative for interactionist thought. *Studies in Symbolic Interaction* 14: 109–24.

Marlowe, Douglas B., David S. Festinger, and Patricia A. Lee. 2004. The judge is a key component of drug court. *Drug Court Review* 4 (2): 128.

McIntosh, James, and Neil McKeganey. 2000. Addict's narratives of recovery from drug use: Constructing a non-addict identity. *Social Science and Medicine* 50: 1501–10.

Miller, Gale, and James A. Holstein. 1991. Social problems work in street-level bureaucracies: Rhetoric and organizational process. In *Studies in organizational sociology: Essays in honor of Charles K Warriner*, edited by G. Miller and C. K. Warriner. Greenwich, CT: JAI Press.

Murray, Tim. 1999. Personal conversation. February 11, 1999.

National Institute on Drug Abuse. 2000. *Approaches to drug abuse counseling.* Washington, DC: National Institute of Health.

Nolan, James L. 2001. *Reinventing justice: The American drug court movement, Princeton studies in cultural sociology.* Princeton, NJ: Princeton University Press.

———. 2002. *Drug courts in theory and in practice: Social problems and social issues.* New York: Aldine de Gruyter.

Peele, Stanton. 1989. *Diseasing of America: Addiction treatment out of control.* Lexington, MA: Lexington Books.

Peters, Roger H., Amie L. Hass, and W. Michael Hunt. 2001. Treatment "dosage" effects in drug court programs. *Journal of Offender Rehabilitation* 33 (4): 63–72.

Peters, Roger H., and Mary R. Murrin. 2000. Effectiveness of treatment-based drug courts in reducing criminal recidivism. *Criminal Justice and Behavior* 27 (1): 72–96.

Peyrot, Mark. 1985. Coerced voluntarism: The micropolitics of drug treatment. *Urban Life* 13 (4): 343–65.

Riemer, Jeffrey. 1977. A review with a special note on research ethics and disguised observation. *The Wisconsin Sociologist* 14 (2–3): 89–97.

Scott, Marvin, and Stanford Lyman. 1968. Accounts. *American Sociological Review* 33 (1): 46–62.

Senjo, Scott, and Leslie Leip. 2001. Testing and developing theory in drug court: A four-part logit model to predict program completion. *Criminal Justice Policy Review* 12 (1): 66–87.

Silverman, David. 2000. *Doing qualitative research: A practical handbook.* London; Thousand Oaks, CA: Sage Publications.

Snow, David A., R. Benford, and Leon Anderson. 1986. Fieldwork roles and information yield. *Urban Life* 14 (4): 377–08.

Spradley, James P. 1979. *The ethnographic interview.* New York: Holt, Rinehart and Winston.

Sykes, Gresham, and David Matza. 1996. Techniques of neutralization: A theory of delinquency. In *Deviant behavior: A text-reader in sociology of deviance*, edited by D. Kelly. New York: St. Martin Press.

Tavuchis, Nicholas. 1991. *Mea culpa: The sociology of apology and reconciliation.* Stanford, CA: Stanford University Press.

Taxman, Faye. 1999. Unraveling "what works" for offenders in substance abuse treatment services. *National Drug Court Institute Review* 2 (2): 93–134.

Taxman, Faye, and Jeff Bouffard. 2003. Drug treatment in the community: A case study of system integration issues. *Federal Probation* 67 (2): 4–14.

Wenzel, Suzanne L., Susan F. Turner, and M. Susan Ridgely. 2004. Collaborations between drug courts and service providers: Characteristics and challenges. *Journal of Criminal Justice* 32 (3): 253–63.

White, William L. 1998. *Slaying the dragon: The history of addiction treatment and recovery in America.* Bloomington, IL: Chestnut Health Systems/Lighthouse Institute.

Wider, D. Lawrence. 1974. *Language and social reality: The case of telling the convict code.* The Hague: Mouton.

Wolf, Elaine, and Corey Colyer. 2001. Everyday hassles: Barriers to recovery in drug court. *Journal of Drug Issues* 31 (1): 233–58.

Yacoubian, George S. 2000. Reassessing the need for urinalysis as a validation technique. *Journal of Drug Issues* 30 (2): 323–34.

17

A Culture of Harm
Taming the Dynamics of Cruelty in Supermax Prisons

CRAIG HANEY

There is now a reasonably large and growing literature on the many ways that so-called "supermax" confinement can adversely affect the overall mental health of prisoners. The long-term absence of meaningful human contact and social interaction, the enforced idleness and inactivity, and the oppressive security and surveillance procedures (and the weapons, hardware, and other paraphernalia that go along with them) all combine to create starkly deprived conditions of confinement. These conditions predictably undermine the cognitive and emotional health of many prisoners who are subjected to them (see, e.g., Cloyes, Lovell, Allen, & Rhodes, 2006; Haney, 2003; Smith, 2006).

Of course, there are better and worse supermaxes, including some that seek to ameliorate these harsh conditions and minimize the harm to prisoners. And there are more and less resilient prisoners, including some who seem able to withstand the painfulness of these environments and to recover from the experience with few if any lasting effects. But neither fact challenges the overall consensus that has emerged on the harmfulness of long-term punitive isolation and the risks to prisoners who are subjected to it.

This consensus has led a number of courts to exclude certain vulnerable groups of prisoners, such as those who are mentally ill—or at especially high risk of becoming so—from supermax confinement (e.g., *Madrid v. Gomez*, 1995), and to express concern and condemnation that prisoners housed there "suffer actual psychological harm from their almost total deprivation of human contact, mental stimulus, personal property and human dignity" (*Ruiz v. Johnson*, 1999, p. 913). National commissions and human rights organiza-

Craig Haney, *Criminal Justice and Behavior*, vol. 35, pp. 956–984, © 2008 by Sage Publications. Reprinted by permission of Sage Publications.

tions also have roundly criticized the use of supermax and called for the practice to end. For example, Human Rights Watch (2000) concluded that "state and federal corrections departments are operating supermax in ways that violate basic human rights" because the conditions of confinement in these facilities "are unduly severe and disproportionate to legitimate security and inmate management objectives; impose pointless suffering and humiliation; and reflect a stunning disregard of the fact that all prisoners . . . are members of the human community" (p. 2). In a report based in part on a series of fact-finding hearings that addressed a wide range of prison issues, the bipartisan Commission on Safety and Abuse in America's Prisons termed supermaxes "expensive and soul destroying" (Gibbons & Katzenbach, 2006, p. 59) and recommended that prison systems "end conditions of isolation" (Gibbons & Katzenbach, 2006, p. 57).

More recently, an international task force of mental health and correctional experts meeting in Istanbul, Turkey, issued a joint statement on "the use and effects of solitary confinement" in which they acknowledged that its "central harmful feature" is the reduction of meaningful social contact to a level that it is "insufficient to sustain health and well being" (International Psychological Trauma Symposium, 2007). Citing various statements, comments, and principles that had been issued previously by the United Nations—all recommending that the use of solitary confinement be carefully restricted or abolished altogether—the Istanbul group concluded that "[a]s a general principle solitary confinement should only be used in very exceptional cases, for as short a time as possible and only as a last resort." Notably, the specific recommendations they made about how such a regime should be structured and operated would, if adopted, end supermax as we know it in the United States.

Even a former supermax warden—one whose writing reflects relatively little sympathy for prisoners in general and for supermax prisoners in particular—acknowledged that "[a]fter long-term confinement and the loss of hope for offenders controlled under [supermax] conditions, mental deterioration is almost assured" (Bruton, 2004, p. 38). Distinguished penologists and correctional legal scholars agree. Thus, Hans Toch (2001) concluded that supermax confinement "is vulnerable to charges that it impairs the mental health of prisoners and that it makes violent men more dangerous" and, in addition, that "[t]he regime is draconian, redolent with custodial overkill, and stultifying" (p. 383). The late Norval Morris concluded that supermax prisons "raise the level of punishment close to that of psychological torture" (Morris, 2000, p. 98). And Fred Cohen (2006) has argued that extreme forms of penal isolation "simply should be banned; in its less onerous forms, isolation should be sharply limited, closely monitored, and very closely regulated," a reform he acknowledged "may well require abandonment of supermax confinement" (p. 296).

Most of the analysis of the harmfulness of supermax is directed at the extreme levels of material deprivation, the lack of activity and other forms of sensory stimulation, and, especially, the absence of normal or meaningful social contact that prisoners experience in these settings. This emphasis is not misplaced. There is no widely accepted psychological theory, correctional rationale, or conception of human nature of which I am aware to suggest that long-term exposure to these powerful and painful stressors is neutral or benign and does not carry a significant risk of harm.

However, in this article I want to concentrate on a closely related but conceptually separate issue—the effects of the supermax environment on correctional staff and the ways in which those effects in turn create a heightened probability of mistreatment, ranging from deliberate indifference to outright brutality. I will suggest that this heightened probability comes about in part as a result of the very assumptions on which supermax prisons are based and in which correctional staff members are more or less steeped—the end product of what I will characterize as "ideological toxicity."

In addition, the toxic or contaminating atmosphere and its perverse and pervasive assumptions about prisoners are reinforced by the specific ways in which many supermax prisons are structured and operated. Thus, what I will term an "ecology of cruelty" is created in many such places where, at almost every turn, guards are implicitly encouraged to respond and react to prisoners in essentially negative ways—through punishment, opposition, force, and repression. For many guards, at least initially, this approach to institutional control is employed neutrally and even-handedly—without animus and in response to actual or perceived threats. However, when punishment and suppression continue—largely because of the absence of any available and sanctioned alternative approaches—they become functionally autonomous and often disproportionate in nature. Especially when these techniques persist in spite of the pain and suffering they bring about, they represent a form of cruelty (notwithstanding the lack of cruel intentions on the part of many of those who employ these harsh techniques).

Finally, I will suggest that there are a number of powerful social psychological processes at work in the confined environment of supermax that amplify the tensions between prisoners and guards. I term these the "dynamics of desperation" because, although they are general processes that can produce interpersonal tension and dysfunction in a variety of settings, they are especially problematic when they occur where psychosocial pressures are at their greatest, personal risks are heightened, and human needs are at their most basic and extreme. These desperate conditions—extreme pressures, significant risks, and dire needs—prevail in the typical supermax prison setting.

I believe that ignoring these aspects of supermax confinement does a disservice to the correctional officers who work in these units as well as to the prisoners subjected to them. Prison administrators who are reluctant to concede that supermax prisons have negative effects on prisoners—and many of them are—also tend to be oblivious to the real psychological costs to guards of working in such a place, as well as the pressures on them to treat prisoners in ways that are at least counterproductive, often painful and provocative, and sometimes truly hurtful to both groups. No comprehensive assessment of the risks of supermax confinement can continue to overlook these issues, and no approach to reforming or meaningfully modifying these units is likely to succeed without taking them into account.

Context Matters

The potential for significant abuse inheres in the very structure of a prison. Whatever its limitations as a literal simulation of an actual prison setting, the venerable Stanford Prison Experiment demonstrated the potentially destructive dynamic that is created whenever near-absolute power is wielded over a group of derogated and vilified others (e.g., Haney, Banks, & Zimbardo, 1973; Haney & Zimbardo, 1977). When the forces that produce that basic dynamic are amplified and intensified, and there are no countervailing pressures introduced into the situation to regulate or moderate their effects, mistreatment is nearly inevitable. Under these conditions, there is great risk that even good, normal people can be led to do bad, sadistic things. Many supermax prisons pose precisely this heightened risk because nearly every negative aspect of the core prison dynamic is amplified and intensified in them.

In fact, there is much disturbing evidence to indicate that this destructive potential has been realized in many of the nation's supermax prisons. Consider the following patterns of mistreatment and specific acts of brutality, all occurring inside supermax prisons run by the nation's three largest prison systems, and all documented by published judicial opinions, court records, or the author's own direct interviews and observations:

> A federal judge in California found that guards working at one of its supermaxes—the Pelican Bay "Security Housing Unit" (SHU)—often "hog tied" prisoners in painful "fetal restraints," were prone to leaving naked or partially dressed prisoners in outdoor holding cages for hours at a time during inclement weather, engaged in unnecessary and unnecessarily violent cell extractions, "routinely" tasered prisoners, fired gas guns at them, and "too quickly" resorted to the use of lethal force (*Madrid v. Gomez*, 1995, p. 1179). In one particularly egregious act of cruelty, guards took a nude, mentally ill prisoner who had smeared himself with feces to the prison infirmary where they forced him into a tub of scalding hot water and held him there for so long that the skin on his lower torso peeled off and hung in "large clumps" around his legs. In what the judge characterized as "a shocking show of indifference," the officers involved "made no attempt to seek any medical assistance or advice" in the face of the injuries they had caused. (p. 1167)

> In many of Florida's supermax units—known as "close management" or "CM" units—guards have resorted to pepper spraying prisoners not just to control but to punish and retaliate against them, sometimes for rule violations as insignificant as talking to inmates housed in nearby cells. At times, the pepper spraying has been rampant and excessive in amount—on many occasions entire canisters of the chemical agent have been emptied into a single prison cell, and prisoners complain that guards some-

times cover up the back windows of their cells to stop ventilation and ensure that the pepper spray lingers in the air inside. In addition to the pepper spraying, there have been numerous allegations that CM prisoners are subjected to severe physical abuse, especially at the Florida State Penitentiary (FSP). The FSP is the facility that houses the largest number of CM prisoners, known as a place that even a former warden testified "had a notorious reputation for the beating of inmates" (*Valdes v. Crosby*, 2006, p. 1240). In one such case a prisoner died inside an FSP supermax unit after a physical altercation with guards. He had 22 broken ribs, fractures in his sternum, spine, and jaw, as well as internal injuries. There were boot marks on his body, and his testicles were badly swollen. Prison guards claimed that the injuries were self-inflicted. (e.g., Word, 2007)

In Texas, a federal judge concluded that even after some 30 years of landmark litigation designed to remedy the problem, a "culture of sadistic and malicious violence" continued to pervade the state's prison system (*Ruiz v. Johnson*, 1999, p. 929). In their equivalent of supermax—Administrative Segregation and "High Security" units—prison staff regularly locked floridly psychotic prisoners and left them to languish nearly around the clock, in what the judge acknowledged was "a frenzied and frantic state of human despair and desperation," without mental health attention or care (p. 913). A number of these prisoners sat in the back corners of feces-smeared cells or in puddles of their own urine. Some of the units erupted—bedlamlike—when outside visitors entered them, as prisoners banged on the walls and doors and screamed out for someone to come help them. Guards were able to accurately point to the severely mentally ill prisoners in their units, sometimes derisively referring to them as "nutters" or "basket cases."

Perhaps the most troubling fact about these documented instances of supermax abuse is that they reflect systemic patterns rather than a "mere collection of isolated and aberrant acts" at these facilities (*Madrid v. Gomez*, 1995, p. 1302). Indeed, although the behavior in question was extreme, there is nothing to suggest that it was aberrational. The supermax units themselves were not being run in an atypical manner, and they were not staffed by especially poorly trained personnel who had been selected for their sadistic tendencies. In fact, until the courts stepped in to condemn them, many guards in the units appeared unaware that they were doing anything wrong, corrections officials ignored many of the worst practices and minimized their consequences, and state attorneys vigorously defended them. In this sense, then, the frightening extremes to which the guards went provided clear and unsettling demonstrations of the inherent power of an unchecked and unregulated supermax environment and the end effect of that power on the behavior of the staff.

Of course, no one would or should attribute this extreme and abusive behavior to a "new generation" of uncaring, sadistic guards (the corrections equivalent of the "new generation" of convicts whose presence in prison systems was said by some—erroneously in my opinion—to require the construction of supermaxes in the first place). The federal court that critically examined the plight of vulnerable prisoners who were suffering inside the Texas supermax units concluded that

> Whether because of a lack of resources, a misconception of the reality of psychological pain, the inherent callousness of the bureaucracy, or officials' blind faith in their own policies, [the state prison system] has knowingly turned its back on this most needy segment of its population. (*Ruiz v. Johnson*, 1999, p. 914)

To be sure, this is an astute analysis of many of the broad structural factors that underlie supermax abuse. But those very structural factors—a lack of resources, a misconception about the nature of psychological pain, a callous bureaucracy, and blind faith in policies that do not work—have helped to create dysfunctional supermax environments in a number of prison systems.

In this article I argue that the destructive potential of supermax is brought to life in large part—although certainly not exclusively—by the staff members who work there. These men and women are themselves very much the captives of the often untenable supermax environment in which they must function. The extreme deprivation, the isolating architecture, the technology of control, and the rituals of degradation and subjugation that exist in supermax prisons are inimical to the mental health of prisoners. But it would be naïve to contend that the nature of the supermax environment does not also affect the staff that works inside. In many such places, an atmosphere of thinly veiled hostility and disdain prevails, and the tension and simmering conflict are often palpable. The stress can be read on the faces of the correctional officers, who seem on edge, hypervigilant, even "pumped up." Among other things, this means that supermax prisoners not only have very few interpersonal interactions of any kind—the essence of this kind of confinement—but that the interactions that they do have are fraught with resentment and recrimination.

The closed nature of the supermax environment amplifies its power and intensifies the dynamics that are generated inside. A cycle of dysfunctional actions and reactions is more likely to occur and less likely to be broken. Thus, the context of many supermax prisons—one that prisoners are admittedly very much a part of—threatens to adversely affect the guards who work there. If and when it does, their behavior, in turn, is negatively affected in ways that typically worsen their treatment of prisoners. The harmful effects of supermax confinement are thereby increased and may spiral out of control.

That supermax units house many troublesome and difficult prisoners is a given. What is not—and what therefore is problematic—is the way in which the structure of supermaxes and the standard procedures by which they operate exacerbate this fact, generate forces that accelerate and amplify the potentially destructive dynamics of prison itself, and drive prisoners and guards even farther apart from one another, increasing the potential for abuse. In the following several sections I discuss some of the ways in which this happens.

A Toxic Ideological Atmosphere

Supermax prisons emerged in the United States during an era in which many politicians and members of the public were indulging a powerful "rage to punish" (Forer, 1994). Indeed, the nation seemed to celebrate (and often demand) rather than merely tolerate (or even lament) official cruelty and the infliction of pain in its criminal justice system. A "punishment wave" swept over us with such force that it ripped citizens, politicians, and courts from the ethical moorings that once served to restrain the severity of criminal sanctions (Haney, 1998). For several decades—the very decades in which many supermax prisons came on-line in the United States—the punishment wave diverted decision makers from considering the consequences of incarceration, obviating a once-recognized need to balance crime control policies with humanitarian considerations.

There were many punitive excesses that characterized this period. Of course, we put unprecedented numbers of people in prison for unheard of amounts of time. But there was more. A county sheriff—the self-proclaimed "meanest sheriff in America"—publicly took pride in running what he termed "a very bad jail" (Mydans, 1995). Some states returned to the use of chain gangs (e.g., Bragg, 1995; Navarro, 1995), whereas others began charging prisoners "room and board" fees for the periods during which they were incarcerated (Pasternak, 1997). So-called "three-strikes" laws were passed that meted out life sentences, often for nonviolent crimes and sometimes for offenses as trivial as stealing a pizza or a loaf of bread (e.g., Zimring, Hawkins, & Kamin, 2001). Conservative commentators coined the term "superpredators" to refer to the hordes of supposedly heartless and dangerous young criminals that they warned were about to overrun us (DiIulio, 1995). In part, in response to this kind of hysterical rhetoric, virtually every state in the country passed laws designed "to get more juveniles into the adult criminal-justice system where they presumably will serve longer sentences under more punitive conditions" (Butterfield, 1997, p. 1A).

And then there were the supermax prisons. I am convinced that the new supermax units were created and proliferated in part in response to what prison authorities perceived as an impending threat the chaos and disorder that might be brought about by unprecedented levels of prison overcrowding. Supermaxes would serve as tightening screws on the pressure cookers that corrections officials worried were being created inside many of their most crowded prisons. Of course, this legitimate concern might have been handled in a number of other ways. Instead, the supermax solution resonated perfectly with the fundamentally punitive ideology that characterized the era—a so-called "penal harm movement" that had become dominant during the "mean season" of corrections, where what passed for "penal philosophy" amounted to little more than devising "creative strategies to make offenders suffer" (Cullen, 1995, p. 340). Supermax confinement was one of those strategies.

Most of the tenets of the penal harm movement—the core assumptions on which the movement was based—can be fairly characterized as "ideological." They were very frequently asserted by political partisans, offered as part of a larger political agenda (e.g., Beckett, 1997), were almost always bolstered by gross exaggerations and inflammatory rhetoric, and based on little or no objective evidence or rational analysis.[1] In any event, they swept across the country and radically changed what many citizens, legal decision makers, and correctional policy makers thought and did about crime and punishment.

There were several important components to the penal harm movement and the underlying logic by which it was justified. For one, crime was decontextualized and depicted as residing entirely in the internal makeup of the persons who engaged in it. That is, criminal behavior was said to be the product of morally blameworthy choices made by individual actors who were presumed to be equally autonomous and free, unencumbered by their social histories or the circumstances in which they acted. Prisoners needed to be incarcerated for long periods of time because they were not only bad—or "wicked," in the formulation of one of the movement's chief architects, James Q. Wilson (1975)—but intractably so. The intractability of their badness or wickedness meant that prison was to be mostly (or exclusively) devoted to the purpose of punishing them; there was no hope for reform, rehabilitation, or redemption.

Thus, what Nils Christie (1993) termed "the whole question of social justice" (p. 134) was excluded from determinations of criminal responsibility as well as from the sentencing calculus by which terms of imprisonment were established. Mental states defenses were drastically limited, consideration of a defendant's social background was deemed irrelevant in sentencing guidelines, and judicial discretion was increasingly limited to legislatively prescribed factors that pertained entirely to the characteristics of the offense, not the social history or context of the person who committed it.

Not surprisingly, these sweeping ideological shifts had profound effects on correctional policies as well as the day-to-day atmosphere inside the nation's prisons. A form of the penal harm movement—devising ways to make offenders suffer—was legitimized and implemented *inside* prison much as it had been on the outside. Obviously, prison systems were freed from the mandate of rehabilitation. As Malcolm Feeley and Jonathan Simon (1992) noted, a "new penology" emerged in which prisons abandoned the attempt to further the social and personal transformation of prisoners and replaced it with correctional strategies aimed at "managing costs and controlling dangerous populations" (p. 465).

Of course, these developments had significant implications for internal prison discipline. By the prevailing ideological view, continued troublemaking inside prison could indicate only one thing: that this particular prisoner was even worse—"more wicked"—than the others and therefore in need of being punished even more. Thus, the only way to respond to continued misbehavior was to make life even more miserable for those prisoners who disobeyed. Just as in the larger criminal justice system, prison-rule violations were viewed in decontextualized terms—they were virtually always the fault of the violators, and rarely if ever produced by the circumstances under which the rule breakers had acted (no matter how dire or coercive those circumstances were). Here, too, the prisoners' bad behavior supposedly stemmed from their internal traits; ones that led certain, especially "wicked" prisoners to freely choose their transgressive, offensive, and predatory behavior. The notion that misbehavior in prison might be a sign or symptom of something else—that the prisoner was struggling with personal problems, had been placed in a dysfunctional prison environment or untenable immediate situation, might be suffering from psychological impairments, or that the system itself might be malfunctioning by failing to anticipate the conflict beforehand—became increasingly inconceivable, irrelevant, or both.

These prevailing ideological views facilitated the creation and proliferation of supermax—a punishing prison-within-a-prison—and also have had a continuing, significant effect on the atmosphere inside the supermax units and the mind-sets of the persons who work there. The especially forceful application of this broad punitive ideology is signified by the term that is routinely applied to supermax prisoners—they are said to be, quite simply, "the worst of the worst." The implications could not be more clear or problematic (or "toxic"): Prisoners in general are bad (indeed, the "worst") but even among this group of "worst" people, there are those who are even more bad—the "worst of the worst." With that as its starting premise, one might ask, what kind of supermax culture could we expect to evolve? Certainly one in which prisoners who are thought to be at the endpoint of irredeemable badness can and must be met with the greatest levels of penal harm that the prison system can muster. The "worst of the worst" designation defines the inhabitants of supermax as fundamentally "other" and dehumanizes, degrades, and demonizes them as essentially different, even from other prisoners. It provides an immediate, intuitive, and unassailable rationale for the added punishment, extraordinary control, and severe deprivation that prevail in supermax.

The fundamental fact or fiction of their essential difference comes to represent them and to organize the mind-set of the people charged with the responsibility of keeping them captive. This allows the compassion and empathy that would otherwise be extended to persons who are held in desperate and degraded conditions, who are in crisis or in need, anguished or disconsolate, to be suspended, so that their pain not only does not register but becomes something that they have earned, asked for, or otherwise simply deserve.

The "worst of the worst" mythology helps to perpetuate another misconception that facilitates the callous and sometimes cruel treatment of supermax prisoners—the notion that they are somehow impervious to the pains of imprisonment. By this view, the tough cons who end up in supermax are constitutionally more capable of standing up to the harshness of life there than the rest of us presumably more sensitive souls. Thus, sociologist David Ward has been quoted as saying about supermax prisoners, "These guys are not like the rest of us. . . . They approach [doing time] in a way that would be completely different for the rest of us. We probably would have mental health problems if we were in there" (Walt, 1999, p. 1). In fact, anyone who has spent a significant time interviewing supermax prisoners and evaluating their backgrounds and social histories understands that the reverse is often true. That is, many supermax prisoners have extensive and extreme childhood and adolescent trauma histories that render them more, not less, vulnerable to psychological stress. The fact that aspects of the prison experience may represent a form of "retraumatization" for many of them means that they are likely to feel the pains of imprisonment especially acutely (something that also may help to account for the dysfunctional patterns of institutional behavior that result in their placement in supermax in the first place).

Lorna Rhodes (2002) is certainly right about the way in which the label "psychopath" affects the judgments of supermax staff about whether certain prisoners under their control "are perceived to be 'human' at all or rather a species—both monstrous and hyperrational—specifically suited to isolation" (p. 444). The only caveat that I would add is that in my experience, many (perhaps most) supermax prisoners—precisely because they already have been designated as the "worst of the worst"—are viewed by many staff members through precisely this dehumanizing lens, whether or not they have been formally labeled as psychopathic. The added, official diagnosis or label is a nicety that is of little real consequence to many correctional officers. They know—because they have been repeatedly told and, for reasons I will develop in subsequent sections of this article, believe that they have seen repeatedly confirmed—the fact that the prisoners under their control are the "worst of the worst." It is as good an operational definition of psychopath as any of them need.

Except, of course, that "worst of the worst" is not a very good operational definition of a psychopath, or anything else for that matter. And it is a terrible description of the diverse group of people who are in supermax.[2] In fact, "worst of the worst" does not lend itself to any precise definition, and a conscientious attempt to create one would lay bare the sloppiness and unreliability of the process by which the label is applied in supermax. Researchers who have looked carefully at the prisoner population in the typical supermax unit or prison are struck by the hodge-podge of persons who are housed there. For example, many supermax units are composed of a plurality of alleged gang members, many of whom are there—often indefinitely—because of an administratively imposed status, irrespective of whether they have committed any other serious disciplinary infractions at all (e.g., Tachiki, 1995).

Perhaps even more troubling, a disproportionate number of supermax prisoners suffer from a wide variety of psychological and psychiatric problems and disorders that range in severity. My own research and that of many others who have now looked carefully at the makeup of supermax populations underscore this fact: A very high percentage of them are truly suffering, and many are deeply disturbed—emotionally and in other ways. Those psychological and psychiatric disturbances may contribute to the disturbing behavior that has resulted in their supermax confinement and certainly render these prisoners more susceptible to the painful stresses of the harsh and deprived environments in which they are housed. They also make it more difficult for these prisoners to conform their behavior to the rigid requirements of supermax well enough to eventually be released. But these things hardly qualify them as the "worst of the worst."

Specifically, several studies have found that nearly a third—29% to be exact—of the prisoners in supermax suffer from a "serious mental disorder" (Hodgins & Cote, 1991; Lovell, Cloyes, Allen, & Rhodes, 2000). In addition, as David Lovell, (2008) points out, "mental health issues, variously conceived" (p. 990) are much broader than the category of those diagnosed or diagnosable with "serious mental illness." In fact, in their study, Lovell and his colleagues (Cloyes et al., 2006; Lovell, (2008) found that some 45% of supermax prisoners suffered from overall "psychosocial impairments"—the cumulative percentage of prisoners suffering serious mental illness (based on prison documentation), marked or severe psychiatric symptoms (based on the administration of a brief psychiatric rating scale), psychotic or self-injurious episodes (derived from prison files), or brain damage (again, as indicated in prison medical charts). In addition, my own direct assessments of supermax prisoners in several jurisdictions indicate that two thirds or more of them are suffering from a variety of symptoms of psychological and emotional trauma, as well as some of the psychopathological effects of isolation (e.g., Haney, 2003).

Despite this high concentration of prisoners suffering from sometimes very severe psychological symptoms and disorders—as I said, suggesting that rather than the "worst of the worst," their behavior may be unusually impaired by pre-existing conditions or the exacerbation of psychological vulnerabilities during confinement—supermax units are uniquely ill-suited to house them and front line correctional officers fundamentally ill-prepared to address their needs. Indeed, as the criminal justice system has become the default placement for the mentally ill in our society, correctional officers in prisons across the country have been increasingly surrounded by disturbed prisoners whose psychiatric problems they were not trained to recognize or understand, and whose needs their prisons often lack the appropriate resources to respond to anyway.

Of necessity, correctional officers have been forced to ignore all but the most flagrantly symptomatic prisoners and instead to interpret their bizarre behavior the only way they could—mistakenly, as willful rule breaking, insolence, or a reflection of the prisoners' dangerousness. Supermax became a repository for these sad, tragic figures—as I say, between a third to a half or more [of] the supermax population—despite the fact that those units cannot humanely house them. Indeed, there are many correctional officers who regard the fact that some supermax prisoners might be, in their view, "mad" as well as "bad" as something that makes them all the more dangerous—rather than an object of sympathetic concern—and they treat them accordingly.

Of course, there is no disputing that many prisoners in supermax have behaved violently in the past and that—at least for those particular prisoners—their violent behavior is what accounts for their placement in disciplinary segregation. Many of them are, in that sense, rightly viewed as "dangerous" by the guards who interact with them and manage their behavior. But very little violence in prison (as elsewhere in society) is independent of the context in which it occurs. Yet as I have noted, the operative framework in supermax prisons views "dangerousness" as an exclusive property of the person—something that is possessed internally, typically in a fixed and largely unmodifiable amount (with supermax prisoners possessing the greatest possible amounts of the trait; one that can only be suppressed but rarely, if ever, eliminated).

Among other things, correctional officers who work for long periods in supermax can easily become oblivious to the indignities of the situations that prisoners routinely endure. This comes about not because of the callousness or insensitivity of the officers, but rather because they have "gotten used to it." From their view, the status quo is simply the way supermax prisoners live, what and how they eat, the minimal, drastically truncated, range of things they are allowed to do, and so on. If prisoners get what the rules say they are entitled to, then there is no reason for them to get frustrated or angry. Their frustrated and angry behavior is produced from within themselves, not their deprived circumstances.

The combination of this routine decontextualizing of rule breaking and the corresponding demonizing of supermax prisoners as categorically the "worst of the worst" means that whatever happens in supermax units—including extreme and abusive behavior on the part of the guards—can be cloaked in a seemingly irrebuttable justification: It is invariably the prisoners' fault, a product of their intrinsic wickedness. Supermax prisoners, thought to be in total command of themselves and their actions, impervious to their surroundings, and invulnerable to intended or unintended provocations, choose to act; correctional officers merely react. It is a clear manifestation of Nils Christie's (1982) insight, here applied to the supermax prison: "It is the [supermax prisoner] who first acted, he initiated the whole chain of events. The pain that follows is created by him, not by those handling the tools for creating such pain" (p. 49).

This mind-set serves to absolve officers of responsibility for day-to-day excesses and overreactions. It also can be employed by prison officials to divert attention from more systemic problems that might implicate groups of officers or the way an entire supermax unit is being run (and correspondingly, to lessen the pressure for reform). Thus, when newspapers in the mid-1990s began reporting stories about brutality at California's second supermax prison—Corcoran State Prison, located in the state's central valley—correctional authorities blamed the prisoners for the abuses they suffered. The allegations were serious, implicated a large number of staff members, and involved behavior that stretched over a number of years:

> In the eight years since the state built the high-tech prison . . . seven
> inmates have been shot dead by officers and more than three dozen have

> been wounded. And in June of last year, 36 inmates bused from [another state prison] were beaten as they arrived at Corcoran. (Lee, 1996, p. 3B)

Those accusations were broadened subsequently to include reports that staff members regularly staged what were billed as "gladiator fights" between rival gang members, ones that terminated with at least some prisoners being killed by prison riflemen (e.g., Fernandez, 1997; Holding, 1996a). Several correctional officers admitted that "[i]t was common practice . . . for guards to pair off rival inmates like roosters in a cockfight, complete with spectators and wagering, then sometimes shoot those who wouldn't stop fighting" (Arai, 1996, p. Al).

The prison warden's explanation for the violence was entirely consistent with the ideology that dominates in supermax: "'I think people lose sight of why we built Corcoran,' he said. 'We house the bad people. And we do the best we can'" (Lee, 1996, p. 3B). When violence at the prison skyrocketed in the midst of the publicity about the gladiator fights—a staggering "almost 50 inmate fights and dozens of shootings on the yards" in a single month in 1996—a Department of Corrections official also blamed the prisoners alone for the problem: "One thing that will change is that inmates who act up at Corcoran will go to Pelican Bay" (Holding, 1996b, p. A17)—the latter facility thought to be an even more harsh and punitive supermax than Corcoran. And, remarkably, as media revelations about these incidents continued to bring adverse publicity to the prison, the Correctional Peace Officers Association, a number of other law enforcement organizations, and a variety of victims' rights groups banded together to take out a full-page newspaper advertisement in support of the guards. "Like the vast majority of California citizens," the ad read, "we stand with you." Why? Because the prisoners who were the victims of these events were, in the words of the ad, "vicious, predatory," "cold-blooded and remorseless," people who "have no conscience," and who, therefore, presumably deserved whatever they got ("We Stand With You," 1997).

There is one final set of beliefs that adds to and exacerbates the operation of the penal harm ideology that pervades the atmosphere in many supermaxes. The beliefs are prevalent among correctional officers generally, but they manifest themselves in a particularly problematic way in many of these particular units. Despite the gender diversity that has been achieved in many prison systems over the past few decades, most correctional officers are influenced by an occupational culture with deeply masculine—"macho"—values and perspectives. They are socialized into (or come already endorsing) an ethos that reveres strength and forcefulness, especially in the face of danger. And, like other occupations that embrace this ethic, higher status tends to be granted to those who encounter the most danger or see the most action.

Thus, in at least some correctional settings, there is a certain caché that comes from handling prisoners alleged to be the "worst of the worst." In some prison systems the supermax staff conceives of itself as an elite force, specially deployed to handle an intractably dangerous group of the system's worst prisoners. The special "combat" uniforms that are worn by the officers in some of the units reinforce that image. Of course, the truest expression of this masculinist ethic requires those worst prisoners to be forcefully dominated and controlled—often literally through the application of sheer physical force or intimidation. To be sure, from this perspective, there is little or no acclaim to be garnered by guards who would go about managing the "worst of the worst" by trying to genuinely understand their needs, effectively administering to their pain, caring deeply about their concerns, or even cleverly manipulating them through guile, verbal skill, or interpersonal sophistication.

I have termed this panoply ideological notions and beliefs—and the atmosphere they create—as collectively "toxic" because of the adverse influence they have on interpersonal relations between supermax guards and prisoners. They have the capacity to contaminate the atmosphere in these units and shape the social relations and interactions that occur between prisoners and guards who live and work there. The extreme version of the penal harm ideology that prevails in supermax creates a set of interpretations, expectations, and stereotypes that, as I will discuss in a subsequent section, have real consequences, not just for the subjective experiences of the participants but for their overt behavior as well.

The toxic ideology that pervades many supermaxes can contribute to the emergence of an atmosphere or culture of harm, one where the risk of mistreatment or brutality is significantly increased. Precisely because there is so little outside monitoring of supermaxes by constituencies who can bring fundamentally different perspectives and mind-sets to bear on what is proper, correct, and humane—the press, prison lawyers, or human rights organizations—there is little meaningful feedback or much possibility for significant self-correction. The toxic ideological environment created inside these isolated and insulated places allows the staff to establish a social reality that is largely immune from critical evaluation, challenge, and debate and exempted from normal forms [of] accountability. Because they are spared ever having to justify the destructive norms that have been created there, whatever toxic atmosphere and abusive norms are engendered are more likely to persist.

An Ecology of Cruelty

Supermax prisons are built on a model of profound deprivation. They are structured to deprive prisoners of most of the things that all but the most callous commentators would concede are basic necessities of life—minimal freedom of movement, the opportunity to touch another human being in friendship or with affection, the ability to engage in meaningful or productive physical or mental activity, and so on. In most prisons—even in maximum security—prisoners retain some small but meaningful freedoms. They can take advantage of admittedly minimal opportunities for programming and activity, and many manage to fashion a semblance of an authentic life, especially in the institutional spaces that remain unregulated. But supermaxes have become places of nearly pure punishment where, by virtue of the totality of the control and the sheer degree of deprivation, there are very few of these interstices left. As a result, it is nearly impossible for supermax prisoners to eke out a meaningful life (as opposed to a mere existence). In such an extreme and extremely deprived environment, whose primary emphasis is on punishment and control, an "ecology of cruelty" is created, where people become inured to the suffering of others.

Elsewhere I have written about the extremes of deprivation and degradation that I saw imposed on prisoners at what was then one of the nation's worst supermax environments (Haney, 1993). Since then I have seen these conditions largely replicated in many such supermax units around the country. Indeed, the published descriptions of the core supermax regime do not vary much. For example, here is how a federal judge in Wisconsin characterized that state's supermax, a facility that she concluded was unfit for mentally ill prisoners but not sufficiently cruel to declare unconstitutional for others:

> Inmates on Level One at the State of Wisconsin's Supermax Correctional Institution in Boscobel, Wisconsin spend all but four hours a week confined to a cell. The "boxcar" style door on the cell is solid except for a shutter and a trap door that opens into the dead space of a vestibule through which a guard may transfer items to the inmate without interacting with him. The cells are illuminated 24 hours a day. Inmates receive no outdoor exercise. Their personal possessions are severely restricted: one religious text, one box of legal materials and 25 personal letters. They are permitted no clocks, radios, watches, cassette players or televisions. The temperature fluctuates wildly, reaching extremely high and low temperatures depending on the season. A video camera rather than a human eye monitors the inmate's movements. Visits other than with lawyers are conducted through video screens. (*Jones 'El v. Berge*, 2001, p. 1098)

> Supermax prisoners experience limited social interaction and almost total idleness, are fed in their cells and have very limited out-of-cell activities. Almost every aspect of daily life is controlled and monitored. Remote controlled doors minimize contact even further. There is little natural light and no access to the outdoors. (*Jones 'El v. Berge*, 2001, p. 1099)

> The institution provides only video visitation. Inmates remain in their cell block and visitors at the front of the institution. Inmates and their visitors see each other on small video screens that are located across the room from the inmate. The audio quality is poor. . . . During the video visits, inmates remain handcuffed, shackled and belly chained. Prison log books show that only 10% of inmates receive visits, an unusually low number. (*Jones 'El v. Berge*, 2001, p. 1101)

Beyond the physical limitations and procedural prohibitions that are central to supermaxes, these places must be "lived in," typically on a long-term basis. Reflect for a moment on what a small space that is not much larger than a king-sized bed looks, smells, and feels like when someone has lived in it for 23 hours a day, day after day, for years on end. Property is strewn around, stored in whatever makeshift way possible, clothes and bedding soiled from recent use sit in one or another corner or on the floor, the residue of recent meals (that are eaten within a few feet of an open toilet) here and there, on the floor, bunk, or elsewhere in the cell.

Ventilation is often substandard in these units, so that odors linger, and the air is sometimes heavy and dank. In some supermaxes, prisoners are given only small amounts of cleaning materials—a Dixie cup or so of cleanser—once a week, making the cells especially difficult to keep clean. Inside their cells, units, and "yards," supermax prisoners are surrounded by nothing but concrete, steel, cinder block, and metal fencing—often gray or faded pastel, drab and sometimes peeling paint, dingy, worn floors. There is no time when they escape from these barren "industrial" environments. Many prisoners sit back on their bunks, look around at what has become the sum total of their entire lives, hemmed in by the tiny space that surrounds them and, not surprisingly, become deeply despondent.

The severe deprivation robs them of large, important things (such as social contact, meaningful stimulation, and activity) and little things (such as sufficient toiletries for personal hygiene). A supermax prisoner in Texas—one with an especially notorious tough-guy reputation—said to me, "Look at me. They have reduced me to an animal. I can't take care of myself, I smell, my hair is matted together, I eat all of my meals just a few feet away from the toilet in my cell. I am living like an animal. I am afraid I am becoming one." And then he began to cry. Other prisoners fight against the threat of lost humanity by acting belligerent, confrontational, and violent, paradoxically taming the fear of becoming like a beast by trying to choose for themselves when and where to act like one.

Indeed, Thelton Henderson, the federal judge who was so critical of the regime in California's Pelican Bay, made several explicit references to the supermax prisoners there being treated like animals. In one instance, the court commented on the practice of leaving prisoners in outdoor cages for a significant period of time "as if animals in a zoo," which the judge concluded "offends even the most elementary notions of common decency and dignity" (*Madrid v. Gomez*, 1995, p. 1172). The second mention came in reference to the concrete-enclosed exercise yards or pens: "[S]ome inmates spend the time simply pacing around the edges of the pen; the image created is hauntingly similar to that of caged felines pacing in a zoo" (p. 1229). Nowadays, of course, the outdoor caging of supermax prisoners that Judge Henderson found so troublesome occurs regularly *inside* supermax housing units all across the country, and supermax prisoners spend a great deal of time pacing around the edges of most of the spaces in which they are confined, including their cells. The comparison to a zoo unfortunately remains apt—places where exotic, presumably dangerous species are caged in so completely, far from their natural environment, kept separate from one another and largely apart, even from their keepers. The haunting similarities are many in number, and one is hard-pressed to name any other place in our society where sentient beings are housed and treated this way.

Consistent with the penal harm ideology I described in the previous section, supermaxes are designed in large part to "make prisoners suffer," whether corrections officials acknowledge this as their intended purpose or not. There is no other way to explain the extremes of deprivation and control to which prisoners in these units are subjected. The touting of supermax confinement as a way to deter misbehavior elsewhere in the prison system is equally telling; the essence of a deterrence model is the implicit threat of pain—the more, supposedly, the better. Moreover, the suffering that occurs in supermax is seen as part of what prisoners housed there deserve, so much so that guards in many supermax units seem ever eager to add more suffering at the slightest provocation.

In fact, there is an unfortunate tendency for environments characterized by such drastic imbalances of power to become even harsher and less forgiving—more cruel—over time. It is as if they generate their own centrifugal force—the limits of what is acceptable continue to be pushed outward, away from the center. Thus, rules are enforced with more rigidity and less concern for their adverse consequences in such extreme environments, those where conditions are so depriving and controlled that they "may press the outer bounds of what most humans can psychologically tolerate" (*Madrid v. Gomez*, 1995, p. 1267). But both groups—prisoners *and* guards—are likely to find the outer limits of their psychological tolerance pressed by these places. Certainly both groups are affected by the stark and severe physical environment in which they live and work—a dominating architecture that is designed to accomplish the goals of surveillance, isolation, and control, and very little else. The staff help to both create and enforce aspects of this ecology, to be sure, but they are also affected by the time spent working in it.

The cruelty of supermax is built into its standard operating procedures and their tendency to produce more suffering. Guards must commit to a rote and routinized application of a pervasive and all-encompassing set of rules, no matter how hurtful or counterproductive the consequences, and are implicitly encouraged to respond and react to prisoners in other essentially negative ways. A kind of institutional obstinance and lack of imagination require them to repeat the same failed strategy of control, again and again, apparently expecting a different result. Because guards are encouraged to punish, repress, and forcefully oppose—by virtue of the fact that they are provided with no alternative strategies for managing prisoners—they have no choice but to escalate the punishment when their treatment of prisoners fails to produce the desired results (as it frequently does). Of course, over time, the correctional staff becomes accustomed to inflicting a certain level of pain and degradation—it is the essence of the regime that they control and whose mandates they implement. They naturally become desensitized to these actions and, in the absence of any alternative approaches (both the lack of conceptual alternatives or the means to implement them), they deliver more of the same.

Not surprisingly, these conditions and forms of treatment lead the prisoners to a "[p]erception of capricious deprivation and custodial overkill" (Toch, 2001, p. 381). In addition to the bitterness and alienation that results, this harsh treatment engenders more than a little "push back" from them, including dangerously assaultive behavior at times—actions that are aimed at degrading and hurting officers and that the officers have every reason to resent and to fear. These responses by the prisoners—some of which are the manifestation of long-standing patterns and others that reflect more immediate adaptations and reactions to the increased repression they experience in supermax—make them an especially difficult group to deal with. The guards have few counterbalancing experiences that leaven or broaden their perspective on the prisoners—they see prisoners acting out or causing problems in these units or they really do not see much of them at all.

Indeed, few of these units allow for the kind of genuine interactions between guards and prisoners that might humanize the prisoners in the eyes of their overseers (or vice versa, for that matter). In fact, the comprehensive network of restrictions imposed in a supermax means that little behavior of any kind can be initiated by prisoners; except, ironically, for rule violations, most the rest of what prisoners can do is to comply with these contingencies, mandates, and directives. Supermax prisoners live minimal existences or worse—obeying orders, or not—and begin to seem like minimal people. In such a place, as Morris (2000) noted, "the prisoners become more dehumanized" to the staff and "the temptation is strong to treat them as less than a human being" (p. 107).

There are other components to the ecology of cruelty that dominates these places. For example, the sophisticated architecture and new generation of technology that enhance the level of punishment and control that can be achieved in supermax are supplemented with more traditional tools from another correctional era. Thus, guards have ready access to and rely heavily on handcuffs, belly chains, leg irons, spit shields, strip cells, four-point restraints, canisters of pepper spray, batons, and rifles to control prisoner behavior in supermax. Indeed, because supermaxes run almost entirely on the norms of punishment and subjugation, guards are vulnerable to what has been termed "the law of the instrument"—the notion that when your only tool is a hammer, everything looks like a nail. Obviously, the narrowly punitive range of "hammers" that the typical supermax guard is given with which to manage problematic prisoners and respond to interpersonal conflict will constrain and constrict the nature of their responses and shape their views of prisoners and their problems. Thus, a particular image of supermax prisoners is forged and repeatedly reinforced by virtue of the manner in which guards are encouraged (or required) to respond to them.

Correspondingly, the guards become increasingly skilled at physically restraining and subjugating prisoners at the expense of controlling them through social interaction and persuasion. Some older correctional officers worry about the "deskilling" of newer generations, ones raised with so much hardware, technology, and other "devices" at their disposal that they never become practiced in or adept at less confrontational methods such as talking and listening to prisoners and persuading them to comply.

The custodial overkill to which Toch (2001) referred can take a number of different forms inside the typical supermax. For example, in many of the units where I have interviewed prisoners, three or more flak-jacketed, helmeted escort officers are required not only to bring certain prisoners to the interview room but also to stand by, visually overseeing the interview itself (despite the fact that the prisoner is typically required to be physically restrained throughout). In addition, some prisoners warrant the presence of several additional guards—sometimes including one who is holding a video camera to create a record of the staff's interaction with him (for whose protection, exactly—theirs or his—is left unclear). Aside from the extraordinary investment of time and resources, consider the effect of this elaborate ritual on the guards themselves. Surely the only inference that can reasonably and in good conscience be made is that these extensive security precautions are absolutely necessary. Enough time spent repeating this process, and the message will surely be internalized.

Moreover, when what supermax staff regard as a real crisis occurs—an obstreperous prisoner refuses to return a food tray, for example—a "cell extraction" or "move team" is assembled and the risk of custodial overkill becomes even greater. The procedures prescribed for these violent encounters have been described elsewhere in the literature (e.g., Haney & Lynch, 1997; Morris, 2000), and I will not belabor them here. Suffice it to say that they involve an elaborately orchestrated physical confrontation in which a team of correctional officers typically wearing shielded helmets, body armor, and padding (and, in units where gas or pepper spray is used, a gas mask), all wielding plastic shields, batons, handcuffs, or chains, forcibly enter a prisoner's cell, subdue and place him in restraints, and take him elsewhere in the prison.

Cell extractions are an important component of the ecology of cruelty that is created in supermax. They can be precipitated by what appear to be disproportionately small provocations or comparatively insignificant infractions, and they are quite frequent in some facilities. In most supermaxes, virtually every prisoner has either been extracted or witnessed others being extracted, and some have been traumatized by the experience. Correspondingly, officers who have engaged in violent cell extractions, or pepper-sprayed or tasered prisoners on numerous occasions—or seen others repeatedly do so—naturally become accustomed to it over time. As they become increasingly desensitized to these uses of force, they are also rendered more susceptible to "behavioral drift"—the tendency in this context for the stress and exigencies of the situation to blur the line between ethical and unethical treatment.

The ecology of cruelty also means that there are very few ways in which a guard can actually reward a prisoner by significantly improving or alleviating the deprived conditions of his confinement. This is in part because there are so few options available with which to do so and in part because this would represent an implicit violation of the punishment-based logic on which the unit is premised. That is, in units based so thoroughly on punishment and deprivation, the act of rewarding prisoners—even for especially meritorious behavior—is highly problematic because it threatens the basic operating assumptions of the unit: After all, if behavior can be effectively shaped through rewards, what purpose supermax? In addition, within this ecology, interventions aimed at de-escalation or compromise may be seen as capitulation, signs of weakness, or "rewarding bad behavior." Guards who violate the norms of punishment by routinely seeking compromise, finding ways to express encouragement, or showing empathy for the prisoners' plight face marginalization, ostracism, and reassignment.

On the other hand, one of the basic principles of any unit premised so completely on domination and punitive control is that no matter how harsh the normative regime, something even harsher must be devised for the recalcitrant. This necessitates the creation of a more punitive and degrading place or unit to which prisoners can be banished, both as punishment for their continuing violations and to send a message to the rest of the prisoners. For example, the Pelican Bay supermax in California devised what they called a "Violence Control Unit" (VCU) to further punish the prisoners who were already being punished by virtue of their presence in the supermax but who nonetheless continued to misbehave. Prisoners in the VCU—many of whom were severely mentally ill when I toured there—were subjected to a number of even more restrictive procedures and rules than the already severely deprived prisoners in the rest of the supermax. For example, a Plexiglas barrier or covering was added to the front of each VCU cell, significantly distorting vision into and out of the cell itself: In fact, the bright lights on the VCU tier reflected off the Plexiglas covering in such a way that it was difficult even to clearly see the faces of prisoners who were standing directly in front. The added barrier on the front of each cell also intensified the perception of confinement and isolation from inside the cell. Perhaps for this reason, the prisoners called the VCU "bedrock."

Other supermaxes have managed to add to the punishment meted out in an already deprived and punitive environment in a variety of other ways. For example, inside New York's version of supermax—what they call Special Housing Units (SHUs)—some 4,500 prisoners are kept under their standard but already very severe supermax regime. The prisoners

> generally live in cells an average size of 56 square feet, behind bars, Plexiglas or thick metal doors. They are "cell-fed" through "feed-up" slots in the doors. Whenever they leave their cells, they are mechanically restrained with handcuffs attached to waist chains and leg irons if they are considered seriously violent or escape-prone. Prisoners in SHU cannot work or go to school. (Correctional Association of New York, 2004, p. 47)

Of course, this is the basic, standard fare in supermax. Again, however, authorities face the problem of what to do when prisoners living in this severely deprived environment act up (as, inevitably, people living under these kinds of harsh conditions do). Prison officials in New York respond by imposing what are called "deprivation orders"—described as "a regimen of increasingly harsh punishments" that include "loss of recreation, showers or haircuts," and can include mechanically restraining prisoners with "handcuffs, waist chains and leg irons during recreation in an outdoor cage" (Correctional Association of New York, 2004, p. 52). Another form of "extra" punishment occurs in the New York supermaxes when prisoners are put "on the loaf"—fed only a "dense, binding, tasteless one-pound loaf of bread that is served to inmates three times a day along with a side portion of raw cabbage" (Correctional Association of New York, 2004, p. 53).

Apparently, these extra punishments are imposed on any supermax prisoner who violates a rule, no matter their mental state or, it would seem, their ability to conform their conduct to the requirements of the unit. Thus, when a sample of mentally ill prisoners was evaluated by an outside monitoring group in New York, they found that nearly 20% of the psychiatrically disturbed prisoners had received 10 or more deprivation orders during their stay in SHU (Correctional Association of New York, 2004, p. 23) Over one third of the mentally ill SHU inmates sampled reported being put on the loaf, and one of them was kept on this restricted diet for 9 months (during which time he lost 65 pounds).

Unfortunately, even the noncustodial supermax staff are contaminated by the punitive, security-obsessed environment in which they must work. They are not immune to the ecology of cruelty that exists in many of these units (and they are powerless to change it). Thus, their professional roles and practices may be distorted and compromised by the pressures and influences that are created inside supermax. In fact, in some supermax units the obsession with security has resulted in the mental health staff's interactions with prisoners becoming increasingly strained and unnatural, sometimes bordering on the bizarre.

Indeed, it is hard to imagine a respectable therapist or clinician anywhere in free society conducting a diagnostic interview or counseling session in an open hallway, while other prisoners in the cellblock listen in and correctional officers—with whom many prisoners have extremely hostile and contentious relationships—stand watching over them, within earshot, from a few feet away. It is hard to imagine a clinician anywhere else in society even attempting a therapeutic interaction with a patient who is standing or sitting inside a thick metal cage—one or another configuration of the so-called "programming cages" that have begun to appear in supermax units across the country. In some supermax units several of these grotesque stand-up cages are arranged in a semicircle—a kind of "only in supermax" parody of an actual "group therapy" session. There are actually some prison clinicians who have arranged to have single steel cages installed inside their offices, so that they can "treat" a caged supermax or administrative segregation "patient" while they sit behind their desks. The sight of these cages is startling and underscores how truly perverse the concept of "mental health" and "treatment" has become in some of these units.

Indeed, whatever routine contact prisoners have with mental health staff in most supermaxes typically occurs through the bars or door of a supermax cell, in so-called "cell-front" therapy (or what prisoners refer to as "drive bys"). But this is not all. The staff member is often required to wear a bulky flak jacket and may even "interact" with his or her patients through the distorting lens of a clear plastic spit shield that is fitted over the staff member's head. Some units have a large plastic protective shield on a metal track so that it can be pushed down the tier, setting up a moving transparent wall between the prisoners in their cells and anyone who enters the cell block— including the clinicians, who must then treat their "patients" through the clear Plexiglas shield between them. Well-intentioned mental health staff make do with these arrangements. It is indisputable, as many of them say, that these bizarre and contorted encounters are "better than nothing." And so, perhaps, they are. But there is little opportunity for genuine interaction, trust, or rapport building, or even a moment of genuine normalization in the interactions that take place between them. Here, too, it would be naïve to assume that these working conditions do not take a toll on the persons who are exposed and become accustomed to them.[3]

Thus, even with mental health staff, there is a powerful psychological message conveyed by the architecture of containment, separation, and isolation that dominates the supermax environment. It wears on the prisoners but surely has a corresponding effect on the staff. When combined with the sheer starkness and deprivation of the environment, the technologies and implements of forceful custodial restraint and control, a special ecology is created. This ecology is fairly described as "cruel" for the simple reason that it inures people to the suffering of others and because it is designed and operated in ways that give staff members little choice but—by merely following procedure—to likely add to that suffering. In the final analysis then, the physical environment and procedural routines that characterize the typical supermax surely have a psychological effect on the thoughts and actions of the people who live and work there, one that unfortunately pulls and pushes the staff in the direction of engaging in—or at least tolerating—more extreme and potentially abusive treatment.

The Dynamics of Desperation

There is an intense interpersonal reciprocity that characterizes the supermax environment, more powerful than in other prison settings. Long-term confinement, in a small space, with high levels of frustration and few degrees of behavioral freedom builds on the basic prison dynamic, creating tensions that are easily magnified as they accumulate and compound. Such pressurized contact not only provides the occasion for conflict and violence, but also precludes the routine "reality testing" that is intrinsic to normal social existence.

Thus, the interactions between guards and prisoners in these units are always at risk of devolving into increasingly tight spirals of negative expectation, conflict, and recrimination. To cite some of the social psychological dynamics at work here is perhaps to belabor the obvious. But the operative mechanisms have been carefully documented in a variety of different settings, and they transpire in supermax with a vengeance.

These processes are set in motion from the outset, upon a prisoner's arrival in supermax. Neither group—not the prisoners nor the guards—starts with a blank psychological slate. In fact, expectations and events that almost always precede supermax confinement are likely to intensify the negative edge on the inter-group interactions that take place in these units. Once the interpersonal processes are set in motion, there is little in the supermax environment to slow down or reverse them. For all of the reasons discussed in the preceding sections, and some that I will identify below, they are likely to gather momentum.

For example, as David Lovell (2008) astutely observes, "[p]unitive or scolding attitudes in a hearing officer can solidify rather than resolve the initial conflict" that led to supermax placement. Moreover, as he also notes, the same conflict can be solidified "when inmates are classified without taking account of their full history, causes of disruptive behavior are misread, along with the inmate's likely response to the strictures of a supermax regime" (Lovell, 2008, p. 1000). Yet these problematic scenarios reflect the normative rather than exceptional cases in most supermax units.

Indeed, the "scolding" attitudes that Lovell rightly questions would be a welcome damping down of the atmosphere and attitudes that actually prevail inside many of the supermaxes with which I am familiar. Moreover, even in those exceptional systems where conscientious hearing officers do attempt to take these complex factors into account, they are subject to disapproval (and stonewalling) by line officers who lack access to the same information and, from their perspective, do not have the luxury of taking it into account in practice anyway. All of this is by way of saying that except in very rare instances—unusually well-run systems, courageous correctional administrators who insist on doing things differently, or court orders that force decision makers to hone in on at least some of these issues—the typical supermax prison is full of prisoners who have come into the unit with the "initial conflicts" that got them there having been "solidified," and then some.

Add to that the fact that most prisoners come to supermax units at the worst moments of their prison careers. In addition to the disproportionate number of mentally ill prisoners there, many new arrivals in supermax are in the throes of a psychological crisis of some sort that helps to account for the behavior that has led to their disciplinary infraction(s). Whatever underlying personal or situational issues that may explain their disturbed or agitated or aggressive state, the prison system has likely ignored them, deciding instead to respond to the prisoner's disruptive behavior by punishing him further. Thus, prisoners who have proven that they are unwilling or unable to conform their conduct to the requirements and rigors of mainline prison life are now expected to do so in a much more severe, punitive, psychologically stressful environment. Many of them will be unable to do so.

Many supermax prisoners find that their temporarily degraded psychological state is worsened by the especially stressful set of situational factors they confront there. However, the resulting behavior is likely to be interpreted by supermax staff entirely in terms of their character traits—a reflection of who they are rather than what they are going through. Social psychologists have long studied the process by which these kinds of judgments are made about the causes of other people's behavior. Fritz Heider (1958) demonstrated years ago that people intuitively attribute motives and intentionality to the actions they see others engage in. The tendency is so deep-seated that Heider's research participants would attach purpose to the otherwise random meanderings of dots on a screen. Attribution theorists broadened the analysis to identify what they termed a "fundamental attribution error" (Ross, 1977)—a widespread tendency to attribute the causes of behavior we observe actors engage in to their presumably stable internal characteristics. We are likely to do this even when there is reason to believe that the behavior in question has been heavily influenced, if not completely determined, by the circumstances under which it occurs—a fact that accounts for it being labeled an attribution "error."

Supermax is an almost perfect environment in which to amplify fundamental attribution error. Prisoners and guards see one another in only one setting—a powerful situation, to be sure, and one that is likely to elicit relatively consistent behavior from both groups within it. It is all too easy to mistake this situationally produced consistency for constancy in character. As would be expected, studies of aggression in various institutional settings find that staff members tend to see the causes of inmate violence primarily as residing inside those who engage in it, whereas the inmates attribute their behavior to external and situational triggers (e.g., Duxbury, 2002; Ilkiw-Lavalle & Grenyer, 2003). Moreover, as Toch (2001) noted, it is tempting "to confuse the effects of problematic behavior—its nuisance value—with its intent, although we ought to recognize that a great deal of acting out consists of helpless outbursts or retaliatory rage" (p. 378).

In any event, the dysfunctional adaptations of supermax prisoners are often attributed to their dispositions—antisocial traits, character flaws, or predatory natures—rather than the characteristics of the setting in which they are forced to live. Those kinds of attributions tend to harden over time. Supermax prisoners are often judged and demonized so effectively that some of them grow into their reputations, and those who acted in ways that warranted those reputations initially find they cannot grow out of them.

Guards make these natural attributional inferences and act accordingly. So, too, do prisoners. Correctional officers are typically performing within the relatively well-defined and enforced strictures of an occupational role, and their behavior is subject to a range of powerful professional and peer pressures, not to mention the many situational forces I have discussed throughout much of this article. Yet prisoners are likely to succumb to the attributional inference that the guards' relatively consistent behavior reflects something enduring about them as people, rather than about the pressures of the job and extreme nature of the environment in which they work. In both instances, the fundamental attribution error works against empathy and understanding and is likely to increase tensions between both groups.

In a related way, the supermax environment is also almost ideally designed to maximize the operation of complex psychological processes through which derogatory social stereotypes are perpetuated and exacerbated. In prisons in general, the stereotypic expectations that prisoners and guards have for one another are fertile ground for what social psychologists have termed "behavioral confirmation" (e.g., Klein & Snyder, 2003; Snyder & Klein, 2005; Snyder, Tanke, & Berscheid, 1977), explaining why stereotypes translate so often into self-fulfilling prophecies. In prison settings, the views that both prisoners and guards hold of each other become intertwined with the behavior in which each group engages. The stereotype-driven behavior that implicitly elicits (and thereby confirms) those pre-existing stereotypes convinces each group that they are "right" about each other.

But the self-fulfilling prophecies that come about are more potent in supermax for several reasons. One is that the initial stereotypes are more uniform and powerful—after all, these prisoners are the "worst of the worst." Everyone says so. Such a uniform and powerful stereotype is more likely to have a controlling effect on behavior. Second, the behavior of prisoners in supermax is more highly dependent on and, therefore, more significantly shaped by the stereotype-driven behavior of the guards. As noted earlier, prisoners in supermax actually "do" almost nothing that is not in some way potentially conditioned—permitted or controlled—by the behavior of the guards. Finally, in a related way, the prisoners have so few degrees of behavioral freedom that opportunities to definitively counter the stereotypes that the guards have of them rarely occur.

This latter point—the way in which supermaxes narrow or constrict the range of possible behavior on the part of prisoners—bears additional emphasis. In their degraded state, brought about by the deprived circumstances under which they live and their absolute dependency on their captors, much of the prisoners' humanity is suppressed, hidden, shielded from view, or disfigured. They are their reputations, regarded in terms of their previous outbursts or the degraded physical and mental conditions to which they have sunk. As I say, it is hard for prisoners to initiate behavior at all in these places, let alone to act and represent themselves as full human beings with true personhood and multidimensional lives and relationships that predate their stay in supermax. To be sure, there is nothing in the day-to-day limited and contorted interactions they have with guards and other staff to remind those in charge of who they really are, were, or could become. A self-fulfilling prophecy is created in which guards see prisoners acting in precisely the degraded terms and within the narrow dehumanized constructs that have been assigned to them, confirming their disparaging views, and justifying—even escalating—their mistreatment.

Pierre Bourdieu (1991) has written about the particular way that an institution communicates—creates—an identity for inmates: "It signifies it to him and imposes it on him by expressing in front of everyone and thus informing him in an authoritative manner of what he is and what he must be" (p. 121). The supermax environment not only reminds the guards who the prisoners are—the guards, after all, are the ones who have to enforce this derogated identity on the prisoners—but also tells them who they are. The way they are dressed, the weapons at their disposal, the limited options they have to resolve conflict primarily through forceful subjugation and increased punishment are all messages about their identities as well.

In addition, because supermax units are often "in crisis"—a weapon has been found, an especially angry and confrontational prisoner has been brought into the unit, a mentally ill prisoner recently attempted suicide, a violent cell extraction has just occurred—they are periodically defined by the staff as places where ordinary rules and norms and standards of decency are suspended. Correspondingly, the staff may come to believe that such rules and norms and standards explicitly do not and should not apply to them. It is not just that "[a]s conflict escalates, cohesion within groups increases, [and] concern for fairness between groups shrinks" (Opotow, 1990, p. 6) but also that the concept of fairness itself is at risk of disappearing. Because the crisis- or exigency-driven nature of supermax means that the rules and norms governing what is decent, proper, and humane are often suspended, staff members can begin to feel over time that they have been given the implicit permission to, in a sense, create their own standards. When this happens, supermax prisoners can be "morally excluded" by staff, placed in a kind of alternative moral universe that is free of the ethical constraints of the larger society, with no accountability to those norms.

As I say, crises are not infrequent in supermax, and both prisoners and guards are implicated both in precipitating them and ensuring that they persist. Toch (2001) has wisely pointed out that "restrictive regimes invite games of cops and robbers. Rules spark efforts to evade them, and regimentation breeds resistance" (p. 382). He also certainly knows that over time, there is nothing at all gamelike about the confrontations that ensue; as he says, "a climate of trench warfare" (p. 382) is often created. Eventually, however, a culture of harm can emerge in which the harsh application of the rules becomes functionally autonomous, pursued for its own sake, the motivation for proceeding having been disconnected from its original purpose. For the guards, the goal becomes simply to enforce one's authority, to subjugate the prisoners to the demands of the unit, no matter the cost, and to dominate them in the end by making them pay for whatever resistance they have demonstrated.

From the prisoners' perspective, what is at stake is sometimes experienced as something different and deeper. Because so much of their identity comes to be defined by the social realities of the supermax environment—indeed, they have no other to fall back on—they come to believe that nothing short of their personhood is in the balance. Just as in closed-ward psychiatric settings, increased punishment is experienced by inmates not as the just imposition of consequences but "as an attack on his/her person" (Whittington & Richter, 2005, p. 385). Over time, these confrontations escalate because both sides lose sight of alternative courses of action:

> The longer the interaction lasts and the more it escalates, the fewer options are available. A very important feature of escalating interactions is the endpoint where one actor only reacts aggressively to the perceived aggression of the other actor. Both actors are thus subjectively defending themselves against the other. (Whittington & Richter, 2005, p. 385)

To illustrate the ways in which some of these dynamics operate to heighten the risk of mistreatment in supermax, consider the following scenario, depicting the kind of problematic interactions that occur routinely—on a weekly if not daily basis—in many of these units. A supermax prisoner who is known to suffer from emotional problems, one who is on the mental health caseload and has attempted suicide in the past, begins to feel anxious and agitated one morning. It has been some time—weeks rather than days—since he has seen his assigned clinician, and he knows that today is one of the times when some of the clinicians who visit the supermax will be coming to the unit to check on their patients. He asks a guard if his particular clinician is coming and, a short time later, is told that she is. The prisoner has no way of knowing whether the guard actually checked and, from his perspective, there have been many times in the past when the staff has lied to him. So his anxiety is not allayed. The prisoner, for his part, is regarded by the staff as especially demanding, sometimes manipulative, and occasionally a troublemaker. The guard may or may not have bothered to check. If he did not, his failure to do so could easily have been an innocent oversight in the course of a busy day, rather than an intentional slight. Neither the guard nor the prisoner will get the benefit of each other's doubt in the events that will follow.

The prisoner waits alone in his cell, experiencing increasing distress. There is nothing to do, of course, no way to distract his racing thoughts or release his tension. Instead, his agitation builds throughout the day. He inquires several more times about the whereabouts of his clinician, and each time is told that she will be there eventually. Of course, the staff is increasingly annoyed by his ceaseless pestering. By the end of the day, when the prisoner asks one final time—this time extremely agitated and upset—the guards tell him, "sorry, I guess she's not coming; all of the clinicians have gone home." The prisoner immediately explodes into a violent spasm of anger, banging his fists and kicking at his cell door in frustration, and screaming and yelling vulgar epithets that he directs at the guards and anyone else he can think of. He demands to see the unit lieutenant, insisting that the lieutenant can contact his clinician and get her to come see him.

The prisoner angrily tells the guard that the situation is desperate and he will not stand down. The guard asks if he is declaring a "crisis"—the magic words that will precipitate a move from his cell to the dreaded suicide observation cell elsewhere in the prison. He says that he is not, that he does not want the unit "move team"—this supermax prison's equivalent of a cell-extraction team—to come for him but is insistent that he wants to see the lieutenant and continues to demand that someone get his clinician and bring her to see him.

This intense exchange continues for several minutes until, finally, the guard—by now exasperated and very angry himself—gives up and calls for the move team. The prisoner is rushed in his cell by a team of helmeted and armored officers who gas him, throw him to the floor, force him into handcuffs and chains, and carry him off, somewhat bruised and battered, to the suicide observation cell. Once there, he is stripped naked (by having his clothes cut off his body), placed in a paper gown, put on the cold, hard concrete "bunk" in four-point restraints. A correctional officer is stationed a few feet outside the cell and keeps visual watch over him for the rest of the night. Of course, the prisoner will be written up and punished for this serious disciplinary infraction, his stay in supermax likely extended as a consequence.

For both the prisoner and the guards involved, the sequence of events no doubt confirms and hardens their most negative beliefs about each other. From the guards' perspective, the prisoner has demonstrated that he is weak, sniveling, overly demanding, and manipulative and someone who not only cannot be reasoned with but also who is capable of violent outbursts in response to the slightest provocation (or no provocation at all). To them, the events once again confirm the wisdom of controlling prisoners like this by applying the maximum amount of force and employing whatever weapons the staff has at their disposal to achieve the necessary domination.

The prisoner, on the other hand, is shamed by his loss of control and humiliated by the public display of his desperate need for mental health attention. He knows that it has made him look weak and vulnerable in front of the other prisoners; he resents the guards for forcing his hand in this way, holds them responsible for this loss of face, and knows he will have to publicly demonstrate his "toughness"—somehow—to make up for this. His sense of helplessness is also deepened. The sequence of events confirms his beliefs that he is surrounded by a sadistic group of guards who not only do not care about his mental illness and the anguish he experiences in supermax but are willing to forcefully repress his desperate calls for help and then add to his punishment in the aftermath. He may privately vow to seek revenge for being treated so badly, or become so despondent over this painful and hopeless situation that he again attempts to take his life.

All too often, supermax brings together a perfect storm of social psychological pressures and influences, and a set of counterproductive interpersonal dynamics that cannot be transcended by either the prisoners or the guards. David Lovell astutely summarizes the way these general processes operate in the case of disturbed supermax prisoners:

> Prisoners classified as disturbed had shown, some more chronically than others, patterns of thinking and feeling that were poorly adapted to their settings; and the predictable response of the institution were sufficiently distressing that they resorted to measures that only made their predicament worse. (p. 999)

Yet precisely this description is often broadly applicable to many prisoners in supermax, regardless of whether they have been classified as disturbed. Most if not all supermax prisoners are "poorly adapted" to this setting, one where the programmed institutional responses frequently make their predicament worse.

Indeed, as I have suggested, these forces combine and coalesce over time to produce a culture of harm—one in which both prisoners and guards become lost in their own animosity toward one another and where guards, in particular (because they have far more power and many more degrees of freedom over whether and how they act) not only become indifferent to the suffering of prisoners but begin to take initiative to worsen it. I have called it a "culture" of harm because the atmosphere in supermax reflects much more than a transitory mood or fleeting set of views. Instead, there is a shared perspective, a commitment to a common set of values, and a set of traditions that are passed along from older to newer guards. Indeed, newcomers to the ranks are inculcated—enculturated—with the supermax ethos. Moreover, the way in which most supermax units are set off from the rest of the prison or complex of prisons where they operate, and the geographical isolation of many of these places, adds to the extent to which a separate world and worldview is often created and maintained inside.

Combating a Culture of Harm

There is some evidence that the penal harm policies of the past several decades have begun to run their course. There is a renewed, surprisingly unapologetic commitment to rehabilitation that has begun to be openly expressed (at least in some quarters), a frank recognition of the need for sentencing reform, and a heightened awareness of the importance of developing effective strategies for reintegrating prisoners into the free world communities to which nearly all of them will return. But the commitment to penal harm is alive and well in supermax prisons. Indeed, supermax may be both the last true vestige of the penal harm movement and perhaps its most extreme expression. It persists despite the condemnations, calls to end the use of solitary confinement, and proposals for drastic reform from distinguished scholars and human rights organizations that I cited at the outset of this article. Supermax has proliferated despite empirical evidence suggesting that its existence has done little or nothing to reduce systemwide prison disorder or disciplinary infractions (Briggs, Sundt, & Castellano, 2003) and more recent evidence that it actually may contribute to elevated rates of recidivism (Lovell, Johnson, & Cain, 2007).

Supermax environments continue to be structured and operated in ways that are designed to deprive, diminish, and punish. In this article I have suggested that just as the degrees of freedom for supermax prisoners are highly constrained and constricted, so too are they for the guards who work inside. Correctional officers get no acknowledgment or consideration for the toll this exposure exacts on them, or appreciation for the ways in which the experience is likely to change them—on the job and off. Yet persons charged with the responsibility of implementing the procedures and enforcing the rules of a regime that deprives people of most of the things that make them human are at grave risk of losing a little humanity themselves. For this reason among others, supermax environments are especially prone to having abusive patterns of behavior become routine and a general atmosphere of inhumane treatment to emerge. It behooves us to take these risks more closely to heart.

Chase Riveland, a corrections expert who has analyzed and assessed many supermaxlike prison settings (Riveland, 1999), has often referred to the "culture of control" that can arise within them. I have argued that the culture of control that is created inside supermax prisons has a tendency to devolve further into a "culture of harm." They are places so devoted to controlling every aspect of a prisoner's behavior primarily (if not exclusively) through deprivation and punishment—the infliction of pain—that staff members are likely to become inured and insensitive to the hurtful consequences of the actions that the environment obligates them to take. They are pushed in the direction of ignoring the suffering of prisoners and routinely blaming them for their own demise. The harm of supermax is minimized, seen as unproblematic, its potentially disabling consequences normalized.

Most proposals to reform supermax include many of the very same elements, expressed in somewhat different ways, with slightly different emphases. They all have much to recommend them. Virtually all of the thoughtful ones concede that the core supermax regime—at least as presently constituted—cannot be operated in a humane way. My focus here has been to underscore the importance of taking guard behavior explicitly into account, both as an element of supermax harm and as a significant target of institutional reform. But the basic lesson of this analysis is that prisoners and guards are locked in a reciprocal embrace in supermax. Overall, conditions of confinement must be taken into account, both in assessing and in reducing the harm created by these units, because they adversely affect both groups.

As I have argued throughout this article, because of the core premises on which they are founded, the way that they are physically structured, and the manner of their operation, there continues to be a heightened potential for abuse in supermax prisons. The culture of harm that results is largely independent of the initial predispositions and preferences of the persons who work there, rendering supermaxes more likely to degenerate into places where various forms of mistreatment—from callous indifference to the suffering of prisoners to their outright physical abuse—become commonplace. The heightened potential of supermax to generate cruelty and mistreatment must be made part of the equation by which these places are reformed, if not eliminated. The ever-present danger that cruelty may emerge must be safeguarded against. Better guards, better training, to be sure, but ultimately better conditions as well.

A little more than a decade ago, Mona Lynch and I reviewed the existing literature on the harmful effects of solitary and supermax-type confinement (Haney & Lynch, 1997). We ended that lengthy discussion with a proposed list of "limiting standards" that we suggested should be enforced in such units (Haney & Lynch, 1997, pp. 558–566), ones that were "rooted in the psychological literature and intended as the basis for a more effective, realistic, and psychologically meaningful oversight" of supermax (Haney & Lynch, 1997, p. 560). Many of our proposed standards were designed to prevent or limit the potential damage of the harsh supermax regime on prisoners, including due process protections for all prisoners in advance of their placement in supermax (irrespective of the purpose for that placement); screening prisoners out of supermax if their medical or mental health conditions made them especially vulnerable to the harmful consequences that we identified; prohibiting the placement of prisoners in supermax whose disciplinary infractions resulted from pre-existing psychiatric disorders; placing severe time limits on the duration of confinement for all prisoners (prohibiting total isolation and extreme segregation of the sort that occurs in "dark cells," while permitting somewhat longer periods of isolation for less draconian segregated housing); monthly mental health evaluations to determine continued fitness for segregated housing; and access to therapy, work, educational, and recreational programs and visitation—comparable to what is offered in mainline units—for prisoners confined in supermax for longer than 3 months.

Of course, the implementation of these prisoner-oriented standards would go a long way toward changing the culture of harm that characterizes many supermax units. It certainly would require prison officials to run a fundamentally different kind of facility, populated by a different group of prisoners than at present. However, we also recommended standards that were designed to address the role of the correctional staff, including requiring specialized staff training that addresses the unique psychological stressors that supermax imposes on prisoners and guards alike; providing instruction in recognizing and responding to signs of psychological trauma and the psychopathological effects of isolation; and carefully monitoring staff not only for the possible use of excessive force but also for indications of deteriorating behavior in the face of adverse working conditions. Finally, we recommended the periodic rotation of staff out of these units "to ensure that they maintain a broader perspective prisoner behavior and the range of potential relationships between staff and inmates" (Haney & Lynch, 1997, p. 566). Unfortunately, no supermax regime of which I am aware has seriously addressed the bulk of our concerns or implemented even a meaningful subset of these important limiting standards.

Much more recently, as I noted at the outset of this article, a group of international trauma experts critically examined supermax-type confinement.

They, too, concluded that it should be drastically limited, and made a series of proposals for reform. Although relatively modest in scope, and eminently reasonable in conception, they are recommendations that, as I noted, would end supermax as we know it in the United States. These reforms included:

> [R]aising the level of prison staff–prisoner contact, allowing access to social activities with other prisoners, allowing more visits, and allowing and arranging in-depth talks with psychologists, psychiatrists, religious prison personnel, and volunteers from the local community. Especially important are the possibilities for both maintaining and developing relations with the outside world including spouses, partners, children, and other family and friends. It is also very important to provide prisoners in solitary confinement with meaningful in cell and out of cell activities. (International Psychological Trauma Symposium, 2007)

Here, too, the goal is to change the ideology and transform the paradigm on which supermax is founded. Nothing short of significantly redesigning the ecology of supermax to emphasize caring over cruelty and drastically reducing or eliminating the level of deprivation that prevails will do. The Istanbul trauma experts understood that with few exceptions, supermax prisoners need more contact not less—contact with caring professionals who can facilitate programming into productive activities, contact with other prisoners with whom they can construct a semblance of normal life in prison, and contact with their families and the outside world and the other people to whom they ultimately will return.

Many supermax units periodically seethe with anger and tension, having become places where outright physical confrontation and abuse simmer just below the surface. The crucible of the typical self-contained supermax unit is filled with difficult-to-manage prisoners and guards who have few options to improve on the prisoners' already problematic track records. Both groups are very much at the mercy of powerful situational forces and pressures around them. To be sure, these distinct and adverse aspects of supermax worsen the experience for prisoners. But they raise as yet empirically unexamined questions about the long-term psychological effects on correctional staff of working under supermax-type conditions as well. And they caution us against what I believe is a naïve view of supermax reform suggesting that modest tinkering with its basic design can produce a meaningful beneficial or palliative response. A comprehensive set of changes or reforms would not only create a more humane environment for prisoners to live and guards to work in but also minimize the inherent potential for cruelty and abuse in supermax.

Endnotes

[1] The "new policies" that were implemented certainly did not stem from any significant scientific breakthroughs or important new data that had surfaced during this period, suggesting that the penal harm approaches were likely to work. In fact, if anything, the underlying scientific paradigms were shifting decidedly in the opposite direction. Had the emerging research on the social historical causes of crime and the importance of immediate social context been

acknowledged and relied on in the development of crime control and penal policy, an entirely different, far more preventive, and much less punitive strategy would have been pursued (Haney, 2006).

[2] It is worth noting that otherwise thoughtful courts have picked up this "worst of the worst" lingo and repeated it, without ever bothering to define it, as in: "Supermax Correctional Institution is a . . . supermaximum security facility . . . designed to incarcerate the worst of the worst offenders" (*Jones 'El v. Berge*, 2001, p. 1096). I cannot speculate on their reasons for doing this, but the fact that the terminology has made its way into judicial opinions means that it has become part of the lexicon by which the apparent legitimacy of supermax is preserved.

[3] It is important to acknowledge that mere contact with mental health workers is no panacea for the debilitating effects of supermax. There are countless caring professionals in these environments who work under conditions that, almost by definition, preclude them from doing their jobs. Eventually, for some, the toxic ideology and ecology of cruelty will begin to take a toll. Thus, Rhodes (2002) reported interviewing mental health workers in supermax who believed a number of their prisoner–patients were not human—indeed, that they were "evil in the biblical sense" (p. 452). Anyone who has spent any considerable time speaking candidly with a wide range of prison clinicians has heard these kinds of comments or worse. Perhaps because the need for adequate mental health services in supermax is so pressing (and too often unmet), we have been content to measure them in terms of the sheer number of available personnel or contact hours. Here, too, the conditions under which clinicians must work and, in turn, how they are changed and affected by them, are often ignored.

References

Arax, M. (1996, August 21). Brutality behind bars. *Los Angeles Times*, p. Al.

Beckett, K. (1997). *Making crime pay: Law and order in contemporary American society.* New York: Oxford University Press.

Bourdieu, P. (1991). *Language and symbolic power.* Cambridge, MA: Harvard University Press.

Bragg, R. (1995, March 26). Chain gangs to return to roads of Alabama. *New York Times*, p. 9.

Briggs, C., Sundt, J., & Castellano, T. (2003). The effect of supermaximum security prisons on aggregate levels of institutional violence. *Criminology, 41,* 1341–1376.

Bruton, J. (2004). *The big house: Life inside a supermax security prison.* Stillwater, MN: Voyageur Press.

Butterfield, F. (1997, May 12). States toughen up juvenile-crime laws. *San Jose Mercury News*, p. 1A.

Christie, N. (1982). *Limits to pain.* Oxford, UK: Robertson.

Christie, N. (1993). *Crime control as industry: Towards gulags, Western style?* London: Routledge.

Cloyes, K., Lovell, D., Allen, D., & Rhodes, L. (2006). Assessment of psychosocial impairment in a supermaximum security unit sample. *Criminal Justice and Behavior, 33,* 760–781.

Cohen, F. (2006). Isolation in penal settings: The isolation-restraint paradigm. *Washington University Journal of Law & Policy, 22,* 295–324.

Correctional Association of New York. (2004). *Mental health in the house of corrections: A study of mental health care in New York State prisons.* Retrieved January 10, 2008, from http://www.correctionalassociation.org/PVP/publications/Mental-Health.pdf

Cullen, F. (1995). Assessing the penal harm movement. *Journal of Research in Crime and Delinquency, 32,* 338, 340.

DiIulio, J. (1995, November 27). The coming of the super-predators. *Weekly Standard,* p. 23.

Duxbury, J. (2002). An evaluation of staff and patient views of and strategies employed to manage inpatient aggression and violence on one mental health unit: A pluralistic design. *Journal of Psychiatric and Mental Health Nursing, 9*, 325–337.

Feeley, M., & Simon, J. (1992). The new penology: Notes on the emerging strategy of corrections and its implications. *Criminology, 30*, 449–474.

Fernandez, E. (1997, December 14). Video of guards killing inmates at state prison. *San Francisco Examiner*, p. D-1.

Forer, L. (1994). *A rage to punish: The unintended consequences of mandatory sentencing.* New York: Norton.

Gibbons, J., & Katzenbach, N. (2006). *Confronting confinement: A report of the Commission on Safety and Abuse in America's Prisons.* New York: Vera Institute of Justice.

Haney, C. (1993). Infamous punishment: The psychological effects of isolation. *National Prison Project Journal, 8*, 3–21.

Haney, C. (1998). Riding the punishment wave: On the origins of our devolving standards of decency. *Hastings Women's Law Journal, 9*, 27–78.

Haney, C. (2003). Mental health issues in long-term solitary and "supermax" confinement. *Crime & Delinquency, 49*, 124–156.

Haney, C. (2006). *Reforming punishment: Psychological limits to the pains of imprisonment.* Washington, DC: American Psychological Association.

Haney, C., Banks, C., & Zimbardo, P. (1973). Interpersonal dynamics in a simulated prison. *International Journal of Criminology and Penology, 1*, 69–97.

Haney, C., & Lynch, M. (1997). Regulating prisons of the future: A psychological analysis of supermax and solitary confinement. *New York University Review of Law and Social Change, 23*, 477–570.

Haney, C., & Zimbardo, P. (1977). The socialization into criminality: On becoming a prisoner and a guard. In J. Tapp & F. Levine (Eds.), *Law, justice, and the individual in society: Psychological and legal issues* (pp. 198–223). New York: Holt, Rinehart & Winston.

Heider, F. (1958). *The psychology of interpersonal relations.* New York: John Wiley.

Hodgins, S., & Cote, G. (1991). The mental health of penitentiary inmates in isolation. *Canadian Journal of Criminology, 33*, 177–182.

Holding, R. (1996a, October 28). Accusations of prison coverup, agency hid staged fights at Corcoran, guards say. *San Francisco Chronicle*, p. Al.

Holding, R. (1996b, December 18). Exercise yards to reopen at Corcoran prison. *San Francisco Chronicle*, p. A17.

Human Rights Watch. (2000). *Out of sight: Super maximum security confinement in the United States.* New York: Author. Retrieved January 10, 2008, from http://www.hrw.org/reports/2000/supermax/index.htm#TopOfPage

Ilkiw-Lavalle, O., & Grenyer, B. (2003). Differences between patient and staff perceptions of aggression in mental health units. *Psychiatric Services, 54*, 389–393.

International Psychological Trauma Symposium. (2007, December 9). *Istanbul statement on the use and effects of solitary confinement*, Istanbul, Turkey.

Jones 'El v. Berge, 164 F. Supp. 1096 (W.D. Wis. 2001).

Klein, O., & Snyder, M. (2003). Stereotypes and behavioral confirmation: From interpersonal to intergroup perspectives. In M. Zanna (Ed.), *Advances in experimental social psychology* (Vol. 35, pp. 153–234). New York: Elsevier North-Holland.

Lee, J. (1996, July 14). Inmates claim brutality at top-security prison. *San Jose Mercury News*, p. 3B.

Lovell, D. (2008) Patterns of Disturbed Behavior in a Supermax Population. *Criminal Justice and Behavior, 35*, 985–1004.

Lovell, D., Cloyes, K., Allen, D., & Rhodes, L. (2000). Who lives in super-maximum custody? A Washington State study. *Federal Probation, 64*, 33–38.

Lovell, D., Johnson, L., & Cain, K. (2007). Recidivism of supermax prisoners in Washington State. *Crime & Delinquency, 53*, 633–656.

Madrid v. Gomez, 889 F. Supp. 1146 (N.D. Cal. 1995).

Morris, N. (2000). Prisons in the USA: Supermax—The bad and the mad. In L. Fairweather & S. McConville (Eds.), *Prison architecture: Policy, design, and experience* (pp. 98–108). London: Architectural Press.

Mydans, S. (1995, March 7). Hard time: What we have here is a failure to tolerate. *San Jose Mercury News*, p. A9.

Navarro, M. (1995, November 21). Florida prisons to revive using chain gangs—But with limits. *San Francisco Chronicle*, p. A7.

Opotow, S. (1990). Moral exclusion and injustice: An introduction. *Journal of Social Issues, 46*, 1–20.

Pasternak, J. (1997, August 7). Prisons are becoming landlords, inmates in some states are being charged monthly rent, though few can pay. *San Jose Mercury News*, p. A8.

Rhodes, L. (2002). Psychopathy and the face of control in supermax. *Ethnography, 3*, 442–466.

Riveland, C. (1999). *Supermax prisons: Overview and general considerations.* Washington, DC: U.S. Department of Justice.

Ross, L. (1977). The intuitive psychologist and his shortcomings: Distortions in the attribution process. In L. Berkowitz (Ed.), *Advances in experimental social psychology* (Vol. 10, pp. 173–220). San Diego, CA: Academic Press.

Ruiz v. Johnson, 37 F. Supp. 2d 855 (S.D. Tex. 1999), rev'd, 178 F.3d 385 (5th Cir. 1999).

Smith, P. (2006). The effects of solitary confinement on prison inmates: A brief history and review of the literature. In M. Tonry (Ed.), *Crime and justice* (Vol. 34, pp. 441–528). Chicago: University of Chicago Press.

Snyder, M., & Klein, O. (2005). Construing and constructing others: On the reality and the generality of the behavioral confirmation scenario. *Interaction Studies, 6*, 53–67.

Snyder, M., Tanke, E., & Berscheid, E. (1977). Social perception and interpersonal behavior: On the self-fulfilling nature of social stereotypes. *Journal of Personality and Social Psychology, 35*, 656–666.

Tachiki, S. (1995). Indeterminate sentences in supermax prisons based upon alleged gang affiliations: A reexamination of procedural protection and a proposal for greater procedural requirements. *California Law Review, 83*, 1117–1149.

Toch, H. (2001). The future of supermax confinement. *The Prison Journal, 81*, 376–388.

Valdes v. Crosby, 450 F. 3d 1231 (11 Cir. 2006).

Walt, K. (1999, March 29). High-control unit may be next battleground for inmate rights. *Houston Chronicle.* Retrieved January 10, 2008, from http://www.chron.com/content/story.html/page1/222960

"We stand with you" [Advertisement]. (1997, January 1). *Fresno Bee.*

Whittington, R., & Richter, D. (2005). Interactional aspects of violent behaviour on acute psychiatric wards. *Psychology, Crime & Law, 11*, 377–388.

Wilson, J. (1975). *Thinking about crime.* New York: Basic Books.

Word, R. (2007, January 18). Deal reached in Florida prison death case. *South Florida Sun-Sentinel.* Retrieved January 10, 2008, from http://www.sun-sentinel.com/news/nationworld/world/wire/sns-ap-prisoner-abuse,0,5284843.story

Zimring, F., Hawkins, G., & Kamin, S. (2001). *Punishment and democracy: Three strikes and you're out in California.* Oxford, UK: Oxford University Press.

18

The Illusion of Structure
A Critique of the Classical Model of Organization and the Discretionary Power of Correctional Officers

MICHAEL J. GILBERT

Early studies of correctional officers did not recognize the rich diversity of work behaviors that these officers possess. Correctional officers were often portrayed in stereotypic terms as if they were part of a monolithic work force characterized by shared traits. Philliber (1987) showed that these characterizations consisted mainly of negative stereotypes. Correctional officers were presented as having limited intelligence, a high threshold for boredom, low self-esteem, a high level of cynicism, extreme alienation, a hostile attitude toward inmates, a willingness to quickly use physical force, and a propensity for the use of excessive force. Recent studies have recognized wide variation in the work behaviors and discretionary power displayed by line correctional officers. These studies have emphasized diversity, complexity, job stress, and individual discretion (Cheek and Miller, 1982; Cullen, Lutze, Link, and Wolfe, 1989; Jurik, 1985; Kauffman, 1988; Lombardo, 1989; Meyerson, 1992; Whitehead and Lindquist, 1989).

Line correctional officers control or deliver services to inmates. These officers strongly influence the lives of the inmates they supervise. Whether a confinement experience is constructive or destructive is largely determined by the actions of line correctional officers. "On the job" behaviors of line officers often determine whether new programs or policies are implemented faithfully or are subverted (Hall and Loucks, 1977; Mazmanian and Sabatier, 1983). There is broad recognition among scholars that the discretionary power of line officers is

Michael J. Gilbert, "The Illusion of Structure: A Critique of the Classical Model of Organization and the Discretionary Power of Correctional Officers," *Criminal Justice Review*, Vol. 22 No. 1, Spring 1997, pp. 49–64. Reprinted by permission of *Criminal Justice Review*.

crucial to policy implementation. However, there is disagreement over the question of how that discretionary power should be guided and managed.

The purpose of this paper is to provide a conceptual framework for understanding the nature and extent of correctional officer discretionary behavior. The primary vehicle for accomplishing this task is Muir's typology of discretionary behavior of police officers (1977). Police officers are viewed as political actors who must exercise individual discretion as an inherent part of their job. Muir describes four work styles:

1. The professional[1] is open and nondefensive, makes exceptions when warranted, prefers to gain cooperation and compliance through communication, but is willing to use coercive power or force as a last resort.

2. The reciprocator wants to help people, assists them in resolving their problems, prefers clinical or social work strategies, may be inconsistent when making exceptions, prefers to "go along to get along," and tends not to use coercive authority or physical force even when it is justifiable.

3. The enforcer practices rigid, "by the book," aggressive enforcement, actively seeks out violations, rarely makes exceptions, has little empathy for others, takes unreasonable risks to personal safety, sees most things as either good or bad, and is quick to use threats, verbal coercion, and physical force.

4. The avoider minimizes offender contact, often does not "see" an offense, avoids confrontation and coercion, views interpersonal aspects of the job as not part of the job, often backs down from confrontation, and blames others.

Theoretical Foundations

Brown (1981:34) identified a set of common organizational conditions that heighten the discretionary power of employees in public sector organizations as "intense political conflict over what [the organization] does, and [pressure to] provide satisfactory solutions to intractable social problems, [while faced with] immense difficulties in rationalizing organizational decision making. Consequently, the latitude for discretion is rather broad and the criteria used to judge different events may be a manifestation of the personal values of the decision maker as much as the priorities and expectations of the administrators." Correctional systems face precisely these conditions. Prisons are embroiled in political conflicts regarding questions of who should be incarcerated, appropriate sanctions, conditions of confinement, resource allocation, overcrowding, site location, operational problems, inmate rights, and many other politically charged issues. Crime is a truly "intractable social problem." There is little public consensus about the social purpose of imprisonment (Durham, 1994; Irwin and Austin, 1994).

While the appropriate role and function of our prisons may be debated, correctional officers have a job to perform. On a daily basis they must translate vague philosophical notions into concerted actions and specific work behaviors. The lack of clarity as to the purpose, role, and function of prisons, the variations between institutions and systems, the inability of correctional managers to communicate consistent philosophical principles and values, and the autonomy that is given to line officers broaden their individual discretionary power. The public image of correctional officers as part of a tightly controlled, paramilitary work force is inconsistent with the discretionary power that these officers possess and exercise; it is assumed that hierarchical and rigid organizational structures afford line officers little independence of action or decision-making authority (Weber, 1971; Wilson, 1941), but this assumption is simply wrong.

The intellectual foundations for understanding the discretionary behavior of correctional officers are found in many of the seminal works on political theory, justice, discretion, organizational behavior, and implementation. Machiavelli (1513/1980), Hobbes (1651/1981), and Locke (1690/1980) provided much of the political theory that guided the formation of modern civil societies. Their works also provided the rationale for the bounded use of coercive power by governments against citizens. The unlimited use of discretionary power by sovereigns gradually gave way to a more circumscribed understanding of the legitimate uses of coercive political power to enforce laws, create police forces, and operate confinement facilities for the common good.

Beccaria provided the conceptual foundation for Western criminal justice, by which legitimately established criminal laws can be enforced by acknowledged political authority (government and public officials) using the coercive powers of the state to maintain social order, peace, and public safety (Beccaria, 1764/1963:87). He recognized that criminal sanctions are political instruments used for social control. Beccaria would also have recognized that correctional officers are employed in a political enterprise serving political interests. However, this perspective was first articulated in 1918 by Max Weber (cited in Gerth and Mills, 1946:77–128) when he argued that public functionaries (i.e., all governmental workers) were employed in a "political vocation" and possessed inherent discretionary power. In this way Weber applied the rationale for bounded use of discretionary power by sovereigns to governmental workers who serve the state.

Muir's Typology

Muir's typology of police discretionary behavior is based on these underlying philosophical and theoretical foundations (Muir, 1977). Muir's typology is shown in table 1.

One of the strengths of Muir's typology is that the characteristics used were derived from Weber's 1918 speech "Politics as a Vocation": In order for political actors to function effectively in a political vocation they need (a) passion for a cause in the interest of public welfare, (b) responsibility to that cause, and (c) a sense of proportionality that enables an actor to calmly and objectively reflect on a situation apart from the people and things involved in

Table 1   Muir's typology of discretionary working styles.

	Human Relations Perspective	
	Tragic	**Cynical**
Integrated morality (Able to use coercion without damage to self-image or values	*Professional* (Reasonable, innovative, able to make exceptions)	*Enforcer* (Aggressive, by the book, unable to make exceptions)
Conflicted morality (Unable to use coercion without damage to self-image or values)	*Reciprocator* (Counseling orientation toward enforcement duties)	*Avoider* (Defines tasks out of the job to limit enforcement activities)

the circumstances (Weber, cited in Gerth and Mills, 1946:115). Weber's work serves as a link between earlier philosophical notions of bounded discretionary power and Muir's work styles in its recognition that public officials, at any level, are practitioners of a political vocation with inherent and irrevocable discretionary power.

One of the determinants of an officer's work style preference (i.e., the manner in which he or she exercises discretionary power) is the ability to resolve the ethical or moral dilemma concerning the use of coercion—a socially negative attribute—to protect public safety and personal property and maintain order (Muir, 1977). The use of coercive authority may be seen as the attainment of "just ends through dubious means." Officers who are able to resolve this quandary are said to have an "integrated morality" that allows them to use coercion appropriately in their professional role without damaging their self-image. Those officers who cannot resolve this quandary are said to have a "conflicted morality" that prevents them from using coercion without damaging their self-image.

Muir's second determinant is the officer's ability to develop a "tragic sense" of the human condition in which offenders find themselves. An ability to have empathy, sensitivity, and compassion for others permits an officer to view human nature (in all its forms) as part of a single continuum encompassing the officer as well as others. Thus most behavioral deviations and aberrations may be viewed as exceptions rather than the norm. Officers with a "tragic sense" usually see deviations in behavior, including their own, as circumstantial abnormalities.

The inability to develop a tragic sense is termed a "cynical perspective" and is characterized by officers who view human nature in dualistic terms (e.g., the good and the bad, victim and victimizer, weak and strong). Such officers tend to focus on extremes of behavior and have difficulty making reasonable allowances for exceptional behavior in anyone, including themselves. From the cynical perspective, once a criminal always a criminal, once a bad cop always a bad cop. Such an officer often sees himself as good and offenders as evil. This dualistic orientation makes empathy for the human condition of others, especially offenders, nearly impossible. Officers with a cynical perspective may deal with offenders in a demeaning, hostile, or aggressive manner.[2]

Lipsky (1973:104) acknowledged the broad discretionary power of line employees in governmental bureaucracies with his definition of "Street Level Bureaucrats" as "government workers who directly interact with citizens in the regular course of their jobs, whose work within the bureaucratic structure permits a wide latitude in job performance, and whose impact on the lives of citizens is extensive." Correctional officers deal directly with citizens who are incarcerated as convicted offenders. The prisons they work in are chronically understaffed and provided with limited resources. Consequently, "wide latitude in job performance" is afforded to these line officers.

It is difficult to define what corrections officers do, let alone assess how well they have done it. Nevertheless, it is clear that the direct work product that these officers produce is not security, control, or safety but personal interactions between themselves and inmates. The affective nature of these interactions directly influences the level of tension between officers and inmates and indirectly influences the safety, security, and control within the prison. The intensely personal nature of 24-hour-a-day supervision and the strong influence of correctional supervision on the daily lives of inmates have been widely noted (Johnson, 1996; Johnson and Price, 1981; Kauffman, 1981, 1988). The importance of the interpersonal aspect of the correctional officer's role in maintaining control of inmates has also been recognized by Gilbert and Riddell (1983:34), who wrote, "Correctional officers must manage the prisoner population, through face to face interactions, in a way that assists in the development and maintenance of a stable, orderly prison in which the living and working environment is safe, secure, and humane; and, where survival with dignity and respect is ensured so that personal growth and self change is possible." From this perspective safety, security, and control may be viewed as byproducts of the personal interactions between officers and inmates that characterize the prison environment. This feature of the job for correctional officers is often unrecognized but is highly consistent with Muir's model of discretionary behavior.

Although the work of both correctional officers and police officers involves the use of state-authorized coercive power and affords officers considerable discretion, these occupations are not identical. The occupations have different job dimensions, and consequently the nature of their discretionary behavior is different. For example, correctional officers are focused on delivery of correctional services to offenders held in confinement, whereas police officers are focused on order maintenance and delivery of law enforcement services to free citizens. Correctional officers also have less opportunity than police officers to pursue interests or initiatives that take them away from their area of responsibility. Patrol officers may retreat to their patrol car and ride. Police officers may also use the patrol car to avoid situations by simply "not seeing them" and driving past them. Consequently, the behavioral descriptors used in Muir's typology for police officers must be modified when applied to correctional officers. Table 2 provides a comparison of behavioral descriptors for police and correctional officers.

Table 2   Discretionary work style descriptors for officers based on Muir's typology

Style Type	Police Officers	Correctional Officers
Professional	Develops the beat	Develops the housing unit
	Takes educated risks	Takes educated risks
	Provides citizens advice on law and government	Provides inmates advice on rules and regulations
	Increases pressure over time to correct behavior	Increases pressure over time to change behavior
	Uses arrest as a last resort	Uses the "write-up" as a last resort
	Tries to preserve the dignity of citizens through the use of non-demeaning behaviors and attitudes	Tries to preserve the dignity of inmates through the use of non-demeaning behaviors and attitudes
	Views offenders as not much different from self	Views offenders as not much different from self
	Empathizes with the human condition of citizens and offenders	Empathizes with the human condition of inmates
	Allows for exceptions in his/her own behavior and that of others	Allows for exceptions in his/her own behavior and that of others
	Uses coercion and force judiciously	Uses coercion and force judiciously
	Calm and easygoing	Calm and easygoing
	Articulate and open	Articulate and open
	Focuses on attaining justice for individuals	Focuses on ensuring the due process and decency in security and control tasks
	Views most other officers as being enforcer-oriented	Views most other officers as being enforcer-oriented
Reciprocator	Allows local "toughs" to keep citizens in line, a mutual accommodation	Allows inmate leaders to keep the unit quiet, a mutual accommodation
	Uses clinical/social work strategies to help people "worthy" of assistance	Uses clinical/social work strategies to help inmates "worthy" of assistance
	Rationalizes situations	Rationalizes situations
	Attempts to educate, cure, or solve the citizen's problems	Attempts to educate, cure, or solve the inmate's problems
	Low tolerance for rejection of offered assistance	Low tolerance for rejection of offered assistance
	Easily frustrated	Easily frustrated
	Often does not use coercion when it should be used	Often does not use coercion when it should be used
	Inconsistent job performance	Inconsistent job performance
	Irrational behavior by citizens stymies the officer	Irrational behavior by inmates stymies the officer
	Often displays a superior attitude toward others	Often displays a superior attitude toward others
	Highly articulate	Highly articulate

Style Type	Police Officers	Correctional Officers
Enforcer	Aggressive law enforcement	Aggressive rule enforcement
	Makes many arrests	Issues many "tickets"
	Actively seeks violations	Actively seeks violations
	Frequently uses force or excessive force	Frequently uses force or excessive force
	Tends to view order maintenance and ser-vice functions as not a part of police work	Tends to view treatment functions as what "others" do with or for the inmates
	Strict enforcement orientation, limits service and order maintenance duties	Strict security and control orientation, limits service delivery duties
	Little or no empathy for the human condition of citizens/offenders	Little or no empathy for the human condition of inmates
	Citizens often complain about this officer's behavior	Inmates often submit grievances over this officer's behavior
	Rigid, rule-bound, makes few exceptions even when appropriate	Rigid, rule-bound, makes few exceptions even when appropriate
	Maintains a dualistic view of human nature (good/bad, cop/criminal, strong/weak)	Maintains a dualistic view of human nature (good/bad, officer/inmate, strong/weak)
	Dislikes management	Dislikes management
	Postures for effect	Postures for effect
	Crazy/brave "John Wayne" behaviors, takes unnecessary risks	Crazy/brave "John Wayne" behaviors, takes unnecessary risks
	Views other officers as "soft" or "weak" if not like him/her	Views other officers as "soft" or "weak" if not like him/her
	Views officers like him/her as being the majority of officers	Views officers like him/her as being the majority of officers
Avoider	Often leaves situations as quickly as possible	Often leaves situations as quickly as possible
	Tends to view most functions as not being "real" police work or part of the job	Tends to view human communications with inmates as not being part of security and control
	Uses the patrol car to reduce contact with citizens	Uses the mechanical aspects of security and control to reduce contact with inmates
	Often the last to arrive in response to an emergency	Often among the last to arrive at an emergency scene
	Likely to seek refuge from the street in the patrol car	Likely to select tower duty/isolated positions away from inmates
	Plays the "phony" tough and frequently backs down	Plays the "phony" tough and frequently backs down
	Tends to blame others for avoidance behaviors or inadequacies	Tends to blame others for avoidance behaviors or inadequacies
	Structures the work to reduce chances of observing offenses and use of coercion	Structures the work to avoid observing infractions and use of coercion
	Avoids confrontations and interactions with offenders and citizens	Avoids confrontations and interactions with inmates

As early as 1982 the Arizona Department of Corrections formally recognized the discretionary power of correctional officers in their training documents. The values-based ends to which correctional officers could appropriately apply their work style preferences were characterized as the following objectives:

1. To maximize cooperation among all participants in the correctional setting—inmates and staff alike.

2. To promote interaction between inmates and staff which demonstrates how individuals should interact in their communities and homes.

3. To harmonize, as much as possible, the need for security with respect for human dignity.

4. To develop a consistent scheme of rewards and deterrents which lead inmates to view the use of your [the officer's] discretion as fair and just. By "fair and just" we mean that the use of rewards and deterrents requires that you balance fitting rules and regulations to the individual with assurance that like situations receive the same response (Arizona Department of Corrections, 1982:4).

The same document goes on to clarify the meaning of "human concern" and provide values-oriented parameters to guide officers in the appropriate use of their discretionary power:

> While it is important for you to develop a sense of human concern for your clients [inmates], you must direct this concern to situations rather than to creating favorites. In short, it is legitimate for you to show human compassion for particular situations (e.g., inmates receiving dear john letters from home), and therefore use your *discretion* [italics added] to work with any inmate who finds himself (herself) in such a situation. However, using your *discretion* [italics added] to make life easier for those inmates you personally like and hard for those who you dislike is not the appropriate way to express your human compassions. (Arizona Department of Corrections, 1982:4)

Prisons are complex organizations that use the symbolic threat of force as the visible means of control to retain inmates within the institution (Etzioni, 1975). They are also "total institutions." Prisoners live, work, sleep, and play within the same general area and under the same authority. All prisoners are treated alike and their activities are preplanned, structured, and strictly scheduled (Goffman, 1961). In short, life in a prison tends to be highly regimented. Controls are placed upon the totality of life for those who are confined and upon the work life of employees.

In order to maintain this regimentation, prisons have typically used paramilitary structures similar to those adopted by police. The military model has historically been viewed as the most appropriate model for the management of formal social control agencies like police forces and prisons (Stinchcombe, 1980). Criminal justice organizations are still characterized by paramilitary structure with strict chains of command, vertical management, centralization, emphasis on formal communication, top-down decision making, written rules for internal control, detailed policies and procedures, limited autonomy, and a view of employees as unwilling workers in need of constant supervision. These features are consistent with Weber's (cited in Gerth and Mills, 1946:196–264) and Wilson's (1887/1941) conceptualization of the "classical model of organization" and are readily observed in most prisons.

Paramilitary organizational structures emphasize strict compliance to orders issued by superiors. Almost every aspect of the paramilitary organization is used in an attempt to reduce or eliminate individual discretion held by employees. The rules, regulations, and policies created are explicitly intended for this purpose. Such efforts are based on faulty assumptions rooted in the classical model of organization. Hierarchy, rules, and regulations do not limit discretionary power; they simply make it more dangerous for employees to openly exercise their discretionary power. Workers who continue to make independent decisions in spite of threats to their careers retain their discretionary power. Each correctional officer must supervise inmates in a wide variety of situations and circumstances that cannot be fully prescribed by formal policies and procedures. Consequently, full 100% enforcement of all rules is impossible. Under these conditions officers are placed in a no-win situation. Attempts to attain full enforcement are among the surest ways to increase hostility, tension, and danger within a prison, because they sharply increase the number of daily confrontations between inmates and staff. On the other hand, selective enforcement exposes officers to censure, discipline, or termination if their decisions backfire and become known to formal authorities (Johnson, 1996:206).

Security and control in prisons are attained mostly through interpersonal communication skills and discretionary application of coercive authority. The line officer's objective is to gain inmate compliance with as little confrontation as possible. Every correctional officer must learn to enforce rules, regulations, and policies in reasonable and appropriate ways given the situations encountered. Officers must also learn to use human relations skills in ways that are appropriate to both the human condition of inmates and the seriousness of the situation.

The classical model of organization used in most prisons ignores the discretionary power held by line officers. Classical organizations also fail to recognize the importance of discretionary decisions by officers to the attainment of a stable, secure, and safe prison. Instead managers in these organizations insist that officers "go by the book." This exhortation is problematic because line officers are greatly outnumbered by the inmates at all times. If inmates decide en masse not to obey these rules, there is little that officers can do about it. The quandary faced by line officers is that rigid enforcement of rules drives up the incentives for inmates to act out in disruptive ways and decreases both officer safety and the security of the institution. When officers are denied authority to decide how and when to exercise their coercive power and prohibited from making reasonable exceptions to rules, there are increased tensions between the reality of their job and the expectations placed upon them by management. Under these conditions officers are likely to become highly frustrated, rule-bound, hostile, demeaning, antagonistic, abusive, neglectful, or avoidance-oriented when dealing with inmates. The negative impacts of such behaviors are exacerbated when officers also have poor interpersonal communication skills. The rigid and unrealistic management expectations imposed by the classical model foster negative discretionary behaviors and attitudes among officers and threaten security and control by undercutting the interpersonal aspects of inmate management performed by correctional officers.

Consequently, the absolute power of the officer is more fiction than reality (Johnson, 1996; Kauffman, 1988; Sykes, 1980). An officer's control over inmates does not depend on strength, imposing stature, threat of force, or rigid application of rules. Rather, as Muir's typology suggests, control over inmates depends on well-developed verbal skills of persuasion, appropriate use of coercive authority, human relations skills, and leadership ability to gain voluntary cooperation of inmates (Johnson, 1996).

Correctional agencies, like other classical organizations, overrely on formal structures such as hierarchy and regulations to control individual discretion. Change is often imposed without direct connection to or commitment from correctional officers. In many cases the philosophy, rationale, and values behind these changes have not been explained or discussed with line officers. In addition, correctional managers tend to view line correctional officers with suspicion similar to that with which line officers view inmates (Johnson, 1996:204–206). As a result, enmity and distrust are easily fostered between managers and line officers. Staff resistance is especially common when formal management controls or operational changes are viewed as being at odds with the values and interests held by line officers. For these reasons, formal bureaucratic controls are unlikely to be effective as a guide for individual discretionary behavior. By default, classical management in a prison leaves the discretionary behavior of correctional officers almost totally unguided under the paramilitary guise of rigid control. Establishing boundaries that structure discretionary behavior among line correctional officers will require that managers provide clearly defined values and ethical structures, establish widely understood and broadly accepted linkages to the values, interests, and concerns of line officers, and hold frequent discussions of the moral and ethical dilemmas regularly faced by line officers.

Correctional organizations are not military organizations. They are primarily social service organizations. In contrast to military organizations, the most important correctional decisions are made by the lowest-ranking members of the institution through their routine and daily interaction with inmates. The meaning of confinement for inmates is determined at the face-to-face level between the line officer and the inmate by the nature of their interpersonal relationships. Effective supervision of inmates depends mostly on the interpersonal communication skills of line correctional officers rather than rank, uniform, military bearing, command voice, or other militaristic attribute. Furthermore, the personal safety of correctional officers depends on their ability to supervise inmates without creating or escalating confrontations with inmates unnecessarily.

The concern of correctional officers for their personal safety provides the underlying rationale for the "passion" dimension needed to apply Muir's model to correctional officers. Uncaring, rigid, and rule-bound enforcement behaviors by officers jeopardize everyone's safety and make voluntary cooperation by inmates unlikely. Furthermore, cynicism, threats, intimidation, physical force, abuse, or neglect by officers toward inmates makes unnecessary enemies among the inmate population, inflames their fears, fosters increased hatred for correctional staff, and drives up the incentives for inmates to attack officers, destroy property, assault each other, and escape. Each of these outcomes is a direct threat to institutional security and control and to the safety of officers. The intuitive but often unstated awareness of officers that their safety depends largely on constructive professional relationships with inmates is the foundation for genuine concern for the human condition of inmates. Such relationships are highly controlling because they are based on human decency, honesty, directness, respectful treatment, and consistent actions that demonstrate the genuineness of an officer's concern for the welfare of inmates. Constructive professional relationships between officers and inmates lead to voluntary cooperation by most inmates.

There will always be some distrust and tension between line officers and inmates because of the officers' rule enforcement responsibilities and the con games that inmates play. Nevertheless, some level of human interaction between officers and inmates beyond that of keeper and kept is an essential aspect of inmate management. It is the collective force of thousands of daily and hourly personal interactions between inmates and officers that drives up tensions and hostilities or quells them, fosters resistance or compliance, and engenders confrontation or cooperation in any prison. The 24-hour-a-day treatment provided inmates by routine interactions with line officers should be recognized as the primary and most influential treatment program offered by any prison. The nature and quality of these interactions will largely determine the extent to which prison security, control, and safety are attained. The character of these routine interactions may also determine the effectiveness of formal treatment programs.

Factors such as classification systems that maintain separation of inmates, grievance systems that resolve inmate complaints, programs and services that reduce idleness and provide treatment opportunities, and adequate resources that minimize conflicts due to scarcity, as well as policies and procedures, are all important elements of prison security and control that are provided or directed by correctional managers. However, these inmate management strategies may be rendered ineffective by a cadre of indecent, disrespectful, insensitive, and rigidly rule-bound correctional officers or by concerted resistance by officers. The effectiveness of formal inmate management strategies is highly dependent on the discretionary power of line officers to either carry them out as envisioned by management or quietly subvert them in subtle ways.

Simon (1976) identified the power of the informal organization within every formal organization. The informal organization is composed of social and professional support networks among employees (e.g., "the locker room") and under some conditions may have more power than the established hierarchy to control the actions of line workers. Therefore, the discretionary power of line workers can be used to oppose as well as support management directives. In prisons, the informal organization of line officers controls inmate movement and therefore inmate access to programs and services. If these officers wish, they can discourage inmate participation in various programs and services simply by retarding the movement of inmates or otherwise "hassling" inmates who do participate.

New employees are socialized to varying degrees into the informal organization during their probationary period as coworkers and supervisors model the work behaviors that they are expected to emulate. As the values, attitudes, and behaviors of new employees increasingly approximate those of coworkers and supervisors, acceptance by their colleagues improves and they are progressively socialized by the informal organization. However, the values, attitudes, and behaviors advocated by the informal organization may not be consistent with those desired by the management team (McGregor, 1978; Simon, 1976).

The policy process by which formal rules are generated is dynamic and fraught with implementation problems. Implementation is dependent on line-level employees who convert written policy and procedure into concerted actions and services delivered. Faithful implementation by line officers (i.e., the informal organization) becomes less likely when a new policy or program is perceived as a confrontation to the values, interests, beliefs, and experiences of line officers (Hall and Loucks, 1977; Mazmanian and Sabatier, 1983). Nevertheless, the paramilitary model of organization has traditionally assumed that policy will automatically be followed by faithful implementation; if not, then faulty employees will be removed and replaced by those who will implement the policy. There is ample theoretical basis to conclude that line correctional officers exercise extensive discretionary power in their professional roles. This power may be exercised in a manner that is either constructive or destructive to inmates, staff, and official policy. The traditional assumptions of faithful and deliberate implementation by line correctional officers are highly questionable.

Conclusions and Implications

Correctional officers, like police officers, are social service personnel. They are required to take independent actions and make independent decisions that affect the lives of clients. They are also expected to use control behaviors that are consistent with both the human conditions of their clients and the enforcement situation. These circumstances require flexibility, reasonable judgment, sensitivity to others, responsible actions, appropriate use of coercion, and, at times, exceptions to formal policy. Unfortunately, the autocratic, authoritarian, and militaristic style used by most correctional organizations attempts to suppress the ability of correctional officers to make reasonable and effective decisions. The militaristic management style also forces officers to make decisions that are not recognized by formal policy and procedure. This structural quandary places line correctional officers in an untenable position. On the one hand, if their decisions turn out well, no one really cares. On the other hand, if their decisions turn out badly, officers may be disciplined or terminated. The inconsistency between such management expectations and the reality of the job for line officers creates tension or conflict that has been linked by some researchers to alienation and cynicism among correctional officers (Cheek and Miller, 1982; Poole and Regoli, 1981).

Correctional supervisors and managers often ignore the critical role that individual decision making by line officers plays in correctional practice. They usually rely on written rules and regulations as the means to structure officer behavior and ignore the underlying values and assumptions that actually guide officer behavior. Rarely do these organizations formally acknowledge that the exercise of discretionary power by line officers is inherent to their occupation and is used to resolve many minor problems before they accumulate to become major management problems. It is therefore ironic that the control-oriented paramilitary structure of prisons should result in line officers being provided little or no guidance for the exercise of their discretionary power over the lives of inmates. In this sense the realities of prison work for line correctional officers are not consistent with the classical (paramilitary) structure of most prisons.

Muir's typology of police discretionary behavior can theoretically be adapted to the study of correctional officers and provide a conceptual framework for understanding their discretionary power. This suggests that correctional executives may need to change the way they have conceptualized prison management if they hope to guide the discretionary power that is applied by those officers who work for them. Correctional managers and supervisors need to formally recognize that full enforcement of prison rules, policies, and procedures is an impossibility and communicate this understanding to line officers. They must also allow correctional officers to make discretionary decisions in complex situations where policy is absent, vague, or inconsistent with the circumstances encountered. Executives, middle managers, and supervisory personnel should also expect variation in work style among line officers. Finally, these managers need to recognize that the discretionary power held by correctional officers is guided less by formal rules and hierarchy than by an explicit understanding of the shared operational values and ethical principles that govern correctional practice (Pollock, 1994).

The development of an ethical framework to guide officers in the application of their discretionary power requires frequent discussion and debate (i.e., formal training experiences) of the operational and ethical quandaries that are found at all levels of prison work. Although managers must allow and expect correctional officers to make ethically defensible exceptions to rules as a routine part of an officer's job, managers are responsible for helping these officers understand the appropriate boundaries of their discretionary power. When the decisions and behaviors of line officers are reasonable (given the situational context they face), consistent with a common set of values and ethical parameters, and legal, they should be supported by those in leadership positions. As a general principle, employees should not be disciplined for making reasonable exceptions to formal rules in complex situations. This is especially important where strict adherence to the rules and regulations would make little sense or would endanger security, control, or safety. Improvements in decision making should be attained through training rather than by disciplinary actions by supervisors and managers.

If future research confirms the efficacy of Muir's typology of discretionary behavior when applied to correctional officers, there will be a need for less rigid models of organization for prisons. Operational policies and procedures and hierarchical supervision are insufficient guides for discretionary behavior because these structures only make it more risky for officers to make discretionary decisions when formal rules do not fit the situations they face. In the absence of values-based ethical principles consistent with management intent, individual discretionary power is largely unguided by management concerns. In classical organizations such as prisons, the discretionary power of line officers is structured mostly by the extent to which officers understand and internalize the values of the formal and informal organization. Because the values of the formal organization are typically vague, abstract, or unstated, it is the values of the informal organization that most influence the work behaviors and attitudes of correctional officers. When the values of the formal organization are perceived to be at odds with those of the informal organization, there are often increased conflicts between management and line officers and greater operational inconsistencies between shifts, work groups, and individual officers. Such outcomes usually conflict with the objectives established by the official hierarchy. Unfortunately, the illusion that the discretionary behavior of line officers is highly structured by the classical organization of prisons persists and will probably continue as long as correctional executives believe it to be the only organizational model suitable for prison management.

Endnotes

1 Neither police officers nor correctional officers are full professionals in the classical sense of that term. Instead they are something less than full professionals (i.e., paraprofessionals), who earn their living applying a specific body of knowledge and skill. Muir's use of this term refers only to a categorization of officers viewed as recognizably different from other types.

2 Testimony in the 1995 trial of O. J. Simpson revealed similar behaviors among Los Angeles police officers in their efforts to "fight crime" by any means possible.

References

Arizona Department of Corrections. (1982). *Channeling discretion in the correctional environment.* Phoenix, AZ: Author.

Beccaria, C. (1963). *On crimes and punishment.* Indianapolis, IN: Bobbs-Merrill Educational Publishing. (Original work published 1764.)

Brown, M. (1981). *Working the street.* New York: Russell Sage Foundation.

Cheek, F., & Miller, M. (1982). *Prisoners of life: A study of occupational stress among state correctional officers.* Washington, DC: American Federation of State, County and Municipal Employees, AFL-CIO.

Cullen, F. T., Lutze, F. E., Link, B. G., & Wolfe, N. T. (1989). The correctional orientation of prison guards: Do officers support rehabilitation? *Federal Probation, 53*(1), 33–42.

Durham, A. M. (1994). *Crisis and reform: Current issues in American punishment.* Boston, MA: Little, Brown & Company.

Etzioni, A. (1975). *A comparative analysis of complex organizations—On power and their correlates.* New York: The Free Press.

Gerth, H., & Mills, C. (1946). *From Max Weber: Essays in sociology.* New York: Oxford University Press.

Gilbert, M. J., & Riddell, J. (1983). Skills for achieving security, control, and public protection. In American Correctional Association (Ed.), *Correctional officers: Power, pressure, and responsibility* (pp. 31–36). College Park, MD: American Correctional Association.

Goffman, E. (1961). *Asylums.* Garden City, NY: Anchor Books.

Hall, G., & Loucks, S. (1977). A developmental model for determining whether a treatment is actually implemented. *American Education Research Journal, 14,* 263–276.

Hobbes, T. (1981). *Leviathan.* New York: Penguin Books. (Original work published 1651.)

Irwin, J., & Austin, J. (1994). *It's about time: America's imprisonment binge.* Belmont, CA: Wadsworth Publishing Company.

Johnson, R. (1996). *Hard time: Understanding and reforming the prison* (2nd ed.). Belmont, CA: Wadsworth Publishing Company.

Johnson, R., & Price, S. (1981). The complete correctional officer: Human service and the human environment of prison. *Criminal Justice and Behavior, 8,* 343–373.

Jurik, N. (1985). Individual and organizational determinants of correctional officer attitudes toward inmates. *Criminology, 23,* 523–539.

Kauffman, K. (1981, July). Prison officers' attitudes and perceptions of attitudes—A case of pluralistic ignorance. *Journal of Research in Crime and Delinquency, 18,* 272–294.

Kauffman, K. (1988). *Prison officers and their world.* Cambridge, MA: Harvard University Press.

Lipsky, M. (1973). Street-level bureaucracy and the analysis of urban reform. In G. Frederickson (Ed.), *Neighborhood control in the 1970s* (pp. 103–115). New York: Chandler Publishing.

Locke, J. (1980). *Second treatise of government.* Indianapolis, IN: Hackett Publishing Company. (Original work published 1690.)

Lombardo, L. (1989). *Guards imprisoned: Correctional officers at work* (2nd ed.). Cincinnati, OH: Anderson Publishing Company.

Machiavelli, N. (1980). *The prince.* New York: The New American Library of World Literature. (Original work published 1513.)

Mazmanian, D. A., & Sabatier, P. A. (1983). *Implementation and public policy.* Dallas, TX: Scott, Foresman and Company.

McGregor, D. M. (1996). The human side of enterprise. In J. S. Ott (Ed.), *Classic readings in organizational behavior* (2nd ed., pp. 57–62). Belmont, CA: Wadsworth Publishing Company.

Meyerson, B. A. (1992). Role definition for the practitioner of correctional supervision: Transcending the role conflict in theory and practice. In C. A. Hartjen & E. E. Rhine (Eds.), *Correctional theory and practice* (pp. 82–96). Chicago: Nelson-Hall Publishers.

Muir, W. (1977). *Street corner politicians.* Chicago: University of Chicago Press.

Philliber, S. (1987). Thy brother's keeper: A review of the literature on correctional officers. *Justice Quarterly, 4*(l), 9–37.

Pollock, J. M. (1994). *Ethics in crime and justice: Dilemmas and decisions* (2nd ed.). Belmont, CA: Wadsworth Publishing Company.

Poole, E., & Regoli, R. (1981, August). Alienation in prison: An examination of the work relations of prison guards. *Criminology, 19,* 251–270.

Simon, H. (1976). *Administrative behavior* (3rd ed.). New York: The Free Press.

Stinchcombe, J. B. (1980). Beyond bureaucracy: A reconsideration of the "professional" police. *Police Studies, 3,* 49–61.

Sykes, G. M. (1980). The defects of total power. In B. M. Crouch (Ed.), *The keepers: Prison guards and contemporary corrections* (pp. 225–246). Springfield, IL: Charles C. Thomas.

Weber, M. (1971). Legitimate authority and bureaucracy. In D. S. Pugh (Ed.), *Organization theory* (pp. 15–30). New York: Penguin Books.

Whitehead, J. T., & Lindquist, C. A. (1989). Determinants of correctional officer's professional orientation. *Justice Quarterly, 6*(l), 69–87.

Wilson, W. (1941, December). The study of administration. *Political Science Quarterly, 56,* 481–506. (Original work published 1887.)

SECTION 4

PROCESSES IN
CRIMINAL JUSTICE ORGANIZATIONS

This section explores the processes found within criminal justice organizations, including the important processes of decision making and addressing organizational effectiveness. Criminal justice administrators are keenly aware of these processes, which bring them under public scrutiny and criticism. How criminal justice officials make decisions and are able to defend them against severe criticism can be a test of their effectiveness. In addition, both decision making and organizational effectiveness are related. Perceived patterns of decision making define, in part, how effective a criminal justice organization is viewed by the public. As a result, it is problematic as to which processes are being evaluated and understood since many processes are inextricably intertwined and difficult to separate. Nevertheless, criminal justice administrators understand outcomes and invariably processes have both general and specific effects. It is these effects that they attempt to control as a critical part of criminal justice administration.

The control of discretion has been a common concern in criminal justice. The dominant view has often been that similar offenders who commit similar crimes should be treated similarly by the criminal justice system. The first chapter in this section examines the impact of a reform that was often regarded as pursuing that goal, federal sentencing guidelines. Keith Wilmot and Cassia Spohn (article 19) present an empirical investigation of the impact of the guidelines and find that in many cases discretion has been transferred from judges to prosecutors. Those officials have leeway in charging decisions and particularly in the number of charges to file. The data show that even though a defendant is convicted of only one charge, multiple charges do increase sanctions. The ability to cooperate with prosecutors also has an impact and may be tied to issues of class and race in the data. The critical point is that the effort to remove discretion by structural reform may have simply transferred influences in decision making to actors in criminal justice other than the judge.

In article 20, Rachel Boba and John Crank examine the record of innovation in policing focusing on the adoption of Problem Oriented Policing

(POP). The authors argue that despite the merits of POP it has often been implemented in a manner inconsistent with the traditional accountability structures of policing. Supervisors are generally removed from the problem-analysis process and have found little role in this innovation. Even community policing and certainly the process of COMPSTAT have reconsidered accountability in a manner consistent with the traditional organization of policing. The authors go on to present a detailed analysis of POP and make recommendations for implementing this process in a manner that engages supervisors and builds on the traditional lines of authoring and accountability in the field.

The final three articles in this section explore decision making by focusing on the exercise of discretion among actors within the criminal justice system. Two of the three are considered classic explorations of the importance of discretion in criminal justice decision making; the third is an application of some of those classic ideas.

William Waegel (article 21) shows how case routinization is essential in detective work. By offering an explanation as to the nature of "interpretive activities" among detectives, Waegel documents how they handle the pressures of their positions while effectively dealing with the uncertainty of tasks, and with the many demands of both victims and other actors in the criminal justice system. His analysis highlights the importance of recognizing a confluence of factors that affect the exercise of discretion among detectives.

Albert Matheny (article 22) applies a similar logic to the practice of plea bargaining. By offering a specific model of plea bargaining, he develops an understanding predicated on how bargain decisions are contextually made and constrained by a number of organizational dictums. First and foremost, he urges for recognition of the importance of uncertainty in the process of plea bargaining. His analysis takes us beyond purely formalistic descriptions of plea bargaining and suggests other directions to pursue for those interested in reforming the plea bargaining process.

In the last chapter in this section Alexes Harris (article 23) extends our analysis of decision making in criminal justice. The author uses the process of juvenile court waiver hearings to explore individual and organization factors as they influence waiver decisions. After a review of research on juvenile waivers, interview data are used to explore how judges consider the degree of a juvenile's sophistication, and the seriousness of the offense, in the construction of a story that supports their decision. It is noted that this decision contains elements similar to those of long hearings but must be made in a much briefer time frame. The process thus culminates with a ceremony of legitimation to support the underlying characterizations of the youth involved. It is a process that combines influences from juvenile justice, criminal justice, and organizational factors. The article extends our understanding of the classic processes discussed in the two previous chapters and allows the reader to apply those ideas in a new setting.

19

Prosecutorial Discretion and Real-Offense Sentencing
An Analysis of Relevant Conduct under the Federal Sentencing Guidelines

KEITH A. WILMOT AND CASSIA SPOHN

With the establishment of the U.S. Sentencing Commission in 1984 and the subsequent enactment of the Federal Sentencing Guidelines Manual (FSGM) in 1987, the major premise guiding federal sentencing was to reduce judicial discretion and unwarranted disparity by prescribing like sentences for like defendants convicted of the same offense (Nagel & Schulhofer, 1992). Under the guidelines, judges are mandated to avoid "unwarranted sentencing disparities among defendants with similar records who have been found guilty of similar criminal conduct" (28 U.S.C. §991[b][1][B]). This transfer of formal sentencing authority from federal judges to the Sentencing Commission replaced the long-standing tradition that had given judges extensive discretion to determine criminal sentences within statutory limits (Stith & Cabranes, 1998). Likewise, the real-offense sentencing system, as opposed to the charge-offense system, was adopted by the Federal Sentencing Commission to reduce prosecutorial discretion in charging (Heaney, 1991; Reitz, 1993; Wilkins, 1992).

Current research, however, suggests that disparity may still exist within the scope of the federal guidelines and, more specifically, that discretion has shifted from the judge to the prosecutor (Albonetti, 1997; Heaney, 1991; Nagel & Schulhofer, 1992; Stith & Cabranes, 1998; Tonry, 1996). As

Keith A. Wilmot and Cassia Spohn, *Criminal Justice Policy Review*, Vol. 15(3), pp. 324–343, © 2004 by Sage Publications. Reprinted by permission of Sage Publications.

Albonetti (1997) explains, the prosecutor can circumvent the guidelines through charging, guilty plea negotiations, and departure motions. The prosecutor's power is further enhanced by the fact that sentences imposed under the federal sentencing guidelines are based not only on the charge of conviction but also on the "real offense" or the offender's "actual behavior," which is identified by the Commission as "relevant conduct" (Tonry, 1996, pp. 42–43). Federal judges, in other words, are required to consider not simply the seriousness of the offense for which the defendant has been convicted but the actual conduct—the relevant conduct—that landed the defendant in court. This can include uncharged conduct, acquitted conduct, conduct described in dismissed counts, and conduct of coconspirators (Lear, 1993).

Consider, for example, the case of an offender who has been convicted of possession of 2 g of crack cocaine. He was initially charged with possession of 5 g of crack cocaine and possession of an unregistered firearm; however, the U.S. Attorney prosecuting the case agreed to reduce the amount of cocaine he would be held accountable for and drop the firearms charge in exchange for a guilty plea. If at the sentencing hearing the prosecutor can prove "by a preponderance of the evidence and not beyond a reasonable doubt" that the offender did, in fact, possess an unregistered firearm and 5 rather than 2 g of cocaine, the judge is required to take this into consideration in determining the offense severity score. As Senior Circuit Court Judge G. W. Heaney of the Eighth Circuit Court of Appeals observed, the guidelines are not mere guidelines, they are sentencing directives, and the judge, when a person has been found guilty of a particular offense, has no alternative but to impose the sentence that is required by the guidelines, including the sentence that is based not only on the conviction charge but also on relevant conduct (G. W. Heaney, personal communication, May 24, 2000).

The relevant conduct principle, which Judge W. Wilkins, the first chairman of the United States Sentencing Commission (USSC), characterized as the cornerstone (Wilkins & Steer, 1990) of the federal sentencing guidelines, is designed to prevent circumvention of the guidelines through charging and plea-bargaining decisions by the prosecutor. According to Judge Wilkins, this feature of the guidelines "significantly reduces the impact of prosecutorial charge selection and plea bargaining by ensuring that the court will be able to consider the defendant's real-offense behavior in imposing a guideline sentence" (Wilkins & Steer, 1990, p. 504). Critics of real-offense sentencing charge that the concept of relevant conduct, which is an "invention of the United States Sentencing Commission" that is unknown outside the federal sentencing guidelines, is "remarkably abstract and difficult to apply" (Stith & Cabranes, 1998, p. 70). They also contended that the system enhances the power of the prosecutor. As Judge Heaney (1991) observed, the prosecutor still determines who will be charged and what charge will be filed; in addition, the prosecutor's collective records substantiate the primary factual basis for establishing a defendant's base offense level and offense characteristics. Therefore, the prosecutor alone controls the charge, the information concerning relevant conduct, and offense characteristics that serve as a basis for a sentence (Heaney, 1991).

The Research Question and Hypotheses

The primary objective of this research was to document the effect of prosecutorial charging decisions on sentencing. Because relevant conduct can include unadjudicated conduct that is part of the same course of conduct or common scheme or plan as the offense of conviction (i.e., acquitted counts and dismissed charges (FSGM §1B1.3[a] [2]), it is important to analyze the original charges for which the defendant was indicted, and not simply the charges of conviction. Because the sentencing guidelines severely constrain the discretion of the judge, charging and plea-bargaining decisions—which determine the charge of conviction—assume a pivotal role in the process. Coupled with the reality of real-offense sentencing, which requires the judge to consider dismissed charges and acquitted charges, this means that the original charges are a key determinant of the eventual sentence and any departures. Two similar offenders convicted of identical crimes, in other words, may receive different sentences based on the presence or absence of relevant conduct. We therefore hypothesize that the number of charges (counts) within the indictment will have a positive and statistically significant effect on the length of sentence imposed on offenders convicted of a single count.

Another key premise of the current study is that the original charges filed by the prosecutor are an important determinant of the eventual sentence and any downward departures. Consistent with the reasoning that guides the first hypothesis, we suggest that similar offenders who have been convicted of the same crime may not have the same likelihood of receiving a departure, and if they do receive a departure, they may receive different sentence discounts based on the effects of the charging decision and the subsequent consequences of relevant conduct and substantial assistance motions. The federal judges interviewed for the current study stated that their sentencing decisions are affected by relevant conduct—relevant conduct that is introduced or not introduced as evidence by the federal prosecutor and considered at sentencing based on a preponderance of the evidence standard.[1]

We suggest that the number of counts the defendant is facing will have a positive effect on the likelihood that the defendant will receive a departure but a negative effect on the magnitude of the sentence discount (for those defendants who do receive a downward departure). Because our sample is composed of offenders convicted of drug offenses, most of the downward departures are departures for substantial assistance. In other words, most of the departures result from the offender's assistance in the prosecution and conviction of another person or persons in the drug distribution network. In these types of cases, defendants who are charged with more than one count are more likely than those facing a single count to be key players in a drug distribution operation. As a result, they would be more likely to have information that they could trade for a more lenient sentence. We therefore hypothesize that the number of charges (counts) within the indictment will have a positive and statistically significant effect on the likelihood that the defendant will receive any downward departure or a substantial assistance departure.

We predict, on the other hand, that the offender's relevant conduct (i.e., dismissed counts or acquitted counts) will have a negative effect on the magnitude of the sentence discount for those offenders who do receive a departure. If, as we contend, judges take relevant conduct into account in determining the appropriate sentence, they would be inclined to give greater sentence discounts to offenders who were originally charged with only one count than to similarly situated offenders who originally faced two or more counts. In other words, two offenders who were convicted of the same crime and who each received a downward departure may get different sentence discounts because of relevant conduct. We therefore test the hypothesis that the number of charges (counts) within the indictment will have a negative and statistically significant effect on the magnitude of the sentence discount for a downward departure or a substantial assistance departure.

Research Design and Method

Data

The data analyzed for this study are a subset of the 1995 Intensive Study Sample (ISS) developed by the USSC. The ISS is a randomly selected 5% sample (approximately 1,925 cases) of the 38,500 defendants who were sentenced between October 1, 1994, and September 30, 1995. The ISS includes variables from a separate data file, the Drug Supplemental Sample (DSS), as well as the monitoring variables routinely collected on all cases. This collection of variables represents one of the most detailed data compilations on cases sentenced under the federal Sentencing Reform Act.

The reason for selecting this data set is that it is the only data set that includes information on the actual criminal conduct that underlies the charges and guideline adjustments applied to the defendant at sentencing (as reported by the probation officer), the initial number of indictments, and the number of counts contained within the indictment (for drug cases only). This information is compiled for a particular year (1995), which should allow us to isolate the effects of guideline procedures for that particular year. Thus, the ISS provides the data necessary for analysis of the relationship between sentence length, prosecutorial decision making at the indictment stage, defendant characteristics, and legally relevant factors.

The ISS/DSS includes information regarding the number of indictments and charges only for offenders convicted of drug offenses. Therefore, in the current study we analyze sentences imposed in cases where the offender was convicted of a single count of a drug offense and where the primary offense type is either drug trafficking (95.7%),[2] use of a communication facility in a drug offense (.6%),[3] or possession of drugs (2.7%). We excluded cases in which the number of indictments and counts within the indictment were unknown, as well as cases involving drugs other than cocaine (powder), crack (cocaine base), heroin, marijuana, methamphetamine, methamphetamine (actual).[4] To eliminate one possible source of variation, we also excluded cases disposed of at trial ($n = 54$). Because our dependent variable is the length of sentence imposed on those who were incarcerated, we eliminated cases that resulted in a sentence of probation ($n = 39$). This left 360 cases for analysis.[5]

Although each of the 360 offenders included in the current study was convicted of a single count of a drug offense, many of them were originally charged with more than one count. As shown in Table 1, 38.9% of the offenders were charged with one count; the remaining offenders originally faced from 2 to 21 counts. For these offenders, then, the conduct included in the original charges—and not simply the conduct referenced in the charge of conviction—will be considered at sentencing. If, for example, a defendant was charged with one count of selling 80 g of cocaine and one count of selling 5 kg of marijuana, the total quantity of drugs involved will be aggregated to determine the seriousness of the offense. If one of the counts is dismissed by plea bargain, the defendant still will be held responsible for the total quantity

Table 1   Frequency Distribution for the Number of Counts within the Indictment (Number of Indictments = 1)

| | Number of Indictments | |
| | 1 | |
Number of Counts Contained Within the Indictment	**N**	**Percentage**
1	140	38.9
2	128	35.5
3	34	9.4
4	22	6.1
5	9	2.5
6	7	2.0
7	6	1.6
8	3	1.0
10	1	.25
11	2	.50
13	1	.25
14	1	.25
16	3	1.0
17	1	.25
19	1	.25
21	1	.25
Total	360	100.0

Source: Intensive Study Sample (U.S. Sentencing Commission, 1995).

of drugs referenced in the two-count indictment. Stated another way, the type and quantity of the drugs specified in the dismissed count will be considered in determining the final offense level.

Dependent Variables

The dependent and independent variables, their codes, and their frequencies are presented in Table 2. The dependent variables are (a) sentence length, (b) whether the defendant received any downward departure or a substantial assistance departure, (c) the magnitude of the sentence discount for a departure, and (d) the ratio between the sentence discount and the presumptive sentence (adjusted guideline minimum). Sentence length is a continuous variable and is operationalized as the length of incarceration in months; the minimum sentence is 3 months and the maximum sentence is life, which has been converted to 490 months. In addition, two dichotomous dependent vari-

Table 2   Descriptive Statistics and Coding of Variables Included in Ordinary Least Squares and Logistic Regression Models

	M	Frequency	Percentage
Dependent variables			
Sentence length in months	66.35		
Independent variables (legal)			
Departures			
No departure (No departure = 1)		188	53.1
Downward departure		166	37.9
Substantial assistance departure		134	9.0
Safety valve provision (yes = 1)		45	12.5
Total number of criminal history points applied	2.82		
Number of counts contained in the indictment	2.51		
Adjusted guideline minimum in months	93.67		
Independent variables—			
Offender characteristics (extralegal)			
Race			
White (White = 1)		92	25.5
Black		131	36.4
Hispanic		137	38.1
Gender			
Female (female = I)		44	12.2
Male		316	87.8
Citizenship			
U.S. citizen (U.S. = 1)		260	72.6
Noncitizen		98	27.4
Age	33.06		

Source: Intensive Study Sample (U.S. Sentencing Commission, 1995).

ables are used to measure the likelihood that a defendant will receive any downward departure or a substantial assistance departure. The magnitude of the sentence discount is the absolute difference (in months) between the presumptive sentence (i.e., the minimum sentence that the judge can impose without departing) and the actual sentence for those defendants who received a downward departure or a substantial assistance departure. If, for example, the presumptive guideline sentence is 90 months but the sentence imposed is 61 months, the magnitude of the sentence discount is 30 months. To control for the fact that defendants facing longer presumptive sentences have the possibility of larger discounts than those facing smaller presumptive sentences,[6] the ratio between the sentence discount and the presumptive sentence also is calculated. In the example above, the ratio would be 30/90 or .33.

Independent Variables: Legal Variables

The legally relevant variables in this study include the number of original counts contained within the indictment (discussed above), the offender's criminal history, the adjusted guideline minimum, and (for the analysis of sentence length) whether the offender received a downward departure. Because very few offenders were charged with more than two counts (see Table 1), in the multivariate analyses we differentiated between offenders charged with one count and those charged with more than one count.

The offender's criminal history is measured by the total number of criminal history points applied.[7] The adjusted guideline minimum or the presumptive sentence is included to control for the seriousness of the offense. Because the presumptive sentence incorporates is included to control for the seriousness of the offense. Because the presumptive sentence incorporates drug weights, specific offense characteristics, enhancements, and discounts for acceptance of responsibility, these factors do not need to be included in the model.[8] In fact, as Engen and Gainey (2000) contend, the presumptive sentence "most closely embodies what the guidelines would have the courts do" (p. 1251).

We also included a set of dummy variables that measure whether the defendant received a downward departure: no departure (reference category), downward departure, substantial assistance departure (those with Title 18 §553[e] motions are not differentiated), and application of the safety valve provision. By statute,[9] departures from the guidelines for defendant cooperation and "substantial assistance in the prosecution of other persons," may be granted only on motion of the government (Hofer & Blackwell, 1999, p. 26). Except for the safety valve provision,[10] these motions are the only means by which a mandatory minimum penalty can be waived (Hofer & Blackwell, 1999). A safety valve departure is available to first-time, nonviolent drug defendants who played a minimal role in the offense, who have a minimal criminal history, and who have minimal information to offer to obtain a substantial assistance departure.

Independent Variables: Extralegal Variables

The sentencing guidelines prohibit judges from taking the offender's race, sex, national origin, creed, or socioeconomic status into consideration when determining the appropriate sentence. Nonetheless, previous research has demonstrated that these extralegal variables may influence sentencing decisions. We therefore included the offender's race/ethnicity, gender, citizenship, and age as controls in the analysis.[11] The offender's race/ethnicity is measured by three dummy variables: Black, Hispanic, and White. White offenders are the reference category. Age is a continuous variable; gender (male/female) and citizenship status (citizen/noncitizen) are categorical variables.

Analytic Techniques

We used multivariate analytical techniques to test our hypotheses. We used ordinary least squares regression to analyze the influence of the independent variables[12] on the continuous sentence-length variable,[13] the magnitude of departures, and the ratio of the sentence discount to the presumptive sentence. We used logistic regression to analyze the effects of the independent variables on the two dichotomous dependent variables—whether the defendant received any downward departure or a substantial assistance departure.

Findings

We hypothesized that the number of charges (counts) within the indictment would have a positive and statistically significant effect on the length of sentence imposed on offenders convicted of a single count of a drug offense. As shown in Table 3, this hypothesis is confirmed. Defendants originally charged with more than one count received about 6 months longer than defendants charged with only one count. Despite the fact that all these offenders were convicted of a single count, in other words, those initially charged with more than one count were sentenced more harshly than those charged with only one count, net of other legally relevant factors.

This finding suggests that decisions made by the prosecutor at charging have an independent effect on sentence severity and confirms the importance of real-offense sentencing. Consider two defendants, each of whom is arrested and charged with possession of a controlled substance. Defendant A is charged with possession of 20 g of cocaine, whereas Defendant B is charged with possession of 20 g of cocaine and possession of 1 kg of marijuana. The prosecutor includes both counts in the original indictment for Defendant B; however, because of concerns about the quality of the evidence, [he] later dismisses the marijuana charge. Both defendants then plead guilty to an identical cocaine charge. At sentencing, the marijuana charge "reappears" as relevant conduct, and Defendant B receives a sentence more severe than Defendant A. Therefore, the charging decision by the federal prosecutor that encompasses the legal criteria to invoke the relevant conduct provision can

Table 3   Ordinary Least Squares Model of Incarceration Length (N = 348)

	Unstandardized Coefficients	Standardized Coefficients		Collinearity Statistics
	b	β	t value	VIF
Counts within the indictment > 1	6.107	.055	1.984*	1.018
Offender characteristics				
Female	−2.826	−.017	−.616	1.048
Hispanic	−1.699	−.015	−.350	2.486
Black	5.647	.050	1.305	1.963
Age	−8.050E-02	−.014	−.487	1.190
U.S. citizen	.974	.008	.218	1.772
Legal characteristics				
Total # of criminal history points applied	.508	.043	1.401	1.259
Downward departure	−24.373	−.129	− 4.909*	1.151
§5K1.1 departure	−49.352	−.439	−14.069*	1.314
Safety valve	−17.400	−.105	−3.537*	1.182
Adjusted guideline range minimum	.695	.830	25.825*	1.389
Hazard rate (prison/probation)	−22.549	.040	.256	1.647
Constant	20.465		.023	

Source: Intensive Study Sample (U.S. Sentencing Commission, 1995).
Note: R^2 = .750. VIF = variance inflation factors. Dependent variable: Total number of months of imprisonment ordered.
*Statistically significant at .05.

lead to disparity in the form of unfairness in sentencing. Similar offenders who have been convicted of identical crimes may, because of dismissed conduct considered at the sentencing hearing under the preponderance of the evidence standard, receive different sentences based on real-offense sentencing.

We also hypothesized that the number of original charges would affect the defendant's likelihood of receiving a downward departure. As shown in Table 4, this hypothesis was not confirmed. The number of counts had no effect on the likelihood that a defendant would receive any type of downward departure. The strongest predictor of a downward departure is the adjusted guideline minimum (i.e., the presumptive sentence). Defendants with longer presumptive sentences were more likely to receive a downward departure or a substantial assistance departure. In addition, the likelihood of a departure is affected by the offender's race/ethnicity and gender.

The fact that the adjusted guideline minimum is a significant predictor of the likelihood of a departure is interesting. It suggests that federal prosecutors and judges attempt to mitigate the harshness of the sentencing guidelines in

Table 4 **Logistic Regression Results and Ordinary Least Squares Regression Results for Defendants Who Received Any Downward Departure and for Defendants Who Received a §5K1.1 Departure**

	Likelihood of Departure (Odds Ratio and Probability Difference)				Sentence Discount (Estimate in Months)			
	Any Departure		§5K1.1		Any Departure		§5K1.1	
	Odds Ratio	Probability Difference (%)	Odds Ratio	Probability Difference (%)	b	β	b	β
Counts within the indictment > 1	.967		.958		−13.837*	−.143	−16.312*	−.169
Offender characteristics								
Female	1.730		2.131*	18.1	4.100	.032	6.676	.053
Hispanic	.867		.328*	−25.3	4.811	.049	7.093	.066
Black	.493*	−17.0	.347*	−24.2	1.450	−.015	1.003	.010
Age	.994		.980		.279	.060	.492	.101
U.S. citizen	1.381		1.191		2.015	.018	.777	.006
Legal characteristics								
Total criminal history points applied	.956		.951		−.963	−.092	−.816	−.084
Adjusted guideline minimum	1.009*	.2	1.014*	.3	.572*	.847		.802
Nagelkerke R^2	.072		.156				.546*	
R^2	.097		.211		.670		.643	
χ^2/df	26.187/8		58.833/8					
Number of Cases	348		134		164		133	

Note: Probability differences reported only for variables that have a statistically significant effect on departures. The formula for converting odds ratios to probabilities is (odds/odds + 1) − .50 (see Hanushek and Jackson, 1977).

*$p \geq .05$.

federal drug crimes. It suggests that judges attempt to circumvent the 100-to-1 difference in the crack cocaine and powder cocaine penalties that create lengthy mandatory minimum sentences under the federal statutes and sentencing guidelines that disproportionately affect Black drug offenders (see McDonald & Carlson, 1993).

The observation that the odds of a downward departure are affected by the offender's race, ethnicity, and gender indicates that these offender characteristics affect sentence length indirectly through their effect on downward departures or substantial assistance departures. For example, women are significantly more likely than men to get a departure for substantial assistance, and Whites are more likely than Blacks and Hispanics to receive a departure for substantial assistance, and receiving a substantial assistance departure decreases the sentence. Therefore, this finding suggests that Black and Hispanic defendants convicted of federal drug crimes are not as likely to be in a position to provide substantial assistance to the government for investigation or prosecution of an unaffiliated individual or organization. In contrast, Whites, convicted of federal drug crimes, may be more likely to have a significant role in the criminal activity, such as organizer, leader, manager, or supervisor; and thus, Whites would be in a better position to offer substantial assistance information to the government. Similarly, women may be in a more favorable position than men, within the context of organized criminal activity, to have access to key information that qualifies as substantial assistance to the government. For example, a woman may maintain a close relationship, that is, girlfriend, with a major player within the criminal organization that allows her the opportunity to obtain critical information. This finding might also imply that courtroom decision making regarding departures is "systematically biased due to institutionalized discrimination" (Zatz, 1987, p. 81), so that the effect of race/ethnicity and gender may be an indirect effect through routine decisions made by federal prosecutors and judges. Alternatively, as Daly and Tonry (1997) noted, the subtle effects of these extralegal variables may be embedded in either the offense and statutory severity categories and/or in criminal history scores.

The results of our analysis of the magnitude of the sentence discount awarded for a substantial assistance departure are presented in Table 5. Consistent with our hypothesis, the magnitude of the sentence discount for substantial assistance is affected by the number of counts in the indictment; defendants charged with more than one count receive a smaller discount for substantial assistance departures than defendants charged with only one count. As indicated by the unstandardized coefficient, defendants originally charged with multiple counts received a discount nearly 10 months smaller than those originally charged with a single count.

The magnitude of the sentence discount also was affected by the defendant's criminal history score and by the presumptive sentence. Defendants with more serious criminal histories got smaller discounts, while those facing longer presumptive sentences got larger discounts. The number of original

Table 5   Ordinary Least Squares Model for the Ratio of the Difference between the Sentence Discount and the Presumptive Sentence for §5K1.1 Departures (N = 133)

	Unstandardized Coefficients	Standardized Coefficients		Collinearity Statistics
	b	β	t value	VIF
Counts within the indictment > 1	–9.617*	–.213	–2.486	1.058
Offender characteristics				
Female	3.823	.065	.760	1.056
Hispanic	1.624	.032	.271	2.074
Black	–3.522	–.078	–.687	1.838
Age	.290	.128	1.345	1.299
U.S. citizen	3.784	.068	.630	1.655
Legal characteristics				
Total # of criminal history points applied	–1.022*	–.225	–2.369	1.293
Adjusted guideline range minimum	5.533E-02	.174	1.775	1.382
Constant	40.961*		3.634	

Source: Intensive Study Sample (U.S. Sentencing Commission, 1995).
Note: R^2 = .138. VIF = variance inflation factors. Dependent variable: Ratio of difference between presumptive sentence and actual sentence (Adjusted guideline range minimum –Total months of imprisonment ordered / Adjusted guideline range minimum). Ratio difference x 100.
*Statistically significant at .05.

charges filed and the presumptive sentence reflect the prosecutorial discretion at charging. The federal prosecutor has nearly unchecked discretion to determine the number of counts within an indictment for each defendant charged with a federal drug crime. Furthermore, the presumptive sentence is made up of legal factors such as mitigating and aggravating circumstances, the weapons enhancement, and the aggregated drug quantity, all of which determine the final offense level from which the adjusted guideline minimum is calculated. Moreover, it is the federal prosecutor who is responsible for establishing the legal criteria that form the basis of the adjusted guideline minimum. As a result, federal prosecutors indirectly control the magnitude of the departure discount based on their charging decisions at the indictment stage and their decision to file or not to file a motion for substantial assistance.

To further explain the results displayed in Table 5, Table 6 provides a descriptive analysis that illustrates the importance of the number of counts in the indictment and the total number of criminal history points. Moreover, Table 6 suggests an explanation for the fact that the offender characteristics did not significantly affect either sentence length or sentence discounts. As the descriptive analysis demonstrates, Black offenders received a smaller sen-

Table 6 Descriptive Statistics for Variables Included in Ordinary Least Squares Model of Sentence Length: Means

Offender Characteristics	Number of Counts Contained Within the Indictment		Total Number of Criminal History Points Applied		Adjusted Guideline Range Minimum (GLMN)		Total Number of Months Imprisonment Ordered (Totprisn)		Difference Between GLMN and Totprisn		Ratio of GLMN – Totprisn/ GLMN	
	All Cases	§5K1.1	All Cases	§5K1.1	All Cases	§5KI.1	All Cases	§5K1.1	All Cases	§5K1.1	All Cases	§5K1.1
Race												
White	2.46	2.43	2.98	2.84	75.10	97.75	48.24	45.59	26.08	52.16	.347	.534
Black	2.56	2.15	4.40	4.25	119.87	144.85	91.88	73.91	28.08	70.94	.234	.489
Hispanic	2.50	3.19	1.23	1.27	80.72	107.46	54.09	50.27	26.08	57.19	.323	.532
Sex												
Male	2.53	2.53	3.04	3.30	95.13	124.45	68.66	62.10	25.82	62.35	.271	.501
Female	2.32	2.52	1.27	1.35	83.45	93.04	49.75	38.70	33.70	54.35	.403	.584
Citizenship												
U.S. citizen	2.55	2.41	3.61	3.50	97.04	118.71	69.93	57.92	26.84	60.79	.276	.512
Noncitizen	2.60	3.00	.81	.85	84.73	120.44	56.51	58.74	27.29	61.70	.322	.512

tence discount for substantial assistance and longer sentences than either Whites or Hispanics; however, Black offenders, on average, also had more serious criminal histories[14] and substantially more severe presumptive sentences.[15] Similar trends are found for men and noncitizens as compared to women and citizens. The harsher sentences and the smaller sentence discounts for Blacks, men, and noncitizens, in other words, can be attributed to the fact that they have more serious prior records and are charged with more serious crimes than Whites, women, and citizens.

Discussion

Although the current study was unable to measure relevant conduct directly, it can be assumed that a defendant who is convicted of a drug offense and who was charged with more than one count in the indictment is potentially subject to the relevant conduct provision. The prosecutor's charging decision, in other words, drives the relevant conduct provision because criminal conduct that is not charged or that is dismissed through plea bargaining or through acquittal at trial must be considered by the judge at the sentencing hearing. Thus, one explanation for the role of relevant conduct in a real-offense sentencing scheme is that defendants who are affected by relevant conduct receive departures that reflect a smaller sentence discount than defendants whose sentences are not affected by dismissed, uncharged, or acquitted conduct. Consequently, defendants convicted of similar crimes who receive downward departures or §5K1.1 departures may receive different sentence discounts because of real-offense sentencing.

The results of the current study provide indirect evidence that relevant conduct does affect sentence severity. Among offenders convicted of a single count, those charged with more than one count are sentenced more harshly than are those charged with only one count; those originally charged with more than one count also receive smaller sentence discounts for downward departures or departures for substantial assistance. Stated differently, the number of counts originally filed by the prosecutor affect sentence severity, despite the fact that some of these charges are dismissed during the plea-bargaining process. This suggests that the goals of those who crafted the real-offense sentencing system have been achieved. Offenders' sentences reflect their actual-offense conduct. It also suggests, however, that offenders may be treated unfairly at sentencing, in that those who are convicted of the same crime do not necessarily receive the same sentence.

The consideration of relevant conduct at sentencing is problematic for at least two reasons. First, defendants who agree to plead guilty if the prosecutor agrees to dismiss all but one count of the indictment probably assume that they will receive a sentence reduction. They assume, in other words, that their sentence will be less harsh than it would have been if they had been convicted of all of the original counts. As the results of the current study indicate, this may not be the case—there is no "bargaining" benefit for dismissed conduct that creates a false illusion for the defendant. A second problem stems from the fact that the standard used to prove relevant conduct at the sentencing hearing is a more lenient standard than the one used to prove the case at trial: preponderance of the evidence rather than proof beyond a reasonable doubt. This suggests that prosecutors can reduce uncertainty by agreeing to dismiss charges with weak evidence and then reintroduce those charges (or at least the criminal conduct on which they were based) at sentencing, where the weakness in the evidence is less problematic.

Conclusion

The findings of this research highlight the important role played by the federal prosecutor in a sentencing guideline system characterized by real-offense sentencing. In addition, because it is the impact of legal factors that affect sentence length and sentence discounts, federal prosecutors, at the indictment stage, can use these legal factors to their advantage while neutralizing the role of the judge in sentencing decisions.

The federal sentencing guidelines were designed to ensure honesty, uniformity and proportionality in sentencing. The major premise guiding the federal sentencing process is that unwarranted disparity can be reduced by structuring judicial discretion. Thus, the guidelines require judges to prescribe identical sentences for identical offenders who engage in the same criminal conduct. To preclude circumvention of the guidelines by prosecutorial charging and plea-bargaining decisions, the sentence is to be based, not on what the offender is convicted of, but rather on what the offender actually did—that is, his relevant conduct.

In an attempt to control judicial discretion and unwarranted sentencing disparity, the federal Sentencing Commission may have created an avenue for injustice at sentencing through the enhanced powers of the federal prosecutor. Perhaps future policy regarding the unchallenged discretion of the prosecutor can best be explained by Sen. Edward T. Kennedy (1979) when he confronted this issue in his sentencing reform package (S. 1437) and stated, "I do not question the need to establish some form of guideline system for prosecutors. . . . A sentencing guidelines, in place and functioning properly, would become a foundation upon which to build similar reforms in the area of prosecutorial decision-making" (p. 381). Future research should address the importance of decision making at different stages of the criminal justice process to expose areas of potential unwarranted disparity or unfairness so that policy makers can act accordingly.

Endnotes

[1] The three federal judges interviewed for this study include a federal district court judge, a senior federal district court judge, and a senior federal circuit court of appeals judge.

[2] §2D1.1. Unlawful Manufacturing, Importing, Exporting, or Trafficking (Including Possession with Intent to Commit These Offenses); Attempt or Conspiracy.

[3] §2D1.6. Use of Communication Facility in Committing Drug Offenses; Attempt or Conspiracy. A communication facility includes any public or private instrument used in the transmission of writing, signs, signals, pictures, and sound; e.g., telephone, wire, radio.

[4] Only those cases that specify a drug type(s) which include gram weights for the following drugs were included in the final sample ($N = 583$): cocaine ($n = 197$, 33.8%). marijuana ($n = 156$, 26.7%), crack ($n = 152$, 26.1%), heroin ($n = 33$, 5.7%), methamphetamine ($n = 28$, 4.8%), and methamphetamine (actual) ($n = 17$, 2.9%).

[5] The sample size for those drug cases which meet the criteria for analysis is $N = 583$; two cases have missing sentence length that makes the sample $N = 581$. In addition, cases disposed of at trial, $n = 54$, and cases that resulted in a sentence of probation, $n = 39$, will be excluded. Of the remaining 488 cases, 360 have one conviction and one indictment.

[6] For example, if the presumptive sentence is only 30 months the sentence discount will typically be smaller than if the presumptive sentence is 90 months.

[7] Criminal history points range from Category I (0 or 1 criminal history points), Category II (2 or 3 points), Category III (4, 5, or 6 points), Category IV (7, 8, or 9 points), Category V (10, 11, or 12 points) and Category VI (13 or more points). In conjunction with the appropriate offense level (not including life sentences), the range in months within each category, from which the judge imposes his or her sentence, varies from a 6-month differential for offense level 13 and Category I, to an 81-month differential for offense level 39 and Category III.

[8] Likewise, aggravating and mitigating roles are already considered in departures.

[9] United States Federal Sentencing Guidelines §5K1.1, "Upon motion of the government stating that the defendant has provided substantial assistance in the investigation or prosecution of another person who has committed an offense, the court may depart from the guidelines" (18 U.S.C. §3553 [e]); "upon motion of the Government, the court shall have the authority to impose a sentence below a level established by statute as minimum sentence so as to reflect a defendant's substantial assistance in the investigation or prosecution of another person who has committed an offense"; "Rule 35(b) of the Federal Rules of Criminal Procedure permits a reduction of a defendant's sentence, triggered by a government motion, within one year after defendant has been sentenced where a defendant provides substantial assistance to the government" (American College of Trial Lawyers. 1999, pp. 3–5).

[10] 18 U.S.C. §3553(0.

[11] Initially, the 12 judicial circuits were used as dummy variables, however, the variance inflation factors (VIF) were high (all above 4.0), thus indicating collinearity. When these variables are eliminated from the models, the explained variance does not change and the models are more stable and parsimonious. The collinearity could be due to the variance in sample size for each circuit, that is, judicial circuits 5.9, and 11 account for 52.8% of all cases; judicial circuits 1.3, and D.C. account for only 4.4% of all cases.

[12] We first tested for multicollinearity among the independent variables. The measure used to test for multicollinearity in this study is the variance inflation factor (VIF), which measures the extent to which a given explanatory variable can be explained by all other explanatory variables in the equation. (Where there is no table of formal critical VIF values, a common rule of thumb is that if $VIF > 5$, the multicollinearity is severe (Studenmund, 1992, pp. 274–275).

[13] The procedures outlined by Heckman (1974) and Berk (1983) were used to correct for potential sample selection bias, which results when some observations (those defendants who receive probation) are systematically removed from the sample being analyzed (see challenging opinion by Stolzenberg & Relles, 1990, p. 395).

[14] Total number of criminal history points applied for substantial assistance departures: Blacks (4.25), Whites (2.84), and Hispanics (1.27).

[15] Total Months of Imprisonment Ordered: Blacks (73.91 months), Hispanics (50.27 months), and Whites (45.59 months).

References

Albonetti, C. (1997). Sentencing under the federal sentencing guidelines: Effects of defendant characteristics, guilty pleas, and departures on sentence outcomes for drug offenses, 1991–1992. *Law and Society Review, 31*, 789–822.

American College of Trial Lawyers. (1999). *Report and proposal on Section 5K1.1 of the U.S. sentencing guidelines.* Irvine, CA: American College of Trial Lawyers.

Berk, R. (1983). An introduction to sample selection bias in sociological data. *American Sociological Review, 48*, 386–391.

Daly, K., & Tonry, M. (1997). Gender, race, and sentencing. In M. Tonry (Ed.), *Crime and justice: A review of research* (pp. 201–252). Chicago: University of Chicago Press.

Engen, R., & Gainey, R. (2000). Conceptualizing legally relevant factors under guidelines: A reply to Ulmer. *Criminology, 4*, 1245–1252.

Hanushek, E., & Jackson, J. (1977). *Statistical methods for social scientists.* New York: Academic Press.

Heaney, G. (1991). The reality of guidelines sentencing: No end to disparity. *American Criminal Law Review, 28*, 161–232.

Heckman, J. (1974). Shadows prices, market wages, and labor supply. *Econometrics, 42*, 679–683.

Hofer, P., & Blackwell. K. (1999). Searching for discrimination in federal sentencing. Washington, DC: U.S. Sentencing Commission.

Kennedy, E. (1979). Towards a new system of criminal sentencing: Law with order. *American Criminal Law Review, 16*, 353–381.

Lear, E. (1993). Is conviction irrelevant? *UCLA Law Review, 40*, 1179–1239.

McDonald, D., & Carlson, K. (1993). *Sentencing in the federal courts: Does race matter?* Washington, DC: Bureau of Justice Statistics.

Nagel, I., & Schulhofer, S. (1992). A tale of three cities: An empirical study of charging and bargaining practices under the federal sentencing guidelines. *Southern California Law Review, 66*, 501–566.

Reitz, K. (1993). Sentencing facts: Travesties of real-offense sentencing. *Stanford Law Review, 45*, 523–573.

Stith, K., & Cabranes. J. (1998). *Fear of judging sentencing guidelines in the federal courts.* Chicago: University of Chicago Press.

Stolzenberg, R., & Relles, D. (1990). Theory testing in a world of constrained research design: The significance of Heckman's censored sampling bias correction for nonexperimental research. *Sociological Methods and Research, 4*, 395–415.

Studenmund, A. (1992). *Using econometrics: A practical guide.* New York: HarperCollins.

Tonry, M. (1996). *Sentencing matters.* New York: Oxford University Press.

U.S. Sentencing Commission. (1995). *Intensive study sample (ISS).* Washington, DC: West Group.

U.S. Sentencing Commission. (2000). *Federal sentencing guidelines manual.* Washington, DC: West Group.

Wilkins, W., Jr. (1992). The federal sentencing guidelines: Striking an appropriate balance. *U.C. Davis Law Review, 25*, 571–586.

Wilkins, W., Jr., & Steer, J. (1990). Relevant conduct: The cornerstone of the federal sentencing guidelines. *South Carolina Law Review, 28*, 495–521.

Zatz, M. (1987). The changing form of racial/ethnic biases in sentencing. *Journal of Research in Crime and Delinquency, 25*, 69–92.

20

Institutionalizing Problem-Oriented Policing
Rethinking Problem Solving, Analysis, and Accountability

RACHEL BOBA AND JOHN P. CRANK

Introduction

This paper presents a model for the integration of problem-oriented policing into contemporary police services through an expansion of accountability across the organizational rank structure. It does not present a new theory per se, in that it does not provide a new terminology to conceptually map existing practices. Instead, it is a paper based on a rethinking of practice, aimed at the institutionalization of extant practices through an expanded accountability structure. The twin ideas underlying the model presented herein are certainly not new—problem-oriented policing has been of substantial interest since Goldstein's seminal development of the notion, and the integration of accountability across the command structure can be traced to Peelian policing in Great Britain in the 1800s. What is new is the melding of these two notions, which is the focus of this paper.

Problem solving has gained traction primarily in Western countries, particularly the USA, Canada, Great Britain, and New Zealand (see, for example, Leigh, Reed, & Tilley, 1998; Mazerolle, 2001; Winfree & Newbold, 1999). However, there is also a move to incorporate problem solving in authoritarian, militarized, and centralized countries such as in the former Soviet bloc (Caparini & Marenin, 2005). For example, the energy and viability of problem solving has begun to be established in Georgia, where US trainers work with local police in the implementation of problem-solving practices

Rachel Boba and John P. Crank, *Police Practice and Research*, Vol. 19, pp. 1–15, © 2008 by Taylor & Francis. Reprinted by permission of Taylor & Francis.

as a component of a broader community policing initiative (see the Rochester/Tbilisi Community Policing Initiative).

It is hoped that this paper will contribute to the literature by proposing a different way to practice problem solving, one that is based on chain-of-command accountability and command reach, but that preserves officer and department integrity. The model presented herein is not a rejection of the notion that police are accountable to citizens, but rather is designed to facilitate intra-organizational dynamics in support of a local police mission. Our notion of accountability is based on the mechanisms by which particular individuals take ownership of problems and thus coordinate or carry out responses to them. Ultimately, we believe, police capacity to respond to local community needs can be best met through this problem-solving model in which the assignment and resolution of problem solving is diffused through the organization within current command structures.

A Brief Overview of Problem-Oriented Policing

The concept of problem-oriented policing (POP) has been of substantial interest to police reformers for over 20 years. First introduced by Goldstein in his seminal 1979 article, "Improving Policing: A Problem Oriented Approach," the notion that police could become more effective by focusing on problems has kindled an increasing body of applied research in police departments in the USA as well as other countries such as the UK and Australia. Furthermore, over the last two decades a significant body of research suggests that problem-oriented policing can lead to more effective control and prevention of crime and disorder (Weisburd & Eck, 2004).

Yet the core ideas of POP have not become routinized into the mission of most police departments and its central element—the distinction between an incident and a problem—has been underdeveloped and often misunderstood (Scott, 2000). Moreover, a lack of inventory of crime prevention responses accompanied by practical guidance for problem solving has slowed the problem-solving movement (Eck, 2003; Goldstein, 2003). An organization-wide strategic orientation to crime prevention advocated by proponents of POP remains, in today's policing, largely untested and unapplied.

Many of the contemporary success stories in crime prevention are based on the ideas associated with problem-oriented policing (see Clarke's *Crime Prevention Studies* Series). Researchers are increasingly recognizing the clustering of similar incidents (Farrell, Sousa, & Weisel, 2002; Sherman, Gartin, & Buerger, 1989; Silverman, 1999; Weisburd & Mazerolle, 2000), the linkages between place and opportunity (Mazerolle, Kadleck, & Roehl, 1998; Pease, 1998; Pierce, Braga, Hyatt, & Koper, 2004), and the causal dynamics of and relevant responses to discrete crime and disorder problems (see Center for Problem-Oriented Policing, 2007, for the *Problem-Oriented Guides for Police* Series). Nonetheless, these ideas have not been routinized into daily police activity (Goldstein, 2003).

In the current era, there is a movement to reinvigorate the ideas and inform the practice of problem-oriented policing movement (Clarke, 1998; Knutsson, 2003; Scott, 2000; Tilley & Bullock, 2003) through publications (Scott, 2000); funding for problem case studies (Clarke & Goldstein, 2002; Sampson & Scott, 2000) and institutionalization of problem analysis (Office of Community Oriented Policing Services, 2003); and the creation of the virtual Center for Problem-Oriented Policing.

The purpose of this paper is to propose a model for the institutionalization of POP. This proposal stems from Scott's (2000) challenge to advocates of POP to take the "next step": develop a model that is useful for the implementation of POP practices in police departments. This model focuses on three key weaknesses identified by Scott:

- *The problem of problem definition:* The term "problem" is easily misunderstood and must be defined precisely and reinforced in practice.

- *The problem of problem analysis:* The quality and use of analysis is weak and underdeveloped.

- *The problem of accountability:* POP has been accountable mostly at the line level. Although Goldstein encouraged line officers' involvement in problem-oriented policing he did not anticipate they would conduct the brunt of the work and in fact had "imagined command-level police officials and research collaborators would lead problem-oriented initiatives" (p. 12).

This paper is a response to Scott's challenge. An integrated model is presented in which problem solving and the use of analysis are expanded through the rank structure of the police organization. The model presented here was developed as part of a project[1] whose goal was to institutionalize problem analysis within the Port St Lucie, FL (PSL) Police Department (Boba, 2005b). Like many agencies, the PSL Police Department had an extensive history of innovation in problem solving and in community policing. The project was a "next stage" in the evolution of PSL Police Department innovation—the institutionalization of problem solving across the rank structure of the organization. This paper focuses on the model developed within the department and sketches the central elements of that model.

The integrated model attempts to link the complexity of problems, conceived on a continuum of relatively narrow incident and incident clusters to general problems, to command reach and resource availability. The purpose of tying problem complexity to command is to provide a strategy, within existing organizational constraints, that allows for the capabilities of those who can muster the staffing and resources to carry out, and to be reasonably held accountable for, problem analysis and their solutions.

Importantly, the recognition of problem complexity requires managerial involvement in all stages of a problem-oriented organizational process. The model also incorporates into its design traditional policing elements of crime suppression such as preventive patrol, responding to calls for service, investigating crimes, and arresting suspects. Crime suppression is not only an end in itself but also contributes the raw information or data that provides the foundation of problem analysis. Finally, the approach of the model is to "meet people where they are" in the organization—to ensure that existing roles and responsibilities are concordant with a problem-oriented policing approach.

That problem complexity and accountability should be tied to organizational rank has been observed in related research in Great Britain. The police in Cleveland sought to implement POP across the command structure and through the civilian component of the organization. The decision to adopt a problem and to close it was initially located at the level of sergeant and constable (Romeanes, 1996). This was amended upward in the command—senior-level officers made the decisions on how to proceed with problem identification and resolution. Decisions were made at weekly meetings designed somewhat like a COMPSTAT model associated with New York (Henry, 2002). Evaluations of the Cleveland model provide several recommendations. Among the most important are those around which the current model is constructed. Perhaps the most important is that of ownership—who carries the responsibility for the identification and resolution of problems? A second problem is that of communication—once a problem is identified at a particular level, how does one communicate appropriate information about it successfully across the rank structure—up for resources and coordination, or back down for the core work carried out by line personnel? Cleveland attempted to resolve this through weekly meetings involving ranking personnel. A third issue is that of "problem." Officers sometimes had difficulty with the meaning of the term "problem" defined as a "cluster of related incidents to which police are frequently called." Many identified problems that did not fall within this definition. The current proposal addresses this issue by developing an expansive definition of problem, one that separates different categories of problems by their scope and complexity and then locates accountability for them to appropriate rank and assignment.

Critique of Current Practice of Problem-Oriented Policing

We believe that a significant problem with the operational practice of problem-oriented policing today is the conflation of problems and incidents. This means that incidents—sometimes solitary, but also occurring in small numbers acted out by a single perpetrator or in a single location—are too often defined as problems. This conflation is a direct consequence of the tendency, in most departments, to make line officers the central actors in problem identification, problem analysis, and problem accountability. Because of this, the scope of problems, described broadly by Goldstein (1990) as crime generators, shifts to a more locally manageable incident-based size, simply conceived in terms of crime suppression and addressable within a short period of time, if at all.

Conceiving of incidents as problems is consistent with traditional line assignments. Historically, the line task has focused on crime suppression through incident response and arrest. Officers respond to incidents and deal with individual crimes and calls for service many times during a shift. The work is usually accomplished alone, sometimes with a back-up officer, and if the task is too large or complex with the assistance of detectives or other specialists. In contemporary POP in many departments, problems are defined and solved within this occupational ask structure (Goldstein, 2003). Because of problem-incident conflation, the problem-oriented model is short-changed at the point of problem definition, inadequately developed at the point of problem analysis, and undermanaged by middle managers who hold line officers accountable for their work. The consequence of this contemporary model is a failure of problem solving as envisioned broadly by Goldstein.

Clearly, line officers in some departments are doing good problem solving of the kind conceived by Goldstein, and are receiving adequate resources to carry out the problem-solving task (see the winners of the Herman Goldstein Awards, www.popcenter.org). But these are exceptional cases. More typically, officers will receive some in-service training funded through a state or national grant, and they will be expected to carry out problem solving on their own, based on that training (Goldstein, 2003). Broader organizational strategy, enacted through an integrated model of problem solving across the chain of command and tied to department resources and command accountability, is missing. This places the burden of organizational change at the lowest ranks, where even the most thoughtful and creative officers will run into resource limitations, the frustrations of working with traditionally oriented commanders, and the need to accumulate information that facilitates promotion.

The Problem of Problem Definition

The primary task in the POP model is the specification of a problem. Goldstein defines a problem as either: (1) a cluster of similar, related, or recurring incidents rather than a single incident, (2) a substantive community concern, or (3) a unit of police business (1990, p. 66). Clarke and Eck (2005, Step 14), similarly define a problem as ". . . a recurring set of related harmful events in a community that members of the public expect the police to address." The problem of problem definition that has emerged from practice lies in how to view the relationship between incidents and problems.

These conceptual definitions have, unfortunately, been difficult to apply to practice. Problems are typically under-specified and are defined much too narrowly. Cordner and Biebel (2005, p. 164), in their study of the San Diego Police Department's practice of problem-oriented policing, found that officers assigned to address problems typically focused on "one person, one address, one building, one parking lot, or one intersection." Why do police tend to define problems so narrowly? The answer, we suspect, is in the task structure assigned to line officers, who are accustomed to carrying out the enforcement of the law and maintenance of the public order on a dispatcher-driven on-call basis. Line officers and detectives are experts in the rapid management of crime and disorder incidents in which they are involved. They may not be aware of what happens on other shifts or on days when they do not work, thus microscoping the problem to a manageable shift identity.

A confounding factor is that when officers are assigned to address problems they are invariably asked to do so as part of their regular patrol or investigative duties. Officers so assigned often say that they have difficulty in balancing problem solving with answering calls and investigating cases (Cordner & Biebel, 2005). Officers in such situations are likely to resolve the tension between POP problem solving and incident-based role structure by redefining problems narrowly, making them solvable on a relatively short-term basis and avoiding the disruption in time a substantial problem would cause. This point is underscored by Scott (2000, p. 13), "Line-level officers lack the requisite resources in most instances to conduct the sort of analysis and effect the sort of responses necessary to bring about substantial improvements in community wide problems."

The Problem of Problem Analysis

The quality and use of analysis in much applied problem solving is frequently weak and underdeveloped (Goldstein, 2003). In Goldstein's POP model, analysis provides an in-depth assessment of antecedent research, the prevalence and underlying causes of the problem, the resources needed for response, and third-party groups that might assist. However, the quality and effectiveness of these aspects of analysis are contingent on the previous stage, problem identification. When problems are underspecified, analysis will underestimate the problem, its causes, and the adequacy of response, sharply increasing the likelihood of failure to control or prevent the problem. A recent study has found that officers relied on experience and observation/interviews for their analysis of problems (Cordner & Biebel, 2005). In other words, analysis, like problem identification, was narrowly focused and carried out with the available time and resources.

In addition, most analysis in police agencies is focused on short-term pattern and series identification and preparation of crime counts for COMP-STAT-like programs (O'Shea & Nicholls, 2003). What evidence there is of broadly conceived problem analysis appears to stem from special projects with independent researchers or from government funding (Police Foundation, 2003; Sampson & Scott, 2000).

The Problem of Accountability

In a traditional patrol assignment, officers are accountable to their immediate supervisors, and their assignments determine their work structure. Accountability is carried out through formal personnel criteria, annual evaluations, and assessments for promotion. Evaluation is based on individual task-related performance, demeanor and attitude, and focuses on daily performance. We are concerned that this accountability structure encourages the treatment of incidents or clusters of incidents as problems. By focusing on incident clusters and redefining them as problems (Cordner & Biebel, 2005), officers can show that they are being productive to their sergeants. Further, supervisors can use these counts to show the chief what they have done. Where managers who evaluate line work are not explicitly brought into the problem-solving process, there will be no motivation for line personnel to view problems more strategically.

Accountability as framed within problem-oriented policing is expansively different. Problem solving requires creativity, innovation, and stand-out individual and group performance (Oettmeier & Wycoff, 1997). POP evaluation focuses on a qualitative notion—the unique characteristics of a problem—and recognizes that there is not always a clear, quantitative solution. One should not, for example, simply count the "number of problems solved" as one author has witnessed, and expect line officers to do anything more than the most simple problem solving. Accountability needs to be carried out through an integrated model so that administrators can also be accountable for—and can comprehend—the work carried out by line personnel and its contribution to the problem-solving process.

Community policing and more recently, COMPSTAT, have reconsidered the accountability structure of police departments. Community policing has emphasized line officer discretion and ingenuity. COMPSTAT has de-emphasized the line discretion. COMPSTAT is characterized by the review of data identifying clustering of incident and related data, and managerial meetings aimed specifically at monitoring efforts to suppress crime. COMPSTAT reinvests authority in the middle ranks, a response to what many critics described as a critical shortcoming of community policing, the location of discretion and accountability at the lower ranks. Only managers, it is argued, have the requisite experience, skill, and authority to deal with larger picture issues (see Henry, 2002).

The COMPSTAT model is an attempt to synthesize an accountability structure and strategic problem solving. Managers are held accountable for both knowing about problems and doing something about the problematic activity in regular scheduled meetings (Weisburd, Mastrofski, McNally, Greenspan, & Willis, 2003). However, in practice, COMPSTAT's problem identification model is driven by analysis of incident patterns, is incident based, and the accountability meetings are often focused on incident suppression. In most agencies, these meetings are held weekly or monthly (Weisburd et al., 2003) and many times the expectations are that what is brought up in one meeting should be solved by the next.

The model proposed in this paper is consistent with the COMPSTAT notion that problems require managerial leadership, and that, throughout the process, managers are central to strategic problem solving and accountability.

However, a more flexible notion of managerial responsibility is put forth, one which (1) aligns managerial responsibility with problem complexity and does not seek short-term correctives to underlying problems through arrest production and (2) continues to emphasize the need for creativity and independence of line activity in the problem-solving process. The model distinguishes among the levels of activity at which problem solving and analysis occur in a police agency, assigns problems to the appropriate ranks/personnel within the organization, and establishes a system in which the appropriateness and effectiveness of problem solving is assessed.

The Integrated Model

To be institutionalized in an organizational setting means to establish as normal or make something a customary and accepted part of the organization. The institutionalization of problem-oriented policing means that the policies, practice, and organizational structure of a police organization contribute to the goal of solving problems. Problem solving is normalized —it is not carried out by a specialist squad or relegated to the lower ranks, but becomes an integral part of the organizational mission.

The integrated model presented here is centered on Goldstein's recognition that "a problem is the basic unit of police work rather than a crime, a case, calls, or incidents" (Scott & Goldstein, 1988). It was developed through a partnership between the researchers and the Port St Lucie, FL Police Department with the goal of making problem analysis routine in the agency (Boba, 2005b). In this model, all crimes and public disorder incidents are recognized to be potentially problem-related. In the model, line officers continue to be integral to problem solving and line ingenuity is encouraged. What the problem-oriented department recognizes is that the incident-oriented work of line officers may stem from problems of unknown scope. Consequently, information on types of crime, nature of arrests, physical environment, and methods of crime are collected in a systematic way that allows for problem identification and resolution at the level originally conceived by Goldstein. It is the codification, analysis, and interpretation of this information, for example, through monthly meetings and annual reviews, that provides the information critical to the successful identification and analysis of problems.

In the model, problem-solving responsibility is distributed across the rank structure. Line officers play a role by assisting middle managers to develop local strategies, from the neighborhood level for small problems, to community-wide strategies for problems requiring broad and complex intervention and prevention strategies. Line officers also play a role on teams addressing large-scale problems. They participate in the data collection, communication, analysis, and implementation of responses of large-scale problems.

Middle managers are managerially engaged in the problem-solving process. They are tuned in proactively, also collecting a variety of data about the everyday workings of the community, reviewing information provided by line, pursuing community contacts, and keeping an eye for the threads that connect incidents and the underlying conditions that might explain *why* they are occurring. Large-scale problems require a strategic response at the command ranks, where budget and strategy are integrated for long-term planning (see Geller & Swanger, 1995). Importantly, the level of aggregation of activity is matched by the level of resources available to analyze and respond to the problem and the same type of activity is addressed simultaneously at different levels of aggregation.

The variable scope of problem solving—from small, incident-centered activity to broad patterns of routine behavior—requires an equally varied but integrated organizational response. Read and Tilley (2000) distinguished incidents and repeat incidents at the beat/ward, sector, district, region, nation, and international levels. They noted that incidents are good predictors of future incidents, particularly in the short term, and they emerge from larger patterns of activity. This suggests a two-stage problem response—one aimed at the specific characteristics of the immediate incident pattern and another aimed at the underlying problem. Incident suppression is a line-level response, while problem identification and response formulation is a command-level product. Importantly, incident suppression is no longer a solitary exercise, but integrated into problem analysis and command-level review.

Levels of activity are distinguished within the model. Problems, according to their complexity, are assigned to specific levels within the police organization. A structure of accountability is introduced that provides supervision and direction for problem-solving efforts. This structure employs the command structure of a traditional police organization: sergeants monitor officers' problem solving as it is carried out at their level, lieutenants monitor sergeants' problem solving, and so forth up the chain of command. The purpose of this accountability structure is not to hold line officers' feet to the fire, as it were—to the contrary, it is to ensure that managers and commander are themselves involved an integrated approach to problem solving. It is through the provision of organizational accountability that the integrated model makes use of managerial skills and command resources, while keeping the agency focused on the mission of problem solving.

Figure 1 illustrates how increases in problem complexity are linked to the rank of those carrying out problem solving within a parallel accountability structure.

The accountability structure is operationalized through regular meetings that facilitate accountability and correspond to the temporal nature of the activity they address. For example, incidents occur on an hourly and daily basis, thus supervisors meet with officers out on the road and have daily meetings or briefings to ensure officers are addressing incidents effectively. On the other hand, problems are manifested over several months or years and meetings that ensure accountability of analysis and problem solving of problems occur monthly, and are carried out by mid-level and command officers.

The role of problem solving is integrated across the rank structure in the model. That is, the problem-solving process can and is used to address problems of different complexity at each organizational level. By separating and distinguishing the levels of activity, problem solving will result in different analyses and responses, and accountability will be facilitated by different personnel within the agency.

Table 1 is an illustration of the model integrated across

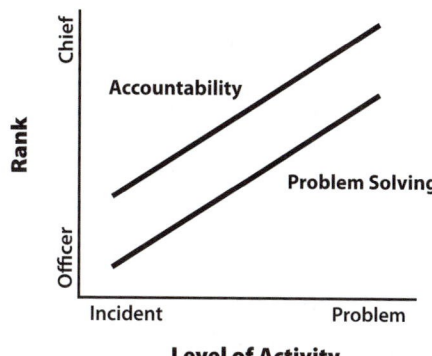

Figure 1   Relationship among level of activity, rank, and accountability.

levels of activity. It highlights specifically who is assigned to conduct problem solving and analysis within the organization, but can be adapted based on the size of the police agency and the amount of activity at each level. For example, a small town with a fairly low crime rate and a police department of 15 officers may focus on lower-level activity because that is what predominantly occurs. Officers may be held responsible for the analysis and problem solving of repeat incidents and patterns because there are a small number of incidents and very few ranks within the department and few large-scale problems. A larger police department serving a community with more crime and disorder would utilize all levels of activity and ranks within the model.

Table 1   Problem complexity by responsibility.

Level of activity	Problem solving	Analysis	Accountability	Meetings
Incidents	Line officers	Line officers	First-line supervisors	Meeting on shift Daily briefings
Serious incidents	Detectives	Detectives	First-line supervisors	Daily/weekly briefings
Repeat incidents	Sergeants	Sergeants	Management	Weekly meetings
Patterns	Detective sergeants Patrol sergeants Lieutenants	Crime analysts Sergeants	Crime analyst supervisor Management	Weekly meetings Monthly meetings
Problems	Team of personnel	Team of personnel	Management	Monthly meetings

Although analysis is part of the problem-solving process, it is distinguished in Table 1 because not all analysis is conducted by those scanning and responding to activity (e.g., crime analysts conducting pattern analysis). The model also illustrates the provision of supervision and accountability for problem solving at each level, as well as the temporal nature of the meeting in which accountability would be facilitated. Following the table is a description of each level of activity and its components.

Incidents and Serious Incidents

Incidents and serious incidents are events to which typically an officer responds to or discovers on patrol or a detective investigates. These types of activities make up a significant amount of the work in a police department. They include crime, disorder, or service-related tasks such as disturbances, robberies, traffic accidents, subject stops, and traffic citations. They happen over a shift or several days if follow-up investigation is necessary and the goal of response is to resolve them according to the laws and policies of the jurisdiction and the police agency.

Police officers and detectives typically conduct both the analysis and responses to these incidents. This is traditional police work. The skills and training come from basic police training, a department's field and in-service training programs, more advanced investigative training, and experience. That officers who lack good incident problem solving and analysis skills are said to have "no common sense" illustrates how fundamental incident analysis is to the practice of policing. Because this is traditional police work, sergeants/first-line supervisors supervise, direct and hold officers accountable for their problem solving and analysis results (i.e., more detailed and insightful police reports) in daily or weekly briefings.

In the integrated problem-oriented model, the work at this level is expanded to include the collection of additional information than what has traditionally been collected (i.e., more that just to establish a crime, name a suspect, or establish probable cause). Data concerning specific methods of the crime (not just general categories, such as "ransacked"), the implications for routine activities (e.g., Sunday night at a bar may be underage night), motivations of the offender (e.g., why did you pick that house to burgle?), and the environment of the place (e.g., the house burgled is isolated in the woods) are collected to be reviewed for their relationship to patterns and problems. For example, in the Port St Lucie, FL Police Department report narrative templates were developed for officers to follow (Port St Lucie, FL Police Department [PSLPD], 2005). The templates outlined specific questions officers are to complete for 13 of their most common crimes (e.g., what are the characteristics of the area around a site where a construction site was burgled). Accountability means that the line supervisors are also trained in problem solving and carry responsibility to ensure that line officers are responding to incidents appropriately and collecting this additional information that contributes to the overall problem orientation of the agency.

Repeat Incidents

Repeat incidents are two or more incidents that are similar in nature and have happened at the same place (typically) or by the same person and are less frequent than incidents. These are usually common non-criminal incidents that do not result in a crime report, such as neighbor disputes, barking dogs, problem juveniles, traffic crashes, etc. Repeat incidents happen within hours, days, and in some cases weeks of one another. The research on repeat victimization indicates that people and places that have been victimized in the past have a higher likelihood of being victimized again than do people and places that have never been victimized (Farrell & Pease, 1993). Repeat incidents are an important level of activity to address because they may represent short-term patterns of opportunity that can focus analysis and problem solving. The goal of problem solving and analysis here is to resolve the immediate issue that is causing the repeat incidents (e.g., neighbor dispute, problem juvenile), but also to look for "patterns in patterns," incident clusters that may be aggregated with other incident clusters. For example, the Port St Lucie Police Department addresses all locations that have had at least three calls (including narcotics, neighbor trouble, juvenile trouble, 911 hang ups, domestic trouble, disturbances, fights, and mentally ill persons) in the last 28 days. Sergeants use this list to identify and prioritize short-term problem addresses and respond to them using tailored approaches (PSLPD, 2006). This type of activity is what has typically been addressed by line officers in departments attempting to conduct problem solving. Although repeat incidents represent an aggregated level of individual incidents, they are narrow in focus and in temporal nature. Consequently, resolving them may not lead to an overall reduction in that type of activity.

First-line supervisors conduct analysis of repeat incidents and are responsible for problem solving this activity, most likely with the help of line officers. First-line supervisors have a broader perspective and have time to conduct repeat incident analysis whereas line officers spend much of their time and focus responding to individual incidents. Supervisors identify and prioritize repeat incidents through analysis reports and discussions with officers, other personnel, and community contacts. In turn, they may assign them to officers to problem solve, or address the activity themselves. Line officers [who] spend most of their time and are focused on incidents thus need encouragement and direction from their supervisors to problem-solve repeat incidents.

Because sergeants/first-line supervisors are responsible for problem solving and analysis of repeat incidents, their supervisors, called "management" in the model, hold them accountable for this work. These supervisors would typically be lieutenants responsible for a shift and/or geographic area who supervise several sergeants. Because repeat incidents occur over days and weeks, the accountability would be facilitated in weekly meetings.

Patterns

Patterns are two or more crimes or serious incidents that seem to be related by victim, offender, location, or property that typically occur over days, weeks, or months. Patterns with the highest public visibility are those in which the victim and the offender do not know one another. Examples include stranger rape, indecent exposure, public sexual indecency, robbery, burglary, and grand theft. Patterns of these crimes are vitally important to police, citizens, businesses, the media, and all members of a community because they are perceived as the most immediate threat to personal safety (i.e., offenders preying on unknown victims).

The main difference between patterns and repeat incidents is the type of data that are analyzed. Both concern activity in the short term, but repeat incidents consist of common quality of life or service calls whereas patterns consist of reported crime. Traditionally, officers, detectives, and sergeants have linked patterns together on an ad hoc basis through informal communication and review of police reports. More recently, analysts with specific training have become central police personnel conducting pattern analysis (Boba, 2005a; O'Shea & Nicholls, 2003).

Unlike the previous levels, patterns are not analyzed and addressed by the same personnel in the organization. First-line supervisors and analysts scan for patterns, but ideally analysts conduct the majority of analysis and disseminate products because of the knowledge of various databases and amount of time it takes for systematic pattern analysis.

Crime analysis supervisors and those using the crime pattern results provide supervision and direction for analysis work. Because first-line supervisors (sergeants) and first-line managers (lieutenants) are responsible for problem solving of patterns, their supervisors, middle managers, hold them accountable for responding to patterns—which means that middle managers are involved in the chain of pattern and problem identification. Similar to repeat incidents, accountability is facilitated in weekly meetings to discuss patterns. However, because certain types of patterns, such as stranger rape, robbery, or homicide, may be of particular concern to the community, or because of interconnections among patterns, the police department may review the analysis and problem solving of the higher priority patterns in monthly meetings.

Commanders and chiefs will answer to media and city officials about these patterns—pragmatically, they have a political stake in these issues—and thus they should be prepared to address the appropriateness and effectiveness of decisions made during the problem-solving process. However, it cannot be overemphasized that these crime patterns may also emerge from an ecological environment conducive to routine crime, and need to be assessed for their linkage to broader problems. For example, the Port St Lucie Police Department holds weekly meetings to ensure patterns are being addressed collaboratively within the agency. Monthly meetings allow the command staff to hold the captains accountable for their response decisions and effectiveness (Boba & Santos, 2006).

Problems

A problem is a set of related activities that occur over several months, seasons, or years that stems from systematic opportunities created by everyday behavior and environment. Problems can consist of common disorder activity (e.g., loud parties or speeding in residential neighborhoods) as well as serious criminal activity (e.g., bank robbery or date rape). Not every repeat incident or pattern is part of a larger problem; however, repeat incidents and patterns may be part of a series of related activities that, over time, become a problem. Problems, conversely, will contain numerous patterns and/or repeat incidents, and by first identifying these lower-level events and the incident-level responses to them, more can be learned about the problem (e.g., interviews with offenders about why they commit those crimes; what works to resolve repeat incidents and what does not).

Consider an example in which 20 separate patterns of street robbery in a particular area are committed by different offenders and have been identified and addressed over a one-year period. Even though some of the offenders are caught, street robberies continue in the area. This suggests that there is something about the structure of opportunity in this area that makes robbery a persistent problem, and line-level suppressive activity is not enough to change what may be favorable environmental conditions. The patterns prove important information about the nature of the robberies, the characteristics of the offenders, and about what works and does not in the way of suppressive activity, but is unlikely to lead to a long-term solution.

Not all incidents of crime and disorder are brought to the attention of the police. Because of this, the ability of police on their own to develop information about some problems may be difficult. That is, problems may not always come to light through the analysis of repeat incidents or patterns. Police–community relations are important to the integrated problem-solving agency, and the input of various community groups through interviews, surveys, and other forms of community outreach are an important source of information. Indeed, as Goldstein has noted, even after the identification of a problem, community information is often central to problem resolution.

The goal of problem analysis is to understand why the problem is occurring. The underlying, situational causes of the problem are examined in terms of the offenders' motivations, the nature of the victims or targets, and the environment of the place(s) where the problem occurs. In addition, the structure of criminal opportunity: the lack of control of offenders by handlers, victims by guardians, and places by place managers are considered (Cohen & Felson, 1979; Eck & Weisburd, 1995). Even though data from incidents collected in a problem-oriented agency are the foundation for problem analysis, primary data collection will be necessary to understand these components and why the problem is persisting (Boba, 2005a; Clarke & Eck, 2005; Schmerler & Velasco, 2002). Responses are tailored to address these causes and reduce/eliminate the opportunities that contribute to the problem.

A team of police personnel, including line officers, conducts both problem solving and analysis. In some cases, non-agency personnel such as researchers or other community professionals with a particular interest in a problem will also participate in the process. The Port St Lucie Police Department brought together a team of personnel and a researcher to analyze and respond to the problem of construction site burglary (Santos, 2006). The team of analysts, officers, and police managers conducted secondary analysis, observed construction site locations, conducted focus groups of home builders, recommended responses to the chief of police, and implemented those responses.

The skills and training necessary to conduct problem solving and analysis at this level vary by problem. Officers who participate and show initiative would be those that, in an integrated problem-oriented agency, would be promoted to become first-line supervisors and managers conducting problem-oriented policing. Over time an agency would contain successful and experienced problem solvers at all levels.

Problem formulation and response is overseen by top levels of upper management and command personnel. Typically, a lieutenant, captain, or other high-level manager will lead the problem-solving team; accountability must consequently be facilitated at an even higher level. Importantly, problem solving at this level may require complex resource management and a broader perspective. For example, one suggested response to the construction site burglary problem in Port St Lucie was to work with the city to change building codes and processes that require the builders to protect their sites more comprehensively. After some discussion, the chief of police decided the team should not pursue this response because the magnitude of the problem did not warrant it (i.e., there were 266 burglaries in 2004 with over 6000 homes under construction on any given day). The chief weighed the importance and potential effectiveness of that response against available resources, using his/her political capital, and decided a more effective response was to work individually with the most victimized builders (Santos, 2006).

Because problems tend to occur over extended and indefinite periods, the review of problem solving and analysis at this level should occur on a monthly basis. The team of personnel would provide monthly updates on the analysis process, response development and implementation, as well as solicit advice and direction. Because problems are defined as the most general level of activity, there would be fewer problems than patterns, repeat incidents, etc. making accountability on a monthly basis manageable at this level.[2]

Conclusion

The model of integrated problem solving developed in this paper is presented to address some of the problems facing the practice of problem-oriented policing. We have considered the shortcomings of current practices involving problem definition, problem analysis, and problem resolution accountability. This model was developed through an ongoing project (Boba,

2005b) and has sought to expand the work of problem-oriented policing by "meeting people where they are." Problem solving is linked in a practical and reasonable way to existing work practices and oversight in terms of existing rank structure. This approach provides a realistic way to define repeat incident, pattern, and problem activity addressed by police and to provide a concrete analysis and accountability structure that, we hope, might help to institutionalize problem-oriented policing as suggested by Scott (2000).

In order to institutionalize problem-oriented policing, an agency must integrate problem solving, analysis, and accountability at all levels. This model builds upon the strengths of traditional policing—its information-gathering capability through call response and crime investigation, the command and accountability structure embedded in its hierarchical design, and the widespread use of structured meetings. However, it goes beyond traditional policing by aligning problem solving, analysis, and accountability with all of these strengths.

Each of these recommendations will require the widespread use of data collection. Additional improvements will involve establishing appropriately timed meetings in which supervisors and managers discuss pattern and problem solutions with commanders; training staff to identify and analyze problems separately than lower-level activity and to collect primary data on particular problems; and adopting new technology that encourages enhanced data collection at lower levels and more capability for analysis, at higher levels.

Ultimately, the goal of problem-oriented policing is to address problems because they are larger and focus the limited resources of police where they can make a more significant impact. However, smaller communities may have fewer problems and thus would focus a significant amount of effort on repeat incidents and patterns. This model provides a framework that can be adapted to any community since effective problem solving at lower levels informs that of higher levels. Our goal is the implementation of effective problem solving, practically applied at all levels in an organization. This notion of problem solving, committed to policing and community safety, carries a great deal of promise for suppressing crime and disorder as well as for addressing the underlying conditions that give rise to problematic activity.

Endnotes

[1] Funded by the Office of Community Oriented Policing Services, #2003-CK-WX-K042. A separate article about the detailed implementation in the Port St Lucie Police Department will be published in the future. Examples from that project are used to illustrate the model here.

[2] An additional level of activity, not incorporated into the model, is the social issue. A social issue is an underlying cause of the routine behavior and opportunities for crime and disorder that have developed over long periods. Social issues fall into the decisional matrix of city, county, and state government, and may involve federal expenditures. Ideally, government works with independent and objective researchers and analysts. Although police often are involved in dealing with unsavory aspects of broad social issues, this is not and cannot be their primary business: such issues are much too broad and are inevitably embodied in ongoing political debate over the proper responsibilities of government.

References

Boba, R. (2005a). *Crime analysis and crime mapping.* Thousand Oaks, CA: Sage.

Boba, R. (2005b). Institutionalization of problem analysis process evaluation/Implementation and problem analysis case study in Port St. Lucie, Florida. Draft site report for *The enhancement of community policing: Institutionalizing problem analysis.* North Carolina State University, Cooperative Agreement #2003-CK-WX-K042.

Boba, R., & Santos, R. (2006). *Institutionalizing problem solving, analysis, and accountability: A case study of Port St. Lucie, FL.* Paper presented at the 14th International Symposium on Environmental Criminology and Crime Analysis, Chilliwack, British Columbia, Canada.

Caparini, M., & Marenin, O. (2005). Reflections on policing in post-communist Europe. *The Journal of Power Institutions in Post-Soviet Societies, 2.* Retrieved March 14, 2007, from http://www.pipss.org/ sommaire271.html

Center for Problem-Oriented Policing. (2007). Retrieved March 14, 2007, from http://www.popcenter.org

Clarke, R.V. (1998). Defining police strategies: Problem-solving, problem-oriented policing, and community-oriented policing. In T. Shelley & A. Grant (Eds.), *Problem-oriented policing: Crime-specific problems, critical issues and making POP work.* Washington, DC: Police Executive Research Forum.

Clarke, R.V. (Ed.). (1993–2007). *Crime prevention studies (Vols. 1–21).* Monsey, NY: Criminal Justice Press.

Clarke, R.V., & Eck, J. E. (2005). *Crime analysis for problem solvers: In 60 small steps.* Washington, DC: US Department of Justice, Office of Community Oriented Policing Services.

Clarke, R.V., & Goldstein, H. (2002). Reducing theft at construction sites: Lessons from a problem-oriented project. In N. Tilley (Ed.), *Analysis for crime prevention.* Monsey, NY: Criminal Justice Press.

Cohen, L., & Felson, M. (1979). Social change and crime rate trends: A routine activities approach. *American Sociological Review, 44,* 588–608.

Cordner, G., & Biebel, E. P. (2005). Problem-oriented policing in practice. *Criminology & Public Policy, 4,* 155–181.

Eck, J. E. (2003). Why don't problems get solved? In W. Skogan (Ed.), *Community policing: Can it work?* (pp. 185–206). Belmont, CA: Wadsworth.

Eck, J. E., & Weisburd, D. L. (1995). *Crime and place.* Monsey, NY: Criminal Justice Press.

Farrell, G., & Pease, K. (1993). *Once bitten, twice bitten: Repeat victimisation and its implications for crime prevention* (Crime Prevention Unit Series Paper 46). London: Police Research Group.

Farrell, G., Sousa, W., & Weisel, D. (2002). The time window effect in repeat victimization: A methodology for its examination, and an empirical study. In N. Tilley (Ed.), *Analysis of crime prevention.* Monsey, NY: Criminal Justice Press.

Geller, W., & Swanger, G. (1995). *Managing innovation in policing: The untapped potential of the middle manager.* Washington, DC: Police Executive Research Forum.

Goldstein, H. (1979). Improving policing: A problem oriented approach. *Crime and Delinquency, 24,* 236–258.

Goldstein, H. (1990). *Problem-oriented policing.* New York: McGraw-Hill.

Goldstein, H. (2003). On further developing problem-oriented policing: The most critical need, the major impediments, and a proposal. In J. Knutsson (Ed.), *Problem-oriented policing: From innovation to mainstream.* Monsey, NY: Criminal Justice Press.

Henry, V. (2002). *The COMPSTAT paradigm*. Flushing, NY: Looseleaf Law.

Knutsson, J. (Ed.). (2003). *Problem-oriented policing: From innovation to mainstream*. Monsey, NY: Criminal Justice Press.

Leigh, A., Reed, T., & Tilley, N. (1998). *Brit POP II: Problem oriented policing in practice* (Police Research Series 93). London: Research Development Statistics.

Mazerolle, L. (2001). *Policing in the 21st century: What works and what doesn't*. Paper presented at the 4th National Outlook Symposium on Crime in Australia.

Mazerolle, L. G., Kadleck, C., & Roehl, J. (1998). Controlling drug and disorder problems: The role of place managers. *Criminology, 36*, 371–404.

Oettmeier, T., & Wycoff, M. A. (1997). *Personnel performance evaluations in the community policing era*. Washington, DC: Community Policing Consortium.

Office of Community Oriented Policing Services. (2003). *Request for proposals: The enhancement of community policing*. Washington, DC: US Department of Justice.

O'Shea, T. C., & Nicholls, K. (2003). Police crime analysis: A survey of US police departments with 100 or more sworn personnel. *Police Practice and Research, 4*, 233–250.

Pease, K. (1998). *Repeat victimization: Taking stock* (Crime Detection and Prevention Series Paper 90). London: Police Research Group.

Pierce, G., Braga, A., Hyatt, R., & Koper, C. (2004). Characteristics and dynamics of illegal firearms markets: Implications for a supply-side strategy. *Justice quarterly, 21*, 391–422.

Police Foundation. (2003). *Advanced problem analysis, crime analysis, and crime mapping training*. Washington, DC: Author.

Port St Lucie, FL Police Department (PSLPD). (2005). *Report narrative templates*. Author.

Port St Lucie, FL Police Department (PSLPD). (2006). *Repeat calls for service report*. Author.

Read, T., & Tilley, N. (2000). *Not rocket science? Problem solving and crime reduction* (Home Office Crime Reduction Research Series Paper 6). London: Police and Reducing Crime Unit.

Romeanes, T. (1996). *Problem-oriented policing: The Cleveland approach*. Unpublished manuscript, Cleveland Constabulary.

Sampson, R., & Scott, M. (2000). *Tackling crime and other public-safety problems: Case studies in problem-solving*. Washington, DC: US Department of Justice, Office of Community Oriented Policing Services.

Santos, R. (2006). *"Bulldozing" construction site burglary in Port St. Lucie, FL*. Herman Goldstein Award Finalist. Retrieved March 14, 2007, from http://www.popcenter.org

Schmerler, K., & Velasco, M. (2002). Primary data collection: A problem-solving necessity. *Crime Mapping News, 4*, 4–8.

Scott, M. (2000). *Problem-oriented policing: Reflections on the first 20 years*. Washington, DC: US Department of Justice, Office of Community Oriented Policing Services.

Scott, M., & Goldstein, H. (1988). *The key elements of problem-oriented policing*. Retrieved December 21, 2005, from http://www.popcenter.org

Sherman, L., Gartin, P., & Buerger, M. (1989). Hot spots of predatory crime: Routine activity and the criminology of place. *Criminology, 27*, 27–55.

Silverman, E. B. (1999). *Innovative strategies in policing*. Boston: Northeastern University Press.

Tilley, N., & Bullock, K. (2003). *Crime reduction and problem-oriented policing*. Cullompton, Devon: Willan.

Weisburd, D. L., & Eck, J. (2004). What can police do to reduce crime, disorder and fear? *The Annals of the American Academy of Political and Social Science, 593,* 42–65.

Weisburd, D. L., Mastrofski, S. D., McNally, A., Greenspan, R., & Willis, J. (2003). Reforming to preserve: Compstat and strategic problem solving in American policing. *Criminology and Public Policy, 2,* 421–456.

Weisburd, D.L., & Mazerolle, L. (2000). Crime and disorder in hot spots: Implications for theory and practice in policing. *Police Quarterly, 3,* 331–349.

Winfree, T., & Newbold, G. (1999). Community policing and the New Zealand police: Correlates of attitudes toward the work world in a community-oriented national police organization. *Policing: An International Journal of Police Strategies & Management, 22,* 589–618.

21

Case Routinization in Investigative Police Work

WILLIAM B. WAEGEL

Discretionary decision making and the nature of the processes by which legal agents structure and manage their handling of persons and events have become central concerns in recent studies of the criminal justice system. Much traditional research on this system has focused on discretion in the context of race and class discrimination. The image is often that of one-person legal units making decisions, but this individualistic conception appears to be substantially misleading. A recent study by Swigert and Farrell (1977) highlights the inadequacy of the use of ostensibly objective criteria of race and class in the analysis of legal processing: they found that social and demographic attributes are filtered through stereotypic conceptions held by legal agents. Their work suggests that conventional research strategies will continue to produce a mass of contradictory findings regarding legal decision making.

Discretion is an irreducible element in the behavior of legal agents. In police work, as in other socially organized activities, members do not always have a set of formal rules which provide an adequate decision-making base for organizing their conduct. Bittner put this succinctly:

> The domain of presumed jurisdiction of a legal rule is essentially open-ended. While there may be a core of clarity about its application, this core is always and necessarily surrounded by uncertainty. . . . No matter how far we descend on the hierarchy of more and more detailed formal instruction, there will always remain a step further down to go, and no measure of effort will ever succeed in eliminating, or even meaningfully curtailing, the area of discretionary freedom of the agent whose duty it is to fit rules to cases. (1970:4)

William B. Waegel, "Case Routinization in Investigative Police Work," *Social Problems*, Vol. 28 No. 3, February, 1981, pp. 263–275. Reprinted by permission of The University of California Press.

Police investigators, prosecutors, public defenders, and presentence case-workers typically must process a steady stream of cases or clients under rather rigid time constraints. In their normal day-to-day activities, these agents do not generally proceed by following a set of codified rules and procedures. However, their discretion is not unlimited nor are their decisions most usefully viewed as individualistic "free choices." The organizational setting in which the work is performed places distinctive constraints and demands on legal agents, producing a specific orientation to case handling and a set of largely shared formulas for dealing with different types of cases.

A more promising approach for understanding legal decision making assigns central importance to occupational typifications and common social stereotypes. Under pressure to observe court schedules or meet paperwork deadlines, and in an effort to reduce problematic features of their tasks at hand, legal agents typically rely on shorthand methods for reaching required decisions.

Typical or "normal case" conceptions have been found to act as a central basis for client treatment in a variety of organizational settings. Sudnow's (1965) study of case processing in a public defender's office found that attorneys did not handle clients and cases in terms of their unique features, but rather used typifications of the normal offense and normal offender as a basis for understanding particular cases and deciding how to handle them. For cases reasonably conforming to a familiar pattern, specific plea bargaining formulas were routinely employed. Stereotypic conceptions have been found to act as guiding imageries for action in the treatment of skid-row residents by patrolmen (Bittner, 1967), in police encounters with juveniles (Piliavin and Briar, 1964) and a "suspect population" (Skolnick, 1967), and in responses to shoplifters (Steffensmeier and Terry, 1973). Swigert and Farrell's (1977) study of the processing of homicide defendants found that critical legal decisions regarding bail, the assignment of counsel, and plea bargaining were based upon the extent to which the person involved conformed to popular criminal stereotypes.[1]

The theoretical implication of these studies is that the decisions made in dealing with a person or event are based not so much on specific features of the actor or situation at hand, but upon the recognition of the person or event as properly belonging to a familiar and typical category and the taken-for-granted understandings built into that category. Stokes and Hewitt (1976) argue for a reflexive relationship between such social constructions and conduct. While meaning structures are a *product* of social action, it is also the case that:

> A great many of the objects that constitute the human world have a "preexisting" meaning, in the sense that people confront such objects with a set of assumptions about them—with a particular preparedness to act in routine, familiar and unquestioned ways. (Stokes and Hewitt, 1976: 841)

Typifications of others and events serve to structure interaction in a provisional way, rendering it more predictable, minimizing its problematic character, and enabling the actor to better manage an ambiguous social environment. Typificatory schemes are used as resources from which to construct a practical solution to the problem at hand.

The corresponding implication for research is that conventional research strategies focusing on decision-making variations between individuals and between functionally similar organizations have severe limitations. A more fruitful approach for studying processing outcomes takes as its focus the shared categorization schemes used by members in organizing their day-to-day activities.

Working Cases: An Overview

In the police department studies,[2] detectives face two practical problems which substantially shape the manner in which cases are handled. They must satisfy the paperwork demands of the organization (referred to as "keeping the red numbers down") by classifying each case and producing a formal investigative report within two weeks after the case is assigned. Sanctions may be applied to those who fail to meet deadlines and who thus accumulate too many "red numbers." At the same time, the detectives are under the same pressure as other employees: they must produce. Specifically, detectives believe they must produce an acceptable level of arrests which will enhance their chances of remaining in the detective division and gaining promotion. While no arrest quota is formalized in the division, there is a shared belief that one should produce roughly two to three lock-ups per week. This arrest level is a practical concern for the detective because most wish to remain in the division and avoid transfer "back to the pit" (i.e., back into uniform in the patrol division). Moreover, the position of detective holds the highest status of any assignment in the department, and a transfer, therefore, generally entails a loss of status.

For the vast majority of cases handled, no explicit procedures exist to indicate what must be done on the case and how to go about doing it. As detectives go about the ordinary business of investigating and processing cases, they can select strategies ranging from a *pro forma* victim interview comprising the total investigative activity devoted to the case, to a full-scale investigation involving extensive interviewing, physical evidence, the use of informants, interrogation, surveillance, and other activities. The selection of a particular handling strategy in most cases is an informal process and not the direct result of formal organizational policy or procedure. This process of selection is grounded in practical solutions to concrete problems faced by the detective; it consists of an assignment of meaning to persons and events in ways that are regarded as proper because they have "worked" in previous cases.

A great deal of actual detective work may thus be seen as a process of mapping the features of a particular case onto a more general and commonly recognized *type* of case. The present work suggests that a detective's interpretation, classification, and handling of cases are guided by a set of occupationally shared typifications. The categorization schemes used by detectives center around specific configurations of information regarding the victim, the offense, and possible suspects. Information pertaining to these three elements constitutes the meaningful unit that detectives deal with: the case.

The most basic dimension of case categorization is that of the routine versus the nonroutine. Where a particular configuration of information regarding the victim, the offense, and possible suspects appears, the competent detective understands the case as a routine one—as an instance of a familiar type—and particular handling strategies are deemed appropriate. Such cases contrast with those which are viewed as nonroutine: that is, where no general type is available to which the case reasonably corresponds, and where the case is vigorously investigated and the detective attends to the unique features of the case. Case routinization is most characteristic for burglaries, which comprise the bulk of cases handled by detectives, but it is also exhibited in the handling of many assault, robbery, rape, and homicide cases.

The categorization schemes used by detectives are derived from concrete experiences in working cases and are continually assessed for their relevance, adequacy, and effectiveness in handling one's caseload. It is because typificatory schemes serve as a solution to practical problems commonly faced by all detectives that they learn to share most of the content of these schemes. Both through direct experience in working cases and through interaction with other members, the detective learns to categorize and handle cases in ways that are regarded as proper by other detectives.

Routine case imageries serve as resources upon which detectives may draw to construct a solution to their problem of interpreting, investigating, and resolving their cases. The features of a specific case are compared with routine case imagery in a process of interpretive interplay. In some instances a correspondence is readily apparent, in others a fit is forced by the detective, and in still others the features of a specific case render the use of the typical imagery inappropriate. The interpretation and handling of a case may also change over the case's history; a routine case may come to be treated as nonroutine upon the receipt of additional information, and vice-versa.

The Organizational Context of Case Routinization

In the department studied, detectives have no formal guidelines for allocating time and effort to different cases and there is little effective monitoring of daily activities by supervisors.[3] In conducting their work, detectives are, however, guided and constrained by two organizational imperatives: 1) the requirement to submit investigative reports, and 2) the requirement to produce arrests. In other words, the work is not organized by formal rules, but rather by the kinds of outcomes that are expected. Both of these expected outcomes generate practical problems leading to routinized solutions.

An investigative report must be produced for each case assigned, and its submission within the prescribed time limit is viewed as a fundamental constraint on how vigorously different cases can be investigated. Departmental policy indicates that each investigative report submitted must be reviewed and signed by a supervisory lieutenant. However, in practice, these reports are often given only a cursory glance, and seldom is the content of a report questioned or challenged by a lieutenant. The primary concern of the supervisor is that the submission of reports complies with time deadlines.

The potential a case appears to hold for producing an arrest also has an important impact on how the case will be handled. Most detectives believe that the number of arrests they produce will be used as a basis for evaluating performance and, therefore, will affect decisions regarding promotions and transfers. Attempts to cope with the practical problems of meeting paperwork demands, while at the same time producing a satisfactory number of arrests, creates a situation in which one burglary case involving a $75 loss may receive less than five minutes investigative effort, yet another case with an identical loss may be worked on exclusively for two or three full days. These two concerns constitute central features of the work setting which structure case handling.

Paperwork

Formal organizational procedure demands that a case be investigated, classified, and a report produced within a specified time period after it is assigned. Detectives experience paperwork requirements and deadlines as central sources of pressure and tension in their job, and stories abound concerning former detectives who "could handle the job but couldn't handle the paperwork."

Most cases are assigned during the daily roll-call sessions. At this point, the information about the incident consists of an original report written by a patrol officer and any supplemental reports submitted by personnel in the evidence detection unit. Each case is stamped with a "red number" which supervisors use to monitor compliance with report deadlines.

Ordinary cases require the submission of two reports within specific time periods. A brief first-day report, consisting essentially of an interview with the victim, is formally required the day after the case is assigned. However, this deadline is generally ignored by supervisors and first-day reports are seldom submitted. The more meaningful deadline for detectives is the fourteen-day limit for the submission of an investigative report. Here, the detective must provide a detailed accounting of the activities undertaken in investigating the incident and assign an investigative status to the case. Compliance with this second deadline is closely monitored: every Sunday a lieutenant draws up a list of each detective's overdue red numbers, and this list is read at the next roll call along with a caution to keep up with one's paperwork.

In the investigative report, the detective must classify the status of the investigation as suspended, closed arrest, or open. The ability to manipulate information about cases to fit them into these categories is of the utmost importance to detectives, for it is through such strategic manipulations that they are able to manage their caseloads effectively.

Of the total cases handled by a detective, a substantial majority are classified as suspended. This means that the steps already taken in the investigation (which may consist merely of a telephone interview with the victim) have not uncovered sufficient information to warrant continued investigation of the incident. Any number of acceptable reasons for suspending a case may be offered, ranging from a simple statement that the victim declines to prosecute up to a fairly elaborate report detailing contacts with the victim, the entry of serial numbers of stolen articles into the computerized crime files, the usefulness of evidence obtained from the scene, and a conclusion that the case must be suspended because there are no further investigative leads. Over 80 percent of the burglary cases assigned in the city are suspended; this percentage drops considerably for robbery cases and even more for assault, rape, and homicide cases.[4]

An investigation is classified as closed when one or more arrests have been made pertaining to the incident and the detective anticipates no additional arrests. A case is classified as open when an investigation extends beyond the fourteen-day limit but it is expected that an arrest eventually will be made. Generally, only major cases may remain classified as open after the fourteen-day investigative period.

Producing Arrests

As organizations become more bureaucratized and their procedures more formalized, there evolves a general tendency to develop quantitative indices or measures of individual performance. In the department studied, most detectives believe that the crude number of lock-ups they make is used as a basis for assessing their performance and competence in doing investigative work. Every arrest a detective makes is entered into a logbook, which is available for inspection by superiors and from which they can compare each detective's arrest level with that of others.

Ambitious detectives in particular are very conscious of producing a steady stream of arrests, feeling that this is an effective way to achieve recognition and promotion. One young detective boasted:

> I've made over forty lock-ups since the beginning of the year and eleven in April alone. Since I don't really have a godfather in here, I gotta' depend on making good lock-ups if I'm gonna' make sergeant.

This detective's use of the term "godfather" reveals a widely shared belief that some individuals are promoted not because of their performance but because they have a friend or relative in a position of power within the department.

Skimming off selected cases from one's workload is widely practiced as a means of achieving a steady stream of arrests. The practice of skimming refers to (1) selectively working only those cases that appear potentially solvable from information contained in the original report, and (2) summarily suspending the remainder of one's ordinary cases. Supervisors are certainly aware of both aspects of this practice, but they recognize its practical value in producing arrests. Moreover, supervisors, to a greater extent than working detectives, find their performance assessed in crude quantitative terms, and they are likely to be questioned by superiors if arrest levels begin to drop sharply. Supervisors support the practice of skimming even though they recognize that it ensures that a majority of ordinary cases will never receive a thorough investigation. The pragmatic work orientation of detectives is further revealed in the lack of attention given to conviction rates both by detectives and supervisors. Competence and productivity are judged by the arrests made, not by the proportion of cases which survive the scrutiny of the judicial process.

The recognition of potentially productive cases and of their utility in effectively managing one's caseload are among the earliest skills taught to the neophyte in the detective division. Moreover, newcomers are taught that their work on burglary cases is the primary basis upon which their performance will be judged. In a sizeable percentage of crimes against persons, the perpetrator is readily identified from information provided by the victim. Since no great investigative effort or acumen is involved, the same credit is not accorded an arrest in this type of case as in burglary cases. Detectives are expected to produce a steady flow of "quality" arrests: that is, arrests involving some effort and skill on the part of the investigator. Straightforward assault cases involving acquainted parties, for example, are often handed out by supervisors along with a remark such as "Here's an easy one for you. "

Interpreting Cases

The preceding observations have suggested that detectives are constrained in their conception and handling of cases not by the formal organization of their work or by supervisory surveillance, but rather by the bureaucratic pressure of writing reports and producing the proper number and quality of arrests. The process of interpreting cases in accordance with these pragmatic concerns may now be considered.

Data derived from observation of detective-victim interviews and from written case reports provide a basis for examining the interpretive schemes used by detectives. In the victim interview, the kinds of questions asked and the pieces of information sought out reveal the case patterns recognized as routine for the different offenses commonly encountered.[5] However, in attempting to make sense of the incident at hand, detectives attend to much more than is revealed in their explicit communications with the victim. Interpretation of the case is also based upon understanding of the victim's lifestyle, racial or ethnic membership group, class position, and possible clout or connections—especially as these factors beat upon such concerns as the likelihood of the victim inquiring into the progress of the investigation, the victim's intentions regarding prosecution, and the victim's competence and quality as a source of information.

The interpretive schemes employed also receive partial expression in the written investigative reports which must be produced for each case. These reports contain a selective accounting of the meaning assigned to a case, the information and understandings upon which this interpretation is based, and the reasonableness of the linkage between this particular interpretation of the case and the handling strategy employed.[6]

Several important features of the process of interpreting cases as routine or nonroutine may be seen in the following incidents.

Case 1: Attempted Homicide

A radio call was broadcast that a shooting had just occurred on the street in a working-class residential area. The victim, a white male, was still conscious when the detectives arrived, although he had been severely wounded in the face by a shotgun blast. He indicated that he had been robbed and shot by three black males, and provided a vague description of their appearance and clothing. This description was broadcast, an area search was initiated, the crime scene was cordoned off, and a major investigation was begun.

The following morning, the victim's employer brought into question the account of the incident that had been provided. He indicated his belief that the incident involved a "lover's triangle" situation between the victim, a male acquaintance of the victim, and a woman. All three were described as "hillbillies." The three parties were interviewed separately and each denied this version of the incident. After further questioning, the victim finally admitted that the story concerning three black males was false, but would say nothing more about the incident. Articles of the woman's clothing believed to show bloodstains and a weapon believed to have been used were obtained, but crime lab analysis would take at least three weeks. The case was now interpreted as a routine "domestic shooting" and little additional effort was devoted to it.

Case 2: Burglary

A detective parked his car in front of an address in a public housing project and pulled out the original burglary report. A new member of the prosecutor's office was riding along to observe how detectives work. The detective read over the report, and after hesitating for awhile decided to go into the residence. He explained to the prosecutor that the loss was an inexpensive record player and added, "This one's a pork chop, like most of the burglaries we get. But we gotta' go and interview the victim before suspending it." The detective asked the victim if she knew who might have committed the burglary or if she had heard about anyone committing burglaries in the area. Negative replies followed both questions. The entire encounter with the victim lasted less than two minutes.

Case 3: Assault and Robbery

A robbery squad detective was waiting for two victims to come in the hall to be interviewed. Both were black, middle-aged, center-city residents who were described by the detective as "dead-end alcoholics." They had been robbed in their residence by a young male who had forced his way in, taken $20 from the pair, and cut the female victim on the hand with a knife. The victims were able to provide the detective with the name of their assailant, and they both picked his photograph out of a number of pictures they were shown. Several minutes later the detective handed them a photograph of a different individual, asking, "Are you sure this is the guy who robbed you?" After inspecting the picture they replied that they knew this person as well but he had not been the one who robbed them. At this point, the detective sat down and took a formal statement from the victims.

When the victims had left, the detective explained his views and usual handling of such "ghetto robberies": "In a case like this, what can we do? To tell you the truth, the only way this kind of thing is going to stop is for the victims or somebody they know to kill this guy off. My involvement in this case is minimal. If the two victims, those two old drunks, if they sober up and if they show up in court, we'll see how they do there. It's up to them here and not up to me."

Case 4: Burglary

A detective entered the center-city residence of a burglary victim in a block where about one-fourth of the row houses were vacant. He examined a large hole in a basement wall that had been made to gain entry, and then sat down to compile a list of articles that had been stolen. The victim had literally been cleaned out, losing every easily transportable item of value she had owned. The woman explained that she worked during the day, that this was the fifth time she had been burglarized in the past four years, and that her coverage had been dropped by the insurance company. She added that she lived in the house for 21 years and was not about to move, and then asked, "What can I do to keep this from happening again?" The detective replied: "Ma'am, I don't know what to tell you. You're the only white family on this block. Most of the people around here work during the daytime and a lot of these people, even if they saw somebody coming out of your house with some of your stuff, they're not going to call the cops anyhow. That's the way it is around here. It's a shame, but that's the way it is." The detective entered the serial numbers of some of the stolen articles into the computerized stolen property files, "to cover myself, just in case." The written report indicated that the pawnshop sheets had been checked but in fact this step was not taken. When the report deadline approached, the case was suspended.

Case 5: Homicides

Two homicides had occurred over the weekend. On Monday morning two detectives who were working on the different cases were discussing the status of their investigations. One detective, who was investigating a shooting death that occurred in a crowded bar in the presence of 100 persons noted that he was on the verge of making a lock-up even though none of the witnesses present had voluntarily come forward. The other detective was investigating a bludgeoning death of a male homosexual whose body had been found by firemen called to extinguish a small fire in the victim's residence. There were as yet no suspects in the case. The second detective took offense to remarks made by the other comparing the lack of progress in the second case to the nearly completed investigation in the barroom case. The second detective remarked, "Anybody can handle a killing like you've got. What we've got here is a murder, not a killing."

The above incidents illustrate detectives' use of a body of accumulated knowledge, beliefs, and assumptions which lead to the interpretation of certain case patterns as common, typical, and routine. Cases are interpreted primarily using conceptions of (1) how identifiable the perpetrators seem to be; (2) the normal social characteristics of the victims; and (3) the settings involved, and behavior seen as typical in such settings. A detective's initial efforts on a case tend to focus on these three aspects, in the process of assigning meaning to the case and selecting an appropriate strategy for handling it.

1.   Conceptions of how different kinds of offenses are typically committed—especially how identifiable the perpetrators seem to be—are routinely used in interpreting incidents. These imageries are specifically relevant to a detective's practical concerns. The ordinary burglary (cases 2 and 4) is seen as involving a crude forced entry at a time of day or at a location where it is unlikely that anyone will witness the perpetrator entering or exiting. A burglary victim's ability or inability to provide information identifying a probable perpetrator constitutes the single feature of burglary cases which is given greatest interpretive significance. In roughly ten percent of these cases, the victim provides the name of a suspected perpetrator (commonly an ex-boyfriend, a relative or a neighboring resident), and vigorous effort is devoted to the case. For the remaining burglary cases, the initial inclination is to treat them as routine incidents deserving of only minimal investigative effort. In these routine cases the victim's race and class position have a decisive impact on whether the case will be summarily suspended or whether some minor investigative activities will be undertaken to impress the victim that "something is being done."

On the other hand, assault, rape, and homicide cases commonly occur in a face-to-face situation which affords the victim an opportunity to observe the assailant. Further, detectives recognize that many personal assault offenses involve acquainted parties. The earliest piece of information sought out and the feature of such cases given the greatest interpretive significance is whether the offense occurred between parties who were in some way known to one another prior to the incident. The interpretation and handling of the shooting incident in case 1 changed markedly when it was learned that the victim and suspect were acquainted parties and that the offense reasonably conformed to a familiar pattern of domestic assaults. Where the victim and perpetrator are acquainted in assault, rape, and homicide cases, the incident is seen as containing the core feature of the routine offense pattern for these cases. In such incidents a perfunctory investigation is usually made for the identity of the perpetrator generally is easily learned from the victim or from persons close to the victim.

The barroom homicide in case 5 was termed a "killing" and viewed as a routine case because the victim and perpetrator were previously acquainted and information linking the perpetrator to the crime could be easily obtained. The term "murder" is reserved for those homicides which do not correspond to a typical pattern.

A somewhat different pattern follows in the category of incidents which detectives refer to as "suspect rapes." Victims having certain social characteristics (females from lower-class backgrounds who are viewed as having low intelligence or as displaying some type of mental or emotional abnormality) are viewed as most likely to make a false allegation of rape. Where a victim so perceived reports a sexual assault by a person with whom she had some prior acquaintance, the initial orientation of the detective is to obtain information which either negates the crime of rape (the complainant actually consented) or warrants reducing the charge to a lesser offense. Where the victim and assailant were not previously acquainted, the case receives a vigorous investigative effort. The level of police resources devoted to the case varies according to the race and social standing of the victim.

2.   Conceptions of the normal social characteristics of victims are also central to case routinization. Victims having different social characteristics are regarded as being more or less likely to desire or follow through with prosecution in the case, to be reliable sources of information about it, and to inquire as to the outcome of the investigation.

The treatment of the assault and robbery in case 3 illustrates how a case may be interpreted and handled primarily in terms of the victim's class position, race, and presumed lifestyle and competencies. The case was cleared by arrest on the basis of information provided by the victims, but the handling of this "ghetto robbery" involved little actual police effort. No attempt was made to locate witnesses, gather evidence from the crime scene, or otherwise strengthen the case against the accused.

Poor and working-class people who are regarded as unlikely to make inquiries regarding the handling and disposition of the case are seen as typical of victims in the category of routine burglaries. Case 2 illustrates how the interpretation of an incident may be accomplished solely on the basis of information contained in the patrol report and prior to an actual interview with the victim. The interview was structured in this case by the detective's expectation of its outcome.

Case 4 illustrates how inconsistent elements in an otherwise routine pattern (in this instance the victim's social status and apparent interest in the handling of the case) are managed to suit the purposes of the detective. Detectives speak of a case "coming back on them" if a respectable victim contacts superiors regarding progress in the case when the incident has received little or no investigative effort. Informing the victim that the case was not solvable largely because of her neighbor's attitudes enabled the detective to suspend the case with minimal problems.

3.   Routinization formulas, finally, contain conceptions of the settings in which different kinds of offenses normally occur and the expected behavior of inhabitants of those settings. While assumptions about victims and perpetrators are derived in part from the nature of the offense involved, the physical and social setting where the incident occurred also contributes to a detective's understanding of these parties. The fact that the burglary in case 2

occurred in a particular public housing project told the detective much of what he felt he had to know about the case. It should be noted that none of these perceptions were communicated to the prosecutor observing the detective work; they were part of the taken-for-granted background upon which the detective based his handling of the case.

With regard to actual and potential *witnesses*, however, a detective's assumptions and beliefs are based primarily on the offense setting, if the witness is seen as a normal inhabitant of that setting. (This latter qualification simply recognizes that detectives attribute different inclinations and sentiments to social workers or salesmen who may have witnessed an incident than to residents of the area who may have witnessed a crime.)

The impact of territorial conceptions may be seen in the handling of case 4. Routine burglaries occur mainly in low-income housing projects, residences in deteriorating center-city areas or, less frequently, in commercial establishments in or near these locations. Residents of these areas are considered unlikely to volunteer that they have witnessed a crime. Although official investigative procedure dictates that neighboring residents be interviewed to determine whether they saw or heard anything that might be of value to the investigation, this step was not undertaken in cases 2 or 4 because it was assumed that the residents would be uncooperative.

Routine cases, then, may be seen as having two components, one at the level of consciousness and cognition, and the other at the level of observable behavior. A detective's interpretation of a case as routine involves an assessment of whether sufficient correspondence exists between the current case and some typical pattern to warrant handling it in the normal way. The criterion of sufficient correspondence implies that not all the elements of the typical pattern need be present for a detective to regard a case as a routine one. Common elements are viewed and used as resources which may be drawn upon selectively in accordance with one's practical concerns and objectives. Further, when certain elements in a case appear inconsistent with the typical pattern, there is a tendency to force and manage a sufficient fit between the particular and the typical in ways that help detectives deal with their caseload management problems and constraints.

These features of the interpretation process mean that the assessments of the routine or nonroutine nature of a case take on more of the character of a dichotomy than a continuum. Once an assessment is made, the case will be handled by means of prescribed formulas unless additional information changes the interpretation. It must be emphasized that the routinization process is not a matter of automatic or unreflective mapping of case features onto more general conceptions of criminal incidents. The interpretation of any particular case is shaped by a detective's understandings of what is required and expected and of how to manage these concerns effectively.

Case Handling

Case handling normally proceeds in accordance with informal under-standings shared among detectives. Routine case patterns are associated with prescribed handling recipes. It is critical to an understanding of investigative police work that interpretation of criminal incidents as routine or nonroutine largely determines which cases will be summarily suspended, which will be investigated, and how vigorous or extensive that investigation will be.

The characteristic behavioral element of a routine case is an absence of vigorous or thorough investigative effort. Two distinct sets of circumstances are ordinarily encountered in routine cases which lead to such a superficial or cursory investigative effort. The first, most common in burglary and robbery cases, is that the available information concerning the incident is seen as so meager or of so little utility that the possibility of making a quick arrest is vir-tually nonexistent. Viewing the case as nonproductive, and not wishing to expend effort on cases for which there are no formal rewards, the detective produces a brief investigative report detailing the routine features of the inci-dent, concludes the case summary with "N.I.L." (no investigative leads were found), and classifies it as a suspended case.

The second set of circumstances associated with an absence of vigorous investigative effort involves assault, rape, and homicide cases which require some investigation because of their seriousness and the possibility of scrutiny by the judicial process. However, in many such incidents the facts of the case are so obvious and straightforward that little actual investigative work needs to be done. In these three types of offenses the victim and perpetrator are often known to one another, and it is not at all uncommon for the victim to name the assailant as soon as the police arrive. Cases in which a spouse or lover is still standing by the victim with weapon in hand when the police arrive, or in which the victim names the perpetrator before expiring, are not unusual. In essence, such cases are solved without any substantial police investigation. The detective is obligated to produce a comprehensive report on the incidence, and the investigation is generally classified as closed in this report if the perpetrator has been apprehended. Indeed, in such obvious and straightforward cases the detective's only difficult task may be that of locating the perpetrator.[7]

Handling recipes associated with routine cases have a practical and instrumental character, reflecting the objective circumstances surrounding the investigation of many criminal events. After all, in the great majority of burglary cases the probability of ascertaining the identity of the perpetrator is rather small. Yet, handling recipes reflect certain *beliefs* and *assumptions* on the part of detectives concerning such matters as a victim's willingness to cooperate fully in the case, whether persons in particular sections of the city are likely to volunteer information about a crime, or the kind of impression a victim or witness would make in court. Such beliefs and assumptions consti-tute integral features in the construction of cases as routine or nonroutine, and they represent a pivotal linkage between specific features of cases and particular handling recipes.

The following incident illustrates the extent to which case handling may be guided by the detective's beliefs and assumptions about the nature of an incident and the parties involved:

> **Case 6:**
> A detective was assigned a case in which a man had stabbed his com-mon-law wife in the arm with a kitchen knife. The patrol report on the incident indicated that the woman had been taken to City Hall to sign an arrest warrant, while the man had been arrested by patrol officers on the charge of felony assault and released on his own recognizance. Nomi-nally, the detective was required to collect additional information and evidence relating to the incident and to write a detailed and comprehen-sive report which would be used in prosecuting the case. However, the detective's interpretation of the incident, based on his understanding of the area in which it occurred and the lifestyles of the persons involved, led him to view any further investigative effort on his part as futile. He remarked: "These drunks, they're always stabbing one another over here. Then you see 'em the next day and they're right back together again. She won't show up in court anyhow. Why waste my time and everybody else's on it." The handling of the case involved only the production of a brief report which concluded: "The victim in this complaint wishes no further investigation by the police department. This complaint is to be classified as closed."

The interpretive schemes used by detectives are not based solely on their experiences as police investigators, but also on their accumulated experi-ences as everyday social actors; they thus reflect commonsense social knowl-edge. Categorizations made by detectives about race, class, ethnicity, sex, and territory parallel wider cultural evaluations of morality and worth. None of the features of the formal organization of detective work substantially reduce this reliance on commonsense knowledge and its typical biases, prejudices, and interpretations.

Summary and Implications

Some general features of case routinization may now be noted in an attempt to clarify the interpretive activities through which detectives achieve order and predictability in their handling of cases and their encounters with victims and other relevant actors.

1.   Shortly after receipt of a case, specific pieces of information are sought out and attended to for use in assessing the typicality of the incident. That is, the fundamental case-working orientation of detectives involves an attempt to establish commonalities between an actual case and typical case patterns. Inci-dents having typical features are interpreted and constructed as some variety of routine case. The orientation to typify and routinize cases is partly traceable

to bureaucratic pressures and constraints to meet paperwork deadlines and produce a certain quantity and quality not of convictions but of arrests.

2. The interpretation of an incident is accomplished by attending to case features having commonly recognized utility as indicators of the type of case at hand. Detectives use such routinization schemes unless some problematic feature of an actual case brings into question their applicability and appropriateness. The interpretation of a case as routine or nonroutine essentially determines whether the case will be quickly closed or suspended or whether it will receive a more vigorous and extensive investigation. However, this initial assignment of meaning is provisional and subject to revision or modification upon receipt of additional information. Most importantly, the handling of cases is directed by these informal categorization schemes, and is not the result of formal organizational policy or procedures. These schemes constitute a taken-for-granted background of decision making.

3. The interpretive schemes shared by detectives represent "successful" solutions to common practical problems, based on experience and shared understandings about the nature of urban crime and about types of urban residents, lifestyles, and territories. These understandings are rooted in socially distributed as well as role-specific knowledge, for both provide a basis for constructing solutions to work problems. Occupationally specific knowledge provides a set of instructions for interpreting case patterns in ways which enable a detective to successfully manage organizational constraints and demands. Commonsense social knowledge provides an understanding of the typical characteristics, attitudes, and action patterns of persons encountered. Identities may be readily assigned to persons by drawing on this stock of knowledge. Such identity assignments structure case handling along race, class, age, sex, and territorial lines in ways that are intended to minimize case handling problems. Because of this reliance on general social knowledge, the treatment of different types of urban residents tends to reflect wider cultural evaluations of social worth.

4. The essential nature of these interpretive processes is phenomenological rather than mechanical or rule-guided. In formulating a particular case, the operative process involves a determination of whether sufficient correspondence exists between the actual case and the paradigmatic case to warrant handling the incident in routine, low-effort ways. Sufficient correspondence assessments are accomplished in ways that serve the practical purposes of detectives, especially those of paper-work compliance and productivity.

5. Accordingly, routine cases are not constituted as a single determinant pattern. A variety of combinations of case features may result in routine handling of the case. For each offense, a core feature or set of features gets maximum interpretive significance. When a core feature is recognized in a particular case, other features which are ambiguous or even contradictory tend to be interpreted in a manner consistent with the identified core feature. Additional interpretive features, particularly the social status of the victim, are used as resources in selecting a safe and workable handling strategy.

6.   In highly routinized case patterns, there is a tendency to squeeze great indicativeness out of a few case features. Detectives often rely upon assumptions to add detail to a case rather than actually gather information to further specify the type of case at hand. In other words, it is frequently taken for granted that certain investigative procedures will have predictable outcomes. Frequently, this process manifests itself in the fudging, doctoring, and manipulation of formal organizational reports.

It is likely that interpretive schemes having similar features will be found in all bureaucratically organized enterprises where large numbers of clients or cases are processed (e.g., social service centers, public hospitals, and other agencies in the criminal justice system). Whenever we find an organizational setting where members deal with similar events time and again, and where there are no features in the formal organization of the work which act to counter stereotyping, we may expect to find routinization schemes in use. These schemes will be used to categorize the population and apply standard patterns of treatment to each category.

These observations have significant implications for the study of decision making by legal agents. Decision making by bureaucratic agents inevitably involves discretion on the part of the agent who must fit general rules to particular cases. This discretionary latitude will be reflected in different forms of decision making in different kinds of organizational settings. The work of Roth (1977), Scheff (1978), Sudnow (1965), and others suggests that caseload size, amount of information readily available about the person or event, the nature of the body of knowledge used, and the expectation of future interaction with the person are crucial features governing the nature of the decision-making process. Where caseloads are high, continued interaction is not anticipated, minimal information is available, and the body of knowledge used by the agent is imprecise—stereotypes tend to become the operative and binding basis for decision making. Accordingly, detective work, presentence casework, public defender work, and medical practice in clinics or emergency rooms may be seen as lying toward the end of a continuum where typifications act as essentially final judgments.

At the other end of the continuum are settings where caseload sizes are smaller, more detailed information about the person is available, future interaction is anticipated, and decision making is grounded in a more substantial body of knowledge. In such settings, typificatory schemes are likely to be used only as provisional hypotheses, to be amplified and modified over the course of the encounter. Thus in probation work, some types of social service work, and the practice of general medicine, we might expect to find interaction only tentatively structured by stereotypic understandings. As interaction proceeds in these latter settings, typifications will begin to fade in importance as the basis for decision making.

Endnotes

[1] The use of shared typificatory schemes to make required decisions appears to be a pervasive phenomenon not only in social control organizations, but in other organizations which process large numbers of people as well. Roth (1977) observed the same basic process in the evaluation, categorization, and treatment of patients by hospital personnel. The differential treatment of clients of public service bureaucracies was likewise found to be rooted in occupational typifications (Gordon, 1975).

[2] The description and the analysis presented here are based on nine months of participant observation fieldwork in a city police detective division. Further, information about access agreements, characteristics of the city and department, the field role adopted, and problems encountered during the research is available from the author.

[3] An exception to this general observation occurs where a supervisor imposes a "major case" definition on an incident. In highly publicized or nonroutine homicide or rape cases, especially those involving higher status victims, a supervisor frequently takes an active part in the investigation and more closely monitors and directs the activities of detectives. With regard to the influence of the victim's social status on case handling, see Wilson's (1968:27) analysis of police perceptions of the legitimacy of complaints made by middle-class versus lower-class victims.

[4] Official nationwide clearance rates are listed as 17.6 percent for burglary, 27.3 percent for robbery, 63.4 percent for felonious assault, 51.1 percent for rape, and 79.9 percent for homicide (Hindelang et al., 1977).

[5] Cf. Sudnow's (1965) argument that public defenders use their first interview with a client to gain an initial sense of the defendant's place in the social structure as well as the typicality or lack thereof of the offense with which the person has been charged.

[6] Garfinkel (1967:186–207) argues that organizational records are not to be treated as accurate or mirror reflections of the actual handling of a client or case by organizational members. However, these records can be employed to examine how members go about constructing a meaningful conception of a client or case and use it for their own practical purposes. Any valid sociological use of such records requires detailed knowledge on the part of the researcher regarding the context in which the records are produced, background understandings of members, and organizationally relevant purposes and routines.

[7] Reiss (1971) makes a similar observation. He found that a great deal of detective work in the department studied merely involves attempting to locate identified perpetrators. The Rand survey of investigative practices in 153 police departments draws conclusions similar to those presented here. It was found that substantially more than half of all serious reported crimes receive no more than superficial attention from investigators (Greenwood and Petersilia, 1975).

References

Bittner, E. (1967, October). The police on skid row: A study of peace keeping. *American Sociological Review, 32,* 699–715.

Bittner, E. (1970). *The functions of the police in modern society.* Chevy Chase, MD: National Institute of Mental Health.

Garfinkel, H. (1967). *Studies in ethnomethodology.* Englewood Cliffs, NJ: Prentice-Hall.

Gordon, L. (1975). Bureaucratic competence and success in dealing with public bureaucracies. *Social Problems, 23*(2), 197–208.

Greenwood, P. W., & Petersilia, J. (1975). *The criminal investigation process* (Vol. 1). Santa Monica, CA: The Rand Corporation.

Hindelang, M., Gottfredson, M., Dunn, C., & Parisi, N. (1977). *Sourcebook of criminal justice statistics.* Washington, DC: National Criminal Justice Information and Statistics Service.

Piliavin, I., & Briar, S. (1964). Police encounters with juveniles. *American Sociological Review, 70,* 206–214.

Reiss, A. (1971). *Police and the public*. New Haven: Yale University Press.

Roth, J. (1977, October). Some contingencies of the moral evaluation and control of clients. *American Journal of Sociology, 77*, 830–856.

Scheff, T. (1978). Typification in rehabilitation agencies. In E. Rubington & M. S. Weinberg (Eds.), *Deviance: The interactionist perspective* (pp. 172–175). New York: Macmillan.

Skolnick, J. (1967). *Justice without trial*. New York: Wiley.

Steffensmeier, D., & Terry, R. (1973). Deviance and respectability: An observational study of reactions to shoplifting. *Social Forces, 51*, 417–426.

Stokes, R., & Hewitt, J. (1976). Aligning actions. *American Sociological Review, 41*, 838–849.

Sudnow, D. (1965). Normal crimes: Sociological features of the penal code in a public defender's office. *Social Problems, 12*(3), 255–276.

Swigert, V., & Farrell, R. (1977). Normal homicides and the law. *American Sociological Review, 42*, 16–32.

Wilson, J. Q. (1968). *Varieties of police behavior*. Cambridge, MA: Harvard University Press.

22

Negotiation and Plea Bargaining Models
An Organizational Perspective

ALBERT R. MATHENY

Plea bargaining seems eminently compatible with the assumptions involved in economic models of resource allocation and decision-theory models of negotiation One can easily picture the choices between trial and negotiated settlement of criminal charges as a matter of utility calculation within the resource constraints of prosecution and defense (Landes, 1971; Forst and Brosi, 1977). Similarly, the settlement itself can readily be interpreted as an "equilibrium point" between competing negotiation strategies based upon the defendant's and prosecutor's expectations of trial outcome (Nagel and Neef, 1976a, 1976b; Fried, 1974). It is no wonder, then, that scholars from several disciplines have recently focused their efforts on "modeling" the plea bargaining process (Lachman and McLauchlan, 1977). A common characteristic of these modeling efforts has been their emphasis on the behavior of individual participants in the criminal process, stressing the "rationality" of that behavior, consistent with the classic assumption of micro-economic theory.

The analysis of the criminal process, and particularly plea bargaining, in terms of economic and decision-theory models, has contributed some powerful insights to our understanding of the actual operation of the criminal justice system and has inspired several empirical efforts aimed at demonstrating the efficacy of a few derivatives from these models (e.g., Landes, 1971, 1974; Forst and Brosi, 1977). Of course, the models are based on a set of simplifying assumptions which necessarily sacrifice descriptive specificity for theoretical generality.

This essay assesses the appropriateness of the dominant models of plea bargaining by introducing certain organizational assumptions into their equations in an attempt to reconcile individual-level behavior of the participants in the criminal process with the collective, administrative demands arising from the peculiar organization of the American criminal justice system. Specifically, we employ "contingency theory" (Thompson, 1967, Thompson, 1973; Carter, 1974a) in order to introduce the concept of *uncertainty*[1] into the plea bargaining equation. Out intent is to temper the economic and decision-theory models with an "organizational model" which can incorporate a broader range of the available empirical information into the practice of plea bargaining. The direction of our analysis is toward greater "descriptive specificity" about plea bargaining, and, as a result, the reasoning used here will be less elegant than that employed by the formal modelers of plea bargaining. Nonetheless, our assertions should enable us to test empirically some of those formal assumptions with available criminal justice data on dispositions and sentencing.

Uncertainty and the Administration of Justice

At the outset, we must conceptualize the criminal process in terms compatible with the language of organization theory. Initially, it is helpful to consider the adversary process as the formally prescribed "technology" of the criminal justice system, used to determine the guilt or innocence of the accused and to establish appropriate punishment.[2] An organization's integrity vis-à-vis its environment depends primarily upon its ability to maintain and enhance the predictability of its technical operations by insulating them from uncertainty in the environment.

The criminal justice system as an organization confronts a peculiar problem. Its formally prescribed technology itself contains elements of uncertainty which contribute to unpredictability in its operation. As noted by Packer (1968), the outcome of a criminal trial is the product of a system of challenge which resists a priori rationalization. The skepticism inherent in the "due process" model of criminal adjudication, replete with its presumptions favoring the defendant, restrictive rules of evidence, and the participation of a lay jury (when requested), injects an essential unpredictability into the determination of guilt or innocence.[3] Because the criminal justice system processes cases despite their unpredictable content, the analyst must explain how the system manages uncertainty in processing criminal cases.

The first step is to examine how the organization actually treats the accused, independent of legal ideals and the formal prescriptions of due process. Then one must describe the way organizational actors make decisions in light of administrative realities and the formal procedures involved in applying criminal sanctions.

Several observers have commented that the actual transformation process of the criminal justice system resembles Thompson's (1967) description of an "intensive technology" (Carter, 1974a; Dill, 1973; Nardulli, 1979).[4]

This type of technology refers to an organizational "treatment" strategy in which treatment is determined by the needs of the typically human "input object." Its distinctive feature is that specific treatments cannot be specified a priori; rather, the choice of various treatment techniques must await diagnosis. In other words, initial treatment depends upon perceived characteristics of the input; subsequent treatments depend upon the perceived outcome of initial treatment. The knowledge or "expertise," of organizational actors consists of an ability to apply a treatment from among techniques available to the organization. "Success" in treatment at all stages of the process is indicated by "appropriate" response from the input object. Obviously, an intensive technology is highly discretionary. Decision makers are usually endowed with professional credentials and given relative autonomy in exercising the discretion necessary for an intensive technology to work.

The criminal process displays many properties of an organization that uses an intensive technology.[5] But the discretionary decision-making in the criminal process is complicated considerably by two factors: (1) *expectations of rationality*, both in terms of procedural rules for establishing guilt or innocence and in terms of consistency in processing defendants; and (2) the *existence of uncertainty* surrounding such decisions as the determination of charges, the development of evidence, the determination of guilt or innocence, and the selection of punishment alternatives. According to Thompson's theory of organizations,[6] intensive technologies are most suitable in decentralized organizations whose actors have a good deal of autonomy, placing them in intimate association with the relevant input so that they can better *monitor* the input, facilitating "diagnosis" and "feedback" Such an arrangement would presumably enable the criminal justice system to attain what Thompson calls "bounded rationality" (1967:76–77).

However, such an organization is incompatible with the "due process" requirements of a criminal justice system based on an adversary model. The criminal trial itself directly conflicts with the tenets of discretionary decision-making by autonomous experts. The defendant's right to trial invokes procedural rules designed to limit the discretionary power of the prosecution, defense, and judge. A system of challenge and potential appellate review further reduces the autonomy, decentralization, and flexibility of these actors, who nevertheless must operate within an intensive technology. In addition, resort to trial increases the risks associated with making decisions about the defendant's guilt and subsequent punishment, well summarized in the following statement:

> No matter how strong the evidence may appear and how well prepared and conducted a trial may be, each side must realistically consider the possibility of an unfavorable outcome. At its best the trial process is an imperfect method of factfinding; factors such as the attorney's skill, the availability of witnesses, the judge's attitude, jury vagaries, and luck will influence the result. (President's Commission on Law Enforcement and the Administration of Justice, 1967:10)

In response to the conflict between procedural prescriptions and administrative necessities, participants in the criminal process routinely resort to plea bargaining. While officially tolerated as an alternative to trial (*Santobello v. New York*, 1971), the practice of plea bargaining enables the participants to establish localized and conditionally autonomous decision-making units consistent with the achievement of bounded rationality in the administration of criminal justice. These plea bargaining units, called "courtroom workgroups" by Eisenstein and Jacob (1977), accommodate nicely the intensive nature of criminal justice operations under conditions of uncertainty.

The Impact of Uncertainty on Models of Plea Bargaining

So far we have only sketched an organizational explanation of plea bargaining and have only addressed tangentially the important concept of uncertainty as it applies to the administration of justice. However, by applying the insights gained from our organizational "model" to the economic and decision-theory models of plea bargaining, we hope to elaborate upon our assumptions, while at the same time strengthening the descriptive reality of the economic and decision-theory models of plea bargaining. The first step is to interpret the concept of uncertainty in the terms of these models.

The Calculus of Uncertainty

Economic and decision-theory models of plea bargaining assume that uncertainty in criminal justice decision-making can be accounted for simply through the adjustment of conditional probabilities of conviction and/or length of sentence. However, Mack (1971) has pointed out that decisions are amenable to rational analysis only if specific attributes of the decisions are consistent with the assumptions of the models involved. Modeling the decision-making process in criminal justice is reasonable only if the goals of that process are clearly defined, if the utilities of the parties to decisions can be identified, and if information on outcomes of the process is available to the parties.

Two models of plea bargaining will be examined here in light of the above discussion. The first is Landes's (1971) economic model of plea bargaining, which attempts to explain the choice between trial and negotiation of criminal charges. The second is Nagel and Neef's (1976a, 1976b) decision-theory model which poses, among other things, a rationale for predicting sentence outcomes resulting from negotiation.

Landes's model assumes that the prosecution and defense maximize their expected utility within respective resource constraints, as they choose between negotiated settlement and trial. Conceptually, that choice is said to depend upon the probability of conviction at trial, the severity of the crime, the availability and productivity of respective resources, trial versus settlement costs, and attitudes toward risk. Crucial assumptions in Landes's model are that the probabilities of conviction entertained by prosecution and defense can be estimated by each and that these probabilities are directly affected by the amount of resources each employs, such that an increase in prosecution resources will increase the probability estimates for both and an increase in defense resources will decrease those estimates. The prosecutor's decision rule is to maximize the expected number of convictions weighted by the severity of the offense, subject to budgetary constraints. The defendant's decision rule is determined by subtracting the costs of obtaining an acquittal from the costs of being convicted at trial, including the transaction costs associated with trial relative to those of a negotiated settlement.

This sketch of Landes's model provides a compelling rationale for why so few criminal cases actually go to trial. Applying the model to actual cases, those few going to trial would be characterized by: (1) relatively serious charges; (2) relatively high levels of resource commitment by both prosecution and defense; (3) differential assessments of conviction probabilities, with the defendant's assessment considerably lower than the prosecutor's; and/or (4) a defendant predisposed to gambling with his future.

Nagel and Neef's model addresses the choice between negotiation and trial in a fashion consistent with Landes's approach, except that their model has the prosecutor maximizing the sentence expected from each conviction, regardless of the severity of charges. Our examination focuses primarily upon Nagel and Neef's efforts to model the dynamics of the plea bargaining process itself. On the assumption that prosecution and defense have opted for negotiation and that both have: (1) an idea of what could have been the outcome at trial and (2) an idea of their respective bargaining limits, Nagel and Neef argue that negotiations will proceed along a stepwise pattern of convergence, characterized by "bluffing" in the exchange of offers and counteroffers. Negotiated settlement occurs only if the bargaining limits of the parties "overlap"; otherwise, the case goes to trial.

The assumptions of both Landes's model and Nagel and Neef's model can be criticized for their failure to recognize the full effect of uncertainty on decision-making in the criminal process. From empirical observation (Carter, 1974a; Mather, 1973; Heumann, 1978), it is obvious that prosecutors do not articulate precisely or consistently the decision rules for choosing between trial and negotiation. The disagreement between the two models (see also Forst and Brosi, 1977) on decision rules of the prosecution is evidence enough on this score. Further, the very unpredictability of the trial process, discussed earlier, makes it extremely unlikely that prosecutors and defendants can develop precise enough estimates of the probability of conviction and sentence length at trial to make a rational choice between trial and settlement or to form a cogent strategy for negotiation. Finally, neither model seems to appreciate the entirely different positions of prosecution and defense with regard to the risk, or personal investment, in the eventual outcome of a given case. For the prosecutor, the outcome of a given trial is simply an individual occurrence in a long series of events to which probabilities might reasonably be attached and used in the development of decision rules governing the choice between trial and settlement. In contrast, the defendant is faced with a "one-shot" outcome involving, at worst, the severest personal consequences, for which probabilities of acquittal offer little comfort or guidance. The defendant's predicament, called "non-seriability" by decision-theorists (Mack, 1971), reflects a fundamental asymmetry in the positions of prosecution and defense (Galanter, 1974). Perhaps this explains why defendants are so often willing to engage in plea bargaining even though empirical evidence demonstrates that, in most cases, no real sentence concessions result, based upon several comparisons of sentencing following plea bargaining and following conviction at trial (Rhodes, 1979; Uhlman and Walker, 1977; Shin, 1973).

By ignoring the effects of uncertainty on criminal justice decision-making suggested above, the two models of plea bargaining project a false precision as well as an illusion of symmetry in accounting for the negotiative strategies of defense and prosecution. While each presents a plausible argument for the prevalence of plea bargaining in the system, an organizational approach achieves the same end with less demanding and more empirically relevant assumptions. Using the presence of uncertainty as a guide, we can easily grasp, in organizational terms, why prosecutors and defendants avoid the trial process and favor negotiation in its place. Uncertainty generally begets conservatism in decision-making. Prosecutors faced with only vague estimates of the probability of conviction at trial will very likely set their bargaining limits unnecessarily low. Likewise, defendants, faced with the same vagueness, compounded by the non-seriability of their decisions, will very likely set unnecessarily with high bargaining limits, thus enhancing the likelihood of "overlap" and the attractiveness of negotiation. Conceptually, of course, this interpretation of the impact of uncertainty on criminal justice decision-making could still be accommodated in the models described above, and, to that extent, these models further our understanding of the criminal process. But these models fail in their precision to grasp the richness of the organizational context of the criminal process and its relevance to the decision to settle or try cases.

Uncertainty and Reciprocity

When it occurs, plea bargaining involves the defendant and members of the "courtroom workgroup," mentioned in our earlier discussion of the organization of the criminal justice system. To understand the dynamics of the plea bargaining process, we must examine the ongoing relationships between the members of the courtroom workgroup, particularly the prosecutor and defense attorney. Bargaining under uncertainty forces prosecution and defense to make exchanges or concessions which are difficult to weigh for their equivalence. Rarely are they simple, balanced, quid-pro-quo deals. Doubts are likely to linger about who is "indebted" to whom when an individual case is resolved through negotiations. Gouldner (1960) has argued that, in general, a "norm of reciprocity" is likely to be invoked to guard against the exploitation of ambiguity by one of the two parties to negotiation. Insofar as the prosecution and defense functions can be characterized as an "exchange relationship" (Cole, 1973) which exists over many cases, the norm of reciprocity is likely to be extended and become generalized into what Carter (1974a:29) calls a "bond of reciprocity":

> These [reciprocal bonds] are built on candor, honesty, and "being realistic." . . . Indeed, instead of depending on exchange of favors—"I'll let you plead X to a reduced charge if you plead Y to the given charge" in the case where a defense attorney represents two clients—the reciprocal bond may facilitate the opposite, the capacity to deny the requests of another or to concede the justness of his position, because each member trusts the other's judgment and can afford to insist or concede without becoming further obligated or threatened.

Under conditions of uncertainty, the mutuality of the exchange relationship between prosecution and defense is likely to be enhanced, as each is particularly vulnerable in negotiations and must rely on trust in the other simply to define the case they are dealing with. This mutuality militates against bluffing, or what might be called "strategic negotiation," and replaces it with a sort of epistemic negotiation, or what Scheff (1968) calls "the negotiation of reality." Within this interpretation, plea bargaining cannot be considered simply haggling in the sentence marketplace between a buyer-defendant and a seller-prosecutor, as characterized by Nagel and Neef (1976b:1). Rather, plea bargaining must be seen as a cooperative venture between two parties, each with limited knowledge, attempting to piece together an acceptable picture of criminal reality.

Ethnographic studies of the American criminal process contribute additional insights to this interpretation of plea bargaining. The gist of these studies is that individual case disposition must be placed within the context of previous dispositions and the ongoing expectations of workgroup members. Rather than bluffing ad hoc about sentence length in a particular case, the parties to negotiation may be engaged in a mutual search for an acceptable way to *categorize* that case among other cases. This categorical bargaining produces "normal crimes," first noted by Sudnow (1965:262):

> Over the course of their interaction and repeated "bargaining" discussions, the P.D. [public defender] and the D.A. [district attorney] have developed a set of unstated recipes for reducing original charges to lesser offenses. These recipes are specifically appropriate for use in instances of normal crimes and in such instances alone. "Typical" burglaries are reduced to petty theft, "typical" ADW's [assaults with a deadly weapon] to simple assault, "typical" child molestation to loitering around a schoolyard, etc.

The plea bargaining recipes represent charge and/or sentence reductions which have proved sufficient in the past to induce the defendant to plead guilty, while at the same time satisfying the prosecution's demands that the defendant "get his due."

Sudnow's approach casts plea bargaining in a new light. It becomes the key to a *learning process* by which the courtroom workgroup as a decision-making unit can reduce uncertainty about the appropriate response to its case input through reliance on past experience with similar cases and on mutual expectations about how each member of the workgroup will react to any given case. Mather (1973) noted such a process in the Los Angeles criminal courts, where defense attorneys and prosecutors implicitly categorize cases in a two-by-two matrix defined by an evidentiary dimension (from "dead-bang" cases to "reasonable-doubt" cases) and a seriousness dimension (from "nonserious" to "serious"). The mode of disposition followed by the Los Angeles prosecutors and defenders depends largely upon the initial, intuitive categorization of each case.

For the individual members of the courtroom workgroup, socialization to workgroup norms is the prerequisite for effective participation. In his study of New Haven criminal courts, Heumann (1978) found that "newcomers" to the plea bargaining process, whether defense attorneys, prosecutors, or judges, were at a distinct disadvantage until they gained a "feel for a case," learned exclusively through experience in negotiation. Battle (1973) found that learning workgroup norms was just as important for private defense attorneys as for public defenders in Denver.

Negotiation as uncertainty reduction rather than convergence through simple haggling and bluffing in a sentence marketplace clearly reveals itself in this summary comment by Eisenstein and Jacob (1977:61):

> Workgroup characteristics heavily influence the techniques used to dispose of cases. When members are familiar with one another, many more cases will be disposed of by negotiation than when they [workgroups] are composed of strangers. Familiarity permits work-group members to reduce uncertainty through bargaining. They know each other well enough to predict reactions to proposals and to achieve some control over outcomes through bargaining.

It should be evident that, from an organizational perspective, plea bargaining enables the decision-making unit of the courtroom workgroup to develop over time the expertise necessary for the operation of an implicit intensive technology in the criminal process. Through something closely akin to "organizational learning" (Cyert and March, 1963), the workgroup develops a diagnostic capacity (with regard to the defendant) and maintains a "repertoire of treatment techniques" which it can apply routinely to transform the defendant's status and to attach an appropriate sanction, while avoiding entirely the inherent uncertainties of the trial process.

Empirical Findings: A Brief Summary

The economic and decision-theory models discussed above suggest that the choice between trial and settlement depends primarily upon the characteristics of the individual cases involved, and, thus, patterns of dispositional choice should remain fairly constant across jurisdictions with similar patterns of criminal activity and prosecution. In their research on urban felony jurisdictions, Eisenstein and Jacob (1977) discovered, on the contrary, a great diversity of disposition rates in different jurisdictions. Using their data for Baltimore and Chicago, we can compare those rates. Table 1 reveals that, aside from dismissals, Baltimore relies most heavily on bench trials for dispositions, while Chicago handles the bulk of its cases through guilty pleas.

The description of the organizational characteristics of the two jurisdictions provides an explanation for the differences in dispositional choice consistent with our organizational "model" of plea bargaining. At the time of Eisenstein and Jacob's analysis (1972), Baltimore had a high turnover among prosecutors, judges served only one-year rotations in given courtrooms, and public defenders were assigned to defendants rather than to courtrooms, on a "man-to-man" basis. All of these factors contributed to the low workgroup stability found there by the authors. In contrast, Chicago's prosecutors held office for longer periods and, with judges, were assigned indefinitely to particular courtrooms, as were public defenders (a "zone" arrangement). In addition, retained counsel were able to direct cases to courtrooms with which they were familiar. These arrangements established very stable workgroups in Chicago (see Eisenstein and Jacob, 1977:224–252).

Data from these two jurisdictions are presented here to illustrate the apparent influence of organizational context upon guilty plea rates. This is not to say that other contextual factors, such as office policies guiding prosecutorial discretion or concerted efforts by a given community's defense bar, have no effect on a jurisdiction's rates of trial and settlement. In fact, data gathered by Brosi (1979) reveal extraordinary variation in the rate of guilty pleas per cases filed, ranging from a low of 28 percent in one jurisdiction to a high of 77 percent in another,[7] suggesting the influence of a variety of factors on plea rates. We are isolating only one of these factors.

Table 1   Disposition Rates for Baltimore and Chicago[a]

	Baltimore		Chicago	
Mode of Disposition	**N[b]**	**Rate**	**N**	**Rate**
Dismissals, etc.[c]	1107	50.5%	188	22.1%
Guilty Pleas	293	13.4	487	57.4
Bench Trials	662	30.2	124	14.6
Jury Trials	130	6.0	50	5.9
Total:	2192	100.1%[d]	849	100.0%

[a] SOURCE: Statistics are based upon original data from the survey by Eisenstein and Jacob (1977).
[b] From analysis of original data.
[c] From *weighted* sample to approximate randomness; the Chicago sample is unweighted and considered random. "Dismissals, etc." includes all cases screened out of the system prior to resolution by one of the other three modes of disposition.
[d] Rounding error.

A reanalysis of the Eisenstein and Jacob data reported elsewhere (Matheny, 1979) employed discriminant function analysis to examine further the differences in patterns of dispositional choice in Baltimore and Chicago. Using variables crucial to the Landes and Nagel and Neef models, such as charge seriousness, evidentiary strength, and extent of defendant resources, it found that, in fact, cases going to bench trials in Baltimore were similar in terms of these variables to ones resolved by guilty pleas in Chicago.[8] Apparently, because of workgroup instability, bench trials were necessary in Baltimore for disposing of cases that would have been resolved as guilty pleas by the more stable workgroups in Chicago. This interpretation is corroborated by Eisenstein and Jacob's (1977:250) observation:

> In Baltimore, bench trials became a functional equivalent to the guilty plea; they were sometimes called a slow plea. Prosecutors and defense counsel presented their evidence to the judge hastily; the formal trial was interspersed with off-the-record remarks which presaged the outcome. Such slow pleas helped reduce uncertainty in the same way negotiations did in Chicago and Detroit, though to a lesser degree.

In support of the economic and decision-theory models, relatively serious cases were, in fact, more likely to be tried before a jury in both jurisdictions. But, with regard to evidentiary strength, cases with relatively weak evidence against the defendant were more likely to go to jury trial in Baltimore, while, in Chicago, evidentiary strength had little or no discriminating effect on the different modes of disposition. While we can only speculate, it appears that evidentiary uncertainties were less problematical for the more stable Chicago workgroups, and could be overcome through informal agreement based upon more well-developed bonds of reciprocity and a richer catalog of normal crimes.

Conclusions

The results from this brief empirical analysis indicate only partial support for the substantive assertions of economic and decision-theory models of choice behavior in negotiating and disposing of criminal cases in two urban felony jurisdictions. A more complete explanation of the *differences* in disposition patterns between jurisdictions requires recognition of contextual factors surrounding the choice behavior of prosecution and defense. We have focused on the structural characteristics of the criminal process to develop a complementary organizational "model" explaining plea bargaining. Our model refines the concept of "uncertainty" and introduces other concepts, such as "technology" and "organizational learning," which, I feel, more accurately describe the operating realities of the criminal justice system than do the formal models discussed above. In addition, our model stresses the significance of key organizational attributes (e.g., courtroom workgroup stability), which may be shown to have an effect on patterns of case disposition across jurisdictions.

The formal models discussed above may mislead those interested in reforming the practice of plea bargaining by creating an illusion of precision surrounding a decision-making process that is, in fact, overwhelmingly uncertain. As models of behavior, they confuse the distinction between calculation and speculation and, thereby, ignore the structural consequences of uncertainty. These are the consequences that must be faced if the operating reality of the criminal courts is to be understood. The "intensive" nature of the criminal process's implicit technology must be appreciated before any effective reform of plea bargaining can be staged. The formal theories of dispositional choice must be tempered by an acknowledgment of organizational factors impinging upon their assumptions. Otherwise, they will be of little practical help in contributing to our understanding of criminal justice decision-making.

Endnotes

[1] As defined in contingency theory, organizational uncertainty is an organization's inability to bring "system-closure" to its operations and is the product of the following conditions:
   (a) inadequate linkage in causal sequence of all variables relevant to the processing of input through the organization
   (b) unpredictable behavior of elements within the organization's environment—elements which vitally affect the organization's operations
   (c) ambiguous standards of evaluation for judging the "quality" of the organization's operations and output vis-à-vis some stated abstract objective
   (d) incomplete decision-premises surrounding the roles of individual decision makers within the organization, such that organizational incentives are incompatible with individual rationality in decision-making.

[2] Basically, an organization's technology is a process of transformation derived from a theory of cause-and-effect relationships which makes assertions of predictability about the organization's output, given certain knowledge about its input (Thompson, 1967).

[3] Max Weber (1958:216–221) emphasized unpredictability as the key feature distinguishing the "empirical" quality of Anglo-American criminal justice from the "rational" quality of Continental criminal jurisprudence. Compare this with the "matter-of-factness" of Continental criminal procedure and its relatively heavy reliance on expertise (Rosett, 1972).

[4] Thompson (1967:17) describes three basic varieties of technology: the *long-linked* technology used in assembly-line mass production processes; the *mediating* technology used in organizations which "pool" resources for the purpose of connecting suppliers and consumers; and the *intensive* technology. In general, organizations employing an intensive technology determine "the selection, combination, and order of application" of elements in the process of transforming input into output on the basis of "feedback" from the input object itself. It is a customized technology.

[5] This is clearly illustrated if one considers what the criminal process actually *does* to the defendant. First, the prosecutor "labels" the defendant by filing criminal charges (the initial treatment) using characteristics of the accused and his or her alleged criminal act as guides. Then, he or she assembles evidence in support of those charges in order to identify subsequent treatments (e.g., defining the elements of the crime for establishing culpability). The defendant is monitored for signs that the treatment is appropriate (e.g., anticipating the arguments in defense of the accused), and adjustments are made on the basis of this information (e.g., through pretrial and trial defense challenges of the prosecutor's case). Virtually any criminal case can be seen as a mutual feedback and adjustment process which culminates explicitly in the selection and application of a form of punishment deemed appropriate for "correction" of the convicted criminal.

[6] Space limitations make it impossible to provide a full development of Thompson's propositional analysis as applied to the organization of criminal justice. For a full treatment of this, see chapter three of my dissertation (Matheny, 1979; see also Carter, 1974a).

[7] Figures are from a nationwide, twelve-jurisdiction sample. The jurisdiction with the 28 percent plea rate was the Florida second circuit; the one with the 77 percent plea rate was Cobb County, Georgia. Taken as a percentage of convictions, the plea rates for these two jurisdictions were 68 percent and 100 percent, respectively (Brosi, 1979:5).

[8] The similarity of Baltimore bench trials and Chicago guilty pleas was indicated by the proximity of the group centroids of the two types of disposition when plotted in discriminant space. For details, see chapter five of my dissertation (Matheny, 1979).

References

Battle, J. B. (1973). Note: Comparison of public defenders' and private attorneys' relationships with the prosecutor in the city of Denver. *Denver Law Journal, 50*(1), 101–136.

Blumberg, A. S. (1967). *Criminal justice*. Chicago: Quadrangle Books.

Brosi, K. B. (1979). *A cross-city comparison of felony case processing*. Washington, DC: Institute for Law and Social Research.

Carter, L. H. (1974a). *The limits of order*. Lexington, MA: D.C. Heath.

Carter, L. H. (1974b, Autumn). Flexibility and uniformity in criminal justice. *Policy Studies Journal, 3*, 18–25.

Cole, G. F. (1973). *Politics and the administration of justice*. Beverly Hills, CA: Sage.

Cyert, R. M., & March, J. G. (1963). *A behavioral theory of the firm*. Englewood Cliffs, NJ: Prentice-Hall.

Dill, F. D. (1973). Bail and bail reform. Ph.D. dissertation, University of California, Berkeley.

Dolbeare, K. M. (1967). *Trial courts in urban politics*. New York: John Wiley.

Eisenstein, J., & Jacob, H. (1977). *Felony justice*. Boston: Little, Brown.

Feeley, M. M. (1973, Spring). Two models of the criminal justice system. *Law and Society Review, 7*, 407–425.

Fried, M. (1974). A decision theoretic model of plea bargaining. Paper presented at the meeting of the Midwest Political Science Association, Chicago.

Forst, B., & Brosi, K. B. (1977). A theoretical and empirical analysis of the prosecutor. *Journal of Legal Studies, 6*(1), 177–191.

Galanter, M. (1974, Fall). Why the "haves" come out ahead. *Law and Society Review, 9*, 95–160.

Gouldner, A. W. (1960, April). The norm of reciprocity: A preliminary statement. *American Sociological Review, 25*, 161–178.

Heumann, M. (1978). *Plea bargaining*. Chicago: University of Chicago Press.

Lachman, J. A., & McLauchlan, W. P. (1977). Models of plea bargaining. In S. Nagel & M. Neef (Eds.), *Modeling the criminal justice system*. Beverly Hills, CA: Sage.

Landes, W. M. (1974, June). Legality and reality: Some evidence on criminal procedures. *Journal of Legal Studies, 3*, 287–337.

Landes, W. M. (1971, April). An economic analysis of the courts. *Journal of Law and Economics, 14*, 61–107.

Mack, R. P. (1971). *Planning on uncertainty*. New York: John Wiley.

Matheny, A. R. (1979). Plea bargaining in organizational perspective. Ph.D. dissertation, University of Minnesota.

Mather, L. M. (1973, Winter). Some determinants of the method of case disposition. *Law and Society Review, 8*, 187–216.

Mohr, L. B. (1976, Summer). Organizations, decision, and courts. *Law and Society Review, 10*, 621–642.

Nagel, S. S., & Neef, M. (1976a, Summer). Plea bargaining, decision theory, and equilibrium models: Part I. *Indiana Law Journal, 51*, 987–1024.

Nagel, S. S., & Neef, M. (1976b, Fall). Plea bargaining, decision theory and equilibrium models: Part II. *Indiana Law Journal, 52*, 1–61.

Nardulli, P. F. (1979). *The courtroom elite*. Cambridge, MA: Ballinger.

Packer, H. L. (1968). *The limits of the criminal sanction*. Palo Alto, CA: Stanford University Press.

Posner, R. A. (1973, June). An economic approach to legal procedure and administration. *Journal of Legal Studies, 2*, 399–458.

Posner, R. A. (1977). *Economic analysis of law*. Boston: Little, Brown.

President's Commission on Law Enforcement and the Administration of Justice. (1967). *Task force report: The courts*. Washington, DC: Government Printing Office.

Rhodes, W. M. (1979). Plea bargaining: Its effect on sentencing and convictions in the District of Columbia. *Journal of Criminal Law and Criminology, 70*(3), 360–375.

Rosett, A. I. (1972, February). Trial and discretion in Dutch criminal justice. *UCLA Law Review, 19*, 353–396.

Scheff, T. J. (1968). Negotiating reality: Notes on power in the assessment of responsibility. *Social Problems, 16*(1), 3–17.

Shin, H. J. (1973). Do lesser pleas pay?: Accommodations in the sentencing and parole processes. *Journal of Criminal Justice, 1*, 27–42.

Sudnow, D. (1965). Normal crimes: Sociological features of the penal code in a public defender's office. *Social Problems, 12*, 255–276.

Thompson, J. D. (1967). *Organizations in action*. New York: McGraw-Hill.

Thompson, V. A. (1973). Organizations as systems. *University Programs Modular Studies*. Morristown, NJ: General Learning.

Trubek, D. M. (1977, Winter). Complexity and contradiction in the legal order. *Law and Society Review, 11*, 529–569.

Uhlman, I. M. & Walker, D. (1977). Pleas no bargains: Criminality, case disposition and defendant treatment. Presented at the meeting of the American Political Science Association.

Weber, M. (1958). *From Max Weber: Essays in Sociology* (Ed. C. W. Mills, Trans. H. H. Gerth). New York: Oxford.

Cases Cited

Santobello vs. New York (1971). 404 U.S. 257.

23

The Social Construction of "Sophisticated" Adolescents
How Judges Integrate Juvenile and Criminal Justice Decision-Making Models

ALEXES HARRIS

People-processing institutions shape individuals' lives by sorting them and conferring a public status (Hasenfeld 1972). Officials employed at institutions such as hospitals, welfare agencies, and university admissions offices are challenged with sets of cases they must assess, categorize, and label for further processing. Similarly, juvenile courts can be analyzed as people-processing institutions because they sort individuals into categories to determine appropriate treatment and sentencing options (Hasenfeld and Cheung 1985). These sorting decisions result in different outcomes and fates for young people, fundamentally changing their legal status.

An interesting example of these institutional sorting processes is the juvenile court waiver hearing. Increasingly sociological and criminological research has investigated the judicial waiver process: the juvenile court practice of transferring young people from the juvenile justice system to the criminal justice system for prosecution and punishment (Fagan and Zimring 2000; Feld 1987). This processing point, which is performed by a juvenile court judge, determines whether youth will be labeled as minors, who will be adjudicated and sentenced in the juvenile justice system, or as adults, who will be adjudicated and sentenced in the (adult) criminal justice system. The legal aim of the hearing is to identify "chronic" and "serious" offenders who are a

Alexes Harris, *Journal of Contemporary Ethnography*, vol. 37, pp. 469–506, © 2008 by Sage Publications. Reprinted by permission of Sage Publications.

threat to society and viewed as no longer rehabilitatable. During the waiver hearing juvenile court judges' assessments are guided by formalized legal criteria that emphasize accountability and give primacy to offense characteristics.

The traditional decision-making model commonly associated with the juvenile justice system is one that emphasizes individualized-assessments and the rehabilitation of young people (Feld 1999; Sutton 1998). The waiver hearing could be viewed as antithetical to the traditional juvenile justice model, in that the goals of the hearing are to assess and identify youth who are no longer amenable to the care and treatment of the juvenile court services (CA WIC 707). In 1966 the United States Supreme Court formalized the judicial waiver process by establishing a set of legal criteria to guide the waiver hearing (*Kent v. the United States*). These criteria focus on an array of social and legal factors including: the seriousness, nature, and extent of the offense, the "sophistication" and maturity of the youth, the record and previous history of the youth, the prospects of the protection of the public, and the reasonable rehabilitation of the youth. While these criteria leave room for individualized assessments of youth, they could possibly change the nature of juvenile justice decision-making by refocusing the emphasis of evaluation away from the offender to the offense.

Much of the current research on the waiver process has focused on the characteristics of cases that are transferred to the criminal system. The research explores the legal and social factors that increase the likelihood of transfer (Bishop and Frazier 1991; Fagan, Forst, and Vivona 1987; Howell 1996; Lee 1994; Poulos and Orchowsky 1994), and the various outcome differences between retained and transferred youth, such as sentences received or recidivism rates (Barnes and Franz 1989; Bishop and Frazier 1997; Jensen and Metsger 1994; McNulty 1996; Winner et al. 1997). In general, the work has found that the process is meeting its legislative intent: "chronic" and "serious" youth are sent to criminal court for prosecution and punishment. However, little is known about how bench officers apply waiver criteria to identify which youth are "chronic" and "serious" offenders, and whether these judges feel the transferred youth should actually be prosecuted in criminal court. Furthermore, while this body of research has investigated legal characteristics associated with youth who move between the two systems, few scholars have framed their research in a way that acknowledges an integration of justice models that are used to assess, label, and process these individuals (for an exception see Kupchik 2003).

The aim of the present study is to investigate how people-processing decisions are made within an institutional setting. I investigate how decision makers engage in practical reasoning by exploring the methods they use to organize information about youth and accomplish their judicial duties (Garfinkel 1967, 2002; Garfinkel and Sacks 1970). An analysis of judicial waiver hearing proceedings is used as an example of institutional processing and will build on previous theoretical explanations for how decisions are made in justice settings. Two research questions are investigated. First, what ideological perspectives about youth and delinquency are judges using to guide their assessments and processing of these adolescents? Second, does the decision-making process used in the judicial waiver hearing suggest a change in the way that juvenile justice is being performed today? The study uses observational and interview data from a case study of three juvenile court-houses in a California county to investigate official case processing and illustrates the type of frameworks and types of information judges use to construct their assessments of youth during judicial waiver hearings.

This process of transferring youth to the criminal system has important consequences for both the individuals involved and for the study of juvenile and criminal justice processing. For example, transferred adolescents have a suicide rate of five to eight times that of youth in juvenile facilities, transferred youth have a higher recidivism rate than retained youth, and there is a vast overrepresentation of youth of color in the criminal system (Bishop et al. 1996). All of these factors warrant the investigation of the implementation of judicial waiver. In addition, the waiver process offers important insight to current understandings of juvenile justice decision-making models (Kupchik 2003; Singer, Fagan, and Liberman 2000; Mears and Field 2000). This process offers a unique opportunity to examine how juvenile court judges have responded to new criminalized procedures, and also how these more punitive policies influence traditional juvenile justice decision making, thus allowing for an investigation of potentially new models of justice. Such an analysis provides a broader understanding of how justice is performed in the juvenile justice system and of the types of youth who are labeled by court officials as "chronic" and "serious" offenders.

This analysis contributes to current sociological and criminological research on institutional processing in general and judicial waiver hearings in particular for two reasons. First, I investigate how judges use legal criteria to create characterizations of young people to determine whether to label them as amenable ("fit" for the juvenile court) or unamenable ("unfit" for the juvenile court) to the juvenile justice system. Previous research has not explored how justice officials interpret and apply these legal criteria to determine which youths will be sent to the criminal justice system. Such insight is important to understand and contextualize quantitative analyses of the transfer process. Second, with an understanding of the approaches judges use to arrive at their legal assessments and characterizations of youth, I show how judges negotiate between the ideal-typical models of juvenile and criminal justice frameworks to arrive at a seemingly logical and individualized assessment while prioritizing offense details over youths' rehabilitative potential. This understanding provides an updated theoretical framework for how juvenile justice decision makers process cases. Overall this study identifies how justice is performed for a segment of young people in the juvenile justice system by uncovering the effects that increasingly punitive juvenile justice statutes have on judicial processing decisions within the juvenile justice system. The findings help juvenile as well as criminal justice researchers, practitioners, and law makers conceptualize the changing nature of juvenile justice processing by illustrating the factors and mechanisms used by decision makers to assess and label young people.

In the following sections I review current research on the judicial waiver process and outline research that investigates models of justice by summarizing research on juvenile and criminal court justice decision-making practices. In the second section I describe the research setting, data collection strategy, and analytic methods used for the present study. The third portion of this article presents the data analysis; I begin with a description of the judicial wavier hearing in California, I analyze how the legal criteria that guide the hearings are interpreted by judges and how these judges construct and present their assessments of youth. Finally, the article concludes with a discussion of the findings, contextualizing the analysis within a framework that contrasts and compares competing models of justice.

Literature Review

Juvenile Waiver

Over the past fifteen years, states have been revamping juvenile statutes to broaden criteria making young people eligible for prosecution in the criminal justice system (Torbet et al. 1996). There are three types of statutes that guide the waiver process: judicial waiver (where a juvenile court judge determines which youth are appropriate for transfer), prosecutorial waiver (where juvenile prosecutors and criminal prosecutors determine which jurisdiction should prosecute youth), and automatic/exclusionary waiver (where certain youth are "automatically" excluded from juvenile court as a result of the type of offenses charged by prosecutors, and age criteria). Research has generally explored one of these types of transfer procedures within one jurisdiction either descriptively or statistically: describing or predicting the types of youth transferred, or investigating differences between retained youth and similarly transferred youth matched on offense and legal characteristics.

The bulk of research on the juvenile waiver process has investigated automated court data with analyses centering on bivariate statistics or on multinomial regressions identifying which offense and offender variables increase the likelihood of transfer. Social characteristics that have been found to be significant predictors of transfer include age (Lee 1994; Poulos and Orchowsky 1994), race (Clement 1997; Keiter 1973; McNulty 1996; Snyder, Sickmund, and Poe-Yamagata 2000), gender (Clement 1997; Storm and Smith 1998), the marital status of parents (Singer 1993 and 1995), and the child's school record (Poulos and Orchowsky 1994; Singer 1993). Youth who are close to the eighteen-year-old mark, who are male and of color, who are from single parent homes, and who are performing poorly in school, tend to be those most likely selected for the transfer process (Howell 1996). In addition, legal factors such as prior juvenile charges, prior incarceration, and the seriousness of the offense, increase the likelihood of transfer (Barnes and Franz 1989; Poulos and Orchowsky, 1994). Such findings have caused some researchers to conclude that juvenile justice personnel appear to be both accurate and consistent in identifying "appropriate candidates" for transfer (Houghtalin and Mays 1991, 405). They find that the transfer process to the adult criminal system is reserved for the "serious few" (p. 405).

In contrast to what these conclusions imply, some researchers have argued that youth transferred via judicial and prosecutorial waiver systems "were not unequivocally dangerous" (Bishop and Frazier 1991, 296). Bishop and Frazier assert this as a result of their descriptive investigation of Florida's prosecutorial waiver system. This study found that a large portion of the rise in Florida's transfer cases in 1987 was as a result of the expansion of the prosecutorial waiver criteria making more youth eligible for transfer. They argue that few youth waived to the criminal system seemed appropriate candidates for adult prosecution: only 35 percent had previously been committed to a juvenile residential program, and 23 percent were first-time offenders where no previous attempts had been made by the juvenile system to rehabilitate them. Bishop and Frazier conclude that "youths transferred via prosecutorial waiver are seldom the serious and chronic offenders for whom prosecution and punishment in criminal court are arguably justified" (Bishop and Frazier 1991, 297).

Another segment of juvenile waiver research has focused on the difference between cohorts of youth who are retained within the juvenile justice system and comparable cohorts of youth who are transferred to the criminal justice system (Bishop et al. 1996; Winner et al. 1997). Researchers have statistically analyzed matched sets of retained and transferred youth and have found, that at least in the short run, transferred youth have higher rates of recidivism than retained youth (Bishop et al. 1996). However, over time, retained youth have the same likelihood of recidivism as transferred youth (Winner et al. 1997, 551). These studies suggest that transfer mechanisms may not be producing the intended result (incapacitation of more serious offenders), but instead may be counterproductive by labeling, stigmatizing, and oversupervising a segment of adolescent offenders (Bishop et al. 1996, Fagan 1996). Some researchers have concluded that the range of legal criteria that are used to sort and label waiver-eligible youth is broad, and the manner in which judges implement the criteria is discretionary (Fagan and Deschenes 1990, 331–2).

A key question then is how are these youth being assessed and labeled by juvenile bench officers? More specifically, how are youths' offenses characterized and understood by court officials? How do court officials evaluate youths' potential for future success, and how much does this rehabilitative promise matter in judicial assessments? Except for a few important studies on the waiver process (Podkopacz and Feld 1995; Singer 1995) we know little about how court officials make their assessments of the social and legal factors during waiver hearings. And thus we know little about how the labels of "serious" and "chronic" offenders are applied.

Justice Decision-Making Frameworks

Criminal Justice Decision Making

The traditional criminal justice decision-making model has been characterized as one that focuses evaluations on offense circumstances and gravity, and has the goals of punishment and retribution (Hagan 1974; Liska and Tausig 1979). Set within the backdrop of this traditional model a wealth of research has investigated how criminal justice officials process cases and create assessments to adjudicate guilt. Research that clarifies criminal justice decision-making models has primarily focused on racial differences in processing (Engen and Steen 2000; Steffensmeier and Demuth 2001). An important theoretical perspective that has emerged in this area is focal concerns theory (Savelsberg 1992). The framework highlights how offenses are prioritized in justice decision making and also demonstrates how characterizations of individuals are used to justify outcome decisions.

The focal concerns perspective suggests that local court communities rely on certain kinds of substantive rationalities that influence their social control decision making (Savelsberg 1992; Steffensmeier, Ulmer, and Kramer 1998; Ulmer 1996). In a statistical analysis of statewide sentencing outcomes in Pennsylvania, Steffensmeier, Ulmer, and Kramer (1998) identify three focal concerns of judicial decision makers in this process: the offender's blameworthiness and degree of harm caused to the victim, the protection of the community, and the practical (constraints and consequences) implications of the potential decisions (organizational and individual). They suggest that in pursuit of these aims judges create a perceptual shorthand to avoid uncertainty about their decisions. This shorthand is linked to race, gender, and age attributions. The researchers use these primary concerns of judicial decision making as a framework to generate hypotheses regarding the effect of these extralegal variables on sentencing decisions.

This framework illustrates the importance of research that conceptualizes how decision makers construct their decisions, identifies their key concerns, and then models processes to acknowledge the complex set of factors in the decision making. Focal concerns theory characterizes the criminal justice decision-making model as one that gives primacy to offenses, harm, and punishment, but that also highlights how justice officials create assessments by relying on characterizations of defendants. If applied to the judicial waiver hearing focal concerns theory predicts that judges would focus on youths' perceived culpability and dangerousness, the severity of the offense (harm done to victim), and the potential adult court outcomes if the case were to be transferred.

Juvenile Justice Decision Making

In contrast to the wealth of analyses of criminal justice processing, few analyses of juvenile justice processing focus on the mechanisms by which officials use to sort through and label individuals; much less provide a theoretical framework from which to understand how justice decisions are made (Mears 1998; Mears and Field 2000). Furthermore, little research has been done to understand the impact that changing legal statutes might have on how juvenile justice officials approach their work.

To augment the criminal justice system, the juvenile justice system was established in 1899 to decriminalize adolescents and focus on treating the causes of juvenile delinquency (Platt 1977; Sutton 1988). Ideologically the system was based on the notion that the causes of adolescent offending were social, and that by separating them from adult criminal offenders, providing youth with individualized assessments and treatment, their delinquent behavior would desist (Feld 1999; Rothman 1980). As a result of this perspective on the nature of juvenile offending, court processing relied on substantive decision making, where judges, social workers, and teachers engaged in deliberative discussions about what dispositions would be in the best interests of the youth (Emerson 1969). To this day, the juvenile justice system is often characterized as having broad judicial discretion (Krisberg and Austin 1993) with decision-making patterns oriented toward rehabilitation (Kupchik 2003).

Previous ethnographic research in the juvenile justice system illustrates this traditional framework and has found that when processing cases court officials explore, interpret, and assess social, legal, and organizational aspects about youth and offenses to arrive at characterizations (Bortner 1986). These characterizations of youth are then used by court officials to logically justify one of several available treatment (punishment) options (Emerson 1969). Both Emerson (1969) and Cicourel (1968) provide substantive insights about how social control decisions are constructed, and the processes by which decisions are made.

For example, Cicourel's discussion of the process by which officials create case histories is a useful concept to understand how decision makers approach cases (1968, 328–9). Cicourel suggests that social control agents (police, probation officers, prosecutors, judges) construct young peoples' legal histories using background expectancies as a framework to understand information (legal "facts," young peoples' actions and statements). These legal histories are used to inform subsequent social control decisions. Key to this process are decision makers' working theories about "how background expectancies render everyday activities recognizable and intelligible" (Cicourel 1968, 329). That is, how social control agents understand social structure and the context of the institution in which they are working matters for how cases are processed. This understanding allows decision makers to make sense of their social world and construct coherent stories about cases and subsequent processing decisions.

Cicourel illustrates that when creating these case histories court officials rely on their background experiences and use previously constructed frameworks to organize the information about offenders into socially and legally relevant categories:

> The officer's tacit knowledge combines with information he has received, and his own observations of the action scene, to provide him with a preliminary mapping, but he invariably asks fairly standardized questions about "what happened" and who were the principal actors involved. (Cicourel 1968, 113)

Cicourel found that frequently probation officers focus on details of the offense in attempt to construct a story to determine the next course of action. Along similar lines, Emerson finds that to construct legal histories processing agents commonly focus on building their evaluations around not "what happened" but rather, "what is the *problem* here?" (Emerson 1969, 87). Emerson finds that decision makers focus on the *problem* to label the behavior and character of the young person. That characterization of the youth is then used to reinterpret the details of the offense and shapes staff's decisions.

In making distinctions among the categories of delinquents, similarly to Cicourel, Emerson finds court officers rely on notions of youths' moral character to guide processing decisions. Initially decision makers make a distinction between trouble[d] and untroubled cases; this categorization helps officials determine whether cases need "special handling" or could be "let go" (Emerson 1969, 90). The assessment of moral character is used by decision makers to determine a second stage of processing, the determination of the *kind* of handling that is required. If youth are labeled as not having trouble than they are assumed to have normal character. If a case is flagged as one involving trouble, youth are described as "hard-core" or "criminal-like" delinquents who are "maliciously or hostilely motivated" (p. 91). A third category of delinquents are labeled as "disturbed" when court officials describe the problem as senseless or irrational. According to previous ethnographies, juvenile justice decision making has relied on substantive rational practices to determine which "type" of youth is before the court and consequently assigns the most "appropriate" disposition. This work suggests that assessments during judicial waiver processes will focus on the social characteristics of the youth.

The above literature review has outlined two decision-making models; one from the criminal justice system and one from [the] juvenile justice system. The following analysis will investigate the extent to which these frameworks are applicable to judicial waiver processing decisions. Focal concerns theory predicts that judges will focus on the culpability and dangerousness of the offender, the seriousness of the offense, and the implications of decisions. Research theorizing juvenile justice decision-making practices outlines the process by which decision makers come to arrive at their characterizations of youth: moving from constructing legal histories about youth, to evaluations of "what happened" during the present offense, to finally arriving at a label of "typical" or "trouble." Driving these juvenile justice assessments is the notion of rehabilitation. These conceptual frameworks will be used to investigate how processing decisions are made and presented in juvenile waiver hearings—is the decision-making process during judicial waiver consistent with either of the models?

Method and Sample Characteristics

The present study is based on observations, interviews and relevant court documents in three juvenile courthouses in Hughes County, California.[1] To provide a demographic context, the total population of this County was 3.7 million in the year 2000 with 46.9 percent being White, 11.2 percent African American, and 10 percent Asian American. In addition, the Latino population (of any race) in this county was 46.5 percent.[2] The field research was conducted between January 2000 and lasted through September 2001.

Three field sites were selected primarily based on access to informants and information as well as the geographic location of the courthouse within the county. The primary field site, "Hughes Juvenile Justice Center" (HJJC), stands in the middle of an impoverished minority community, historically African American, but because of rapid demographic shifts has become increasingly Latino. The two commissioners at this courthouse are African American males in their sixties. The second field site, "Garfield Juvenile Hall" (GJH), was selected because it is the "Flagship" operations—as one prosecutor describes the courthouse—it is the central juvenile hall for the county. The majority of the fitness hearings within the county are held here. This courthouse is located in a predominantly Latino community where many immigrants and poor families live. The five courtrooms at GJH are staffed with an Asian American female judge, a Latino male judge, two White male referees, and a White female commissioner. The third site, "Williams Juvenile Courthouse" (WJC), was selected primarily for diversity reasons.[3] This courthouse is located in the northern area of the county in a racially mixed area, but primarily White community. This courthouse holds the fitness hearings for youth charged within the radius of this courthouse and holds the fitness hearings for youth processed in the Northern most courthouse of the County. There are four courtrooms in this courthouse with two White male judges and two White male commissioners.[4]

I observed twenty-nine waiver hearings at these three courthouses. The charges for these crimes ranged from molestation, armed robbery, assault, attempted murder, and murder. All of the youth I observed during these fitness hearings, except four, were waived to adult court. The youth were of color, primarily Latino and African American. They ranged from fourteen to twenty-one years of age.[5] Only two of the youth observed during the waiver hearings were female. During the observations, I recorded field notes of attorneys' presentations of youths' cases, judges' concluding remarks, and final decisions, as well as informal comments made before, during, and after the hearings.

I conducted forty-one formal interviews with judges (sixteen), prosecutors (fifteen), probation officers (three), defense attorneys (six), and a social worker (one). The interviews lasted between forty-five to ninety minutes. The selection of the interviewees was purposive and also occurred through snowballing. All but one person contacted and asked to be interviewed agreed to participate—one prosecutor refused. The interviews consisted of a set of open-ended questions that were designed to begin a dialogue about court officials' roles during the fitness process. For example, I asked, "What is your position in the courtroom? What are your responsibilities and daily duties? What kinds of things do you consider when making an assessment about a youth before the court?" I made an effort to elicit how the court officials assess the legal criteria for transfer through discussion of past and recent cases. I attempted to read any documents that pertained to the waiver hearings of the youth observed including probation reports, prior records, psychiatric evaluations, and police reports of the alleged incidents. After transcribing all handwritten notes, field notes were hand coded for main themes and memos were written on topical areas. Efforts were made to comb data for counterfactual examples adding further dimensions to the main themes.

The analytical strategy for the analysis of this article involved the coding of descriptive field notes with themes, concepts, and events that appeared frequently or seemed to be particularly important to the courts observed. For example, the following codes were created in regards to the assessment of youth: criteria applied, "sophistication," adult-like, child-like, "bad" character, and "good" kids. Once the codes were created and the notes were reviewed, memos on key themes were developed, guided, and infused by theoretical questions about people-processing patterns such as how stories are negotiated, depictions of "what happened," and the effects of such labeling. The resulting article is an analysis of representative data taken from field notes and guided by current theoretical concepts and questions centered on the nature of court actors' assessments and labeling of youth.

California Judicial Waiver Hearing

The Fitness Hearing

Over the past ten years, states have been revamping juvenile statutes to broaden criteria making young people eligible for prosecution in the criminal justice system (Torbet et al. 1996). California's juvenile court judicial waiver system will be used as an example of a setting where court actors process cases based on legal criteria and present arguments to justify their decisions. The developing criminalization policies in California are representative of changes occurring nationwide in juvenile justice policy (Torbet et al. 1996). Such criminalization policies include blended sentencing, extended jurisdiction, "strike-able" offenses, lack of confidentiality during hearings and in reporting of sustained charges, and expanding waiver eligibility to younger offenders and less serious offenses. The waiver process is a further example of juvenile legislation that criminalizes youthful offenders treating them more as traditional adults than children under the law.

More specifically, under California's judicial waiver process, juvenile prosecutors have the option to petition for waiver hearings if they believe the youth "is not a "fit" and proper subject to be dealt with under the juvenile court law" (CA WIC 707 b).[6] During the hearing, judges determine whether youth are either "fit" to remain in the juvenile justice system, or are "unfit" to the juvenile system, and will be transferred to the criminal system for adult prosecution. When Deputy District Attorneys (DDAs) file juvenile court charges against youth that include acts labeled as violent felony offenses, they have the discretion to also file an accompanying petition for a waiver hearing. Once a DDA files a waiver petition the fitness hearing is held.[7]

Legal Criteria

During this amenability hearing court officials evaluate offenses according to five legal criteria. The legal term of amenability "refers to the likelihood of an individual desisting from crime and/or being rehabilitated when treated with some sort of intervention" (Steinberg and Cauffman 2000, 399). In the context of waiver hearings, judges determine whether youth are amenable to treatment, and if they are found not to be, then the youth will be transferred to the criminal court system. The legal criteria are number: (1) the degree of criminal sophistication; (2) whether the youth can be rehabilitated prior to the expiration of the juvenile courts' jurisdiction (twenty-five years of age); (3) previous delinquent history; (4) success of previous attempts by the juvenile court to rehabilitate the youth; and (5) the circumstances and gravity of the offense (see the appendix).[8] In practice these criteria were measured by (1) the apparent amount of planning used to commit the offense, a youth's level of participation in the offense, any evident remorse; (2) the youth's assessed level of maturity as an individual and as a criminal; (3) any formal and informal petitions brought against the youth, and also any sort of contact he/she had with the juvenile justice system; (4) the youth's previous delinquent history after contact had been made with the juvenile system and performance while on probation; (5) the type of offense and circumstances alleged and the context within which it was committed.

Because of the legal presumption of unamenability, or "unfitness," in order for a judge to make a decision that a youth is "fit" to remain in the juvenile justice system, evidence must be presented by defense attorneys in a way that shows mitigating circumstances. Thus, if a youth has not overcome her burden to rebut the "unfit" presumption, and is found to be "unfit" on any one of the five criteria, then she is deemed "unfit" to remain in the juvenile justice system. For example, when a youth is found to be sophisticated—she is "unfit" on criterion one, but found "fit" on all the other criteria; she still must be assessed as "unfit" to the juvenile justice system as a whole by the juvenile court judge. Substantial mitigating evidence must be stated by judges in their summation to support a finding that an individual has met their burden and demonstrated fitness to the juvenile court.[9]

At the beginning of waiver hearings judges "read in" to the record information from past minute orders, previous probation reports regarding youths' behavior while under court supervision, psychiatric recommendations and the district attorney's complaint.[10] Defense attorneys present arguments pertaining to the five criteria explaining why youth are "fit" to remain in the juvenile system. Prosecutors offer counterarguments as to why the youth are "unfit" to remain in the juvenile system. Both sides have the opportunity to rebut the others' arguments before the judge makes the final decision of fitness.[11] Legally, judges must state the reasoning for their findings on each of the five criteria.

Findings

Focal Concerns during Judicial Waiver

The key focus of judicial attention during waiver hearings was on the legal criterion of "sophistication." Factors used by judges to create assessments of "sophistication" were partially consistent with focal concerns theory; judges relied on perceptions of youths' culpability and dangerousness, as well as the severity of the offense to inform processing decisions. However, inconsistent with the third focal concern, judges were not overly concerned with either practical limitations or with the future implications of their decisions (in terms of what would happen to the youth).[12] The following subsection illustrates judges' focal concerns during judicial waiver hearings. These concerns include the "sophistication" of the youth and the offense, the circumstances of the offense, and the "lifestyle" of the youth.

Sophistication

During waiver hearings bench officers, prosecuting attorneys, and defense attorneys primarily focused on criterion number one, the degree of criminal "sophistication." Assessments of the "sophistication" criterion involved evaluations of youths' level of participation in offenses, their amount of planning, remorse, intent, and assessments of their social characteristics (school performance, family, and social lifestyle). Practically bench officers defined "sophistication" in terms of youths' motives for committing offenses. The "sophistication" of the offense and the youth were assessed at the same time. For example, in the following waiver hearing the judge found three Latino male youth aged fourteen, sixteen, and seventeen years, as "unfit" to remain in the juvenile court because of their perceived level of "sophistication" and the "sophistication" of the offense. The three cousins were charged with the murder and conspiracy to commit murder of the mother of the sixteen-year-old and the aunt of the fourteen- and fifteen-year-olds. Granted this is an extreme case involving a violent murder. The point is to demonstrate how judges focused and assessed the legal criterion of "sophistication" when little or no prior delinquency existed. All three of the youth had minimal previous contact with the juvenile justice system. The prosecuting attorney argued that the murder was planned in order for the youth to obtain money to purchase materials to replicate scenes from a popular teen murder movie. The judge concluded:

> Therefore, I find that each minor, because of their involvement in the planning and strategic organization involving the surrounding of the circumstances, and how they were going to equate the circumstances of the movie to the actual carrying out of the homicide, makes all three of them not amenable to juvenile court under criteria [sic] one and I find each of them unfit.

During the summation of the waiver hearing, this judge concluded the youths' planning prior to the offense indicated a high level of criminal "sophistication." As others have found, when a crime appears to be planned or is accompanied by the use of professional or sophisticated techniques, judges will often view such circumstances as indicators of youths' "exposure to criminal ways of doing things and criminal purposes" (Emerson 1969, 116). This information is used as evidence of "sophistication" and when coupled with the gravity of the offense, was used by the judge to overshadow the youths' lack of previous delinquent involvement, and also served to indicate their lack of amenability to the court.

To contrast this example with a less extreme case, the following fitness hearing illustrates how two youth charged with armed robbery, which resulted in no injury to the victim, was assessed. Both youth were sixteen years of age and Asian American; one was male and one was female. The judge relied on evidence indicating the offense was planned, that the youth had obtained tools to hide their identity, and the youth had associated with an adult criminal street gang member to arrive at his decision:

> I've analyzed each case [minor] individually, but I have come to the same conclusion, each is unfit [for the juvenile court] at 16 years old. With [criterion] number one [sophistication], some points in time these three people sat down and planned this crime. Both were active participants. They planned it with each other and a member of a notorious Asian gang. Gloves were used. All of this goes to the criminal sophistication. A weapon was used—not by these individuals—but at this robbery [by the adult defendant]. It is not the type of callous sophisticated crime that we would see with other minors [who are unfit], but it is sophisticated.

In this example the judge acknowledged differing levels of seriousness in the notion of "sophistication." He stated that while these youth may not be as callous as some other youth, the case still can be labeled as sophisticated. The judge inferred information from the way the offense appeared to be conducted to assess the type of youth and level of "sophistication" and used this "legal" information to justify why the youth should not be processed in the juvenile justice system.

The Circumstances of the Offense

Clearly related to the criterion of "sophistication" is criterion five, the circumstances and gravity of the offense. At times judges would explore the context of the offense in attempts to shape an understanding about individuals' motives, thus shaping images about the level of "sophistication." In the following example, details of the offense were actually shaped by the judge to create a positive image of the individual. In this case a judge determined that Erin, a seventeen-year-old Latino male, was "fit" to remain in juvenile court. Erin was charged with assault with a deadly weapon: the police report stated that Erin was spray painting on the side of a building when a resident holding a beer can came out and challenged him to stop. In response, Erin asked the man for the beer. When the man denied his request and began moving toward Erin, Erin threw the paint can and hit the man on his forehead. The judge concluded:

> I find the minor fit [for the juvenile court] under [the] criteria as indicated by criminal sophistication. It would appear that this is a crime of opportunity, the crime was committed on impulse . . . [continues to explain why he finds Erin fit on criteria 2–4]. . . . [In terms of the] circumstances and gravity, clearly, this is an unprovoked attempt, it could have caused significant harm. This instance the court has to decide was the minor in a position to willfully and wantonly to perform this crime . . . the minor who by his admission had been sniffing paint was high and appeared so, and demanded beer. When that was declined, the minor reacted violently and the minor hit the victim in the eye. Clearly, the gravity of the offense is a serious offense. The circumstances when viewed in totality, I find the minor has borne the burden [presumption of unfitness]; he is fit to be dealt with by the juvenile court law.

The judge claimed that Erin was not criminally sophisticated because it did not appear to the judge that Erin had planned to assault the victim. To support this judgment, the bench officer used information about Erin's state of mind to inform his evaluation of criterion five. The judge relied on evidence that Erin was high on paint fumes at the time of the offense as an indication of the presence of mitigating factors—suggesting that Erin was unable to form intent to hurt the individual. Because he was intoxicated, Erin was assessed as not "willfully or wantonly" able to carry out this offense. Furthermore, the judge labeled Erin's previous delinquent history as one that was successful; he had gone through a probationary run camp program and was released, apparently indicating that he had no further behavioral problems. The judge could have just as easily assessed the evidence that Erin had been high on paint fumes as aggravating the gravity of the offense. Similarly, his prior record could have been seen as escalating in severity; processed as evidence indicating his lack of control and regard for his probation. However, information about the offense—particularly the weapon usage—coupled with offender information was used by the judge to construct a positive assessment, or at least one where criminal culpability and "sophistication" were lacking.

Lifestyle

In addition to investigating the apparent circumstances and motives for youth having committed offenses, bench officers also relied on information about youths' lifestyles to construct arguments about amenability. Indicators used to create assessments about youths' lifestyles included school involvement and performance, family interactions, and gang membership. In an exploration of these lifestyle dimensions, bench officers established images that led to judgments of the quality of the youth before the court; essentially asking, is this a "good" or "bad" kid? During an interview a judge told me he begins evaluating cases by asking himself the following questions:

> I look to see if the minor is himself sophisticated. Is he emancipated, living on his own? Does he have his own address? Is he on his own with his own source of shadow income? Is he under the supervision of an adult, or just living in their house?

As illustrated in this excerpt, bench officers would often treat the absence of adult guardianship as negative qualities of adolescents. Youth who were living on their own, taking care of their own finances and not attending school were viewed by judges as qualitatively different from youth living with their parents. In a discussion with a judge following a fitness hearing for a youth who was charged with arson and murder, the judge justified how she came to the conclusion that the youth was sophisticated.

> He went out to the adult world, he worked, he didn't go to school. He has been acting in our emancipated way. [To me] You are an adult right? [Yes.] And, you have to pay rent? [Yes.] And you have to do your laundry and things like that? People will hold you responsible.

The youth this judge was referring to was an immigrant and was working to help financially support his mother and younger brother. He and his brother had been playing with matches near an abandoned mattress in their apartment building. When the mattress accidentally caught on fire the older brother told his younger brother to run and tell their mother that the building was on fire while the older brother ran throughout the building to warn people. A woman died as a result from being trapped in the burning building. This judge chose to focus her assessment on evidence that the youth was working to support his family as evidence that he was criminally sophisticated—"unfit" for the juvenile justice system.

Even when youth appear to be successfully managing their lives with or without adult supervision, judges inferred a tainted image of their lives. Judges concluded that because adolescents were employed and paying rent, they were living in "adult worlds." Youth who lived on their own, for whatever reasons, were characterized by the court as no longer having childlike dispositions, and therefore are no longer deserving of treatment by the juvenile court.

Another important lifestyle aspect that bench officers weighed heavily was the extent of youths' gang involvement. Individuals who were identified as gang members were viewed by most judges as street wise, criminal-like, and inherently of bad moral character.[13] A basic assumption many court officials held about street gangs is that they were crime-involved and a violent threat to society. Cases that involved youth labeled as gang members were viewed as quick and simple assessments of criminal-like behavior. During an interview, the following judge candidly described an effortless waiver hearing decision.

> There was a bar-b-que that some gang bangers weren't invited to but they crashed it. They were told to get out. They came back with a gun and shot two or three people. They already had an assault. That was a slam-dunk. Very easy.

Based on the label of "gang," judges quickly made determinations of youths' characters. Thus, fitness hearings involving youth labeled as gang members were discussed by judges as being relatively "easy" or "slam-dunks." In fact, many of the public defenders interviewed stated that defending youth who were associated with gangs was almost useless: "anytime you have something cloaked in anything that looks like gang, you can forget about" trying to defend the client.

It is important to note that while the primary focus of judges during waiver hearings centered on the degree of criminal "sophistication" and the circumstances and gravity of the offense, bench officers did at times spend time discussing the other three criteria; whether the youth could be rehabilitated prior to the expiration of juvenile court jurisdiction (age twenty-five), the extent of the youth's previous delinquent history, and the success of previous attempts by the juvenile justice system to rehabilitate the youth. Many times these three criteria were irrelevant to youths' amenability evaluations because of a lack of prior contact with the juvenile justice system (thus no previous attempts to rehabilitate), and because their ages (all youth were under seventeen years of age which left a minimum of seven years for treatment within the juvenile justice system). The defense attorneys would often cite youths' lack of previous delinquent histories and either minimal or no contacts with juvenile court services as evidence of their potential for rehabilitation. Yet, I never observed a waiver hearing where a positive assessment of the middle three criteria—a youth was evaluated as having high rehabilitative potential—was used to outweigh, or mitigate, a negative assessment of criteria one ("sophistication") or five (circumstances and gravity).

This section illustrates how bench officers applied the five legal criteria outlined in the juvenile law to arrive at their assessments of youths' amenability during the judicial fitness hearings. Judges would primarily focus on criteria numbers one and five, the "sophistication" of the offense and the youth, and the circumstances and gravity of the offense. However, bench officers relied on a combination of information about youths' lives and offense circumstances to justify their findings of "sophistication" or lack of "sophistication." Assessments overtly prioritized issues of dangerousness, culpability, and harm done to the victim, over rehabilitation or perceptions of what might happen to the case if/when sent to the criminal justice system. The following section illustrates how bench officers merged traditional models of juvenile justice decision making—one focused on individualized rehabilitative-oriented evaluations—with a criminal justice decision-making model—one focused on the offense and punishment.

Constructing What Happened

Similarly to Cicourel's (1968) and Emerson's (1969) descriptions of juvenile court officials, judges during waiver hearings relied on their perceptions of "the problem" or "what happened" to arrive at a fitness finding. Judges created a legal history, in a sense a story, about who the youth was, and the type of life he/she was living, to bolster either a "fit" or "unfit" finding. In the following analysis, constructions of youths' legal histories are highlighted during court officials' exploration of "what happened" during the offense, which is used subsequently to construct characterizations of normalcy or seriousness.

The waiver hearing illustrates a subtle change in the emphasis of judicial assessments in juvenile justice. As further illustrated below, judges combined individualized assessments (commonly associated with the traditional juvenile court) with offense-driven concerns (commonly associated with the traditional criminal justice model). Judges would approach cases with an understanding of how "typical" youth behave—an image based on prior cases. All youth were measured against this ideal-typical model. What is interesting is that the image changed for youth depending on the decision maker. There was no consistent image of a "typical" child; rather this notion was context specific.

The "Typical" Delinquent Youth

Frequently during waiver hearings judges would construct images of ideal delinquents (ones who made bad decisions, but ultimately were viewed as "good" kids) with a discredited image of youth who were criminally sophisticated. Typical waiver-eligible cases were assessed as "fit" for the juvenile court, and troubled cases are labeled as "unfit" for the juvenile courts. The legal criteria making youth waiver-eligible, and the legal assumptions that presume such youth as unamenable, pre-assign all of these cases as trouble[d], however, judges relied on substantive offender and offense factors during their required assessments to sort through the youth, and to support and finalize their legal assessments.

Past research in the juvenile justice system has found a similar shorthand method that officials use to sort and process cases. Cicourel defines "normal" delinquency as actions typical to young people's behavior on a weekend at a party or school gathering where drinking, sexual activity, curfew violations, or fighting might occur; actions oftentimes expected of adolescents. These actions, as translated into offenses, would include "petty theft, malicious mischief, joyriding, shooting in the city limits, battery" (Cicourel 1968, 119). Cicourel finds that probation officers are less concerned with the actions, but more with their regularity and frequency. "Serious" offenses are any type of offenses but are committed by young people labeled as "hard core" or "gangster" (p. 120). These characterizations are based on the family structure, youth demeanor, or official past record, and are used to indicate the need for serious dispositions, such as placement in the Youth Authority.

Within the courts observed crimes of the typical offenders would oftentimes be described by judges as occurring by happenstance or on the spur of the moment. Bench officers often described youth who were found "fit" to remain in the juvenile court as participating in offenses that occurred by happenstance. This explanation would often be coupled with information describing the youth as having "good [family] backgrounds," having "so much going for them," and having "potential" for the future. Amenable youth were often labeled by court officers as not being too far gone from the rehabilitative arm of the juvenile court or the control of their parents. These types of youth were seen as "typical"—ones deserving of treatment within the juvenile justice system.

Unamenable or atypical offenders would be described as having planned their offenses; having outlined their tactics for achieving success (gaining access to money or jewelry and successfully evading detection). A youth's deliberation prior to engaging in illegal activity was viewed by judges as very different from the normal kid-like behavior seen in juvenile court. For example, judges often compared a youth snatching a bike from another kid at the park to a robbery with a handgun as a kid-like versus adult-like offense. Through the use of this typical-kid framework judges moved back and forth between information about the offense and the offender to construct images of either child-like youth—deserving of treatment in the juvenile justice system—or criminal-like youth—deserving of adult punishment.

Assigning Moral Character

The dialectic judges used to frame their analyses of typical and criminal offenders surrounded the notion of moral character. What is interesting about the waiver hearings is the focus of judicial assessments on the *type* of the youth before the court. Essentially, judges searched to construct the character of the youth. At all other points in judicial processes (juvenile and adult), while the character of the individual may be an underlying issue, the past and prior record and severity of the offense are taken into discussion and are the center of open court deliberation. However, during fitness hearings the offense is legally presumed to have occurred as illustrated by police and probation officers in their reports, and as a result, the character of the youth is at the forefront of discussion and analysis, not the determination of guilt.

In their concluding remarks at fitness hearings judges would present stories about youths' character and use these images as justifications for either "fit" or "unfit" decisions. While direct comments about "character" or "nature" of young people were not stated, implicitly in the summation of their evaluations of the legal criteria judges indicated the "type" of youth. For example, the following waiver hearing was for two Latino males, both sixteen years old, who were labeled as gang members and charged with attempted murder. During the delivery of her evaluation the judge concluded that both youth were "unfit" to the juvenile court because of their predatory behavior.

> The court [the judge] finds both minors 16 years of age or older; the minors are not amenable. Criteria [sic] number one [sophistication]: I find this a situation where two youth, Cherry Street Gang members, already under injunction of the Superior Court [informing them that their gang membership was illegal], went out looking for the rival gang member. They choose to go there. I am diminished as a person to speak these words that human beings would go out to a neighborhood to seek out other human beings. If the police weren't there, Miguel would have been dead. The neighbors were so scared they wouldn't have helped him. They attacked an innocent person. I don't care if he [the victim] is a gang member. They were willful acts. [A] car club [was used to] bludgeoned him almost to death. The fact that Miguel did not die does not matter [in terms of the gravity of the offense]. They are fit [on criteria] 2, 3, 4. Criteria [sic] number five: the circumstances and gravity are so severe that they do not belong in juvenile court.

Judicial analyses of the "sophistication" and gravity of the offense were commonly used to shape a story about offenders—who they are as members of society. In this case, the judge understood the youth as having purposefully chosen the location of the offense and victim. The judge characterized the youth as violent predators who "attacked" people during "willful acts." This information was used by the judge to construct a vision of criminally responsible offenders. The two youth in this fitness hearing had minimal involvement with the juvenile justice system prior to this offense, making them "fit" on criteria two, three, and four. Despite this finding, the judge meshed the concept of "sophistication"—the characterizations of who these youth were inherently—with notions about the circumstances and gravity of the offense to support a finding of unfitness to the juvenile court.

As the above example illustrates, during their assessments judges created an understanding about the case through a combination of information about the offender and the offense. The decision makers' emphasis on "sophistication" was a judgment about both the nature of the youth and how their related offense was understood and labeled. Young people were assessed in light of the offenses they were charged. Similarly, offense type and gravity were assessed in light of the type of youth viewed to be before the judge. Garfinkel's (1967) description of the documentary method of interpretation clarifies this process. Essentially, "fact production" is created by using one piece of evidence about the youth and/or their offenses to interpret another piece of information; each substantiates the other in the creation of knowledge of the case (p. 79). Through a reflexive process, information about the offender sheds light on the offense, and evidence about the offense sheds lights on the nature of the offender.[14] The stories about youth and their offenses that result from the process of fact production develop into case histories that are used to inform subsequent processing decisions.

Decision makers processed information about offenses through understandings of the youth and in other cases processed information about youth through understandings of the offense. In the example involving the Cherry Street youth above the judge situated the offenders and offense in a gang context, highlighting their legal predicaments prior to the offense, and then used this characterization to illustrate the "sophistication" of the offenders and their current offense. The judge believed that the youth knew their gang activities (participation) were illegal, and in spite of this sought out other human beings to attack in the name of their gang. By characterizing this offense as a gang-related act—the offense was labeled as willful and predatory—the judge created an image of a victim being hunted down and savagely beaten. This representation connotes a fully culpable criminal offender. For the judge, this characterization of the context of the life circumstances of the offenders, as well as the context of the offense, lead to an obvious legal determination of the nature of the offenders as unamenable to the juvenile system. Understanding the offense in this light, leads to an apparently rational judicial determination that the offender is a sophisticated criminal. While the offense drives judicial assessments of amenability, the focus of the discussion during the hearing is about the nature of the individual giving an impression of an individualized assessment of the youth.

While judges often had initial reactions to offenses and used these reactions to create assessments of the youth, judges also at times had initial reactions about the nature of the youth, and then used this understanding to assess the offenses. The following example is a further illustration of how judicial assessments of youths' moral character were used to assess whether or not youth were typical or criminal. In the following example the judge described a case of an adolescent who was originally charged with murder. He and his friend had been jumping on a bed, horsing around, when the youth at one point picked up a loaded shotgun in the corner of the room and shot and killed his friend. The judge had found the youth "fit" to remain in juvenile court and in an interview described her impression of him as she conducted the adjudication of his case:

> It was a young boy, 17 years old, that killed his best friend at gunpoint range. He was a good student, church going . . . This was reckless and wanton, [but] not like driving down the street drunk and hitting someone inside a crosswalk. It wasn't like that. It was an accident. The problem [in finding him fit] was he was an intelligent young boy; he had fired the gun and knew that it was defective.

Despite characterizing the offense as "reckless and wanton," and indicating that she believed the youth knew and understood that he was playing with a volatile weapon (the judge said that the youth had been warned by his father not to play with the gun because it was loaded), the judge characterized the youth as lacking "sophistication" and was essentially amenable to the juvenile system. The dilemma for this judge was that in the face of a grave crime, she viewed the youth as intelligent; someone who should have known not to play with the gun. However, this judge decided to rely on information about the youth's positive behavior in school and community to characterize him as a "typical" youth who was amenable to the juvenile justice system; one who had made a horrible decision, but was reachable.

This judge used reports from family members and the probation officer to generate facts about the youth's life which in turn were used to create a case history about the youth, an understanding about the character and aptitude of the youth. This case history was then used by the judge as evidence that the youth was a typical kid who made a bad decision. This bench officer could have framed her decision in a dramatically different way had she chosen to do so. One could have argued that the youth knew the gun was loaded and because he picked it up and shot at his friend he meant to kill him. The gravity and circumstances of the offense—the death of a young man—could have easily been used to justify finding the youth "unfit" to remain in the juvenile system. This example demonstrates how subjective the characterizations of youths' amenability are and how case information is shaped to support a judge's characterization of youth.

Context Specific Typicality

As evident from the above examples, an important point to make is that the notion of a typical delinquent was not consistent across the courtrooms observed. The following remarks by a judge during a fitness hearing illustrates how the same type of offense and offender information that have been used in previous examples to justify an "unfit" finding are used by a different judge to support a decision to retain two youth in juvenile court. In the following example two friends, who were both African American males and seventeen years old, had been living in a neighborhood with heavy gang activity. The youth, who had been labeled by probation and police officers as being gang members, were charged with attempted murder. They had been walking down the street and a car full of rival gang members slowed down and drove past them. One of the youth walking down the street yelled out his gang name and the other youth pulled out a gun and shot at the car. The judge concluded in the fitness hearing that the youth were amenable to remain in the juvenile system.

> [Criteria] number one, there is no criminal sophistication. None. Guys are walking down the street; one says Neighborhood Crips the other pulls out a gun. What is sophisticated about that? It doesn't seem to me that there is anything inherently sophisticated about this act. It is stupid, lacks judgment . . . So, the offense itself I don't find it to be criminally sophisticated. And the youth is not criminally sophisticated.

In contrast to the Cherry Street Gang case, the circumstances of this offense and the context of the youths' lives were characterized by the judge as being unsophisticated.[15] In this case, the youth were charged with attempted murder (no one was physically injured)—shooting a gun at a car loaded with rival gang members. The judge relied on the criterion of "sophistication" and determined that none existed. Essentially, the youth were viewed as not criminally culpable because they were characterized as having "lacked judgment." The individuals were also found "fit" on criteria two through five, consequently, the judge found the youth amenable to the juvenile system. The same law and criteria were applied to this case as in the Cherry Street case, yet the judge found no criminal "sophistication," and as a result allowed the youth to remain in the juvenile court system.

This is an important similarity with Cicourel's (1968) work. With these two gang examples we see how "legal histories" are applied to cases differently. In the examples illustrating judicial characterizations of the Cherry Street and the Neighborhood Crips, none of the youth involved had prior legal contacts with the juvenile court. Yet, in the first instance, involving the Cherry Street youth, their prior legal history was not presented by the judge as important information to the presentation of their character. However, in the second example, a different judge relied on the legal history, the lack of legal priors, to support his evaluation of these being "typical" youth who made stupid decisions. In addition, this judge used information obtained from a letter one of the youth had written to the judge to further develop a characterization about the youth. The following excerpt from the judge's statement during the fitness hearing illustrates how he chose to represent these youth:

> On behalf of Karl, perhaps under [the criterion of the] circumstances and gravity [of the offense] we had testimony [a letter] of his feelings about someone who died. His letter—and Ms. Washington [district attorney] you have his letter—again whether you believe it or not to be self serving—it shows mitigation. He talks about the neighborhood he has been living [in], fear of streets, people he knows who have been killed. [Quoting from letter] "Sir, I had the weapon because I felt I needed to protect myself." Whether you agree or not, I'm certain it was mitigation.

The judge cited one of the youth's statements of being fearful to live in his neighborhood as evidence of mitigation. The youth wrote in the letter that he was fearful of rival gang members: a fear recently reinforced by the loss of a cousin who had been killed. To this judge, within the context of the community [in which] the courthouse was located, these offenders were typical, and their actions, while "stupid" and "lacking judgment," were not sophisticated, but rather a reasonable response to a perceived threat (a car slowing down when it drove past them).

This analysis extends previous ethnographic work that described juvenile court decision making (Cicourel 1968; Emerson 1969) by illustrating a more context-specific version of typicality in judicial categorization. This last example illustrates how substantive rationalities that guide decision making are embedded in the culture and organization of local court communities (Savelsberg 1992). As one can see in these examples, some youth were evaluated in light of the context of impoverished inner-city communities (gangs, gun availability, and drug/alcohol usage), and were viewed as characteristic of juvenile delinquents to that court. In the Neighborhood Crips example the judge assessed the youths' behavior in light of his understanding of gang-entrenched communities. The judge gave validity to a youth's claim that he needed to carry and use a gun because he felt threatened.

In other instances, youth labeled as gang members, or who used weapons, were assessed within the context of a broader, maybe more idealistic society, where "normal" youth do not engage in such behavior. Under these latter conditions the youth were assessed as atypical; more criminal-like and sophisticated. Thus, while the same gang-like characteristics were used to construct a characterization of youth who were non-typical and in need of criminal punishment in earlier examples, here a judge used the very same information to construct a characterization of youth who carry and use weapons out of fear and self-defense.

One may argue the circumstances of the offense varied: in one case a victim was beaten and in the other the victims were not harmed. These differences could have influenced the judges' assessment of the youth. However in the Neighborhood Crips example the judge did not rely on the lack of injury as a mitigating factor to support his evaluation. These youth, at least in the Neighborhood Crips case, were labeled as typical youth in this court jurisdiction, and as a result were found "fit" to remain in the juvenile justice system. In all of the examples, the primary focus of judges' evaluations is on the offense and how information about the youth can be used to justify the overall evaluation.

Discussion and Conclusion

Partially consistent with the criminal justice framework outlined above, judges' focal concerns during judicial waiver hearings centered on perceptions of youths' culpability, dangerousness, and the severity of the offense. However, there were no discussions of what might happen to the case once transferred to criminal court or if the case was retained in juvenile court. Instead, there was an implicit assumption that transfer to the criminal justice system meant accountability and punishment for the youth, and safety for society.[16]

While the criminal justice decision-making framework was somewhat applicable to the jurisdiction under study, the traditional juvenile model, which centers on individualized assessments, was also applicable. However, rehabilitation took a back seat to offense-based focal concerns. Thus, the traditional juvenile court process of individualized evaluations occurred, yet this process was embedded in criminal-like conversations about offense details and notions of law and order.

What is distinctive about the waiver hearing in terms of other processing points in both juvenile and criminal justice systems is that judges have to decide at one point in time many issues that they normally have a longer period of time to formulate; moral character, youths' amenability to rehabilitation, and remorse. In addition, they assume youths' guilt in the process as outlined in the waiver statute. What culminates is a ceremony of legitimacy where the subject under evaluation, the youth, "becomes in the eyes of his condemners literally a different and *new* person. . . . He is not changed, he is reconstituted" (Garfinkel 1956, 421). The above analysis demonstrates how these assessments represent a legal formulation of nonlegal characteristics that primarily focus on the notion of "sophistication," producing a new legal label for many young people. Judges relied on local notions of rationality to achieve a sense of justice. The following three subsections discuss the changing organizational decision-making patterns of juvenile justice officials, the type of justice model that is produced, and what these decision-making practices imply for youth who are labeled as unamenable to the juvenile court.

Models of Justice: Not Juvenile or Criminal, but Sophisticated

This analysis found that similar juvenile court decision-making patterns that have been identified in past juvenile and criminal justice systems are being used in current courts. The traditional juvenile justice model emphasizing individualized assessments and focusing on the character of the youth was employed. Judges determine whether youth are salvageable by the juvenile court system based on characterizations of youths' lives coupled with an understanding of the offense and context. These images of youth are then reinforced during the waiver process in two manners. First, when making their evaluations of the five waiver criteria judges construct characterizations of the youth based on images of typical juvenile behavior. Judges make evaluations, determining their initial feelings about youth, and then use this image to process the remaining criteria. In contrast to past descriptions of court categorizations of normal and serious cases, the current research found a new version of typicality, one where judges at times rely on the structural circumstances of youth to help explain or describe their actions.

Second, how judges portray offense details will determine whether or not youth will be labeled as typical or serious. Through this reflexive process, judges construct justifications using characterizations and offense information to justify or support their findings with a rational and non-subjective appearance. Constructions of offender culpability are used to support these findings. Thus, "legal histories" as described by Cicourel (1968) are used selectively in judges' creation and portrayal of youths' moral characters. Ultimately, what are driving these characterizations are youths' assessed culpability and dangerousness, and the seriousness of the offense. We thus see a blending of juvenile and criminal justice models—individualized assessments determining the character of the youth which are driven by offense-based concerns.

This decision-making model blended both juvenile and criminal justice frameworks was consistent with two of the three focal concerns outlined in previous research (Steffensmeier, Ulmer, and Kramer 1998); judges were chiefly concerned with youths' blameworthiness and the extent of harm done to victims and with the protection of the community. However, few judges mentioned concerns about the practical consequences of their decisions for either the juvenile or criminal justice systems or for the youth. The judges expressed very clear notions of youth who were "unfit" to remain in the juvenile justice system versus youth who were "fit" to remain. There was no discussion of uncertainty of how cases should be handled—either the youth was "fit" or "unfit" for the juvenile justice system. Furthermore, the findings are consistent with focal concerns theory in that judges did rely on attributions—characterizations imputed to the young people that were used as reasons for why the offense occurred—in their processing decisions. They used stereotypes (although none that could be analyzed as connected to race, ethnicity, or gender) about "typical" kids to inform their decisions.

As a result of criminalization policies like the judicial waiver hearing, what we see is a blend between the "principle of individualized justice" and the "principle of the offense" (Matza 1964). At least among the cases observed, there was not a clear line between the traditional rehabilitative model of the juvenile court relying on informal processing, offender-based evaluations, rehabilitative treatment, and lower standards of culpability (Emerson 1969; Feld 1999; Platt 1977), and the criminal justice model for adult offenders, involving formal processing, offense-based evaluations, and punishment-oriented sentencing (Hagan 1974; Mears and Field 2000). Rather, a simultaneous combination of assessments driven by offense information, but coupled with offender information, guided judgments of waiver-eligible youth. Judges created a short hand, or rule of thumb, account of the typical amenable youth to bring order to the various pieces of information about the case to guide the waiver hearing process.

Substantive Rationality in the Performance of "Justice"

Through a socially constructed process, one that involved judgments, morals, and stereotypes, judges realized the law. The outcome of this accomplishment was that judges acted in a way that demonstrated rationality and objectivity. It is important to note the importance of the notion of youths' lifestyles in judicial creation of youths' case histories. Judges applied legal categories of "sophistication" and gravity not only to offenses, but also to the social categories of school, family, and lifestyle, to guide their assessments of youths' amenability to the court. This analysis illustrates that the legal criterion of "sophistication" is amorphous and ill defined. Court actors were granted the discretion to apply the criteria relying on their norms, morals, assumptions, and stereotypes about the youth before them. In a circular reasoning pattern, judges' assessments of youths' life circumstances went hand in hand with their evaluation of the details of the acts committed.

While relying on characterizations of youths' life circumstances to inform notions of "sophistication" offenders living nontraditional lifestyles are assessed as being sophisticated, when in actuality many show no indication of lacking control over their lives. The waiver hearings become contradictory in that the behavior of youth used to identify them as sophisticated are these very actions of which mark them as "immature" youth: for example, such youth often are teen parents, do not listen to the direction of adults, seek out the security of gang ties and fall under their persuasion, and are failing in school. Judges, nevertheless, deem these offenders sophisticated. Consequently, youth who are raised in nontraditional life circumstances are viewed in an unfavorable light and are very likely to be transferred to criminal court. As previous research has found, and as witnessed, these youth will typically be of color and from lower socioeconomic backgrounds (Bishop and Frazier 1996; Leiber 2002; Leiber and Mack 2003; Podkopacz and Feld 1995).

These depictions of youths' daily lives incorporate legal categories to frame analyses. Information about structural factors of offenders' neighborhoods (level of poverty, crime, violence and gang activity, nature of schools and families) informs analyses about the types of youth before the court. Similar to Albonetti and Hepburn's findings (1996) that prosecutors develop a complex model that considers how ascribed and achieved status interact to affect prosecutorial decision making, judges combine youths' ages, family life, and offense characteristics to label and process waiver-eligible youth. Furthermore, judges rely on their own values about how typical youths should be living, and which youths are salvageable or valuable, to arrive at their overall evaluations. These decision makers evoke ideologies to "reread the 'facts', character structure, family structure, mental stability, and the like" (Cicourel 1968, 327). All of these factors are evaluated during the construction of cases and lead to seemingly appropriate and logical outcomes within the institution. This analysis illustrates the mechanisms by which substantive factors and concerns enter into legal reasoning and is an example of how practical reasoning occurs.

Organizationally Situated Justice

It is important to note that the processing of young people in the courts observed was dependent on the local courthouse norms, values, and types of cases observed. This is a similar process that others have found in the study of justice decision making (Maynard and Manzo 1993). The above analysis shows the local rationality of judges' accounting procedures. In certain settings judges offered accounts that justified their findings of amenability, however, in other court settings such analyses might be unacceptable. Some judges would be labeled as abusing their discretion for making such "fit" decisions and have their decisions legally challenged (Harris 2007). Thus, these people-processing assessments were situationally dependent. This finding raises important questions about justice and fairness. Should youth be assessed within the context of the communities they come from? Should considerations be made to the level of acceptable violence, or at least acceptable weapons presence, in certain communities? Who should be able to create and judge such standards? Future studies should investigate how the cultures of court communities might vary in terms of attitudes toward different categories of offenses and offenders.

Conclusion

This study is about organizational decision making; how decision makers "historicize" legal cases, which in turn determine the course of action regarding social control, the label attached to the youth, and the subsequent rights, punishment, and/or treatment youth will receive (Cicourel 1968, 328–9). The focus of this study is not about the outcomes of cases, but instead how judges selectively take parts of case histories to construct their justifications for deciding if a youth is "fit" or "unfit" for the juvenile justice system. The decision-making process outlined in this study reveals how youth are processed within certain frames of reference and provides an illustration of the mechanisms through which elite actors in judicial institutions incorporate social factors into judicial decision making. Once legal and social concepts are unpacked, examining members' meanings and applications of the law, a dynamic and multifaceted decision-making process involving members' evaluation of structural, value-based, and legal factors associated with characterizations of offenders' lifestyles is revealed.

Because this study involves ethnographic research methods within one jurisdiction the findings of the study in terms of generalizability are limited. The courthouses and waiver hearings were selected purposively and on convenience. Other researchers have found that outcomes in juvenile courts often depend on the jurisdiction that the offenders reside (Feld 1999), thus similar studies should be performed in the future. In addition, while attempts were made to attend hearings where youth were found "fit" it was difficult to make these observations because roughly only twenty percent of the waiver hearings result in such a finding.[17] Similarly, efforts were made to identify courthouses where White youth attended waiver hearings, yet the researcher was unable to locate or attend such hearings. Thus, comparisons between characterizations of White youth and youth of color could not be made: in particular investigations about racial stereotypes and attributions.

Despite these limitations, the study offers three important theoretical insights; a revised theoretical framework for understanding juvenile justice decision making that incorporates criminal justice frameworks, an analysis of how substantive factors (e.g., values, stereotypes, assumptions) can enter into decision making, and an illustration of how decision making is organizationally situated. This analysis adds to existing sociological and criminological research by demonstrating the applicability of criminal justice theorizing to juvenile justice by illustrating a complex processing framework that prioritizes focal concerns about offense-related details.

Future research should focus on juvenile court decision making in other jurisdictions, paying particular attention to how state legislation guiding the hearings may allow for variations in processing. Furthermore, research should investigate the extent to which the imposition of punitive policies on the juvenile court disrupts the juvenile court workgroup—how might some judges attempt to retain more discretion in the face of these more structured guidelines? Research should also investigate how transferred cases are assessed and processed in criminal court. Studies such as this (see Kupchik 2003) would help to illustrate how varying decision-making models often associated with either the juvenile or criminal justice system might operate within the same setting. As noted earlier future research should examine how processing decisions, in various types of institutions, are contextually situated. What types of local factors—organizationally, value-based, informal legal practices—may impact how individuals are assessed and labeled?

Appendix

Legal and Working Definitions of California's Judicial Waiver Criteria

Formal Criteria	Working Definition
1 Degree of criminal "sophistication."	Amount of planning, level of participation, remorse, intent, and offender characteristics.
2 Whether minor can be rehabilitated prior to the expiration of the juvenile courts' jurisdiction.	The minor's assessed level of "sophistication" or maturity as an individual and a criminal. Whether or not the minor is "criminal-like" versus "kid-like."
3 Previous delinquent history.	Formal and informal charges brought against the minor resulting in contact with the juvenile court.
4 Success of previous attempts by the juvenile court to rehabilitate.	Minor's previous delinquent history after contact with the juvenile system and performance on probation.
5 Circumstances and gravity of the offense.	The type of offense and circumstances alleged and the context within which it was committed.

Endnotes

[1] The names of the juvenile courts and individuals observed and interviewed have been changed to protect the confidentiality of individuals.

[2] U.S. Census, Census 2000 Redistricting Data (Public Law 94-171) Summary File, Matrices PL1, PL2, PL3, and PL4.

[3] When selecting this courthouse my aim was to be able to observe waiver hearings involving White youth. However, because White youth are a rarity in the jurisdiction observed none were observed.

[4] Throughout the time I conducted observations in the courthouses judges rotated between courthouses—especially in and out of GJC. Thus, the descriptions of the judges here were the judges I had the most contact with. The two commissioners at HJJC were consistently on the bench while this research was conducted, as was the White male judge at HJJC.

[5] At times youth charged as co-defendants would have their fitness hearings held together, thus thirty-seven youth were observed during these hearings. One waiver hearing was attended at a fourth courthouse because an informant at Hughes County was involved with the case. All cases observed, except one, dealt with youth under the age of eighteen. The waiver hearing for the fourteen-year-old was a 707E, which involved the minor personally killing his mother. The waiver hearing for the twenty-one-year-old was moreso a formality. This man had committed a crime when he was a minor; because of the nature of the crime (the victim was mentally disabled and was the victim of sexual assault) the victim had waited to press charges, thus legally a fitness hearing had to be held for the court to waive jurisdiction of the juvenile case to criminal court.

[6] There are actually four types of waiver hearings DDAs can petition for, depending on the age of the minor and the type of offense alleged to have been committed. Under CA WIC 707A, the prosecution can file for a waiver hearing for any violation for minors sixteen and seventeen years of age; however, the burden is on the DDA to show that the minor is "unfit" for the care of the juvenile court. This type of waiver is directed at the chronic offender and is rarely used because of the difficulty for the prosecution to rebut the presumption that minors are "fit" for the juvenile court. CA WIC 707 C outlines the criteria for 707 B, it is not in itself a separate type of waiver petition. CA WIC 707 D and E outline the criteria for fitness hearings for youth fourteen and fifteen years of age. Under 707 D, prosecution may file for a waiver hearing if it is alleged that youth have committed one of twenty-four offenses, similar to the 707 B offenses. However, in contrast to 707 B, these younger youth are presumed "fit" for the juvenile justice system. The final type of waiver hearing, 707 E, is for children fourteen or fifteen years of age, who are charged with "personally" committing or aiding in the commission of a murder. Under this last statute, youth are presumed "unfit" for the juvenile court. CA WIC 707 A and D are rarely used because of the difficulty the prosecution has in rebutting the presumption that minors are "fit" to remain under the jurisdiction of the juvenile court. For purposes of this article I focus on the most commonly used and observed fitness hearing, 707 B.

[7] Prior to the fitness hearing a preliminary hearing is held to establish a prima facie case exists involving the offender. This hearing is called an Edsel P. hearing (*Edsel P. v. Superior Court* 165 Cal.App. 3d 763, 78 2[1985]). At this hearing, usually held the day of the fitness hearing, the prosecution has the burden to demonstrate it has established probable cause that the youth committed the offense as alleged. In light of the minimum standards for guilt, which prosecutors must demonstrate, defense attorneys must show evidence exists indicating their clients did not commit the offense, or at least at the level charged. After probable cause is established, the court assumes the youth committed the offense and the youth is presumed to be "unfit" to remain in the juvenile court system. The Edsel P. hearing is an unusual procedure in that it leads to a cursory determination of guilt. In no other hearing in juvenile or criminal court prior to adjudication are individuals assumed to be guilty of offenses. Rather, youth in juvenile court and defendants in criminal court are viewed as innocent and the prosecutor must prove their guilt. However, in waiver hearings, youth are assessed in light of having committed the offense, prior to any type of trial or adjudication of guilt is held. Ironically, after Edsel P. is established, the youth cannot present an argument of innocence. In fact, a guiding principle during waiver hearings is the legal concept of presumption of guilt and the accompanying presumption of youths' unfitness to the juvenile court.

[8] These criteria come directly from the Supreme Court decision *Kent v. United States*, 383 U.S. 541 9 (1966). This case provided uniform guidelines for determining youths' amenability to the juvenile court system.

[9] Furthermore, the evidence that judges are allowed to consider as mitigating is limited. In the face of the usual gravity of the types of crimes that make youth eligible for waiver hearings in the first place, demonstrating mitigating circumstances that overcome the presumption of unfitness for the juvenile system is very difficult for defense attorneys. For example, see the appellate courts' discussion of legal criteria, mitigating evidence and the youths' burden of presumption in *People v. Jones*, 958 P.2d 393 (Cal. 1998). The circumstances of mitigation include: the youth participated under coercion or duress, the minor exercised caution to

avoid harm to person or damage to property, amounts of money or property taken were deliberately small, the defendant was motivated by a desire to provide necessities for his/her family. See Rule 423, "Superior Court's Sentencing Rules." West's CA Codes Penal Code, 1997 Compact Ed. (1971). The result of the California legislation listing specific offenses which make youth eligible for transfer, coupled with the shift in the presumption of unamenability, create "a dramatic increase in the number of youths who were tried as adults after having been charged with one of the enumerated offenses" within California (Feld 1987, 509).

[10] Minute orders are court reports indicating: past charges, progress reports, and outcomes of hearings. The district attorney's complaint is the formal outline of charges filed by the district attorney's office. Judges also have access to waiver petitions submitted by prosecution, probation reports detailing present offenses and social backgrounds of youth, probation recommendations of fitness to each of the five legal criteria, and probation recommendations of youths' overall fitness to the juvenile court.

[11] Infrequently, defense attorneys will present clinical witnesses to testify. Among the hearings observed I witnessed only one where a licensed clinical psychiatrist presented testimony to the fitness of the youth. Judges then determined the fitness of minors to the juvenile court.

[12] Prior work does show that judges were very much concerned with the practical implications of their decisions organizationally (Harris 2007).

[13] The identification of youth as "gang members" is in itself problematic. Proof of gang membership is often subjective on the part of the police, prosecution or judge and is commonly treated as a universal identifier of a "bad kid." At times youth openly identify themselves as belonging to certain gangs, using certain words, tattoos, or other symbols to signify their membership. However, in other cases youth were labeled as gang members by police and probation officers for simply living in a certain neighborhood, or having been seen associating with a certain group of individuals. For further discussion see Bjerregaard (2002), Takata and Zewitz (1990), and Vigil (1988).

[14] Similarly to the work of an ethnographer, court officials' examination of cases are reflexive: "The analysis is at once inductive and deductive . . . like a carpenter alternately changing the shape of a door and then the shape of the door frame to obtain a better 'fit'" (Emerson, Fretz, and Shaw 1995, 144).

[15] Obviously, the extent of injury to the victims is different between the two examples. However, the comparison of the assignment of "sophistication" between the two cases is interesting. In both cases there are gang identified youth who are actively fighting/shooting at rival gang members.

[16] It is important to note that while there was no explicit discussion of the implications of case processing in terms of outcomes for the youth themselves, there were several organizational conditions that shaped court actors' assessments of youths' amenability or "sophistication"; (1) a stronger legal and cultural environment that emphasizes transferring youth up to the adult court; (2) a process initiated and largely controlled by prosecutors; and (3) youth who were effectively established as guilty prior to any adjudicatory process (Harris 2007).

[17] At times court clerks would know beforehand if the case was a "borderline"—the probation officer's report recommended the youth be retained in juvenile court, the offense lacked any physical harm to the victim, the judge had given some indication that he/she was thinking of retaining the youth. The clerk may have had this information because the case was on calendar (thus the court file was pulled), but later postponed to another date. It is difficult to observe a "fit" hearing because of the nature of the waiver hearings. Once a youth is petitioned by the DDA for transfer, most likely the youth will be found unamenable to the juvenile court. Thus, the vast majority of the cases observed were found "unfit" to remain in the juvenile court.

References

Albonetti, C. A., and J. R. Hepburn. 1996. Prosecutorial discretion to defer criminalization: The effects of defendant's ascribed and achieved status characteristics. *Journal of Quantitative Criminology* 12:63–81.

Barnes, C., and R. Franz. 1989. Questionably adult: Determinants and effects of the juvenile waiver decision. *Justice Quarterly* 6 (1): 117–35.

Bishop, D., and C. Frazier. 1991. Transfer of juvenile to criminal court: A case study and analysis of prosecutorial waiver. *Notre Dame Journal of Law, Ethics and Public Policy* 5 (2): 281–302.

———. 1996. Race effects in juvenile justice decision making: Findings from a statewide analysis. *Journal of Criminology and Criminal Law* 86 (3): 392–414.

———. 1997. The influence of race in juvenile justice processing. *Journal of Research in Crime and Delinquency* 25 (3): 242–63.

Bishop, D., C. Frazier, L. Lanza-Kaduce, and L. Winner. 1996. The transfer of juveniles to criminal court: Does it make a difference? *Crime and Delinquency* 42 (2): 171–91.

Bjerregaard, B. 2002. Self definitions of gang membership and involvement in delinquent activities. *Youth and Society* 34 (1): 31–54.

Bortner, M. A. 1986. Traditional rhetoric, organizational realities: Remand of juveniles to adult court. *Crime and Delinquency* 32 (1): 53–73.

Cicourel, A. 1968. *The social organization of juvenile justice.* New Brunswick: Transaction.

Clement, M. 1997. Five-year study of juvenile waiver and adult sentences: Implications for policy. *Criminal Justice Policy Review.* 8:201–19.

Emerson, R. 1969. *Judging delinquents: Context and process in juvenile court.* Chicago: Aldine.

Emerson, R., R. Fretz, and L. Shaw. 1995. *Writing ethnographic field notes.* Chicago: University of Chicago Press.

Engen, R., and S. Steen. 2000. The power to punish: Discretion and sentencing reform in the war on drugs. *American Journal of Sociology* 105 (5): 1357–95.

Fagan, J. 1996. The comparative advantage of juvenile criminal court sanctions on recidivism among adolescent felony offenders. *Law and Policy* 18:77–114.

Fagan, J., and E. Deschenes. 1990. Determinants of judicial waiver decisions for violent juvenile adolescent felony offenders. *Journal of Criminal Law and Criminology* 81 (2): 314–47.

Fagan, J., M. Forst, and T. S. Vivona. 1987. Racial determinants of the judicial decision: Prosecuting violent youth in criminal court. *Crime and Delinquency* 33 (2): 259–86.

Fagan, J., and F. Zimring. 2000. *The Changing borders of juvenile justice: Transfer of adolescents to the criminal court.* Chicago: The University of Chicago Press.

Feld, B. 1987. The juvenile court meets the principle of the offense: Legislative changes in juvenile waiver statutes. *The Journal of Criminal Law and Criminology* 78 (3): 471–533.

———. 1999. *Bad kids: Race and the transformation of the juvenile court.* New York, Oxford Press.

Garfinkel, H. 1956. Conditions of successful degradation ceremonies. *American Journal of Sociology* 61 (5): 420–24.

———. 1967. *Studies in ethnomethodology.* Englewood Cliffs, NJ: Prentice-Hall.

———. 2002. *Ethnomethodology's program.* Englewood Cliffs, NJ: Prentice-Hall.

Garfinkel, H., and H. Sacks. 1970. On formal structures of practical action. In *Theoretical sociology: Perspectives and developments,* edited by J. C. Tiryakian and E. A. McKinney, 337–66. New York: Appleton-Century-Crofts.

Hagan, J. 1974. Extra-legal attributes and criminal sentencing: An assessment of a sociological viewpoint. *Law and Society Review,* 8:357–83.

Harris, A. 2007. Diverting and abdicating judicial discretion: Cultural, political, and procedural changes in California juvenile justice. *Law & Society Review* 41 (2): 387–428.

Hasenfeld, Y. 1972. People processing organizations: An exchange approach. *American Sociological Review* 37:256–63.

Hasenfeld, Y., and P. Cheung. 1985. The juvenile court as a people-processing organization: A political economy perspective. *American Journal of Sociology* 90 (4): 801–24.

Houghtalin, M., and G. L. Mays. 1991. Criminal dispositions of New Mexico: Juveniles transferred to adult court. *Crime and Delinquency* 37 (3): 393–407.

Howell, J. 1996. Juvenile transfers to the criminal justice system: State of the art. *Law and Policy Review* 18:17–60.

Jensen, E., and L. Metsger. 1994. A test of the deterrent effect of legislative waiver on violent juvenile crime. *Crime and Delinquency* 40:96–104.

Keiter, R. 1973. Criminal or delinquent? A study of juvenile cases transferred to the criminal court. *Crime and Delinquency* 19:528–38.

Krisberg, B., and J. Austin. 1993. *Reinventing juvenile justice.* Thousand Oaks, CA: Sage.

Kupchik, A. 2003. Prosecuting adolescents in criminal courts: Criminal or juvenile justice? *Social Problems* 50 (3): 439–60.

Lee, L. 1994. Factors determining waiver in a juvenile court. *Journal of Criminal Justice* 22 (4): 329–39.

Leiber, M. 2002. Disproportionate Minority Confinement (DMC) of youth: An analysis of state and federal efforts to address the issue. *Crime and Delinquency* 48 (1): 3–45.

Leiber, M., and K. Y. Mack. 2003. The individual and joint effects of race, gender, and family status on juvenile justice decision-making. *Journal of Research in Crime and Delinquency* 40 (1): 34–70.

Liska, A., and M. Tausig. 1979. Racial differentials in legal decision-making for juveniles. *Sociological Quarterly* 20:18.

Maynard, D., and J. Manzo. 1993. On the sociology of justice: Theoretical notes from an actual jury deliberation. *Sociological Theory* 11 (2):171–93.

Matza, D. 1964. *Delinquency and drift.* New York: Wiley.

McNulty, E. 1996. The transfer of juvenile offenders to adult court: Panacea or problem? *Law and Policy Review* 18 (1 and 2):61–75.

Mears, D. 1998. The sociology of sentencing: Reconceptualizing decision-making processes and outcomes. *Law and Society Review* 32 (3): 667–724.

Mears, D., and S. Field. 2000. Theorizing sanctioning in a criminalized juvenile court. *Criminology* 38 (4): 983–1019.

Platt, A. M. 1977. *The child savers: The invention of delinquency.* Chicago: University of Chicago Press.

Podkopacz, M., and B. Feld. 1995. Judicial waiver policy and practice: Persistence, seriousness and race. *Law and Inequality* December (1): 73–178.

Poulos, T., and S. Orchowsky. 1994. Serious juvenile offenders: Predicting the probability of transfer to criminal court. *Crime and Delinquency* 40 (1): 3–17.

Rothman, D. J. 1980. *Conscience and convenience: The asylum and its alternatives in progressive America.* Boston, MA: Little, Brown and Company.

Savelsberg, J. 1992. Law that does not fit society: Sentencing guidelines as a neoclassical reaction to the dilemmas of substantivized law. *American Journal of Sociology* 97 (5): 1346–81.

Singer, S. 1993. The automatic waiver of juveniles and substantive justice. *Crime and Delinquency* 39 (3): 253–61.

———. 1995. *Recriminalizing delinquency: violent juvenile crime and juvenile justice reform.* Cambridge, MA: Cambridge University Press.

Singer, S., J. Fagan, and A. Liberman. 2000. The reproduction of juvenile justice in criminal court: A case study of New York's juvenile offender law. In *The changing boarders of juvenile justice,* edited by Jeffrey Fagan and Franklin E. Zimring, 353–77. Chicago: University of Chicago Press.

Steinberg, L., and E. Cauffman. 2000. Developmental perspectives on jurisdictional boundary. In *The changing boarders of juvenile justice: Transfer of adolescents to the criminal court,* edited by Jeffrey Fagan and Franklin Zimring, 379–406. Chicago: University of Chicago Press.

Steffensmeier, D., and S. Demuth. 2000. Ethnicity and sentencing outcomes in U.S. federal courts: Who is punished more harshly? *American Sociological Review* 65:705–29.

———. 2001. Ethnicity and judges' sentencing decisions in Pennsylvania: Hispanic-Black-White comparisons. *Criminology* 39:145–78.

Storm, K., and S. Smith. 1998. Juvenile felony defendants in criminal courts. Washington DC: U.S. Department of Justice, Bureau of Justice Statistics (NCJ 165815).

Sutton, J. 1998. *Stubborn children: Controlling delinquency in the United States, 1640–1981.* Berkeley, CA: University of California Press.

Snyder, H., M. Sickmund, and E. Poe-Yamagata. 2000. *Juvenile transfers to criminal court in the 1990's: Lessons learned* from *four studies.* Washington, DC: U.S. Department of Justice, Office of Justice Programs, Office of Juvenile Justices and Delinquency Prevention.

Takata, S., and R. Zwitz. 1990. Divergent perceptions of group delinquency in a Midwestern community: Racine's gang problem. *Youth and Society* 21 (3): 282–305.

Torbet, P., R. Gable, H. Hurst, I. Montgomery, L. Szymanski, and D. Thomas. 1996. State responses to serious and violent juvenile crime. Washington, DC: Office of Juvenile Justice and Delinquency Prevention.

Ulmer, J. 1996. Sentencing disparities and departures from guidelines. *Justice Quarterly* 13 (1): 81–106.

Vigil, D. 1988. Group processes and street identity: Adolescent Chicano gang members. *Ethos* 16 (4): 421–45.

Winner, L., L. Lanza-Kaduce, D. Bishop, and C. Frazier. 1997. The transfer of juveniles to criminal court: Reexamining recidivism over the long run. *Crime and Delinquency* 43 (4): 548–63.

CHANGE IN
CRIMINAL JUSTICE ORGANIZATIONS

No other topic has generated more discussion and debate among citizens, politicians, and criminal justice administrators over the past decade than change and reform. Initiatives have been proposed across the country to address a myriad of criminal justice problems. Whether the issue is jail overcrowding, the police use of force, or appropriate sentencing schemes, both critics and reformers have proposed some interesting and controversial reforms for the criminal justice system. The primary concern for criminal justice administrators is *how* these change efforts will affect their organizations. History is replete with examples of how intended consequences are very rarely realized in criminal justice reform movements. Instead, what has been produced is a host of unintended consequences and bad results. While reformer intentions generally have been good, the aphorism that the road to hell is paved with good intentions applies particularly well to criminal justice reform and change platforms.

The first article in this final section explores the dangers of criminal justice reform. Eugene Doleschal (article 24) provides an excellent analysis of how reforms tend to fall into circularity. Over time, today's reforms can resemble the practices of the past; and in some cases the reforms actually do more harm than good. Criminal justice administrators are aware of this unavoidable consequence, yet in many cases they are powerless to do anything about reforms, particularly those efforts that are externally imposed and politically charged. Doleschal warns both the criminal justice administrator and the reformer that all change programs have consequences, and that if reform is to have any real and long-lasting impact, the implementation process should be based more on circumspection rather than zeal.

In the second piece in this section, Rhonda Allen (article 25) examines the impediments to changing police organizations from a traditional, top-down hierarchy to the more flexible and open organizational structure found within a community policing model. She documents not only the impediments to change, but more importantly those factors that seem to facilitate change. Of particular importance to the change process within police organizations are individual attitudes and pressure to change. Police administrators have the ability to influence both of these variables if they desire change within their organizations. The process of change is enhanced by police administrators' commitment to the change process and the influence they can engender toward accepting change among officers in the rank and file. Planning for change is a long-term process and a commitment. If this is not recognized by administrators, then the possibility of promoting and instituting significant change within criminal justice organizations is drastically reduced.

A major unintended change in the criminal justice system during the last two decades is the influx of mentally ill inmates into prisons and jails. The change came about after the deinstitutionalization of mental hospitals. There were no doubt good reasons to close the old mental asylums, and the plan was to support those released through a system of community mental health. However, the released clients soon found their way into the nation's prisons, especially the jails. The criminal justice system has been slow to respond to this challenge, but during the last several years mental health courts have been created in jurisdictions across the nation. Allison Redlich, Henry Steadman, John Monahan, Pamela Clark Robbins, and John Petrila (article 26) surveyed jurisdictions across the nation to learn the extent to which mental health courts have been created, and how the local jail populations have been affected by the use of the courts. Drug courts are distinguished from traditional courts in that (1) their dockets are for mentally ill offenders only, (2) their goal is to divert mentally ill offenders from the system, (3) community mental health treatment can be mandatory along with continuous supervision, and (4) noncompliance of the terms of supervision is sanctioned. The authors found that during the last eight years, mental health courts have been created in 34 states and manage over seven thousand clients. Most courts used jail as a sanction for clients who did not comply with the terms of supervision. The authors conclude that the use of mental health courts will continue to grow.

Community policing, broadly construed, asks law enforcement officers to take an active role in the community the serve to ensure order and reduce criminal activity. This role can take on many forms. Edmund McGarrell, Steven Chermak, Jeremy Wilson, and Nicholas Corsaro (article 27) describe a "lever pulling" strategy to reduce homicides and gun-related violence in high-crime areas. The approach combines face-to-face communication of a deterrence message to youth gang members as well as a crackdown on gangs. The approach had success in Boston and Minneapolis. The city of Boston, for example, realized a 60% drop in youth violence following the intervention. Given such successes, the authors did a replication study in Indianapolis, Indiana, and found that the deterrent effect of the strategy combined with social service interventions did serve to reduce youth crime and violence.

Samuel Walker, Geoffrey Alpert, and Dennis Kenney (article 28) suggest that so-called early warning systems (EW) have become a new tool for law enforcement administrators to reduce officer misconduct and enhance accountability. The EW system is a departure from traditional police personnel systems that relied on punishment for officer misconduct. Essentially, the EW system is data driven and records problematic performance such as citizen complaints and use of force. The interventions in the EW system rely on counseling and corrective actions rather than the traditional reliance on punitive actions against officers. The authors provide a brief overview of EW programs in a number of jurisdictions, including the Miami police department that established the first permanent EW system. The authors conclude that EW systems have emerged as a popular remedy for police misconduct, providing a good tool for control of police officer misconduct and promoting accountability standards.

Beyond individual and organizational interests, change must be understood within the context of a developing body of scientific knowledge. Jennifer Ferguson (article 24) provides an interesting and compelling justification for the use of research in correctional organizations. She notes how in the correctional treatment literature there have been many scientifically documented successful interventions with offender populations. How a correctional administrator incorporates this knowledge into an organization becomes another matter. Ferguson notes the importance of understanding knowledge in the organizational context and framing change contingent upon the many factors that affect the implementation of knowledge within correctional organizations.

Hundreds of prisoners have been exonerated since 1989. Death row inmates in Illinois who were there by virtue of their confessions were released when DNA evidence proved their innocence. As a result of such travesties of justice, major movements are robustly occurring across the nation to find and release innocent individuals from prisons. Marvin Zalman provides an excellent overview of the "innocence movement" that has been instrumental in freeing innocent people from prison as well as raising the consciousness of policy makers and criminal justice practitioners. While the author supports efforts to reform the justice system, he finds the development of new policy to do so is limited. He argues that the recent method is to discover errors and wrongdoing in the system and create new rules to prevent their recurrence. Zalman encourages criminal justice scholars to look more deeply into the process to see why practitioners may misuse their power or perhaps are not cognizant of the outcomes of their actions.

Rick Lovell (article 31) concludes this section by examining how research influences reform in criminal justice organizations. He goes to the core of organizational analysis by looking at how information is collected and used by correctional organizations. In this case, he describes how information serves the interests of prison administrators. Through a revealing analysis, Lovell demonstrates what many researchers are hesitant to face or discuss, namely, that research must have some instrumental purpose for correctional administrators in order for it to be useful to them. By emphasizing bureaucratic and organizational constraints, Lovell makes clear that research use (and nonuse) is highly structured and contingent upon specific demands in the work setting. He shows how research is critical to reformers who seek to change criminal justice organizations.

24

The Dangers of
Criminal Justice Reform

EUGENE DOLESCHAL

Several years ago, Robert Martinson startled the criminal justice community by presenting convincing evidence that "nothing works"—that no type of correctional effort is capable of reforming offenders, of reducing recidivism. Although he has had many critics, and volumes of comments on his main work[1] have been written, his basic point is driven home again and again. Almost every day, the Information Center of the National Council on Crime and Delinquency receives evidence from evaluative studies that Martinson was indeed correct. One solution to this discouraging and humbling finding was well expressed by Edwin Schur, in his *Radical Non-Intervention*: That is, people should be left alone as much as possible. They and society are better off if we intervene as little as possible and then only when absolutely necessary.[2]

Evidence is also accumulating about the effects of efforts to reform the criminal and juvenile justice systems. The highly disturbing findings of evaluations show that well-intentioned humanitarian reforms designed to lessen criminal justice penalties either do not achieve their objectives or actually produce consequences opposite those intended. In other words, it may be said that "nothing works" in criminal justice reform, as in offender rehabilitation. Worse than this, criminal justice reforms tend to backfire, making things worse from the reformer's point of view, not better.

This review will examine some of the literature on the untoward effects of criminal justice reforms, draw on evidence from other disciplines exhibiting similar patterns, and attempt to point a way out of the dilemma.

Adult Criminal Justice Reforms

During the recent past an increasing number of criminal justice researchers and writers have expressed concern over the direction of diversion and similar "alternatives to incarceration." Those who helped develop pretrial diversion programs are deeply troubled by the way they have worked out. Programs have had a minimal effect on defendants, and judges and prosecutors are using them to widen the net of social control.[3]

The Vera Institute of Justice of New York studied the effects of the oldest and largest pretrial diversion program, New York's Court Employment Project. The report concluded that the project was accomplishing none of its goals: It was not reducing pretrial detention time; it was not reducing the number of stigmatizing criminal convictions; it was not having any effect on the behavior, employment, educational status, or life styles of its clients; and it was not reducing its clients' recidivism. Above all, almost half the diverted defendants, the report found, would not have been prosecuted had there been no court Employment Project.[4]

How local enforcement agencies responded to and influenced the direction of the San Pablo (California) Adult Diversion Project (SPAD) was examined in a study using randomly placed experimental and control groups. Both groups were followed for a 36-month period to test SPAD's effects on recidivism, costs, and social control.

Five distinct stages of reform were found to emerge during the SPAD experiment: (1) resistance, (2) accommodation, (3) transformation, (4) dissolution, and (5) rebirth. Each of these phases resulted in major change in the content and direction of the reform. Impact results show that SPAD had no effects in reducing recidivism, that it proved to be much more expensive than traditional processing, and that it failed to curb the level of criminal justice intervention.

The dismal results are explained by process analysis. Local officials interpreted diversion as a means of increasing control over misdemeanant defendants. Consequently, they selected defendants for the program unlikely to be severely sanctioned by the courts. Such a population was found to engage infrequently in criminal acts regardless of the court's intervention. By locating diversion at the pretrial stage and within the lower courts, the program diminished the potential for reducing social control. By working with such a population, the program diminished the potential for reducing crime and costs. More important, pretrial diversion placed the value of intervention and control ahead of a determination of the defendant's guilt or innocence, thereby compromising the basic values of a due process model of justice. Instead of correcting the deficiencies of the justice system itself, diversion extended an irrational system. As one writer has concluded in his review of such alternatives: "Instead of justice, there is diversion."[5]

Further similar evidence comes from a national assessment of restitution programs in the Untied States. The theme is the same: Restitution projects have been unable to divert substantial numbers of offenders from severe penalties; they, too, exhibit a tendency to increase the degree of social control exercised over offenders. Instead of helping to reduce rates of incarceration as intended, such projects increase the number of persons under custodial confinement.[6]

The results of a national evaluation of community service programs funded by the Law Enforcement Assistance Administration also demonstrated that community service is only marginally effective, if effective at all, as a means of reducing institutional overcrowding, correctional costs, recidivism, or probation caseload. The reader may be left wondering what it is good for except to widen the net of social control.[7]

A study of community correction programs in Saskatchewan found that a great expansion of such programs produced no corresponding decrease in the use of correctional institutions. On the contrary, the use of institutions increased steadily; thus, the establishment of community programs permitted the correctional system to expand at a tremendous rate, placing an ever larger proportion of the population under some form of state supervision. During the 18 years under study, the rate of persons under supervision nearly tripled.

It is clear that, had community programs not been introduced as humanitarian "reform," the cost of supervising an increasing volume of offenders would have been enormous. If the state had been unable or unwilling to sustain these additional expenditures, the correctional system could not have expanded, and some offenders would have been released outright without supervision. In effect, community programs have not been alternatives to incarceration but alternatives to release. Social control, once concentrated in the institutions is now being dispersed into the community.[8]

There is wide agreement among students of criminal justice that the trend during the first three-quarters of the twentieth century has been a consistent movement toward community programs in lieu of penal institutions as the mode of correction. A study aptly entitled "Alternatives to Incarceration: From Total Institutions to Total Systems" takes issue with this common perception of correctional history, using California as the focus of a time series analysis of correctional reform. California was chosen for many reasons, chiefly because that state has been a pioneer in criminal justice reform. It was in California that the substitution of other penalties for imprisonment reached its extreme, with the introduction of the probation subsidy program. Moreover, the state of California has made a greater investment in research than has any other state. Massachusetts was used as the control state. Unlike California, that state introduced very few correctional reforms after 1900; most criminologists and other experts, including those who served on the prestigious President's Crime Commission of 1966, regarded criminal justice in Massachusetts as "mediocre."

The study found the same pattern of reform effects: Alternatives to incarceration in California did not reduce prison populations, but they increased the control of populations previously left alone. Providing the first hint of what may be responsible for this development, the study found that

California, the inventor of innumerable "alternatives" to incarceration, kept considerably more people in prisons, in jails, and on probation and parole than did "mediocre" Massachusetts, which did very little during the same 80 years under study, even if crime rates are taken into account. When declines in some measures of incarceration did occur in California, they did not follow the introduction of any particular new alternative: Declines in incarceration appear to have resulted from increases in control rather than from the process of substitution. Faster increases in other forms of control reduced the proportion of offenders incarcerated but there were no declines in the rates of offenders committed to institutions.

Overwhelming evidence was found in the comparison of the two states for the proposition that the twentieth century has witnessed a process of extension of control, whereby offenders have been shifted from mechanisms that exerted very little control, or no control at all, to mechanisms with more social control. Sharp increases in control immediately after the introduction of major alternatives, such as probation, the split sentence, and the probation subsidy, strongly suggest that active reforms are responsible for this development. After probation was introduced in California around 1900, the risk of incarceration did not decline, and a large group of probationers was simply added to the ranks of the controlled population. Similarly, split sentences legislation expanded probation and jail populations without reducing prison populations, and the probation subsidy program did more to enhance superior court probation populations than it did to decrease commitments to prisons.

The study is a powerful addition to the growing body of literature indicating a relationship between correctional innovations and reforms and the extension of criminal justice control over populations previously not controlled—through formalizing available types of control, and incorporating them into the criminal justice process. Early probation laws in California replaced several forms of informal control and suspended sentences. Split sentences led to increases in sentences to institutions as well as to probation. The California probation subsidy program was instrumental in the transition from traditional forms of incarceration to less traditional ones, while at the same time it led to a substantial increase in probation.

The study concludes that (1) new alternatives to incarceration will draw most of their clientele not from institutions but from populations not previously incarcerated, and (2) relatively successful alternatives that divert offenders from institutions involve some modified form of institutionalization, such as civil commitments and split sentences. Extension of control occurs in liberal systems more than in conservative ones, in innovative and activist states more than in those where change is slow.[9] In its conclusion, the study serves to remind us of the Netherlands, which is generally regarded as having the world's most humane criminal justice system, as well as the world's lowest rate of incarceration and the lowest average length of stay in prison among offenders worldwide—but which is absolutely without "innovative" correctional programs.

Criminal justice reform enthusiasts have argued that the widespread adoption of community-based programs would benefit the criminal justice system in a number of ways. The alternative programs, it is argued, are more effective than correctional institutions in rehabilitating offenders. Therefore, they will reduce crime rates and ease requirements for correctional programming. The literature is also replete with statements, as mentioned above, that such programs are an important means of coping with the mounting volume of offenders and that they provide a substitute for the institution.

A paper by John Hylton presents convincing evidence refuting arguments for the effectiveness, humaneness, and economy of community-based programs. Such programs, Hylton points out, have a range of highly undesirable effects on the justice system and on society—effects that have been largely ignored. The failure to reduce reliance on institutions is not restricted to the United States. No country in the world in which community-based programs have been widely adopted has experienced substantial reductions in imprisonment rates. This is equally true in those countries where elimination or curtailment of the use of institutions has been an explicit goal.[10]

There is also a substantial and growing body of evidence indicating that community programs have been associated with a variety of outcomes that can hardly be termed humane. A number of studies have shown that community programs, particularly those housing participants, tend to reproduce in the community the very features of the system they were designed to replace. They serve not only as alternatives to incarceration but rather as alternative forms of confinement. Community resistance to such programs is one reason why they are apt to reproduce institutional environments in the community. The community, Hylton stresses, is not necessarily a more humane environment than the correctional system; we may be in the process of creating a monster of a new system.

Modern correctional programming has blurred the boundaries between the institution and the community and left the community susceptible to entirely new strategies of supervision and control. The "correctional continuum" that extends from the institution to the community makes it difficult to discern where the social control apparatus begins and ends. This blurring is a natural outgrowth of the community correction philosophy. The dangerous system we are creating, a system that will be able to track and influence our activities at almost all times and places, may not seem to be an outgrowth of the "humane" community care movement until the significance of blurring the boundaries between the institution and community is recognized.[11]

If Hylton is right, if this is the cure we are devising, perhaps we should prefer the disease. The dream of criminal justice reform come true can readily become the nightmare of the benevolent state gone mad.

The phenomenon of untoward effects of reforms has been observed in other countries as well: The experience of foreign countries demonstrates convincingly that the criminal justice system has a life of its own, independent of and oblivious to the intent of administrative or legislative reform. In

Britain, the suspended sentence of imprisonment was introduced in 1968 as a way to reduce prison populations. As in the United States, the effect was the opposite. Courts used suspended sentences not only in place of imprisonment but also in place of fines and probation, sentences that in Britain carry no threat of incarceration. In addition, courts imposed longer suspended sentences than sentences of actual imprisonment. As suspendees reoffended, they had their old sentences activated and served those and their new sentences consecutively instead of concurrently. England's prison population increased as a result of this reform, in direct contrast to what was intended.[12]

A similar phenomenon has been observed in state subsidies to local correction. Although promoted as a means of reducing prison populations and allowing countries and cities to supervise offenders in their own communities, the intent has not been fulfilled.

An official report on the Minnesota Community Corrections Act (CCA), a model adopted later by many states, sums up the experience of most of the states that introduced correctional subsidies. In 10 of 11 geographic areas analyzed in the evaluation, there was no evidence that the CCA had had an effect on the adult sanctions meted out. The CCA's failure to affect the diversion from prison of significant numbers of offenders is the major explanation for this finding. Costs increased compared with the costs of pre-CCA policy because of the development of 12 new organizational structures at the local level without corresponding decreases in the cost of state-level administration.

The major failure of the Minnesota program has been the inability of state correctional legislation to alter judges' sentencing policies. Judges responded to the reform by using local incarceration to a greater extent for types of offenders previously sentenced to the community. In addition, the alternative to state prison tended to the local jail.[13] Finally, in none of the areas was there improved public protection as measured by arrests of crime rates.

Of the various subsidies, none has been analyzed and evaluated more frequently than has the California probation subsidy. Perhaps the most thorough is an evaluation by Edwin Lemert and Forrest Dill. Under the California subsidy, probation departments built their strategies on the hope that careful use of special supervision caseloads would reduce commitments. Departments sought to bring about commitment reductions simply by opening their doors to more probationers. This strategy broke down early, and departments began to lean more on local institutions and quasi-institutional programs as methods of reducing commitments. While the California probation subsidy promoted somewhat liberalized use of probation, it also increased the use of facilities for local incarceration. As in all the other criminal justice "reforms," the program helped to augment the capacity of the correctional system in California.

With regard to reduced probation caseloads, the subsidy experiment confirmed earlier findings: They accomplish little, and officers accustomed to large caseloads do not know how to handle small caseloads. In some departments, particularly in Los Angeles, growth was measured by earnings from the state subsidy, and a great deal of entrepreneurial energy was applied to push them upward. This produced uneven development and disorganization in the sense that almost any means were deemed valid to reduce commitments.

A system of control based on rewards, the researchers conclude, presents great administrative difficulties. They draw a useful comparison between the California probation subsidy and the Stakhanovite movement in Soviet industry in 1935, which greatly increased productivity but reduced product quality, caused disruption among the workers, and distorted human values.[14]

In adult criminal justice reform, the phenomenon of the distortion and frustration of the original purposes of reforms is evident in the efforts to decriminalize victimless crimes, including such offenses as public drunkenness. Removal of victimless crimes from criminal justice jurisdiction and law enforcement scrutiny as advocated by the President's Crime Commission of 1966 and numerous criminal justice reform agencies is another example of a criminal justice reform that has not worked out as intended. In 1969, victimless crime arrests in the United States were 51.5 percent of all arrests; in 1980, they were 32.4 percent of all arrests. In 1960, 36 percent of all arrests nationally were for public drunkenness alone; in 1980, they were just over 10 percent. However, the law enforcement community was shifting its attention not from victimless crimes to (serious) index crimes, as reformers wanted them to do, but to the less serious part II crimes. Although victimless crime arrests declined from 51.5 percent of all arrests in 1969 to 32.4 percent of all arrests in 1980, part II crimes (minus victimless crime arrests) increased from 29.5 percent to 45.2 percent of all arrests, rising in almost the same proportion as the fall in victimless crime arrests. Arrests for the more serious index crimes remained relatively stable at around 20 to 22 percent of all arrests throughout this period.

As in so many other reforms, the decline in victimless crime arrests nationwide was accomplished through widening of the net in part II crimes and through "label switching" from one type of offense to another. For instance, public drunkenness or disorderly conduct can easily become simple assault. In addition, a substantial increase in arrests in "all other" category of offenses occurred: They increased from 12 percent of all arrests in 1970 to 17 percent in 1980.[15]

How the intent of the reform to decriminalize public drunkenness was frustrated is illustrated by two case studies, one in Massachusetts and one in New Mexico. Both states abolished the crime of public drunkenness in 1973, yet both experienced an increase in the number of drinking-related jail detention: While "arrests" were abolished, the same activity continued under the label "protective custody." In Massachusetts, protective custody detentions increased 19 percent, and disorderly conduct charges increased 27 percent after the reform.[16] In 1979, the city of Gallup, New Mexico, population 18,000, checked drunken persons into its jail for protective custody 26,000 times. An immense drunk tank was built in 1970 as part of a new jail after living conditions in the old one were declared unconstitutional by a federal court. Conditions in the new jail are worse: Gallup officials view the protective custody law as exempting them from minimum standards for the treatment of jail inmates because drunk tank inmates are not formally arrested and therefore technically not inmates. While the old jail provided inmates with mattresses and blankets, most drunks in the new jail sleep on cement floors.[17] The original intent of the reform that decriminalized drunkenness was for inebriates to be placed in a detoxification center, not in a jail under "protective custody."

The History of Reform

Our fathers and forefathers tried to reform criminal justice according to varying diagnoses of the system's problems. After almost 200 years of criminal justice reform, we should know what has to be done. This is not, however, the case. Historical analyses of criminal justice reforms provide substantial evidence of their ill effects, as well as of the circularity and repetitiveness of reform. The harmful consequences of good intentions are only now beginning to be understood.

Stanley Cohen notes that decarceration as a correctional policy is currently hailed with as much enthusiasm as was its opposite, the concept of asylum and of the penitentiary, when it was first introduced 150 years ago. On the surface, large-scale reaction against institutions may appear to stem from ideological opposition to state intervention. Yet ironically, the major results of the new movements toward "community" and "diversion" have been increases rather than decreases in the amount of intervention directed at many groups of deviants and offenders in the system, expanding rather than lowering the total number of persons brought into the system. "Alternatives" are not alternatives at all but new programs that supplement or expand the existing system by attracting new populations. The "new" move into the community, Cohen observes, is merely a continuation of the pattern established in the nineteenth century. It is only the scale of the operation and the technologies enabling the expansion of social control that are new. [18]

David Rothman, in his *Conscience and Convenience*, documents that notwithstanding the good intentions of reformers, convenience was a major factor in the implementation of their reforms; administrators used the reforms to their own advantage. Historically, all progressive reforms share one outstanding feature: They expanded the power of the state, thus enlarging the freedom of action of public officials. Rothman's basic finding is by now familiar: Innovations that appeared to be substitutes for incarceration became supplements to incarceration.[19]

Another characteristic of reform is its circularity. Two hundred years ago, much of criminal justice was community justice, and it was often brutal and inhumane. To counteract this inhumanity, Quakers invented the penitentiary in the early 1800s; this was quickly accepted as the model institution for correcting offenders in North America and Western Europe. Instead of being exposed to a vindictive and cruel community, the Quakers argued, criminals would be placed in a quiet cell of their own, there to engage in penance, meditation, and prayer, and through their actions to reform. It did not take the Quakers long to regret their invention. The penitentiary turned out to be no more humane than the pillory or the whipping post. Two hundred years later, the new reformers have discovered that the community has not become more humane, more accepting, or less vindictive toward its offenders, even though the physical expression of that vindictiveness is no longer tolerated.

The circularity of criminal justice reform is also documented in a study of women's prison reform. Nineteenth century women prison reformers proclaimed a sisterhood with the imprisoned woman, explicitly identifying with her plight inside prisons run by and for men. After a long and hard-fought campaign by nineteenth century feminists, a sexually segregated penal system was established with separate prisons run by and for women. The reformers clung to a definition of woman's separate nature that limited the reformers' own power and stifled the inmates they sought to aid. In the 1970s began an experiment with a "new" correctional reform: sexual integration of the prisons. The circle is complete.[20]

Juvenile Justice Reform

Evaluations of efforts to reform juvenile justice consistently yield results identical to those documented in criminal justice reform.

In a review of evaluations of juvenile diversion programs, Thomas Blomberg finds net widening reported again and again. Virtually all diversion projects expanded control by selecting the major proportion of their clients from a population never before adjudicated. The widening of control has had as its practical consequence double prosecution jeopardy, increased rearrest rates, intrusion into the family, and accelerated movement of youths into the justice system. Juvenile justice reform has resulted in a continuing sprawl of the correctional system.[21]

An analysis of a California juvenile court's implementation of a diversion program found that it expanded the organization and service function of the juvenile court, extending services beyond problem youths to include whole families. Data collected on five years of the court's diversion program showed it to produce expanded control as measured by larger numbers of youths receiving some form of juvenile court service, as well as accelerated control as determined by out-of-home placement of youths whose families were unable or unwilling to respond to family intervention. Diversion has enlarged the scope of the juvenile court and the proportion of the population under its control.[22] An evaluation of a Dade County (Florida) prevention and diversion program reported the familiar pattern of findings: The five programs, which provided counseling, recreational, educational, and employment services, widened the net of intervention and control without demonstrating any reduction in delinquency.[23]

An evaluation of 15 juvenile diversion projects funded by the California Office of Criminal Justice Planning found that, of all the clients served, 49 percent would not have been processed within the traditional juvenile justice system had the diversion projects not existed. The findings with respect to recidivism were mixed: Recidivism was not reduced for youths who had no or two or more arrests. Among youths with one prior arrest, clients did better than comparisons.[24]

Another interesting example of juvenile justice reform is the fate of Youth Service Bureaus (YSBs). YSBs were originally promoted by the President's Crime Commission in 1966 and by many agencies such as the National Council on Crime and Delinquency as a "key to delinquency prevention." The primary functions of YSBs were to be service brokerage, advocacy, resource development, and systems modification. YSBs were not to engage in direct service.

Three selected evaluations of YSBs (a national evaluation, an evaluation of two Illinois YSBs by the National Council on Crime and Delinquency, and a local evaluation of a YSB in Minneapolis) had similar results and led researchers to identical conclusions. Contrary to the original intent, YSBs provided direct service. The advocacy function was nonexistent in all YSBs, and no YSB was engaged in systems change. In Minneapolis, diversion from juvenile justice via YSBs was negligible, as suburban communities had few youths to divert and central city police did not refer juveniles to YSBs.[25]

The development of the YSBs has been so contrary to their original purpose that, for the past five years, the literature has remained remarkably silent about this type of reform. No new evaluations are reported since 1977, and agencies such as the National Council on Crime and Delinquency long ago ceased advocating them as a means to reduce delinquency or reform juvenile justice.

By far the most revealing analysis of a juvenile justice reform concerns the effort to deinstitutionalize status offenders. The first example is a federally funded attempt to remove status offenders from institutions in ten states. The result was an easily documented and considerable widening of the net. In one site, enthusiastic practitioners were found to be canvassing neighborhoods for clients to populate the programs. Many youths who were "diverted" had had no contact with the law at all.

The second example of an effort to deinstitutionalize status offenders was in California, where legislation mandated the removal of all status offenders from locked institutions, a dramatic and uncompromising move. No youths officially labeled status offenders were found in public correctional institutions after the law went into effect. However, there was considerable circumvention of the mandate, through relabeling, which took three forms: from status offender to criminal offender, from status offender to neglected or dependent child, and from status offender to psychiatrically troubled youth. All three forms of relabeling enabled status offenders to be incarcerated in spite of the legislation. They were more stigmatized than would have been the case under the old law, and the seriousness of their official records in the system was increased.[26]

An evaluation of the Illinois Status Offender Services project (ISOS) also documents a pronounced widening of the net. Contact with ISOS increased the youths' penetration into the justice system and the public social service system. That is, it increased court processing of status offenders and their subsequent referral to the Illinois Department of Children and Family Services. The findings were that 10.3 percent of pre-program youths but 76.3 percent of ISOS program youths came to the attention of the department. Comparison of secure detention and the community-based program did not reveal differences in their effects on youths' subsequent contacts with the juvenile justice system.[27]

Edwin Lemert is generally credited with being the "father" of modern diversion. Yet Lemert, as well as others who have developed diversion programs, is deeply troubled by the way they worked out. A salient and unintended consequence of the diversion movement, Lemert maintains, has been its substantial preemption by police and probation departments, which, in many areas, have set up in-house programs, hired their own personnel, and programmed cases in terms of the departments' special needs and circumstances. This development is diametrically opposed to the main idea of diversion—that is, that movement should be away from the juvenile justice system. The effect has been little more than an expansion in the intake and discretionary powers of police and a shuffling of such powers from one part of their organization to another.

Cases selected for diversion include large numbers of youths who formerly would have been screened out. Diversion projects have included disproportionately large numbers of younger juveniles, those with trivial offenses, youngsters without prior records, females, and status offenders.

What began as an effort to reduce discretion in juvenile justice has become a warrant to increase discretion and extend control where there was none before.[28] Lemert reflects on the failure of the diversion movement he helped to create:

> The cooptation of the diversion movement by law enforcement leaves the rather sour impression that not only have the purposes of diversion been perverted but, moreover, police power has been extended over youths and types of behavior not previously subjected to control. . . . It may be argued that police never should have been involved in the programmatic aspects of diversion and that the way to make diversion work is to take it out of the juvenile justice system.[29]

James Austin and Barry Krisberg conclude that all the frantic activity in criminal and juvenile justice reform has resulted in an unchanged system or an extension of its reach. Reform movements have widened, strengthened, or created different nets of social control as organizational dynamics resist, distort, and frustrate the reform's original purpose. Reformers have ignored the surrounding political, social, economic, and ideological context in which their reforms occur. Future efforts at change, the authors recommend, must include detailed analyses of the larger political structure and its connections with the social control apparatus if more substantive results are to be realized.

Austin and Krisberg's explanation for the failure of reform emphasizes the interactive and dialectic nature of the criminal justice system as an organization. The system is interactive in the sense that changes in one part of it trigger reactions among others, reactions that may take the form of resistance, modification, or efforts to defeat the intended reform. Crime control ideology, agency values, power, and authority are sources of conflict among police, prosecutors, the courts, and correctional officials. Agencies compete with one another, and reactions to a given reform depend upon the perceived value of that reform to the agency's survival. In addition, the criminal justice system is dialectic in the sense that it is affected by contradictions in the larger society and is subject to the ideological currents that support the structure. Research on an earlier period of intense criminal justice reform shows that the interplay of ideology, social change, and reform in criminal justice today is an extension of previous patterns.[30]

Criminal Justice Statistics Creation of Illusions

So far in this paper we have examined the effects of liberal reform efforts designed to decrease penalties or reduce the number and the rate of persons incarcerated or under control by the criminal justice system, and we have noted their failure to do so. Readers of a review ("Social Forces and Crime") published in a previous issue of this journal will recall that it examined many studies of efforts designed largely to achieve the opposite, namely, an increase in penalties or an increase in the number or rate of persons to be subjected to criminal sanctions. Without exception, they, too, were failures: The evaluations showed that discretion removed from one point of justice simply reappears elsewhere; punishment increased at one point is nullified in practice at another point.[31] It was shown that juries might defeat or nullify the purpose of legislators, parole release the effects of plea bargaining, judges the intent of prosecutors, police the intent of a governor, and courts the purpose of a city council.

An example taken from the experience of the federal prison system deserves to be repeated here. Over the years, legislators at the federal level have passed ever more punitive criminal laws. Federal judges have reflected the increasingly punitive trend and increased the average length of prison sentences. In 1960, the average sentence to prison meted out to federal offenders was 29.6 months; in 1965, it was 33.5 months; in 1970, 41.1 months; in 1975, 45.5 months; in 1979, 49.0 months.

Charts in the federal prison system's latest annual reports graphically illustrate how flexible indeed a prison system can be, how instantaneous is its population-regulating mechanism, and how meaningless it is to use length of sentences as a tool for gauging reform: The charts trace the average sentence length of released inmates from 32 months in 1965 to 40 months in 1975, then following it to an apparently temporary drop back to 32 months during

1976 and 1977. As the chart traces the average length of sentence, it shows a *simultaneous* and *immediate* decline in the percentage time actually served of the average sentence from about 60.5 percent in 1965 to 46.5 percent in 1975. As sentence lengths declined in 1976 and 1977, the prison system adjusted immediately by simultaneously increasing the percentage of time served from 46.5 percent to about 50.1 percent. The overall result was a remarkable constancy in the average time served of roughly 19 months throughout the 12-year period. Unusual highs in average time served (21 months in 1967) were immediately followed by declines; unusual lows (15 months in 1976) were immediately followed by increases during the following year.[32]

The overall national patterns are not as easily traced and not quite as pronounced but nevertheless clearly discernible. Throughout the depression years of the 1930s the incarceration rate in the United States steadily increased until it reached a high of 137 per 100,000 population. It then sharply decreased during World War II to reach a low of 100 in 1946. The late 1940s and 1950s experienced a slow increase except for a slight dip during the Korean War. It reached a high of 121 in 1961, only to decline again during the Vietnam War years to a historic low of 94 in 1968. Beginning with 1973 the rate experienced its sharpest increase and is now about 150 per 100,000 population.

The national median time served to first parole is available for only a few years, but the data are enough to show a distinct pattern: During most of the period the National Prisoner Statistics report a typical median time served of around 21 months. But there are important exceptions: During World War II the median jumped to 25 months, and during the Vietnam War year of 1966 it was 26 months, 4 to 5 months longer than the norm. In 1977, 1978, and 1979, the national median dropped to its lowest level ever: 17 months, or 9 months less than during 1966.

The clear and logical pattern is that as the incarceration rate decreases the length of stay in prison increases, and as the rate of incarceration increases the length of stay in prison decreases. It is one of the many population-regulating mechanisms the system uses to deal with underpopulated or overcrowded prisons.[33] An additional mechanism is prison returns: According to the *Uniform Parole Reports* a smaller and smaller percentage of parolees are returned to prison for new convictions or technical violations. To the question, are we more punitive today than we were in the past, the answer is clearly yes and no: We incarcerate more offenders, but we keep them locked up for shorter periods and return fewer of them once they are released on parole.

The many examples cited in this paper and the previous review mentioned above lead to the conclusion that there is a dynamic equilibrium in criminal justice which prevents those attempting to reform criminal justice by reducing penalties or incarceration rates from succeeding. Conversely, the studies also support the conclusion that those who attempt the opposite, an increase in penalties, are also ultimately, if not immediately, frustrated in their efforts. Furthermore, an increase in one type of punitiveness (incarceration rates) is accompanied by a decrease in another type of punitiveness (time served). The powers of both groups are thus extremely limited, if not nonexistent. Although incarceration rates fluctuate from decade to decade to a greater or lesser extent, they have the tendency to return to previous highs or previous lows, not rising much beyond apparently predetermined limits or going much below them. When unusual highs or lows are reached, they are compensated for by other factors, such as inmates' increased or decreased lengths of stay in prison and increased or decreased returns to prison of released and paroled offenders.

Shooting the Wolves

Man and society are thus not exempt from the checks and balances that have been observed in many other disciplines. There is no reason why such an equilibrium should not work to man's advantage and for his survival, as it does in nature. Ecologists, to use one example, speak of a balance between predator and prey that assures neither will die out. They speak of an equilibrium in nature within which all living things exist.

Historians, to use another example, long ago discovered the balance of power that exists between nations. History is full of examples of its mechanism: When France emerged as Europe's superpower three centuries ago, alliances between unlikely partners, such as England and tsarist Russia, quickly nullified France's predominance. The balance was quickly restored. When Nazi Germany and Japan threatened the world's balance of power, the world quickly and automatically united to thwart the threat. After World War II, America stood on the pinnacle of unchallenged nuclear power, but the balance was soon restored by the rise of Soviet Russia and the Chinese power. Today, the Soviet Union seems to pre-dominate militarily, but its very success has triggered the balancing mechanism, which is tilting the world once again toward a restoration of the balance of power. In the process the two most unlikely societies, China and the United States, as have so many nations so many times before, find themselves drawn to one another. A Sino-American alliance grows closer with each new Soviet threat. Once again, the USSR's very success has caused the world to realign itself to nullify Russia's increased might: Now 900 million Chinese are added to the economic and technological power of the United States, Japan, and Western Europe.

A program on educational television showed herds of caribou that migrate north across Canada and Alaska during the summer and south again in the winter. Their steady companions are packs of wolves. While wolves reach a top speed of about 25 miles an hour and can run for short spurts only, caribou have a top speed of over 40 miles an hour and can maintain it for long distances. A healthy caribou thus has nothing to fear from the slower wolf, who has to wait patiently until a member of the herd becomes sick or is injured or too old. The constant presence of the wolf makes the caribou alert, his running away from his predator keeps him set on his journey and in shape to face the cold and the arduous trek.

Along comes man, who shoots the pack of wolves to protect the caribou. What happens to the herd? Since wolves no longer kill the caribou, the herd grows in size. Instead of a fast, merciful death, many caribou die a slow death of starvation and disease. Man has done the herd no favor. He has increased its suffering. Nature would maintain the balance, but man has intervened, disrupting a healthy exchange.

Eventually other wolves from other parts of Canada rejoin the herd and the ecological balance is restored. Man learns his lesson: The cruelty of the wolf is in fact merciful. His quick kill in eliminating the sick and the injured has a vital role in the survival of the herd and its fitness. The caribou *needs* the wolf as much as the wolf needs the caribou. They are in ecological balance.

The next point has already been hinted at. Man is not exempt from a system of balances. The Sierra Club and other organizations whose job it is to protect nature are hammering away at their theme: Man may study and observe, but he must leave nature alone; he must not upset the balance; he must not shoot the wolves. Science fiction writers and futurists speculate, in writing about visitors to earth from outer space, that if such visitors are beings of superior intelligence they will come only as observers, never intervening in anything we do, never taking sides. The same thought is expressed in many religions: If there is a God, He does not intervene in man's activities directly, but works indirectly, allowing man to make his mistakes and to learn from them; "God helps those who help themselves" is a proverb that expresses the same idea.

Accumulating evidence shows that crime and punishment are also in social balance, in an equilibrium assuring that neither can get out of hand in the long run, that both have their distinct limits. It means that "criminals" cannot expand their activities indefinitely, and neither can society increase its punishments without triggering counterforces which reduce crime and punishment to their former levels and keep them in balance. A new level of thinking in criminal justice is taking Schur's principle one step farther, urging that we leave the *system* alone and allow each society to find its own level of crime and punishment. *We are learning that that is in fact the most humane level.* Criminal justice reforms that ignore the balance of social, political, and economic forces in society make things worse, not better; they increase suffering, rather than diminishing it. You don't shoot the wolves.

In an essay written in 1894, sociologist William Sumner reflected on the "Absurd Effort to Make the World Over":

> If we puny men by our arts can do anything to straighten [the world] it will be only by modifying the tendencies of some of the forces at work, so that, after a sufficient time, [it] may be changed a little. . . . This effort, however, can at most be only slight, and it will take a long time. In the meantime spontaneous forces will be at work, compared to which our efforts are like those of a man trying to deflect a river, and these forces will have changed the whole problem before our interferences have time to make themselves felt. . . . The things that will change [the world]

are ... the new reactions inside the social organism. ... The utmost [men] can do by their cleverness will be to note and record their course as they are carried along, which is what we do now, and is that which leads us to the vain fancy that we can make or guide the movement. That is why it is the greatest folly of which man can be capable, to sit down with a slate and pencil to plan out a new social world.[34]

In 1892, H. Spencer applied the idea of regressive effects to a variety of governmental programs. In his view, legislative intrusion into natural evolutionary processes almost always produces destructive results:

> Acts of Parliament do not simply fail; they frequently make worse. Moreover, when these topical remedies applied by statesmen do not exacerbate the evils they were meant to cure, they constantly induce collateral evils; and these are often graver than the original ones.[35]

There is no dearth of contemporary authors who are discovering "new reactions inside the social organism" and "forces that will have changed the whole problem before our interferences will have time to make themselves felt." Sam Sieber, in his book *Fatal Remedies—The Ironies of Social Intervention*, examines null effects, side effects, and reverse effects not only in criminal justice reforms but in innumerable other social reforms as well, noting that good intentions have very often made matters far worse for the very people for whom the help was intended. A wide variety of causes of ironic outcomes are analyzed, in education, political behavior, criminal justice, welfare, warfare, health care, public administration, and economic development. Sieber proposes a theory of "social devolution" as a counterbalance to Parsonian theory of social evolution.[36]

Similarly, Robert Merton refers to "unanticipated consequences as self-amplifying social problems in which efforts to do away with one social problem introduce other damaging problems."[37] And D. Bell has a profound message for social reform and criminal justice reform groups who demand to be heard or are encouraged to expect full participation in the social process:

> There is probably more participation today than ever before in political life, at all levels of government, and that very increase in participation leads to the multiplication of groups that "check" each other, and this to a sense of impasse. Thus increased participation paradoxically leads, more often than not, to increased frustration.[38]

The groups, in other words, "monitor" each other and are in antagonistic balance with one another.

That we should leave the system alone, intervening as little as possible and only when absolutely necessary, is an idea whose time has come, and an increasing number of authors are expressing it. A Canadian author, looking at Canadian and foreign data and experiences with diversion, concludes that formalized diversion will increase rather than decrease social control; in effect, he urges the Canadian Parliament not to pass pending legislation on diversion. If Parliament does decide to go ahead with the proposed legislation, it should at least acknowledge that doing nothing with an offender may be preferable.[39]

One of the strongest arguments for allowing the criminal justice system to operate in a marketlike fashion is aptly entitled "The Desirability of Goal Conflict within the Criminal Justice System." Radicals, liberals, and conservatives alike, it is observed, agree on the desirability of a unified, rational, and well-integrated system of criminal justice in which a common set of goals can be pursued through a compatible set of strategies and techniques. Taking a contrary point of view, the article argues that such positions ignore the political environment in which criminal justice operates. There are at least three reasons why goal conflict and fragmentation, rather than unification of the system, are advantageous to the system's processes and functioning: Conflict makes it possible to represent and protect different societal interests; conflict establishes a system of checks and balances; and conflict promotes a smoothly operating offender-processing system. The dynamic equilibrium of a fragmented justice system promotes a balance of power between antagonistic interests as it encourages adaptation and change. As social attitudes and values change, the system can make corresponding changes.[40] A study of a prosecutor's office found that it operated in a marketlike fashion and the decision to prosecute or not to prosecute was often based on the influence of a variety of officials and groups. Any system that exhibits high diversity, even in the form of fragmentation, allows conflicts to be played out and resolved on a continuing basis. Centralization and unification, on the other hand, promote rigidity and create a bureaucracy that is an inefficient structure for change.

Seen in this light, the principle of planned and judicious nonintervention in the operation of the criminal justice system assumes new meaning. Direct intervention and interference become the social equivalent of "shooting the wolves" by producing the kind of untoward consequences discovered by studies of the full effects of criminal justice reforms. The principle of nonintervention allows the system to make its mistakes because the social balance between antagonistic forces renders those mistakes relatively harmless and allows for evolutionary change.

By allowing small conflicts and confrontations to be resolved on a continuing basis society in effect maintains a healthy and steady equilibrium of forces and avoids major conflict and confrontation. The ritual of criminal justice thus becomes a useful, functional safety valve designed to prevent more violent conflict.

Endnotes

1. Lipton, D., Martinson, R., & Wilks, J. (1975). *The effectiveness of correctional treatments.* New York: Praeger. Martinson's and two of his main critics' points of view were reprinted in a 1976 NCCD pamphlet entitled Rehabilitation, Recidivism, and Research.
2. Schur, E. (1973). *Radical non-intervention.* Englewood Cliffs, NJ: Prentice-Hall.
3. Potter, J. (1981). The pitfalls of pretrial detention. *Corrections Magazine, 7*(1), 5–7, 10–11, 36.

4 Ibid.; U.S. National Institute of Justice. (1981). *Diversion of felony arrests: An experiment in pretrial intervention. An evaluation of the court employment project.* Washington, DC: Government Printing Office.

5 Austin, J. F. (1980). *Instead of justice: Diversion.* Ph.D. dissertation, University of California, Davis.

6 University of Minnesota, School of Social Development. (1980). *National assessment of adult restitution programs: Final report.* Duluth: University of Minnesota.

7 Cooper, G., & Anita, S. (1981). *An evaluation of the community service restitution program: A cluster analysis.* Denver, CO: West University of Denver, Denver Research Institute.

8 Hylton, J. H. (1980). *Community corrections and social control.* Regina, Saskatchewan: University of Regina.

9 Miller, D. (1980). *Alternatives to incarceration: From total institutions to total systems.* Ph.D. dissertation, University of California, Berkeley.

10 Hylton, J. H. (1981). *Rhetoric and reality: A critical appraisal of community correction programs.* Regina, Saskatchewan: University of Regina.

11 Ibid.

12 Bottoms, A. E. (1981). The suspended sentence in England, 1967–1978. *British Journal of Criminology, 21*(1), 1–26.

13 Minnesota Corrections Department. (1981). *Minnesota community corrections act evaluation: General report.* St. Paul: Minnesota Corrections Department.

14 Lemert, E. M., & Dill, F. (1978). *Offenders in the community: The probation subsidy in California.* Lexington, MA: Lexington Books.

15 Doleschal, E. (1981). 1980 victimless crime arrests. Unpublished memorandum to National Council on Crime and Delinquency.

16 Daggert, L. R., & Rolde, E. J. (1980). Decriminalization of drunkenness: Effect on the work of suburban police. *Journal of Studies on Alcohol, 41*(9), 819–828.

17 Katel, P. (1980). Sleeping it off in Gallup, N.M. *Corrections Magazine, 6*(4), 16–23.

18 Cohen, S. (1979). The punitive city: Notes on the dispersal of social control. *Contemporary Crises, 3*(4), 339–363.

19 Rothman, D. J. (1980). *Conscience and convenience: The asylum and its alternatives in progressive America.* Boston: Little, Brown.

20 Freedman, E. B. (1981). *Their sisters' keepers: Women's prison reform in America, 1830–1930.* Ann Arbor: University of Michigan Press.

21 Blomberg, T. G. (1980). Widening the net: An anomaly in the evaluation of diversion programs. In M. W. Klein & K. S. Teilmann (Eds.), *Handbook of criminal justice evaluation* (pp. 572–592). Beverly Hills, CA: Sage Publications.

22 Blomberg, T. (1977). Diversion and accelerated social control. *Journal of Criminal Law and Criminology, 68*(2), 274–282; Blomberg, T. (1978). *Social control and the proliferation of juvenile court services.* San Francisco, CA: R & E Research Associates.

23 Dade County Human Resources Department. (1979). *An evaluation of the impact of five juvenile delinquency prevention/diversion programs.* Miami, FL: Dade County Human Resources Department.

24 Palmer, T., & Lewis, R. V. (1980). *An evaluation of juvenile diversion.* Cambridge, MA: Oelgeschlager, Gunn and Hain.

25 Minnesota Center for Sociological Research. (1974). *Evaluation of seven youth service bureaus in the Twin Cities region.* Minneapolis: University of Minnesota; National Council on Crime and Delinquency, Survey Services. (1973). *Youth services bureaus in Rock Island and Henry Counties, Illinois.* Austin, TX: National Council on Crime and Delinquency, Survey Services; U.S. National Institute of Law Enforcement and Criminal Justice. (1977). *National evaluation program youth service bureaus—Phase 1 assessment.* A. Schuchter & K. Polk (Eds.). Boston: Boston University.

26 Van Dusen, K. T. (1981). Net widening and relabeling: Some consequences of deinstitutionalization. *American Behavioral Scientist, 24*(6), 801–810.

27 Spergel, I. A., Reamer, F. G., & Lynch, J. P. (1981). Deinstitutionalization of status offenders: Individual outcome and system effects. *Journal of Research in Crime and Delinquency, 18*(1), 4–33.

[28] Lemert, E. M. (1981). Diversion in juvenile justice: What hath been wrought. *Journal of Research in Crime and Delinquency, 18*(1), 34–46.

[29] Ibid., p. 43.

[30] Austin, J., & Krisberg, B. (1981). Wider, stronger, and different nets: The dialectics of criminal justice reform. *Journal of Research in Crime and Delinquency, 18*(1), 165–196.

[31] Doleschal, E. (1978). Social forces and crime. *Criminal Justice Abstracts, 10*(3), 395–410.

[32] U.S. Federal Prison System. (1977). *Statistical Report, 1975 and 1977.* Washington, DC: Government Printing Office.

[33] Incarceration rates and median time served are taken from the National Prisoner Statistics published by various bureaus of the U.S. Justice Department for the past 40 years. Median time served since 1977 is taken from NCCD's annual Uniform Parole Reports.

[34] Sumner, W. G. (1919). The absurd effort to make the world over. In W. G. Sumner & A. K. Keller (Eds.), *War and other essays* (pp. 209–210). New Haven, CT: Yale University Press.

[35] Spencer, H. (1946). *The man versus the state.* Caldwell, ID: Caxton Printers.

[36] Sieber, S. D. (1981). *Fatal remedies: The ironies of social intervention.* New York: Plenum Press.

[37] Merton, R. K. (1978). Unanticipated consequences and kindred sociological ideas. Paper delivered at the annual meetings of the Society for the Study of Social Problems, San Francisco.

[38] Bell, D. (1973). *The coming of post-industrial society* (p. 469). New York: Basic Books.

[39] Trepanier, J. (1981). La déjudiciarisation des mineurs délinquants au Canada et les projets législatifs du gouvernement fédéral [The removal of juvenile offenders from juvenile court jurisdiction in Canada and legislative projects of the federal government]. *Canadian Journal of Criminology, 23*(3), 279–289.

[40] Wright, K. N. (1981). The desirability of goal conflict within the criminal justice system. *Journal of Criminal Justice, 9*(3), 209–218.

25

Assessing the Impediments to Organizational Change
A View of Community Policing

RHONDA Y. W. ALLEN

Introduction

With the advent of reengineering, rightsizing, reorganizing, and reinventing government, one of the greatest challenges facing public organizations is the process of change. Change implies a fundamental difference or a substitution of one thing for another. Organizational change involves, by definition, a transformation of an organization between two points in time (Barnett and Carroll, 1995).

In the context of American policing, change is particularly difficult. Although the structures of most police departments conform to the quasi-military, hierarchical model of organization, police officers are not closely supervised (Blau, 1994; Sewell, 1986). This social arrangement in which the police work results in a highly fragmented, internalized, and isolated environment (Stamper, 1993). As a result, the police tend to band together and exclude outsiders. This tendency to close ranks develops into a police culture that makes it extremely difficult to make changes within police departments.

This study addressed the issue of impediments to organizational change within police agencies. More specifically, this research identifies and assesses the impediments to implementing community-oriented policing (COP) in three southwestern police departments. Identifying the impediments to change across departments provide a theoretical basis for informing the kinds of management decisions that will inevitably transform police departments into healthy productive organizations.

Reprinted from *Journal of Criminal Justice*, Vol. 30, Rhonda Y. W. Allen, "Assessing the Impediments to Organizational Change: A View of Community Policing," pp. 511–517, 2002, with permission from Elsevier.

Background

Resistance to change has been discussed in the current organization development (OD) literature at great length (Damanpour, 1991; Delacroix and Swaminathar, 1991; Greenwood and Hinings, 1996). Many models and theoretical frameworks had been used to explore, describe, explain, and predict what will aid in the change process. The literature on organizational change examined several schools of thought about organizations' abilities to change and the characteristics that impede or assist in the change process (Halliday, Powell, and Granfors, 1993; Huber, Sutcliffe, Miller, and Glick, 1993; Kelly and Amburgey, 1991). A variety of insightful arguments has been advanced regarding characteristics that produce positive change. Little has been done, however, to compare the implementation of programs across departments and identify the major forms of resistance that remain constant across them. Largely missing are integrative models that have the ability to examine and explain the multidimensional phenomenon of organization change (Klein and Sorra, 1996). Therefore, by examining the underlying dimensions of change and ascertaining, if there are any impediments that remain constant across the various departments, the present study expands the current literature and opens the door for greater knowledge about resistance to change and impediments to program implementation.

COP-Designated Patrol Assignment

The concept of COP began with the community relations programs of the 1950s and 1960s, which developed in order to increase interaction between the community (especially the minority community) and the police, and continued through the 1970s with the team policing concept (Greene, 1987). Team policing was a patrol method from the late 1960s to the early 1970s. Team policing focused on efficient and effective policing, improved police-community relations, assigned patrol of police teams, and enhanced police officer morale (Sherman, 1973). Despite the failure of the team-policing concept in some organizations, the idea of a community context of policing remained strong.

More recently, the proliferation of community policing has been initiated as a result of the increasing evidence that the reactive model and conventional police practices have not been effective (Bayley, 1994; Goldstein, 1990; Greene, 1987; Rohe, Adams and Arcury, 2001; Smith, Novak and Frank, 2001). Therefore, programs that focused on dealing with specific problems faced by communities and reducing community fear of crime continued to develop (Brown and Wycoff, 1987; Eck and Spelman, 1987; Goldstein, 1987; Skolnick and Bayley, 1987). Although community policing is widely believed to be important by those involved with or affected by community policing, the term means different things to different people (Bayley, 1988). For example, under the rubric of community policing, police departments are developing crime prevention seminars, storefront and mini-police stations, newly designed patrol beats, community advisory groups, neighborhood watch programs, increased foot patrols, patrol-detective teams, and door-to-door visits by police officers (Bayley, 1988; Rohe et al., 2001; Skogan, 1994).

Although the initial idea of COP was to institute programs that allowed the police to become familiar with people in the community, the definition has been expanded to include almost any program that serves as an instrument to improved police service and better community relations. This expansion of the community policing definition, however, has resulted in much confusion concerning what the term community policing actually means and how to implement it. Implementing community policing has many difficulties. As indicated previously, police organizations are inherently reluctant to accept and try new ideas (Scheingold, 1991). Thus, many police organizations resist the notion of community policing because it represents a change from the traditional reactive policing model.

This research examined the patrol assignment aspect of community policing. In police organizations where community policing is not the standard philosophy, police officers are assigned to a beat that covers an extensive area of the city. In police organizations that share in the community policing philosophy, police officers are often assigned to a small community area to allow officers to become familiar with the community (citizens) so that they can proactively solve problems together. Patrol assignment includes the selection and placement of officers in newly designed community policing areas, as well as the tasks assigned to them. Much of the success or failure of community policing efforts rests on the actions of the individual officers who translate community-policing philosophy into reality (Brown, 1989; Friedmann, 1992).

The cross-case comparison of the impediments to COP implementation revealed that COP is a complex and complicated philosophy and the methods used to implement COP programs will vary. Focusing on designated patrol assignment, however, has isolated key impediments to COP implementation.

Methodology

The agencies selected for study were three municipal police departments located in a large metropolitan area of Arizona: the Phoenix Police Department (PPD), the Mesa Police Department (MPD), and the Tempe Police Department (TPD). The agencies selected were all self-defined as engaged in designated officer assignments to implement some form or variation of COP.

At the time of this study, the PPD had approximately 2,310 sworn police officers and served a population of 1,149,417. The MPD had approximately 634 sworn police officers and served a population of 338,117. The TPD had approximately 260 sworn police officers and served a population of 153,821. The three police departments had similar organizational structures in terms of personnel and operating units. Each department had slightly over 90 percent White, non-Hispanic, male officers.

In-depth interviews were conducted with 126 employees of the three municipal police agencies, including three different levels (executive, middle, and street-level) of police practitioners identified as being responsible for or involved with the specific aspects of the change program being studied—community-based patrol assignment. Interviews were conducted at the three different levels in order to collect data from different perspectives. The interviews included ninety street-level officers, twenty-six mid-level officers, and ten executive-level officers. Participants were assured of confidentiality and written permission was received from each agency. The interviews were in a structured, open-ended format and a comprehensive protocol ensured standardization of data collection across sites.

Interviews were conducted over a four-month period. Interviews were approximately one to three hours in length and extensive field notes were taken. The interview time varied depending on interviewees' availability and willingness to give information. The data collected from each interview was recorded with as much detail as possible; interviews were taperecorded when possible.

Each interview session began with a general set of questions regarding interviewees' length of time in the department, current and past positions, and overall length of time in the field of law enforcement. Police personnel were asked about the role they played in the change effort, major problems of program implementation, ease of implementation, most effective methods of implementing change, organizational attitude toward community policing, and the relationship between management and employees during the change process. In conjunction with the interviews, supporting data were gathered through observations while in the police stations, on patrol ride-alongs, and through police records and official documents.

The Study Variables

Dependent Variable

Resistance to organizational changes—more specifically, resistance to designated officer assignment for community policing. Resistance to change includes both the overt (obvious) and covert (subtle) actions that affect implementation of the change programs (Recardo, 1995).

Independent Variables

Based on the organizational change literature (Allen, 1999; Barnett and Carroll, 1995; Porras and Silvers, 1991), factors that impede or facilitate change fall into two general categories—structure or process. Structural variables deal with division of labor and the arrangements of organizational parts. Process variables relate to the way the transformation occurs—the speed, the planning, the sequence of activities, and the communication systems. Structural variables for this study included complexity, centralization, and formalization. Process variables included pressure, individual attitudes, departmental attitude, and communication.

Complexity referred to the number of structural components (horizontal differentiation, vertical or hierarchical differentiation, and spatial dispersion) that required coordination and control (Hall, 1996). A highly complex organization is characterized by many occupational roles, subunits (division and departments), levels of authority (rank structure, i.e., chiefs, captains, lieutenants, and sergeants), and operating sites. Complexity is perceived as beneficial in the planning stage of change, but a problem for implementation. In short, complexity adds to the difficulty of implementing change.

Centralization described the locus of decision making within an organization (Hall, 1996). Centralization was measured by the level and variety of participation in strategic decisions by groups relative to the number of groups in the organization (Hage, 1980). Resistance to change is minimized when organizations involve employees in the decision-making process (Covin and Kilmann, 1990).

Formalization referred to the use of rules in an organization and involved organizational control over individuals (Hall, 1996). Formalization is also related to the number of new programs added in an organization. Formalization has been shown to be negatively associated with the adoption of new programs (Hall, 1996). In the more formalized organizations, there is likely to be less time, support, or incentive for involvement in change and innovation. Measures of formalization included job codification and rule observation.

Pressure described the perceived or real pressure for the change (reasons). The literature notes the concept of pressure as being an important factor in the implementation of change (Guyot, 1991; Slack and Sigelman, 1987).

Individual attitude described the respondents' (top-management, mid-management, and street-level officers) attitudes toward the underlying issues (i.e., the role of the police—COP) of the particular change programs. Attitudes toward COP have been reported as being related to the motives underlying individuals' resistance to change (Skogan, 1994).

Departmental attitude described the departments' (command staff) attitudes toward the underlying issues of the particular change programs. It should be noted that the individual attitude and departmental attitude variables were separated during the initial data collection stage. Respondents made clear distinctions between their individual attitudes and their department's overall attitude toward change.

Communication referred to the exchange of information and the transmission of meaning (Hall, 1996). Communication occurs in three directions: upward, downward, and horizontal; it also includes omission, distortions, and overload of information. Lack of organizational communication or poor communication can result in an unclear purpose of the program and misplacement of program responsibility (Covin and Kilmann, 1990).

Case Analysis

Miles and Huberman's (1994) pattern coding and case analysis strategy were used for this study. The names of the variables were used as categories (subject headings) to code and analyze the data collected from the open-ended interviews. This method initially organized data into separate categories that corresponded with the variable names. The coding scheme included complexity, centralization, formalization, pressure, individual attitudes, departmental attitude, and communication. During the course of the field research, however, the coding scheme was revised and subcodes were developed.

Coding was done after each wave of interviews by transcribing and reviewing the collected data and then tagging the most relevant pieces. Coded data were condensed (summarized) and categorized under the previous stated subject headings. The codes were used to retrieve and organize the data. This grouping assisted in identifying and clustering the segments related to the impediments of implementing COP. Clustering then set the stage for the analysis and conclusions.

The analysis was aimed at understanding both individual case dynamics and cross-site comparisons. First, recurring patterns and themes were noted (pattern coding). There was an expectation that patterns involving similarities and differences among categories and processes involving implementation would surface. The second stage of analysis pulled together the separate pieces of data. Once the data were clustered, they were reviewed to see which pieces of data went together and which did not. Clustering by similar patterns or characteristics assisted in gaining a better understanding of the factors affecting the change process.

Findings

This study revealed that centralization, complexity, and formalization (the structural variables) could be impediments to change. Themes related to the structural variable surfaced in all three police departments. For example, although the command staff of the PPD tried to push discretion and authority down to the street-level officers in an attempt to implement COP, it was met with skepticism and mistrust. This was also true with the MPD and the TPD. Street-level officers, in all three departments, reported being unable to trust that their departments would support their decisions, if and when something went wrong. Therefore, street-level officers did not take full advantage of their new level of authority and discretion. Command staff from each department believed that the many years of working under a quasi-military, bureaucratic structure made officers unable to accept a more decentralized departmental structure. The effects of the structural variables, however, were not strong and varied depending on the stage of implementation and size of the organization. This finding supported earlier literature that examined the effect of structure on organization change (Amburgey, Dawn, and Barnett, 1993; Delacroix and Swaminathan, 1991).

Although, in many cases, strong themes did not emerge related to the three structural variables, there was enough evidence to show that these factors may influence many of the process variables. For example, in the PPD, complexity affected communication. Within all three of the police departments, formalization affected departmental and individual attitudes. By influencing the process variables, the structural variables had a greater ability to affect organizational change.

Of the process variables, the pressure variable surfaced consistently as a major factor in facilitating the implementation of COP. All three levels of police practitioner responded to external pressure and reported that, without it, organizational change may not have occurred. Additionally, respondents from all three police departments and at all three levels did cite that environmental changes (change in crime rates and city demographics) acted as an impetus for change. This emerging theme was consistent with earlier studies that argued that organizational change occurs mainly through the adaptive responses of existing individual organizations to natural changes in technology and environment (Burt, 1992; DiMaggio and Powell, 1983; Zucker, 1983). Although the majority of these studies were directed at the private sector, the current study found that this was also true for the police organizations.

Of all the variables studied, individual attitudes were among the most important factors in COP implementation. Proponents of the COP philosophy, in all three departments, had embraced the concept, but reported that it was the opponents of COP who made implementation difficult. Mid-level managers who did not buy into the COP concept always found "other things" for their officers to do, instead of assignments related to community policing. Street-level officers, who were resistant to the change, went through the motions, but never put forth any real effort of implementing community-based programs. It was mentioned repeatedly by street- and mid-level officers that someone from the command rank must champion the COP concept to facilitate the change process.

As was found in the MPD, proponents still struggle with the initial phases of implementation because of the department's lack of strong support from the command staff. The TPD implemented COP throughout the department, and while no one openly resisted the change, covert resistance was rampant throughout the organization. The lack of overt resistance was reported as being the result of strong COP support from command staff.

Discussion

Police organizations are complex social systems that are grounded in democracy, operate within a "fishbowl," and are funded primarily by tax dollars. To use tax dollars more efficiently and effectively, it is imperative that police organizations understand the change process and the difficulties that they might encounter. This study identified several factors that could potentially impede the change process within complex settings.

To mobilize and motivate employees, trust must be established before managers can transfer the necessary decision-making authority. To establish trust, employees must exhibit competence and prove they are knowledgeable; that is, understand the assigned tasks and can do their job. There must also be managers who support employees and will not punish them if they voice their own opinions. Once trust is attained and authority transferred, employees must learn how to use their newly acquired power. There were several examples, within this study, where command staff had attempted to empower street-level officers, but officers did not trust or believe that they had discretion to make decisions. As a result, officers refused to accept the decision-making power and followed the standard hierarchy of decision-making. In these instances, command staff never asked why officers did not accept their new authority, nor did street-level officers communicate their concerns to the supervisors.

Clearly, communication must be honest and open. Anything less than sincere conversation will result in a false sense that progress is being made. Without clear understanding through open communication and training, change may not take place. It is, however, extremely important to note that public sector agencies have multiple constituents, thus complicating the process of change and making it more difficult to implement.

In terms of policing, it is important to understand that those who attempt to introduce change programs within police departments often fail to take into account the constant effects of the police setting and culture. That is, new programs are planned and implemented without a sufficient understanding of the effects of the context on the likelihood of successful change.

The police agencies used in this study were well aware of the potential benefits of employee participation in planning, organizing, and decision-making. The police departments understood that a lack of support from line officers, as well as upper- and mid-level managers, could slow down or, worse yet, stop the change process. The police agencies also knew the importance of training and clear communication throughout the organization. When it came time to getting the job done, however, they immediately fell back into their standard operating procedures: (1) command staff makes the decisions, (2) command staff delegates to middle management, (3) middle management orders rank and file to do the job. In sum, police organizations must apply their knowledge to their current practices.

The journey through organizational change is challenging and difficult, yet it is possible to achieve a balance between the goals of the organization and the needs of the employee. The best strategies of successful change are not only in the literature, but are in organizations that have tried and tested many approaches to making their organizations more effective and efficient. The goal is to continue finding successful change organizations in order to collect and disseminate their information that will assist other agencies in making positive change and eliminating the forces of resistance. This information will contribute to the knowledge and practice regarding organizational change.

Conclusion

The ability to plan for and identify impediments to change is an important issue for law enforcement administrators. In an attempt to use a more integrative model to examine and explain the phenomenon of organizational change, this study identified potential impediments to implementing COP. Results indicated that pressure and individual attitudes toward change were the factors that remained consistent across departments. Individual attitudes were impediments to implementing change, while pressure acted as a facilitator of change. Additionally, communication surfaced as a necessary factor when implementing change and was intertwined with all of the study variables.

By examining the underlying dimensions of change and ascertaining impediments that remained constant across departments, the present study expands the current literature and opens the door for greater knowledge about resistance to change and impediments to program implementation.

References

Allen, R. Y. W. (1999). Analyzing organizational change: Characteristics, structure and process. *Journal of Public Management and Social Policy, 5*, 1–17.

Amburgey, T., Dawn, K., & Barnett, W. (1993). Resetting the clock: The dynamics of organizational change and failure. *Administrative Science Quarterly, 38*, 51–73.

Barnett, W., & Carroll, G. (1995). Modeling internal organizational change. *Annual Review of Sociology, 21*, 217–236.

Bayley, D. (1988). Community policing: A report from the devil's advocate. In J. R. Green & S. D. Mastrofski (Eds.), *Community policing—rhetoric or reality* (pp. 225–237). New York: Praeger.

Bayley, D. (1994). *Police for the future.* New York: Oxford University Press.

Blau, T. (1994). *Psychological services for law enforcement.* New York: Wiley.

Brown, L. P., & Wycoff, M. A. (1987). Policing Houston: Reducing fear and improving service. *Crime and Delinquency, 33*, 71–89.

Brown, M. (1989). *Working the street: Police discretion and the dilemmas of reform.* New York: Russell Sage.

Burt, R. S. (1992). *Structural holes.* Cambridge: Harvard University Press.

Covin, T. J., & Kilmann, R. H. (1990). Participant perceptions of positive and negative influences on large-scale change. *Group and Organization Studies, 15*, 233–248.

Damanpour, F. (1991). Organizational innovation: A meta-analysis of effects of determinants and moderators. *Academy of Management Journal, 34*, 555–590.

Delacroix, J., & Swaminathan, A. (1991). Cosmetic, speculative, and adaptive organizational change in the wine industry: A longitudinal study. *Administrative Science Quarterly, 36*, 631–661.

DiMaggio, P. J., & Powell, W. W. (1983). The iron cage revisited: Institutional isomorphism and collective rationality in organizational fields. *American Sociology Review, 48*, 147–160.

Eck, J. E., & Spelman, W. (1987). Who ya gonna call? *American Journal of Police, 6*, 45–65.

Friedmann, R. (1992). *Community policing: Comparative perspectives and prospects.* New York: St. Martin's Press.

Goldstein, H. (1987). Toward community-oriented policing: Potential, basic requirements, and threshold questions. *Crime and Delinquency, 33*, 6–30.

Goldstein, H. (1990). *Problem-oriented policing*. Philadelphia: Temple University Press.

Greene, J. R. (1987). Foot patrol and community policing: Past practices and future prospects. *American Journal of Police, 6,* 1–15.

Greenwood, R., & Hinings, C. R. (1996). Understanding radical organizational change: Bringing together the old and the new institutionalism. *Academy of Management Review, 21,* 1022–1054.

Guyot, D. (1991). *Policing as though people matter*. Philadelphia: Temple University Press.

Hage, J. (1980). *Theories of organizations*. New York: Wiley.

Hall, R. (1996). *Organizations, structures, processes, and outcomes*. Englewood Cliffs, NJ: Prentice Hall.

Halliday, T. C., Powell, M. J., & Granfors, M. W. (1993). After minimalism: Transformations of state bar associations from market dependence to state reliance, 1918 to 1950. *American Sociology Review, 58,* 515–535.

Huber, G. P., Sutcliffe, K. M., Miller, C. C., & Glick, W. H. (1993). Understanding and predicting organizational change. In G. P. Huber & W. H. Glick (Eds.), *Organizational change and redesign* (pp. 215–263). New York: Oxford.

Kelly, D., & Amburgey, T. L. (1991). Organizational inertia and momentum: A dynamic model of strategic change. *Academy of Management Journal, 34,* 591–612.

Klein, K. J., & Sorra, J. S. (1996). The challenge of innovation implementation. *Academy of Management Review, 21,* 1022–1054.

Miles, M. B., & Huberman, A. M. (1994). *Qualitative data analysis*. Thousand Oaks, CA: Sage Publications.

Porras, J., & Silvers, R. (1991). Organization development and transformation. *Annual Review of Psychology, 42,* 51–58.

Recardo, R. (1995, Spring). Overcoming resistance to change. *National Productivity Review, 14,* 5–12.

Rohe, W. M., Adams, R. E., & Arcury, T. (2001). Community policing and planning. *Journal of the American Planning Association, 67,* 78–82.

Scheingold, S. A. (1991). *The politics of street crime—criminal process and cultural obsession*. Philadelphia: Temple University Press.

Sewell, J. (1986). Administrative concerns in law enforcement stress management. In Reese & Goldstein (Eds.), *Psychological services for law enforcement: A compilation of papers submitted to the National Symposium on police psychological services* (pp. 153–159). Quantico, VA: FBI Academy.

Sherman, L. (1973). *Team policing: Seven case studies*. Washington, DC: Police Foundation.

Skogan, W. G. (1994). The impact of community policing on neighborhood residents: A cross-site analysis. In D. P. Rosenbaum (Ed.), *The challenge of community policing* (pp. 167–180). Thousand Oaks, CA: Sage Publications.

Skolnick, J. H., & Bayley, D. (1987). *Community policing: Issues and practices around the world*. Washington, DC: National Institute of Justice.

Slack, J. D., & Sigelman, L. (1987). City managers and affirmative action: Testing a model of linkage. *Western Political Quarterly, 40,* 668–673.

Smith, B. W., Novak, K. J., & Frank, J. (2001). Community policing and the work routines of street-level officers. *Criminal Justice Review, 26,* 17–37.

Stamper, N. (1993). Workshop given at the International Association for Civilian Oversight of Law Enforcement (IACOLE) Eighth Annual Conference—Law Enforcement Issues, San Diego, CA.

Zucker, L. G. (1983). Organizations as institutions. In S. B. Bacharach (Ed.), *Perspectives in organizational sociology: Theory and research: Vol. 2* (pp. 1–14). Greenwich, CT: JAI Press.

26

Patterns of Practice in Mental Health Courts
A National Survey

ALLISON D. REDLICH, HENRY J. STEADMAN, JOHN MONAHAN,
PAMELA CLARK ROBBINS, AND JOHN PETRILA

Introduction

The emergence of mental health courts (MHCs) in the last decade is an important new development at the interface of the criminal justice and mental health systems (Petrila, 2003). MHCs are specialty criminal courts with dockets usually exclusive to individuals with mental illnesses. MHCs developed as one of a number of strategies designed to stop the revolving door of repeated cycling through the criminal justice system of persons with mental illnesses. MHCs are, in essence, a response to the large numbers of persons with severe mental illness incarcerated in jail and prison, their special needs while incarcerated, the difficulties courts face in effectively addressing mental illness issues, and the strains that involvement with the criminal justice system places on individuals with mental illness and their families.

The courts are proliferating rapidly (Steadman, Davidson, & Brown, 2001). Today, the number of MHCs in the United States approaches 100, whereas only a couple existed in 1997 (GAINS Center for People with Co-Occurring Disorders in the Justice System, 2005). Congress recently appropriated 7 million dollars to the development of new MHCs (Public Law 106-515, *America's Law Enforcement and Mental Health Project* (Nov. 13, 2000; 114 Stat. 2399). However, research on these specialty courts has not kept pace with their growth. There are a few multisite studies available to date that describe the structures and operations of a limited number of MHCs (Gold-

Allison D. Redlich et al., *Law and Human Behavior*, vol. 3, pp. 347–362, © 2006 by Springer Publications. Reprinted by permission of Springer Publications.

kamp & Irons-Guynn, 2000; Griffin, Steadman, & Petrila, 2002; Steadman, Redlich, Griffin, Petrila, & Monahan, 2005). There also are several single-site studies reporting on MHC-related outcomes (Boothroyd, Calkins Mercado, Poythress, Christy, & Petrila, 2005; Cosden, Ellens, Schnell, Yasmeen, & Wolfe, 2003). However, there has yet to be a comprehensive examination of more than a few MHCs.

In this study, we present survey data from all U.S. mental health courts existing at the time of our survey. This rare opportunity to study a population (as opposed to a sample) is especially important given the pressing number of unanswered questions and controversies surrounding MHCs.

Mental Health and Other Specialty Courts

Mental health courts are a relatively new addition to "specialty courts" or "problem-solving courts" and are predated by other problem-solving courts such as juvenile justice courts (1899) and drug treatment courts (1989). As stated by Casey (Casey, 2005), "Problem-solving courts address juvenile delinquency, drug abuse, domestic violence, and mental health by promoting programs of treatment designed to address the root causes of criminal behavior. In each of these contexts, treatment presents an attractive alternative to the standard criminal justice system" (p. 1462). Usually, a team approach to legal decision-making is taken, which can involve the judge, the prosecuting and defense attorneys, case manager and other treatment providers, and the defendant.

Despite the rapid growth of these courts—both in terms of number and type (e.g., there are now teen smoking cessation courts [Petrila, 2003])—they are not without controversy. Opponents cite problems such as the increased and inappropriate discretionary power of the judge (e.g., in that judges in nonspecialty courts have standardized sentencing guidelines) and that judges are becoming social workers without the concomitant training. In regard to MHCs specifically, opponents are concerned that the mere existence of courts for persons with mental illness will exacerbate rather than ameliorate the problem of this population's involvement with the justice system. This problem, referred to as net-widening (in that the police will cast a wider net and arrest more people in order to get people-in-need into treatment), to date is speculative and in need of firm data (Seltzer, 2005). In contrast, advocates of specialty courts, generally, and MHCs specifically, contend that the courts are an innovative and therapeutic way to handle people who do not fit into the traditional and inflexible criminal justice model. Indeed, there is evidence to suggest that MHCs "work" for some individuals (Boothroyd et al., 2005; Herinckx, Swart, Ama, Dolezal, & King, 2005). Regardless of the controversies surrounding MHCs and other problem-solving courts, the courts are growing nationally and internationally. Empirically collected data can provide further insight into some of these contentious issues.

Characteristics of Mental Health Courts

At least six characteristics operationally define mental health courts (Goldkamp & Irons-Guynn, 2000; Redlich, 2005; Steadman, Davidson, & Brown, 2001). First, MHCs are criminal courts with separate dockets for persons with mental illness. Some MHCs are exclusive to persons with serious and persistent mental illness, whereas others have less stringent criteria requiring only "demonstrable mental health problems." In addition, the amount and type of formal clinical screening that occurs prior to referral to an MHC varies across courts; however, the core characteristic of maintaining a separate docket, generally with a single judge presiding over the docket, is at the heart of an MHC.

Second, MHCs share the goal of diverting persons with mental illness (PMIs) from the criminal justice system into community mental health treatment, thereby reducing the detrimental cycle of revolving in and out of jail (CMHS 1995; Torrey, Stieber, Ezekiel, Wolfe, Sharfstein, Noble, et al., 1992). Empirical outcome data from specific courts are beginning to emerge (Boothroyd et al., 2005; Trupin & Richards, 2003) suggesting that MHCs can be somewhat successful in (1) obtaining access to treatment for at least some individuals before the court and (2) lessening recidivism.

Third, MHCs mandate community mental health treatment, typically requiring that participants engage in treatment, take prescribed medications, and adhere to any other conditions imposed by the court or the treatment system. MHCs often create incentives for the individual to adhere to treatment involving the criminal charge; for example, providing that the initial charge may be dropped or reduced or the conviction vacated (in addition to avoiding jail or prison) per successful completion of treatment. In addition, MHCs may impose other conditions that vary by court and by defendant, such as requiring the individual to find and maintain employment, and other, more idiosyncratic mandates (e.g., physical exercise).

Fourth, MHCs provide continuing supervision via judicial status review hearings conducted by the court and through direct supervision in the community. Judicial status hearings, where participants' compliance is monitored, may praise or sanction the individual depending on the individual's progress or lack thereof. The type and frequency of both judicial and community supervision can depend on the court and on the defendant. Griffin et al. (2002) described three types of MHC community supervision: (1) community treatment providers are responsible for supervision and for reporting back to the court; (2) probation officers and court personnel are responsible; and (3) a combination of community treatment providers and criminal justice personnel are jointly responsible (see also Redlich, Steadman, Monahan, Petrila, & Griffin, 2005).

Fifth, as mentioned, MHCs typically offer praise and encouragement for compliance and impose sanctions for noncompliance. Many MHCs work under the model of therapeutic jurisprudence (Winick & Wexler, 2003), and as such recognize small and large successes. After sustained periods of success and stability, participants may graduate from MHC, at which point the original charges may be dropped or the conviction vacated, with formal oversight by the criminal justice system ending. Commonly used sanctions include admonishments from the judge, increases in supervision and in the number of status hearings, and when necessary, returning people to jail. If noncompliance is ongoing, participants may be dismissed from the MHC and returned to regular criminal court processing and/or to their jail or prison sentence. Finally, all MHCs are voluntary, that is, it is for potential participants to choose whether to enroll in the court or not (Redlich. 2005).

Mental Health Court Issues and Controversies

As noted, our research knowledge of MHCs is limited. As a result, a number of important policy issues have been debated on the basis of assumptions about the characteristics and operations of MHCs that may be faulty. We sought in this study to address some of these pressing issues. For example, one outstanding concern is the proportion of misdemeanants versus felons enrolled in mental health courts. For some, this is controversial. The Bazelon Center (Bazelon Center for Mental Health Law, 2003) has argued that misdemeanants are ill-suited for MHCs because they should be diverted from the criminal justice system entirely (e.g., through prebooking diversion programs). The Center states "To avoid becoming the entry point for people abandoned by the mental health system, mental health courts should close their doors to people charged with misdemeanors" (p. 7). Further, Redlich et al. (2005) found that newly established MHCs are more likely to accept felons, whereas early MHCs tended to focus on, or be exclusive to, misdemeanants. Thus, our survey of all known mental health courts was designed to provide a comprehensive answer to this question.

A second issue concerns the potential factors that drive the number of clients MHCs serve, over and above the capacity of the jail. That is, after the size of the community's criminal population has been accounted for, what other pertinent factors predict the size of the MHC capacity? For example, does the frequency with which clients have to return to see the judge affect capacity? Or if the MHCs accept more felony defendants, is the size of the court smaller? These are the questions that to our knowledge have not been addressed.

Two related issues concern the percentage of mental health courts that exist in communities where there are other types of criminal justice diversion programs for defendants with mental illnesses, and the percentage of MHCs that are dual-diagnosis courts, that is, courts that only accept defendants with co-occurring mental health and substance abuse disorders. In the larger context of diversion programs that extend beyond mental health courts (Draine & Solomon, 1999; Steadman, Morris, & Dennis, 1995), it is important to know whether the MHC is a stand-alone effort by the community or part of a larger array of programs that include pre- and postbooking diversion and/or other types of specialty courts. Because MHCs have continuing judicial and community supervision, they tend to have small caseloads relative to the number of persons with mental illness involved in the justice system (Steadman et al., 2005). Most MHCs simply do not have the resources and capacity to serve all—or even nearly all—people in need in the community. As such, knowledge about whether the communities with MHCs have other options for diverting persons with mental illness from the justice system into treatment can help to contextualize mental health courts.

In regard to dual-diagnosis MHCs, it is well known that the prevalence of co-occurring mental and substance use disorders among people involved in the justice system is high (Peters & Hills, 1993; Steadman, Fabisiak, Dvoskin, & Holohean, 1987), and that this subpopulation is at higher risk for criminal justice encounters. In a prospective 3-year study, 83% of persons with co-occurring disorders had nonarrest interactions with the police, and 58% had at least one formal arrest (Clark, Ricketts, & McHugo, 1999). Thus, it is useful to know how many MHCs serve only dual-diagnosed defendants. Further, dual-diagnosis exclusive MHCs may be qualitatively different than non-dual-diagnosis exclusive MHCs. For example, because all defendants in a dual-diagnosis court will, by definition, have substance use problems, these courts may be more similar to drug treatment courts than non-dual-diagnosis MHCs, insofar as they are more punitive and carry out more intense monitoring.

A third and more contentious issue is the frequency with which MHCs use jail as a sanction for nonadherence to judicial and treatment orders. Drug treatment courts, which provide at least part of the foundation on which MHCs rest, routinely use jail as a sanction to gain treatment adherence (National Drug Court Institute, June 2000). However, the use of jail as a sanction has been more controversial with MHCs. To some, returning people to jail for treatment noncompliance is counter to the therapeutic philosophy of mental health court and seemingly punishes people for their mental illness. Others see the utilization of jail time as a necessary evil and in the long-term best interests of the defendant, on the basis of the assumption that measures (in this case, jail time) that increase treatment adherence produce positive outcomes. The available data suggest that MCGs differ on their use of jail as a sanction. In its report on 20 mental health courts, Bazelon Center (Bazelon Center for Mental Health Law, 2003) found that 64% were willing to place people in jail for noncompliance, but the Center's report did not specify the frequency of use.

Finally, relations between the courts' knowledge of when and to what degree participants are noncompliant and levels of supervision has also been unclear. As mentioned, MHCs utilize both judicial (periodic status review hearings) and community (via probation, treatment providers, court personnel, etc.) supervision. Previous research on the supervision of offenders with and without mental illness has revealed a consistent picture: offenders who receive more intensive monitoring (e.g., via Assertive Community Treatment teams) have higher re-incarceration rates (most often for technical probation/parole violations) than those receiving less intensive monitoring (Gott-fredson, Mitchell-Herzfeld, & Flanagan, 1982; Solomon & Draine, 1995; Solomon, Draine & Marcus, 2002; Tonry, 1990). In other words, the more intense the monitoring, the more likely one's transgressions are to be (1) noticed and (2) dealt with. In our study, we sought to address the question of monitoring in MHCs by examining relations between type and frequency of supervision and the use of jail as a sanction.

The Present Study

A main goal of the study was to address a number of important operational questions that lie at the heart of the current policy debates regarding MHCs. More specifically, we first set out to describe the population of currently operating mental health courts on a number of heretofore understudied variables, such as number of active clients and whether the communities have other types of diversion programs in place for PMI. Second, we were interested in determining what variables predicted (1) the number of active MHC clients, over and above the capacity of the community's jail, and (2) the use of jail as a sanction. Of importance, our findings have the potential to inform MHC understanding and practice.

Methods

Identification of the Universe of Mental Health Courts

To determine our survey population, we first identified MHCs using a list compiled by the National GAINS Center, the TAPA Center, the National Alliance for the Mentally Ill, and the mental health/criminal justice consensus project [Council of State Governments] (cited as GAINS Center 2005), http://www.mentalhealthcourtsurvey.com/ At the time of our retrieval, this list included 98 courts. After first surveying these 98 courts, we learned from a survey recipient of 14 potential additional MHCs in Ohio that had not been included in the GAINS publication and in our initial survey. In all, 116 courts were contacted, but as we describe in detail later, not all of the courts we surveyed were actually MHCs.

Survey Instrument

A brief survey was designed to facilitate completion (see appendix). In the survey, we asked for the name, location, and starting date of the MHC. We also asked for the number of MHC clients newly enrolled in the 12 months prior to receipt of the survey, the number of active MHC clients, and whether the court had a maximum number of clients it could serve. Additional questions were included on the percentages of misdemeanants and felons served, whether their court was a co-occurring mental health/substance use court (i.e., the court would only accept defendants with mental health *and* substance abuse problems), and whether other diversion programs for PMIs existed in the community. We also asked about the size of the jail in their community.

In the next section of the survey, we inquired about supervision. Specifically, we asked (1) who was responsible for community supervision (e.g., probation officers, community treatment providers), (2) what was the usual schedule of status review hearings, (3) how this schedule was adapted when defendants were noncompliant, and (4) the use of jail as a sanction for noncompliance. In regard to the use of jail as a sanction, respondents were given five options: never, less than 5% of all cases, between 5 and 20%, between 20 and 50%, and more than 50% of cases. And finally, we asked MHCs if they thought they would sustain for another 3 years.

Survey Procedures

We followed several procedures, some noted previously, to capture the entire universe of MHCs. First, the survey was e-mailed and/or mailed to the 98 mental health courts obtained from the GAINS list. The survey was sent to mental health court judges and/or the contact listed for the court. The court contact is often the MHC coordinator, but may be someone who plays another important role in the court, such as probation officer, defense attorney, or community treatment provider. Our initial response rate was 53%. Only one survey per court was received. A second round of surveys was then sent to the nonresponders and to courts that had not been included in the initial GAINS list. Lastly, phone calls were made to the courts that had not responded. The survey was either conducted over the phone or resent. Through these efforts, we obtained information from 100% of the courts surveyed. Data collection lasted approximately 4 months, ending in January 2005.

Results

We contacted 116 *possible* MHCs. We were able to establish contact with and obtain information from all of the courts. We do not include 26 of the 116 courts contacted in our analyses because (1) some were once an MHC but funding and operations had stopped ($n = 6$); (2) some that we thought were existing MHCs in fact were not ($n = 16$; e.g., plans had been initiated but the court was [not] yet operational or the court was a civil commitment court); or (3) some were MHCs serving juveniles ($n = 4$). Because juvenile mental health courts are likely to qualitatively differ from adult mental health courts, and because we were unable to ensure that we surveyed all juvenile mental health courts, we also excluded these four courts from our database. Thus, our final data set included all 90 operational adult mental health courts in existence in the United States in January 2005.

In Fig. 1, we display the number of mental health courts by state. Thirty-four states have at least one mental health court, with Ohio having the largest number. Nineteen states have only one mental health court presently.

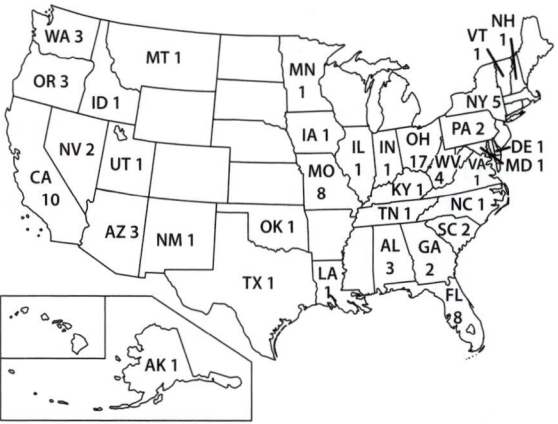

Figure 1   Number of mental health courts in each U.S. State

Length of Court's Existence

The first U.S. mental health courts were established in January (Marion County, Indiana) and June (Broward County, Florida) 1997, and still exist today. The length of MHC existence ranged from 3 months to 8 years; mean = 2.61 years, SD = 1.7; median = 2.18. As shown in Table 1, nearly one-fifth of the courts have been in operation for 4 years or longer.

Table 1   MHC characteristics

	N	Valid percentage
Length of MHC existence	89	
1 year or less	12	14
Between 1 and 2 years	31	35
Between 2 and 4 years	31	35
More than 4 years	15	17
Misdemeanor—felony	87	
Misdemeanor exclusive	35	40
Misdemeanors and felonies	43	49
Felony exclusive	9	10
Other diversion in community	89	
No	48	54
Yes	41	46
Co-occurring disorders court	89	
No	69	78
Yes	20	23
Sustainable for next 3 years	90	
No	7	8
Yes	78	87
Do not know	5	6

MHC Capacity

The number of newly enrolled clients in the past 12 months ranged from 3 to 1,977 with a median of 36 clients. (For courts that were in existence for less than 1 year, we annualized their rates by multiplying the number of clients by the proportion of months/years they had been in operation.) The high end of the range—1,977—was an outlier, with the next highest number being 400. Relevant to the courts' capacity is the size of their jail from which eligible MHC court clients are drawn. We asked each jurisdiction to provide the capacity of their local jail. As would be expected, jail capacity ranged broadly from 25 to 18,600; mean = 2,080; median and mode = 1,000.

The number of active clients (i.e., clients currently on the court's docket) ranged from 3 to 852 with a median of 36 and a mode of 30 clients. Summing the number of active clients across the courts, an estimated 7,560 defendants with mental illness are currently participating in a U.S. mental health court.

Half of the courts stated that they had a maximum number of clients they could potentially serve (5% stated they were unsure if they had a maximum). Of the courts that had a limit to the number of clients they could serve, the maximum number ranged from 10 to 250; median and mode = 40 clients. Finally, the majority of courts (66%) responded they had plans to increase the number of clients they could serve in the next year (6% did not know).

Misdemeanor–Felony Ratios

Approximately one-half of the courts surveyed enrolled both misdemeanants and felons. However, more courts were misdemeanant-exclusive than felony-exclusive (see Table 1). If we expand the parameters to include courts that were primarily comprised of misdemeanants or felons (i.e., 95–100% of the caseload was misdemeanants or felons), 49% (43 courts) were primarily misdemeanor and 14% (12 courts) were primarily felony. A closer examination revealed that these data are somewhat dependent upon the state in which the court operated. For example, of the 17 Ohio courts in our database, 15 primarily served misdemeanants. Also, in Florida, six of the eight courts were primarily for misdemeanants. A trend that we observed in our previous research and that seems to be supported from data here, is that courts in the same state tend to be similar to each other as the newer courts in the state will visit, observe, and replicate the older courts. Thus, because Ohio and Florida have large numbers of mental health courts relative to other states, the number of courts serving misdemeanants may seem skewed.

Other Diversion Programs and Co-Occurring Courts

Nearly half of the courts were in communities that had other forms of diversion for PMIs involved in the criminal justice system (Table 1). About one-quarter of the courts reported that they were co-occurring mental health-substance abuse courts in that all of their participants were required to have both types of problems.

Community Supervision and Judicial Status Review Hearings

MHCs are expected to monitor participants in the community. Only one court (1%) reported that it did not supervise MHC participants in the community. As seen in Table 2, the use of mental health professionals was the most prevalent way of monitoring participants in the community, with 79% of the MHCs citing this use. The use of probation officers was also quite prevalent, with 70% of courts citing their use. Overall, 70% (62 courts) had more than one form of community supervision (41 courts had two forms, 19 courts had three forms, and 2 courts had four forms). Thus, the majority of courts do not rely on one model of supervision to the exclusion of another.

We also inquired about the frequency of judicial status review hearings. Almost all of the courts adjusted their schedule to have the client appear in court less frequently if s/he was doing well (i.e., complying with judicial, court, and treatment orders), or alternatively appear more frequently if doing poorly. Table 2 displays the percentages of the frequency of status review hearings when the defendant first enters the court. For example, if the court stated "bi-weekly, then monthly," we coded this as "bi-weekly."

A few courts had MHC participants return to court as frequently as several times a week or as infrequently as four to six times a year. Thus, the range of judicial hearings upon enrollment was quite wide. However, the majority of the courts had their clients return either weekly or monthly at the onset of their participation (see Table 2).

Table 2   Community and judicial supervision and jail sanction use

	N	Valid percentage
Community supervision[a]	90	
Probation officers	63	70
Mental health treatment providers	70	79
MHC personnel	34	38
Police/jail/pretrial services	7	8
Judicial status hearings upon enrollment	87	
More than once a week	5	6
Once a week	36	41
Every other week (or twice a month)	13	15
Once a month	30	35
Every 2 or 3 months	3	3
Use of jail as a sanction	90	
Never	7	8
Less than 5% of cases	30	33
Between 5 and 20% of cases	35	39
Between 20 and 50% of cases	16	18
More than 50% of cases	2	2

[a] Percents add to more than 100% because respondents were allowed to endorse more than one option.

Use of Jail as a Sanction for Noncompliance

Courts were given five options for rating their use of jail as a sanction for noncompliance, ranging from never to use in more than 50% of cases. As shown in Table 2, seven courts (8%) indicated that they never put people in jail in order to gain compliance, whereas two courts (2%) indicated that they used jail as a sanction in more than half of their cases. One-third (30 courts) report using jail in less than 5% of their cases, whereas 39% (or 35 courts) report using jail as a sanction between 5 and 20% of cases, with 18% (or 16 courts) reporting the use of jail between 20 and 50% of their cases.

Predictors of Number of Active Clients and the Use of Jail as a Sanction

Two multivariate regression analyses were performed. The first predicted the number of active MHC clients using the variables listed in Table 3 as predictors. This regression was significant, $F(8, 76) = 2.93$, $p < .01$, $R^2 = .26$. The number of active clients was positively predicted by three factors (see Table 3). In comparison to courts with fewer active participants, courts with larger numbers of participants (1) were in operation longer, (2) required their participants to return to see the judge less frequently, and (3) had more forms of supervision in the community. The capacity of the local jail from which eligible MHC defendants are drawn was not a significant predictor. Although intuitively the size of the MHC and the size of the jail would be positively related (indeed the bivariate correlation between the two was significant, $r = .23$, $p < .05$), when other factors were considered, the community jail capacity was not predictive of the actual capacity of the mental health court.

The second regression, predicting the use of jail as a sanction was also significant, $F(8, 76) = 3.20$, $p < .01$, $R^2 = .27$. MHCs that more often used jail as a sanction for noncompliance allowed in more felons and had their participants return for judicial status hearings more frequently (Table 4). Size of the local jail was not a significant predictor of the use of the jail as a sanction in the MHC.

Table 3   Multivariate regression predicting number of active clients

Predictors	B	SE(B)	β
Length of court existence	19.70	9.37	.23*
Capacity of local jail	0.01	0.01	.11
Percent of felons	0.29	0.51	.07
Other diversion programs	17.93	32.84	.06
Co-occurring MHC	24.22	38.95	.07
Frequency of initial status reviews (lower = more frequent)	41.86	19.87	.29**
Number of forms of community supervision	54.11	21.54	.28**
Use of jail as sanction	26.48	19.87	.16

*$p< .05$. **$p <.01$.

Table 4 Multivariate regression predicting use of jail as sanction (higher = more use)

Predictors	B	SE(B)	β
Number of active clients	0.001	0.001	.16
Length of court existence	−0.05	0.06	−.09
Capacity of local jail	0.00	0.00	−.04
Percent of felons	0.009	0.003	.39**
Other diversion programs	0.00	0.20	.00
Co-occurring MHC	0.02	0.24	.01
Frequency of initial status reviews (lower = more frequent)	−0.26	0.10	−.29**
Number of forms of community supervision	0.03	0.14	.03

$**p < .01$.

Discussion

We designed this study to describe the current universe of adult mental health courts in the United States. To our knowledge, this is the first time data have been examined on more than a handful of mental health courts. We were also interested in addressing controversies surrounding the courts and examining relations between certain MHC characteristics.

It has been said that MHCs are idiosyncratic and are not yet easily categorized by model in the manner in which drug courts may be (Goldkamp & Irons-Guynn, 2000; Steadman et al., 2001). Some of our data support this notion. The number of new enrollments and the number of active clients varied widely across the courts, from just a few to upwards of 1,000 active clients, and for one court, upwards of 2,000 new enrollees over a 12-month period. It is likely that these numbers reflect the size of the community (e.g., urban vs. rural) and capacity of the court and attendant treatment system, the length of operation, and the resources available to the court, county, and/or state. However, when the size of the local jail was examined in conjunction with other MHC-relevant factors, jail size was not a significant predictor of MHC size. Insofar that jail size is an accurate proxy of community size (or at least the size of the community's criminal problems), our data suggest that the intake capacity of the MHC is not influenced by the size of the community, per se.

We also found the frequency of judicial status review hearings to vary widely, from approximately four times a week to four times a year. Of importance, the frequency of going before the judge predicted both the number of active clients and the use of jail as a sanction. MHCs with more clients required their clients to return to see the judge less frequently. In contrast, MHCs that required their clients to see the judge more frequently were more likely to report using jail as a sanction.

Our data indicate that at this one point in time there are over 7,500 active MHC clients in the United States. Our data also indicate that the number of mental health court participants is likely to grow, as two-thirds of the courts stated they had plans to increase the number of clients they could serve. The issue of sustainability is also related to the question of capacity. On the one hand, in conducting the survey, we found six MHCs (five in California) whose doors closed after funding ended. (We also note that if a court had closed down and had been deleted from, or never appeared in, the GAINS publication, we would not have surveyed this court; thus the number of six courts is likely to underestimate the number of MHCs that had ceased operation.) Anecdotally, one of the courts that had shut down indicated that the defendants who were active participants in the MHC at the time of the closing were returned to regular court processing using the standard process of alphabetical assignment by last name to a judge.

On the other hand, when asked if they thought they could exist for another 3 years, most currently operating MHCs said they could, although nearly 1 out of 10 believed they could not. Additionally, 17% of the courts have been in operation for more than 4 years and 52% for more than 2 years. Thus, the majority of courts have found ways to sustain and even grow.

A controversial issue we noted above concerned the acceptance of misdemeanants versus felons. MHCs are only one form of diversion for persons with mental illnesses involved in the criminal justice system. Other forms include prebooking police diversion programs and crisis intervention teams (Steadman & Morris, 1995), in which the person is diverted from the criminal justice system almost entirely. Many MHCs today require guilty pleas and process their cases post-adjudication (Redlich et al., 2005). It has been argued that MHCs should be reserved for persons with mental illness who commit more serious crimes (Bazelon Center for Mental Health Law, 2003). We found that there were more MHCs that only allowed misdemeanants than those that only allowed felons, although about half of the courts' populations were comprised of both misdemeanants and felons. We also found that 46% of communities with MHCs also had other criminal diversion programs in place for PMI.

Redlich et al. (2005) noted a trend toward courts established more recently (which they characterized as "second generation" MHCs) being more likely to accept felons. In the present study, we did not find a significant relation between length of a court's existence and the percentage of felons on the caseload. An important caveat, though, is that we did not measure changes in a court's procedures over the length of its existence. Thus, it is possible that earlier courts were once misdemeanant exclusive, but over time changed their eligibility criteria to allow for defendants charged with felonies. Our data would not reflect this possibility.

Another MHC controversy is the use of jail as a sanction for noncompliance. MHCs are less formal and less adversarial than regular criminal courts (Petrila, 2003). The roles of judges, district attorneys, and public defenders are often blurred. In general, most courts follow a therapeutic jurisprudence approach (Winick & Wexler, 2003); thus, placing people in jail is controversial and to some, goes against the nature of the courts. Redlich et al. (2005) had also argued that second generation MHCs are more likely to use jail as a sanction. Although the same caveat noted in the paragraph above is relevant, the data presented here when compared to earlier data seem to support Redlich et al.'s argument. Specifically, earlier research (Bazelon Center for Mental Health Law, 2003) found that 64% of MHCs were willing to place people in jail for nonadherence. We found 92% of courts willing to do. But, we also found that 33% said they put noncompliant participants in jail less than 5% of the time.

Additionally, we found a significant and positive predictor of placing people in jail for noncompliance was the percentage of felons in the court. Is this because PMI charged with felonies are less compliant than PMI charged with misdemeanors? Or is this because the MHCs have fears about threats to public safety when felons are not complying with the courts' judicial and treatment orders? Naples and Steadman (2003) examined self-reported rates of arrest (violent and nonviolent), violent acts, hospitalization, and emergency room use among jail-diverted persons with co-occurring disorders with and without violent charges (i.e., the charges that led to the diversion). They did not find significant differences between the two groups at a 12-month follow-up on any of these outcome measures. In other words, in comparison to PMI without violent charges, PMI with violent charges were no more likely to pose a public threat as measured by direct and indirect assessments of (potential) violence. Thus, if the reason MHCs tend to use jail as a sanction more with felons is because of public safety, Naples and Steadman's data would suggest this is unnecessary because in their study, the two groups had comparable rates of future violence. However, clearly more data are needed on why we found a significant relation between number of felons in the courts and the use of jail as a sanction, as well as more data on the outcomes experienced by individuals diverted by MHCs.

Perhaps the more intriguing findings from the present data are the significant findings concerning judicial and community supervision. We found the number of clients MHCs served to be influenced by these two types of supervision, but in different directions. That is, MHCs with larger caseloads was negatively predicted by supervision but positively predicted by community supervision. In other words, MHCs with large clienteles relied on professionals like probation officers, case managers, etc., to supervise the defendants, thereby reducing the load of the judge and allowing the court to serve more clients.

However, irrespective of the number [of] active clients, we also found that MHCs that had their participants return more often for judicial review hearings used jail as a sanction more frequently. One interpretation of this finding is that MHC clients who are subject to more intense judicial supervision are more likely to be "caught" in acts of noncompliance and then placed in jail as a consequence. This is consistent with a growing literature indicating that offenders with mental illness who are subject to intense supervision fare worse (in terms of returning to jail) as an artifact of the supervision (Solomon & Draine, 1995; Solomon, Draine, & Meyerson, 1994; Tonry, 1990). For example, Solomon et al. (2002) reported that probationers/parolees with mental illness who had received intensive case management services were six times more likely to be incarcerated on technical violations compared to those who did not receive intensive case management. However, inconsistent with this interpretation, we did not find supervision in the community to predict the use of jail as a sanction.[1]

What we cannot infer from our data is whether jail sanction use is an effective method of gaining compliance with MHC orders and engaging participants in treatment, and if so whether it is associated with other outcomes, for example, a reduction in recidivism. Nor do our data resolve the broader debate regarding the appropriateness of using jail as a sanction for nonadherence to treatment. Although it is therefore possible that MHCs that use jail as a sanction for nonadherence produce better outcomes for their clients, this is a question for future research.

Conclusions and Implications

Although our findings are largely descriptive in nature, we describe a number of important characteristics of the entire universe of mental health courts. We also provide heretofore unknown data on MHCs (such as the number of active U.S. MHC participants) and address several unexamined, but controversial, issues. We discovered that MHCs quite commonly place treatment nonadherents in jail and that this is associated with more intense judicial supervision. Of importance, our findings have the potential to inform larger, more comprehensive studies on the outcomes associated with mental health court participation (e.g., whether and what types of impacts MHCs have on recidivism, adherence with treatment, and quality of life, for whom, and by what mechanisms).

However, certain limitations should be mentioned. Our data were collected at one point in time and do not reflect changes in MHC operations over time. MHCs appear to be highly adaptive and are likely to find what works best for them and their clients through trial and error, and then continue to make alterations as necessary. Another possible limitation is that our data came directly from the MHC programs and not from objective sources such as jail records or MHC records. However, the perspective of the courts on these issues is important and is a necessary complement to the use of archival data. Finally, although we examined several controversial and understudied issues, there are many other issues we did not address such as the frequency of requiring guilty pleas as a condition of entry to an MHC, the impact on treatment provision, and the open questions of net-widening and whether the courts "Do justice well". These are also issues in need of future research.

It is likely that the number of MHCs will continue to grow as jurisdictions struggle with creating responses to the number of individuals with mental illnesses entering the criminal justice system. A consensus has emerged in recent years that diversion is a worthy goal (see Council of State Governments' Criminal Justice/Mental Health Consensus Report [Council of State Governments, 2002]) and MHCs represent an important development in attempting to attain that goal. However, much more data are necessary before we can answer the questions "Do mental health courts work? If so, for whom? And why?"

Appendix

MacArthur Mental Health Court Survey

1. What is the name of your Mental Health Court (MHC): _____
   Where is your MHC located? City: _____ County: _____ State: _____

2. Please provide the following about your MHC capacity:
   Approximate number of clients newly enrolled in the past 12 months: _____
   Approximate number of active participants in your MHC: _____
   Do you have a maximum # of clients that you can serve?   YES   NO
   If yes, what is the maximum #? _____
   Does your court have plans to increase the number
   of clients served in the next year?   YES   NO

3. Date of your first MHC participant: ____/ ____/ _____
                                        mm   dd   year

4. What is the approximate % of defendants charged with misdemeanors currently enrolled in
   your MHC? _____
   What is the approximate % of defendants charged with felonies currently enrolled in your
   MHC? _____

5. Does your community/jurisdiction have other types of diversion programs for defendants
   with mental illness, such as prebooking police diversion programs, or a Co-occurring Drug
   Treatment/Mental Health court? (*note, do not include Drug Treatment Courts if persons with
   mental illness are not eligible*)   YES   NO

6. Is your MHC considered a Co-Occurring Drug/Mental Health Court? (*i.e., do you **only** accept
   defendants with substance abuse **and** mental health issues?*)   YES   NO

7. What is the approximate capacity of your local/county jail? _____

8. Who is responsible for the community supervision of your MHC participants?
   (*circle all that apply*)
            a. Probation officers   b. Community treatment providers
            c. Court personnel   d. Other, please specify: _____
            e. We do not supervise clients in the community   _____

9. What is your usual schedule of status review hearings (e.g., once a week, once a month)?
   _____

10. How, if at all, do you adapt this schedule if participants are or are not fulfilling their MHC
    requirements? _____
    _____

11. Within the last year, approximately what was the percentage of MHC cases in which participants
    were returned to jail to obtain compliance with judicial and/or treatment provider orders?
             a. Never
             b. Less than 5% of cases
             c. Between 5 and 20% of cases
             d. Between 20 and 50% of cases
             e. More than 50% of cases

12. Do you believe that your MHC will be able to be sustained for the next 3 years? YES   NO

    **Please provide the name and contact information of the person best able to answer
    additional questions:**

    NAME: _____
    TELEPHONE: _____ **E-MAIL:** _____

Endnote

[1] Judicial supervision (lower scores indicate more frequent supervision) and community supervision (higher scores indicate more forms of supervision) were significantly correlated, $r = -.23$, $p = .03$. Thus, it is possible, in the regression predicting jail sanction use, the two forms of supervision did not provide unique variance.

References

Bazelon Center for Mental Health Law (2003). Criminalization of people with mental illnesses: The role of mental courts in system reform. *Jail Suicide/Mental Health Update, 12,* 1–8, 10–11.

Boothroyd, R., Calkins Mercado, C., Poythress, N. P., Christy, A., & Petrila, J. (2005). After mental health court: Do diverted defendants experience improved clinical outcomes. *Psychiatric Services, 56,* 829–834.

Casey, T. (2005). When good intentions are not good enough: Problem-solving courts and the impending crisis of legitimacy. *SMU Law Review, 57,* 1459–1519.

Clark, R. E., Ricketts, S. K., & McHugo, G. J. (1999). Legal system involvement and costs for persons in treatment for severe mental illness and substance use disorders. *Psychiatric Services, 50,* 641–647.

CMHS. (1995). *Double jeopardy: Persons with mental illnesses in the criminal justice system.* A report to Congress. Rockville, MD: U.S. Department of Health and Human Services, Substance Abuse and Mental Health Services Administration, Center for Mental Health Services.

Cosden, M., Ellens, J., Schnell, J., Yasmeen, Y., & Wolfe, M. (2003). Evaluation of a mental health treatment court with assertive community treatment. *Behavioral Sciences and the Law, 21,* 415–427.

Council of State Governments. (2002). *Criminal justice/mental health consensus project.* Retrieved October 10, 2002, from http://www.consensusproject.org.

Draine, J., & Solomon, P. (1999). Describing and evaluating jail diversion services for persons with serious mental illness. *Psychiatric Services, 50,* 56–61.

GAINS Center for People with Co-Occurring Disorders in the Justice System. (2005). *Survey of mental health courts.* Delmar, NY. Available online at http://www.mentalhealthcourtsurvey.com/

Goldkamp, J. D., & Irons-Guynn, C. (2000). *Emerging judicial strategies for the mentally ill in the criminal caseload: Mental health courts in Fort Lauderdale, Seattle, San Bernardino, and Anchorage.* Washington, DC: U.S. Department of Justice, Office of Justice Programs, Bureau of Justice Assistance Monograph, pub. no. NCJ 182504.

Gottfredson, M. R., Mitchell-Herzfeld, S. D., & Flanagan, T. J. (1982). Another look at the effectiveness of parole supervision. *Journal of Research in Crime and Delinquency, 19,* 277–298.

Griffin, P., Steadman, H. J., & Petrila, J. (2002). The use of criminal charges and sanctions in mental health courts. *Psychiatric Services, 53,* 1285–1289.

Herinckx, H. A., Swart, S. C., Ama, S. M., Dolezal, C. D., & King, S. (2005). Rearrest and linkage to mental health services among clients of the Clark County mental health court program. *Psychiatric Services, 56,* 853–857.

Naples, M., & Steadman, H. J. (2003). Can persons with co-occurring disorders and violent charges be successfully diverted? *International Journal of Forensic Mental Health, 2,* 137–143.

National Drug Court Institute. (June 2000). *The critical need for jail as a sanction in the drug court model. Drug Court Practitioner Fact Sheet, 2.* Alexandria, VA. Available online at http://www.nadcp.org/publications/

Peters, R. H., & Hills, H. A. (1993). Inmates with co-occurring substance abuse and mental health disorders. In H. Steadman & J. Cocozza (Eds.), *Mental illness in America's prisons.* Seattle, WA: National Coalition for the Mentally Ill in the Criminal Justice System.

Petrila, J. (2003). An introduction to special jurisdiction courts. *International Journal of Law and Psychiatry, 26,* 3–12.

Public Law 106-515, *America's Law Enforcement and Mental Health Project* (Nov. 13, 2000; 114 Stat. 2399).

Redlich, A. D. (2005). Voluntary, but knowing and intelligent? Comprehension in mental health courts. *Psychology, Public Policy, and Law, 11,* 605–619.

Redlich, A. D., Steadman, H. J. Monahan, J., Petrila, J., & Griffin, P. (2005). The second generation of mental health courts. *Psychology, Public Policy, and Law, 11,* 527–538.

Seltzer, T. (2005). Mental health courts: A misguided attempt to address the criminal justice system's unfair treatment of people with mental illnesses. *Psychology, Public Policy, and Law, 11,* 570–586.

Solomon, P., & Draine, J. (1995). One-year outcomes of a randomized trial of case management with seriously ill clients leaving jail. *Evaluation Review, 19,* 256–273.

Solomon, P., Draine, J., & Marcus, S. C. (2002). Predicting incarceration of clients of a psychiatric probation and parole service. *Psychiatric Services, 53,* 50–56.

Solomon, P., Draine, J., & Meyerson, A. (1994). Jail recidivism and receipt of community mental health services. *Hospital and Community Psychiatry, 45,* 793–797.

Steadman, H., Davidson, S., and Brown, C. (2001). Mental health courts: Their promise and unanswered questions. *Psychiatric Services, 52,* 457–458.

Steadman, H. J., Fabisiak, S., Dvoskin, J., & Holohean, E. J. (1987). A survey of mental disability among state prison inmates. *Hospital and Community Psychiatry, 38,* 1086–1090.

Steadman, H. J., Morris, S. M., & Dennis, D. L. (1995). The diversion of mentally ill persons from jails to community-based services: A profile of programs. *American Journal of Public Health, 85,* 1630–1635.

Steadman, H. J., Redlich, A. D., Griffin, P., Petrila, J., & Monahan, J. (2005). From referral to disposition: Case processing in seven mental health courts. *Behavioral Sciences and the Law, 23,* 1–12.

Tonry, M. (1990). Stated and latent functions of ISP. *Crime and Delinquency, 36,* 174–191.

Torrey, E. F., Stieber, J., Ezekiel, J., Wolfe, S. M., Sharfstein, J., Noble, J. H., et al. (1992). *Criminalizing the mentally ill: The abuse of jails as mental hospitals.* Washington, DC: Public citizen's health research group.

Trupin, E., & Richards, H. (2003). Seattle's mental health courts: Early indicators of effectiveness. *International Journal of Law and Psychiatry, 26,* 33–53.

Winick, B. J., & Wexler, D. B. (2003). *Judging in a therapeutic key: Therapeutic jurisprudence and the courts.* Durham, NC: Carolina Academic Press.

27

Reducing Homicide through a "Lever-Pulling" Strategy

EDMUND F. MCGARRELL, STEVEN CHERMAK,
JEREMY M. WILSON, AND NICHOLAS CORSARO

Introduction

The decade of the 1990s witnessed significant declines in firearms-related violence. Indeed, rates of homicide declined from 9.4 per 100,000 in 1990 to 5.5 in 2000 (Federal Bureau of Investigation, 2005). In absolute numbers, homicides declined from 23,438 to 15,586, a 34 percent decline through the decade. Yet, debate continues over the causes of the decline in rates of violence (Blumstein & Rosenfeld, 1998; Blumstein & Wallman, 2000). Some have suggested criminal justice policies such as increased incarceration and proactive policing. Others point to the healthy economy and improved employment prospects experienced throughout the decade.

One planned criminal justice intervention that appears to have had an impact on firearms violence, at least with respect to youth firearms violence, was the so-called "lever-pulling" strategy implemented by criminal justice officials in Boston in the mid-1990s (Braga, Kennedy, Waring, & Piehl, 2001; Kennedy, 1997, 1998; Kennedy & Braga, 1998; Kennedy, Piehl, & Braga, 1996; McDevitt, Braga, Nurge, & Buerger, 2003). A series of meetings were held with gang members thought to be at risk of being involved in gun violence. The meetings included a deterrence-based message that essentially said that if the groups continue to be involved in violence, all potential sanctions, or levers, would be applied to the group. The communication strategy was coupled with a crackdown on a violent gang in which the adult gang members were prosecuted in federal rather than state court. This crackdown was believed to have given credibility to the deterrence message.[1] The city of

Edmund F. McGarrell, Steven Chermak, Jeremy M. Wilson, and Nicholas Corsaro, *Justice Quarterly*, Vol. 23(2), pp. 214–231, © 2006 by Taylor & Francis. Reprinted by permission of Taylor & Francis.

Boston experienced over a 60 percent decline in youth homicides following the intervention. This strategy was then applied in a very similar fashion in Minneapolis, and a federal crackdown on one of the city's violence-involved gangs was followed by a substantial reduction in homicide (Kennedy, 1998; Kennedy & Braga, 1998).

Based on the apparent success in Boston and Minneapolis, criminal justice officials in Indianapolis decided to implement a very similar strategy in late 1998 and early 1999. This paper is based on an evaluation of the Indianapolis project. Consequently, it provides an opportunity to test whether the lever-pulling strategy had an impact on homicide in a third city.

Assessing the potential impact of the lever-pulling strategy is critical because, despite the significant declines in firearms violence, it remains a significant problem in the United States. Moreover, recent studies indicate that violence is back on the rise in some communities (e.g., Wilson & Riley, 2004; Wilson, Hiromoto, Fain, Tita, & Riley, 2004). National Crime Victimization figures indicate that approximately 6 million individuals are victimized by crimes of violence annually (Bureau of Justice Statistics, 2001), and the Uniform Crime Reports show that there were approximately 1.4 million violent offenses reported to the police in 2003 (Federal Bureau of Investigation, 2005). Over 10,000 victims were murdered with guns, and guns were involved in over one-third of violent crimes in 1999 (Project Safe Neighborhoods, 2001). Miller, Cohen, and Wiersema's (1996; Cook & Ludwig, 2000) study of the costs of crime finds that personal crimes cost over $100 billion annually in tangible losses, such as property damage and loss, medical and mental health care, productivity losses, and costs related to providing assistance to victims. Adding intangible losses, such as the amount of pain, suffering, and reduced quality of life caused by crime, increases the costs of victimization to over $450 billion annually.

Lever-Pulling and Focused Deterrence

One of the most intriguing criminal justice interventions implemented in the 1990s was "Project Ceasefire" that was part of a problem-solving initiative known as the "Boston Gun Project." Starting in 1995, a multi-agency working group of officials and researchers in Boston met to analyze, design, implement, and assess responses to violent crime (Braga et al., 2001; Kennedy, 1997, 1998; Kennedy & Braga, 1998; Kennedy, Braga, Piehl, & Waring, 2001; Kennedy et al., 1996; McDevitt et al., 2003). Analyses indicated that gang members with prior criminal justice system involvement committed most homicides. Indeed, the data suggested that approximately 1,200 gang-involved, chronic offending youths were responsible for at least 60 percent of the city's youth homicides. These chronic offending youths constituted approximately 1 percent of the city's youth population. The multi-agency working group attempted to deter future violent behavior of chronic offenders by informing them that violence would not be tolerated and would be met with an unprecedented law-enforcement response. The message was communicated directly to gang members through forums that have subsequently been referred to as "offender notification" meetings or "lever-pulling" meetings in cities that have adopted these practices. The gang members were told to report to the meeting by their probation officer and sometimes included gang members not on probation who were brought to the meeting by a streetworker member of the clergy. The agencies backed up the message by using all legally available sanctions against the targeted offenders. The meetings were coupled with crackdowns on several gangs that remained involved in gun crime. One high-profile crackdown involved the Intervale Posse gang and included federal prosecution of the adult gang members. Although this action was not a planned component of the intervention, officials used this crackdown as evidence that they were serious about reducing violence and that the illegal use and possession of firearms by chronic offenders could result in long sentences in federal prison.

The results from research analyzing the impacts of this intervention are impressive. Violent gang offending slowed dramatically, and youth homicide in Boston fell by two-thirds after the strategy was put into place (Kennedy, 1998, p. 3). The intervention also produced significant reductions in shots fired, gun assaults, and youth gun assaults. Braga et al.'s time-series analysis (1991–1998) examining monthly counts of youth homicide before and after the implementation of Project Ceasefire indicates a significant reduction in youth homicides. The results show a 63 percent reduction in the number of monthly homicides. Moreover, when comparing the results to 39 other cities, Boston experienced the largest statistically significant decline in youth homicide between 1991 and 1997 (Braga et al., 2001).

As noted above, following the Boston experience, Minneapolis officials implemented a very similar process whereby groups of chronic offending probationers were called into offender-notification meetings. City officials used the example of the federal prosecution of the "Boguz Boys" in much the same way that Boston officials presented the crackdown on the Intervale Posse. Minneapolis also experienced sharp reductions in homicide after having implemented the "pulling levers" strategy (Kennedy, 1998; Kennedy & Braga, 1998).

The Boston and Minneapolis lever-pulling interventions can be considered focused deterrence strategies that are based on several characteristics of both offending and the system response to offending. First, the strategy takes advantage of the long-established conclusion that a small number of offenders account for a disproportionate number of crimes (Moore, 1984). Thus, chronic offenders "le[ave] themselves open to an enormous range of sanctions, exactly because they [are] so highly criminal" (Kennedy, 1997, p. 461). Second, because the strategy is implemented and supported by a multi-agency working group, there are a variety of sanctions available to be used against the offenders. The involvement of many agencies focused on a specific problem should increase the severity and the certainty of penalties. Third, the approach includes directly confronting offenders by providing what Kennedy calls a "retail deterrence message" (Kennedy, 1998, p. 4). Offenders are told that gun-related offending will not be tolerated and informed about how the system will respond to violations of these new standards. Meeting with offenders is an important first step in altering their perceptions about sanction risk (see Homey & Marshall, 1992; Nagin, 1998). Fourth, such a strategy attempts to influence the informal communication networks of offenders. Interactions between offenders in jail and court, and on the streets may help spread information about new initiatives in place to respond to crime and how such programs might directly affect their activities. Deterrence scholars discuss how offenders are constantly revising theft perceptions of the risks and rewards of criminal behavior based on new information (see Nagin, 1998; p. 16). The lever-pulling meetings and an affirmative follow-up response are the types of new information that may cause offenders to reassess the risks of committing crime.

Thus, there appears to be a theoretical basis for linking the declines in homicide in Boston and Minneapolis to the lever-pulling intervention. Consequently, it is important to assess similar interventions in other jurisdictions.

The Indianapolis Lever-Pulling Initiative[2]

In late 1997, Indianapolis officials, including the Mayor, US Attorney, County Prosecutor, and Chief of Police, convened a meeting of all criminal justice agency heads to discuss the record-setting levels of homicide the city had experienced during the 1994–1997 period. Indianapolis had experienced success in reducing firearms violence in specific neighborhoods through a directed patrol experiment (McGarrell, Chermak, & Weiss, 2002; McGarrell, Chermak, Weiss & Wilson, 2001), and officials were thus sympathetic to the focused deterrence components of the lever-pulling strategy. They thus decided to implement the problem-solving strategy employed in Boston including the offender-notification meetings.

The lever-pulling program was part of what became known as the Indianapolis Violence Reduction Partnership (IVRP). The key components of the IVRP included a multi-agency working team, collaboration with a research partner, and application of formal problem-solving techniques to the homicide and gun assault problem. Since early 1998, a multi-agency coalition of criminal justice agencies, working with a variety of community partners, and committed to employing a strategic problem-solving approach, has been collaborating to assess the violent-crime problem and implement strategies in response to it. The coalition studied patterns of homicide and firearms violence in Indianapolis, crafted various interventions, assessed the impact of these interventions, and revised the strategy.

The analysis that supported the problem-solving approach initially focused on homicide patterns. Homicides from 1997 through August 1998 were analyzed based on official police records as well as through incident reviews. The incident reviews involved case-by-case reviews by homicide investigators, street and special unit (gang and drug) officers, federal law enforcement, federal and local prosecutors, and probation and parole officers. Members of the research team recorded the information shared during these meetings with particular attention to gang or group affiliations, drug involvement, and prior involvement in the criminal justice system by homicide suspects and victims.

The basic picture that emerged from these analyses was one of a high use of firearms involvement and considerable victim-offender overlap in terms of group involvement and prior criminal histories. Nearly 80 percent of homicide victims died of a gunshot wound. Homicide victims averaged 12.5 prior arrests, and homicide suspects averaged 11.5 prior arrests. The initial 206 victims and suspects from 1997 had been arrested over 1,600 times including 500 violent crime arrests and had over 800 convictions. Approximately 60 percent of the homicides involved a suspect, victim, or both who could be linked to a group of known, chronic offenders (gang or neighborhood crew). Over half the incidents were drug-involved, not necessarily drug-motivated, but involving a known user, seller, or located at a known drug house.[3]

The problem analysis suggested to the IVRP working group that a focused deterrence strategy aimed at illegal gun carrying and use among known groups of chronic offenders, often involved in the drug trade, made sense. A key element of the strategy was communicating a deterrent message to high-risk offenders with the hope that they would in turn communicate it throughout their network of chronic offenders. A key component of the implemented strategy, borrowed from Boston's Ceasefire, was what became known as "lever-pulling" meetings. These meetings involved face-to-face meetings with groups of high-risk probationers and parolees. At the meetings, criminal justice officials and community members described their concern that the probationers/parolees were at high risk of either committing a violent crime or being a victim of a violent crime. A deterrence message was communicated with an explanation of the severe penalties available under federal law for felons in possession of a firearm and the commitment of local, state, and federal law enforcement to impose severe sanctions for firearms crimes. In addition, probationers and parolees were urged to take advantage of a range of services and opportunities including mentoring from ex-offenders, employment, housing, substance abuse, education, and vocational training. For over two and a half years, at least one lever-pulling meeting was held per month.

The initial lever-pulling meetings began in fall of 1998. From October 1998 through early summer 1999, nine lever-pulling meetings involving approximately 160 probationers and parolees along with eight follow-up meetings[4] with the same individuals were conducted. These meetings were complemented with a major federal-local intervention targeted at a criminal gang operating in the Brightwood section of Indianapolis. The coupling of the lever-pulling meetings, the arrests, and federal prosecution of a major gang was very similar to the lever-pulling strategy that included arrests and prosecution of the Intervale Posse in Boston and the Bogus Boyz in Minneapolis.

The Brightwood Investigation[5]

On April 5th, 1999, a joint federal-local investigation culminated in a series of arrests of members of what was known as the Brightwood Gang. The group of offenders targeted had ties to criminal activity throughout the city, but the investigation focused primarily on the drug market situated in an area of the city known as Brightwood. The Brightwood neighborhood had long been a violent crime hot spot. The arrest, indictment, and eventual conviction of offenders controlling the Brightwood drug market was the product of a 10-month investigation conducted by a task force of law enforcement personnel from federal and local agencies. The United States Attorney's Office, the FBI, the IPD, the Marion County Sheriff's Department, local prosecutors, and several other local police departments were involved. The investigation included long-term surveillance of the major players, controlled drug purchases, and the use of wiretaps. The investigation concluded with the execution of 33 search warrants, the arrest of 16 individuals, and the seizure of 78 firearms, 12 kg of powdered cocaine, 500 g of crack, and over $150,000 in cash.

Although this investigation was not a direct product of the IVRP, many of the law-enforcement officials responsible for this successful investigation were members of the IVRP working group. It also provided a good example of the potential of collaborative efforts between agencies. In addition, the "Brightwood Gang" provided an excellent example of the key factors driving the increases in the Indianapolis homicide problem in the 1990s—factors that were substantiated with the analysis of homicide and gun assaults patterns conducted by the IVRP research team. The Brightwood Gang was a tightly organized group of individuals working together to distribute crack and cocaine. Suppliers, mid-level distributors, and street-level sellers were arrested. This gang also used several "police spotters" to warn street-level distributors of police presence with cell phones. It was documented that they distributed nearly 50 kg of cocaine during the investigation period—a street value of about $1.5 million. The primary objective of this group was profit-making, and they protected their turf and product with threats and acts of violent crime. These offenders had assault weapons, semi-automatic handguns, shotguns, pistols, and revolvers. The members of the gang were chronic offenders, well known as major players by federal and local authorities as well as the offending population. The individuals arrested had over 20 prior convictions for violent felonies, and nearly 70 convictions for other offenses.

The arrests and prosecution of this gang were exploited by members of the IVRP to accomplish its objective of communicating a "zero tolerance of violence" message to the offending population. Working-group members made a significant effort in the neighborhood where the arrests occurred to suppress activities of rival groups attempting to replace the significant gaps in drug supply. This included increased police patrol and outreach to several key community leaders to communicate directly with gang members about the increased law enforcement attention. In addition, they communicated to people living in these neighborhoods that the arrest was part of a new commitment to reducing violence in the neighborhood and across the city. Several lever-pulling meetings were held following the arrests. Working-group members that presented at these sessions used the Brightwood crackdown to describe how law enforcement was using a new collaborative approach to respond to violence in Indianapolis. The United States Attorney, for example, described how the case against the Brightwood Gang was going to be heard in Federal District Court and described the amount of prison time that the defendants faced when convicted. Other law-enforcement officials and members of the community described how they were not going to stand for gangs terrorizing neighborhoods. This message, however, was coupled with concern for the probationers and parolees in attendance. Other speakers presented a message of hope and opportunities for change, encouraging the attendees to take advantage of the community resources and support that were present at the meeting.

Method

To assess the impact of the crackdown on the Brightwood Gang and the associated lever-pulling meetings, we employed time-series analyses of the trends in homicide across Indianapolis. The greatest threat to the validity of our Indianapolis findings is a main history effect, which we control for by examining homicides in six additional "no-treatment" cities.[6] Homicide data for these comparison sites were obtained using the Supplementary Victim-Level Homicide Database. The comparison sites (Cincinnati, OH, Cleveland, OH, Columbus, OH, Kansas City, MO, Louisville, KY, and Pittsburgh, PA) were chosen based on their Midwestern location and population. These seven cities run along a border from Interstate Highway 64 in the south to Interstate 80 in the north from Pittsburgh to Kansas City. They range in population from Louisville with a population of 256,231 to Columbus at 711,470. Due to its consolidated city-county government structure, Indianapolis is the most populous of the seven cities at 791,926. However, its center city, patrolled by the Indianapolis Police Department and accounting for approximately 80 percent of homicides, is just under 400,000 in population and thus quite similar to the comparison cities. We describe the time-series method in more detail as we present the findings.

Time-Series Analyses—Homicide in Indianapolis

Time-series analyses were conducted for Indianapolis as well as six comparison sites to examine the changes in homicide patterns.

Indianapolis had experienced 149 homicides in the 12 months prior to April 5th. This declined to 101 in the next 12 months. The average number of homicides declined from 2.9 per week to 1.9 per week following the Brightwood crackdown. To further assess the potential impact of the IVRP lever-pulling strategy on firearms-related violence, we conducted an interrupted time series quasi-experiment. The analysis was conducted in accordance with modeling techniques developed by Box and Jenkins (1976). This entails identifying, estimating, and diagnosing autoregressive integrated moving average (ARIMA) models in order to find the most appropriate stochastic model of the series prior to estimating the impact of the intervention.

The initial analysis examined the trend in homicides. The data allowed for aggregation into either weekly or monthly intervals. Monthly intervals allow for the detection of seasonality in the data and are not plagued by problems associated with frequencies of zeros. Attempts were made to model the series at both interval levels, and ultimately monthly intervals were chosen.

Each month was operationalized as running from its first through its last day. Utilizing data from January 1, 1997 to June 30, 2001 yielded a total of 54 months. Figure 1 shows the trend in homicides across both the pre-intervention and post-intervention periods, which comprised 27 months (the intervention was month 28).

The number of monthly homicides was plotted over the assessment period. The time plot indicated that the variance of the series was nonstationary in that it reduced over time. This could suggest that the trend in homicide was regressing to the mean and would have declined absent the intervention. To address this possibility, the data were transformed into their natural-logarithm form and replotted. By using the natural logarithm of the data in the time-series analysis, the trend was eliminated prior to our subsequent analyses.

This plot illustrated a considerable improvement in stabilizing the variance. Although the plot suggested that the data might have been following a

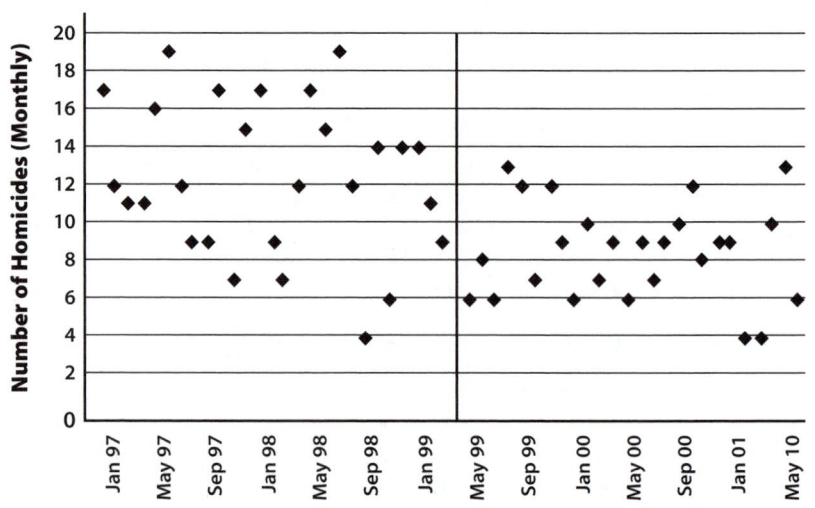

Figure 1   Number of homicides in Indianapolis, Indiana between January 1997 and June 2001.

downward trend over time, the autocorrelation function (ACF) and partial autocorrelation function (PACF) of the logged series indicated that there was no trend requiring to be modeled. In addition, the ACF and PACF revealed that there were no significant correlations at key lags, suggesting neither autoregressive nor moving average components (standard or seasonal) needed to be modeled.

Estimation of the impact of the intervention requires coupling both the noise parameters to account for autocorrelation in the data and a transfer function to capture the impact. Based upon the time plots and the ACF and PACF, the tentative model of this series requires no components to account for autocorrelation in the data. Therefore, the model contains only the transfer function to estimate the impact. Given the expectation that the intervention would reduce homicides immediately and sustain the reduction over the course of the evaluation period (which is also consistent with the time plot of monthly homicides), an abrupt, permanent transfer function was used to estimate the impact of the intervention. This entails introducing a dummy variable into the model, where 0 represents all pre-intervention time periods and 1 all post-intervention time periods.

Since there were no noise parameters to include with the transfer function, this model simply reduced to a bivariate regression of the natural logarithm of homicides each month on the dummy intervention variable. The F-test of this model was statistically significant ($p < .001$), indicating that the model statistically explained variation in the natural logarithm of homicides per month. The R^2 revealed that this model explains approximately 22 percent of the variation in the natural logarithm of homicides per month. The intervention was also statistically significant ($p < .001$). The estimate of the impact, $-.42$, signifies that at the time of the intervention, homicides declined immediately by 34.3 percent,[7] per month (see Table 1). Moreover, this reduction was sustained over the evaluation period.[8] By logging, or compressing the data, to fit the assumptions of the test, the analysis was essentially a mean comparison without the impact of a trend within the data. The finding of a significant reduction suggests that there was an immediate and abrupt reduction in the number of homicides in Indianapolis.

Table 1   Time-series analysis for homicides in Indianapolis

City	Pre-intervention mean	Post-intervention mean	Mean difference post–pre	ARIMA model			Intervention coefficient	SE
				p	d	q		
Indianapolis, Indiana	2.46 (ln)	2.04 (ln)	–.42 (ln)	—	—	—	–.42***	0.11

***p < .001.

The appropriateness of this model was diagnosed by calculating the ACF and PACF of the model residuals. There were no significant spikes in either the ACF or PACF, and accordingly, the Box-Ljung Q-statistic, testing whether the residuals as a whole are random, was not significant. Demonstrating that there was no autocorrelation remaining to be modeled, these tests established that the estimated model was proper, and no further adjustments were required.

Homicide in Comparison Sites

First, we conducted an extensive number of estimated models, parameters, and transfer functions, using a systematic interactive process, for each of the cities. The findings presented in Table 2 represent the most appropriate model for each comparable homicide series. An advantage to this approach is that we were able to find the most appropriate estimated model for every site because each series is inevitably different. Similar to Indianapolis, we plotted data for each site over the assessment period in order to adjust for nonstationarity series. If a series had components of variance nonstationary, we used the natural logarithm of homicides in each month (Indianapolis and Pittsburgh). If a series suffered from mean nonstationarity, we used both first-order differencing (Louisville) and seasonal differencing (Cincinnati), if necessary.

Following the Box and Jenkins (1976) approach, we identified, estimated, and diagnosed ARIMA model parameters that best fit each independent series during the same time period as the Indianapolis study. In addition to the stationary adjustment, some models required autoregressive components white others required moving average components. We selected the most parsimonious series for each site. Additionally, we diagnosed the appropriateness for each series by examining the ACF and PACF model residuals and found that there were no significant spikes indicating there are no white noise parameters in any of the models. Among these sites, only Indianapolis had a statistically significant decline over this period.

It is also important to note that the findings presented in Table 2 represent a zero-order transfer function that assesses whether an abrupt, permanent change is found between pre-intervention and post-intervention. It begs the question, what if national homicide frequency gradually declined over this same period, perhaps more rapidly in Indianapolis, and that this could be an alternative explanation to the reduction in estimated homicides. We conducted a number of first-order transfer functions, or pulse functions that measure a gradual temporary change, for each city. We did not find any significant models for any of the series using this method.[9] The data presented in Appendix B, however, do indicate that the greatest reduction in homicide in Indianapolis occurred in the month following the Brightwood intervention. The impact had an immediate effect, which was sustainable over time. This is consistent with an explanation that attributes the decline in homicide to the impact of the intervention.[10] When coupled with the prior analysis of the Indianapolis time series using the natural logarithm of the data, the results suggest an abrupt decline in homicides beyond that attributable to regression to the mean.

Table 2 Time-series analyses for homicide by month across six cities plus Indianapolis

City	Pre-intervention mean	Post-intervention mean	Mean difference post–pre	ARIMA model			Intervention coefficient	SE
				p	d	q		
Cincinnati, Ohio	0.89	3.15	2.26	1	1, (12)	—	.08	.45
Cleveland, Ohio	7.07	6.85	−.22	—	—	—	−.22	.71
Columbus, Ohio	1.70	7.22	−.48	—	—	—	−.48	.88
Indianapolis, Indiana	2.46 (ln)	2.04 (ln)	−.4	—	—	—	−.42***	.11
Kansas City, Missouri	11.19	11.96	−1.23	—	—	—	−1.22	1.22
Louisville, Kentucky	6.75	6.61	−.1	—	1	1	.03	.11
Pittsburgh, Pennsylvania	2.06 (ln)	1.90 (ln)	−.1	—	—	—	−.15	.11

***$p < .001$.

Summary

As noted above, the strategies developed by the IVRP involved a focused deterrence approach coupled with increased linkage to services for high-risk offenders. This included both suppression and intervention components that have been included in prior crime-reduction initiatives (e.g., see Decker, 2003; Sherman et al., 1997). The distinguishing characteristic of the IVRP approach was the attempt to use a problem-solving framework to focus these components on the key dimensions of the local firearms violence problem. What emerged was a focused deterrence lever-pulling strategy (Kennedy, 1998) that sought to focus limited criminal justice resources on firearms violence, to use both state and federal sanctions to deter illegal gun carrying and use, to communicate this strategy through as many venues as possible to those individuals believed to be most at risk for involvement in violence, and to link potential offenders to legitimate opportunities and services.

The evaluation of the IVRP intervention provides evidence that the IVRP process did lead to reduced levels of homicide. Specifically, the time-series analysis indicated that monthly homicides were reduced by 34.3 percent following the April 1999 intervention. When compared to the homicide trend in six other cities, Indianapolis was the only one that experienced a statistically significant change. Additionally, the impact was greatest during the month following the Brightwood gang crackdown, thus suggesting an intervention effect.

The most significant threat to the finding that the lever-pulling intervention had an impact on homicide is that the pre-intervention rates were exceptionally high and that the numbers were likely to decline absent any intervention ("regression to the mean"). This threat does not seem likely given that homicides had been at a fairly stable level from 1994 through early 1999. Yet, the data suggested a potential downward trend. Consequently, the time-series analyses that were conducted eliminated the trend in the data from the intervention assessment and continued to find a significant reduction in homicide. Thus, it does not appear to be the case that the results capture a short-term "peak" in homicides.

The additional factor that suggests that homicides were substantially reduced is the sudden decline in homicides following the intervention. Homicides dramatically declined in the spring and summer of 1999 and have been relatively stable since that time. We would anticipate that a regression to the historic mean would have resulted in a more gradual decline in homicides. This interpretation is supported by the analysis presented in Table 2 whereby the Indianapolis findings were consistent with a zero-order transfer function that tests for an abrupt shift in the series trend. It is also supported by the results reported in Appendix B that showed the greatest reduction was in the month following the intervention.

These findings are suggestive when considered in the context of recent studies finding that directed police patrol aimed at violent-crime hot spots may reduce firearms crime (Cohen & Ludwig, 2003; McGarrell, Chermak, Weiss, & Wilson, 2001; Sherman & Rogan, 1995). More directly, the findings of this study are also promising when read in light of the experience in Boston and Minneapolis (Braga et al., 2001; Kennedy & Braga, 1998; Kennedy et al., 2001). Combining Boston, Minneapolis, and Indianapolis, we see evidence from three cities experiencing group-related firearms violence that a lever-pulling strategy involving face-to-face communication of a deterrence message and a federal crackdown on a violent gang resulted in immediate and significant reductions in homicide. All three cities experienced what Kennedy has referred to as a "light-switch" impact on homicide.[11]

In addition to the nature of the specific interventions in Boston, Minneapolis, and Indianapolis, an additional common feature is that all three were part of a problem-solving approach whereby researchers were paired with practitioners. Patterns of homicide specific to each city were analyzed, and a focused deterrence strategy targeting these patterns of violence was implemented. These findings should be considered in light of other promising problem-solving crime-reduction interventions (e.g., Braga et al., 1999; Decker, 2003; Green, 1996; Weisburd & Green, 1995).

Given the threats to single-city evaluations of multiple component interventions, caution is appropriate in interpreting the results of the present study. On the other hand, the results across these three cities are quite consistent and promising in terms of the potential for reducing homicide. Clearly, there is a need for systematic experimentation[12] on the impact of lever-pulling interventions on homicide.

Appendix A   Demographic, crime, and employment comparison for the seven cities used in the time series analyses

City, State	Population (2000)	Homicide total (January 1997-June 2001)	Homicide rate per 100,000 (average per year)	Violent-crime rate per 100,000 (1999)	Percent non-White (2000)	Percent persons below poverty (1999)	Unemploy-ment rate (2000)
Cincinnati, Ohio	331,285	109	7.31	732.6	47	21.9	3.4
Cleveland, Ohio	478,403	376	17.46	1214.9	58.5	26.3	4.4
Columbus, Ohio	711,470	403	12.59	854.6	32.1	14.8	4.7
Indianapolis, Indiana	781,870	558	15.86	992.3	30.9	11.9	2.5
Kansas City, Missouri	441,545	679	34.17	1749.1	39.3	14.3	3.3
Louisville, Kentucky	256,231	236	20.47	862.9	37.1	21.6	3.3
Pittsburgh, Pennsylvania	334,563	423	28.01	877.6	32.4	20.4	4.1

Note. The general population and demographic figures, from the US Census Bureau, can be found at http://quickfacts.census.gov. The unemployment estimates, from the US Dept of Labor, can be found at http://www.bls.gov/lau/lamtrk00.htm. The homicide data are from the Supplementary Victim-Level Homicide Database. The violent-crime-rate measure is from the Sourcebook of Criminal Justice Statistics, 2000.

Appendix B
Examining the successive effect of the intervention

In order to assess the successive effect after the intervention month (month 28), we attempted to run a first-order transfer function model with the logged homicide data from Indianapolis. No model successfully estimated the logged data, so we relaxed the assumption of variance stationarity and used the first-order transfer function on the *raw count* of Indianapolis homicides. In order to address some of the nonstationarity problem, we differenced the series. This, we believe, gives us a good estimate of the successive effect. We were then able to model a first-order transfer function using homicide data in Indianapolis. We estimated the gradual effect on the raw number of homicides using the following equation, $Yt = (\omega 0/1 - d\ B)/t$, where Yt is the expected number of homicides per month in Indianapolis; ($\omega 0$ is the maximum likelihood estimated effect between pre-intervention and post-intervention at month 28 (–8.09); $\delta\ B$ (.605) represents the gradual rate of decline over the successive months starting in month 29; and $/t$ is the transfer function. From this, we are able to determine that the greatest effect is at month 28, which is an estimated mean difference of –8.09 in the raw number of homicides between pre-intervention and post-intervention. At month 29, it is –4.89 and continues to decline. Figure B1 represents the decline over the subsequent 6 months after month 28 using this model. The important point is that the greatest reduction is at month 28, the initial post-intervention month. The reduction then gradually declines. This is consistent with explanations that the violence-reduction intervention produced the observed effect.

Because we were more comfortable drawing our conclusions from the logged series, as it accounts for variance nonstationarity, we present the logged series in the main findings section.

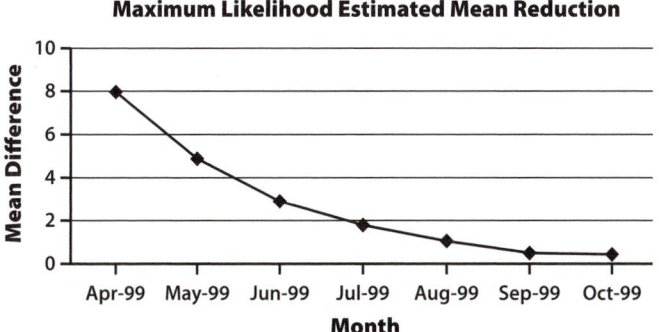

Maximum Likelihood Estimated Mean Reduction

Figure B1   Estimated effect after intervention.

Endnotes

[1] The specific crackdown on the Intervale Posse gang was preceded by a crackdown on another gang and followed by several additional crackdowns on gangs believed to be involved in gun crime (Kennedy et al., 2001).

[2] The Indianapolis initiative eventually became part of the Department of Justice's Strategic Approaches to Community Safety (SACSI) Initiative. The cities involved in SACSI ultimately implemented some variation of the lever-pulling strategy (Dalton 2003).

[3] Details on the homicide analysis are available in McGarrell and Chermak (2003b).

[4] The follow-up meetings were shorter, with fewer speakers. They reinforced the message of the original meeting. Where violence associated with the group or neighborhood had continued, the meetings often included the arrest of individuals who had violated conditions of probation or parole. Where there was no violence associated with the group or neighborhood, the meeting was held in a community setting and tended to have a more positive tone with community speakers likely to express their appreciation with the improved conditions in the neighborhood.

[5] See also McGarrell and Chermak (2003a).

[6] See Appendix A for a comparison of the seven Midwestern cities included in this study.

[7] Since the data are in natural-logarithm form, we follow the following mathematical rule that transforms the coefficient to read as a raw percentage change: [exponent $(-.42)$] $- 1.00 =$ .343 or 34.3 percent.

[8] See Appendix B for a detailed discussion of the estimated time series parameters in Indianapolis.

[9] The only city that had a marginal effect was Indianapolis, Indiana. See Appendix B.

[10] We also examined pre- and post-patterns of the characteristics of homicides. Homicides were less likely to involve guns, gangs, and drugs in the post-intervention period. They were also less geographically concentrated. Interviews with jail inmates suggested an increase in perceived certainty and severity of sanctions for gun crimes in the post-intervention period. The magnitude of these effects were all marginal but suggestive of an intervention effect. The findings are presented elsewhere (Chermak & McGarrell, 2004; McGarrell & Chermak, 2003a, 2003b).

References

Blumstein, A., & Rosenfeld, R. (1998). Explaining recent trends in US homicide rates. *Journal of Criminal Law and Criminology*, 88, 1175–1216.

Blumstein, A., & Waltman, J. (2000). *The crime drop in America*. New York: Cambridge University Press.

Box, G. E. P., & Jenkins, G. M. (1976). *Time series analysis: Forecasting and control*. San Francisco: Holden-Day.

Braga, A., Kennedy, D. M., Waring, E. J., & Piehl, A. M. (2001). Problem-oriented policing, deterrence, and youth violence: An evaluation of Boston's operation ceasefire. *Journal of Research in Crime and Delinquency*, 38, 195–226.

Braga, A., Weisburd, D., Waring, E., Mazerolle, L. G., Spelman, W., & Gajewski, F. (1999). Problem-oriented policing in violent crime places: A randomized controlled experiment. *Criminology*, 37, 541–580.

Bureau of Justice Statistics (2001). *Criminal victimization 2000: Changes 1999–2000 with trends 1993–2000*. Washington, DC: US Department of Justice.

Chermak, S., & McGarrell, E. F. (2004). Problem-solving approaches to homicide: An evaluation of the Indianapolis violence reduction partnership. *Criminal Justice Policy Review*, 15, 161–192.

Cohen, J., & Ludwig, J. (2003). Policing crime guns. In J. Ludwig a P. J. Cook (Eds.), *Evaluating gun policy* (pp. 217–250). Washington, DC: Brookings.

Cook, P. J., & Ludwig, J. (2000). *Gun violence: The real costs*. New York: Oxford University Press.

Cook, P. J., & Ludwig, J. (2003). Pragmatic gun policy. In J. Ludwig & P. J. Cook (Eds.), *Evaluating gun policy* (pp. 1–37). Washington, DC: Brookings.

Dalton, E. (2003). *Lessons in preventing homicide.* [On-line] Project Safe Neighborhoods Report, Michigan State University. Retrieved June 22, 2005, from http: // www.cj.msu.edu/%7Eoutreach/psn /erins_report jan_2004.pdf

Decker, S. H. (2003). *Policing gangs and youth violence.* Belmont, CA: Wadsworth. Federal Bureau of Investigation. (2005). *Uniform Crime Reports* [On-line]. Available: www.fbi.giv/ucr/civs_03/xl/03tbl01.xls (accessed 9/23/05)

Green, L. (1996). *Policing places with drug problems.* Thousand Oaks, CA: Sage.

Horney, J., & Marshall, I. H. (1992). Risk perceptions among serious offenders: The role of crime and punishment. *Criminology, 30,* 575–594.

Kennedy, D. (1997). Pulling levers: Chronic offenders, high-crime settings, and a theory of prevention. *Valparaiso University Law Review, 31,* 449–484.

Kennedy, D. (1998). Pulling levers: Getting deterrence right. *National Institute of Justice Journal,* July, 2–8.

Kennedy, D., & Braga, A. A. (1998). Homicide in Minneapolis: Research for problem solving. *Homicide Studies, 2,* 263–290.

Kennedy, D., Piehl, A. M., & Braga, A. (1996). Youth violence in Boston: Gun markets, serious youthful offenders, and a use-reduction strategy. *Law and Contemporary Problems, 59,* 147–196.

Kennedy, D. M., Braga, A. A., Piehl, A. M., & Waring, E. J. (2001). *Reducing gun violence: The Boston gun project's operation ceasefire.* Washington, DC: United States Department of Justice, National Institute of Justice.

McDevitt, J., Braga, A. A., Nurge, D., & Buerger, M. (2003). Boston's youth violence prevention program: A comprehensive community-wide approach, In S. Decker (Ed.), *Policing gangs and youth violence* (pp. 77–101). Belmont, CA: Wadsworth.

McGarrell E. F., & Chermak, S. (2003a). Problem solving to reduce gang and drug-related violence in Indianapolis. In S. H. Decker (Ed.), *Policing gangs and youth violence* (pp. 77–101). Newbury Park, CA: Wadsworth.

McGarrell E. F., & Chermak, S. (2003b). Strategic approaches to reducing firearms violence: Final report on the Indianapolis violence reduction partnership. Final Report submitted to the National Institute of Justice. Retrieved June 17, 2005, from http://www. ncjrs.org/pdffilesl/nij/grants/203976.pdf

McGarrell, E. F., Chermak, S. M., & Weiss, A. (2002). *Reducing gun violence: Evaluation of the Indianapolis police department's directed patrol project.* Washington, DC: United States Department of Justice, National Institute of Justice.

McGarrell, E. F., Chermak, S., Weiss, A., & Wilson, J. (2001). Reducing firearms violence through directed police patrol. *Criminology and Public Policy, 1,* 119–148.

Miller, T. R., Cohen, M. A., & Wiersema, B. (1996). *Victims costs and consequences: A new look.* Washington, DC: National Institute of Justice.

Moore, M. (1984). *Dangerous offenders: The elusive target of justice.* Cambridge, MA: Harvard University Press.

Nagin, D. S. (1998). Criminal deterrence research at the outset of the twenty-first century. In M. Tonry (Ed.), *Crime and justice: A review of research* (pp. 1–42). Chicago: University of Chicago Press.

Project Safe Neighborhoods. (2001). *Project safe neighborhoods: America's network against gun violence. Implementation guide for PSN partners.* Washington, DC: United States Department of Justice.

Sherman, L. H., & Rogan, D. P. (1995). Effects of gun seizures on gun violence: "Hot spots" patrol in Kansas City. *Justice Quarterly, 12,* 673–693.

Sherman, L. W., Gottfredson, D., MacKenzie, D., Eck, J., Reuter, P., & Bushway, S. (1997). *Preventing crime: What works, what doesn't, what's promising.* Washington, DC: US Department of Justice, National Institute of Justice.

Weisburd, D., & Green, L. (1995). Policing drug hot spots: The Jersey City DMA (drug market analysis) experiment. *Justice Quarterly, 12,* 711–742.

Wilson, J. M., Hiromoto, S., Fain, T., Tita, G., & Riley, K. J. (2004). *Homicide in San Diego: A case study analysis.* Santa Monica, CA: RAND, WR-142-OJP.

Wilson, J. M., & Riley, K. J. (2004). Violence in East and West Oakland: Description and intervention. RAND Working Paper WR-129-OJP. Santa Monica, CA.

28

Early Warning Systems for Police
Concept, History, and Issues

SAMUEL WALKER, GEOFFREY P. ALPERT, AND DENNIS J. KENNEY

Early warning (EW) systems have emerged as a new law enforcement administrative tool for reducing officer misconduct and enhancing accountability. EW systems are data-driven programs designed to identify officers whose behavior appears to be problematic and to subject those officers to some kind of intervention, usually in the form of counseling or training designed to correct the problematic behavior. Because of their potential for providing timely data on officer performance and giving police managers a framework for correcting unacceptable performance, EW systems are consistent with the new demands for performance evaluation raised by community policing (Alpert & Moore, 1993) and for the effective strategic management of police departments (Moore & Stephens, 1991).

The purpose of this article is to explore the concept of EW systems, the history of EW systems in American policing, and issues related to the program elements of EW systems. It reports the initial findings of a national evaluation of EW systems (Walker, Alpert, & Kenney, 1999). The evaluation involved a mail survey; municipal and county law enforcement agencies serving populations more than 50,000 people; and case studies of EW systems in three large, urban police departments.

The basic concept of EW systems is that law enforcement agencies should use data on problematic officer performance (e.g., citizen complaints, use-of-force incident reports, etc.) to identify those officers who appear to be having recurring problems or apparent problems interacting with citizens. As a retrospective, performance-based approach, an EW system is not designed

Samuel Walker, Geoffrey P. Alpert, and Dennis J. Kenney, *Police Quarterly,* Vol. 3, pp. 132–153, © 2000 by Sage Publications. Reprinted by permission of Sage Publications.

to prospectively predict officer performance based on officer characteristics (Stix, 1994). An EW system is "early" in the sense that it attempts to identify officers before their performance results in more serious problems (e.g., civil litigation, police-community relations crisis, etc.). An EW system itself does not involve formal discipline (although an officer may be disciplined for particular actions that led to identification by the system); rather, it is an attempt to warn an officer and/or correct his or her behavior. Some EW systems explicitly state that their purpose is to help officers improve their performance (New Orleans Police Department, 1998).

The intervention phase of EW systems generally consists of individual counseling by a supervisor or in a training class. It is informal in the sense that as explained above, it is not defined as a discipline within the terms of the agency's personnel procedures or collective bargaining agreement. Generally, no record of participation in an EW program per se is placed in an officer's personnel file, although the incidents that originally identified the officer (e.g., citizen complaints, use-of force reports) do remain in the officer's file and can be considered for discipline. A separate record of participation in the EW system is generally maintained by the internal affairs or professional standards unit of the police department.

EW systems have been endorsed by the U.S. Commission on Civil Rights (1981), the International Association of Chiefs of Police (1989), private consultants on police internal investigations (Reiter, 1998), and the 1996 Justice Department conference on Police Integrity (U.S. Department of Justice, 1997a). An EW system is incorporated in the consent decree negotiated by the Civil Rights Division of the Justice Department and the city of Pittsburgh (*United States v. City of Pittsburgh,* 1997). By 1999, an estimated 27% of all municipal and county law enforcement agencies serving populations greater than 50,000 had EW systems in place, and another 12% were planning to implement one (Walker et al., 1999).

The EW concept represents a departure from traditional police practice in which departments have been seen as punishment oriented, with innumerable rules and regulations that can be used against an officer (Westley, 1970, pp. 24–30) but with few procedures for rewarding good conduct. Alpert and Moore (1993, p. 129) argued that under community policing, police departments must develop performance measures that identify and reward "exemplary service to the community and the reduction or diffusion of violence," actions that have been essentially ignored by traditional performance evaluation systems. Apart from employee assistance programs designed to address substance abuse or family problems, police departments have done relatively little in a formal way to correct problem behavior. In the private sector, by comparison, personnel issues have become defined in terms of human resource development, with a specific emphasis on helping employees correct behavior that is not consistent with the organization's goals (Mathis & Jackson, 1999, p. 102).

The Problem Police Officer

Empirical Evidence

Interest in EW increased in response to growing evidence that in most law enforcement agencies, a small percentage of officers are responsible for a disproportionate share of citizen complaints, use-of-force incidents, or other problematic incidents. The phenomenon of the "problem officer" who receives a high rate of citizen complaints was first recognized in the 1970s. Toch, Grant, and Galvin (1975) developed a program in which Oakland, California, police officers with records of use-of-force incidents were counseled by peer officers. Goldstein (1977, p. 171) cited this program in a discussion of the need for identifying officers with a propensity for wrongdoing.

The U.S. Commission on Civil Rights (1981) published data indicating that a small group of Houston, Texas, police officers received extraordinarily high numbers of citizen complaints. In the aftermath of the 1991 Rodney King incident in Los Angeles, the Christopher Commission (1991) identified 44 problem officers in the Los Angeles Police Department (LAPD) with extremely high rates of citizen complaints. The commission commented that these officers were "readily identifiable" on the basis of existing LAPD records.

Investigative journalists have found the problem officer phenomenon in other police departments. In Kansas City, Missouri, 2% of the sworn officers were responsible for 50% of citizen complaints ("Kansas City Police," 1991). In Boston, 11% were responsible for 61.5% of complaints ("Wave of Abuse," 1992), and in Washington, D.C., a small number of officers were responsible for a large proportion of multiple discharge of firearms ("DC Police," 1998). With the exception of Kansas City, all of these reports found that police managers ignored patterns of repeated involvement in critical incidents and failed to take any kind of action against the officers with the worst records.

From Informal Knowledge to Management Tool

The concept of EW is consistent with the basic principles of personnel management and human resource development (Mathis & Jackson, 1999; Poole & Warner, 1998). Employers recruit, select, and train employees to serve effectively the goals and objectives of the organization. Effective personnel management assumes that employee performance is assessed and evaluated on a regular basis, and that the organization collects and analyzes performance data relevant for that purpose. It is also assumed that on an informal basis, each employee's immediate supervisor is familiar with the quantity and quality of the subordinate's performance (Mathis & Jackson, 1999, p. 102). Presumptively, systematic performance evaluations and supervisors' firsthand knowledge of employees is sufficient to identify those employees whose performance does not meet the organization's standards (Redeker, 1989).

Identifying problematic employees is a legitimate management goal as organizations seek to enhance the quality of the service they deliver and maintain positive relations with clients and customers. This is particularly important in human service organizations such as the police that routinely engage in a high level of interactions with citizen-clients (Bittner, 1970; Reiss, 1971). Alpert and Moore (1993, p. 130) argued that the goals of community policing require police departments to develop personnel evaluation systems that reward officers who avoid using force without justification (and by implication identify and properly discipline those who use excessive force).

Police personnel evaluation systems, however, have generally failed to provide meaningful assessments of performance. As Westley (1970, pp. 24–30) noted, police departments have been punishment oriented, with few formal programs for helping individual officers improve performance and little organizational focus on officers with recurring performance problems. Standard in-service training programs are generally directed at all sworn officers and not just officers with special performance problems. Employee assistance programs (EAPs), meanwhile, are generally voluntary and directed toward officers with marital, psychological, or substance abuse problems, not officers with on-the-street performance problems (Ayers, 1990; Finn & Tomz, 1997). Thus, for example, an overly aggressive officer who receives a high rate of citizen complaints but has no off-the-job personal problems would fall outside the scope of standard EAPs.

A review of police personnel evaluation systems nearly 25 years ago found that they had serious deficiencies. In particular, the formal categories for performance assessment were vague and global (e.g., "initiative," "dependability") (Landy, 1977). A more recent report, reflecting the concerns of community policing, rendered an equally critical assessment. Oettmeier and Wycoff (1997) concluded that "most performance evaluations currently used by police agencies do not reflect the work officers do" (p. 5). In particular, they fail to address the most critical aspects of police work, notably the exercise of discretion under conditions of uncertainty and stress, with the most important decisions involving the use of deadly or physical force. The neglect of these aspects of the job is particularly important because of the unique role of the police (Bittner, 1970). And, as Alpert and Moore (1993) argued, community policing creates the need for even more comprehensive and sophisticated performance evaluation systems.

The historic failure to address problem officers is particularly notable because, as Goldstein (1977) observed, those officers "are well known to their supervisors, the top administrators, to their peers, and to the residents of the areas in which they work"; nonetheless "little is done to alter their conduct" (p. 171). Insofar as law enforcement agencies took any kind of action, anecdotal evidence suggests that they "dumped" problem officers on racial minority neighborhoods (Reiss, 1971, pp. 167–168).

Two recent examples illustrate the extent to which some contemporary police departments have failed to collect, much less utilize, relevant data on potential officer misconduct. Prior to the 1997 consent decree with the U.S. Department of Justice (*United States v. City of Pittsburgh*, 1997), the Pittsburgh

Police Bureau did not have a comprehensive department-wide database on citizen complaints, use-of-force incidents, and other problematic behavior. Similarly, prior to 1999, the LAPD did not ensure that all citizen complaints brought to the attention of the department were in fact officially recorded and eventually forwarded to a centralized office (Office of the Inspector General, 1997).

History of the EW Concept

Emergence of the Concept

The first EW programs appear to have developed independently in a number of different departments in the late 1970s. The process of development was ad hoc and experimental, without the guidance of recommended or model programs. And because these initial programs appear to have been short lived, few records survive. Several departments began using indicators of activities to monitor officers' involvement in citizen contacts that involved use of deadly force and in response to growing public concern about that particular issue (Milton, Halleck, Lardner, & Albrecht, 1977). These initial approaches included review of arrest reports and identification of situations that involved the use of force by officers.

In Oakland, for example, records were kept on individual officers to determine whether any officers showed early signs of trouble. In addition, computers were used to determine whether any officer characteristics such as age, length of service, or education correlated with their use of force (Milton et al., 1977, p. 96). Toch et al. (1975) developed an experimental peer-counseling program directed toward officers with recurring performance problems.

In New York City, information on each officer's use of force, use of firearms, complaints, discipline, sick leave, and off-duty employment was used to determine whether that officer needed further monitoring or intervention. Officers who entered the information into the files were responsible for noting trends in behavior or activities and reporting them to a supervising officer (Milton et al., 1977, p. 96).

The Kansas City Police Department, meanwhile, cross-referenced officers with their supervisors "on the theory that particular supervisory officers may be tolerating abusive behavior" (Milton et al., 1977, p. 97). The department also participated in a Police Foundation experiment in peer counseling designed to improve the performance of officers with recurring problems (Pate, McCullough, Bowers, & Ferrara, 1976).

The concept of EW systems received its first official endorsement in 1981 by the U.S. Commission on Civil Rights in its report *Who Is Guarding the Guardians.* The report was based largely on hearings with regard to police misconduct in Philadelphia, Memphis, and Houston. It included data on Houston police officers indicating that a small percentage of officers received a disproportionate share of complaints. The commission recommended that police departments create and utilize early warning systems, arguing that the careful maintenance of records based on written complaints is essential to indicate officers who are frequently the subject of complaints or who demonstrate identifiable patterns of inappropriate behavior. Some jurisdictions have "early warning" information systems for monitoring officers' involvement in violent confrontations. The police departments studied routinely ignore early warning signs. (U.S. Commission on Civil Rights, 1981, p. 159)

The First Permanent EW Systems

The initial experiments with EW systems appear to have been short lived, and none of those identified by Milton et al. (1977) have survived to the present. The first EW systems known to have been maintained from their inception to the present were created in the Miami Police Department and in the Miami-Dade Police Department in the late 1970s.

Miami Police Department. The Miami Police Department became concerned with its officers' behavior that generated citizen complaints in 1979, in response to a major police-community relations crisis (Porter, 1984; U.S. Commission on Civil Rights, 1984). In a May 29, 1979, memorandum to the chief, the commander of the internal security unit suggested an EW system based on the principle of organizational development. That is, the development of the organization's capacity to provide better service to the public and to reduce both citizen complaints and the perception of poor service required attention to those officers and/or department practices that created real or perceived problems with the public. This memorandum proposed a "cyclical model where the problem is diagnosed, outside professionals are consulted, strategies are developed, programs are implemented and evaluated, and results are fed back to begin the cycle again" (Ross, 1979, p. 1).

To demonstrate his idea, Commander John S. Ross had identified a list of officers, by assignment, who had two or more citizen complaints during a two-year period (1976–1978). Ross also compiled a list of officers who had received five or more civilian complaints during that period. Armed with those data and the internal security monthly activity reports, Ross computed some interesting statistics. He found that the average number of complaints filed against a Miami police officer was .65 per year and 1.3 complaints for two years. He found that 5% of the officers accounted for 25% of all complaints. He noted, "If this group were suddenly removed from our department, our complaint picture could be reduced by as much as one-fourth. Obviously, this group should warrant some special attention, if we are to reduce our complaint incidence" (Ross, 1979, pp. 2–3).

At the midpoint in the study, the average Miami police officer was 32 years old with 8 years of service. The officers with five or more complaints were 27.5 years old with 4.2 years of service. The officers with the most complaints were disproportionately assigned to midnight shift. The complaint of excessive force made up 9% of complaints against all officers, but for those with two to four complaints, the complaint of excessive force made up 13% of complaints, and for those with five or more complaints, the figure increased to 16%. A similar relationship was found with complaints for harassment.

Ross (1979) suggested that commanders and supervisors should be systematically provided with information "that can be used to identify problem officers" (p. 7). He also noted that off-duty employment, including rock concerts, wrestling matches, and football games, generates a high number of citizen complaints. He reasoned that fatigue may "heighten an officer's opportunity to react in an aggressive manner" (p. 10). Ross suggested that the department should respond to these officers before they become involved in self-destructive activities or develop a trend of violating departmental orders. His proposal included more intensive supervision, counseling by outside professionals, and training in tactics and strategies. Ross (1979) concluded,

> The problem will not vanish, but it can be reduced through constant attention. The solutions will not be cheap, they will be time consuming, and may be difficult to implement. However, the potential is there to make a significant impact on the citizen complaint's [*sic*] against police officers. (p. 12)

The Miami EW system evolved into one of the more comprehensive approaches to monitoring police officers in the United States. Most important, it currently uses a broader range of performance indicators than other EW systems, many of which rely solely on citizen complaints as performance indicators (Walker et al., 1999). As officers are identified by the system, their supervisors are notified by official memorandum. The supervisor is then responsible for meeting with the officer and determining whether he or she needs any assistance, counseling, training, or other intervention.

The Miami EW system uses four categories of behavior as selection criteria for identifying officers (Departmental Order 2, Chap. 8). These data, which are routinely collected by the department and entered into a department-wide database, include the following:

1. Complaints—A list of all officers with five or more complaints, with a finding of sustained or inconclusive, for the previous two years

2. Control of persons (use of force)—A list of all officers involved as principals in five or more control-of-persons incidents for the previous two years

3. Reprimands—A list of all employees with five or more reprimands for the previous two years

4. Discharge of firearms—A list of all officers with three or more discharge of firearms within the previous five years.

An officer who is identified by the EW system is subject to a performance review by his or her supervisor. The internal affairs unit provides the supervisor with a report of each incident that caused the officer to be placed on the EW system. The supervisor evaluates these reports to determine whether the officer's behavior was consistent with professional standards (e.g., use of force justified by the circumstances, citizen complaint without merit) or whether there are behavior problems (e.g., unjustified use of force) that require attention. In this respect, the EW system is discretionary and not mandatory. Not all officers identified by the performance indicators will be referred for intervention.

In the case of officers requiring formal intervention, the supervisor then writes a memorandum recommending one of the following: reassignment, retraining, transfer, referral to an employee assistance program, fitness-for-duty evaluation, or dismissal pursuant to civil service rules and regulations. The supervisor's memorandum goes to the commander of internal affairs through the chain of command. Each reviewing supervisor must agree or disagree with the recommendation. It is important to note that, unlike some other EW systems, a number of supervisors are involved in decisions related to potential problem officers, with the result that these decisions represent a consensus of opinion.

Miami-Dade Police Department.   Several events took place in the Miami area during the late 1970s that created problems for police officers in the Miami-Dade Police Department, formerly the Metro-Dade Police Department, and Dade County Sheriff's Office. The beating of an African American school teacher and the beating death of another African American (insurance agent Arthur McDuffie) by Miami-Dade officers aggravated existing racial tensions in the Miami area. On May 17, 1980, the four officers accused of the death of McDuffie were acquitted by an all-White jury in Tampa. Upon notification of the verdict, three days of riots broke out that resulted in civilian deaths and millions of dollars in property damage (Porter, 1984; U.S. Commission on Civil Rights, 1982).

As a result of the problems, the Dade County Commission enacted local legislation that made public the internal investigations conducted by the Miami-Dade Police Department. In addition, an employee profile system was adopted to track formally all complaints, use-of-force incidents, commendations, discipline, and disposition of all internal investigations. As an offshoot of the employee profile system, the Miami-Dade Police Department implemented the early identification system (EIS) under the supervision of the Internal Review Bureau. This system was created because early signs of potential problems are often not apparent to officers and may be missed by some supervisors. It is not clear what role the city of Miami's EW system had in the development of the system for the Metro-Dade Police Department.

In 1981, a system of quarterly and annual EIS reports was instituted. Quarterly reports listed officers who had received two or more complaints that had been investigated and closed, or who were involved in three or more use-of-force incidents during a three-month reporting period. Annual reports listed employees who had been identified in two or more quarterly reports. The requirement that complaints be investigated and closed before they would qualify to be included in the quarterly report created a timing problem, because many complaints would take months before they were investigated and closed. Because of this problem, monthly reports were issued in 1992, which listed employees who had received two or more complaints during the past 60 days (regardless of disposition). It is these monthly reports that have identified officers with the most recent complaints or behavioral concerns. Major Dan Flynn (n.d., p. 2) reported that

> patterns of certain kinds of officer behavior, such as serious disputes with citizens and/or co-workers, or an above-average rate of using force, can be very predictive of more serious stress-related episodes to follow. Even though not all complaints and disputes are the fault of the involved officer, a process that enables a review of those events is invaluable. It makes it possible to reach officers who may be experiencing an escalating level of stress, before it gets out of hand and results in serious misconduct.

The monthly, quarterly, and annual reports are disseminated to the supervisors of the listed officers. The information on the list is "utilized by supervisors as a resource to determine if job stress or performance problems exist. They are designed as a resource in evaluating and guiding an employee's job performance and conduct" (Charette, n.d., p. 5). The information included in these reports is used by supervisors as one resource about an officer's performance and in conjunction with other information to provide a comprehensive picture of that officer's performance.

The immediate supervisor of any officer identified by the system receives a report on that officer. The supervisor then discusses the report with the officer and determines what further action is needed. The options include no further action or referral to departmental or outside programs, including psychological services, stress abatement programs, and specialized training programs. In 1981, 150 employees were identified in the two initial reports. In 1982, 46 employees were identified in all four quarterly reports. This decline is due to a number of factors, including the improved recruitment and selection procedures in the agency, not just the EIS. Between 1981 and 1992, departmental strength increased approximately 96%, but complaints remained at an average of approximately 300 per year. Charette (n.d.) concluded his report by noting: "A department's ability to monitor and control its employees [sic] conduct in a formalized tracking system, instills confidence in the employees, the organization, and the public it serves" (p. 12).

Issues Related to EW Systems

The national evaluation of EW systems found that they are complex administrative tools, with a number of different goals, program elements, and potential impacts (Walker et al., 1999). There is presently no consensus of opinion among professionals with regard to any of these issues. EW systems are also high-maintenance operations requiring careful planning and a high level of ongoing administrative attention. The following section discusses the various issues related to the development and ongoing administration of EW systems.

Program Goals

EW systems are widely understood to be directed toward so-called problem officers, with the goal of reducing on-the-street police misconduct (U.S. Commission on Civil Rights, 1981). The national evaluation, however, found that the goals of EW systems must be understood in broader terms. This interpretation follows developments in private sector employment where human resource development is seen as operating at three levels: individual, group, and organization (Poole & Warner, 1998, p. 93). Consistent with that approach, law enforcement EW systems can be understood to have separate program goals related to individual officers, supervisors, and departments as a whole.

Individual Officers. EW systems are directed in part toward individual rank-and-file officers. The anticipated impact on an individual officer involves learning theory, deterrence theory, or some combination of the two.

Many EW systems are officially conceptualized as a means of helping officers. The New Orleans Professional Performance Enhancement Program (PPEP), for example, explicitly states that it is designed to help and not punish officers. The intervention phase includes a stress reduction component and a training session designed to help officers understand how to handle potentially volatile situations without incurring citizen complaints. In this respect, the anticipated impact of EW systems on officers may be characterized in terms of a learning effect.

At the same time, an implicit assumption of EW systems is that they will deter future misconduct. That is, the intervention phase will communicate to subject officers the threat of punishment in the future if their present behavior continues (Zimring & Hawkins, 1973). There is also an implicit assumption that an EW system will have some general deterrent effect on officers not subject to the system. The system theoretically communicates the threat of punishment should their performance warrant placement on the EW system.

In at least one observed police department, the EW system had a labeling effect, and officers were observed to refer to themselves as "bad boys" and to the program as "bad boys school" and "politeness school" (Walker et al., 1999). Thus, one of the dangers of EW systems is that through a labeling process (Schur, 1972), they will reinforce undesirable attitudes (and perhaps undesirable performance) among subject officers.

Deterrence theorists point out that deterrence is a communication system and that research to date has not adequately explored the extent to which a threat of punishment is perceived by its intended audience (Nagin, 1998). The same problem applies to EW systems, whether conceptualized in terms of deterrence, learning, or labeling. Thus, it is possible that some officers will be readily deterred by an EW system, some will learn from the counseling or training they receive, and some will not be affected by either process. By the same token, some officers may embrace the label of bad boy whereas others will not.

The national evaluation found that EW systems in three sites are effective in reducing citizen complaints and use-of-force reports among officers subject to intervention. The data are reported in Walker et al. (1999).

Supervisors.   EW systems also have some impact on supervisors. This goal was explicitly acknowledged in two of the sites in the national evaluation (Miami-Dade and New Orleans), although in different ways, but not in the third (Minneapolis, Minnesota). The New Orleans PPEP requires the supervisor of a subject officer to monitor that individual for 6 months and to file performance evaluations every 2 weeks. Thus, the system has a formal mechanism for holding supervisors accountable for their behavior. New Orleans officials responsible for the PPEP expressed their belief that some supervisors would aggressively urge subject officers to improve their performance because further indicators of poor performance would reflect badly on them (Walker et al., 1999).

In Miami-Dade, several officials associated with the EW system explained that it "keeps things from slipping through the cracks." That is, the formal requirements of the program help ensure that a supervisor will pay closer than normal attention to an officer who is having performance problems and recognize that without such a safeguard the necessary attention may be lost in the rush of normal day-to-day work. The Minneapolis EW system paid little explicit attention to the behavior of supervisors (but see the subsequent changes in the program discussed below).

The potential impact of EW systems addresses an important issue in police management. Moore and Stephens (1991, p. 92) argued that one "particularly troubling deficiency" of traditional police management has been the lack of systems for monitoring the performance of supervisors. EW systems offer one potential remedy for that deficiency by defining specific activities related to holding officers under their command accountable. As is the case with the impact of EW systems on individual officers, however, there are a number of important but unresolved issues related to the impact of an EW system on supervisors. It is not known whether a formal monitoring process has a positive effect on supervisors or whether it is counterproductive because of the paperwork demands and a perceived intrusion into a supervisor's autonomy.

Departments.   EW systems also have some impact on the organizations in which they function. Organizational development is seen as one of the key goals of human resource management (Mathis & Jackson, 1999, pp. 98–102; Poole & Warner, 1998, p. 93). The national evaluation, however, found that this was the least well-articulated aspect of EW systems. In theory, an EW system improves the overall quality of police service to the extent that it effects improvements in the behavior of individual officers. At the same time, to the extent that an EW system changes the behavior of supervisors, it has some broader impact on the department. Finally, to an unknown extent, the existence of an EW system communicates a general message about a department's values, indicating that misconduct will not be tolerated. From this perspective, an EW system can be conceptualized as one means of controlling police department use of authority in the service of a comprehensive strategic management of police departments (Moore & Stephens, 1991).

With respect to organizations, the national evaluation found that instead of affecting organizations, EW systems are more likely to be affected by the organization in which they operate. At one extreme, an EW system is not likely to be effective in a police department that has no serious commitment to accountability and integrity and where serious forms of misconduct are not punished. In this context, the EW system may well become little more than a formal bureaucratic procedure, empty of meaningful content. The potential contributions of an EW system will simply be overwhelmed by the failure of the department to investigate alleged misconduct and discipline officers appropriately. It is also possible that a poorly managed EW system will generate hostility and cynicism among officers to the extent that it harms the larger organizational environment (Omaha Police Union, 1992).

At the other end of the continuum, an EW system is most likely to be effective in a department that has high standards of accountability and, as a part of that commitment, has in place a personnel data system that captures the relevant data on police officer performance. In one of the sites in the national evaluation (Miami-Dade), the EW system was found to be simply one part of a larger personnel data system that, in turn, is part of a broader commitment to accountability. In this context, the EW system functions as a management tool that converts the data into a usable form.

The vast majority of police departments undoubtedly fall somewhere in the middle of this continuum. In many of those instances, the EW system has the potential for helping to change the organizational culture and enhancing standards of accountability. Investigating the impact of EW systems on organizations was not part of the design of the national evaluation, and no systematic data on this issue exist (Walker et al., 1999). Further research is needed on this subject.

Program Components

EW systems consist of three basic components: selection criteria, intervention, and postintervention monitoring. The national evaluation found considerable variation in each of these components. There is also at present no consensus of opinion among law enforcement specialists as to the ideal components of an EW system.

Selection Criteria.   EW systems operate on the basis of a set of formal criteria for identifying problem officers and selecting them for intervention. The national evaluation found considerable variation in the selection criteria currently being used and a lack of consensus within the law enforcement community with regard to the appropriate set of criteria.

Some EW systems rely solely on citizen complaints (e.g., Minneapolis), whereas others rely on a broad range of performance indicators (e.g., Miami-

Dade and New Orleans). The indicators include but are not limited to official use-of-force reports, involvement in civil litigation, and violations of administrative rules (e.g., neglect of duty).

The use of multiple indicators provides a broader base of information about an officer's performance compared with reliance on citizen complaints alone. Citizen complaints are highly underreported (Walker & Graham, 1998) and therefore are unlikely to lead to the identification of officers whose behavior legitimately requires intervention. In a number of law enforcement agencies, citizen complaints are received by an independent citizen oversight agency (Walker, 2000). In these jurisdictions, it is not necessarily the case that the law enforcement agency receives timely or complete reports on all complaints filed.

Multiple indicators are more likely to identify officers whose performance is genuinely problematic and in need of some official intervention. Departmental use-of-force reports are widely used by EW systems, but their reliability depends on the scope of a department's reporting requirements, the extent of officer compliance with those requirements, and the existence of a data system that ensures that all relevant reports are entered into the EW database.

In sum, there are a number of unresolved issues related to selection criteria, including the best set of performance indicators to be used and the management infrastructure necessary to ensure that the relevant data are entered into the EW system. The national evaluation drew no conclusions with regard to the relative effectiveness of different selection criteria.

Intervention.   The intervention phase of an EW system may consist of either an informal counseling session between the officer and his or her immediate supervisor or a training class involving a group of officers (e.g., New Orleans).

With respect to individual counseling sessions, there are a number of issues related to the delivery and content of the counseling. In Minneapolis, for example, the requirement that supervisors document the counseling session was abolished after a few years. In the absence of documentation and close supervision, there is no guarantee that counseling sessions will in fact occur, that supervisors will deliver the appropriate message, or that counseling sessions will be consistent across supervisors. It is entirely possible that some supervisors simply tell their officers not to worry about it, with the result being that the goals of the EW system are undermined. Some EW systems involve higher ranking command officers (e.g., commander of professional standards or internal affairs unit) in the counseling sessions, thereby ensuring consistency and guarding against the delivery of inappropriate messages.

Group training sessions, such as the PPEP classes in New Orleans, have the advantage of ensuring consistency of content. At the same time, however, a group approach inhibits the delivery of the appropriate message to officers who may have very different performance problems. The group approach also runs the risk of creating solidarity among officers in the class, causing them to embrace the bad boys label and reinforcing inappropriate attitudes (Schur, 1972). This effect occurred in at least one known instance (Omaha Police Union, 1992).

The national evaluation was not able to determine whether one form of intervention is more effective than other forms (Walker et al., 1999). More research on this issue is needed.

Postintervention Monitoring.   Extreme variations are found among EW systems with respect to postintervention monitoring of subject officers. At one extreme are highly formal systems with considerable required documentation. At the other extreme are highly informal systems with no documentation.

The New Orleans PPEP represents a highly formal system. Subject officers are monitored for 6 months following intervention. Supervisors are required to observe subject officers on duty and to file a signed evaluation of officers' performance every 2 weeks (New Orleans Police Department, 1998). As noted above, this approach has the effect of putting supervisors on notice that their behavior is being monitored. Whether this approach has a positive effect on supervisors or is dysfunctional because of the increased paperwork requirements is not known.

Informal postintervention monitoring approaches rely on supervisors to monitor subject officers' performance and, in the event of further indicators of poor performance (e.g., citizen complaints), take whatever steps they deem necessary. In the absence of documentation or close supervision by higher ranking officers, however, there is no guarantee that the expected informal monitoring will occur.

One of the unresolved issues related to postintervention monitoring involves striking the proper balance between a formal bureaucratic approach designed to hold supervisors accountable and an informal approach designed to enhance efficiency and flexibility.

Program Administration

The national evaluation found that EW systems are complex, high-maintenance operations, requiring a significant investment by the department in planning, personnel, data collection, and administrative oversight.

The national evaluation found that in two of the sites (Miami-Dade and New Orleans), the system was established with considerable initial planning and ongoing administrative attention, whereas in the third site (Minneapolis), the EW system had received little in the way of administrative attention. Yet, in that third site, developments subsequent to the evaluation period indicate that considerable new attention has been given to the EW system and that it has been substantially strengthened as a result.

The administrative demands of an EW system are illustrated by the New Orleans Police Department's PPEP, the most elaborate EW system of the three case studies in the national evaluation. The department's Public Integrity Division employs one full-time (nonsworn) data analyst and uses part of the time of two other full-time employees (one of whom is sworn) for the purpose of data entry. The Miami-Dade EW system, meanwhile, is an integral part of a sophisticated data system on police officer performance that has been developed over the course of two decades.

Conclusion

EW systems have emerged as a popular remedy for police misconduct. The national evaluation has found that EW systems exist in slightly more than one fourth of all law enforcement agencies and are spreading rapidly. The national evaluation also found that EW systems vary considerably in terms of their formal program content, specifically with respect to selection criteria, the nature of the intervention, and postintervention follow-up. There are many unresolved issues related to these program elements, however, and it is not possible at present to specify any one approach that is the most effective.

EW systems are a potentially important management tool for the control of police officer misconduct and for promoting standards of accountability within a law enforcement agency. The national evaluation found, however, that EW systems are expensive, complex, high-maintenance operations, requiring a significant investment of administrative resources. There is evidence that some EW systems are essentially symbolic gestures with little substantive content. There is also some preliminary evidence that well-run EW systems are effective in reducing the number of citizen complaints and problematic behavior.

An EW system is no panacea for problems of misconduct and a lack of accountability. An EW system should be seen as part of a system of accountability. In a law enforcement agency without effective accountability measures in place, it is unlikely than an EW system will have much, if any, effect. At the same time, in an agency that has made a commitment to accountability, an EW system can serve as one of several management tools designed to curb misconduct and raise the quality of services delivered to the public.

References

Alpert, G., & Moore, M. H. (1993). Measuring police performance in the new paradigm of policing. In *Performance measures for the criminal justice system.* Washington, DC: Government Printing Office.

Ayers, R. M. (1990). *Preventing law enforcement stress: The organization's role.* Washington, DC: Government Printing Office.

Bittner, E. (1970). *The functions of the police in modern society.* Washington, DC: National Institute of Mental Health.

Charette, B. (n.d.). *Early identification of police brutality and misconduct.* Unpublished manuscript, Metro-Dade Police Department, Miami, FL.

Christopher Commission. (1991). *Report of the independent commission on the Los Angeles Police Department.* Los Angeles: City of Los Angeles.

DC police lead nation in shootings. (1998, November 15). *The Washington Post,* p. 1.

Finn, P., & Tomz, J. E. (1997). *Developing a law enforcement stress program for officers and their families.* Washington, DC: Government Printing Office.

Flynn, D. (n.d.). *Reducing incidents of officer misconduct: An early warning system.* Unpublished manuscript, Metro-Dade Police Department, Miami, FL.

Goldstein, H. (1977). *Policing a free society.* Cambridge, MA: Ballinger.

International Association of Chiefs of Police. (1989). *Building integrity and reducing drug corruption in police departments.* Washington, DC: Government Printing Office.

Kansas City police go after their "bad boys." (1991, September 10). *The New York Times,* p. 1.

Landy, F. (1977). *Performance appraisal in police departments.* Washington, DC: Police Foundation.

Mathis, R. L., & Jackson, J. H. (Eds.). (1999). *Human resource management: Essential perspectives.* Cincinnati, OH: Southwestern College.

Milton, C., Halleck, J., Lardner, J., & Albrecht, G. (1977). *Police use of deadly force.* Washington, DC: Police Foundation.

Moore, M. H., & Stephens, D. W. (1991). *Beyond command and control: The strategic management of police departments.* Washington, DC: Police Executive Research Forum.

Nagin, D. (1998). Criminal deterrence research at the outset of the twenty-first century. In M. Tonry (Ed.), *Crime and justice: A review of research* (Vol. 23). Chicago: University of Chicago Press.

New Orleans Police Department. (1998). *Professional Performance Enhancement Program (PPEP).* New Orleans, LA: Author.

Oettmeier, T. N., & Wycoff, M. A. (1997). *Personnel performance evaluations in the community policing context.* Washington, DC: Police Executive Research Forum.

Office of the Inspector General. (1997). *Six-month report.* Los Angeles: Los Angeles Police Commission.

Omaha Police Union. (1992, April). Bad boy/girl class notes shared. *The Shield,* p. 1.

Pate, T., McCullough, J. W., Bowers, R. A., & Ferrara, A. (1976). *Kansas City peer review panel: An evaluation.* Washington, DC: Police Foundation.

Poole, M., & Warner, M. (1998). *The IEBM handbook of human resource management.* London: International Thomson Business Press.

Porter, B. (1984). *The Miami riot of 1980.* Lexington, MA: Lexington Books.

Redeker, J. (1989). *Employee discipline: Policies and practices.* Washington, DC: Bureau of National Affairs.

Reiss, A. J. (1991). *The police and the public.* New Haven, CT: Yale University Press.

Reiter, L. (1998). *Law enforcement administrative investigations* (2nd ed.). Tallahassee, FL: Lou Reiter and Associates.

Ross, J. S. (1979, May 29). Citizen complaints against police officers (Memorandum from Commander John S. Ross to Chief Kennith I. Harms).

Schur, E. (1972). *Labelling deviant behavior.* New York: Harper & Row.

Stix, G. (1994, December). Bad apple picker: Can a neural network help find problem cops? *Scientific American,* 44–45.

Toch, H. J., Grant, D., & Galvin, R. T. (1975). *Agents of change.* New York: John Wiley.

United States v. City of Pittsburgh (W. D. PA., 1997).

U.S. Commission on Civil Rights. (1981). *Who is guarding the guardians.* Washington, DC: Author.

U.S. Commission on Civil Rights. (1984). *Confronting racial isolation in Miami.* Washington, DC: Government Printing Office.

U.S. Department of Justice. (1997a). *Police integrity: Public service with honor.* Washington, DC: Government Printing Office.

U.S. Department of Justice. (1997b). *Police use of force: Collection of national data.* Washington, DC: Government Printing Office.

Walker, S. (2000). *Police accountability: The role of citizen oversight.* Belmont, CA: Wadsworth.

Walker, S., Alpert, G. P., & Kenney, D. (1999). *Responding to the problem police officer: A national evaluation of early warning systems.* Interim final report, National Institute of Justice.

Walker, S., & Graham, N. (1998). Citizen complaints in response to police misconduct: The results of a victimization survey. *Police Quarterly, 1,* 65–90.

Wave of abuse claims laid to a few officers. (1992, October 4). *The Boston Globe,* p. 1.

Westley, W. A. (1970). *Violence and the police.* Cambridge, MA: MIT Press.

Zimring, R. E., & Hawkins, G. J. (1973). *Deterrence: The legal threat in crime control.* Chicago: University of Chicago Press.

29

Putting the "What Works" Research into Practice
An Organizational Perspective

JENNIFER L. FERGUSON

Over the past decade, significant advances have been made in correctional research. This research has resulted in an increased sense of optimism that correctional assessment and treatment can be effective. "What works" has emerged as a popular theme to describe effective correctional services. Some attempt has been made to describe how organizations can take this research and implement it into daily practice (Bonta, 1997). However, the focus has been on what should be done and the steps that need to be taken without giving attention to how to implement these steps or the challenges that might be experienced while doing so. The lack of attention to the practical implementation of what works is problematic for organizations that wish to engage in effective correctional services. This article aims to address this issue by describing how one probation department implemented research-based practice as part of the daily routine of the organization.

What Works

In the 1970s, the phrase "nothing works" took hold with the publication of Martinson's (1974) article titled "What Works? Questions and Answers About Prison Reform." This phrase was used to describe the apparent lack of effectiveness of correctional rehabilitation and helped steer correctional practice in a more punitive direction, with an increased reliance on sanctions as a means of crime control. Since that time, the research has been reviewed again and new research has been conducted, resulting in a recognition that criminal

Jennifer L. Ferguson, *Criminal Justice and Behavior*, Vol. 29 No. 4, copyright © 2002 by Sage Publications. Reprinted by permission of Sage Publiations.

sanctions alone have a minimal effect on recidivism (Andrews et al., 1990). This research has also found that treatment can be effective and can reduce recidivism. The key ideas of correctional research have changed and the focus is now on what works.

What has emerged as key principles of effective correctional intervention are the principles of risk, need, and responsivity (Andrews and Bonta, 1994; Andrews, Bonta, and Hoge, 1990). These principles help define the appropriate targets for treatment and how treatment should be delivered. They also help link assessment to treatment and highlight the importance of assessment to the delivery of effective treatment programs (Gendreau, 1996).

The risk principle states that treatment services should be matched to the risk level of the offender (Andrews and Bonta, 1994; Andrews, Bonta, and Hoge, 1990). Individuals who are high risk should receive the most intensive services, whereas those who are low risk should receive minimal intervention and services. This principle is supported by research that has found that low-risk individuals who have received intensive services have had no change or increases in their level of recidivism, whereas high-risk individuals who receive intensive services show reductions in levels of recidivism (Andrews, Bonta, and Hoge, 1990).

The need principle focuses on the factors that should be targeted through intervention and states that appropriate targets for correctional intervention are criminogenic needs. Criminogenic needs are dynamic risk factors that can be changed through treatment and where change is known to reduce recidivism (Andrews and Bonta, 1994).

The responsivity principle suggests that characteristics of the offender, such as personality and learning style, influence how he or she responds to different types of treatment. As a result, for treatment to be more effective, the style and mode of services should be matched to the individual. For example, clients who are anxious may do better in a supportive, nonconfrontational treatment environment.

Assessment is a key component to effectively implementing the risk, need, and responsivity principles. Because advances have been made in learning what is needed for effective correctional intervention, advances have also been made in the type of assessment that should be conducted to help with the delivery of effective treatment programs. Bonta (1996) has identified different generations of assessment to highlight the advances that have been made. The first generation of correctional assessments conducted was primarily based on the professional judgment, intuition, and gut-level feelings of the individual conducting the assessment. The information collected and the way that information was interpreted could vary from person to person.

The second generation of assessment moved toward a more standardized assessment. Specific criteria were identified to be included in each assessment conducted. However, the focus was primarily on static risk factors, which are factors that contribute to an individual's risk to reoffend but cannot be changed. For example, an individual's age at first juvenile adjudication is a factor that is often measured through risk assessment tools. However, no intervention can be conducted that will change the age the first juvenile adjudication occurred. During this generation of assessment, the information provided by the risk assessment was used primarily to determine appropriate levels of supervision.

The second generation of assessment also gave some attention to assessing an individual's needs to identify potential targets for treatment. These assessments were conducted independently of the risk assessment, and risk and needs were viewed as separate concepts.

Building on the second generation of assessment, a third generation of risk and needs assessment has been identified. In the third generation of assessment, risk and needs are viewed as related concepts that should be included in a single assessment tool. Needs are recognized as dynamic risk factors that contribute to an individual's overall risk to reoffend. When both static and dynamic risk factors are included within a single assessment tool, the assessment is strengthened and can help direct offenders to the type of services they should receive and also to the appropriate level of services.

Recent research also has identified key predictors of recidivism. Both static (historical) and dynamic (changeable) factors have been found to be significant predictors of recidivism, although some factors are stronger predictors than others. The strongest predictors have been identified as adult criminal history, antisocial personality, criminal attitudes, and companions (Andrews and Bonta, 1994; Gendreau, Little, and Goggin, 1996). The research has also found that composite risk scores, which combine information from several predictor domains (as is usually done in a combined risk and needs assessment), are the strongest predictors of recidivism (Gendreau et al., 1996).

Along with the advances in assessment, the correctional research highlights characteristics of effective treatment programs. This research has found that when certain characteristics are present, reductions in recidivism can range from 25 to 60 percent (Gendreau, 1996). Effective treatment programs are those that adhere to the principles of risk, need, and responsivity; provide cognitive behavioral programming; enforce program rules in a firm but fair manner; provide more positive reinforcers than punishers; use therapists that respond in sensitive and constructive ways; and use therapists who have appropriate training and supervision.

The shift in research findings away from "nothing works" to a focus on "what works" means that correctional practice also must shift from a get-tough law-and-order focus, relying strictly on sanctions, to a more balanced approach that includes both sanctions and treatment. There is some evidence that organizations that are in the business of correctional practice are willing to make this shift. For example, in its position paper on probation, the American Probation and Parole Association (APPA, 1987) stated that "probation . . . views itself as an instrument for both control and treatment appropriate to some, but not all, offenders" (p. 1). However, although the knowledge base of what contributes to effective correctional services has grown and organizations appear committed to implementing what works, there has been little practical guidance on how organizations can take this research and implement it in daily practice. The title of Bonta's (1997) recent article, "Offender Rehabilitation: From Research to Practice," suggests that this type of guidance exists. In that article, Bonta identified three steps that should be followed to put research findings on assessment and treatment into practice. First, there needs to be an organizational commitment to the value of rehabilitation. This commitment must include the dedication of time and resources. Second, valid instruments need to be used to accurately assess offender risk and needs. The final step is to use cognitive-behavioral approaches to improve the effectiveness of treatment. Although these are necessary steps, little guidance is provided about how to achieve them. There is no discussion of the practical challenges that might be experienced while trying to implement any of the steps. These shortcomings pose problems for organizations that wish to implement research findings and engage in effective correctional services.

The Maricopa County Adult Probation Department (MCAPD)

The MCAPD is an organization that is trying to take the current findings of correctional research and implement them in the daily practice of the organization. The current strategies being used to accomplish this include conducting a combined risk and needs assessment and providing programs that attempt to adhere to the principles of effective correctional intervention.

A primary responsibility of the MCAPD is to provide supervision to individuals sentenced to probation through the Superior Court of Arizona, in Maricopa County. At any given time, active supervision is provided to approximately 23,000 individuals on standard probation and 1,800 individuals on intensive probation supervision. The department also provides presentence recommendations for all individuals coming through the Superior Court of Arizona, in Maricopa County. Approximately 15,000 presentence investigations are conducted each year.

In addition to the supervision and presentence investigation services provided by the department, efforts are made to provide a number of programs that meet the needs of the offenders. These programs may be provided internally by the department, or other agencies may be used to provide these services.

A key component that shapes how the MCAPD operates is the use of a combined risk and needs assessment tool. The remainder of this article focuses on how the department implemented this tool as part of everyday practice of the organization and includes a discussion of how it was developed and implemented, the challenges faced, and the lessons learned.

Implementing a Risk and Needs Assessment Tool

Organizational Commitment to Research-Based Practice

As a first step toward implementing a risk and needs assessment tool and similar to the first step that Bonta (1997) identified for putting research into practice, the MCAPD made a commitment to implementing research-based practice and to using the findings of research to guide the strategies used by the organization. The importance of organizational commitment has been cited as important to obtaining quality work (Crosby, 1984; General Accounting Office, 1993; Hunt, 1993). If something is important to management, it will be viewed as important to staff.

The MCAPD made the commitment to conducting research-based practice by incorporating it in the strategic plan of the department, which outlines the priorities of the organization. The commitment to research-based practice first appeared in the strategic plan developed in 1996. This commitment could be seen in statements such as "All department programs will be based on empirically validated research" and "The department will use (a risk/needs assessment tool) and individual screening tools to assess client needs."

The organizational commitment to research and to implementing research-based practice was maintained and strengthened when the strategic plan was revisited at the end of 1999. One of the strategies identified for accomplishing the mission of the department was "working in partnership with the community to provide research-based prevention and intervention services." Although providing prevention and intervention services was part of the 1996 strategic plan, the words "research-based" were added, demonstrating the commitment to putting research into practice.

New goals were also developed that highlighted the commitment to research. One goal was "to utilize proven and effective methodology to assess and change behavior of offenders through effective case management." A goal specific to research was also added that stated that the department wanted "to increase our use of internal research-based information to make quality decisions."

Selecting an Assessment Tool

The commitment to implementing research-based practice also included conducting the type of assessment that was supported by the research literature. The MCAPD wanted to conduct meaningful assessments of the individuals coming through the department that would allow assessment information to guide decisions about its level of supervision an individual should receive and also to guide program planning. However, in 1996, when the department reviewed the current assessment practices, it recognized that there were some problems with the assessments that were being conducted.

First, different instruments were being used to assess risk and to assess needs. The risk assessment and the needs assessment were modeled after the

Wisconsin risk and needs assessment tools (Baird, 1981). Although the instruments were standardized and allowed the same information to be gathered on each individual, risk and needs were treated as separate entities. An individual's risk level was not being used to inform decisions about the level of treatment services that should be received.

Second, the risk assessment conducted focused primarily on static factors. Whereas conducting both the risk and the needs assessment allowed static and dynamic factors to be assessed, the dynamic risk factors were not considered when determining the individual's overall risk level, and they did not inform the level of services needed.

Finally, concerns existed about the quality with which the assessments were being conducted. The risk and needs assessments were often conducted as an afterthought and completed quickly at the last minute. They were viewed as something that had to be done, and the information contained in the assessment was not necessarily viewed as useful to staff. Staff generally did not use the assessment information that was available to make decisions.

As a result of the review of existing assessment practices, the MCAPD recognized a need to change the assessment tool that was being used. In particular, an assessment tool was desired that would provide a broad, overall assessment of the risk and needs of the offender. The assessment tool should contain both static and dynamic risk factors that focus on the key predictors of criminal behavior. Also, the assessment tool should allow the information to be used to determine the overall risk the individual posed to reoffend, the appropriate targets for services or intervention, and the appropriate level of services. The department also wanted to select an assessment tool and develop an assessment process that would make risk-needs assessment more meaningful and valuable to staff.

The MCAPD considered two options when selecting an assessment tool that would meet its needs. One was to use an existing validated risk and needs assessment tool, and the other was to create a new tool that incorporated the existing research. The advantages and disadvantages of each approach were considered before making a decision.

Assessment tools do exist that would meet the needs of the MCAPD. One of the most commonly used assessment tool is the Level of Service Inventory-Revised (LSI-R) (Andrews and Bonta, 1995). There are a number of advantages to using an existing assessment tool. An existing tool is likely to have many resources already in place, such as the forms, training curriculum, a pool of trainers, and software. It is also likely that an existing tool has already been validated, increasing the amount of confidence that people have in the instrument. For example, a significant body of research literature exists that discusses the reliability and validity of the LSI-R (Andrews, Kiessling, Mickus, and Robinson, 1986; Loza and Simourd, 1994) and that discusses its use with different offender populations (Bonta and Motiuk, 1987; D. J. Simourd and Malcolm, 1998). One of the disadvantages is the cost of purchasing the tool, which may be an ongoing expense.

Developing a new assessment tool also has advantages and disadvantages. When developing a new tool, staff can be involved in the process, which may help increase staff willingness to use the information provided by the assessment. There may also be fewer ongoing costs. However, developing a new tool has the disadvantage of not being validated, and more work is required to develop the instrument, the training curriculum, and to train trainers.

The Offender Screening Tool (OST)

The MCAPD made the decision to develop its own tool, called the OST. One reason for the decision was the cost required to use an existing tool given the large number of assessments the department conducts each year, along with the department's desire to engage in reassessment. Another key factor was a concern about resistance of staff to a change in the way assessment was being conducted. Because there was a desire to conduct assessment that was meaningful to staff, the decision was made to involve staff in the development of the OST.

At the same time that a decision was made to develop the OST, the decision was also made to reengineer the presentence division. The reengineering decision was made because the presentence process had become complex and labor intensive. There were also a number of areas where work was being duplicated. The redesigned process would eliminate the duplication of effort and also introduce the OST as the risk and needs assessment tool of the department.

The current version of the OST was developed and implemented in 1998. The OST is administered at the presentence level, and information used to score the OST is gathered as part of a larger presentence interview. The presentence interview is automated, so interviewers enter the information directly into the computer. At the end of the interview, the OST is automatically scored.

The content of the OST incorporates the existing research on assessment. The OST gathers information in 10 categories that are supported by the research as predictors of an offender's criminal behavior. The 10 categories are (a) physical health/medical, (b) vocational/ financial, (c) education, (d) family and social relationships, (e) residence and neighborhood, (f) alcohol, (g) drug abuse, (h) mental health, (i) attitude, and (j) criminal behavior. The items on the OST include both static and dynamic criminogenic risk factors.

The OST also focuses on those factors that are the strongest predictors of recidivism. Although all the factors included in the OST are predictors of recidivism, those categories that are stronger predictors are weighted more and contribute more to the offender's composite risk score. For example, where an individual lives and who an individual lives with can influence criminal behavior. This is measured through the residence and neighborhood category of the OST. However, residence and neighborhood is not as strong a predictor as attitudes that may be supportive of criminal behavior. As a result, the residence and neighborhood section of the OST contains two items, whereas the attitude section contains seven items and makes a greater contribution to the overall risk score.

Once scored, the OST provides information about an offender's risk and needs. All the items on the OST are used to create a composite risk score. Cutoff scores have been statistically determined based on Maricopa County's offender population to identify risk levels of low, medium, and high. Need scores also exist for each category. A rational cutoff has been created to highlight those areas where an individual may need treatment or intervention. The risk score, in combination with the information provided in each category, can also help identify the level of services needed. Preliminary validation research (Grobe, Simourd, Lessard, and Ferguson, 2000) has been conducted on the OST, which suggests the tool has considerable promise as an appropriate risk and needs assessment instrument.

The risk and need information generated by the OST is used by staff throughout the MCAPD. The OST is implemented as part of the presentence investigation and can be used, along with other information, to inform the recommendations of presentence officers. It is also intended for probation officers in the field to inform their case management and supervision plans.

Training on the OST

Once the OST was developed, a key to successful implementation was to provide staff with enough information and training to allow them to incorporate the assessment and its results into their daily work. Multiple trainings were developed. The presentence division was trained on both the administration of the OST and how to interpret the results. The rest of the department, from support staff to probation officers to upper management, was trained on how to interpret the OST and how to use it to develop case management and supervision plans. What was important in developing each training was to tailor the training as much as possible to the needs of the group being trained.

The most significant training component was the training provided to the entire department on how to interpret the OST and use it for case plans. To help this training go more smoothly, the MCAPD developed a written training curriculum to ensure the essential information was consistently provided to staff. The key information the department hoped to convey through the training included (a) a discussion of the history of assessment and the advances that have been made; (b) specific information about the OST, including how it was developed and the categories that were assessed; (c) a discussion of OST scores and the information they provide; and (d) a discussion of how to interpret the OST and use the information to guide decisions. Sample cases were included, so training participants could practice interpreting the scores.

At the end of the training, a training assessment was conducted. The assessment was designed to gather information in two areas. One was to test participants' knowledge of the information provided during the training. In general, it was important to know if the participants understood the concepts that were presented. Some of the issues tested through the MCAPD's assessment included the following questions; (a) Is the difference between static and dynamic risk factors understood? (b) Is the importance of assessing multiple risk factors understood? (c) Do participants understand how to interpret the composite risk score? (d) Do participants understand how to identify areas in need of treatment or intervention? (e) Do participants understand how risk level influences the level of services an individual should receive?

The second type of information that was gathered was participants' perceptions of the OST. For example, do participants believe they could explain the purpose of the OST to others? Questions were also asked about whether probation staff believe the OST will help them in their jobs. Finally, the training assessment asked staff to identify any concerns they had about the OST or about using the information the OST provides to guide decisions.

The training assessment conducted by the MCAPD provided administrative staff with confidence that the trainers did a good job of conveying the essential information of the training. However, the assessment also highlighted which concepts were most difficult for people to understand. One of the most difficult concepts was the idea that someone who poses a low risk to reoffend may not need to receive intensive services, even if they do have a need that should be addressed. Receiving this information helped the trainers identify some different ways to present this information so it could be more easily understood.

The training assessment also highlighted the concerns that staff had about using the OST to do their jobs. Some of the common concerns were potentially receiving inaccurate information through client self-report and the loss of professional judgment. Receiving this information helped highlight some of the potential obstacles that may interfere with staff using the information provided by the OST to guide their decisions. With this information, the department could work to identify strategies to help address these concerns.

Another component of the implementation of the OST and the reengineered presentence process was the creation of the Quality Assurance Council (QAC). The QAC was created to help demonstrate the commitment to quality, which has been identified as a key to success (Crosby, 1984; General Accounting Office, 1993; Hunt, 1993). The purpose of the QAC was to help identify where errors could occur in the presentence process and to identify ways to minimize or eliminate those errors. The MCAPD wanted to be sure that quality information was gathered through the presentence interview and used to make informed decisions. It also wanted to be sure there was a mechanism in place to address questions and concerns about the OST and about the presentence process. The QAC addressed issues such as the need for ongoing training, workload concerns, and the need for technical support. It was in the meetings of the QAC that many of the challenges faced during the implementation of the OST were discussed.

Challenges

The MCAPD has been successful in developing and implementing the OST as the risk and needs assessment being conducted by the department. As a result, the MCAPD has achieved its goal of incorporating research-based assessment in the daily practice of the organization. However, the implementation of the OST did not occur without significant challenges, some of which are still ongoing. Some of the challenges experienced by the MCAPD, as well as the strategies used to address them, are described in this section.

Perceived Loss of Discretion

Research on assessment acknowledges that structured assessments are better predictors of criminal behavior than clinical judgment (Glaser, 1987; Meehl, 1954). As a result, assessments are better when they are structured and objective, ensuring that all clients are assessed using the same criteria. This shift to a more structured assessment resulted in concerns of probation staff that they no longer had any discretion when making presentence recommendations or when developing case management plans. The following quotes describe the essence of their concerns: "It (the OST) will be too standardized so that individual judgment will be lost." Another person expressed a concern "that the professional judgment aspect will slowly fade out." This perceived loss of discretion poses a significant challenge when implementing research-based assessment because it can contribute to a resistance to change.

While implementing the OST, it was important for the MCAPD to acknowledge this concern of staff. As one staff member commented, "Officers need to be reassured the OST does not replace professional judgment, it complements it." Trainers tried to respond to this concern. They drew on the work of Andrews and Bonta (1994) when presenting this message. Andrews and Bonta highlighted that in addition to the principles of risk, need, and responsivity, professional judgment plays a role in effective assessment. Trainers presented the message that the information provided by the OST, along with their professional judgment, was a powerful tool. Trainers also acknowledged that the information provided by the OST was not the only information that needed to be considered when making a decision. For example, when making a presentence recommendation, the officer also needs to consider the seriousness of the offense and the concerns of the victims so that there is a balance between the needs of the victim, the offender, and the community. These messages helped staff feel they were still a valued part of the assessment process and that their experience was still valued. It also helped to reassure them that the department would still support them if they used their professional judgment.

Obtaining Quality Information

Another area that posed a challenge was obtaining quality information. Quality assessment information is essential if the assessment tool is going to be used to inform decisions. Two challenges were experienced related to quality information. One was a concern of probation staff about the quality of the information contained in the OST The second challenge was making sure that probation staff gathered quality information.

Probation staff members were concerned that the information provided by the OST would not be meaningful because it was gathered through self-report. They were concerned that the offender may not be honest and that information provided by the offender may not be accurate or give a true picture of the client. Trainers acknowledged that sometimes offenders are not honest or provide misleading information. They also emphasized that although information is initially gathered from the offender through an interview, the offender should not be the only source of information used to gather information for the OST. Information should still be verified through official records. Trainers stated that when there were inconsistencies between the information provided by the client and the information obtained from other sources, the information should be changed to reflect the official records.

Staff also expressed a concern that the OST does not address all factors. As an example of this concern, one person commented that "human behavior is more complex than a questionnaire." Related to this, staff was concerned that the OST would not provide enough information for specialized caseloads, such as sex offenders. To address this concern, several key messages were presented. One was to emphasize that the OST was designed to be a general risk and needs assessment tool that could be administered to a broad offender population. The assessment tool would become too long and cumbersome if all potential risk factors were included. However, the OST did consider multiple risk factors and incorporated those that were considered some of the strongest predictors of criminal behavior.

Another message was that there was value in having a general assessment conducted on each offender. There are common risk factors across offender groups that contribute to the risk to reoffend (D. J. Simourd and Malcolm, 1998; L. Simourd and Andrews, 1994). A general assessment tool can help identify areas in need of treatment or intervention that may not be recognized if the only assessment conducted was related to the offending behavior. At the same time, there is value to specialized assessment, and a general assessment can identify areas where there might be a need for further assessment. For example, when there is an elevated score in the drug category of the OST, a more detailed substance abuse assessment is conducted. Additional assessments are also conducted when there is an elevated score in the attitude category of the OST.

Although staff members were concerned about the quality of the information provided by the offender, the MCAPD also wanted to ensure that quality data were collected and maintained by probation staff. Having quality data was viewed as important not only for the case-by-case decisions but also for research that would be done to validate the OST. One issue was making sure staff members were conducting quality interviews. A number of strategies were used to address this. Prior to conducting any interviews, the presentence screeners were provided training that included a component on interviewing skills. The training addressed issues such as how to listen effectively, how to treat the offender with respect, and how to ask probing questions to obtain more detailed information. Once a number of interviews were conducted, focus groups were held with interviewers to obtain feedback. The key questions for the focus groups were whether there were any questions that the offenders had difficulty understanding and whether there were any questions where the interviewers were uncertain about the question's intent. Clarifying item intent was important to ensure that everyone was interpreting and answering the questions the same way. The feedback provided during the focus group was used to develop refresher training.

Another step taken to verify consistency across interviewers was to have an independent observer attend a number of interviews and record responses to the questions. The similarity between the interviewer's OST scores and the observer's OST scores were then compared. The close relationship that was found between the two scores gave the department confidence that when properly trained, the OST could be administered consistently.

Mechanisms were also built into the automated system to help ensure quality. One feature was to make each question that contributed to the OST score a required question. If the question was not asked and answered, a drop-down menu box would appear on the computer screen informing the interviewer that he or she had missed a question. The interviewer was prevented from continuing until the question had been answered. This was important because the OST was designed as a structured assessment, and it helped ensure that each person was assessed using the same questions.

It was also important to ensure that all staff members were using the same version of the automated system because enhancements or corrections were occasionally made. To do this, whenever a change had been made, staff members were prompted to update their version of the program. They could not access the system until it had been updated.

Maintaining Appropriate Levels of Resources and Support

The changes that were made to the presentence process, which included the implementation of the OST, were significant. The process was reengineered in part to help use existing resources more effectively and efficiently. At the same time, it was important that the number of resources and support that were dedicated to the effort were sufficient to ensure its successful implementation. The resources and support included organizational commitment, staff, time, training, equipment (e.g., computers, software, printers), and technical support. The OST was initially implemented as a pilot project in the presentence division. The intent of the pilot project was to help manage the change and to help identify the resources that would be needed. Once the department was comfortable with the new presentence process and the implementation of the OST on a small scale, it was implemented departmentwide.

One of the biggest challenges was anticipating and maintaining resource levels once the project was implemented. It was difficult to anticipate the ongoing resource needs. The Quality Assurance Council played a key role in identifying those needs because it provided a forum to raise concerns and identify problems so resources could be directed to the issue.

Managing Workload

It has been noted that the OST was implemented as one part of a reengineered presentence process. One of the reasons for undertaking the reengineering project was to minimize the duplication of effort that previously existed. One description of the presentence process called it a "a complex process that is difficult to describe and labor intensive." The example that was often used to highlight the duplication of effort that occurred was that an individual name had to be entered into the system 20 different times. Although an exaggeration, it highlighted the problem. As a result, there was a concern with managing workload. This was also a concern of staff who were trained in the OST. They expressed concerns about the amount of time it would take to complete and that it would add more paperwork.

It was difficult to address concerns about workload. Trainers tried to emphasize that this was a new and different way to look at risk and needs rather than something additional that needed to be done. However, trainers also had to acknowledge that it might require more time. What trainers tried to emphasize was how the OST could benefit staff and help them do their job. Based on responses to a training assessment item, it appears that trainers were effective in conveying this message. Staff members were asked to state in their own words why the department was using the OST. One of the top responses was to help officers do their job. Other responses also identified ways the OST could help, such as by identifying levels of treatment supervision, prioritizing treatment needs, and developing case management plans. They also stated it could help supervise clients better and help officers make better decisions.

Resistance to Change

By definition, reengineering involves making radical changes in the way work is done. As a result, significant changes were taking place that staff needed to adjust to. Comments made during the training acknowledge staff concern about the changes being made. One comment was "It will be a major shift in the way we do business and that will be difficult for officers to adjust to the change." Staff also raised a concern about continual change and suggested that by the time they adjusted to this change, it would be changed again. One staff person said, "I'll get used to it and be told there is a new tool to use."

As with the other concerns raised by staff, it was important to acknowledge this concern. It was more difficult to respond to it because change can be necessary to remain a vital organization. What was emphasized was the need for this change and how it would add value to the work that staff members do.

Lessons Learned

With all the challenges experienced, an important question to ask is whether the investment of time and resources was worth the effort. To answer that question, it is important to go back and review what the MCAPD hoped to accomplish by reengineering the presentence process and implementing the OST. The MCAPD hoped to develop a process that would allow it to use resources wisely while responding to growth in the number of cases coming through the presentence division. The MCAPD also wanted to conduct a more systematic assessment that would be meaningful to probation staff.

Some noticeable changes have occurred that suggest the investment made was worth the effort. The workload of the presentence division has continued to grow, but the increase in workload has been managed with the existing resource levels. Information is also being gathered more systematically at the presentence level, and assessment is a routine part of the staff's job. The information gathered also appears to be meaningful and is allowing more time to be devoted to the high-risk and high-needs cases.

Because of the positive results, the MCAPD will continue its efforts to implement research into practice. At the same time, the MCAPD hopes to remember some key lessons learned from this experience. First, it is important to have the commitment of the organization, especially the top levels of management, for implementation to be successful. The support of management will help address other challenges experienced along the way, such as the need for sufficient resources, how to manage the changes that are taking place with the organization, and providing a consistent message to staff about the need for the change.

Second, once a commitment has been made, sufficient resources need to be committed to the effort. Resource needs should be anticipated beyond the initial implementation and should include the resources needed to sustain the project or program.

Third, it is important to invest in good-quality training. Devoting resources to training, such as developing a written training curriculum and developing a pool of quality trainers, will help sustain the project.

Fourth, as something new is implemented, be sure to acknowledge the concerns of staff as they adjust to the change. This includes providing them with opportunities to voice their concerns and planning for ways to respond to those concerns.

Finally, be prepared to face challenges and anticipate what those challenges may be. It will not be easy to implement the findings of research into practice and organizations need to be prepared for that. The experience of the MCAPD in implementing risk and needs assessment helps highlight the practical steps needed to implement the findings of research in the daily practice of an organization. While specifically applied to the implementation of risk and needs assessment, they can also be applied to the implementation of other research findings, such as appropriate treatment programs. MCAPD's experience helps fill a gap that has existed in the literature by addressing how to implement research findings. The lessons learned can help organizations committed to implementing effective correctional service and research-based practice achieve that goal.

References

American Probation and Parole Association. (1987). *Probation*. Retrieved July 26, 2001, from the American Probation and Parole Association Web site: http://www.appa-net.org.

Andrews, D. A., & Bonta, J. (1994). *The psychology of criminal conduct.* Cincinnati, OH: Anderson.

Andrews, D. A., & Bonta, J. (1995). *The level of service inventory—revised.* Toronto, Canada: Multi-Health Systems.

Andrews, D. A., Bonta, J., & Hoge, R. D. (1990). Classification for effective rehabilitation: Rediscovering psychology. *Criminal Justice and Behavior, 17,* 19–52.

Andrews, D. A., Kiessling, J. J., Mickus, S., & Robinson, D. (1986). The construct validity of interview-based risk assessment in corrections. *Canadian Journal of Behavioral Science, 17,* 19–52.

Andrews, D. A., Zinger, I., Hoge, R. D., Bonta, J., Gendreau, P., & Cullen, F. T. (1990). Does correctional treatment work? A clinically relevant and psychologically informed meta-analysis. *Criminology, 28,* 369–404.

Baird, C. (1981). Probation and parole classification: The Wisconsin model. *Corrections Today, 43,* 36–41.

Bonta, J. (1996). Risk-needs: Assessment and treatment. In A. T. Harland (Ed.), *Choosing correctional options that work: Defining the demand and evaluating the supply* (pp. 18–32). Thousand Oaks, CA: Sage.

Bonta, J. (1997). Offender rehabilitation: From research to practice. Retrieved October 21, 1998, from the Solicitor General Canada Web site: http://www.sgc.gc.ca/epub/corr/e199701/e199701.htm.

Bonta, J., & Motiuk, L. L. (1987). The diversion of incarcerated offenders to correctional halfway houses. *Journal of Research in Crime and Delinquency, 24,* 302–323.

Crosby, P. B. (1984). *Quality without tears: The art of hassle free management.* New York: McGraw-Hill.

Gendreau, P. (1996). Offender rehabilitation: What we know and what needs to be done. *Criminal Justice and Behavior, 23,* 144–161.

Gendreau, P., Little, T., & Goggin, C. (1996). A meta-analysis of the predictors of adult offender recidivism: What works! *Criminology, 34,* 575–607.

General Accounting Office. (1993). *An audit quality control system: Essential elements.* Washington, DC: Author.

Glaser, D. (1987). Classification for risk. In D. M. Gottfredson & M. H. Tonry (Eds.), *Prediction and classification: Criminal justice decision making.* Chicago: University of Chicago Press.

Grobe, B., Simourd, D. J., Lessard, S., & Ferguson, J. (2000, July). *The offender screening tool: One department's answer to risk assessment.* Paper presentation at the annual convention of the American Probation and Parole Association, Phoenix, AZ.

Hunt, V. D. (1993). *Quality management for government: A guide to federal, state and local implementation.* Milwaukee, WI: ASQC Quality Press.

Loza, W., & Simourd, D. J. (1994). Psychometric evaluation of the Level of Supervision Inventory (LSI) among male Canadian federal offenders. *Criminal Justice and Behavior, 21,* 468–480.

Martinson, R. (1974). What works? Questions and answers about prison reform. *The Public Interest, 35,* 22–54.

Meehl, P. E. (1954). *Clinical versus statistical prediction: A theoretical analysis and a review of the literature.* Minneapolis: University of Minnesota Press.

Simourd, D. J., & Malcolm, P. B. (1998). Reliability and validity of the Level of Service Inventory-Revised among federally incarcerated sex offenders. *Journal of Interpersonal Violence, 13,* 261–274.

Simourd, L., & Andrews, D. A. (1994). Correlates of delinquency: A look at gender differences. *Forum on Correctional Research, 6,* 26–31.

30

Criminal Justice System Reform and Wrongful Conviction
A Research Agenda

MARVIN ZALMAN

The exoneration of hundreds of prisoners since 1989, and the plausible belief that thousands of wrongful convictions occur each year, underlie the importance of wrongful conviction as a policy issue (Gross, Jacoby, Matheson, Montgomery, & Patil, 2005). "Wrongful conviction" is not only the conviction of a factually or "actually" innocent person.[1] It also describes an emerging movement and an evolving multidisciplinary academic subject. Paradoxically, although wrongful conviction has generated extensive legal, psychological, and forensic science research, the subject has not been significantly addressed by criminal justice scholars (Leo, 2005). This article highlights the issue's policy significance and suggests avenues for research by criminal justice scholars.

Wrongful Conviction as a Policy Issue

This section describes the policy salience of wrongful conviction, the nature of the emerging innocence movement, the movement's reform and research agenda, and the limited nature of innocence research by criminologists and criminal justice scholars. This discussion sets the stage for discussing potential avenues of criminal justice innocence research.

Wrongful Conviction on the Public and Policy Agendas

Fear of convicting the innocent is intrinsic to justice systems and predates the wrongful conviction (or innocence) movement (Blackstone, 1769/1979, p. 352; Volokh, 1997). Several 20th century books and films identified wrong-

Marvin Zalman, *Criminal Justice Policy Review,* Vol. 17, pp. 468–492, © 2006 by Sage Publications. Reprinted by permission of Sage Publications.

ful convictions but had little influence on criminal justice thinking or practices prior to the mid-1980s (Borchard, 1932; Frank & Frank, 1957/1971; Leo, 2005).[2] Erle Stanley Gardner (1952), creator of the fictional defense attorney Perry Mason, failed in the late 1940s to institutionalize a short-lived "Court of Last Resort" created to correct miscarriages of justice. In political science terms, wrongful conviction was not on the public or governmental agendas.

The innocence movement that now exists is based in part on research that significantly undermined faith in the accuracy of the criminal justice process, especially DNA testing, first used to exonerate a defendant in 1989 (Leo, 2005, pp. 205–206; Medwed, 2005, p. 1117). Its ability to prove with astronomically high probability that likely perpetrators deposited biological evidence, and its power to absolutely rule out DNA donors among convicted defendants, shattered social and professional disinterest in miscarriages of justice and created traction for wrongful conviction as a public issue (Connors, Lundregan, Miller, & McEwan, 1996; Leo, 2005, p. 205). In addition to DNA testing, the cumulative work of psychologists since the 1970s has cast doubt on the unerring accuracy of eyewitness identification (Doyle, 2005, pp. 129–132; Wells et al., 1998). The "DNA revolution" forced a reevaluation of the criminal justice system's capacity to function according to Packer's (1968, pp. 160–161) crime control model, in which factual errors are thought to be minuscule.

Two factors were especially salient in putting wrongful conviction on the public and policy agendas. First, Attorney General Janet Reno authorized an influential Justice Department study that highlighted the ability of DNA testing to undermine convictions, especially those based on eyewitness identification (Connors et al., 1996; Doyle, 2005, pp. 127–130, 165–167). The Justice Department followed up with a report on improved methods of interviewing witnesses and conducting lineups (Doyle, 2005, pp. 169–187; Technical Working Group for Eyewitness Evidence, 1999). Second, *Actual Innocence* was published (Scheck, Neufeld, & Dwyer, 2000). To their great credit, the lawyer and journalist authors of this popular book went beyond empathetic storytelling about the innocent people they helped free. They conceptualized the wrongful conviction project in terms of specific kinds of errors and organized the chapters of *Actual Innocence* around them. These were drawn together in an appendix—a "Short List of Reforms to Protect the Innocent"—which was slightly expanded in the 2003 edition (Scheck et al., 2000; Scheck, Neufeld, & Dwyer, 2003, pp. 351–362). The book's lack of academic refinement is an advantage in reaching a mass audience. The inclusion of sources, however, acknowledges the debt owed by the innocence movement to varied and expanding fields of knowledge outside the law. To a significant degree, the innocence movement's policy and research agenda is set out in *Actual Innocence* and has been shaped by Scheck and Neufeld's leadership in opening new arenas, including programs to assist exonerees.[3]

Wrongful conviction is now an issue on the public agenda. The news media, long supportive of prosecutors, are now sensitized to miscarriages of justice, and their continuing reports of exonerations keeps the issue in the public eye (Tulsky, 2006; Warden, 2003). A stream of popular books and documentaries attest to a market for true accounts (Blakeslee, 2005; Edds, 2003; Holden, 2005; Humes, 1999; Johnson, 2003; Junkin, 2004). Novels and dramas portray wrongful convictions (Barnes, 2005; Feige, 2006a; Patterson, 2005). *The Exonerated* (Blank & Jensen, 2004) not only played off Broadway and on tour but was made into a television production and shown on Court TV. This publicity is not entirely happenstance, as innocence projects (described in the next section) have promoted some of it (Scheck et al., 2000; Vollen & Eggers, 2005). The movement's leaders appear to understand that innocence reforms require public opinion support.

Innocence movement reforms are on the governmental agenda (see Zalman, 2005). The *Innocence Protection Act*, passed after four years in the congressional hopper, was a most significant movement victory (Leahy, 2004a, 2004b). This watered-down part of the 2004 *Justice for All Act* provides, inter alia, standards and funding for DNA testing of potential exonerees (Weich, 2005). At least 38 states and the District of Columbia have passed innocence statutes allowing appeals by prisoners with claims based on DNA evidence but who have exhausted appellate remedies (C. E. Jones, 2005, p. 1249; Zacharias, 2005, pp. 193–195). The videotaping of police interrogations is spreading (Sullivan, 2005). Several states and a number of police departments have begun to adopt lineup reforms (Lindo, 2000). The *Justice for All Act* "increased the amount of compensation for those wrongfully convicted of federal crimes to up to $100,000 a year for death row exonerees, and $50,000 a year for non-death row exonerees" (Innocence Project, n.d.), and bills to compensate exonerees have been introduced in several state legislatures, including those of Georgia, Michigan, and Utah (Hunt, 2006; "State Should Offer," 2006; C. Tucker, 2005).

The most notable item on the innocence reform agenda is capital punishment. In what is arguably the best known wrongful conviction story, by 2000, 13 men on death row in Illinois had been exonerated, prompting then-Governor George Ryan to impose a moratorium on executions, appoint a commission to study the death penalty, and, before leaving office in 2002, commute the death sentences of all Illinois death row inmates. The 207-page report of the Illinois Governor's Commission on Capital Punishment (2002) made 85 recommendations that have become blueprints for reform. Other states have considered or imposed death penalty moratoria, and the American Bar Association (ABA) established a Death Penalty Moratorium Implementation Project. Widespread knowledge of death row exonerations is credited with reenergizing the anti-death penalty movement and with a decline in capital sentences and executions since 2000 (Kirchmeier, 2002; Steiker & Steiker, 2005; Warden, 2005).

The Innocence Movement

Unlike Gardner's (1952) abortive efforts to create a court of last resort, an institutional response has emerged to do the legal work needed to exonerate prisoners and the policy work designed to promote the issue. It began with a law school-based clinical program in 1992 led by Barry Scheck and Peter Neufeld (Scheck et al., 2000, 2003), which has grown into a multipurpose nonprofit organization—the Innocence Project (n.d.). About 40 law school clinical programs or other legal organizations (e.g., public defenders' offices), half of them established after 2000, now screen and litigate cases for prisoners claiming innocence (Medwed, 2003; Stiglitz, Brooks, & Shulman, 2002). These projects reflect an American penchant for grassroots solutions to contentious issues that involve governmental impropriety (Zalman, 2005, pp. 187–189).

Two innocence projects, the Innocence Project (n.d.) at Cardozo Law School and the Center for Wrongful Conviction (n.d.) at Northwestern University, have expanded into multifunction organizations designed to promote systemic reforms.[4] The Center for Wrongful Conviction has three stated functions: legal representation, research into the systemic problems that cause wrongful convictions, and community service to raise awareness of the causes and costs of wrongful conviction. The latter goal includes assisting exonerees to reintegrate into the community after years in prison (Center for Wrongful Conviction, n.d.).

Beginning in 2001, Scheck and Neufeld and other innocence project leaders met annually to consider their collective interests. The National Innocence Network was formalized in 2005 with membership limited to innocence projects. Its three goals are to represent potential exonerees in court, to provide assistance for exonerees on release, and to work for policy reforms designed to reduce wrongful convictions. To advance the latter goal, the Innocence Project hired a policy director to manage legislative and policy reform and to train local innocence projects' personnel in lobbying skills (National Innocence Network Conference, 2005). In one policy area for example—improving the accuracy and integrity of forensic laboratories—the Innocence Project has worked to create audit oversight committees in a number of states to ensure laboratory quality, to suggest improvements, "and possibly to evaluate wrongful convictions and assist in determining what went wrong" (Cromett & Thurston Myster, 2005).

The innocence movement is not limited to innocence projects. It includes cognitive psychologists who have tested new lineup methods in thousands of experiments (Wells et al., 1998) and innocence commissions established to investigate the wrongful conviction issue (Mumma, 2004). It includes nonprofit organizations designed to promote the goals of criminal justice reform (Justice Project, n.d.), to investigate cases (Centurion Ministries, n.d.), or to report wrongful conviction news (Justice Denied, n.d.). It includes authors who write about miscarriages of justice, documentary filmmakers, lawyers who take appeals on behalf of potentially innocent appellants, therapists who help exonerees, and scholars who research wrongful conviction issues. Exonerees such as Kirk Bloodsworth have become part of the movement by working for innocence reform or by participating in publicity events. The innocence movement has some attributes of a reformist social movement, a point of departure for potential research initiatives discussed below.

The Innocence Movement's Reform and Research Agenda

If wrongful conviction is viewed as a multidisciplinary academic subject, its backbone of knowledge is contained in a list of topics that are deemed to be causes of wrongful conviction. This perspective makes the innocence movement's reform agenda coterminous with the wrongful conviction research agenda. Leo (2005) notes that the "standard list" of causes began with Borchard's (1932) tally of factors associated with wrongful convictions. A version is found in the chapter outline and appendices of Scheck et al. (2003, pp. 205, 212–213), and it may have achieved canonical status with its adoption by an ABA committee (Gianelli & Raeder, 2006). The ABA report includes separate chapters with analyses and recommendations on six causes of wrongful conviction: false confessions, eyewitness identification procedures, forensic evidence, jailhouse informants, defense counsel practices, investigative policies and personnel, and prosecution practices. It concludes with a chapter on compensation for the wrongly convicted. Similar lists and parallel analyses are found in many sources, including the Illinois Governor's Commission on Capital Punishment (2002), the Innocence Commission for Virginia (2005), and a scholarly anthology (Westervelt & Humphrey, 2001). The basic list of causes and remedies can be expanded. Scheck et al. (2003, pp. 358–362), for example, include creating statewide innocence commissions and the creation of an innocence network, reflecting the Innocence Project's goals.

A point worth noting is that some rhetoric of innocence advocates is radically transformative. Neufeld asserted that the larger goals of innocence projects "is 'nothing less than the complete overhaul of the criminal justice system with a new awareness of how to make it more reliable" (Vollen & Eggers, 2005, p. 256). A lawyer who litigated cases for exonerees believes that large judgments in civil lawsuits for exonerees might bring "diverse actors together to collaborate on systemic change in our criminal justice system," leading to "widening ripple effects throughout the policing industry . . . [having] a great impact on law enforcement" and "the most far-reaching and effective criminal justice system reform that our country has experienced since the Warren Court's criminal procedure revolution" (Garrett, 2005, pp. 45, 7–8, 111).[5] Although not all rhetoric by the movement's leaders is so transformative,[6] it suggests that emotions among innocence activists are akin to those of participants in reformist social movements. Transformative rhetoric may be driven by a belief that urgent action is needed because widespread DNA testing in criminal cases will eliminate easily observable miscarriages; this may cause publicized exonerations to decline and so undermine popular support for innocence reforms before the problems that cause wrongful convictions are corrected (Scheck et al., 2003, p. 323; Steiker & Steiker, 2005, p. 622).[7] This fear is belied by the high proportion of exonerations not based on

DNA testing and by the plausibility that thousands of miscarriages of justice occur every year (Gross et al., 2005).

Each component of the standard list of innocence reform is itself a major area of research, whose scholars and scientists command daunting bodies of recondite knowledge and research. This poses potential tensions between activists eager to implement reforms based on existing knowledge and scholars who argue for continuing research. A legal scholar eager for implementation, for example, has incautiously suggested that "the scholarly work on false confessions, faulty eyewitness identifications, and other predictable problems of proof is largely complete" (Siegel, 2005, p. 1222). Few doubt that imposing best-practices laboratory standards, videotaping interrogations, improving lineup procedures, or the like will reduce errors and improve criminal justice practices, but it seems risky to shut the door on continuing research in these areas. In addition, further research may qualify or enrich earlier findings, necessitating updating and modification. Conflicting research findings or challenges to the quality of innocence research can be expected to generate controversy.[8]

The wrongful conviction research agenda is curiously incomplete. It fails to acknowledge the adversary system itself as a source of error despite recent innovative scholarship on comparative trial and justice systems and on evidence law theory and practice (Burns, 1999; Damaka, 1986, 1997; Lerner, 2001). Perhaps such studies are so theoretical and so unlikely to change constitutionally embedded practices as to be irrelevant to the innocence movement. But more practical jury research exists on issues such as the comprehensibility of jury instructions, juror note taking and witness questioning, and jurors discussing cases before formal deliberations begin (Dann & Hans, 2004). Jury research has been underway for decades and has generated proposals adopted in several jurisdictions, so it is unlikely that innocence movement leaders are unaware of it. These practical jury reforms might plausibly reduce wrongful convictions and yet are not found on the standard list of wrongful conviction issues.

Speculation as to why the innocence movement has largely overlooked the adversary trial includes the fact that the innocence narratives did not make a connection between trial procedures and erroneous verdicts. Such connections are not as easily observed as the effects of mistaken eyewitness identification and the like. Trial errors are embedded in trial transcripts (which are expensive and not automatically provided), and it requires painstaking legal analysis to sift through them to identify errors, as was done by pro bono lawyers for the Innocence Commission of Virginia (2005). In addition, the innocence movement's leaders are litigators who are not conditioned to see a properly operating trial as a problem, even while documenting such failures as a prosecutor, acting within the bounds of professional propriety, befuddling an honest witness on cross-examination (Scheck et al., 2003, pp. 25–27).

Trial issues were not entirely ignored by legal scholars concerned with wrongful convictions. An early and insightful article explored but did not completely answer the questions of whether the adversary jury trial, when working properly, can be a source of error and why trials often fail to filter out errors occurring earlier in the criminal justice process (Givelber, 1997). More recently, an evidence law theorist has generated an intriguing potential solution to trial-generated error by proposing two kinds of adversary system jury trial procedures (Risinger, 2004). The usual criminal trial would be reserved for cases involving "polyvalent facts" (e.g., intent in a homicide or rape case) where the criminal act is stipulated and a jury is well-suited to explore issues of motive and intent. For "who-done-it" cases, where a jury is called on to determine what happened ("binary facts"), Risinger (2004) sketches a stipulated procedure in which the adversaries agree to forego the rich storytelling tradition of adversary advocacy and instead focus on the facts (pp. 1307–1313). He also suggests adopting an "unsafe verdict" standard of guilt under such a procedure that has been adopted for appeals in England (pp. 1313–1333). Additional recent analyses by legal scholars have explored trial issues and wrongful conviction including acquittals (Givelber, 2005), the pretrial process (Leipold, 2005), an archaic and arguably unconstitutional South Carolina procedure that allows prosecutors to control criminal trial dockets (Siegel, 2005), and the preservation of evidence (C. E. Jones, 2005).

A final point about the wrongful conviction policy agenda, related to its partial focus, is the practicality of the standard list of reforms. The list was derived from counting factors associated with miscarriages of justice in the wrongful conviction narratives, beginning with Borchard (1932; see Harmon, 2001; Leo, 2005). Given the terrible consequences of wrongful convictions, there is an urgency to establish policies to correct such deficiencies as inadequate defense counsel, poorly equipped and operated forensic laboratories, and the like. There is little premium on conducting theoretical or basic research into the items on the innocence agenda, although some exists (e.g., Cole, 2005). Many items on the agenda are the special preserve of lawyers (e.g., prosecution and defense counsel issues), and most of the law review writing on innocence-related subjects is aimed at generating policy rather than legal theory. Issues concerning forensic science require major input from forensic scientists, laboratory directors, and forensic examiners, and innocence activists are not competent to generate innovation but only to lobby to ensure that proper procedures are followed. Police investigation intersects with important matters on the innocence agenda, but the study of the investigative process had its heyday in the 1970s, and there has been little research focusing on investigation by criminal justice scholars in recent years. In sum, much of the research on wrongful conviction is fragmented into various specialties, is mostly applied research, and is not within the competence of most criminal justice scholars.

The Paucity of Criminal Justice Innocence Research

Richard Leo (2005, pp. 208–211), noting that most wrongful conviction research has been conducted by lawyers and psychologists, identified three specialized areas of empirical research: eyewitness identification, child suggestibility, and false confessions. Significantly, this work has led to proposed reforms. Leading research psychologists, for example, made their findings about eyewitness identification accessible to policy makers and have assisted in policy reform efforts (Doyle, 2005; Wells, 2001; Wells et al., 1998). Research by child witness experts has led to substantial improvements in how police and courts treat child witnesses (ABA Task Force on Child Witnesses, 2002; Ceci & Bruck, 1995; Gilstrap, Fritz, Torres, & Melinder, 2005). Leo, a leading authority on confessions, has helped to make the study of false confessions an area of sociolegal and criminal justice scholarship (Drizin & Leo, 2004; Leo & Ofshe, 1998) and a concern of psychologists (Gudjonsson, 2003; Wrightsman & Kassin, 1993). As a result, many police departments have begun to videotape interrogations (Sullivan, 2005).

In contrast, Leo (2005, p. 214) identified only two or three studies by criminologists that have explored the causes of wrongful conviction (Harmon, 2001; Huff, Rattner, & Sagarin, 1986; Lofquist, 2001).[9] Although a few others can be located (Denov & Campbell, 2005; Poveda, 2001; Schehr, 2005; Schoenfeld, 2005), this is remarkable when considering that Wells et al. (1998) estimated that more than 2,000 psychological research articles on eyewitness identification were in print almost a decade ago. I estimate that several hundred law review articles have been published on wrongful conviction topics in recent years, with a few based on empirical analysis (e.g., Campbell & Denov, 2004; Gross et al., 2005).[10] Leo does not ask why so few criminologists have studied wrongful conviction but seeks to stimulate empirical research by urging criminologists to eschew research into the "legal causes" and instead study the "actual root causes" of wrongful convictions. In this perspective, it is a simplistic or unexamined assumption that once the causes of wrongful conviction are identified "we will know how and why the problem of wrongful conviction occurs" (Leo, 2005, p. 213). Deeper causal and theory-generating research is needed to determine why the causes of wrongful conviction occur in the first place. Criminologists, for example, should ask, "What are the causes of eyewitness misidentification?" and the like (Leo, 2005, p. 213). Leo cites Lofquist (2001) as an exemplary study. Lofquist explored the structural dynamics within a police department that led to the identification of an innocent suspect as the perpetrator. Note that Leo's conclusion that the deeper "criminological" research called for relies on organizational methods and theory.

Leo (2005) concludes by urging criminologists to move beyond legal categories and to draw on "existing social science frameworks" to build theories of miscarriages of justice. He specifically references psychological, sociological, and organizational frameworks for research. For example, psychological research could "study how the process of memory and perception formation" and the like "underlie a variety of psychological errors . . . and how those errors then lead to wrongful prosecution and conviction" (p. 215). "Sociologically, [criminologists] . . . need to study how the institutions of criminal justice . . . are structured and how the decision making, actions, and ideologies of these social actors are patterned in the production of both accurate and inaccurate outcomes" (p. 215). As for an organizational perspective, Leo recommends that "criminologists need to look at the microlevel and macrolevel forces, contexts, and structures that underlie the normal processes and production of perception, belief, and error in American criminal justice" (p. 216). He ends by tempering enthusiasm of potential wrongful conviction scholars by specifying the huge obstacles to this research: the lack of a database, the unlikelihood of police and prosecution support, and the inherent difficulties of determining whether wrongful convictions occurred from assembled case files (pp. 217–218).

A Criminal Justice Wrongful Conviction Research Agenda

Leo's (2005) insightful depiction of the state of wrongful conviction research misspecifies the target audience by directing his remarks to criminologists and suggests too narrow a model of empirical innocence research, oriented mainly toward generating theories of the causal dynamics of wrongful convictions. He then suggests that this worthy goal is virtually unattainable because no database exists, primary case materials are very difficult to assemble, and it is inherently difficult to prove that a conviction was erroneous (pp. 216–217). Curiously, by holding up Lofquist (2001) as a model of wrongful conviction research, Leo glosses over the fact that it is more aptly categorized as organizational rather than criminological research. Analysts in business schools and in departments of public administration, organizational psychology, sociology, and criminal justice are better equipped to pursue such studies. Leo may be using criminology as shorthand for criminology and criminal justice, a reasonable assumption as these disciplines are coming to be housed in the same departments and as their research foci overlap to a greater extent than heretofore. If so, Leo takes a narrow view of criminological research. Kraska (2006), by contrast, posits criminal justice as a multifaceted discipline that, like criminology, has generated a variety of theoretical constructs. The theories generated by the subdisciplines within criminal justice may be macro theories of the entire criminal justice system (e.g., systems theory, late modernity), micro theories of system components (e.g., a theory of police management, of investigator behavior), or normative theories (e.g., democracy and policing, criminal jurisprudence).

Building on this broader foundation, I propose a number of innocence research strategies that could be pursued by "justician" scholars, whether their academic roots are in criminology, criminal justice, or allied disciplines. This perspective diverges from Leo's (2005) hint that undervalues existing lines of innocence research because of the "simplistic assumption" that the standard list of causes provides a theoretically robust explanation of wrongful convictions. I agree that the kind of empirical and theory-building research conducted by Harmon (2001) and Lofquist (2001) ought to be pursued. In addition, however, criminal justice scholars capable of conducting eyewitness identification experiments, for example, or adept at the legal analysis of recent bills designed to strip federal courts of habeas corpus jurisdiction (Bergman, 2005) ought to attend to these and other areas where research questions need to be refined and resolved. Likewise, American scholars of police and prosecution need to explore the construction of the truth in criminal cases, an understudied area, in the light of recent knowledge of miscarriages of justice (Fisher, 1993; Martin, 2001; McConville, Sanders, & Leng, 1991; Schoenfeld, 2005). That said, much of the research agenda proposed in this article is aimed not only at understanding wrongful convictions but also at understanding the reform process (i.e., the innocence movement and its research agenda).

The Context of Reform

The DNA revolution is used as a shorthand explanation for the emergence of the innocence movement. This kernel of truth masks other likely reasons for why the movement emerged when it did. Edwin Borchard (1932), Jerome Frank (Frank & Frank, 1957/1971), and Gardner (1952) understood the deep problems of criminal justice, but their failure to establish lasting reforms such as widespread exoneree compensation or prisoner review tribunals suggests that structural factors impeded progress on the wrongful conviction issue.

A social history of wrongful conviction that goes beyond a description of the 20th-century wrongful conviction literature is needed (Leo, 2005, pp. 203–205). The current innocence reform movement presupposes a criminal justice system with national prosecutorial standards, criminalistics labs in every jurisdiction, managerial-style police departments, and the like. The criminal justice system of the early 21st century is a product of major changes that began in the 1960s. Police are far more professional today, as measured by increased education, less corruption, a managerial mentality among ranking officers, a legacy of constitutional reform that makes policing relatively law abiding, and a growing commitment to community policing (Silverman, 1999; S. Walker, 2005). Another structural change critical to the existence and operation of innocence projects is the rise of law school clinical education in the 1970s (Panel Discussion, 1987). A research question amenable to social historical inquiry is whether the 2006 innocence research agenda (Gianelli & Raeder, 2006) was feasible, or even conceivable, in the middle of the 20th century. A study of these kinds of institutional innovations would have to be placed in the context of evolving social expectations such as Lawrence Friedman's (1985) sociolegal theory of total justice.

Understanding the Innocence Movement

Study of the innocence movement itself can shed light on the capacity of the criminal justice system to change. Several large, well-developed, and partially overlapping subfields of sociology and political science—social movements, interest groups, policy analysis—provide models of inquiry (Burstein, 1999; Burstein & Linton, 2002; Heinz & Manikas, 1992; Mack, 1997, pp. 18–24; Weed, 1995; Zalman, 2005). Characterizing the innocence movement as a social movement may be odd as the latter category typically applies to the collective behavior of masses of people with common grievances who are typically excluded from political decision making and who coalesce to protest policies and to promote various interests (Eyerman & Jamison, 1991; Green & Bigelow, 2005; Morris & Mueller, 1992). It may be more accurate to describe the Innocence Network (n.d.) as an association type of interest group because of its organizational membership (31 innocence projects; Lowery & Brasher, 2004, p. 5). The lawyer leaders of the innocence movement seem to fit the model of interest group participants in that they are highly educated and well positioned to get results in various policy venues. They can marshal arguments before legislative committees, newspaper editorial boards, and a host of places where public opinion is shaped and policy decisions made. They are adept at working with scientists and experts and in mobilizing recondite information and techniques to gain attainable ends. The innocence movement, however, promotes a highly generalized interest—justice—and is marked by the kind of fervor encountered in reformist social movements. This is seen in the prodigious efforts of pro bono litigators on behalf of truly innocent (Blakeslee, 2005) and ultimately guilty defendants (Dao, 2006; J. C. Tucker, 1997). This zeal also motivates movement participants toward criminal justice system reform efforts.

Research strategies and themes from sociology and political science can produce useful insights about the movement. Methodological modifications may be necessary as the innocence movement can be viewed as a species of social movement organization (SMO) without a mass social movement as a foundation (McCarthy & Zald, 1977). The sociology of social movements, which prior to the 1960s emphasized the social psychology of collective behavior, has been eclipsed by newer theoretical models. The resource mobilization model, although perhaps not the focus of recent sociological analyses, provides useful research themes. Researchers could explore, among other themes, the constellation of innocence SMOs as organizations, studying their mobilization patterns, the confederated structure of the movement, modes of cooperation and competition, alliances with congruent groups (e.g., NAACP-Legal Defense Fund, ACLU; Death Penalty Information Center, n.d.), strategies for survival and growth, and the division of labor among innocence projects in regard to different areas of policy innovation (McCarthy & Zald, 1977, pp. 1226–1227; Minkoff, 2002). These kinds of organizational studies can be categorized under Kraska's (2004, pp. 177–213) theoretical orientation of criminal justice as a "growth complex." This list is meant to be suggestive of the wide variety of issues that could be explored through the resource mobilization lens.

Successful social movements often generate countermovements (Marx, 1979; Meyer & Staggenborg, 1996). Recent writings indicate some outright prosecutorial opposition to the innocence movement's policy goals (Marquis, 2005) and potential rifts among those supportive of the innocence movement's aims (Steiker & Steiker, 2005).[11] Although prominent conservatives have strongly supported and even led innocence reforms (Mumma, 2004; Sessions, 2003), the dogged opposition by many prosecutors to postconviction DNA testing (Medwed, 2004) suggests an ideological component among prosecutors at the core of a countermovement. Defense lawyers and prosecutors are natural enemies. However much they may cooperate in plea negotiations, they are combatants in an adversary system, reflexively wary and initially antagonistic to any proposal coming from the "other side" (Doyle, 2005, pp. 169–187).

Research at this point can explore whether the oppositional themes sounded by Marquis (2005) are widespread among prosecutors, what threats are perceived by potential opponents that could mobilize a countermovement, whether the innocence movement has framed its agenda in a way to avoid opposition, and the elite sponsorship of both the movement and any countermovement that arises (Loge, 2005). Given the relatively high status of innocence movement leaders, they may be able to win the allegiance of political elites.

More recent social movement research has focused theory-building energies on individuals within social movements, examining the social psychology of recruitment patterns into SMOs and the influence of social movements on individuals' political activities (Eyerman & Jamison, 1991; Morris & Mueller, 1992). This is linked to the emergence of "new social movements," such as the environmental movement, that are largely postindustrial, middle-class movements that focus on contemporary quality of life issues (Pichardo, 1997). Such approaches may yield useful insights as innocence movement participants for the most part are middle class. More recent attention to broader theoretical themes in social movement research, including mobilizing political opportunity structures and cultural dynamics and emphases on tactical solutions, movement leadership, and the impact of transformative events, readily suggests applications to the study of the innocence movement (Morris, 2000).

Studies of SMOs can also be approached from the political science interest group perspective. Some studies examine the mobilization of individuals and institutions through the lenses of niche theory and exchange theory to explain organizational maintenance (Lowery & Brasher, 2004, pp. 29–69). Given the newness of the innocence movement, it may be premature to study its environment (a parallel concept to that of a social movement "industry"). The logic of studying the innocence movement's organizations as interest groups is that they seek policy changes in government agencies and from legislatures and courts. Although the study of interest groups has waxed and waned within political science, there is no doubt that interest groups are a large and important sector in the public policy universe (Baumgartner & Leech, 1998). A variety of issues are open to innocence movement researchers. One is the way in which the news and popular media have promoted the movement's interests or how the movement has utilized the media (i.e., "lobbied the public"; Browne, 1998, pp. 84–108; Kingdon, 1984, pp. 61–64; Molotch, 1979); this parallels the sociological category of frame analysis. Given the salience of legal issues, attention can be paid to legal strategies used by innocence groups to influence judicial bureaucracies and to use litigation as a policy lever (Smith, 1997; Wasby, 1983). As a small movement consisting mostly of tiny organizations, it is worth examining the nature of the lobbying or influence strategies employed (e.g., inside vs. outside strategies; Green & Bigelow, 2005; Kingdon, 1984; State & Zalman, 2003). These approaches could be applied to a case study of the passage of the Innocence Protection Act or to studies of other policy advances.

Network analysis, described as "a powerful new approach to the study of social structure" (Emirbayer & Goodwin, 1994, p. 1411), is used by interest group and social movement researchers. Network analysis examines relationship patterns to overcome the limits of explaining human behavior "solely in terms of the categorical attributes of actors." Its central insight is that networks of social relations ("nodes" or behavioral networks), which can be precisely described, constrain and enable "patterned relationships among social actors within systems" (Emirbayer & Goodwin, 1994, pp. 1414–1418). Two "conceptual strategies" used to explain patterned relationships are (a) a social cohesion approach "that focuses on the direct and indirect connections among actors" (Emirbayer & Goodwin, 1994, pp. 1419–1422) and (b) a "positional" strategy that explores "actors' ties not to one another, but to third parties," so as to define an actor's position relative to other actors in a social system (Emirbayer & Goodwin, 1994, pp. 1422–1424).

A number of methods used in conjunction with network analysis could help describe and explain the behavior of innocence movement participants when acting as policy entrepreneurs (Diani, 2002; D. Friedman & McAdam, 1992). Scheck, one of the most prominent figures in the innocence movement, has, for example, placed himself in existing policy networks as past president of the National Association of Criminal Defense Lawyers and as a commissioner on the New York Forensic Science Review Board. By deliberately pursuing a networking strategy, Scheck has almost perfectly followed the script of a policy entrepreneur who creates opportunities to "persuade others to support their policy ideas" (Mintrom, 1997) and thus stimulate the diffusion of innovation (discussed below; Kingdon, 1984, pp. 188–193; Ward, 1998).[12] The quantity and intensity of network ties could, when combined with substantive knowledge of policy events, produce the kind of rich understanding that has illuminated elite criminal justice networks in one jurisdiction (Heinz & Manikas, 1992).

Studying the Innocence Reform Agenda

In addition to studying the innocence movement itself, criminal justice scholarly analysis and research can improve the understanding of the innocence reform agenda and its prospects for success. The focus of such research can include studies of established reforms and evaluations of claims about the innocence research agenda.

Diffusion of Innocence Innovations

The diffusion of innovation is an autonomous research tradition employed in many disciplines and is reported in more than 5,000 publications in the social and behavioral sciences and in other disciplines (Rogers, 2003, pp. 43–45, 477). "*Diffusion* is the process in which an innovation is communicated through certain channels over time among the members of a social system" (p. 5). The four elements of innovation, communication, time, and social system have been the focus of much diffusion research (pp. 11–38), and much research has also been devoted to the process of making innovations decisions, focusing on the elements of knowledge, persuasion, decision, implementation, and confirmation (pp. 168–218). The unit of analysis in most diffusion research has been individuals, but in recent years diffusion research has focused more on organizations (pp. 402–435) and can include states of the union in political diffusion studies (Mintrom, 1997; J. Walker, 1969).

An opportunity exists to capture the recent spread of innovations such as videotaping interrogations and lineup reforms because the ability to "gather data at several points during the diffusion process" (Rogers, 2003, p. 129) can be helpful in resolving causality issues. Of special importance to innocence reform studies are the existence of diffusion networks. This can allow criminal justice scholars to move away from the study of the innocence movement and to focus on more familiar venues such as police agencies. Political and policy analysts among criminal justice scholars could examine the spread of state innocence laws (C. E. Jones, 2005), perhaps analyzing the role of policy entrepreneurs (Kingdon, 1984, pp. 188–193; Mintrom, 1997). An important concept of diffusion research is the critical mass, akin to the idea of a "tipping point," which is "the point after which further diffusion becomes self-sustaining" (Rogers, 2003, p. 343). This concept, interestingly, was borrowed from social movement research. Given the tendency of proinnovation bias in innovation research, innocence movement scholars should be cautious in finding that a critical mass has occurred and should be sensitive to the existence of reinvention of innovations, which is common (Rogers, 2003, pp. 106, 180–189).

Diffusion methods could be applied to the spread of state innocence commissions (Mumma, 2004; Scheck & Neufeld, 2002) or to a group of specific issues on the standard list of reforms. Correcting errors caused by lying jailhouse informants, for example, requires not one but a variety of solutions. Diffusion research could measure the spread of (a) jail procedures regarding the placement and control of prisoners, (b) police and prosecutors' policies on screening panels and evaluative techniques for properly evaluating the use of informants' testimonies, (c) judicial precedents allowing or requiring cautionary instructions to juries concerning the weighing of informants' testimonies, (d) prosecutorial policies requiring prosecutors to divulge any inducements to informants and procedures to ensure compliance, and (e) rules requiring extensive discovery when informants' testimonies are used (Gianelli & Raeder, 2006, pp. 63–78). One can imagine a legal analysis of appellate judicial precedents concerning jury instructions that sheds light on that rule. Such a study, however, would not fully cover the more important question of whether policies have been adopted that in combination may reduce wrongful convictions caused by jailhouse snitches. Awareness of diffusions research could stimulate such broader studies.

Criminal justice researchers should be aware of political fragmentation in the United States as an impediment to the diffusion of innovations within criminal justice agencies. Consider, for example, the videotaping of interrogations. Sullivan (2005, p. 1128) reported that all police departments in Alaska and Minnesota and more than 300 additional departments have adopted the innovation. As of this writing, seven states and the District of Columbia have required electronic recording by statute or judicial decision, with a variety of conditions and limitations.[13] Sullivan (2005) noted that although many police departments have voluntarily adopted a recording requirement, "they represent only a small percentage of all law enforcement departments in the country" (p. 1136). A recent study indicates that 40% of big city police department administrators oppose videotaping, suggesting considerable potential resistance (Zalman & Smith, 2005). This finding, in light of the existence of 3,070 sheriff's offices, 12,666 local police departments, and 49 state police agencies in the United States, suggests at least that the diffusion of recording interrogations will be a major undertaking (Hickman & Reeves, 2003, p. 1). The fragmentation of the American polity refers not only to the large number of jurisdictions but to the relative autonomy of local units of government. With no centralized authority over local police departments or sheriffs, the adoption of an innovation such as the recording of interrogation will be made on a department-by-department basis.

Case Studies of Innocence Legislation

A few law review articles have described the federal Innocence Protection Act of 2004, which was a watered-down version of its original proposal and was passed as part of the comprehensive Justice for All Act that included support for law enforcement. In addition, almost 40 states have passed laws that authorize postconviction appeals on the grounds of innocence, typically where DNA evidence can be found. Legal writing tends to be instrumental and practical, and legislative surveys published in law journals are useful to innocence policy advocates in understanding the strengths and limitations of the legislation (C. E. Jones, 2005; Kleinert, 2006). A retrospective case study of the efforts needed to pass the Innocence Protection Act, perhaps utilizing network analysis, ought to lead to a more theoretically robust understanding of the innocence movement and shed more light on the nature of the movement's policy goals. Indeed, Sen. Patrick Leahy's statement on passage of the act names the Justice Project (n.d.) and a number of individuals and legislators who were instrumental in the passage of the act (Leahy, 2004b). The discrepancy between the act's initial goals and the act as passed could be analyzed in terms of the incrementalism that is characteristic of American politics and policy making (Haller, 2001; Kingdon, 1984, pp. 83–88).

Critiquing the Innocence Reform Agenda

As noted above, some of the descriptive, legal, or policy-oriented innocence movement rhetoric is often transformative. Criminal justice scholars can analyze the innocence reform agenda, applying what is known about change in criminal justice, to suggest the possible shape and limits of reform. However sympathetic researchers may be to the aims of innocence reforms, deep knowledge of the nature of justice bureaucracies suggests that claims of imminent criminal justice transformation may be premature.

The limits of litigated reform.   Garrett (2005), for example, asserted that criminal justice can be transformed through civil litigation on behalf of exonerees. Because defendants' constitutional rights are viewed negatively as "truth-defeating" in criminal cases by a conservative judiciary, few defendants win retrials based on police or prosecution error. Federal civil rights actions by exonerees against the police under 42 U.S.C. § 1983, however, reverse the "guilt paradigm." In civil cases, "fair trial rights vindicate the truth, while government misconduct is revealed as having concealed evidence of a person's innocence, leading to a gross miscarriage of justice" (Garrett, 2005, p. 38). Many such cases have resulted in large monetary awards. Garrett's legal tour de force, proposing that the cost of civil lawsuits will force wholesale criminal justice reforms and even restore the Warren Court-era respect for defendant's rights, is a rationalistic idea that needs to be subjected to empirical testing.

Sociolegal and political science research offers at best a tempered view of the ability of court cases to effect social change. Some political scientists have written well-researched books positing that Supreme Court cases have had limited or no effect on important areas of social life (Horowitz, 1977; Rosenberg, 1991). Other authors counter that litigation strategies have a place in social action as, for example, catalyzing correctional reform (Epstein & Kobylka, 1992; Feeley & Rubin, 1998; Zalman, 1991, 1998). Even if a view that the law has no effect is too extreme, empirical evaluations of the law's impact simply do not find that litigation itself can institute radical institutional change. A program of sustained litigation can initiate and highlight problems, but without other levers of change, it is unlikely that deep policy modifications will occur (Feeley & Rubin, 1998). Cross-sectional research could compare innocence reforms in police departments that have been hit with large awards (and perhaps in close-by departments) to a matched set of police departments that have not been subjected to such suits to find whether the suits have had a policy effect.

Implementing reforms.   Most legal writing on innocence reforms is conceptual and descriptive and tends to equate reform with rule creation. The formal adoption of a policy by legislation, court decision, or administrative rule, however, is only the beginning of reform; to be effective, a policy must be implemented. Implementation is only one step in the policy process, which extends conceptually from problem perception and agenda building, to policy formulation, legitimation, adoption, and budgeting, and to implementation, evaluation, and termination or redesign (C. O. Jones, 1984).[14] Every step of the policy process may be the subject of policy analysis, and this author has previously called for a public policy approach to understanding the innocence movement's agenda (Zalman, 2005). Criminal justice researchers, with their knowledge of criminal justice system functioning, are well positioned to engage in implementation research at a time when a number of agencies are formally adopting innocence reforms.

Implementation is a well-developed area of policy analysis that provides a variety of methodological and conceptual tools. Criminal justice scholars contemplating the study of agency adoption of lineup procedural changes or the like should be aware of the consensus among policy scholars that implementation is itself a political process that is intimately connected to earlier policy design stages. In other words, implementation is not a mechanical process but a continuation of policy making. The inevitable gap between early policy designs and the programs that emerge led early policy researchers to view the entire policy process in harshly negative terms. On mature reflection, they have come to accept such gaps not as policy failures per se but as evidence of a dynamic policy process that endures through the implementation phase (Hill & Hupe, 2002; C. O. Jones, 1984, pp. 164–195; Palumbo & Calista, 1990).

Again using the electronic recording of interrogation as an example, case studies of implementation could apply qualitative and quantitative methods. Researchers would have to define what is meant by implementation (the dependent variable). For example, if a state law mandated recording, the statutory elements can provide measures of compliance. Independent variables could include such organizational features as the strength of the chief's policy support, officer training and monitoring, the means interrogating detectives might have to evade recording, and internal sanctions for rules violations. Such research potentially transcends the innocence issue and provides the foundation for theory-oriented research about police agencies.

Conclusion

Wrongful conviction narratives have exposed serious flaws in the investigation, prosecution, and adjudication of felony cases. As a result of the DNA revolution, it is now thought that wrongful convictions are so numerous as to constitute a major policy concern that poses a serious challenge to the fairness and accuracy of the criminal justice process. Most innocence research has been conducted by psychologists and lawyers and has focused on specific subprocesses such as lineups. This research has been oriented toward understanding the ways in which these processes have failed and have caused wrongful convictions. Innocence research that goes beyond these specific areas can potentially provide a better understanding of the way in which the criminal justice systemically generates errors. Unfortunately, the difficulties in collecting and evaluating case materials and unresolved issues in defining a wrongful conviction limits this kind of research at the present time.

This article has proposed a broad research agenda addressing the new innocence movement that works to exonerate wrongly convicted inmates and to generate and publicize policy changes that logically should reduce miscarriages of justice. The innocence research agenda sketched here is primarily useful for understanding the innocence movement, itself a worthy object of research. Beyond this, the proposed kinds of research into the innocence movement and its reform agenda will possibly illuminate the capacity of the criminal justice system to reflect on its own shortcomings and to correct them. This wider goal should be of interest to the community of criminal justice policy scholars.

Endnotes

[1] A strict legalist differs:

> I count myself among those who use the term "wrongful conviction" to refer not only to the conviction of the [factually] innocent but also to any conviction achieved in part through the violation of constitutional rights or through the use of systems and procedures that render the proceedings fundamentally unfair. (Siegel, 2005, p. 1219)

Factual innocence can include a "wrong person" error (i.e., the person had no involvement with the facts of a criminal event) and legal innocence under substantive criminal law:

> An acquittal is historically accurate whenever the jury correctly determines that the defendant either did not engage in the prohibited conduct or, if he did so engage, he either lacked the state of mind required to make the conduct criminal or his action was the product of appropriate beliefs that justify it. (Givelber, 2005, p. 1175)

Forst (2004) describes two broad kinds of errors of justice: errors of due process, which can range from violations of a defendant's rights to the conviction of a factually innocent person, and errors of impunity, which range from the failure to apprehend a criminal to the acquittal of a factually guilty defendant. The latter kinds of cases have caused dismay in recent decades (Fletcher, 1995). Nevertheless, it seems improper to speak of "wrongful acquittals," however logical the term. This reflects the common law balance that accepts such acquittals as a necessary price to be paid, however grudgingly, for a fair trial.

Take the following hypotheticals. (a) A defendant whom the police investigator thinks is guilty is acquitted. Depending on the crime's heinousness, different reactions are deemed acceptable. In a drug case, for example, the chagrined officer can expect the defendant to recidivate and get caught in the future, thinking, "We will put together a stronger case and get a conviction." Another reaction to a vicious crime, say the rape and murder of a child, is to have the acquitted defendant closely monitored as a means of individualized crime prevention. A third approach, arguably improper but facially lawful, is to monitor the defendant to catch him or her in any criminal act for which some punishment can be imposed. This may have happened to Oreste Fulminante (*Arizona v. Fulminante*, 1991). This is the strategy of organized crime enforcement. In contrast to these acceptable reactions, if beyond the pale, even after acquittal for a vicious crime, for the officer to engage in private retribution. (b) After a conviction the investigating officer is left with a belief that the wrong man was convicted. Although not obliged to do so, the officer investigates the case on her own time. This results in an exoneration. Such action is deemed noble. The different societal reactions to private retribution in (a) and private investigation in (b) bring out the essential difference between social acceptance of an acquittal of the factually guilty and the moral imperative to free the factually innocent. Incidentally, the error of wrongful conviction can be compounded if police in hypothetical (a) wrongly believe that an innocent defendant has been acquitted and add the person to a list of usual suspects in later criminal investigations. This can lead to a wrongful conviction (Johnson, 2003).

[2] Films based on actual cases include *The Wrong Man* (1956), directed by Alfred Hitchcock, starring Henry Fonda, and *Call Northside 777* (1948), starring James Stewart (see Mnookin & West, 2001). "From the time Borchard published his book . . . until the early 1990s, there was typically one big-picture book or major article published every decade or so on the subject of miscarriages of justice" (Leo, 2005, p. 203).

[3] They learned to their surprise that exonerees face many adjustment problems and helped to establish a framework for action—the establishment of the Life after Exoneration Program (n.d.), an organization that provides assistance for exonerees (Vollen & Eggers, 2005).

[4] A comparable organization in Canada is AIDWyC, Association in Defence of the Wrongly Convicted (http://www.aidwyc.org).

[5] Brandon Garrett practiced with law firms headed by innocence movement leaders (Cochran Neufeld & Scheck, LLP) and with Beldock Levine & Hoffman LLP, one of whose partners, Myron Beldock, represented Rubin "Hurricane" Carter (Hirsch, 2001). The acknowledgments in Garrett (2005, p. 35) include many leaders in the wrongful conviction movement.

[6] Scheck (2005), in a more restrained vein as president of a national defense lawyer's association, expressed "cautious optimism" for reforms emanating for the innocence movement.

[7] The "policy window" for innocence reforms can be the subject of more sustained discussion or analysis (Kingdon, 1984, pp. 173–204).

[8] News accounts discuss a rare 2006 field experiment of lineup methods in Chicago that purportedly finds more error using sequential compared to simultaneous lineups, contrary to the general findings of lab experiments. Some claim that this undermines reform efforts; others claim that the study was flawed (Feige, 2006b; Paulson & Llana, 2006; Zemike, 2006).

[9] A number of studies can be bundled into a frequency-of-wrongful-conviction category: Bedau and Radelet (1987), Huff, Rattner, and Sagarin (1986, 1996), Rattner (1988), Poveda (2001), Ramsey and Frank (in press), and Zalman, Smith, and Kazaleh (2006).

[10] A Lexis search for the terms *wrongful conviction* or *innocence* in the titles of U.S. and Canadian law journals produced 226 articles, and a search for the term *wrongful conviction* anywhere in the article produced 1,455 articles (June 7, 2006). The author's personal bibliography on the subject is extremely long.

[11] Some defense lawyers worry that an emphasis on actual innocence will make jurors and appellate courts even more hostile to procedural claims of defendants who are or appear to be "factually guilty" (Siegel, 2005, p. 1221).

[12] The practice of networking is not the focus of network analysis; network analysis assumes that networks arise "naturally from contacts between individuals and organizations and studies the nature and intensity of those contacts and their influence on behavior.

[13] Alaska: *Stephen v. State* (1985); District of Columbia: D.C. Code (2006); Illinois: 20ILCS (2006); Maine: 25 M.R.S. (2005); Massachusetts: *Commonwealth v. DiGiambattista* (2004); Minnesota: *State v. Scales* (1994); New Mexico: Michie's Ann. Stat. (n.d.); Texas: Tex. Crim. P. Code Ann. (2005).

[14] Diffusion of innovation research has also examined implementation by individuals and organizations and has generated findings about the "re-invention" of innovations as implementers modify the innovation or how it is used in a number of ways (Rogers, 2003, pp. 179–180, 424–433).

References

ABA Task Force on Child Witnesses. (2002). *The child witness in criminal cases.* Chicago: American Bar Association.

Arizona v. Fulminante, 499 U.S. 279 (1991).

Barnes, J. (2006). *Arthur & George.* New York: Knopf.

Baumgartner, F. R., & Leech, B. L. (1998). *Basic interests: The importance of groups in politics and in political science.* Princeton, NJ: Princeton University Press.

Bedau, H. A., & Radelet, M. L. (1987). Miscarriages of justice in potentially capital cases. *Stanford Law Review, 40,* 21–120.

Bergman, B. E. (2005, September/October). From the president: Great writ endangered. *Champion, 29*(4), 68.

Blackstone, W. (1979). *Commentaries on the laws of England, Volume IV. Of public wrongs.* Chicago: University of Chicago Press. (Original work published 1769)

Blakeslee, N. (2005). *Tulia: Race, cocaine, and corruption in a small Texas town.* New York: Public Affairs.

Blank, J., & Jensen, E. (2004). *The exonerated: A play.* New York: Faber & Faber.

Borchard, E. M. (1932). *Convicting the innocent: Sixty-five actual errors of criminal justice.* Garden City, NY: Garden City Publishing.

Browne, W. P. (1998). *Groups, interests, and U.S. public policy.* Washington, DC: Georgetown University Press.

Burns, R. (1999). *A theory of the trial.* Princeton, NJ: Princeton University Press.

Burstein, P. (1999). Social movements and public policy. In M. G. Giugni, D. McAdam, & C. Tilly (Eds.), *How social movements matter* (Vol. 10, pp. 3–21). Minneapolis: University of Minnesota Press.

Burstein, P., & Linton, A. (2002). The impact of political parties, interest groups, and social movement organizations on public policy: Some recent evidence and theoretical concerns. *Social Forces, 81,* 381–408.

Campbell, K., & Denov, M. (2004). The burden of innocence: Coping with a wrongful imprisonment. *Canadian Journal of Criminology and Criminal Justice, 46*(2), 139–163.

Ceci, S. J., & Bruck, M. (1995). *Jeopardy in the courtroom: A scientific analysis of children's testimony.* Washington, DC: American Psychological Association.

Center for Wrongful Conviction. (n.d.). Retrieved February 23, 2006, from http://www.law.northwestern.edu/wrongfukonvictions/

Centurion Ministries. (n.d.). Retrieved June 19, 2006, from http://www.centurionministries.org/

Cole, S. A. (2005). More than zero: Accounting for error in latent fingerprint identification. *Journal of Criminal Law & Criminology, 95*(3), 985–1078.

Commonwealth v. DiGiambattista, 813 N.E. 2d 516, 533 (Mass, 2004).

Connors, E., Lundregan, T., Miller, N., & McEwan, T. (1996). *Convicted by juries, exonerated by science: Case studies in the use of DNA evidence to establish innocence after trial* (NCJ 161258). Washington, DC: National Institute of Justice.

Cromett, M. F., & Thurston Myster, S. M. (2005, October/November). The work of an innocence project. *Forensic Magazine.* Retrieved February 23, 2006, from http://www.forensicmag.com/articles.asp?pid=60

Damaška, M. (1986). *The faces of justice and state authority: A comparative approach to the legal process.* New Haven, CT: Yale University Press.

Damaška, M. (1997). *Evidence law adrift.* New Haven, CT: Yale University Press.

Dann, B. M., & Hans, V. P. (2004). Recent evaluative research on jury trial innovations. *Court Review, 41,* 12–19.

Dao, J. (2006, January 13). DNA ties man executed in '92 to the murder he denied. *New York Times,* p. A14.

D.C. Code § 5-116.01-.03 (2006).

Death Penalty Information Center. (n.d.). Retrieved Jan. 15, 2006, from http://www.deathpenaltyinfo.org/

Denov, M. S., & Campbell, K. M. (2005). Criminal injustice: Understanding the causes, effects, and responses to wrongful conviction in Canada. *Journal of Contemporary Criminal Justice, 21,* 224–249.

Diani, M. (2002). Network analysis. In B. Klandermans & S. Staggenborg (Eds.), *Methods of social movement research* (pp. 173–200). Minneapolis: University of Minnesota Press.

Doyle, J. M. (2005). *True witness: Cops, courts, science, and the battle against misidentification.* New York: Palgrave Macmillan.

Drizin, S. A., & Leo, R. A. (2004). The problem of false confessions in the post-DNA world. *North Carolina Law Review, 82,* 891–1007.

Edds, M. (2003). *An expendable man: The near-execution of Earl Washington, Jr.* New York: New York University Press.

Emirbayer, M., & Goodwin, J. (1994). Network analysis, culture, and the problem of agency. *American Journal of Sociology, 99,* 1411–1454.

Epstein, L., & Kobylka, J. F. (1992). *The Supreme Court & legal change: Abortion and the death penalty.* Chapel Hill: University of North Carolina Press.

Eyerman, R., & Jamison, A. (1991). *Social movements: A cognitive approach.* Cambridge, UK: Polity.

Feeley, M. M., & Rubin, E. L. (1998). *Judicial policy and the modern state: How the courts reformed America's prisons.* Cambridge, UK: Cambridge University Press.

Feige, D. (2006a, January 1). We find the defendant not guilty (if that's O.K. with everyone). *New York Times,* p. 23.

Feige, D. (2006b, June 6). Witnessing guilt, ignoring innocence? *New York Times,* p. Al.

Fisher, S. Z. (1993). "Just the facts, ma'am": Lying and the omission of exculpatory evidence in police reports. *New England Law Review, 28,* 1–62.

Fletcher, G. (1995). *With justice for some: Victims' rights in criminal trials.* Reading, MA: Addison-Wesley.

Forst, B. (2004). *Errors of justice: Nature, sources, and remedies.* Cambridge, UK: Cambridge University Press.

Frank, J., & Frank, B. (1971). *Not guilty.* New York: DaCapo Press. (Original work published 1957)

Friedman, D., & McAdam, D. (1992). Collective identity and activism: Networks, choices, and the life of a social movement. In A. D. Morris & C. M. Mueller (Eds.), *Frontiers in social movement theory* (pp. 156–173). New Haven, CT: Yale University Press.

Friedman, L. M. (1985). *Total justice.* New York: Russell Sage.

Gardner, E. S. (1952). *The court of last resort.* New York: W. Sloane.

Garrett, B. L. (2005). Innocence, harmless error, and federal wrongful conviction law. *Wisconsin Law Review, 2005,* 35–114.

Gianelli, P., & Raeder, M. (Eds.). (2006). *Achieving justice: Freeing the innocent, convicting the guilty. Report of the ABA Criminal Justice Section's Ad Hoc Committee to Ensure the Integrity of the Criminal Process.* Washington, DC: American Bar Association.

Gilstrap, L. L., Fritz, K., Torres, A., & Melinder, A. (2005). Child witnesses: Common ground and controversies in the scientific community. *William Mitchell Law Review, 32,* 59–79.

Givelber, D. (1997). Meaningless acquittals, meaningful convictions: Do we reliably acquit the innocent? *Rutgers Law Review, 49,* 1317–1396.

Givelber, D. (2005). Lost innocence: Speculation and data about the acquitted. *American Criminal Law Review, 42,* 1167–1199.

Green, J. C., & Bigelow, N. S. (2005). The Christian right goes to Washington: Social movements resources and the legislative process. In P. S. Herrnson, R. G. Shaiko, & C. Wilcox (Eds.), *The interest group connection: Electioneering, lobbying, and policymaking in Washington* (pp. 189–211). Washington, DC: CQ Press.

Gross, S. R., Jacoby, K., Matheson, D. J., Montgomery, N., & Patil, S. (2005). Exoneration in the United States, 1989 through 2003. *Journal of Criminal Law & Criminology, 95,* 523–60.

Gudjonsson, G. (2003). *The psychology of interrogation and confessions: A handbook.* Chichester, UK: Wiley.

Haller, R. L. (2001). Notes & comments: The Innocence Protection Act: Why federal measures requiring post-conviction DNA testing and preservation of evidence are needed in order to reduce the risk of wrongful executions. *New York Law School Journal of Human Rights, 18,* 101–132.

Harmon, T. R. (2001). Predictors of miscarriages of justice in capital cases. *Justice Quarterly, 18,* 949–968.

Heinz, J. P., & Manikas, P. M. (1992). Networks among elites in a local criminal justice system. *Law & Society Review, 26,* 831–861.

Hickman, M. J., & Reaves, B. A. (2003). *Local police departments 2000* (NCJ 196002). Washington, DC: Bureau of Justice Statistics.

Hill, M., & Hupe, P. (2002). *Implementing public policy: Governance in theory and in practice.* London, UK: Sage.

Hirsch, J. S. (2001). *Hurricane: The miraculous journey of Rubin Carter.* New York: Houghton Mifflin.

Holden, S. (2005, October 21). Highlighting a tragic chink in the criminal justice system (movie review, *After Innocence*). *New York Times,* p. E1.

Horowitz, D. L. (1977). *The courts and social policy.* Washington, DC: Brookings Institution.

Huff, C. R., Rattner, A., & Sagarin, E. (1986). Guilty until proved innocent. *Crime & Delinquency, 32,* 518.

Huff, C. R., Rattner, A., & Sagarin, E. (1996). *Convicted but innocent: Wrongful conviction and public policy.* Thousand Oaks, CA: Sage.

Humes, E. (1999). *Mean justice.* New York: Simon & Schuster.

Hunt, S. (2006, January 15). Bill seeks to pay for wrongful conviction. *Salt Lake Tribune,* p. B1.

Illinois Governor's Commission on Capital Punishment. (2002, April). *Report.* Retrieved February 23, 2006, from http://www.idoc.state.il.us/ccp/ccp/reports/commission report/index.html

Innocence Commission for Virginia. (2005, March). *A vision for justice: Report and recommendations regarding wrongful convictions in the Commonwealth of Virginia.* Retrieved February 23, 2006, from http://www.icva.us

The Innocence Network. (n.d.). Retrieved June 12, 2006, from http://www.innocencenetwork.org/

The Innocence Project. (n.d.). Retrieved February 23, 2006, from http://www.innocenceproject.org/

Johnson, C. C., Jr. (with Hampikian, G.). (2003). *Exit to freedom.* Athens: University of Georgia Press.

Jones, C. O. (1984). *An introduction to the study of public policy* (3rd ed.). Monterey, CA: Brooks/Cole.

Jones, C. E. (2005). Evidence destroyed, innocence lost: The preservation of biological evidence under innocence protection statutes. *American Criminal Law Review, 42,* 1239–1270.

Junkin, T. (2004). *Bloodsworth: The true story of the first death row inmate exonerated by DNA.* Chapel Hill, NC: Algonquin Books.

Justice Denied. (n.d.). *Justice denied: The magazine for the wrongly convicted.* Retrieved June 19, 2006, from http://www.justicedenied.org/index.htm

The Justice Project. (n.d.). Retrieved June 19, 2006, from http://ccjr.policy.net/

Kingdon, J. W. (1984). *Agendas, alternatives and public policies.* New York: HarperCollins.

Kirchmeier, J. L. (2002). Another place beyond here: The death penalty moratorium movement in the United States. *University of Colorado Law Review, 73,* 1–116.

Kleinert, M. E. (2006). Note: Improving the quality of justice: The Innocence Protection Act of 2004 ensures post-conviction DNA testing, better legal representation, and increased compensation for the wrongfully imprisoned. *Brandeis Law Journal, 44,* 491–508.

Kraska, P. (2004). *Theorizing criminal justice: Eight essential orientations.* Long Grove, IL: Waveland Press.

Kraska, P. (2006). Criminal justice theory: Toward legitimacy and an infrastructure. *Justice Quarterly, 23*(2), 167–185.

Leahy, P. (2004a). *Justice for All Act of 2004: Section-by-section analysis.* Retrieved February 23, 2006, from http://leahy.senate.gov/press/200410/100904E.html

Leahy, P. (2004b). *Statement of Senator Patrick Leahy—The Justice For All Act of 2004.* Retrieved February 23, 2006, from http://leahy.senate.gov/press/200410/100904B.html

Leipold, A. D. (2005). How the pretrial process contributes to wrongful convictions. *American Criminal Law Review, 42,* 1123–1165.

Leo, R. A. (2005). Rethinking the study of miscarriages of justice: Developing a criminology of wrongful conviction. *Journal of Contemporary Criminal Justice, 21*(3), 201–223.

Leo, R. A., & Ofshe, R. J. (1998). The consequences of false confessions: Deprivations of liberty and miscarriages of justice in the age of psychological interrogation. *Journal of Criminal Law & Criminology, 88,* 429–496.

Lerner, R. L. (2001). The intersection of two systems: An American on trial for an American murder in the French cour d'assises. *University of Illinois Law Review, 2001,* 791–856.

Life after Exoneration Program. (n.d.). Retrieved February 23, 2006, from http://www.exonerated.org/

Lindo, J. L. (2000). Note: New Jersey jurors are no longer color-blind regarding eyewitness identification. *Seton Hall Law Review, 30,* 1224–1254.

Lofquist, W. S. (2001). Whodunit? An examination of the production of wrongful convictions. In S. D. Westervelt & J. A. Humphrey (Eds.), *Wrongly convicted: Perspectives on failed justice* (pp. 174–196). New Brunswick, NJ: Rutgers University Press.

Loge, P. (2005). How to talk crimey and influence people: Language and the politics of criminal justice policy. *Drake Law Review, 53,* 693–709.

Lowery, D., & Brasher, H. (2004). *Organized interests and American government.* Boston: McGraw-Hill.

Mack, C. S. (1997). *Business, politics, and the practice of governmental relations.* Westport, CT: Quorum.

Marquis, J. (2005). The myth of innocence. *Journal of Criminal Law & Criminology, 95*(2), 501–521.

Martin, D. L. (2001). The police role in wrongful convictions: An international and comparative study. In S. D. Westervelt & J. A. Humphrey (Eds.), *Wrongly convicted: Perspectives on failed justice* (pp. 77–93). New Brunswick, NJ: Rutgers University Press.

Marx, G. (1979). External efforts to damage or facilitate social movements: Some patterns, explanations, outcomes, and complications. In M. N. Zald & J. D. McCarthy (Eds.), *The dynamics of social movements* (pp. 94–125). Cambridge, MA: Winthrop.

McCarthy, J. D., & Zald, M. N. (1977). Resource mobilization and social movements: A partial theory. *American Journal of Sociology, 82,* 1212–1241.

McConville, M., Sanders, A., & Leng, R. (1991). *The case for the prosecution: Police suspects and the construction of criminality.* London: Routledge.

Medwed, D. S. (2003). Actual innocents: Considerations in selecting cases for a new innocence project. *Nebraska Law Review, 81,* 1097–1151.

Medwed, D. S. (2004). The zeal deal: Prosecutorial resistance to post-conviction claims of innocence. *Boston University Law Review, 84,* 125–183.

Medwed, D. S. (2005). Looking foreword: Wrongful convictions and systemic reform. *American Criminal Law Review, 42,* 1117–1121.

Meyer, D. S., & Staggenborg, S. (1996). Movements, countermovements, and the structure of political opportunity. *American Journal of Sociology, 101,* 1628–1660.

Michie's Ann. Stat. N. M. §§ 29-1-16.

Minkoff, D. (2002). Micro-organizational analysis. In B. Klandermans & S. Staggenborg (Eds.), *Methods of social movement research* (pp. 260–285). Minneapolis: University of Minnesota Press.

Mintrom, M. (1997). Policy entrepreneurs and the diffusion of innovation. *American Journal of Political Science, 41,* 738–770.

Mnookin, J. L., & West, N. (2001). Theaters of proof: Visual evidence and the law in *Call Northside 777. Yale Journal of Law & the Humanities, 13,* 329–390.

Molotch, H. (1979). Media and movements. In M. N. Zald & J. D. McCarthy (Eds.), *The dynamics of social movements* (pp. 71–93). Cambridge, MA: Winthrop.

Morris, A. D. (2000). Reflections on social movement theory: Criticisms and proposals. *Contemporary Sociology, 29,* 445–454.

Morris, A. D., & Mueller, C. M. (Eds.). (1992). *Frontiers in social movement theory.* New Haven, CT: Yale University Press.

Mumma, C. C. (2004). The North Carolina actual innocence commission: Uncommon perspectives joined by a common cause. *Drake Law Review, 52,* 647.

National Innocence Network Conference. (2005). *Conference information packet.* Retrieved November 9, 2005, from http://www.regonline.com/Checkin.asp?EventId=20222

Packer, H. (1968). *The limits of the criminal sanction.* Stanford, CA: Stanford University Press.

Palumbo, D. J., & Calista, D. J. (Eds.). (1990). *Implementation and the policy process: Opening up the black box.* Westport, CT: Greenwood.

Panel Discussion. (1987). Panel discussion, symposium on clinical legal education. Clinical legal education: Reflections on the past fifteen years and aspirations for the future. *Catholic University Law Review, 36,* 337–365.

Patterson, R. N. (2005). *Conviction.* New York: Random House.

Paulson, A., & Llana, S. M. (2006, April 24). In police lineups, is the method the suspect? *Christian Science Monitor,* p. 1.

Pichardo, N. A. (1997). New social movements; A critical review. *Annual Review of Sociology, 23,* 411–430.

Poveda, T. G. (2001). Research note: Estimating wrongful convictions. *Justice Quarterly, 18,* 689–708.

Ramsey, R. J., & Frank, J. (in press). Wrongful conviction: Perspectives of criminal justice professionals regarding the frequency of wrongful conviction and the extent of system errors. *Crime & Delinquency.*

Rattner, A. (1988). Convicted but innocent: Wrongful conviction and the criminal justice system. *Law and Human Behavior, 12,* 283–293.

Risinger, D. M. (2004). Unsafe verdicts: The need for reformed standards for the trial and review of factual innocence claims. *Houston Law Review, 41*, 1281–1336.

Rogers, E. M. (2003). *Diffusion of innovations* (5th ed.). New York: Free Press.

Rosenberg, G. N. (1991). *The hollow hope: Can courts bring about social change?* Chicago: University of Chicago Press.

Scheck, B. (2005, April). A time for cautious optimism. *The Champion, 29,* 4.

Scheck, B. C., & Neufeld, P. J. (2002, September/October). Toward the formation of "innocence commissions" in America. *Judicature, 86*(2), 98–105.

Scheck, B., Neufeld, P., & Dwyer, J. (2000). *Actual innocence and other dispatches from the wrongly convicted.* New York: Doubleday.

Scheck, B., Neufeld, P., & Dwyer, J. (2003). *Actual innocence: When justice goes wrong and how to make it right.* New York: Penguin/New American Library.

Schehr, R. C. (2005). The Criminal Cases Review Commission as a state strategic selection mechanism. *American Criminal Law Review, 42*, 1289–1302.

Schoenfeld, H. (2005). Violated trust: Conceptualizing prosecutorial misconduct. *Journal of Contemporary Criminal Justice, 21*, 250–271.

Sessions, W. S. (2003, September 21). DNA tests can free the innocent. How can we ignore that? *Washington Post*, p. B2.

Siegel, A. M. (2005). Moving down the wedge of injustice: A proposal for a third generation of wrongful convictions scholarship and advocacy. *American Criminal Law Review, 42*, 1219–1237.

Silverman, E. (1999). *NYPD battles crime: Innovative strategies in policing.* Boston: Northeastern University Press.

Smith, C. (1997). The capacity of courts as policy-making forums. In B. S. Hancock & P. M. Sharp (Eds.), *Public policy: Crime and criminal justice* (pp. 232–248). Upper Saddle River, NJ: Prentice Hall.

State should offer compensation to the exonerated. (2006, February 8). *Detroit Free Press*, p. 10A.

State v. Scales, 518 N.W.2d 587 (Minn. 1994).

Steiker, C. S., & Steiker, J. M. (2005). The seduction of innocence: The attraction and limitations of the focus on innocence in capital punishment law and advocacy. *Journal of Criminal Law & Criminology, 95*, 587–624.

Stephen v. State, 711 P.2d 1156 (Alaska 1985).

Stiglitz, J., Brooks, J., & Shulman, T. (2002). The hurricane meets the paper chase: Innocence projects new emerging role in clinical legal education. *California Western Law Review, 38*, 413–430.

Strate, J., & Zalman, M. (2003). Interest group lobbying on a morality policy issue: The case of physician-assisted suicide. *American Review of Politics, 24*, 321–342.

Sullivan, T. P. (2005). Recent developments: Electronic recording of custodial interrogations: Everybody wins. *Journal of Criminal Law & Criminology, 95*, 1127–1140.

Technical Working Group for Eyewitness Evidence. (1999). *Eyewitness evidence: A guide for law enforcement* (NCJ 178204). Washington, DC: National Institute of Justice.

Tex. Crim. P. Code Ann. 38.22(3)(4) (West 2005).

Tucker, J. C. (1997). *May God have mercy: A true story of crime and punishment.* New York: Norton.

Tucker, C. (2005, December 14). Let's arrest wrongful convictions. *Atlanta Journal-Constitution*, p. 15A.

Tulsky, F. (2006, January 21–26). Tainted trials, stolen justice. *San Jose Mercury News.* Retrieved January 28, 2006, from http://www.mercurynews.com/mld/mercurynews/news/special_packages/stolenjustice/

20 ILCS 3930/7.2 (2006).

25 M.R.S. § 2803-B (1) (K) (2005).

Vollen, L., & Eggers, D. (Eds.). (2005). *Surviving justice: America's wrongfully convicted and exonerated.* San Francisco: McSweeny's.

Volokh, A. (1997). Aside: n guilty men. *University of Pennsylvania Law Review, 146,* 173–216.

Walker, J. (1969). The diffusion of innovations among the American states. *American Political Science Review, 63,* 880–899.

Walker, S. (2005). *The new world of police accountability.* Thousand Oaks, CA: Sage.

Ward, J. D. (1998). Public policy entrepreneur. In J. M. Shafritz (Ed.), *The international encyclopedia of public policy and administration* (Vol. 3, pp. 1850–1851). Boulder, CO: Westview.

Warden, R. (2003). The revolutionary role of journalism in identifying and rectifying wrongful convictions. *UMKC Law Review, 70,* 803.

Warden, R. (2005). Illinois death penalty reform: How it happened, what it promises. *Journal of Criminal Law & Criminology, 95,* 381–426.

Wasby, S. L. (1983). Interest groups in court: Race relations litigation. In A. J. Cigler & B. A. Loomis (Eds.), *Interest group politics* (pp. 251–274). Washington DC: CQ Press.

Weed, F. (1995). *Certainty of justice: Reform in the crime victim movement.* New York: Aldine de Gruyter.

Weich, R. (2005, March). The Innocence Protection Act of 2004: A small step forward and a framework for larger reforms. *The Champion, 29,* 28–31.

Wells, G. L. (2001). Police lineups: Data, theory and policy. *Psychology, Public Policy and Law, 7,* 791–801.

Wells, G. L., Small, M., Penrod, S., Malpass, R. S., Fulero, S. M., & Brimcomb, C. A. E. (1998). Eyewitness identification procedures: Recommendations for lineups. *Law & Human Behavior, 22,* 603–647.

Westervelt, S. D., & Humphrey, J. A. (Eds.). (2001). *Wrongly convicted: Perspectives on failed justice.* New Brunswick, NJ: Rutgers University Press.

Wrightsman, L., & Kassin, S. (1993). *Confessions in the Courtroom.* Newbury Park, CA: Sage.

Zacharias, F. C. (2005). The Role of prosecutors in serving justice after convictions. *Vanderbilt Law Review, 58,* 171–239.

Zalman, M. (1991). *Wayne County Jail Inmates v. Wayne County Sheriff:* The anatomy of a lawsuit. *The Prison Journal, 71*(1), 4–23.

Zalman, M. (1998). Juricide. In D. A. Schultz (Ed.), *Leveraging the law: Using the courts to achieve social change* (pp. 293–318). New York: Peter Lang.

Zalman, M. (2005). Cautionary notes on commission recommendations: A public policy approach to wrongful convictions. *Criminal Law Bulletin, 41*(2), 169–194.

Zalman, M., & Smith, B. (2005). *The attitudes of police executives toward Miranda and interrogation policies.* Unpublished manuscript.

Zalman, M., Smith, B., & Kazaleh, A. (2006, March). *Officials' estimates of the prevalence of wrongful convictions.* Paper presented at the annual meeting of the Academy of Criminal Justice Sciences, Baltimore.

Zernike, K. (2006, April 19). Questions raised over new trend in police lineups. *New York Times,* p. Al.

31

Research Utilization in Complex Organizations
A Case Study in Corrections

RICK LOVELL

Nearly 50 years have passed since Robert S. Lynd (1939) posed the question to social scientists: "Knowledge for what?" During the past two decades in particular there has been increasing interest in the potential of social science research information, or information developed through the use of social science methods, to "routinely guide policy and practice in people-changing organizations" (Glaser, 1973:2). As in other areas of public policy, importance has been attached to the possibility of empirical information serving as a significant input, if not as the predominant basis, for policy development and decision making in corrections and in other criminal justice agencies (Glaser, 1973; Gottfredson and Gottfredson, 1980).

The literature on research utilization (RU) is growing. Most of the available literature points to the "general failure" of research information to "affect decision making in a significant way" (Patton, 1978:2). The perceived lack of effect of empirical information on decision making in public agencies has led to much discussion and to some research. In criminal justice, particularly in corrections, there is scant research on the use of empirical information and too little consideration of the potential role of research information as an input in decision making and policy formulation.

It has long been assumed that research information is underutilized in correctional decision making and policy development. Yet, as noted, there is little empirical evidence about the level or scope of utilization in corrections: what information is used, by whom, for what purposes, and with what result.

Rick Lovell, "Research Utilization in Complex Organizations: A Case Study in Corrections," *Justice Quarterly* Vol. 5 No. 2, 1988, pp. 257–280. Reprinted by permission of the Academy of Criminal Justice Sciences.

This article reports and discusses an exploratory study on the use of research information by upper-level administrators and staff members in a state department of corrections. The purposes of the study were 1) to examine the use of social science research information in policy development and decision making and 2) to develop an understanding of factors which influence or shape use in the department. The aims of the following discussion are 1) to stimulate consideration of the predominant expectations about research use in corrections and 2) to encourage dialogue on possible directions for further inquiry and on the development of an adequate integrative model of the research utilization process in corrections.

Defining Utilization

Asking questions about research utilization proves to be difficult. Many of our images of RU are conditioned, if not determined, by rigorous and demanding notions rooted in the analytic paradigm of decision making in complex organizations. Many common images are associated with normative expectations derived from viewing social science research information as "conclusive," "useful," and "authoritative."

The most rigorous conceptualization of RU is defined operationally in terms of documentable or observable changes in programs or policies, based directly on the information supplied by empirical studies (Patrick, 1979). Such a conception generally is described by the terms *instrumental use* or *impact*. The predominant expectation about instrumental use is that research information would enter into an analytic, rational decision-making process and that the findings and/or conclusions would be incorporated directly into the outcome. In short, the empirical information would affect the outcome significantly.

Scholars, researchers, and practitioners have recognized the shortcomings of simply assuming that research information will achieve instrumental use regularly. Such expectations and their resultant definitions, according to Weiss and Bucuvalas (1980:10), "identify what program directors in the applied research offices of [The National Science Foundation] used to call 'nuggets,' those occasional gems of direct application that they mined and cherished for their value in proving the utility of their research programs to a hostile Congress." Weiss also states, "It probably takes an extraordinary concatenation of circumstances for research to influence policy *directly*" (1979:428).

An awareness that empirical findings seldom achieve instrumental use has led to broader conceptualizations. Many scholars now find it acceptable to define utilization in terms of consideration. From this perspective, research information is seen as a tool for enlightenment "in sorting out assumptions, clarifying logic, or arriving at a better understanding of the range of activities and constraints involved in a particular decision [or set of decisions]" (Rich, in Grosskin, 1981:9). In other words, research information is used to guide and clarify the decision-making process. Such application generally is termed *conceptual use.*

Now it is also recognized generally that utilization may include symbolic functions; that research information may be put to *persuasive use*. In other words, empirical information may be used to "substantiate a previously held position, marshal support, or cast doubt on propositions at odds with those of the user, among other such possibilities" (Knorr quoted in Weiss, 1977:152).

Broader operational definitions of utilization corresponding to the latter conceptualizations (conceptual use and symbolic use) must emphasize research information as a competing rather than a dominating input among other sources of information. Furthermore, the corresponding view of the utilization process may need to replace the rational, analytic image, and admit to a dynamic process in which individuals with diverse interests and unequal influence affect actively the process of utilization.

Perspectives on Research Utilization

Even among those who employ broad definitions of use there remains an overall impression and a rather pervasive belief that research information is underutilized in decision making in public agencies. Several perspectives have been employed by those seeking to account for the modest levels of use observed in most studies.

Relying on a belief that differences in the culture of science and the culture of government (following Snow, 1962) lead to less effective utilization, some scholars have focused on the processes of knowledge production and transfer to locate the major variables that account for use or nonuse of research information (see Caplan, 1979; Weiss and Bucuvalas, 1980:17–23). "Proponents [of this approach] assume that bridges need to be constructed to link the worlds of policymakers and researchers and analysts" (Rich, 1981:12). The reasons offered for the alleged lack of effect of research information have been summarized in long lists which include such items as poor methodological quality of the research, lack of relevance of research information to decision making, and inadequate, ineffective, and untimely communication of results (Grosskin, 1981:1).

Scholars also have employed varying perspectives (often presented as mutually exclusive) to explore barriers to utilization associated with individual characteristics and/or orientations of decision makers, political constraints, and the linkage system for transmitting results. It is reasonable to expect that barriers to utilization can arise in any or all of these areas (for excellent discussions see Glaser, Abelson, and Garrison, 1983 and Weiss and Bucuvalas, 1980). No adequate theoretical framework exists yet, however, to integrate the various perspectives.

A few students of utilization have focused on the nature of organizational decision making and on the processes through which use of research information may occur in complex, bureaucratic organizations. Lindblom and Cohen (1979) attempt to come to an understanding of use/nonuse by conceptualizing the potential role of such information in the problem-solving process of complex organizations. They remind us that decision makers always have a choice between trying to find "solutions" by arranging to have a given problem frontally attacked by persons who will think it through to a solution, or by managing to set in motion interaction, that will, with the help of analysis adapted to the interaction, eventuate in a solution or a preferred outcome. (25)

Further, Lindblom and Cohen provide a critical insight in suggesting that research information must compete with a "mountain of ordinary knowledge which it cannot replace but only reshape here and there" (32). Their insights are crucial in directing our attention to the interactive nature of the decision-making process and in sensitizing us to the descriptive inaccuracy of the images associated with the rational, analytic paradigm of decision making. As emphasized in the quote above, Lindblom and Cohen point out the need to consider the potentially active focus of decision makers regarding information requirements. They also suggest the need to pay attention to patterns of information search and to the bureaucratic decision making norms of tailoring the search for information to problems at hand and of addressing problems sequentially, as these arise and become important enough to require resolution.

Robert Rich (1981) focuses on *bureaucratization* to locate a set of variables associated with internal agency control and with bureaucratic interests as important factors in utilization. According to Rich, one can assume that the characteristics of knowledge—its quality or perhaps its conclusiveness— establish a necessary but not a sufficient condition in accounting for its application or utilization (159). He concludes that research information is less likely to be used because of its quality or its appropriateness to the substantive policy or problem area than because of its value in enhancing bureaucratic interests (158–64).

Scholars disagree on what the important determinants of utilization may be. No completely adequate theoretical framework exists from which to investigate it. As noted, much of the discussion of utilization has been impressionistic, and empirical work to date has been exploratory.

Framework for This Study

Corrections policy presents a challenge to the study of utilization. Decision makers in corrections operate in complex, bureaucratic environments, in a rather visible and competitive policy arena. They occupy the unenviable position of needing to be "successful" (perhaps in terms of loyalties to the organization, perhaps in other ways); at the same time, these administrators are the focal points for scrutiny and review by a number of outside sources, including legislative bodies, state executives, the judiciary, reform groups, and other significant parties. Decisions and policies in this context emerge from compromise, confusion, and conflict among many actors, engaged in some version of what Allison (1971) would term "bureaucratic politics." Because powerful external elites may be important in shaping use within correctional agencies, attention to the overall decision-making and policy-making context is required.

The array of findings and thought on utilization suggests a variety of possibilities for organizing a study of this subject. The most promising perspectives are suggested in work by Lindblom and Cohen (1979) and by Rich (1981); their conceptualizations and findings urge consideration of the context in which utilization is expected to occur. The complexity of the issues to be addressed, the possibility that relevant variables will be influenced by or will stem directly from the decision-making context, and the lack of available evidence or use in corrections argue for an exploratory, qualitative approach. This study proceeded with a framework of basic concepts derived from a review of the RU literature and the literature on complex organizations and decision making. The empirical intent of the study was 1) to ascertain patterns of use (with particular attention to availability of research information as well as types and scope of use) and 2) to determine whether factors associated with the bureaucratization of the decision-making process would prove important in understanding use in the department under study here.

Methods

This study examined the use of social science research information at the upper levels of management in a state department of corrections. The author used a qualitative design to provide depth and variety within a limited context and to allow for examination of foci that emerged as the author moved toward grounded theory.

The study interviewed a sample of 27 top-level administrators, major division managers, and research/information-producing personnel in the central headquarters of the organization. The respondents were responsible for or contributed directly to systemwide planning and decision making for the department. The working universe consisted of all persons in the groups defined above.

The author employed a semistructured interview schedule. The procedure was flexible; it permitted respondents to develop their thoughts and allowed the interviewer to pursue leads that emerged. The tape-recorded interviews averaged 90 minutes in length.

In addition to the interview data, a variety of other sources provided evidence on utilization and on the processes and context in which use might occur. These sources included agency records, project memoranda and documents, and illustrative material such as study reports, journals, and other information provided by respondents. This material was used in examining the flow of research information within the department, to document use where possible, and to provide information on organization structure and relevant formal policies within the department.

Setting

The chief executive officer of a state department of corrections (DOC) granted access for the study; this is a medium-sized DOC located in a southern state. The organization is headed by a chief executive appointed by and primarily accountable to the governor of the state. Upper-level management positions are unclassified and appointed.

The department has a complex mission to perform and is highly differentiated structurally. The operating environment and the projected operating environment at the time of the study were turbulent. Leaders of the department faced stiff competition for resources in a state struggling to reconcile large budget deficits with expectations of an uncertain economic future. The operating environment was one of fiscal retrenchment stemming from economic crises.

In addition, the department was experiencing a major problem with overcrowding, it had come under increasing scrutiny from an array of outside observers including the judiciary, the state legislature, the governor's office, the news media, and special interest groups. The external pressures compounded the usual difficulties found in the internal environment of a large, complex public organization.

Gaining access for this study required that a research understanding be reached. The agreement involved a promise that the author would control the data developed in this study and would assure confidentiality regarding the data and the respondents. To comply with the request, the author has generalized descriptions of the organization and the respondents. He has made an effort to avoid using names, titles, and other designations which may reveal identities.

Analysis of the Data

The interviews provided the bulk of the data concerning use in the department. Collateral evidence in the form of agency documents, project memoranda, and other material provided verification of some responses, data on use, and data concerning the dissemination networks and structural features of the department.

The data were submitted to a qualitative analysis. The coding of interview responses corresponded to categories established on the basis of subjective analysis of the content of responses, together with basic questions established and a general conceptual framework rooted in the utilization literature.

The following basic questions were addressed:

Category	Questions
1. type of information	Is research information available? If so, what information is available?
2. type of use	If research information is used, how is it used? What types of use occur? Is use immediate or does it occur in a diffuse way?
3. user's identity	Who uses research information? Individuals? Groups? Who is more likely to use research information?

Category	Questions
4. scope of use	Is research information systematically used? Is it put to greater/equal/less use than other types of information? Are there certain individuals/ groups/areas where research information is more likely to be used? To be ignored?

A portion of the data collection was devoted to investigating the information dissemination process in the department and to obtaining data on the possible bureaucratization of the utilization process. To suggest possible categories for analysis the author drew on the work done by Rich (1981) in his assessment of use of Continuous National Survey information in federal policy making. In addition, the author left leeway to explore emerging foci and to allow for creation of categories based on content analysis of the data.

Discussion of Findings

The following discussion is organized (1) to address the basic questions concerning use in the department and (2) to present findings of primary interest in coming to understand utilization in the department; such findings may be important in considering the RU process in general.

Availability of Research Information

Members of the department had access to research information in a number of forms and from a variety of sources. A substantial amount of research-based information was physically present and at least ostensibly was available for use. In many instances this information had not been acquired for specific purposes; in most instances no discernible attempt had been made to categorize or evaluate it in terms of potential identifiable use by members of the department. In other words, a great deal of research-produced knowledge was merely present and might possibly be put to some use ad hoc and rather haphazardly. Most of this "information" could be said more appropriately to consist of pieces of knowledge which happened to be present in the department.

Externally Produced Information

Much of the research-based information in the department could be characterized as "routinely encountered material." Various individuals in the department received such information rather regularly. Research-based information was received routinely from a variety of sources:

1. professional journals and publications (e.g., ACA *Journal* and *Federal Probation*); psychological journals; juvenile justice publications; professional business journals.

2. material disseminated from national clearing houses and from federal agencies such as NIC and NCJRS.

3. material disseminated by other agencies, such as studies on risk prediction or on riot situations in other states.

The department, as an organization, was on no dissemination lists; only individuals were included on such lists. There was no central coordination of information resources and no centralized process for acquiring, assessing, or disseminating such resources. In fact, the department had no formal policies regarding the dissemination or potential use of this type of information. It was left to the discretion of individual department members to decide whether to acquire certain research-based information or any information, and whether (as well as to whom) to pass along information.

One administrator reflected the organization's short-term focus and summarized management's views on routinely encountered material:

> A lot of this material is looked on as a frivolous encumbrance. No, we do not centrally acquire this material on a day-to-day basis and distribute it. There is actually little forethought about this. [We] do not acknowledge the utility of acquiring this kind of information in doing business. There is a large body of knowledge out there, but a lot is not valuable. There is little utility in it in addressing day-to-day problems.

A member of the in-house research staff assessed this issue as follows:

> Information [of this type] comes in at different points. It may be sent on to so and so, but this is [done] purely on personal initiative. Information sent on to an individual is done on the basis of who you think might be interested. If information comes in to [the chief executive's] office it might be disseminated. A lot of information comes in. We do crisis-oriented search.

Regarding routinely encountered empirical knowledge, the department could be said to have a *distributed-information problem*. No formal policies governed the acquisition, assessment, dissemination, or use of such information; consequently, much potentially useful information simply was shelved and disregarded. The author found no formal decision rules which would encourage use of research information.

In-House Research: Internally Produced Empirical Information

Members of the department visualized "research" with a great deal of variability. The participants in this study evidenced widely differing conceptions of research and notions of the processes and outcomes associated with research. The term "research" might be applied to activities ranging from tightly designed and rather rigorously conducted empirical investigations to compiling basic data (as in daily census totals and counts on bed space); decision makers were expected to evaluate this material heuristically and to put it to some use. Most respondents, with the notable exception of the in-house research personnel, tended to refer to any "special" or specific data collection activity as research. In this study the interviewer had to be specific about the meaning of the term "research information"; perhaps the same would be true in other studies.

Tangible evidence showed that members of the department conduct empirical studies using social science research methods. Most of the studies would fall loosely into the category of program evaluation. The department's structure included a program evaluation section which had been in existence for two years at the time of the study. This section had completed three major studies, each involving survey techniques combined with collection of collateral evidence and qualitative analysis, as well as some descriptive quantitative analysis. A separate statistics section also developed a limited amount of empirical information, primarily descriptive analyses intended for use by top-level administrators.

The mental health division of the department also engaged in empirical research. The division administrator, a clinical psychologist with a Ph.D., provided evidence of several projects completed or under way. This administrator also provided evidence of recent publication in a professional journal and furnished a copy of an article submitted for publication.

Again, research-based information was present. There were no formal policies regarding the dissemination or potential use of the information produced in-house. None of the work reviewed included a utilization scheme or plan. The author noted evidence, however, of an informal but quite explicit policy regarding the products of the program evaluation section. Respondents, including administrators and research personnel, stated that information developed by this section would be disseminated on a "need-to-know" basis. "Need to know" would be determined situationally by the chief executive officer.

Knowledge Possessed by Individuals

The study could not ascertain how much scientific knowledge was possessed by individual respondents. The respondents' credentials were impressive; many possessed considerable experience in corrections as well as substantial educational attainment. As one top-level administrator observed, "Many of these people are experts in their own minds." The primary base of information in the department existed in the form of the knowledge and expertise possessed by the individual members of the department.

Use of Research Information

The primary evidence of use in the department was drawn from responses of the participants in the study. Very little evidence of use was present in agency documents, project memoranda, or other material.

It is impossible to make absolute statements about levels of use of research information, but relative to the use of other forms of information, the use of this information for decision making or policy formulation was minimal. Even so, some research information was used in what must be termed circumscribed ways, and the diversity of types of use was somewhat surprising.

Instrumental Use

Interviews and review of documents covering a two-year period revealed only three instances of instrumental use. Even these instances, although documentable, arguably could be placed in the category of symbolic use. In one instance where documentation revealed instrumental utilization of study findings, a researcher explained:

> We were assigned to do this study. But you have to understand that the decision had already been made. The outcome was obvious. We knew what we were going to find, and that is why we were asked to do what we did. We didn't have time for adequate study, but it didn't matter anyway.

An administrator noted further:

> Recommendations, findings, from [that study] were made use of in making the change. They [the legislature] already knew what they wanted, so the study didn't decide that. It helped to justify the changes.

The other two instances of instrumental use were surrounded by circumstances that also could have led to categorization as symbolic use. The data collection in the present research was centered on the upper levels of management in the department; that focus could be significant in considering the small amount of instrumental use and the circumstances surrounding the instances noted.

Conceptual Use

Most of the evidence for use of research information in this study was provided by respondents who discussed instances of conceptual use. The accounts of conceptual use often were cloudy or nonspecific in the sense that respondents were attempting to describe instances in which they considered research information in coming to understand the issues confronting them. Research/information-producing personnel more often were able to point out specific instances of conceptual use by referring to studies completed or under way which involved a preliminary review of literature or collection of research information as a foundation for a study or project. Administrators' responses were less specific; their responses conveyed the idea that even conceptual use was minimal, although several indicated a *belief* that conceptual use occurred.

The following statements represent the range of responses among administrators:

> Administrator: For the most part, I think there is strong consideration of research results. I can name areas where we look at research of a general nature. The process of using this information is more informal. We rely heavily on other kinds of information-practical information.

> Administrator: Sometimes there are so many recommendations. They tell you too much. You get tired. Research can become word-of-mouth. Something gets translated, becomes part of what someone believes, gets used in this way.

> Administrator: I can't point to anything right now.

Specifically mentioned instances of conceptual use included consideration of research information concerning work on a hostage policy, reviews of crowding and risk prediction studies, design work for a pilot study using the M-C inkblot test to detect inmates faking psychoses, review of recent findings on the Rorschach method, design work on education evaluations, and review of studies on riots and riot situations to identify possible policy needs. In addition, research information produced in house was put to conceptual use. One administrator noted:

> Like this one study program evaluation did. If nothing else, it enlightened me. I used it to critique some of the things we were doing. I also looked at information from other states. I put these things together, and if it's reasonable, we might try some tests.

Symbolic Use

Most administrators reported that their primary use of research information involved supporting budget requests, justifying grant or funding requests, or strengthening policy recommendations already formulated. One administrator noted:

> We use research mostly in our budget requests; to get funding—as a justification.

Another administrator summarized the statements made by most respondents:

> We'll recommend what we *feel*—but that won't be without as much backup as we can get.

Yet another administrator commented on the products of the program evaluation section:

> Program evaluation is used as a management tool—to get budget increases.

Type of Use in Perspective

This study focused on diversity in types of use, not on quantity. In view of all the data, however, it is possible to form a rather clear picture of use. It is apparent that symbolic or persuasive use of research information was the primary mode of use among administrators in the department. Among research/information-producing personnel, however, conceptual use was the primary application; conceptual use was described by all respondents. Instrumental use was minimal.

Scope of Use

Systematic use of research information was found to be limited in the department. Yet a pattern emerged which was supported both in the responses of study participants and to some degree in agency documents and memoranda.

The respondents agreed that the operational (program) level in the department contained the areas where the greatest amount of use had probably taken place, and certainly where the greatest levels of use had probably taken place, and certainly where the greatest levels of use could be expected. Small program sections, such as those involved with mental health, classification, and certain treatment interventions, were seen as the areas where research information could find consistent application.

One administrator provided a summary of most respondents' perceptions:

> Research is going to be useful in program areas—almost any treatment program. From my level [division manager] on up, almost everything is geared for planning for budget. If we had more time, maybe it would be different. Here we live from day to day, and here there are value choices.

Another administrator addressed the scope of use in the following way:

> It depends on the issue. At the operational level, the decision is going to be based about 60 percent on experience. The other 40 percent depends on reviewing policies and regulations. We *need* a body of knowledge—a statistical base to draw on. If we had that we might use it. Managers are not acclimated to research. I don't know that many researchers who are top-line managers. Empirical data is *boring* to legitimate power brokers.

During the study and in analyzing the data it became rather obvious that persons in certain subunit sections at the operational level were most likely to be seen as the users of research information. Also it was clear that use could vary among individuals and groups within hierarchical levels. Respondents perceived the use of research information as more appropriate in certain subsections with limited "scientific" missions. In addition, it was clear that use—both type of use and the degree of reliance on research information—would vary between hierarchical levels. At the division-manager level and particularly at the top management level, the likelihood of instrumental or strictly conceptual use was diminished greatly, whereas the use of research information for symbolic or persuasive purposes was somewhat more likely, when it was considered necessary. Stated in another way, an inverse relationship exists between hierarchical level and research utilization. In the agency studied, the higher an individual ascends in the hierarchy, the less that individual uses research information. At the upper levels, research information might prove useful only for symbolic or persuasive purposes.

Moreover, the use of research information was a matter of individual determination in the department. Most respondents were rather pessimistic about the likelihood that research information would affect policy or decision in a significant way. Further, evidence of any concerted effort to use research information in a systematic way (formal policies, decision rules or structure, systematic procedures) was totally absent.

Research Information versus Other Forms of Information

Relative to reliance on other forms of information, research information was used only minimally, except for certain circumscribed purposes. As noted earlier, Lindblom and Cohen (1979:32) hypothesize that research information must compete with a "mountain of ordinary knowledge which it cannot replace but only reshape here and there." Consideration of the data in regard to this notion sheds light on the role accorded to research information in the department.

With little variation, the respondents described the preference for practical policy without research. The separation of research data from policy data or data for decision making was pervasive; with few exceptions (notably among the researchers) the respondents did not recognize a direct relationship between research information and the development of policy. The issue of reliance on research information compared to other forms of information is illuminated by the following representative comments:

> Administrator: The need for policy takes priority over the need to review research. The kinds of information decision makers look to are not necessarily what you would call research. Definitely the need for policy takes priority over the need for evaluation.

> Researcher: I don't think we use research. I may be biased. We use historical data. We use aggregate data: looking at today, last week, last year—strictly numbers. I think these numbers have a stronghold on the formulation of policy and on making decisions in general.

> Administrator: Research, even reviewing research, is a luxury—whatever the source. Needs and resource-oriented constraints and the personal time factor make it so.

> Administrator: Decisions are political. To have the greatest impact for research information, you have to learn the secret; learn how to market it in a political environment—to influence decision makers to change their behaviors.

> Administrator: Expertise is used more than any other source of information for policy and decisions.

> Administrator: Whatever information supports the budget, we use that and go that way.

Finally,

> Administrator: We use the resources at hand: experience, expertise, and the legislature.

The study participants made it quite clear that information drawn from experience and expertise dominated decision making and policy development in the department. Even though one might argue that individuals may have knowledge of specific research findings and conclusions, and might put these to conceptual use in a diffuse way, the respondents generally distinguished individual knowledge and expertise from research information. The role accorded to individual knowledge and expertise, together with other forms of "ordinary" information (e.g., "strictly numbers"), was patently greater than that accorded to research information except where the use of research information received validation for limited purposes.

Factors Which Emerge as Important in Understanding Use/Nonuse in the Department

The department studied here is a complex, bureaucratic organization in which more than 5,000 persons are employed. The department has a differentiated structure and is characterized by the generally accepted features of a bureaucratic organization.

Every participant in the study characterized the management climate in the department as "crisis-oriented." All the participants characterized the department's external environment as uncertain; perceptions of a turbulent environment were pervasive. It appeared to the author that the respondents viewed "crisis" as a general, understandable rationale for an overall management approach based on incrementalism. Administrators interviewed gave little indication that rational analysis would be important for decision making unless the appearance of rationality would assist in persuading a particular audience.

Concern with established routine and with safe, incremental adaptation was evident in the responses of top administrators in the department. "Success" for the department was linked to preservation of staff and budget in the face of what the participants perceived to be an uncertain future. Understanding research utilization (or the lack of it) in the department requires the realization that the potential role of research information is limited by the orientation of the decision system (incrementalism as opposed to rational, analytic process) and by the corresponding logic and processes which facilitate decision making and policy formulation.

The department is structured along functional lines; problem solving is partitioned across and among subelements, as well as being ordered hierarchically. Members of the department were left relatively free to create what may be described best as "information spaces," based on the selective perception of information considered (on whatever basis) to be relevant to task accomplishment and/or to the resolution of immediate or anticipated problems.

One must suggest that the partitioning of problems, coupled with the absence of any formal forethought concerning information resources, was important in understanding the patterns of use noted previously. Members of the department viewed research information as relevant for certain limited purposes. In other words, the types of problems to be addressed and the perceptions of the nature of problems (technical as opposed to involving questions of value) contributed at least in a basic way to perceptions of the appropriateness of research information as an input; thus they must be seen as contributing to the pattern of circumscribed use.

The hierarchical ordering of problems also must be considered. At upper management levels, where intra-organizational interests, external interests, and questions of value were emphasized by respondents as more important, it is apparent that the potential role for research information diminished significantly and changed from perceptions of potential instrumental and conceptual use to a role with more practical importance for symbolic or persuasive purposes.

This study developed data on the patterns of search for information in problem solving. Overall, problem solving in the department could be described best as "problemistic" (Cyert and March, 1963). In other words, it appeared that the general tendency was to address immediate problems sequentially and to tailor the search for information to perceptions of what would be necessary to resolve the problem or problems at hand.

All respondents except research/information-producing personnel evidenced a strong inclination to rely on the expertise and experience of department staff members as the primary source of information for problem solving. As identified, the sources of information for problem solving fell into six categories, ranked as follows: 1) staff (experience/expertise); 2) standards and laws; 3) other systems' activities (direct observation of practices); 4) in-house research information; 5) research information from external sources; 6) review by consultants.

The crisis orientation of management appeared to reinforce perceptions of the need to address immediate problems sequentially. Respondents perceived that resource and time constraints related to crisis would preclude most attempts to use research information as a basis for decision. Review of research information or in-house production of empirical information was viewed in general as a "luxury" or, as one administrator put it, "a waste of time better applied to other pursuits." Conducting in-house research was perceived in general as a way to supplement problem-specific interactions aimed at resolving immediate problems, primarily to gain leverage for budget requests or for other symbolic purposes.

Bureaucratic Interests

It could not be said that as a group, the administrators had discounted research information completely as a possible input. They did show a preference for receiving information which already had been digested and evaluated by persons trusted to apply expertise and experience in determining its relevance and importance. Consider the following comments:

> Administrator: I always staff the problem. I expect the staff to use whatever resources are available—whether that means journals, the library, civil service regulations, other states, get in touch with universities—whatever. After that they give me a summary. I write a decision and distribute it for consideration. That usually generates a response. Then I act on it.

> Administrator: I prefer statistics to back up a decision. My people give me a capsule version and their recommendations. I look at what is necessary. You have to have a feel for the politics of it. I seldom look at an entire study.

Rich (1981) draws attention to the "selective utilization" of research information within complex organizations. His work emphasizes the need to examine the upward dissemination of research information as a process in which "trusted aides" are relied on to select safe and bureaucratically useful information. In the department under study, some evidence indicated that upper-level administrators relied on trusted staff to send them appropriate information. One researcher stated quite directly:

> Reliability is the key. It depends on the subject matter, but if you find the "right ear" [to transmit information], then you get this halo effect.

In pursuing the issue of "selective utilization," the author asked all respondents whether research information that comes directly to a decision maker through a trusted staff aide would be of great importance, of some importance, or of no importance in understanding utilization in the department. Twenty of the 27 respondents had an opinion on this issue; 12 stated that they would judge the issue to be of great importance and eight considered it to be of some importance, reflecting a strong perception of the possible importance of selectivity in transmitting information in the department. Future studies may attend to this issue quite fruitfully. It is intriguing and important to consider the possibility that the use of research information is influenced by implicit, informal information policies concerning what administrators may want to see. It may be an important possibility that certain information is used or ignored because it is transmitted by "trusted staff," as opposed to others, especially when (as this study finds) upper-level administrators use research information more for symbolic than for other purposes.

The issue of bureaucratic interest and research use/nonuse was more pronounced in another vein. It is natural that upper-level decision makers place faith in reliable subordinates; delegation of authority demands such an attitude. In addition, however, upper-level administrators discussed the potential nonuse of research information (any information) in connection with risk avoidance and perceptions of uncertainty. Candid comments from two administrators were ominous in their possible effect on RU:

> Administrator: Our biggest problem is, do we even want to develop certain information? If we are not prepared to handle it—deal with the results—do we even want to develop it? If we can't handle what they want to tell us, I don't even want to generate it right now. Because if you do there is a tremendous push from the outside, from the legislature, from do-gooders, from the media, saying, "You mean you were aware of this all the time and didn't do anything about it?"
>
> We'll back-burner things. That's a terrible thing to admit, but it's true. We have limited resources. If a federal judge says, "You will do this," then we'll do that. We've got state laws and regulations to respond to. Then we can get to other things.
>
> Administrator: All you have to do is have one disgruntled employee. The information becomes a matter of public record. If I don't like you or you don't like me, all you have to do is call this reporter and say, "Hey, go check on this." This has happened. Frankly, I don't want some of our

employees to have the information they request . . . People do not know some of the information that does exist, and we can't make it available to them.

The respondents associated issues of bureaucratic interest particularly with the possible use of products of the in-house evaluation section. One top administrator characterized evaluation information as a "management tool." Respondents expressed concern that research information produced by the in-house evaluation section might be used to promote bureaucratic interests and therefore would become suspect.

A researcher commented on perceived conflict regarding evaluation information:

You have to consider that there are adversary relationships within the department.

An administrator noted:

There is some defensiveness about evaluation research. It loses credibility when you have the feeling that it is promoted to do somebody in. The research in this department has not been formative. Many administrators are concerned with boundary maintenance. Hidden agendas discourage the circulation of some information.

Another administrator stated:

People react to evaluation with some apprehension. It's like sending out eyes and ears. Their reaction may be antagonistic. Any utilization may be antagonistic utilization.

The attitudes expressed above indicate a belief among some respondents that certain research information (particularly that produced in house) could have an adverse effect. As the comments show, this effect could be associated (1) with uncertainty as to the possible use of research information by powerful external elites, especially the legislature and the judiciary, and/or (2) with the conflict resulting from internal bureaucratic antagonisms.

All the study respondents appeared to understand decision making and policy development as part of a larger political process. It was apparent during the study that bureaucratic politics and bureaucratic interest, both internal and involving external relationships, were important in influencing perceptions of research and the use of research information. The comments above, other responses, and the general attitude about crisis support an inference that uncertainty, risk avoidance, and bureaucratic interest could constitute a critical overlay in understanding use/nonuse. Future studies might address the possibility that uncertainty over the ability of external elites to request or commission research and to use research information in a challenging manner could result in implicit or explicit information policies affecting use. In addition, future inquiry should take into account the possibility that internal bureaucratic struggles may lead to similar potential effects on the role for research and on use. The existence of implicit or explicit informal information policies could be very important in understanding the RU process.

The Findings in Perspective

This study was undertaken to contribute to the development of a body of data and to increase our basic understanding of the role and the potential of research information in order to help identify possibilities for conceptual development. Generalizing from limited data can be risky; the critic of information presented in this paper could ask whether the empirical base—a southern DOC facing a state of crisis—is atypical. One must suggest that the limitations of coverage do not invalidate the utility of the findings. The core features of this DOC—its bureaucratic arrangements—are similar to most if not all state DOCs. The most important question is whether the crisis overlay contributes to a characterization of this DOC as idiosyncratic.

Considering nationwide trends, one must think not. As Jurik and Musheno (1986:457) observe, "The 1980's mark a new era of crises for correctional systems in the United States." They point out appropriately that "the instability of corrections today revolves around a reconsideration of system goals with a renewed emphasis on deterrence and incapacitation, and on an exploding population of inmates unaccompanied by adequate fiscal support for correctional bureaucracies" (457). This statement describes aptly the situation in the DOC studied here.

Nonetheless, it is important to realize that "crisis" and crisis perceptions are relative. Perhaps one should compare these findings to expectations about use in state DOCs that are not characterized by perceptions of crisis. Yet demarcating possible differences places one in the realm of speculation; ultimately, comparing these findings in a series of further studies is the only sure way to know how valid they may be. (The author hopes that this research will encourage further efforts.) Such consideration may help clarify the limits and the value of this research.

As explained earlier, the existing literature on RU points out the strong expectation that research information will not have a direct influence on policy-making or decision-making outcomes. The findings in this study are in accord with such an expectation. Even in the "noncrisis" situation, if the RU literature is to be believed, instances of instrumental use will be minimal.

What differences, then, can one expect? One might find a more generally positive attitude toward use. The participants in this study indicate that research information assumes a very low priority as an input to policy making and decision making ("It is a luxury to review research"; "There is actually very little forethought"). What one could expect is that a state DOC with adequate resources and a more research-oriented leadership might invest both energy and dollars in coordinating inputs of information, including research information. In such a situation one might find more commitment to in-house and external studies and more forethought about the potential use of the resulting information, as well as more attention to the acquisition, assessment, dissemination, and use of the type of information characterized in this study as routinely encountered material. In general, one might expect a great deal more attention to conceptual use and possible instrumental use, primarily because one would conceive of a situation where time and resource constraints were not presented as a rationale for a lack of attention. Even so, one hardly could conceive of a reality approaching normative expectations for a research-oriented, rationalistic decision system.

Even when resources are plentiful enough to allow an agency to be characterized as "fat," they do not necessarily ensure a great deal of instrumental research use. Questions of policy—in fact, most decisions at the upper levels of management—involve the resolution of questions of value or preference. The participants in this study recognize their environment as political; accordingly one must consider the ways of doing business in complex, bureaucratic organizations that operate within complex, bureaucratic systems. In view of the research on corrections organizations and systems which addresses these issues (e.g., Conley, 1981; Jacobs, 1983; McEleney, 1985), it appears that this DOC is not unusual.

Conclusion

The findings and the insights obtained in this study point to the need for further research examining utilization in corrections and other criminal justice agencies. Baseline data must be established and effort must be devoted to understanding the potential role of research information in corrections agencies. The state of knowledge concerning RU in criminal justice requires additional explanation and conceptual development before we attempt quantitative cross-sectional studies of determinants and outcomes (Ellickson, 1981:54).

This study yields several points that are worth consideration. First, it cannot be assumed simply that patterns of research use will be consistent throughout an organization. This statement seems obvious, but much of the literature on RU fails to emphasize this issue. Use may vary within and between hierarchical levels.

The literature on RU attends to the possibility that use may be affected by the substantive issue, but it does not direct sufficient attention to the possibilities of variability in uses within the organization. In the department under study here, levels and types of use appeared to be associated with the hierarchical ordering and the partitioning of problems. Utilization appeared to be associated with perceptions of the appropriateness of research information to fulfill limited purposes.

In addition, the parceling out and the incremental, sequential ordering of problems contributed to the creation of information spaces and to variation in attention to information resources. These are important foci in constructing a useful conceptual framework for inquiry; they point to the need to turn to the rich literature on organizations and decision making in order to develop sets of propositions to be addressed in studying utilization.

Second, this study supports the contention that bureaucratic interests constitute a key overlay in developing an understanding of use. Again the literature on organizations and decision making may provide the basis for propositions about the relationship of uncertainty, risk avoidance, and associated concepts to the use/nonuse of research information. This study supports Rich's (1981) contention that "bureaucratization," as expressed in terms of informal policies and selective use, is crucial in understanding use. Evidence in this study points to the possibility that intentional control of information and intended control of the decision process deserve attention in further research. These points are important in developing an adequate model of the RU process; they indicate a major direction for incorporating related variables, such as individual interest, and for developing hypotheses.

Finally, the study suggests that those who develop prescriptions about systematic use of research information must attend to the structure and the dynamic nature of the decision system and to the overlay of bureaucratic interests. The patterns of circumscribed use noted in the study seem to be regularized. Perhaps conceptual development must proceed to identify characteristic modes of organizational learning and related processes in criminal justice agencies. This direction may be promising in attempts to clarify basic assumptions and expectations about use and in locating sets of variables from an integrative perspective.

References

Allison, G. T. (1971). *Essence of decision.* Boston: Little, Brown.

Caplan, N. S. (1979). The two-community theory and knowledge utilization. *American Behavioral Scientist, 22,* 459–470.

Conley, J. (1981, Winter). Beyond legislative acts: Penal reform, public policy, and symbolic justice. *The Public Historian, 3,* 26–39.

Cyert, R. M., & March, J. G. (1963). *A behavioral theory of the firm.* Englewood Cliffs, NJ: Prentice-Hall.

Ellickson, P. (1981). *Knowledge utilization in local criminal justice agencies: A conceptual framework.* Santa Monica: Rand.

Glaser, D. (1973). *Routinizing evaluation: Getting feedback on the effectiveness of crime and delinquency programs.* Rockville, MD: NIMH.

Glaser, E. M., Abelson, H. H., & Garrison, K. N. (1983). *Putting knowledge to use: Facilitating the diffusion of knowledge and the implementation of planned change.* San Francisco: Jossey-Bass.

Gottfredson, M., & Gottfredson, D. (1980). *Decision making in criminal justice: Toward the rational exercise of discretion.* Cambridge, MA: Bellinger.

Grosskin, R. (1981). Toward the integration of evaluation in criminal justice policy: Constructing alternative interpretational models of the evaluation utilization process. Unpublished paper.

Jacobs, J. (1983). *New perspectives on prison and imprisonment.* Ithaca, NY: Cornell University Press.

Jurik, N. C., & Musheno, M. C. (1986). The internal crisis of corrections: Professionalization and the work environment. *Justice Quarterly, 4*, 457–480.

Lindblom, C., & Cohen, D. (1979). *Usable knowledge.* New Haven, CT: Yale University Press.

Lynd, R. S. (1939). *Knowledge for what?* Princeton, NJ: Princeton University Press.

McEleney, B. L. (1985). *Correctional reform in New York: The Rockefeller years and beyond.* Lanham, MD: University Press of America.

Patrick, M. S. (1979). Utilizing program evaluation products: A rational choice approach. Paper presented at the annual meeting of the Midwest Political Science Association, Chicago.

Patton, M. (1978). *Utilization-focused evaluation.* Beverly Hills, CA: Sage.

Rich, R. (1981). *Social science information and public policy making.* San Francisco: Jossey-Bass.

Snow, C. P. (1962). *Science and government.* New York: New American Library.

Snow, C. P. (1979, September/October). The many meanings of research utilization. *Public Administration Review,* 426–431.

Weiss, C. (1977). *Using social science research in public policymaking.* Lexington, MA: Heath.

Weiss, C., & Bucuvalas, M. (1980). *Social science research and decision-making.* New York: Columbia University Press.

DATE DUE
